CCNA Self-Study
CCNA ICND
Exam Certification Guide

Wendell Odom, CCIE No. 1624

Cisco Press

Cisco Press
800 East 96th Street
Indianapolis, IN 46240 USA

CCNA ICND Exam Certification Guide

Wendell Odom

Copyright© 2004 Cisco Systems, Inc.

Published by:
Cisco Press
800 East 96th Street
Indianapolis, IN 46240 USA

Printed in the United States of America   13 14 15

Thirteenth Printing May 2006

Library of Congress Cataloging-in-Publication Number: 2002116060

ISBN: 1-58720-083-x

Warning and Disclaimer

This book is designed to provide information about selected topics for the ICND Exam for the CCNA certification. Every effort has been made to make this book as complete and accurate as possible, but no warranty or fitness is implied.

The information is provided on an "as is" basis. The author, Cisco Press, and Cisco Systems, Inc. shall have neither liability nor responsibility to any person or entity with respect to any loss or damages arising from the information contained in this book or from the use of the discs or programs that may accompany it.

The opinions expressed in this book belong to the author and are not necessarily those of Cisco Systems, Inc.

Feedback Information

At Cisco Press, our goal is to create in-depth technical books of the highest quality and value. Each book is crafted with care and precision, undergoing rigorous development that involves the unique expertise of members of the professional technical community.

Reader feedback is a natural continuation of this process. If you have any comments regarding how we could improve the quality of this book, or otherwise alter it to better suit your needs, you can contact us through e-mail at feedback@ciscopress.com. Please be sure to include the book's title and ISBN in your message.

We greatly appreciate your assistance.

Trademark Acknowledgments

All terms mentioned in this book that are known to be trademarks or service marks have been appropriately capitalized. Cisco Press or Cisco Systems, Inc. cannot attest to the accuracy of this information. Use of a term in this book should not be regarded as affecting the validity of any trademark or service mark.

Corporate and Government Sales

Cisco Press offers excellent discounts on this book when ordered in quantity for bulk purchases or special sales. For more information, please contact:

U.S. Corporate and Government Sales 1-800-382-3419 corpsales@pearsontechgroup.com

For sales outside of the U.S. please contact:

International Sales international@pearsoned.com

Publisher: John Wait

Editor-In-Chief: John Kane

Executive Editor: Brett Bartow

Managing Editor: Patrick Kanouse

Development Editor: Christopher Cleveland

Project Editor: Marc Fowler

Copy Editor: Gayle Johnson

Team Coordinator: Tammi Barnett

Book and Cover Designer: Louisa Adair

Compositor: Mark Shirar

Indexer: Tim Wright

Cisco Representative: Anthony Wolfenden

Cisco Press Program Manager: Nannette M. Noble

Technical Editors: Elan Beer, Lynn Maynes, Martin Walshaw

CISCO SYSTEMS

Corporate Headquarters
Cisco Systems, Inc.
170 West Tasman Drive
San Jose, CA 95134-1706
USA
www.cisco.com
Tel: 408 526-4000
   800 553-NETS (6387)
Fax: 408 526-4100

European Headquarters
Cisco Systems International BV
Haarlerbergpark
Haarlerbergweg 13-19
1101 CH Amsterdam
The Netherlands
www-europe.cisco.com
Tel: 31 0 20 357 1000
Fax: 31 0 20 357 1100

Americas Headquarters
Cisco Systems, Inc.
170 West Tasman Drive
San Jose, CA 95134-1706
USA
www.cisco.com
Tel: 408 526-7660
Fax: 408 527-0883

Asia Pacific Headquarters
Cisco Systems, Inc.
Capital Tower
168 Robinson Road
#22-01 to #29-01
Singapore 068912
www.cisco.com
Tel: +65 6317 7777
Fax: +65 6317 7799

Cisco Systems has more than 200 offices in the following countries and regions. Addresses, phone numbers, and fax numbers are listed on the
Cisco.com Web site at www.cisco.com/go/offices.

Argentina • Australia • Austria • Belgium • Brazil • Bulgaria • Canada • Chile • China PRC • Colombia • Costa Rica • Croatia • Czech Republic
Denmark • Dubai, UAE • Finland • France • Germany • Greece • Hong Kong SAR • Hungary • India • Indonesia • Ireland • Israel • Italy
Japan • Korea • Luxembourg • Malaysia • Mexico • The Netherlands • New Zealand • Norway • Peru • Philippines • Poland • Portugal
Puerto Rico • Romania • Russia • Saudi Arabia • Scotland • Singapore • Slovakia • Slovenia • South Africa • Spain • Sweden
Switzerland • Taiwan • Thailand • Turkey • Ukraine • United Kingdom • United States • Venezuela • Vietnam • Zimbabwe

About the Author

Wendell Odom, CCIE No.1624, is a senior instructor with Skyline Advanced Technology Services (http://www.skyline-ats.com), where he teaches courses on QoS, CCNA, and storage networking. He has worked in the networking arena for 20 years, with jobs in pre- and post-sales technical consulting, teaching, and course development. He has written portions of more than 12 courses, covering topics such as IP routing, MPLS, Cisco WAN switches, SNA protocols, and LAN troubleshooting. He is the author of three prior editions of the *CCNA Exam Certification Guide*, the DQOS and QoS Exam Certification Guides, and *Computer Networking First-Step*.

About the Technical Reviewers

Elan Beer, CCIE No. 1837, CCSI No. 94008, is a senior consultant and Certified Cisco Instructor. His internetworking expertise is recognized internationally through his global consulting and training engagements. As one of the industry's top internetworking consultants and Cisco instructors, Beer has used his expertise to design, implement, and deploy multi-protocol networks for a wide international clientele. As a senior instructor and course developer, Beer has designed and presented public and implementation-specific technical courses spanning many of today's top technologies. He can be reached at elan@CiscoConsultants.com.

Lynn Maynes, CCIE No. 6569, is a senior network engineer with Sprint Managed Network Services specializing in network design, architecture, and security for large-scale networks worldwide. He has more than 9 years of experience in computer networking and is a co-author of the Cisco Press book, CCNA Practical Studies. He holds a bachelor's degree in international business from Westminster College.

Martin Walshaw, CCIE No. 5629, CISSP, CCNP, CCDP, is a systems engineer working for Cisco Systems in the Enterprise line of business in South Africa. His areas of specialty include convergence, security, and content delivery networking. Over the last 15 years, Walshaw has dabbled in many aspects of the IT industry, ranging from programming in RPG III and COBOL to PC sales. When Walshaw isn't working, he likes to spend all his available time with his patient wife, Val, and his sons, Joshua and Callum. Without their patience, understanding, and support, projects such as this would not be possible.

Brent Stewart is a certified Cisco Systems instructor for Global Knowledge. With Global Knowledge, he has participated in the development of ICND, BSCI, BCMSN, BCRAN, and CIT for Internet-based delivery and served as SME (Subject Matter Expert) for the CD-based ICND and CIT titles. He helped author the BSCI 2.0 update and served as the lab development engineer. Before working for Global Knowledge, Brent owned an ISP and worked as an IT consultant. Brent holds the CCNP, CCDP, and MCSE certifications. Brent lives in Hickory, North Carolina, with his wife, Karen, and beautiful but mischievous children, Benjamin, Kaitlyn, and Madelyn.

Dedication

The nature of the book-writing process requires some long and odd work hours. My darling wife, Kris, never complains about it, picks up my slack, and makes our lives run smoothly—all so I can write. Kris, the first time you read this dedication, you're entitled to a whole week of "Honey do" tasks from me at home. Thanks for making it all possible!

Acknowledgments

The technical editing team for this book and its companion volume were fantastic. Not only did they find where I had written wrong technical facts, they also helped me find new, more interesting, and clearer ways to convey certain facts about networking. Lynn was particularly helpful with comments that helped keep small sections in line with the overall theme of the chapter—a skill I'm sure he developed as a result of having written books himself. Martin helped a lot with technical details and perspectives from what customers see every day. And Elan excelled at noticing both small, nitpicky errors and significant technical problems. (And that's not an insult—every technical author loves help in finding the small problems!) Also, Brent Stewart assisted greatly with reviews and new exam questions related to the ongoing updates to Appendix D (also posted at http://www.ciscopress.com/ccna). Together, these gentlemen formed a great team with complementary skills. Thanks so much, guys!

The production team, headed by Patrick Kanouse, did their usual excellent job. Like the "behind-the-scenes" people in many businesses, their specific efforts might not be obvious to the public, but they are no less appreciated by me. In particular, Marc Fowler, the project editor, did an incredible job working through these two books on a very tight schedule, with his usual excellent work. You folks make me look good on paper. If only you could be in charge of my wardrobe too, I'd look good all the time!

Brett Bartow, Executive Editor, did his usual New-York-Yankees-like job of helping steer these two projects toward completion. In between talking about sports, Brett worked through the many changes in direction with this book and helped guide us to the right product. And yes, so the whole world knows, he did pick an Atlanta Braves player, John Smoltz, for his fantasy league baseball team—again proving he's a really smart guy.

Chris Cleveland developed this book and the *CCNA INTRO Exam Certification Guide.* He's simply the best. He also works way harder than I do to get these books to market. You da man, Chris C!

Contents at a Glance

Contents

Icons Used in This Book

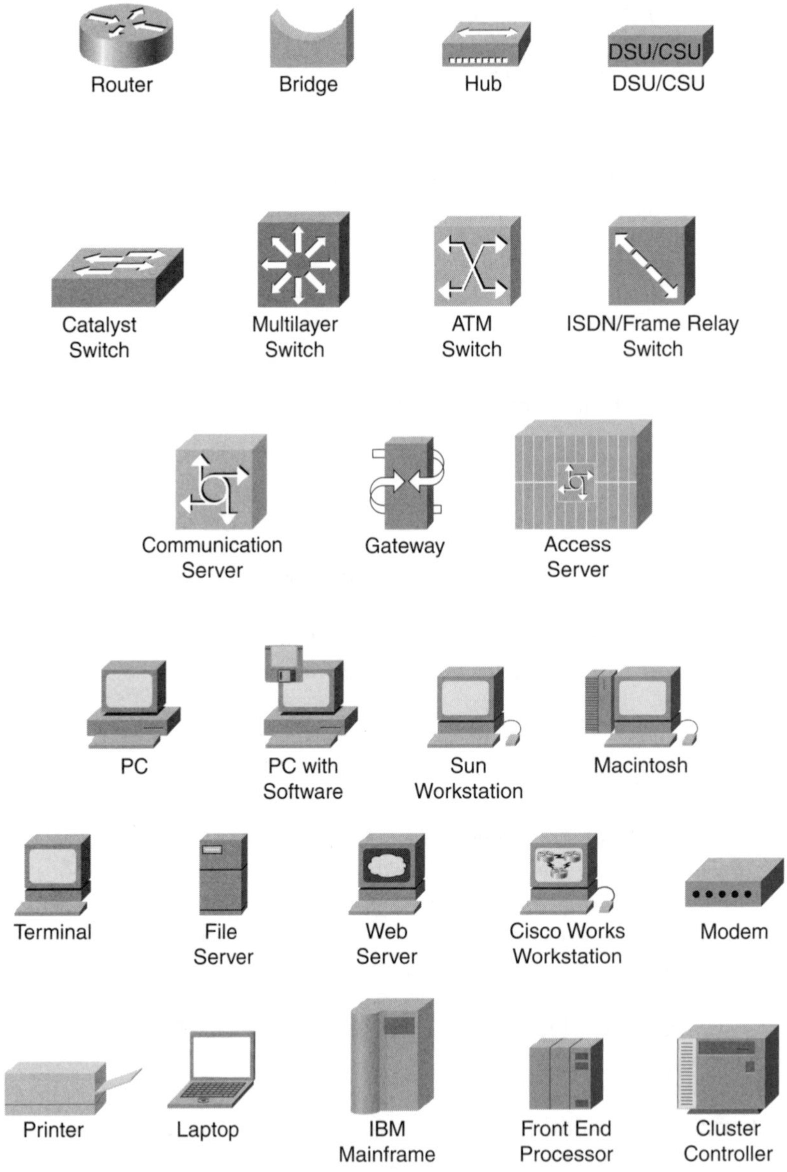
Router
Bridge
Hub
DSU/CSU
DSU/CSU
Catalyst Switch
Multilayer Switch
ATM Switch
ISDN/Frame Relay Switch
Communication Server
Gateway
Access Server
PC
PC with Software
Sun Workstation
Macintosh
Terminal
File Server
Web Server
Cisco Works Workstation
Modem
Printer
Laptop
IBM Mainframe
Front End Processor
Cluster Controller

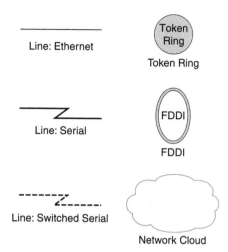

Line: Ethernet

Token Ring

Line: Serial

FDDI

Line: Switched Serial

Network Cloud

Command Syntax Conventions

The conventions used to present command syntax in this book are the same conventions used in the IOS Command Reference. The Command Reference describes these conventions as follows:

- Vertical bars (|) separate alternative, mutually exclusive elements.

- Square brackets ([ ]) indicate an optional element.

- Braces ({ }) indicate a required choice.

- Braces within brackets ([{ }]) indicate a required choice within an optional element.

- Bold indicates commands and keywords that are entered literally as shown. In actual configuration examples and output (not general command syntax), bold indicates commands that are manually input by the user (such as a show command).

- Italic indicates arguments for which you supply actual values.

Introduction: Overview of Certification and How to Succeed

Congratulations! If you're reading this Introduction, you've probably decided to go for your Cisco Certified Network Associate (CCNA) certification. Cisco Systems' entry-level certification, CCNA, has a reputation as one of the most valuable entry-level certifications in the computing industry. Although getting your CCNA does not guarantee you your first networking job, or a new job, it will certainly help convince others that you know what you're talking about!

Cisco's CCNA certification proves that you have a firm foundation in the most important components of the Cisco product line—routers and switches. It also proves that you have broad knowledge of protocols and networking technologies. CCNA is not an easy certification to get, but it is well worth the effort. In a booming economy, CCNA is the first step toward getting a higher salary than your noncertified peers. In a difficult economy, it could determine whether a prospective employer even looks at your resume. Regardless of your local economy, CCNA improves how people in the marketplace view your skill level!

People occasionally ask me for career advice, and my answer is typically the same: If you want to be in the networking industry, you need to know Cisco. Cisco has some amazing market shares in the router and switch industry, with more than 80% market share in some markets. In many markets, networking equals Cisco. If you want to be taken seriously as a network engineer, you need a CCNA certification. Frankly, you probably also need to work toward a more advanced Cisco certification—but first things first! CCNA requires some time and effort.

Cisco's Motivation: Certifying Partners

Cisco's primary motivation for creating CCNA and most of the other Cisco certifications is to help determine the skill levels of their partners. Cisco fulfills only a small portion of its orders through direct sales; most often, a Cisco reseller is involved. (Cisco calls resellers channel partners.) Also, Cisco encourages partners to perform most consulting and implementation services relating to Cisco products. While working heavily with partners, Cisco needed to know which partners truly had the right skills. So it created many certifications, including CCNA.

Cisco measures the technical readiness of channel partners (resellers) and professional services partners in part by requiring specific numbers of Cisco certified employees. For instance, Premier, Silver, and Gold Channel Partners are required to have either two or four CCNAs on staff, along with Cisco professional and expert-level certified individuals.

So what does this mean to you? Well, if you already have some Cisco certifications on your resume, you are more valuable to Cisco partners. In today's competitive environment, every edge counts, so having the right Cisco certifications can help you get that next job! In particular, the CCNA certification is a prerequisite for almost every Cisco certification, so this is the right place to start!

The CCNA Certification Exams (What? There's More Than One Exam?)

For the first time since Cisco announced CCNA in 1998, the CCNA certification has an option for multiple exams. Before Cisco announced these latest changes in 2003, to get your CCNA certification, you passed a single "CCNA exam." With this latest generation of the CCNA, you can take a single exam to get your CCNA, or you can take two exams—with each of these exams covering a subset of the CCNA exam topics. Table I-1 lists the exams.

Table I-1 *CCNA Exam Names and Numbers*

Exam Name	Exam Number	Description
INTRO exam	640-821	A subset of the CCNA topics. It should be taken before the ICND exam.
ICND exam	640-811	A subset of the CCNA topics. It should be taken after the INTRO exam.
CCNA exam	640-801	Can be taken instead of the INTRO and ICND exams. It covers the same content as the other two exams combined.

So you either take the CCNA exam, or you take both the INTRO and the ICND exams, to pass CCNA.

Like most Cisco certification exams, the names of the INTRO and ICND exams come from two Cisco Authorized courses. Cisco's INTRO course covers a broad range of topics, from Ethernet cabling to virtual private networks (VPNs). The Interconnecting Cisco Network Devices (ICND) course delves more deeply into core Cisco technology and protocols—in particular, switching and routing. The INTRO course covers a broader range of topics in less depth, and the ICND course covers fewer topics in more depth. Like their namesakes, the INTRO and ICND exams cover similar depth and breadth.

The CCNA exam covers everything on both the INTRO and ICND exams. So if you want to save some cash, and you are confident that you are ready to answer questions across the whole range of topics for CCNA, you can take just the CCNA exam. Alternatively, you can focus on the INTRO exam first, master those topics, pass the exam, and then move on to the ICND exam.

Format of the CCNA Exams

The INTRO, ICND, and CCNA exams all follow the same general format. As soon as you get to the testing center and check in, the proctor will give you some general instructions and then take you to a quiet room with a PC. After you sit down at the PC, you have a few things to do before the timer starts on your exam. For instance, you can take a sample quiz to get accustomed to the PC and the testing engine. Anyone who has user-level skills in getting around a PC will have no problems with the testing environment.

As soon as you start the exam, you will be asked a series of questions. You answer the question and then move on to the next one. The exam engine does not let you go back and change your answer. As soon as you move on to the next question, that's it for the preceding question.

The exam questions can be in the following format:

- Multiple choice
- Fill-in-the-blank
- Drag and drop
- Simulated lab

The multiple-choice format requires that you click a circle beside the correct answer(s). If more than one answer is required, the question probably will tell you how many answers to choose. Fill-in-the-blank questions require that you enter the answer, so you must get the answer exactly right.

Drag-and-drop questions require you to click and drag a button or icon to another area and then release the mouse button to place the object—typically in a list. For some questions, you might need to put a list of five things in the proper order.

The type of question that gives most people a scare before the exam is the simulated lab question. The exam engine gives you an interface into a network with several routers, and you must log in and troubleshoot a scenario. To solve the problem, you need to be able to navigate through the user interface, know several commands, and possibly configure something that has been misconfigured. You should also save your configurations, unless the question tells you not to, just in case.

The best way to prepare for simulated lab questions is to practice with real gear. You can use the Internet to find sites that offer free CCNA lab access. I searched for "free CCNA labs," and the first three hits were (seemingly) legitimate offers for free lab access for CCNA study. You can also use a simulator product, such as Cisco Press's CCNA Router and Switch eSIM. A special version of Boson's Netsim product, compiled specifically for this book, is also included on the CD that comes with this book.

What's on the CCNA Exams

Ever since I was in grade school, whenever the teacher announced that we were having a test soon, someone would always ask, "What's on the test?". Even in college, people would try to get more information about what would be on the exams. The goal is to know what to study a lot, what to study a little, and what to not study at all.

Cisco wants you to know what topics to study, and it wants you to be well-prepared for your exams. However, Cisco does not want to be so specific that you can just memorize a very specific set of facts and pass the exams. In short, Cisco wants you to pass the exams because you know your stuff, not because you memorized a set of questions that someone (possibly illegally) posted on an Internet site.

What can be said about the content of the exams? First, Cisco posts exam topics for each exam. This official posting is the basis of what Cisco intends to put on the exams, so you should pay close attention to this list. Also, the breadth and depth of topics on the exams tend to match the Cisco Authorized courses with which they are associated, so it is useful to know the outlines for those courses. Finally, Cisco designs the Cisco Networking Academy Program (CNAP) course materials with CCNA in mind. Looking at all these sources can give you insight into CCNA.

ICND Exam Topics

Carefully consider the exam topics Cisco posts on its website as you study, particularly for clues as to how thoroughly you should know each topic. The exam topics use action words that follow a quasi-standard called "Bloom's Taxonomy of the Cognitive Domain." Bloom's Taxonomy defines a standard for word usage for when educators create objectives for courses. Objectives written according to Bloom's Taxonomy define what the student should be able to accomplish after taking the class. So, when you look at an exam topic, look for the action word. It gives you a good hint about the level of knowledge and skill you will need before taking the exam. (If you want to see a description of Bloom's Taxonomy, search the Internet. My favorite quick list of terms is at http://chiron.valdosta.edu/whuitt/col/cogsys/bloom.html.)

The action word in the exam topic gives you a good hint about the level of knowledge and skill you will need to have before taking the exam. For instance, a course objective that uses the word *list* as the action word means that you should be able to list the features. An action word such as *configure* means that you should know all the related configuration commands and how to use them. *Troubleshoot* might mean that you need to know what all the **show** and **debug** commands do for a particular topic.

What does Bloom's Taxonomy mean in terms of how you study for the exam? It means that you should focus on the action words in the exam topics and make sure you can do those things for the stated topics. For instance, if an exam topic says something like "Configure RIP...," don't just study RIP concepts. Also study the configuration details, because the exam topic specifically tells you that you need to know how to perform configuration.

Cisco adds a disclaimer that the posted exam topics for all its certification exams are *guidelines*. Cisco tries to keep the exam questions within the confines of the stated exam objectives, but doing this for every question and every exam is difficult. Thus, you could see questions that fall outside both the scope and depth implied by the exam topics. However, if you follow the Cisco exam topic guidelines, you should have a good understanding of the breadth and depth of topics on the exam.

Table I-2 lists the exam topics for the ICND exam. You can find these topics in the Introduction to the *CCNA ICND Exam Certification Guide* and on www.cisco.com. Note that although Cisco's posted exam topics are not numbered, they are numbered in the Exam Certification Guide series for easier reference. Also note that Cisco has historically changed exam topics without changing the exam number, so do not be alarmed if small changes in the exam topics occur over time. When in doubt, go to www.cisco.com, click Learning & Events, and select Career Certifications and Paths.

Table I-2 *ICND Exam Topics*

Exam Topic Reference Number	Exam Topics
	Planning and Design
1	Design or modify a simple LAN using Cisco products
2	Design an IP addressing scheme to support classful, classless, and private addressing to meet design requirements
3	Select an appropriate routing protocol based on user requirements
4	Design a simple internetwork using Cisco products
5	Develop an access list to meet user specifications
6	Choose WAN protocols to meet design requirements
	Implementation and Operation
7	Configure routing protocols given user requirements
8	Configure IP addresses, subnet masks, and gateway addresses on routers and hosts
9	Configure a router for additional administrative functionality

Table I-2 *ICND Exam Topics (Continued)*

Exam Topic Reference Number	Exam Topics
10	Configure a switch with VLANS and inter-switch communication
11	Implement a LAN
12	Customize a switch configuration to meet specified network requirements
13	Implement access lists
14	Implement simple WAN protocols
	Troubleshooting
15	Utilize the OSI model as a guide for systematic network troubleshooting
16	Perform LAN and VLAN troubleshooting
17	Troubleshoot routing protocols
18	Troubleshoot IP addressing and host configuration
19	Troubleshoot a device as part of a working network
20	Troubleshoot an access list
21	Perform simple WAN troubleshooting
	Technology
22	Describe the Spanning Tree process
23	Evaluate the characteristics of LAN environments
24	Evaluate the characteristics of routing protocols
25	Evaluate rules for packet control
26	Evaluate key characteristics of HDLC, PPP, Frame Relay, DDR, and ISDN technologies

Cross-Reference Between Exam Topics and Book Parts

Table I-3 provides a cross-reference between the exam topics and the book parts in which they are covered.

Table I-3   *ICND Exam Topics Cross-Reference to Parts in the CCNA ICND Exam Certification Guide*

Exam Topic	Part	Exam Topic	Part
1	1	14	3
2	2	15	1-4
3	2	16	1
4	1-3	17	2
5	4	18	2
6	3	19	1-4
7	2	20	4
8	2	21	3
9	2	22	1
10	1	23	1
11	1	24	2
12	1	25	4
13	4	26	3

CCNA Exam Topics

Interestingly, the CCNA (640-801) exam topics posted by Cisco are not simply the combination of the INTRO exam topics and the ICND exam topics. If you look closely, the CCNA exam topics match more closely to the ICND exam topics than they do to the INTRO exam topics.

So, for those of you planning to take the single CCNA exam, what does that mean? Well, for practical purposes, the CCNA exam covers all the topics covered on both the INTRO and ICND exams. However, the length of the CCNA exam does not allow Cisco to ask you about every possible fact. So, you should expect the CCNA exam to include questions that cover more advanced topics, many of which require that you know the more basic facts. For instance, rather than ask a question about how to do binary math, which is specifically mentioned for the INTRO exam topics, you might have to derive subnet numbers – which requires you to use binary math. Another example: instead of describing LAN cabling, you might have a question about troubleshooting a LAN topology, and need to decide if an incorrect type of cable was used. So, while the exam topics do not exactly match up, but you essentially need to know all the same concepts on both the INTRO and ICND exams in order to succeed on the CCNA exam.

Table I-4 lists the CCNA exam topics at time of publication. As always, look to www.cisco.com for the latest posted information about the CCNA, INTRO, and ICND exams!

Table I-4 *CCNA Exam Topics*

Exam Topic Reference Number	Exam Topic
	Planning and Design
1	Design a simple LAN using Cisco Technology
2	Design an IP addressing scheme to meet design requirements
3	Select an appropriate routing protocol based on user requirements
4	Design a simple internetwork using Cisco technology
5	Develop an access list to meet user specifications
6	Choose WAN services to meet customer requirements
	Implementation and Operation
7	Configure routing protocols given user requirements
8	Configure IP addresses, subnet masks, and gateway addresses on routers and hosts
9	Configure a router for additional administrative functionality
10	Configure a switch with VLANS and inter-switch communication
11	Implement a LAN
12	Customize a switch configuration to meet specified network requirements
13	Manage system image and device configuration files
14	Perform an initial configuration on a router
15	Perform an initial configuration on a switch
16	Implement access lists
17	Implement simple WAN protocols
	Troubleshooting
18	Utilize the OSI model as a guide for systematic network troubleshooting
19	Perform LAN and VLAN troubleshooting
20	Troubleshoot routing protocols
21	Troubleshoot IP addressing and host configuration
22	Troubleshoot a device as part of a working network

continues

Table I-4 *CCNA Exam Topics (Continued)*

Exam Topic Reference Number	Exam Topic
23	Troubleshoot an access list
24	Perform simple WAN troubleshooting
	Technology
25	Describe network communications using layered models
26	Describe the Spanning Tree process
27	Compare and contrast key characteristics of LAN environments
28	Evaluate the characteristics of routing protocols
29	Evaluate TCP/IP communication process and its associated protocols
30	Describe the components of network devices
31	Evaluate rules for packet control
32	Evaluate key characteristics of WANs

INTRO and ICND Course Outlines

Another way to get some direction for the topics on the exams is to look at the course outlines for the related courses. Cisco offers the Introduction to Cisco Networking (INTRO) and Interconnecting Cisco Network Devices (ICND) courses through its Certified Learning Solutions Providers (CLSPs). CLSPs in turn work with other learning partners as well.

The INTRO course covers a much broader set of topics than ICND, but for the topics it covers, ICND covers the topics in much greater detail. In particular, ICND includes a lot more information about commands used on routers and switches to configure and troubleshoot the various features.

These outlines can be found at www.cisco.com.

About the *CCNA INTRO Exam Certification Guide* and *CCNA ICND Exam Certification Guide*

As mentioned earlier in this Introduction, you can take both the INTRO and ICND exams to pass CCNA, or you can take a single CCNA exam. Because of the significantly expanded topics as compared with the previous CCNA exam, there was simply too much material for a single book. So we created two books—one for the INTRO exam and one for the ICND exam.

The contents of the two books were designed for both the single-exam and dual-exam audience. If you're preparing for just the ICND exam, you can read just this book. Because the ICND exam covers topics more deeply than the INTRO exam, you should probably pass the INTRO exam first. Use the *CCNA INTRO Exam Certification Guide* to help with that task.

If you are studying for the CCNA exam, you can use both books and alternate reading each book to optimize your efforts in preparing for the exam. This Introduction includes a reading plan for anyone taking the CCNA exam, telling you in what order to read the chapters in the two books. Essentially, you read the first three parts of this book and then read part of the other book, come back here for a part, go back to the other book, and so on, for most of the parts of both books. The parts are named so that it is obvious which sections to read as you move between the books. By doing so, you complete all the coverage in a particular technical area before moving on to another.

Objectives and Methods

The most important and somewhat obvious objective of this book is to help you pass the ICND exam or the CCNA exam. In fact, if the primary objective of this book were different, the book's title would be misleading! However, the methods used in this book to help you pass the exams are also designed to make you much more knowledgeable about how to do your job.

This book uses several key methodologies to help you discover the exam topics on which you need more review, to help you fully understand and remember those details, and to help you prove to yourself that you have retained your knowledge of those topics. This book does not try to help you pass the exams only by memorization, but by truly learning and understanding the topics. The CCNA certification is the foundation of many of the Cisco professional certifications, and it would be a disservice to you if this book did not help you truly learn the material. Therefore, this book helps you pass the CCNA exam by using the following methods:

- Helping you discover which exam topics you have not mastered

- Providing explanations and information to fill in your knowledge gaps

- Supplying exercises that enhance your ability to recall and deduce the answers to test questions

- Providing practice exercises on the topics and the testing process via test questions on the CD

Book Features

To help you customize your study time using these books, the core chapters have several features that help you make the best use of your time:

■ **"Do I Know This Already?" Quizzes**—Each chapter begins with a quiz that helps you determine the amount of time you need to spend studying that chapter. If you follow the directions at the beginning of the chapter, the "Do I Know This Already?" quiz directs you to study all or particular parts of the chapter.

■ **Foundation Topics**—These are the core sections of each chapter. They explain the protocols, concepts, and configuration for the topics in that chapter. If you need to learn about the topics in a chapter, read the "Foundation Topics" section.

■ **Foundation Summary**—Near the end of each chapter, a summary collects the most important information from the chapter, summarized in lists, tables, and figures. The "Foundation Summary" section is designed to help you review the key concepts in the chapter if you scored well on the "Do I Know This Already?" quiz. This section is an excellent tool for last-minute review. The "Foundation Summary" sections of each chapter are available in printable format from the main menu of the CD-ROM.

■ **Q&A**—Each chapter ends with a "Q&A" section that forces you to exercise your recall of the facts and processes described in that chapter. These questions generally are harder than those on the exam, partly because they are in "short answer" format instead of multiple-choice. These questions are a great way to increase the accuracy of your recollection of the facts.

■ **CD-based practice exam**—The companion CD contains a large number of questions not included in the book, as well as all the questions from the "Do I Know This Already" quizzes. You can answer these questions by using the simulated exam feature or the topical review feature. This is the best tool for helping you prepare for the test-taking process.

■ **Hands-on practice using Boson NetSim™ LE**—The CD also includes the Boson NetSim for CCNA ICND Learning Edition network simulator software, supporting the ability to perform many of the commands covered in the book. In particular, you can perform many of the practice scenarios and hands-on lab exercises also included on the CD, as well as several from the book. Appendix C details how to access the simulator, and what lab exercises can be performed. (The version of the Boson NetSim™ software included with this book is a limited functionality version. In order to access all functions and features of the software, you must purchase a full license for the software from Boson Software, Inc.)

■ **CD-based practice scenarios**—The companion CD contains a CD-only appendix B (which is a totally different appendix as compared with the printed appendix B in the book) which has several practice scenarios. These scenarios include several problem statements, with solutions, in order to help you pull both concepts and configuration commands together. These scenarios are useful for building your hands-on skills, even if you do not have lab gear. You can also perform some of these scenarios using the Boson NetSim LE network simulator, or using your own lab gear.

- **CD-based lab exercises**—The companion CD contains a CD-only appendix C (which is a totally different appendix as compared with the printed appendix C in the book) which has several lab exercises. These lab exercises guide you through the steps used to perform the most popular configuration tasks. Like the scenarios, CD-only appendix C includes the answers to the labs, making it useful to just read the materials for extra reinforcement of the commands. You can also perform these labs using the Boson NetSim LE network simulator, or using your own lab gear.

- **CD-based subnetting practice**—The companion CD contains an appendix that has 25 additional subnetting practice problems. Each problem shows the solutions for the subnet number, broadcast address, and valid IP addresses in each subnet. With this extra practice, you can be ready to answer subnetting questions quickly and accurately on the INTRO, ICND, and CCNA exams.

- **Companion website**—The website http://www.ciscopress.com/158720083X posts up-to-the-minute materials that further clarify complex exam topics. Check this site regularly for new and updated postings written by the author that provide further insight into the more troublesome topics on the exam.

How This Book Is Organized

This book contains 12 core chapters—Chapters 1 through 12. Chapter 13 includes some summary materials and suggestions on how to approach the exams. Each core chapter covers a subset of the topics on the ICND exam. The core chapters are organized into four parts. The chapters cover the following topics:

Part I: LAN Switching

- **Chapter 1, "LAN Switching Review and Configuring Cisco 2950 LAN Switches"**—If you've taken the INTRO exam, you might have forgotten some of the details. This chapter reviews the basics of LAN switching. It also covers some basic administrative configuration on the 2950 series switches.

- **Chapter 2, "Spanning Tree Protocol"**—The *CCNA INTRO Exam Certification Guide* covers Spanning Tree Protocol (STP) briefly; this chapter takes a deeper look, including an explanation of the newer Rapid STP (RSTP).

- **Chapter 3, "Virtual LANs and Trunking"**—This chapter reviews the concepts of VLANs and VLAN trunking and explains the VLAN Trunking Protocol (VTP). It also covers VTP configuration.

Part II: TCP/IP

- **Chapter 4, "IP Addressing and Subnetting"**—This chapter gets into the depths of IP addressing and subnetting. The Boolean math operations required for analyzing IP addresses are explained, and several examples are used to detail how IP subnets are created, what IP addresses are in the same subnet, and the math required to answer exam questions about subnetting. This chapter is actually a subset of Chapter 12 in *CCNA INTRO Exam Certification Guide*, with only some differences in the questions at the beginning and end of the chapter. See the later section "How to Use These Books to Prepare for the CCNA Exam" for suggestions on how to use this chapter.

- **Chapter 5, "RIP, IGRP, and Static Route Concepts and Configuration"**—Routing Information Protocol (RIP) and Interior Gateway Routing Protocol (IGRP) are two long-standing IP routing protocols. This chapter explains their underlying logic, called distance vector, and shows you how to configure the protocols in a Cisco router.

- **Chapter 6, "OSPF and EIGRP Concepts and Configuration"**—Open Shortest Path First (OSPF) and Enhanced IGRP (EIGRP) are two more advanced and more powerful IP routing protocols. This chapter explains their underlying logic and shows you how to configure them in a Cisco router.

- **Chapter 7, "Advanced Routing Protocol Topics"**—Many IP routing protocols have similar features. This chapter covers some of the more complicated similar features of these routing protocols, including variable-length subnet masking (VLSM) support and route summarization.

- **Chapter 8, "Advanced TCP/IP Topics"**—In this final chapter on topics related specifically to TCP/IP, several small but important topics are covered, including Classless Interdomain Routing (CIDR) and Network Address Translation (NAT).

Part III: Wide-Area Networks

- **Chapter 9, "Point-to-Point Leased Line Implementation"**—This chapter covers the two popular data-link protocols used on point-to-point links—HDLC and PPP.

- **Chapter 10, "ISDN and Dial-on-Demand Routing"**—This chapter covers ISDN concepts and configuration, with a fair number of samples covering dial-on-demand routing (DDR), which is one way of causing a dialed ISDN connection to be established between routers.

- **Chapter 11, "Frame Relay"**—Engineers deploy Frame Relay more than any other WAN protocol today. This chapter reviews the details of how Frame Relay accomplishes its goal of delivering frames to multiple WAN-connected sites. This chapter also describes Frame Relay configuration, with its many options.

Part IV: Network Security

- **Chapter 12, "IP Access Control List Security"**—IP Access Control Lists (ACLs) filter IP packets as they pass through a router. This chapter explains the concepts and the configuration.

Part V: Final Preparation

- **Chapter 13, "Final Preparation"**—This chapter includes a variety of suggestions for taking the exam. It also provides several exercises that help you review some of the material in the book.

When you are finished with the core chapters, you have several options as to how to finish your exam preparation. Additional questions and exercises in Chapter 13 provide a method of final preparation. You can review the questions at the end of each chapter, and you can use the CD's testing software to practice the exam.

Part VI: Appendixes

- **Appendix A, "Answers to the "Do I Know This Already" Quizzes and Q&A Sections"**—Includes the answers to all the questions from Chapters 1 through 12. This appendix is available in printable format from the main menu of the CD-ROM.

- **Appendix B, "Binary to Decimal Conversion Table"**—Lists decimal values 0 through 255, along with the binary equivalents.

- **Appendix C, "Using the Simulation Software for the Hands-On Exercises"**—Provides instructions for accessing the NetSim network simulator that comes with the book. This appendix also lists the labs and scenarios from this book that can be performed using NetSim.

- **Appendix D, "Comparisons of Dynamic Routing Protocols"**—For those of you that do not also have a copy of the CCNA INTRO Exam Certification Guide, Appendix D holds a reprint of Chapter 14 from that book. This appendix summarizes the various features of routing protocols, and provides some basic comparisons.

- **Appendix E, "Configuring Cisco 1900 Switches"**—Although highly unlikely to be on the exam, many people still have old Cisco 1900 series switches for practicing their LAN skills for the exam. This appendix is included for reference for people that do not have access to a 2950 switch.

- **Appendix F, "ICND Exam Updates: Version 1.0"**—This appendix covers a variety of short topics that either clarify or expand upon topics covered earlier in the book. This appendix is updated from time to time, and posted at http://www.ciscopress.com/ccna, with the most recent version available at the time of printing included here as Appendix F. (The first page of the appendix includes instructions on how to check to see if a later version of Appendix F is available online.)

To study for the ICND exam, you can simply take this book and start reading. This study plan is simple. However, if you have some experience in or knowledge of Cisco products and networking protocols, you might be able to save some study time while taking small risks. Figure I-1 shows the progression you should take through the books as you prepare for the INTRO exam.

Figure I-1 *How to Approach Each Chapter of This Book*

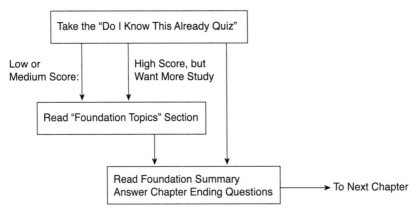

In each chapter, an assessment quiz called the "Do I Know This Already?" (DIKTA) quiz helps you decide if you already know a lot of the material in the chapter. The DIKTA quiz does not quiz you on every topic in the chapter. It focuses on a representative sample from that chapter. Doing well on the DIKTA quiz indicates how much you already know about the topic.

Based on your DIKTA score and your confidence level, you can decide whether to skip the "Foundation Topics" section. Regardless, everyone should at least read the "Foundation Summary" section and answer all the questions at the end of the chapter. If you get a good score on the DIKTA quiz and then miss a lot of the open-ended questions at the end of the chapter, you might still consider reading the "Foundations Topics" section of that chapter.

After you have completed Chapters 1 through 12, you can move on to your final preparation. Several activities help you with your final preparation:

■ Read Appendix D for the *CCNA INTRO Exam Certification Guide* and Appendix F for the *CCNA ICND Exam Certification Guide*. These appendixes clarify and expand upon key topics from the books.

■ Read Chapter 13. It contains some exam-taking tips and exercises that reinforce materials from all parts of the book.

■ Answer the chapter-ending questions again. These questions are generally harder than those on the CD because they are open-ended.

■ Review the "Foundation Summary" sections of each chapter.

- Prepare for hands-on questions on the exam. You should definitely perform all simluated questions using the exam engine on the CD. Also, you may want to either read or perform the scenarios in chapter 13, the scenarios in CD-only appendix B, and the labs in CD-only appendix C. Appendix C in this book (not the CD-only appendix C), titled, "Using the Simulation Software for Hands-on Exercises", both summarizes all the hands-on exercises included with the book that can be performed on the simulator.

- Practice subnetting. If needed, use the subnetting appendix on the CD. You get 25 more subnetting questions, with answers worked out, most using difficult subnet masks.

- Using the exam engine on the CD, select "Questions from the Book" instead of "Questions only on the CD." By doing so, you are quizzed from the CD, but with questions that appear in the DIKTA quizzes. Use practice mode, and drill on these questions until you can answer them automatically.

- Finally, using the CD, deselect Book Questions, and select New Questions. Then use exam mode and take a couple of simulated exams. This should be the final step in preparation.

For any questions you miss, read the relevant sections of the book for a refresher.

At this point, you should be well-prepared for the ICND exam!

How to Use These Books to Prepare for the CCNA Exam

If you are using this book to study for the ICND exam, just follow the plan outlined in the last few pages. However, to use this book to study for the CCNA exam, you really should use both this book and the *CCNA INTRO Exam Certification Guide*. (By the way, if you haven't bought this book yet, and you want both, you can generally get the pair cheaper by buying a set, called the *CCNA Certification Library*.) These two books were designed to be used together to help those who want to get their CCNA certification by taking a single exam.

Notice that the names of four of the six parts in the *CCNA INTRO Exam Certification Guide* match the names of all five parts in the *CCNA ICND Exam Certification Guide*. Essentially, when you complete a part in the first book, if there is a like-named part in the second book, you read that part next. After finishing that part in the CCNA ICND Exam Certification Guide, you move back to the *CCNA INTRO Exam Certification Guide*. Figure I-2 outlines the process.

Moving back and forth between books helps you focus on one general topic at a time. Each time you transition to the ICND book, you read a lot of additional material about that topic, plus a few things that seem like review. (Those review items are included for those who are using the ICND book for their ICND exam preparation.) As a result, you complete the coverage of each major topic before moving on to the next.

Figure I-2 *Reading Plan When Studying for the CCNA Exam*

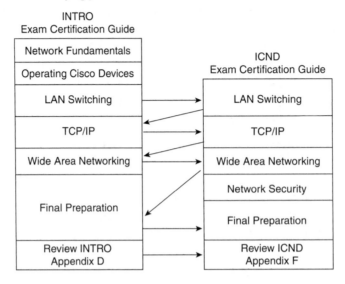

There is one point in this reading plan for the CCNA exam for which you should consider a couple of options. Cisco includes one major topic, IP addressing and subnetting, on both the INTRO and ICND exams. So that topic is covered in both books for those who are studying for the INTRO and ICND exams. Chapter 12 in the *CCNA INTRO Exam Certification Guide* covers subnetting, and Chapter 4 in the *CCNA ICND Exam Certification Guide* does as well. If you are studying for the CCNA exam, you should keep in mind that the "Foundation Topics" of the ICND book's Chapter 4—the core part of the chapter—is a subset of the INTRO book's Chapter 12. So there's no need to read this material twice!

When reading the books, you should take a few minutes to look at the ICND book's Chapter 4. The DIKTA quiz has some new questions, and some new questions appear at the end of the chapter that are different from the INTRO book's Chapter 12. You might also make some adjustments in the order in which you read the chapters. Figure I-3 outlines two suggested options for your IP subnetting study with these two books.

By choosing the first of the two options shown in the figure, you can review IP subnetting after you have finished all the TCP/IP topics from the first book. If you choose the second option, you can inundate yourself with IP addressing all at once, finish all the TCP/IP-specific coverage in the first book, and then move back to the second book for the rest of the TCP/IP coverage. Either plan can work well; it's just a matter of personal preference.

Figure I-3 *Study Plan Options for Studying IP Addressing When Preparing for the CCNA Exam*

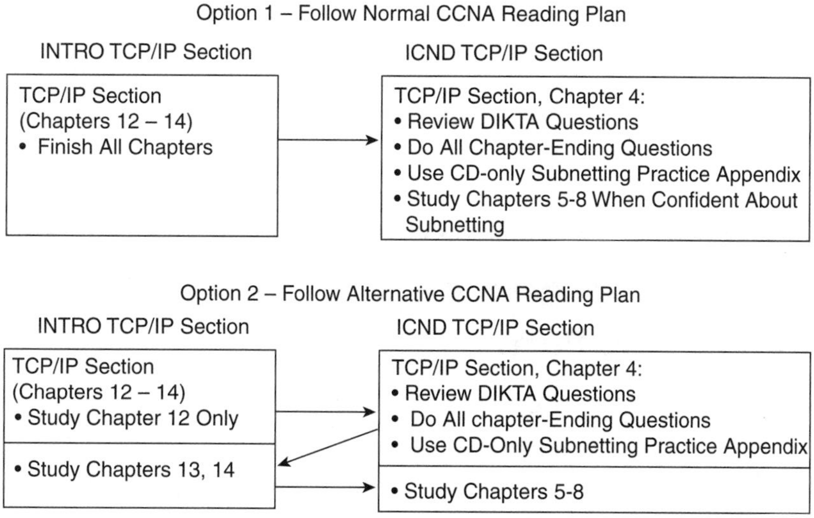

Option 1 – Follow Normal CCNA Reading Plan

INTRO TCP/IP Section   ICND TCP/IP Section

TCP/IP Section
(Chapters 12 – 14)
• Finish All Chapters

TCP/IP Section, Chapter 4:
• Review DIKTA Questions
• Do All Chapter-Ending Questions
• Use CD-only Subnetting Practice Appendix
• Study Chapters 5-8 When Confident About
  Subnetting

Option 2 – Follow Alternative CCNA Reading Plan

INTRO TCP/IP Section   ICND TCP/IP Section

TCP/IP Section
(Chapters 12 – 14)
• Study Chapter 12 Only

• Study Chapters 13, 14

TCP/IP Section, Chapter 4:
• Review DIKTA Questions
• Do All chapter-Ending Questions
• Use CD-Only Subnetting Practice Appendix

• Study Chapters 5-8

For More Information

If you have any comments about this book, you can submit them via the www.ciscopress.com website. Just go to the website, select Contact Us, and enter your message.

Cisco occasionally might make changes that affect the CCNA certification. You should always check www.cisco.com for the latest details.

Over time, reader feedback allows us to gauge which topics readers are having the most problems with when taking the exams. To assist with those topics, the author posts new materials clarifying and expanding upon these exam topics, in PDF documents at http://www.ciscopress.com/ccna. That living document is printed in this book as Appendix F, "ICND Exam Updates: Version 1.0". To make sure you have the latest version, visit http://www.ciscopress.com/title/158720083x, and click **Downloads** in the **More Information** box on the left side of the page. If the version number shown with the appendix on the web page is later than the version in this book, you should download the one from the website, and use it. This appendix gives the author a chance to provide more insight into the more troublesome topics on the exam.

The CCNA certification is arguably the most important Cisco certification. It certainly is the most popular. It's required for several other certifications, and it's the first step in distinguishing yourself as someone who has proven knowledge of Cisco.

This book is designed to help you attain CCNA certification. It is the CCNA INTRO certification book from the only Cisco-authorized publisher. We at Cisco Press believe that this book can help you achieve CCNA certification, but the real work is up to you! I trust that your time will be well spent.

Cisco Published ICND Exam Topics*
Covered in This Part:

1   Design or modify a simple LAN using Cisco products

4   Design a simple internetwork using Cisco products

10   Configure a switch with VLANS and inter-switch communication

11   Implement a LAN

12   Customize a switch configuration to meet specified network requirements

15   Utilize the OSI model as a guide for systematic network troubleshooting

16   Perform LAN and VLAN troubleshooting

19   Troubleshoot a device as part of a working network

22   Describe the Spanning Tree process

23   Evaluate the characteristics of LAN environments

* Always re-check www.cisco.com for the latest posted exam topics

Part I: LAN Switching

This chapter covers the following subjects:

- Brief Review of LAN Switching

- Basic Configuration and Operation Commands for the Cisco 2950 Switch

CHAPTER 1

LAN Switching Review and Configuring Cisco 2950 LAN Switches

This chapter covers two different major topics. It starts with some basics about how LAN switches work. The second, and by far larger, part of this chapter covers some basic LAN switch configuration on the Cisco 2950 switch.

If you are planning on taking the two-exam approach to CCNA, and you are reading this book, you should already have passed the INTRO exam, and you are beginning to study for the ICND exam. The first part of this chapter, which reviews LAN basics, reminds you of a few details you should already know pretty well. Depending on how much you remember about LAN switching and Ethernet addresses, you might want to skip this first section.

If you're taking the one-exam approach to CCNA and you're following the reading plan described in the Introduction to this book, you already have LAN switching concepts firmly in mind from Chapter 9, "Cisco LAN Switching Basics", of the *CCNA INTRO Exam Certification Guide*. So you too can skip this first section as well.

If you want a brief review of LAN switching concepts, definitely take a few minutes to read over the first section of this chapter.

"Do I Know This Already?" Quiz

The purpose of the "Do I Know This Already?" quiz is to help you decide if you need to read the entire chapter. If you intend to read the entire chapter, you do not necessarily need to answer these questions now.

The 12-question quiz, derived from the major sections in the "Foundation Topics" section, helps you determine how to spend your limited study time.

Table 1-1 outlines the major topics discussed in this chapter and the "Do I Know This Already?" quiz questions that correspond to those topics.

Table 1-1 *"Do I Know This Already?" Foundation Topics Section-to-Question Mapping*

Foundations Topics Section	Questions Covered in This Section
Brief Review of LAN Switching	1–4
Basic Configuration and Operation Commands for the Cisco 2950 Switch	5–12

CAUTION The goal of self-assessment is to gauge your mastery of the topics in this chapter. If you don't know the answer to a question or you're only partially sure of the answer, you should mark this question as wrong for purposes of the self-assessment. Giving yourself credit for an answer you guess correctly skews your self-assessment results and might give you a false sense of security.

1. Which of the following statements describes part of the process of how a switch decides to forward a frame destined for a unicast MAC address?

   a. It compares the unicast destination address to the bridging, or MAC address, table.

   b. It compares the unicast source address to the bridging, or MAC address, table.

   c. It forwards out all interfaces, except the incoming interface, every time.

   d. It forwards based on the VLAN ID.

   e. It compares the destination IP address to the destination MAC address.

   f. It compares the frame's incoming interface to the source MAC entry in the MAC address table.

2. Which of the following statements describes part of the process of how a LAN switch decides to forward a frame destined for a broadcast MAC address?

   a. It compares the unicast destination address to the bridging, or MAC address, table.

   b. It compares the unicast source address to the bridging, or MAC address, table.

   c. It forwards out all interfaces, except the incoming interface, every time.

   d. It forwards based on the VLAN ID.

   e. It compares the destination IP address to the destination MAC address.

   f. It compares the frame's incoming interface to the source MAC entry in the MAC address table.

3. Which of the following statements best describes what a switch does with a frame destined for an unknown unicast address?

    a. It forwards out all interfaces except the incoming interface.

    b. It forwards based on the VLAN ID.

    c. It compares the destination IP address to the destination MAC address.

    d. It compares the frame's incoming interface to the source MAC entry in the MAC address table.

4. Which of the following comparisons does a switch make when deciding whether to add a new MAC address to its bridging table?

    a. It compares the unicast destination address to the bridging, or MAC address, table.

    b. It compares the unicast source address to the bridging, or MAC address, table.

    c. It compares the VLAN ID and source MAC address to the bridging, or MAC address, table.

    d. It compares the destination IP address's ARP cache entry to the bridging, or MAC address, table.

5. In which of the following CLI modes could you configure the duplex setting for interface fastethernet 0/5?

    a. User mode

    b. Enable mode

    c. Global configuration mode

    d. Setup mode

    e. Interface configuration mode

6. In which of the following CLI modes could you issue a command to erase the switch's initial configuration?

    a. User mode

    b. Enable mode

    c. Setup mode

    d. Global configuration mode

    e. Interface configuration mode

7. What type of switch memory is used to store the configuration used by the switch when the switch first comes up?

    a. RAM

    b. ROM

    c. Flash

    d. NVRAM

    e. Bubble

8. What command copies the configuration from RAM into NVRAM?

    a. **copy running-config tftp**

    b. **copy tftp running-config**

    c. **copy running-config start-up-config**

    d. **copy start-up-config running-config**

    e. **copy startup-config running-config**

    f. **copy running-config startup-config**

9. You configure the **enable secret** command, followed by the **enable password** command, from the console. You log out of the switch and log back in at the console. Which command defines the password you had to enter to access privileged mode again from the console?

    a. **enable password**

    b. **enable secret**

    c. Neither **enable password** nor **enable secret**

    d. You cannot configure both the enable secret password and the enable password at the same time.

10. What command is used on a switch to set the switch's IP address for in-band management to 10.1.1.1, subnet mask 255.255.255.0?

    a. **ip address 10.1.1.1 255.255.255.0**

    b. **ip address 10.1.1.1 mask 255.255.255.0**

    c. **address 10.1.1.1 255.255.255.0**

    d. **set ip address 10.1.1.1 255.255.255.0**

    e. **set ip address 10.1.1.1 mask 255.255.255.0**

11. Imagine a 2950 switch with a PC plugged into interface fastethernet 0/1 and a router plugged into interface fastethernet 0/2. The PC needs to use TCP/IP to communicate through the router with other TCP/IP hosts. In what configuration mode could you enter the switch's IP address?

    a. User mode

    b. Enable mode

    c. Setup mode

    d. Global configuration mode

    e. Interface configuration mode for fastethernet 0/1

    f. Interface configuration mode for fastethernet 0/2

    g. None of the above

12. What interface subcommand tells the switch to take an interface out of service?

    a. down

    b. admin down

    c. shutdown

    d. admin shutdown

    e. disable

The answers to the "Do I Know This Already?" quiz appear in Appendix A. The suggested choices for your next step are as follows:

- **10 or less overall score**—Read the entire chapter. This includes the "Foundation Topics," "Foundation Summary," and "Q&A" sections.

- **11 or 12 overall score**—If you want more review on these topics, skip to the "Foundation Summary" section and then go to the "Q&A" section. Otherwise, move to the next chapter.

Foundation Topics

Cisco's LAN switch revenues surpassed router revenues about the time the CCNA exam was first announced, in 1998, so there is little doubt about the importance of LAN switches to Cisco. Not surprisingly, both CCNA exams cover LAN switching concepts extensively.

This chapter starts with a brief review of LAN switching topics. The majority of this chapter is devoted to basic switch configuration for a Cisco 2950 switch.

Brief Review of LAN Switching

LAN switches forward Ethernet frames—they just have to decide when to forward them and when not to. Most switch logic relates somehow to the source and destination MAC addresses inside the Ethernet frame headers of the frames sent through the LAN. Switch logic is also dependent on the type of MAC addresses used. So, a brief review of Ethernet addresses can help shed some light on how LAN switches work.

The IEEE defines three general categories of MAC addresses on Ethernet:

- **Unicast addresses**—A MAC address that identifies a single LAN interface card. Today, most cards use the MAC address that is burned into the card.

- **Broadcast addresses**—The most often used IEEE group MAC address, the broadcast address, has a value of FFFF.FFFF.FFFF (in hexadecimal notation). The broadcast address implies that all devices on the LAN should receive and process a frame sent to the broadcast address.

- **Multicast addresses**—Frames sent to unicast addresses are destined for a single device; frames sent to a broadcast address are sent to all devices on the LAN. Frames sent to multicast addresses are meant for all devices that care to receive the frame, meaning that all devices might receive the frame, none, or some number in between. Some applications need to communicate with multiple other devices. By sending one frame, all the devices that care about receiving the data sent by that application can process the data, and the rest can ignore it.

With these reminders of the three types of Ethernet MAC addresses, you can appreciate the logic used by a LAN switch. A switch listens for frames that enter all its interfaces. After receiving a frame, a switch decides whether to forward a frame and, if so, out which port(s). Switches basically perform three tasks:

- **Learning**—The switch learns MAC addresses by examining the source MAC address of each frame the bridge receives. By learning, the switch can make good forwarding choices in the future.

- **Forwarding or filtering**—The switch decides when to forward a frame or when to filter (not forward) it based on the destination MAC address. The switch looks at the previously learned MAC addresses in an address table to decide where to forward the frames.

- **Loop prevention**—The switch creates a loop-free environment with other bridges by using Spanning Tree Protocol (STP). Having physically redundant links helps LAN availability, and STP prevents the switch logic from letting frames loop around the network indefinitely, congesting the LAN.

The next few sections take you through the first two tasks a switch performs. The third task, loop prevention, is performed using STP, which is covered in depth in Chapter 2, "Spanning Tree Protocol."

The Forward-Versus-Filter Decision

Switches reduce network overhead by forwarding traffic from one segment to another only when necessary. To decide whether to forward a frame, the switch uses a dynamically built table called a *bridge table* or *MAC address table*. The switch examines the address table to decide whether it should forward a frame.

For example, consider the simple network shown in Figure 1-1. Fred first sends a frame to Barney and then one to Wilma.

The switch decides to filter (in other words, to not forward) the frame that Fred sends to Barney. Fred sends a frame with a destination MAC address of 0200.2222.2222, which is Barney's MAC address. The switch overhears the frame, because it is attached to Hub1. The switch then decides what common sense tells you from looking at the figure—it should not forward the frame, because Barney, attached to Hub1 as well, already has received the frame. (Hubs simply repeat the signal out all ports, for all frames, so the switch receives everything sent by either Barney or Fred.) But how does the switch know to not forward the frame? The switch decides to filter the frame because it received the frame on port E0, and it knows that Barney's MAC is also located out E0.

Conversely, the switch decides to forward the frame that Fred sends to Wilma in the bottom part of the figure. The frame enters the switch's E0 interface, and the switch knows that the destination address, 0200.3333.3333, is located somewhere out its E1 interface. So the switch forwards the frame.

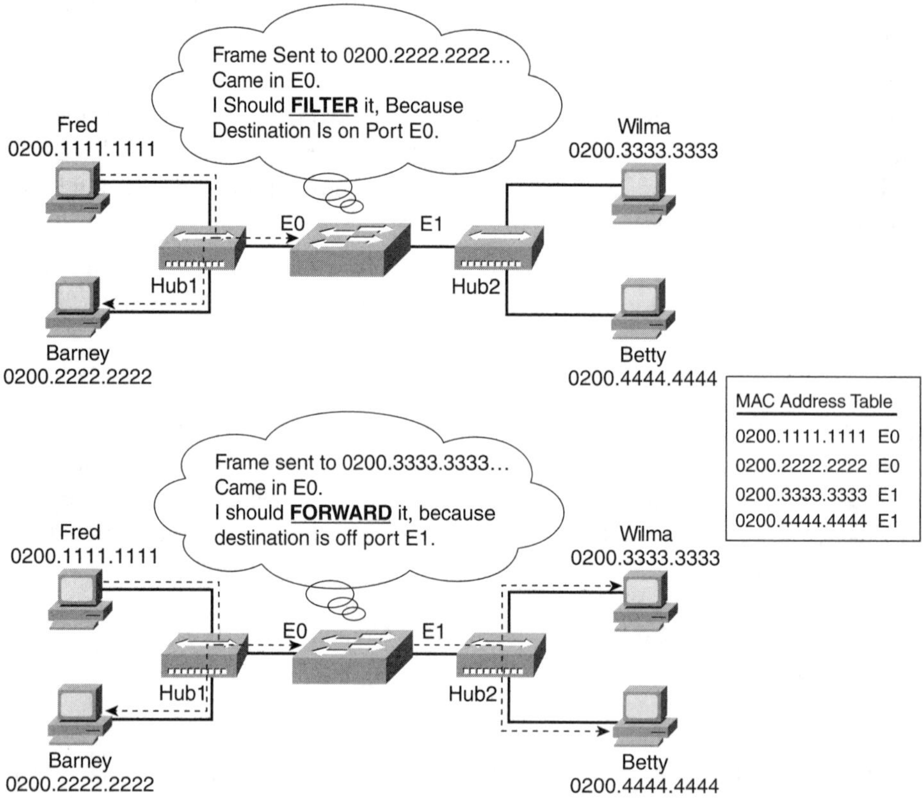

Figure 1-1 *Switch Forwarding and Filtering Decision*

How Switches Learn MAC Addresses

The filter-versus-forward decision works best when the switch knows where all the MAC addresses are in the network. Switches dynamically learn the MAC addresses in the network to build its MAC address table. With a full, accurate MAC address table, the switch can make accurate forwarding and filtering decisions.

Switches build the MAC address table by listening to incoming frames and examining the frame's source MAC address. If a frame enters the switch, and the source MAC address is not in the address table, the switch creates an entry in the table. The MAC address is placed in the table, along with the interface in which the frame arrived. Switch learning logic is that simple!

Figure 1-2 shows the same network as Figure 1-1, but before the switch has built any bridge table entries. This figure shows the first two frames sent in this network—a frame from Fred, addressed to Barney, and then Barney's response, addressed to Fred.

Figure 1-2 *Switch Learning: Adding Two Entries to an Empty Table*

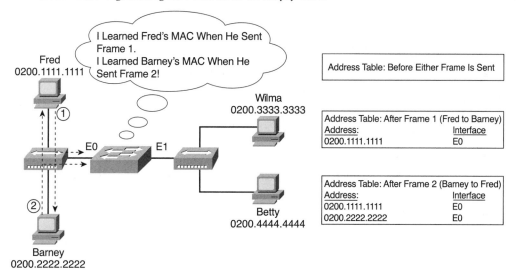

As shown in the figure, after Fred sends his first frame to Barney, the switch adds an entry for 0200.1111.1111, Fred's MAC address, associated with interface E0. When Barney replies in Step 2, the switch adds a second entry, this one for 0200.2222.2222, Barney's MAC address. Learning always occurs by looking at the source MAC address in the frame.

Forwarding Unknown Unicasts and Broadcasts

Bridges forward LAN broadcast frames, and unknown unicast frames, out all ports. LAN broadcasts, by definition, are received by all devices on the same LAN. So the switch simply forwards broadcasts out all ports, except the one on which the broadcast was received. Switches forward *unknown unicast frames*, which are frames whose destination MAC addresses are not yet in the bridging table, out all ports as well. The switch floods the frame with the hope that the unknown device will be on some other Ethernet segment, it will reply, and the switch will build a correct entry in the address table.

Generally speaking, switches also forward LAN multicast frames out all ports, just like they do for broadcasts. However, a few multicast features in switches limit the flooding of multicasts, such as Internet Group Management Protocol (IGMP) snooping.

LAN Switch Logic Summary

The following list provides a quick review of the basic logic a switch uses:

1. A frame is received.

2. If the destination is a broadcast or multicast, forward on all ports except the port on which the frame was received.

3. If the destination is a unicast, and the address is not in the address table, forward on all ports except the port on which the frame was received.

4. If the destination is a unicast, and the address is in the address table, and if the associated interface is not the interface on which the frame arrived, forward the frame out the one correct port.

5. Otherwise, filter (do not forward) the frame.

With this brief review of LAN switching concepts, you should now be ready to read the LAN materials for the ICND exam, as covered in the first three chapters of this book.

Basic Configuration and Operation Commands for the Cisco 2950 Switch

If you know how to navigate a Cisco router, you know how to navigate a Cisco 2950 switch. This chapter covers some of the more common configuration and operational commands in the switch. Chapters 2 and 3 cover some additional commands for STP and VLAN configuration, respectively.

For reference, Table 1-2 lists the switch configuration commands referred to in this section. Table 1-3 lists the commands used for operation and troubleshooting.

Table 1-2   *Commands for Catalyst 2950 Switch Configuration*

Command	Description
interface vlan 1	Global command. Moves the user to interface configuration mode for a VLAN interface.
ip address *address subnet-mask*	Interface configuration mode command that sets the IP address for in-band switch management.
ip default-gateway *address*	Global command that sets the default gateway so that the management interface can be reached from a remote network.
interface fastethernet 0/*x*	Puts the user into interface configuration mode for that interface.

Table 1-2 *Commands for Catalyst 2950 Switch Configuration (Continued)*

Command	Description
duplex {auto | full | half}	Interface configuration mode command that sets the duplex mode for the interface.
speed {10 | 100 | 1000 | auto | nonegotiate}	Interface configuration mode command that sets the speed for the interface.
switchport port-security mac-address *mac-address*	Interface configuration mode command that statically adds a specific MAC address as an allowed MAC address on the interface.
switchport port-security mac-address sticky	Interface subcommand that tells the switch to learn MAC addresses on the interface and add them to the configuration for the interface as secure MAC addresses.
switchport port-security maximum *value*	Global command that sets the maximum number of static secure MAC addresses that can be assigned to a single interface.
switchport port-security violation {protect | restrict | shutdown}	Global configuration command that tells the switch what to do if an inappropriate MAC address tries to access the network through a secure switch port.
hostname *name*	Sets the switch's host name.
line con 0	Global command that places the user in console configuration mode.
line vty 0 15	Global command that places the user in vty configuration mode.
login	Console or vty configuration mode command that tells the switch to ask for a password for a console user or Telnet user, respectively.
password *password*	Console or vty configuration mode command that sets the password required.
enable secret *password*	Global command that sets the switch's enable password. The password is stored in a hashed format, meaning that someone reading the configuration file will not see the correct text password.
enable password *password*	Global command that sets the switch's enable password. The enable secret password is used if both are configured.

Table 1-3 *Commands for Catalyst 2950 Switch Operation*

Command	Description
configure terminal	Places the user in configuration mode.
show interfaces fastethernet 0/*x*	Displays the interface status for a physical 10/100 interface.
show interfaces vlan 1	Displays the IP address configuration.
show interfaces [*interface-id* | vlan *vlan-id*] [description | etherchannel | pruning | stats | status [err-disabled] | switchport | trunk]	Generic command, with many options, for displaying information about specific interfaces.
show running-config	Shows the currently active configuration.
show startup-config	Shows startup-config, which is used the next time the switch is reloaded.
show mac-address-table [aging-time | count | dynamic | static] [address *hw-addr*] [interface *interface-id*] [vlan *vlan-id*]	Displays the MAC address table. The security option displays information about the restricted or static settings.
show port-security [interface *interface-id*] [address]	Shows information about security options configured on an interface.
erase startup-config	Erases the startup-config file.
show version	Lists information about the version of software in the switch.
reload	Re-initializes all software and hardware in the switch.

Basic Switch Operation

You can order a Cisco 2950, take it out of its box, plug it in, and it works! So, rather than starting with configuration, this section begins with a basic examination of switch **show** commands. Almost every command that helps you look at the status of a switch—or a router, for that matter—starts with the word **show**, so most people just call troubleshooting commands **show** commands. Example 1-1 shows the output of several popular **show** commands on a 2950 switch that has no added configuration.

Example 1-1 *Popular* show *Commands on a 2950 Switch*

```
Switch>
Switch>enable

Switch#show interfaces fastEthernet 0/13
FastEthernet0/13 is up, line protocol is up
  Hardware is Fast Ethernet, address is 000a.b7dc.b78d (bia 000a.b7dc.b78d)
  MTU 1500 bytes, BW 100000 Kbit, DLY 100 usec,
     reliability 255/255, txload 1/255, rxload 1/255
```

Example 1-1 *Popular* show *Commands on a 2950 Switch (Continued)*

```
     Encapsulation ARPA, loopback not set
     Keepalive set (10 sec)
     Full-duplex, 100Mb/s
     input flow-control is off, output flow-control is off
     ARP type: ARPA, ARP Timeout 04:00:00
     Last input never, output 00:00:01, output hang never
     Last clearing of "show interface" counters never
     Input queue: 0/75/0/0 (size/max/drops/flushes); Total output drops: 0
     Queueing strategy: fifo
     Output queue :0/40 (size/max)
     5 minute input rate 0 bits/sec, 0 packets/sec
     5 minute output rate 0 bits/sec, 0 packets/sec
        0 packets input, 0 bytes, 0 no buffer
        Received 0 broadcasts, 0 runts, 0 giants, 0 throttles
        0 input errors, 0 CRC, 0 frame, 0 overrun, 0 ignored
        0 watchdog, 0 multicast, 0 pause input
        0 input packets with dribble condition detected
        20 packets output, 2291 bytes, 0 underruns
        0 output errors, 0 collisions, 1 interface resets
        0 babbles, 0 late collision, 0 deferred
        0 lost carrier, 0 no carrier, 0 PAUSE output
        0 output buffer failures, 0 output buffers swapped out

Switch#show interfaces status

Port    Name            Status         Vlan       Duplex  Speed Type
Fa0/1                   notconnect     1             auto   auto 10/100BaseTX
Fa0/2                   notconnect     1             auto   auto 10/100BaseTX
Fa0/3                   notconnect     1             auto   auto 10/100BaseTX
Fa0/4                   notconnect     1             auto   auto 10/100BaseTX
Fa0/5                   connected      1           a-full  a-100 10/100BaseTX
Fa0/6                   notconnect     1             auto   auto 10/100BaseTX
Fa0/7                   notconnect     1             auto   auto 10/100BaseTX
Fa0/8                   connected      1           a-full  a-100 10/100BaseTX
Fa0/9                   notconnect     1             auto   auto 10/100BaseTX
Fa0/10                  notconnect     1             auto   auto 10/100BaseTX
Fa0/11                  notconnect     1             auto   auto 10/100BaseTX
Fa0/12                  notconnect     1             auto   auto 10/100BaseTX
Fa0/13                  connected      1           a-full  a-100 10/100BaseTX
Fa0/14                  notconnect     1             auto   auto 10/100BaseTX
Fa0/15                  notconnect     1             auto   auto 10/100BaseTX
Fa0/16                  notconnect     1             auto   auto 10/100BaseTX
Fa0/17                  notconnect     1             auto   auto 10/100BaseTX
Fa0/18                  notconnect     1             auto   auto 10/100BaseTX
Fa0/19                  notconnect     1             auto   auto 10/100BaseTX
Fa0/20                  notconnect     1             auto   auto 10/100BaseTX
Fa0/21                  notconnect     1             auto   auto 10/100BaseTX
```

continues

Example 1-1 *Popular* show *Commands on a 2950 Switch (Continued)*

```
Fa0/22                         notconnect  1        auto   auto 10/100BaseTX
Fa0/23                         notconnect  1        auto   auto 10/100BaseTX
Fa0/24                         notconnect  1        auto   auto 10/100BaseTX
Gi0/1                          notconnect  1        auto   auto unknown
Gi0/2                          notconnect  1        auto   auto unknown

switch#show mac-address-table dynamic
          Mac Address Table
-------------------------------------------

Vlan    Mac Address     Type     Ports
----    -----------     ----     -----
   1    0007.8580.71b8  DYNAMIC  Fa0/5
   1    0007.8580.7208  DYNAMIC  Fa0/8
   1    0007.8580.7312  DYNAMIC  Fa0/13


Total Mac Addresses for this criterion: 2
Switch#
Switch#show running-config
Building configuration...

Current configuration : 1451 bytes
!
version 12.1
no service pad
service timestamps debug uptime
service timestamps log uptime
no service password-encryption
!
hostname Switch
!
ip subnet-zero
!
spanning-tree extend system-id
!
interface FastEthernet0/1
 no ip address
interface FastEthernet0/2
 no ip address
interface FastEthernet0/3
 no ip address
interface FastEthernet0/4
 no ip address
interface FastEthernet0/5
 no ip address
interface FastEthernet0/6
 no ip address
```

Example 1-1 *Popular* show *Commands on a 2950 Switch (Continued)*

```
interface FastEthernet0/7
 no ip address
interface FastEthernet0/8
 no ip address
interface FastEthernet0/9
 no ip address
interface FastEthernet0/10
 no ip address
interface FastEthernet0/11
 no ip address
interface FastEthernet0/12
 no ip address
interface FastEthernet0/13
 no ip address
interface FastEthernet0/14
 no ip address
!
! (Lines omitted for brevity)
!
interface Vlan1
 no ip address
 shutdown
!
ip classless
ip http server
!
line con 0
line vty 5 15
!
end
Switch#show startup-config
%% Non-volatile configuration memory is not present
```

Although Example 1-1 is rather long, the more important points to consider are highlighted. To begin, the user at the console is immediately placed in user mode, as implied by the command prompt that ends in a >. The switch has no enable password set, so the **enable** command places the user in enable mode without the need for a password. For security reasons alone, you will want to learn enough to be able to do basic configuration in a Cisco switch!

Next, the **show interfaces fastethernet 0/13** command lists basic status and configuration information about fastethernet interface 0/13. That interface cable connects to a working PC, so the status in the first line of the command output shows a status of "up" and "up." An interface is not yet operational if both status words do not say "up."

A more practical command for looking at all interfaces at once comes next in the example—the **show interfaces status** command. This command lists the status of each interface in a single line, including the speed and duplex settings negotiated on that interface. In this example, only three working devices are cabled to the switch. You can tell from the command output which interfaces are currently active (0/5, 0/8, and 0/13).

Next, the **show mac-address-table dynamic** command lists all the dynamically learned entries in the bridging table. (Note: the **show mac address-table** command performs the same function, so either is valid.) One MAC address has been learned on each of the three interfaces that showed up as "connected" in the **show interfaces status** command output earlier in the example. The **show mac-address-table dynamic** command, as seen in the example, shows only the dynamically learned MAC addresses. The **show mac-address-table** command shows both static and dynamic entries.

Next in the example, the **show running-config** command lists the default configuration. (The output has been edited slightly to save a little space.) Notice that each interface is listed, as well as an interface called Vlan1. The switch's management IP address will be configured on that interface, as shown later in this chapter.

The **show startup-config** command at the very end of the example lists some very interesting output. It says that nothing has been saved! To build this example, I started by erasing the startup-config with the **erase startup-config** command, and then I reloaded the switch (with the **reload** command). I did not configure anything, but the switch did indeed come up and start working. Because I had not done a **copy running-config startup-config** command since erasing the startup-config earlier, nothing has been stored in NVRAM, so the file is empty, as implied by the message shown in the example. Later, after changing the configuration, you would typically want to save the configuration using the **copy running-config startup-config** command, and the startup-config would then have something in it.

The switch is now up and working. Next you will see some of the more typical basic switch configuration commands.

Typical Basic Administrative Configuration

The switch comes up and works, with all the ports in VLAN 1, without any configuration. However, you typically want to configure something. Example 1-2 shows a typical initial configuration session on a 2950 switch, along with some other commands that point out what the configuration has accomplished.

Example 1-2   *Basic Configuration of a 2950 Switch*

```
Switch>enable
Switch#
Switch#configure terminal
Enter configuration commands, one per line.  End with CNTL/Z.
Switch(config)#hostname fred
fred(config)#enable secret cisco
fred(config)#line con 0
fred(config-line)#password barney
fred(config-line)#login
fred(config-line)#line vty 0 15
fred(config-line)#password wilma
fred(config-line)#login
fred(config-line)#interface fastethernet0/5
fred(config-if)#speed 100
fred(config-if)#duplex half
fred(config-if)#
00:23:49: %LINEPROTO-5-UPDOWN: Line protocol on Interface FastEthernet0/5, changed
  state to down
00:23:52: %LINK-3-UPDOWN: Interface FastEthernet0/5, changed state to up
00:23:54: %LINEPROTO-5-UPDOWN: Line protocol on Interface FastEthernet0/5, changed
  state to up
fred(config-if)#
fred(config-if)#shutdown
fred(config-if)#
00:24:33: %LINK-5-CHANGED: Interface FastEthernet0/5, changed state to
  administratively down
00:24:34: %LINEPROTO-5-UPDOWN: Line protocol on Interface FastEthernet0/5, changed
  state to down
fred(config-if)#
fred(config-if)#no shutdown
fred(config-if)#
fred(config-if)#
00:24:42: %LINK-3-UPDOWN: Interface FastEthernet0/5, changed state to up
00:24:45: %LINEPROTO-5-UPDOWN: Line protocol on Interface FastEthernet0/5, changed
  state to up
fred(config-if)#exit
fred(config)#interface vlan 1
fred(config-if)#ip address 10.1.1.1 255.255.255.0
fred(config-if)#no shutdown
00:25:07: %LINK-3-UPDOWN: Interface Vlan1, changed state to up
00:25:08: %LINEPROTO-5-UPDOWN: Line protocol on Interface Vlan1, changed state
  to up
fred(config-if)#exit
fred(config)#ip default-gateway 10.1.1.2
fred(config)#^Z

fred#copy running-config startup-config
```

continues

Example 1-2 *Basic Configuration of a 2950 Switch (Continued)*

```
Destination filename [startup-config]?
Building configuration...
[OK]

fred#show startup-config
Using 1613 out of 393216 bytes
!
version 12.1
no service pad
service timestamps debug uptime
service timestamps log uptime
no service password-encryption
!
hostname fred
!
enable secret 5 $1$sgBC$CWUWtIwBJ1G1zedlEIYr5/
!
spanning-tree extend system-id
!
interface FastEthernet0/1
 no ip address
!
interface FastEthernet0/2
 no ip address
!
interface FastEthernet0/3
 no ip address
!
interface FastEthernet0/4
 no ip address
!
interface FastEthernet0/5
 no ip address
 duplex half
 speed 100
!
!
! Lines omitted for brevity
!
interface Vlan1
 ip address 10.1.1.1 255.255.255.0
!
ip classless
ip http server
!
line con 0
 password barney
```

Example 1-2   *Basic Configuration of a 2950 Switch (Continued)*

```
 login
line vty 0 4
 password wilma
 login
line vty 5 15
 password wilma
 login
!
end

fred#quit

fred con0 is now available

Press RETURN to get started.

User Access Verification

Password:
fred>enable
Password:
fred#
```

Rather than just listing the configuration commands, this example shows you everything that appears on the screen when you enter the commands in configuration mode.

The example begins with the user logging in to the switch. Because no configuration is added at this point, the switch does not ask for a console password or enable password. Next, the user enters configuration mode, setting the switch's name with the **hostname fred** command. Notice that the command prompt immediately changes to begin with **fred**, because the prompt starts with the host name. This is more proof that that the switch IOS accepts configuration commands immediately—so be careful out there!

Next, the user sets the enable secret password to **cisco**, the console password to **barney**, and the vty (Telnet) password to **wilma**. The **login** commands tell the switch to require a password at the console and for Telnet sessions, respectively, and the **password** commands tell it what passwords to expect. Often, the console and Telnet passwords are the same value, because both let you enter user mode; I used two different passwords in the example just to make the point that they can be different.

With this configuration, when a user Telnets to the switch, the switch prompts the user for a password, expecting **wilma**. Similarly, the switch prompts the user for a password at the console and expects **barney**. Both methods put the user into user mode. To enter privileged mode, the user uses the **enable** command and enters the enable secret password of **cisco** when prompted. (An example of that process at the console is shown at the end of the example.)

> **NOTE** Both the **enable secret** and **enable password** commands define the password needed to enter enable mode. **enable password** also defines the enable password. If only one of these two commands is in the configuration, that password is used. If both are configured, the **enable secret** password is used. Why two commands? The **enable password** command came first, but even with encryption, breaking the password was easy to do. The **enable secret** command uses a hash algorithm to store the password value in the configuration, which makes breaking the password very difficult, and more secure.

Next, the user issues the **interface Fastethernet 0/5** command to enter interface configuration mode. While there, the **duplex** and **speed** commands tell the switch to force these settings rather than use the autonegotiated settings. But the PC on the other end of the cable on interface fastethernet 0/5 has already negotiated for 100 Mbps, full-duplex—and the new duplex setting of half-duplex takes effect immediately! So that interface will no longer work for a short time.

The messages that clutter the example, immediately after the changing of the speed and duplex settings, actually confirm that interface fastethernet 0/5 was temporarily unusable. The switch issues informational messages when events occur and sends them to the console by default. So these messages tell you that the switch brought the interface down because of the duplex mismatch. The next message tells you the interface is back up again as a result of the switch and the device negotiating to use half duplex.

Next, the example just shows the basic operation of the **shutdown** and **no shutdown** commands. **shutdown** puts an interface in a down status administratively so that the interface cannot pass traffic. The **no shutdown** command brings the interface back up. The example shows the informational messages that tell you that the interface has changed status after each command.

The switch needs an IP address to allow people to Telnet to and manage the switch. The switch also needs to know a default gateway, just as an end-user PC would. The default gateway is the IP address of a router connected to the switch; the switch sends IP packets to that router to send them to IP hosts that are not on the LAN created by the switch.

To configure the IP address, you first use the **interface vlan 1** command, because the IP address of the 2950 switch is configured on that interface. Next, the **ip address** command sets the IP address and subnet mask. (IP subnet masks are covered in Chapter 4, "IP Addressing and Subnetting.") Finally, the **ip default-gateway** command, a global command, sets the default IP gateway for the switch.

Now that the configuration has been changed, you should save the configuration so that it will not be lost when the switch is reloaded. The **copy running-config startup-config** command does just that, as shown in the example.

Finally, the **show startup-config** command lists the newly stored startup configuration. Remember, the previous **show startup-config** command at the end of Example 1-2 implied that the startup-config was empty; now, the startup-config has a configuration that will be used at the switch's next reload. The **show startup-config** output highlights the configuration commands added earlier in the example.

Port Security Configuration

The last major topic for this chapter revolves around something Cisco calls *port security*. Because the network engineer knows what devices should be cabled and connected to particular interfaces on a switch, the engineer can restrict that interface so that only the expected devices can use it. If the wrong device attempts to use the interface, the switch can issue informational messages, discard frames from that device, or even shut down the interface.

To configure port security, you need to configure several things. You enable port security using the **switchport port-security** interface configuration command. Also, the 2950 switch IOS allows port security only on ports that do not connect to other switches. To designate an interface as not connecting to another switch, you use the **switchport mode access** command. Then you can statically configure the MAC addresses using the **switchport port-security mac-address** *mac-address* command.

For example, in Figure 1-3, Server 1 and Server 2 are the only devices that should ever be connected to interfaces Fastethernet 0/1 and 0/2, respectively. You can use port security to ensure that only those MAC addresses connect to those ports, as shown in Example 1-3.

Figure 1-3   *Port Security Configuration Example*

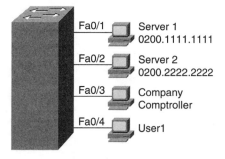

Example 1-3   *Using Port Security to Define Correct MAC Addresses of Particular Interfaces*

```
fred#show running-config
(Lines omitted for brevity)


interface FastEthernet0/1
 switchport mode access
 switchport port-security
 switchport port-security mac-address 0200.1111.1111
 no ip address
!
interface FastEthernet0/2
 switchport mode access
 switchport port-security
 switchport port-security mac-address sticky
 no ip address


fred#show port-security interface fastEthernet 0/1
Port Security : Enabled
Port status : Err-Disabled
Violation mode : Shutdown
Maximum MAC Addresses : 1
Total MAC Addresses : 1
Configured MAC Addresses : 1
Sticky MAC Addresses : 0
Aging time : 0 mins
Aging type : Absolute
SecureStatic address aging : Disabled
Security Violation count : 1


fred#show port-security interface fastEthernet 0/2
Port Security : Enabled
Port status : SecureUp
Violation mode : Shutdown
Maximum MAC Addresses : 1
Total MAC Addresses : 1
Configured MAC Addresses : 0
Sticky MAC Addresses : 1
Aging time : 0 mins
Aging type : Absolute
SecureStatic address aging : Disabled
Security Violation count : 0


fred#show running-config
(Lines omitted for brevity)
interface FastEthernet0/2
 switchport mode access
 switchport port-security
```

Example 1-3 *Using Port Security to Define Correct MAC Addresses of Particular Interfaces (Continued)*

```
switchport port-security mac-address sticky
switchport port-security mac-address sticky 0200.2222.2222
no ip address
```

This example uses two styles of port security configuration. For fastethernet 0/1, Server 1's MAC address is configured with the **switchport port-security mac-address 0200.1111.1111** command. For port security to work, the 2950 must think that the interface is an access interface rather than a trunk interface, so the **switchport mode access** command is required. And to enable port security on the interface, the **switchport port-security** command is required. Together, these three interface subcommands enable port security, and only MAC address 0200.1111.1111 is allowed to use the interface.

Port security uses a default of a single allowed MAC address per interface; you can configure up to 132 per interface using the **switchport port-security maximum** command. Also, by default, the action taken if a different MAC address tries to use the interface is to shut down the interface. You can change that default action using the **switchport port-security violation** command.

Interface fastethernet 0/2 uses a feature called *sticky secure MAC addresses*. The configuration still includes the **switchport mode access** and **switchport port-security** commands for the same reasons as on fastethernet 0/1. However, the **switchport port-security mac-address sticky** command tells the switch to learn the MAC address from the first frame sent into the switch, and then add the MAC address as a secure MAC to the running configuration. In other words, the first MAC address seen "sticks" to the configuration. So the engineer does not have to know the MAC address of the device connected to the interface ahead of time.

As it turns out, a security violation has occurred on fastethernet 0/1, while all is well on fastethernet 0/2. The **show port-security interface fastethernet 0/1** command shows that the interface is in an err-disabled state, which means that the interface has been disabled. The device connected to interface fastethernet 0/1 does not use MAC address 0200.1111.1111, so the switch receives a frame in that interface from a different MAC and takes the interface out of service.

For interface fastethernet 0/2, the interface is in "secureup" state as far as the port security feature is concerned. Notice that in the final portion of the **show running-config** output, Server 2's MAC address (0200.2222.2222) has been learned and added to the running configuration in the command **switchport port-security mac-address sticky 0200.2222.2222**. If you wanted to save the configuration so that only 0200.2222.2222 is used on that interface from now on, you would simply need to use the **copy running-config startup-config** command to save the configuration.

Foundation Summary

The "Foundation Summary" section lists the most important facts from the chapter. Although this section does not list everything that will be on the exam, a well-prepared CCNA candidate should at a minimum know all the details in each Foundation Summary before taking the exam.

Switches basically perform three tasks:

■ **Learning**—The switch learns MAC addresses by examining the source MAC address of each frame the bridge receives. By learning, the switch can make good forwarding choices in the future.

■ **Forwarding or filtering**—The switch decides when to forward a frame or when to filter (not forward) it based on the destination MAC address. The switch looks at the previously learned MAC addresses in an address table to decide where to forward the frames.

■ **Loop prevention**—The switch creates a loop-free environment with other bridges by using the Spanning Tree Protocol (STP). Having physically redundant links helps LAN availability, and STP prevents the switch logic from letting frames loop around the network indefinitely, congesting the LAN.

The following list is a quick review of the basic logic used by a switch:

1. A frame is received.

2. If the destination is a broadcast or multicast, forward on all ports except the port on which the frame was received.

3. If the destination is a unicast, and the address is not in the address table, forward on all ports except the port on which the frame was received.

4. If the destination is a unicast, and the address is in the address table, and if the associated interface is not the interface on which the frame arrived, forward the frame out the one correct port.

5. Otherwise, filter (do not forward) the frame.

Q&A

As mentioned in the Introduction, you have two choices for review questions. The following questions give you a bigger challenge than the exam because they are open-ended. By reviewing with this more-difficult question format, you can exercise your memory better and prove your conceptual and factual knowledge of the topics covered in this chapter. The answers to these questions are found in Appendix A.

For more practice with exam-like question formats, including multiple-choice questions and those using a router simulator, use the exam engine on the CD.

1. Describe how a switch decides whether it should forward a frame, and tell how it chooses the output interface.

2. How does a switch build its address table?

3. What configuration command causes the switch to require a password from a user at the console? What configuration mode context must you be in? (That is, what command(s) must you enter before this command after entering configuration mode?) List the commands in the order you must enter them while in config mode.

4. What configuration command is used to tell the switch the password that is required at the console? What configuration mode context must you be in? (That is, what command(s) must you enter before this command after entering configuration mode?) List the commands in the order in which you must enter them while in config mode.

5. What command sets the password that is required after you enter the **enable** command? Is that password encrypted by default?

6. Is the password required at the console the same one that is required when Telnet is used to access a switch?

7. Name two commands used to view the configuration to be used at a 2950 switch's next reload. Which one is the more-recent addition to IOS?

8. Name two commands used to view the configuration that is currently used in a 2950 switch. Which one is the more-recent addition to IOS?

This chapter covers the following subjects:

- Spanning Tree Protocol

- Rapid Spanning Tree (IEEE 802.1w)

- Spanning Tree Protocol Configuration

CHAPTER 2

Spanning Tree Protocol

When LAN designs require multiple switches, most network engineers include redundant Ethernet segments between the switches. The goal is simple. The switches might fail, and cables might be cut or unplugged, but if redundant switches and cables are installed, the network service might still be available for most users.

LAN designs with redundant links introduce the possibility that frames might loop around the network forever. These looping frames would cause network performance problems. Therefore, LANs use Spanning Tree Protocol (STP), which allows the redundant LAN links to be used while preventing frames from looping around the LAN indefinitely through those redundant links. This chapter covers STP, along with a few configuration commands used to tune how STP behaves.

This chapter covers the details of STP, plus a newer variation called Rapid Spanning Tree Protocol (RSTP). The end of the chapter covers STP configuration on 2950 series switches.

"Do I Know This Already?" Quiz

The purpose of the "Do I Know This Already?" quiz is to help you decide if you need to read the entire chapter. If you intend to read the entire chapter, you do not necessarily need to answer these questions now.

The ten-question quiz, derived from the major sections in the "Foundation Topics" section, helps you determine how to spend your limited study time.

Table 2-1 outlines the major topics discussed in this chapter and the "Do I Know This Already?" quiz questions that correspond to those topics.

Table 2-1 *"Do I Know This Already?" Foundation Topics Section-to-Question Mapping*

Foundations Topics Section	Questions Covered in This Section
Spanning Tree Protocol	1–6
Rapid Spanning Tree (IEEE 802.1w)	7 and 8
Spanning Tree Protocol Configuration	9 and 10

> **CAUTION**   The goal of self-assessment is to gauge your mastery of the topics in this chapter. If you don't know the answer to a question or you're only partially sure of the answer, you should mark this question as wrong for purposes of the self-assessment. Giving yourself credit for an answer you guess correctly skews your self-assessment results and might give you a false sense of security.

1. Which of the following are the port states when STP has completed convergence?

   a. Blocking

   b. Forwarding

   c. Listening

   d. Learning

   e. Discarding

   f. Disabled

2. Which of the following are transitory port states used only during the process of STP convergence?

   a. Blocking

   b. Forwarding

   c. Listening

   d. Learning

   e. Discarding

   f. Disabled

3. Which of the following bridge IDs would win election as root, assuming that the switches with these bridge IDs were in the same network?

   a. 32768:0200.1111.1111

   b. 32768:0200.2222.2222

   c. 200:0200.1111.1111

   d. 200:0200.2222.2222

   e. 40,000:0200.1111.1111

   f. 40,000:0200.2222.2222

4. Which of the following facts determines how often a root bridge or switch sends a BPDU message?

   a. The hello interval configured on a nonroot switch

   b. The hello interval configured on the root switch

   c. It is always every 2 seconds.

   d. The switch reacts to BPDUs received from the root switch by sending another BPDU 2 seconds after receiving the root BPDU.

5. What feature causes an interface to be placed in forwarding state as soon as the interface is physically active?

   a. STP

   b. RSTP

   c. Root Guard

   d. 802.1w

   e. PortFast

   f. EtherChannel

   g. Trunking

   h. 802.1q

6. What feature combines multiple parallel Ethernet links between two switches so that traffic is balanced across the links, and so that STP treats all links as one link?

   a. STP

   b. RSTP

   c. Root Guard

   d. 802.1w

   e. PortFast

   f. EtherChannel

   g. Trunking

   h. 802.1q

7. What name represents the improved STP standard that lowers convergence time?

    a. STP

    b. RSTP

    c. Root Guard

    d. 802.1w

    e. PortFast

    f. Trunking

    g. 802.1q

8. Which of the following RSTP port roles have the same name as a similar role in STP?

    a. Blocking

    b. Forwarding

    c. Listening

    d. Learning

    e. Discarding

    f. Disabled

9. On a 2950 switch, what command lets you change the value of the bridge ID without having to configure a specific value for any part of the bridge ID?

    a. **spanning-tree bridge-id**

    b. **spanning-tree vlan** *vlan-number* **root {primary | secondary}**

    c. **spanning-tree priority**

    d. **set priority**

10. What command lists spanning-tree status information on 2950 series switches?

    a. **show spanning-tree**

    b. **show stp**

    c. **show spantree**

    d. **show span-tree**

    e. **debug span**

The answers to the "Do I Know This Already?" quiz appear in Appendix A. The suggested choices for your next step are as follows:

- **8 or less overall score**—Read the entire chapter. This includes the "Foundation Topics," "Foundation Summary," and "Q&A" sections.

- **9 or 10 overall score**—If you want more review on these topics, skip to the "Foundation Summary" section and then go to the "Q&A" section. Otherwise, move to the next chapter.

Foundation Topics

Spanning Tree Protocol

Without Spanning Tree Protocol (STP), frames would loop for an indefinite period of time in networks with physically redundant links. To prevent looping frames, STP blocks some ports from forwarding frames so that only one active path exists between any pair of LAN segments (collision domains). The result of STP is both good and bad. Frames do not loop infinitely, which makes the LAN usable, which is good. However, the network does not actively take advantage of some of the redundant links, because they are blocked to prevent frames from looping. Some users' traffic travels a seemingly longer path through the network, because a shorter physical path is blocked, which is bad. However, the net result (yep, I wrote that on purpose!) is good. If frames looped indefinitely, the LAN would be unusable. So, STP has some minor unfortunate side effects compared to the major benefit of letting you build redundant LANs.

For the INTRO exam, you need to know why STP is necessary, and a few details about how it works. For the ICND exam, you need to know the details of STP, as defined in IEEE 802.1d, in more detail. This chapter includes a more-detailed explanation of how 802.1d STP works, including root election and how ports are placed in the forwarding and blocking states. This chapter also covers the newer Rapid Spanning Tree Protocol (RSTP), as defined in IEEE 802.1w.

What IEEE 802.1d Spanning Tree Does

The spanning tree algorithm places each bridge/switch port in either a forwarding state or a blocking state. All the ports in forwarding state are considered to be in the current *spanning tree*. The collective set of forwarding ports creates a single path over which frames are sent between Ethernet segments. Switches can forward frames out ports and receive frames in ports that are in forwarding state; switches do not forward frames out ports and do not receive frames in ports that are in blocking state.

Figure 2-1 shows a simple STP tree with one port on SW3 in blocking state.

Figure 2-1   *Network with Redundant Links and STP*

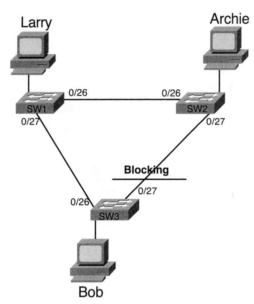

When Larry sends a broadcast frame, the frame does not loop. SW1 sends a copy to SW3, but SW3 cannot forward it to SW2 out its port 0/27 because it is blocking. SW1 sends the broadcast to SW2, who forwards it to SW3, but SW3 ignores frames that enter port 0/27. However, STP causes some frames to use a longer physical path for the sake of preventing loops. For instance, if Archie wants to send a frame to Bob, the frame has to go from SW2 to SW1 and then to SW3—a longer path than is physically required. STP prevents the loops, but you then have to live with a less-efficient path for some traffic. Of course, at LAN speeds, a user typically wouldn't notice any difference in performance unless the network was also badly congested as a result of the traffic patterns.

If the link between SW1 and SW3 fails, STP converges so that SW3 no longer blocks on its 0/27 interface. For instance, in Figure 2-2, that link has failed, and STP has converged.

Figure 2-2 *Network with Redundant Links and STP After Link Failure*

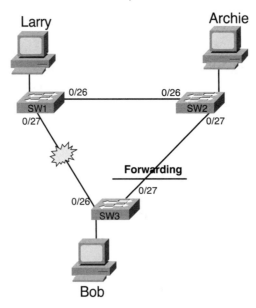

How does STP manage to make switches block or forward on each interface? And how does it converge to change state from blocking to forwarding to take advantage of redundant links in response to network outages? The following sections answer these questions.

How Spanning Tree Works

The STP algorithm creates a spanning tree of interfaces that forward frames. The tree structure creates a single path to and from each Ethernet segment, just like you can trace a single path in a living, growing tree from the base of the tree to each leaf. STP actually places interfaces in forwarding state or blocking state; if an interface has no specific reason to be in forwarding state, STP places the interface in blocking state.

In other words, STP simply picks which interfaces should forward and which shouldn't.

STP uses three criteria to choose whether to put an interface in forwarding state:

- STP elects a root bridge. STP puts all interfaces on the root bridge in forwarding state.

- Each nonroot bridge considers one of its ports to have the least administrative cost between itself and the root bridge. STP places this least-root-cost interface, called that bridge's *root port*, in forwarding state.

- Many bridges can attach to the same Ethernet segment. The bridge with the lowest administrative cost from itself to the root bridge, as compared with the other bridges attached to the same segment, is placed in forwarding state. The lowest-cost bridge on each segment is called the *designated bridge,* and that bridge's interface, attached to that segment, is called the *designated port.*

All other interfaces are placed in blocking state. Table 2-2 summarizes the reasons why STP places a port in forwarding or blocking state.

Table 2-2   *STP: Reasons for Forwarding or Blocking*

Characterization of Port	STP State	Description
All the root bridge's ports	Forwarding	The root bridge is always the designated bridge on all connected segments.
Each nonroot bridge's root port	Forwarding	The root port is the port receiving the lowest-cost BPDU from the root.
Each LAN's designated port	Forwarding	The bridge forwarding the lowest-cost BPDU onto the segment is the designated bridge for that segment.
All other ports	Blocking	The port is not used for forwarding frames, nor are any frames received on these interfaces considered for forwarding.

Electing the Root and Discovering Root Ports and Designated Ports

STP begins with each bridge claiming to be the root bridge by sending STP messages. STP defines these messages used to exchange information with other bridges, which are called *bridge protocol data units (BPDUs).* Each bridge begins by sending a BPDU specifying the following:

- **The root bridge's bridge ID**—The bridge ID is the concatenation of the bridge's priority and a MAC address on that bridge (unless it is explicitly configured as another number). At the beginning of the root-election process, each bridge claims to be root, so each bridge advertises itself as root using its own bridge ID. For instance, Example 2-1 later in this chapter shows output from a switch with a priority of 32768 and a MAC address 0050.f035.a940, combined to form the bridge ID. The lower the priority, the better chance of being root. The IEEE 802.1d STP specification allows for priorities between 0 and 65,535, inclusive.

- **The cost to reach the root from this bridge**—At the beginning of the process, each bridge claims to be root, so the value is set to 0, which is this bridge's cost to reach itself. The lower the cost, the better the path, with the range of costs being between 0 and 65,535, inclusive.

■ **The bridge ID of the sender of this BPDU**—This value is always the bridge ID of the sender of the BPDU, regardless of whether the bridge sending the BPDU is the root.

The bridges elect a root bridge based on the bridge IDs in the BPDUs. The root bridge is the bridge with the lowest numeric value for the bridge ID. Because the two-part bridge ID starts with the priority value, essentially the bridge with the lowest priority becomes the root. For instance, if one bridge has priority 100, and another bridge has priority 200, the bridge with priority 100 wins, regardless of what MAC address was used to create the bridge ID for each bridge/switch.

If a tie occurs based on priority, the bridge with the lowest MAC address used in the bridge ID is the root. The MAC addresses used to build the bridge IDs should be unique. Bridges and switches use one of their own burned-in MAC addresses as their bridge ID, so the bridge IDs are unique, because MAC addresses are supposed to be unique. So if the priorities tie, and one switch uses a MAC address of 0020.0000.0000 as part of the bridge ID, and the other uses 0FFF.FFFF.FFF, the first switch (MAC 0200.0000.0000) becomes the root.

The message used to identify the root, its bridge ID, and cost is called a hello BPDU.

STP elects a root bridge, in a manner not unlike a political election. The process of choosing the root begins with all bridges claiming to be the root by sending hello BPDUs with their bridge IDs and priorities. If a bridge hears of a better candidate, it stops advertising itself as root and starts forwarding the hello sent by the better bridge. It works like a political race in which a candidate gives up and leaves the race: The lesser candidate throws his support behind another candidate. Eventually someone wins, and everyone supports the elected switch—which is where the political race analogy falls apart.

Figure 2-3 outlines part of the process. Imagine that SW1 has advertised itself as root, as have SW2 and SW3. SW2 now believes that SW1 is a better root, but SW1 and SW3 still believe that they each are the best, so they still advertise themselves as root.

Figure 2-3 *Root Election Process*

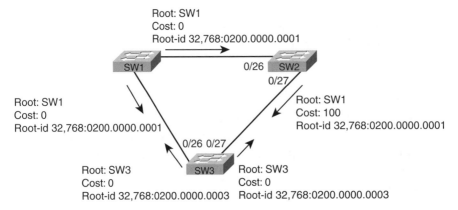

Two candidates still exist in Figure 2-3—SW1 and SW3. So who wins? Well, from the bridge ID, the lower-priority switch wins; if there is a tie, the lower MAC address wins. As shown in the figure, SW1 has a lower bridge ID (32768:0200.0000.0001), so it wins, and SW3 now also believes that SW1 is the better bridge. Figure 2-4 shows the resulting hello messages sent by the switches.

Figure 2-4   *SW1 Wins Election*

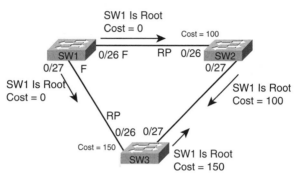

SW1's interfaces are placed in forwarding state because SW1 won the election. All interfaces on the root switch forward. But what about SW2's and SW3's interfaces? Well, the second reason that STP places an interface in forwarding state is if it is the root port on that switch. Each switch has one root port, which is the port receiving the least-cost BPDU from the root. In Figure 2-4, SW2's best cost is seen in the hello entering its port 0/26. Likewise, SW3's best cost is seen entering its 0/26 port. Therefore, the figure places "RP" beside each of those ports. SW2 and SW3 place those ports in forwarding state.

The final reason that STP places interfaces in forwarding state is if they advertise the lowest-cost hello onto a LAN segment—in other words, if the bridge becomes the designated bridge on a segment. In Figure 2-4, both SW2 and SW3 forward hello messages onto the link between them. The cost is calculated by adding the cost in the received hello (0 in this case) to the cost of the interface on which the hello was received. So SW2 adds cost 100 to 0, and SW3 adds 150 to 0. (The costs of those interfaces are listed in Figure 2-4.) The costs can be configured, or they can default. So, because SW2 advertises the lower-cost hello, SW2's 0/27 port is the designated port on the LAN segment between SW2 and SW3. SW2 places its port 0/27 in forwarding state because it is the designated port on that segment. (If the costs were the same, the lower bridge ID of the switch sending the BPDUs to the segment would become the designated bridge. In this case, SW2 would win, with bridge ID 32768:0200.0000.0002 versus SW3's 32768:0200.0000.0003.)

The only interface on the three switches that does not forward is SW3's 0/27 port, which is the same spanning-tree topology shown in Figure 2-1. The process is now complete, with all ports in forwarding state except SW3's E0/27 interface.

Table 2-3 outlines the state of each port and shows why it is in that state.

Table 2-3   *State of Each Interface*

Bridge Interface	State	Reason That the Interface Is in Forwarding State
SW1, E 0/26	Forwarding	The interface is on the root bridge
SW1, E 0/27	Forwarding	The interface is on the root bridge
SW2, E 0/26	Forwarding	The root port
SW2, E 0/27	Forwarding	The designated port on the LAN segment to SW3
SW3, E 0/26	Forwarding	The root port
SW3, E 0/27	Blocking	Not the root bridge, not the root port, and not designated port

Port costs can be configured, or you can use the default values. Table 2-4 lists the default port costs defined by IEEE; Cisco uses these same defaults. The IEEE revised the cost values because the original values, set in the early 1980s, did not anticipate the growth of Ethernet to support 10-Gigabit Ethernet.

Table 2-4   *Default Port Costs According to IEEE*

Ethernet Speed	Original IEEE Cost	Revised IEEE Cost
10 Mbps	100	100
100 Mbps	10	19
1 Gbps	1	4
10 Gbps	1	2

Reacting to Changes in the Network

After the STP topology has been set, it does not change unless the network topology changes. This section covers STP, but if you want more information, the Cisco Press book *Cisco LAN Switching,* by Kennedy Clark and Kevin Hamilton, explains STP in great depth. It is worth the time to think about a single example of how STP changes its topology when reacting to network changes, because you can learn a couple of important terms that you will see in real life when working with STP.

The root bridge sends a new hello BPDU every 2 seconds by default. Each bridge forwards the hello, changing the cost to reflect that bridge's added cost to reach the root. Each bridge uses this repetitive hearing of hellos from the root as a way to know that its path to the root is still working, because the hello follows the same path as all the data frames. When a bridge ceases to receive the hellos, something has failed, so it reacts and starts the process of changing the spanning tree.

The hello BPDU defines the timers used by all the bridges when choosing when to react:

■ **Hello Time**—How long the root waits before sending the periodic hello BPDUs, which then are forwarded by successive switches/bridges. The default is 2 seconds.

■ **MaxAge**—How long any bridge should wait, after beginning to not hear hellos, before trying to change the STP topology. Usually this is a multiple of the hello time; the default is 20 seconds.

■ **Forward Delay**—Delay that affects the time involved when an interface changes from blocking state to forwarding state. A port stays in listening state and then learning state for the number of seconds defined by the forward delay. This timer is covered in more depth shortly.

As a quick review, when the network is stable, the STP process works like this:

1. The root sends a hello BPDU, with a cost of 0, out all its interfaces.

2. The neighboring bridges forward hello BPDUs out their nonroot designated ports, identifying the root, but with their cost added.

3. Each bridge in the network repeats Step 2 as it receives these hello BPDUs.

4. The root repeats Step 1 every hello time.

5. If a bridge does not get a hello BPDU in hello time, it continues as normal. If a bridge fails to receive a hello BPDU for an entire MaxAge time, the bridge reacts.

For example, imagine that the link between SW1 and SW3 fails, as shown in Figure 2-5.

Figure 2-5 *Reacting to Link Failure Between SW1 and SW3*

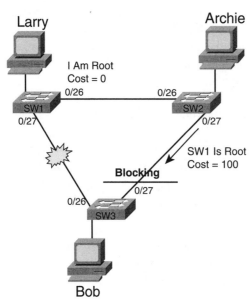

SW3 reacts to the change, but SW2 does not. SW3 ceases to receive the hello message in its root port, interface 0/26. Remember, when a switch ceases to hear its best hello message after the MaxAge amount of time, it reacts; however, SW2 continues to receive its best hello BPDU, so it does not react.

After MaxAge expires on SW3, SW3 either advertises itself as root again or believes the next-best claim of who should be root. Because SW2 forwards SW1's claim to be root and SW1 was already root, SW1 must have a better (lower) priority or better (lower) MAC address than SW3. In other words, in this case, SW3 already knows that it loses compared to SW1, so SW3 does the following:

■ Decides that its 0/27 interface is now its root port because SW3 is receiving a hello with lower bridge ID. So SW3 places 0/27 in forwarding state.

■ Interface 0/26 probably has physically failed, so it is in blocking state.

■ SW3 flushes its address table for those two interfaces because the location of MAC addresses, relative to itself, might have changed. For instance, Larry's MAC address formerly was reachable out 0/26 and now is reachable out 0/27.

However, SW3 cannot immediately transition from blocking to forwarding on its 0/27 port. If SW3 immediately transitioned to forwarding on 0/27, and other bridges/switches also were converging, loops could occur. To prevent this, STP uses two intermediate interface states.

The first, *listening,* allows each device to wait to make sure that there are no new, better hellos with a new, better root. The second state, *learning,* allows the bridge to learn the new location of MAC addresses without allowing forwarding and possibly causing loops. These states help prevent the switches from flooding frames until all the switches have converged and learned the new MAC addresses.

Using default timers, SW3 requires 50 seconds before it can place port fastethernet 0/27 in forwarding state. First, SW3 waits MaxAge seconds before deciding that it is no longer receiving the same root BPDU in its root port (20 seconds is the default). At that point, SW3 places port fastethernet 0/27 in listening state for Forward Delay seconds (15 seconds is the default). After that, SW3 places fastethernet 0/27 in learning state for another Forward Delay seconds before transitioning the port to forwarding state. So, a total of MaxAge plus twice Forward Delay, or 50 seconds, is required.

Table 2-5 summarizes spanning tree's intermediate states.

Table 2-5   *Spanning-Tree Intermediate States*

State	Forwards Data Frames?	Learns MACs Based on Received Frames?	Transitory or Stable State?
Blocking	No	No	Stable
Listening	No	No	Transitory
Learning	No	Yes	Transitory
Forwarding	Yes	Yes	Stable

SW3 also must tell the other switches to timeout the entries in their bridging tables. For instance, SW2's bridging table lists Bob's MAC address as being out port 0/26, but now it will be out port 0/27. So, SW3 sends a special Topology Change Notification (TCN) BPDU out port 0/27. When SW2 receives the TCN, it decides to timeout all MAC table entries based on the Forward Delay timer (default 15 seconds). Because SW3 sends the TCN BPDU as soon as it puts its interface into a listening state, SW2 has removed the entry for Bob's MAC address before SW3 begins forwarding. (SW2 forwards the TCN to the root switch as well, who makes sure all other bridges/switches know to timeout MAC table entries quickly as well.)

Spanning Tree Protocol Summary

Spanning trees accomplish the goal of allowing physical redundancy, but with only one currently active path through a bridged network. Spanning tree uses the following features to accomplish the goal:

■   All bridge interfaces eventually stabilize at either forwarding or blocking state. The forwarding interfaces are considered a part of the spanning tree.

- One of the bridges is elected as root. The election process includes all bridges claiming to be the root, until one bridge is considered best by all. All root bridge interfaces are in forwarding state.

- Each bridge receives hello BPDUs from the root, either directly or forwarded by another bridge. Each bridge can receive more than one such message on its interfaces. The port on which the least-cost BPDU is received is called the bridge's root port. That port is placed in forwarding state.

- For each LAN segment, one bridge sends the forwarded BPDU with the lowest cost. That bridge is the designated bridge for that segment. That bridge's interface on that segment is placed in forwarding state.

- All other interfaces are placed in blocking state.

- The root sends BPDUs every hello time seconds. The other bridges expect to receive copies of these BPDUs so that they know that nothing has changed. The hello time is defined in the BPDU itself, so all bridges use the same value.

- If a bridge does not receive a BPDU for MaxAge seconds, it begins the process of causing the spanning tree to change. The reaction can vary from topology to topology. (MaxAge is defined in the BPDU itself, so all bridges use the same value.)

- One or more bridges decide to change interfaces from blocking to forwarding, or vice versa, depending on the change in the network. When moving from blocking to forwarding, the interim listening state is entered first. After the Forward Delay amount of time (another timer defined in the root BPDU), the state is changed to learning. After another Forward Delay amount of time, the interface is placed in forwarding state.

- When a switch first transitions to a listening state, the switch sends a TCN BPDU over the new path to the root, forcing switches to quickly remove invalid entries from their MAC address tables.

- The Spanning Tree Protocol includes these delays to help ensure that no temporary loops occur.

Optional STP Features

STP has been around for 20 years. It was designed to solve a very specific need, but networking has changed over the years. Likewise, vendors and standards bodies alike have made changes to STP. In fact, Cisco has added several proprietary enhancements to STP and to the logic used by its switches. Also, the IEEE, which owns the STP specifications, has made other enhancements, some similar to Cisco's proprietary enhancements.

If you plan to work on a production campus LAN network, you should learn more about STP features. Cisco documentation for the 2950 covers many of the details. Go to Cisco.com and search for the document "Catalyst 2950 Desktop Switch Software Configuration Guide, 12.1(11)EA1," especially for the coverage of STP, RSTP, and optional STP features.

EtherChannel

The best way to lower STP's default 50-second convergence time is to avoid convergence altogether. EtherChannel provides a way to prevent STP convergence from being needed when only a single port or cable failure occurs.

EtherChannel combines from two to eight parallel Ethernet trunks between the same pair of switches, bundled into an EtherChannel. STP treats an EtherChannel as a single link, so if at least one of the links is up, STP convergence does not have to occur. For instance, Figure 2-6 shows the familiar three-switch network, but now with two FastEthernet connections between each pair of switches.

Figure 2-6 *Two-Trunk EtherChannels Between Switches*

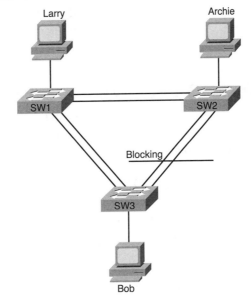

With each pair of Ethernet links configured as an EtherChannel, STP treats each EtherChannel as a single link. In other words, both links to the same switch must fail for a switch to need to cause STP convergence. Without EtherChannel, if you have multiple parallel links between two switches, STP blocks all the links except one. With EtherChannel, all the parallel links can be up and working at the same time, while reducing the number of times STP must converge, which in turn makes the network more available.

EtherChannel also provides more network bandwidth. All trunks in an EtherChannel are either forwarding or blocking, because STP treats all the trunks in the same EtherChannel as one trunk. When an EtherChannel is in forwarding state, the switches forward traffic over all the trunks, providing more bandwidth.

PortFast

PortFast allows a switch to place a port in forwarding state immediately when the port becomes physically active. However, the only ports on which you can safely enable PortFast are ports on which you know that no bridges, switches, or other STP-speaking devices are connected. So PortFast is most appropriate for connections to end-user devices. If you turn on PortFast for end-user devices, when an end-user PC boots, as soon as the Ethernet card is active, the switch port can forward traffic. Without PortFast, each port must wait MaxAge plus twice Forwarding Delay, which is 50 seconds with the default MaxAge and Forward Delay settings.

Although it isn't required, you can also figuratively "buy insurance" against someone's putting a bridge or switch on a PortFast-enabled port. The Cisco BPDU Guard feature, if enabled, tells the switch to disable PortFast ports if a BPDU is received on those ports. This prevents someone from accidentally or maliciously forcing STP convergence in your network.

Rapid Spanning Tree (IEEE 802.1w)

As mentioned earlier in this chapter, the IEEE defines STP in the 802.1d IEEE standard. The IEEE has improved the 802.1d protocol with the definition of Rapid Spanning Tree Protocol (RSTP), as defined in standard 802.1w.

RSTP (802.1w) works just like STP (802.1d) in several ways:

- It elects the root switch using the same parameters and tiebreakers.
- It elects the root port on nonroot switches with the same rules.
- It elects designated ports on each LAN segment with the same rules.
- It places each port in either forwarding or blocking state—although RSTP calls blocking state "discarding" instead of "blocking."

RSTP can be deployed alongside traditional 802.1d STP bridges and switches, with RSTP features working in switches that support it, and STP features working in the switches that support only STP.

With all these similarities, you might be wondering why the IEEE bothered to create RSTP in the first place. The overriding reason is convergence. STP takes a relatively long time to converge (50 seconds with the default settings). RSTP improves network convergence when topology changes occur.

STP convergence has essentially three time periods, each of which RSTP improves upon. First, a switch must cease to receive root BPDUs for MaxAge seconds before it can begin to transition any interfaces from blocking to forwarding. For any interfaces that need to transition from blocking to forwarding, the interface must endure Forward Delay seconds in listening state and Forward Delay more seconds in learning state before being placed in forwarding state. These three waiting periods of (by default) 20, 15, and 15 seconds create STP's relatively slow convergence.

RSTP convergence times typically take less than 10 seconds. In some cases, they can be as low as 1 to 2 seconds. Before examining how RSTP reduces convergence time, you should know some RSTP terminology and concepts.

RSTP Link and Edge Types

RSTP characterizes the types of physical connectivity in a campus LAN into three different types:

- Link-type point-to-point
- Link-type shared
- Edge-type

Figure 2-7 shows each type.

Figure 2-7   *RSTP Link and Edge Types*

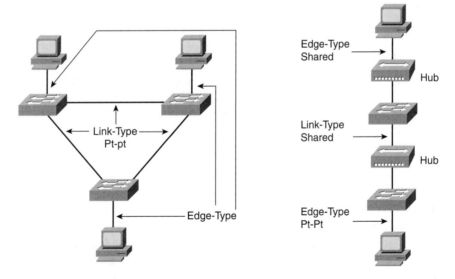

Figure 2-7 shows two sample networks. The network on the left is a typical campus design today, with no hubs. All the switches connect with Ethernet cables, and all the end-user devices also connect with Ethernet cables. The IEEE defined RSTP to improve convergence in these types of networks.

In the network on the right side of the figure, hubs are still in use for connections between the switches, as well as for connections to end-user devices. Most networks do not use hubs anymore. The IEEE did not attempt to make RSTP work in networks that use shared hubs, and RSTP would not improve convergence in the network on the right.

RSTP calls Ethernet connections between switches *links* and calls Ethernet connections to end-user devices *edges*. Two types of links exist—point-to-point, as shown on the left side of Figure 2-7, and shared, as shown on the right side. RSTP does not distinguish between point-to-point and shared types for edge connections, although the Cisco ICND course (upon which CCNA is partially based) makes this distinction.

RSTP reduces convergence time for link-type point-to-point and edge-type connections. It does not improve convergence over link-type shared connections. However, most modern networks do not use hubs between switches, so the lack of RSTP support for link-type shared doesn't really matter.

RSTP Port States

You should also be familiar with RSTP's new terms to describe a port's state. Table 2-6 lists the states, with some explanation following the table.

Table 2-6 *RSTP and STP Port States*

Operational State	STP State (802.1d)	RSTP State (802.1w)	Port Included in Active RSTP Topology?
Enabled	Blocking	Discarding	No
Enabled	Listening	Discarding	No
Enabled	Learning	Learning	Yes
Enabled	Forwarding	Forwarding	Yes
Disabled	Disabled	Discarding	No

Similar to STP, RSTP stabilizes with all ports either in forwarding state or discarding state. *Discarding* means that the port does not forward frames, process received frames, or learn MAC addresses—but it does listen for BPDUs. In short, it acts just like the STP blocking state. RSTP uses an interim learning state, which works just like the STP learning state. However, RSTP needs to use learning state for only a short time.

RSTP Port Roles

RSTP defines a set of port roles. STP also uses port roles, such as root port and designated port. RSTP adds three more port roles, two of which are shown in Figure 2-8. (The disabled state is not shown in the figure.)

Figure 2-8 *RSTP Port Roles*

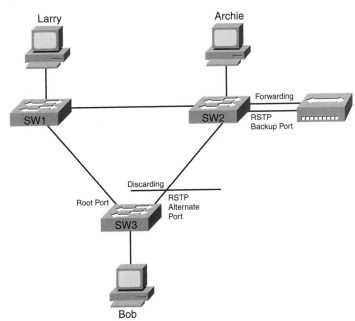

Switch SW3 has a root port, just as it would with STP. SW3 also considers its link to SW2 an RSTP alternate port. RSTP designates ports that receive suboptimal BPDUs (BPDUs that are not as "good" as the one received on the root port) as alternate ports. If SW3 stops getting hellos from the root bridge, RSTP on SW3 chooses the best alternate port as the new root port to begin the speedier convergence process.

The other new RSTP port type, backup port, applies only when a single switch has two links to the same segment. To have two links to the same segment, the switch must be attached to a hub, as shown in Figure 2-8. For instance, switch SW2 places one of the two ports in forwarding state and the other in discarding state. SW2 forwards BPDUs out the port in forwarding state and gets the same BPDU back on the port that is in discarding state. So SW2 knows it has an extra connection to that segment, called a *backup port*. If the port in forwarding state fails, RSTP on SW2 can immediately place the backup port in forwarding state.

Table 2-7 lists the port role terms for STP and RSTP.

Table 2-7 *RSTP and STP Port Roles*

RSTP Role	STP Role	Definition
Root port	Root port	A single port on each switch in which the switch hears the best BPDU out of all the received BPDUs.
Designated port	Designated port	Of all switch ports on all switches attached to the same segment/collision domain, the port that advertises the "best" root BPDU.
Alternate port	—	A port on a switch that receives a suboptimal root BPDU.
Backup port	—	A nondesignated port on a switch that is attached to the same segment/collision domain as another port on the same switch.
Disabled	—	A port that is administratively disabled.

RSTP Convergence

This section on RSTP started by telling you how similar RSTP is to STP—how they both choose a root using the same rules, choose designated ports using the same rules, and so forth. If RSTP did only the same things as STP, there would have been no need to update the original 802.1d STP standard with the new 802.1w RSTP standard. The main reason for the new standard is to improve convergence time.

The next section provides a glimpse of the detailed workings of RSTP and how it improves convergence.

Edge-Type Behavior and PortFast

RSTP improves convergence for edge-type connections by immediately placing the port in forwarding state when the link is physically active. In effect, RSTP treats these ports just like Cisco's proprietary PortFast feature. In fact, on Cisco switches, to enable RSTP on edge interfaces, you simply configure PortFast.

Link-Type Shared

RSTP doesn't do anything differently from STP on link-type shared links. However, because most of the links between switches today are not shared, but full-duplex point-to-point links, it doesn't matter.

Link-Type Point-to-Point

RSTP improves convergence over full-duplex links between switches—the links that RSTP calls "link-type point-to-point." The first improvement made by RSTP over these types of links relates to how STP uses MaxAge. STP requires that a switch that no longer receives root

BPDUs in its root port must wait for MaxAge seconds before starting convergence. MaxAge defaults to 20 seconds. RSTP recognizes the loss of the path to the root bridge, through the root port, in 3 times the hello timer, or 6 seconds with a default hello timer value of 2 seconds. So RSTP recognizes a lost path to the root much more quickly.

RSTP removes the need for listening state and reduces the time required for learning state by actively discovering the network's new state. STP passively waits on new BPDUs, and reacts to them, during the listening and learning states. With RSTP, the switches negotiate with neighboring switches. When ports that can be transitioned immediately to forwarding state are discovered, they are transitioned immediately. In many cases, the process takes only a second or two for the whole RSTP domain.

An Example of Speedy RSTP Convergence

Rather than explain every nuance of RSTP convergence, one example will give you plenty of knowledge about the process. Figure 2-9 shows a network that explains RSTP convergence.

Figure 2-9   *RSTP Convergence Example: Steps 1 and 2*

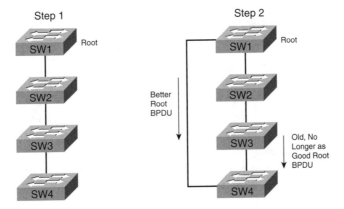

Figure 2-9 sets up the problem. On the left, in Step 1, the network has no redundancy. RSTP has placed all link-type point-to-point links in forwarding state. To add redundancy, the network engineer adds another link-type point-to-point link between SW1 and SW4, as shown on the right. So, RSTP convergence needs to occur.

The first step of convergence occurs when SW4 realizes that it is receiving a better BPDU than the one that entered from SW3. Because both the old and new root BPDUs advertise the same switch, SW1, the new, "better" BPDU coming over the direct link from SW1 must be better because of lower cost. Regardless of the reason, SW4 needs to transition to forwarding state on the new link to SW1, because it is now SW4's root port.

At this point, RSTP behavior diverges from STP. RSTP on SW4 now temporarily blocks all other link-type ports. By doing so, SW4 prevents the possibility of introducing loops. Then SW4 negotiates with its neighbor on the new root port, SW1, using RSTP Proposal and Agreement messages. As a result, SW4 and SW1 agree that they can each place their respective ends of the new link into forwarding state immediately. Figure 2-10 shows this third step.

Figure 2-10 *RSTP Convergence Example: Steps 3 and 4*

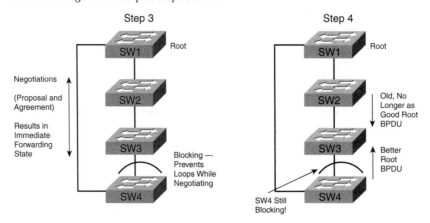

Why can SW1 and SW4 place their ends of the new link in forwarding state without causing a loop? Because SW4 blocks on all other link-type ports. In other words, it blocks on all other ports connected to other bridges or switches. That's the key to understanding RSTP convergence. A switch knows it needs to change to a new root port. It blocks on all other links and then negotiates to bring the new root port to forwarding state. Essentially, SW4 tells SW1 to trust it and start forwarding, because SW4 promises to block all other ports until it is sure that it can move some of them back to forwarding state.

The process is not yet complete, however. The RSTP topology currently shows SW4 blocking, which in this example is not the final, best topology.

SW4 and SW3 repeat the same process that SW1 and SW4 just performed. In Step 4, SW4 still blocks, preventing loops. However, SW4 forwards the new root BPDU to SW3, so SW3 hears two BPDUs now. In this example, assume that SW3 thinks that the BPDU from SW4 is better than the one received from SW2—which makes SW3 repeat the same process that SW4 just performed. It follows this general flow from this point:

1. SW3 decides to change its root port based on this new BPDU from SW4.

2. SW3 blocks all other link-type ports. (RSTP calls this process *synchronization*.)

3. SW3 and SW4 negotiate.

4. As a result of the negotiation, SW4 and SW3 can transition to forwarding on their interfaces on either end of the link-type point-to-point link.

5. SW3 maintains blocking state on all other link-type ports until the next step in the logic.

Figure 2-11 shows some of these steps in the Step 5 portion on the left and the resulting behavior in Step 6 on the right.

Figure 2-11 *RSTP Convergence Example: Steps 5 and 6*

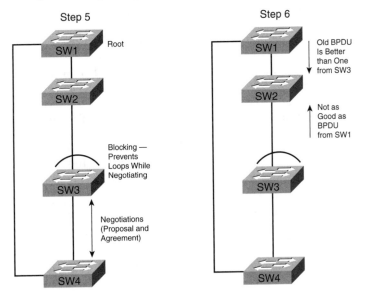

SW3 stills blocks on its upper interface at this point. Notice that SW2 is now receiving two BPDUs, but the same old BPDU it had been receiving all along is still the better BPDU. So SW2 takes no action. And RSTP is finished converging!

Although it took several pages to explain, the process in this example might take as little as 1 second. For the ICND exam, you should remember the terms relating to RSTP, as well as the concept that RSTP improves convergence time compared to STP.

Spanning Tree Protocol Configuration

Cisco switches use STP by default. You can buy some switches, connect them with Ethernet cables in a redundant topology, and STP will ensure that no loops exist. And you never even have to think about changing any of the settings!

You might want to change some of STP's default settings. You might also want to use different settings for different virtual LANs (VLANs, which are covered in Chapter 3, "Virtual LANs and Trunking"). This section lists configuration and **show** commands for STP on the 2950 series switches. It also shows a simple example of how to examine STP parameters and change some common STP parameters.

Table 2-8 lists some of the 2950 commands relating to STP.

Table 2-8   *Configuration and Operations Commands from This Chapter for 2950 Switches*

Command	Description
spanning-tree vlan *vlan-number* root {primary | secondary}	Global configuration command that changes this switch to the root switch. The switch's priority is changed to the lower of either 24,576 or 100 less than the priority of the current root bridge when the command was issued.
spanning-tree vlan *vlan-id* {priority *priority*}	Global configuration command that changes the bridge priority of this switch for the specified VLAN.
spanning-tree cost *cost*	Interface subcommand that changes the STP cost to the configured value.
channel-group *channel-group-number* mode {auto | desirable | on}	Interface subcommand that enables EtherChannel on the interface.
show spanning-tree	EXEC command that lists details about the state of STP on the switch, including the state of each port.
show spanning-tree *interface interface-id*	EXEC command that lists STP information only for the specified port.
show spanning-tree vlan *vlan-id*	EXEC command that lists STP information for the specified VLAN.
debug spanning-tree	EXEC command that causes the switch to provide informational messages about changes in the STP topology.
show etherchannel [*channel-group-number*] {brief | detail | port | port-channel | summary}	EXEC command that lists information about the state of EtherChannels on this switch.

The following examples were taken from a small network with two switches, as shown in Figure 2-12.

Figure 2-12 *Two-Switch Network*

The examples in the rest of this chapter use the network as shown in the figure. Two 2950s connect using crossover cables. The cables are plugged into interfaces 0/16 and 0/17 on both switches.

Basic STP show Commands

Example 2-1 lists information about the current state of STP in this network, with all default STP parameters.

Example 2-1 *STP Status for the Network Shown in Figure 2-12 with Default STP Parameters*

```
sw1-2950#show spanning-tree

VLAN0001
  Spanning tree enabled protocol ieee
  Root ID    Priority    32768
             Address     0050.f035.a940
             Cost        19
             Port        16 (FastEthernet0/16)
             Hello Time   2 sec  Max Age 20 sec  Forward Delay 15 sec

  Bridge ID  Priority    32769  (priority 32768 sys-id-ext 1)
             Address     000a.b7dc.b780
             Hello Time   2 sec  Max Age 20 sec  Forward Delay 15 sec
             Aging Time 300

Interface        Port ID                         Designated            Port ID
Name             Prio.Nbr      Cost Sts      Cost Bridge ID            Prio.Nbr
---------------- --------      --------- ---  -------- ------------------- --------
Fa0/16           128.16         19 FWD        0 32768 0050.f035.a940 128.26
Fa0/17           128.17         19 BLK        0 32768 0050.f035.a940 128.27

sw1-2950#show spanning-tree interface fastethernet 0/17

Vlan             Port ID                         Designated            Port ID
Name             Prio.Nbr      Cost Sts      Cost Bridge ID            Prio.Nbr
---------------- --------      --------- ---  -------- ------------------- --------
VLAN0001         128.17         19 BLK        0 32768 0050.f035.a940 128.27
```

This example lists the output of the **show spanning-tree** command on SW1. At the beginning of the example, the SW1 output lists the root bridge ID, comprised of the priority and MAC address, first. The bridge ID combines the priority and the MAC address used to identify each bridge or switch. Next, the output lists SW1-2950's own bridge ID. Notice that the root bridge ID is different from SW1-2950's bridge ID.

The topology in this example ends up with SW2 as the root bridge, so it forwards on both interfaces. SW1-2950 receives BPDUs on FastEthernet ports 0/16 and 0/17. From the topology, you know that the two BPDUs are both from SW2, and both tie in every respect. However, SW1 must choose one interface to put into forwarding state and one into blocking state to avoid a loop. You can see from the in the example that the port cost is 19 on each interface, the default IEEE port cost for FastEthernet interfaces. So SW1 breaks the tie by using the lowest internal interface number, which is FastEthernet 0/16. So, in the example, you see SW1 port 0/16 in forwarding state and 0/17 in blocking state.

Changing STP Port Costs and Bridge Priority

In Example 2-2, the configuration changes to affect the spanning tree. First, on SW1-2950, the port cost is changed on fastethernet 0/17, which makes SW1-2950 transition that port from blocking state to forwarding state and interface fastethernet 0/16 to blocking state. Next, SW1-2950 becomes the root by changing its bridge priority.

Example 2-2   *Manipulating STP Port Cost and Bridge Priority*

```
sw1-2950#debug spanning-tree

Spanning Tree event debugging is on

sw1-2950#configure terminal
Enter configuration commands, one per line.  End with CNTL/Z.
sw1-2950(config)#interface fastethernet 0/17
sw1-2950(config-if)#spanning-tree cost 2
sw1-2950(config-if)#^Z
sw1-2950#
00:23:19: STP: VLAN0001 new Root Port Fa0/17, cost 2
00:23:19: STP: VLAN0001 Fa0/17 -> listening
00:23:34: STP: VLAN0001 Fa0/17 -> learning
00:23:49: STP: VLAN0001 Fa0/17 -> forwarding

sw1-2950#show spanning-tree

VLAN0001
  Spanning tree enabled protocol ieee
    Root ID    Priority    32768
               Address     0050.f035.a940
               Cost        2
               Port        17 (FastEthernet0/17)
               Hello Time   2 sec  Max Age 20 sec  Forward Delay 15 sec
```

Example 2-2 *Manipulating STP Port Cost and Bridge Priority (Continued)*

```
  Bridge ID  Priority    32769  (priority 32768 sys-id-ext 1)
             Address     000a.b7dc.b780
             Hello Time   2 sec  Max Age 20 sec  Forward Delay 15 sec
             Aging Time 300

Interface        Port ID                        Designated          Port ID
Name             Prio.Nbr    Cost Sts    Cost Bridge ID             Prio.Nbr
---------------- --------- --------- --- --------- ------------------- --------
Fa0/16            128.16         19 BLK       0 32768 0050.f035.a940 128.26
Fa0/17            128.17          2 FWD       0 32768 0050.f035.a940 128.27

sw1-2950#configure terminal
sw1-2950(config)#spanning-tree vlan 1 root primary
 vlan 1 bridge priority set to 24576
 vlan 1 bridge max aging time unchanged at 20
 vlan 1 bridge hello time unchanged at 2
 vlan 1 bridge forward delay unchanged at 15
sw1-2950(config)#^Z
sw1-2950#
00:24:49: setting bridge id (which=1) prio 24577 prio cfg 24576 sysid 1 (on) id
  6001.000a.b7dc.b780
00:24:49: STP: VLAN0001 we are the spanning tree root
00:24:49: STP: VLAN0001 Fa0/16 -> listening
00:24:49: STP: VLAN0001 Topology Change rcvd on Fa0/16
00:25:04: STP: VLAN0001 Fa0/16 -> learning
00:25:19: STP: VLAN0001 Fa0/16 -> forwarding
```

This example starts with the **debug spanning-tree** command on SW1-2950. This command tells the switch to issue informational messages whenever STP performs any significant work. These messages show up in the example as a result of the commands shown later in the example output.

Next, the port cost of the SW1-2950 interface fastethernet 0/17 is changed using the **spanning-tree cost 2** command. (The default cost on a 100-Mbps link is 19.) Immediately following this command, you see the first meaningful **debug** messages. SW1-2950 issues a message each time an interface transitions to another state, and it includes a time stamp. Notice that the message stating that fastethernet 0/17 moves to listening state is followed by a message stating that fastethernet 0/17 has been placed in learning state—and the time stamp shows that this message was issued 15 seconds after the first one. Similarly, the message stating that fastethernet 0/17 was placed in forwarding state happens 15 seconds after that. So the debug messages simply reinforce the notion of the Forward Delay timer.

Following the debug messages, the output of the **show spanning-tree** command lists fastethernet 0/16 as blocking and fastethernet 0/17 as forwarding, with the cost to the root bridge now only 2, based on the changed cost of interface fastethernet 0/17.

The next change occurs when the **spanning-tree vlan 1 root primary** command is issued on SW1-2950. This command changes the bridge priority to 24,576, which makes SW1-2950 the root. The **debug** messages that follow confirm this fact.

EtherChannel Configuration

Finally, the two switches do have parallel Ethernet connections that could be configured for EtherChannel. By doing so, STP does not block on either interface, because STP treats both interfaces on each switch as one link. Example 2-3 shows the SW1-2950 configuration and **show** commands for the new EtherChannel.

Example 2-3 *Configuring and Monitoring EtherChannel*

```
sw1-2950#configure terminal
Enter configuration commands, one per line.  End with CNTL/Z.
sw1-2950(config)#int fa 0/16
sw1-2950(config-if)#channel-group 1 mode on
sw1-2950(config)#int fa 0/17
sw1-2950(config-if)#channel-group 1 mode on
sw1-2950(config-if)#^Z

sw1-2950#show spanning-tree

VLAN0001
  Spanning tree enabled protocol ieee
  Root ID    Priority    24577
             Address     000a.b7dc.b780
             This bridge is the root
             Hello Time   2 sec  Max Age 20 sec  Forward Delay 15 sec

  Bridge ID  Priority    24577  (priority 24576 sys-id-ext 1)
             Address     000a.b7dc.b780
             Hello Time   2 sec  Max Age 20 sec  Forward Delay 15 sec
             Aging Time 15

Interface        Port ID                         Designated           Port ID
Name             Prio.Nbr    Cost Sts   Cost Bridge ID               Prio.Nbr
---------------- -------- ---------- --- --------- -------------------- --------
Po1              128.65          12 LIS       0 24577 000a.b7dc.b780 128.65

sw1-2950#

00:32:27: STP: VLAN0001 Po1 -> learning
00:32:42: STP: VLAN0001 Po1 -> forwarding
```

Example 2-3   *Configuring and Monitoring EtherChannel (Continued)*

```
sw1-2950#show etherchannel 1 summary
Flags:  D - down         P - in port-channel
        I - stand-alone  s - suspended
        R - Layer3       S - Layer2
        u - unsuitable for bundling
        U - port-channel in use
        d - default port
Group Port-channel  Ports
-----+------------+-----------------------------------------------------------
1     Po1(SU)      Fa0/16(P)  Fa0/17(P)
```

At the beginning of this example, you see the configuration on SW1-2950. On the 2950, any port can be part of an EtherChannel, with up to eight on a single EtherChannel, so the EtherChannel commands are interface subcommands. The **channel-group 1 mode on** interface subcommands enable EtherChannel on interfaces fastethernet 0/16 and 0/17. Both switches must agree on the number for the EtherChannel—1 in this case.

The **channel-group** command uses the **on** parameter on both switches to ensure that the two links are placed in an EtherChannel. If for some reason SW2 was not configured correctly for EtherChannel, the ports could not be used. Alternatively, the EtherChannel configuration commands on each switch could use parameters of **auto** or **desirable** instead of **on**. With these other parameters, the switches negotiate whether to use EtherChannel. If negotiated, an EtherChannel is formed. If not, the ports can be used without forming an EtherChannel, with STP blocking some interfaces.

The use of the **auto** and **desirable** parameters can be deceiving. If you configure **auto** on both switches, the EtherChannel never comes up! The **auto** keyword tells the switch to wait for the other switch to start the negotiations. If both switches are waiting, it's a long wait! As long as one of the two switches is configured with the keyword **desirable**, the EtherChannel is negotiated.

In the rest of Example 2-3, you see several references to **port-channel** or **Po**. Because STP treats the channel as one link, the switch needs some way to represent the entire EtherChannel. The 2950 IOS uses the term **Po**, short for "port channel," as a way to name the EtherChannel. (EtherChannel is sometimes called "port channeling.") For instance, near the end of the example, the **show etherchannel 1 summary** command references **Po1**, for port channel/EtherChannel 1.

Foundation Summary

The "Foundation Summary" section lists the most important facts from the chapter. Although this section does not list everything that will be on the exam, a well-prepared CCNA candidate should at a minimum know all the details in each Foundation Summary before taking the exam.

Table 2-9 summarizes the reasons why spanning tree places a port in forwarding or blocking state.

Table 2-9 *Spanning Tree: Reasons for Forwarding or Blocking*

Characterization of Port	Spanning Tree State	Description
All the root bridge's ports	Forwarding	The root bridge is always the designated bridge on all connected segments.
Each nonroot bridge's root port	Forwarding	The root port is the port receiving the lowest-cost BPDU from the root.
Each LAN's designated port	Forwarding	The bridge forwarding the lowest-cost BPDU onto the segment is the designated bridge for that segment.
All other ports	Blocking	The port is not used for forwarding frames, nor are any frames received on these interfaces considered for forwarding.

Table 2-10 lists the default port costs defined by IEEE; Cisco uses these same defaults.

Table 2-10 *Default Port Costs According to IEEE*

Speed of Ethernet	Original IEEE Cost	Revised IEEE Cost
10 Mbps	100	100
100 Mbps	10	19
1 Gbps	1	4
10 Gbps	1	2

Table 2-11 summarizes spanning tree's intermediate states.

Table 2-11   *Spanning-Tree Intermediate States*

State	Forwards Data Frames?	Learns MACs Based on Received Frames?	Transitory or Stable State?
Blocking	No	No	Stable
Listening	No	No	Transitory
Learning	No	Yes	Transitory
Forwarding	Yes	Yes	Stable

Table 2-12 lists the various RSTP and STP states.

Table 2-12   *RSTP and STP Port States*

Operational State	STP State (802.1d)	RSTP State (802.1w)	Port Included in Active RSTP Topology?
Enabled	Blocking	Discarding	No
Enabled	Listening	Discarding	No
Enabled	Learning	Learning	Yes
Enabled	Forwarding	Forwarding	Yes
Disabled	Disabled	Discarding	No

Spanning trees accomplish the goal of allowing physical redundancy, but with only one currently active path through a bridged network. Spanning tree uses the following features to accomplish the goal:

- All bridge interfaces eventually stabilize at either forwarding or blocking state. The forwarding interfaces are considered a part of the spanning tree.

- One of the bridges is elected as root. The election process includes all bridges claiming to be the root, until one bridge is considered best by all. All root bridge interfaces are in forwarding state.

- Each bridge receives hello BPDUs from the root, either directly or forwarded by another bridge. Each bridge can receive more than one such message on its interfaces. The port on which the least-cost BPDU is received is called the bridge's root port. That port is placed in forwarding state.

- For each LAN segment, one bridge sends the forwarded BPDU with the lowest cost. That bridge is the designated bridge for that segment. That bridge's interface on that segment is placed in forwarding state.

- All other interfaces are placed in blocking state.

- The root sends BPDUs every hello time seconds. The other bridges expect to receive copies of these BPDUs so that they know that nothing has changed. The hello time is defined in the BPDU itself, so all bridges use the same value.

- If a bridge does not receive a BPDU for MaxAge seconds, it begins the process of causing the spanning tree to change. The reaction can vary from topology to topology. (MaxAge is defined in the BPDU itself, so all bridges use the same value.)

- One or more bridges decide to change interfaces from blocking to forwarding, or vice versa, depending on the change in the network. When moving from blocking to forwarding, the interim listening state is entered first. After the Forward Delay amount of time (another timer defined in the root BPDU), the state is changed to learning. After another Forward Delay amount of time, the interface is placed in forwarding state.

- When a switch first transitions to a listening state, the switch sends a TCN BPDU over the new path to the root, forcing switches to quickly remove invalid entries from their MAC address tables.

The Spanning Tree Protocol includes these delays to help ensure that no temporary loops occur.

Q&A

As mentioned in the Introduction, you have two choices for review questions. The following questions give you a bigger challenge than the exam because they are open-ended. By reviewing with this more-difficult question format, you can exercise your memory better and prove your conceptual and factual knowledge of the topics covered in this chapter. The answers to these questions are found in Appendix A.

For more practice with exam-like question formats, including multiple-choice questions and those using a router simulator, use the exam engine on the CD.

1. What routing protocol does a transparent bridge use to learn about Layer 3 address groupings?

2. What settings does a bridge or switch examine to determine which should be elected as root of the spanning tree?

3. If a switch hears three different hello BPDUs from three different neighbors on three different interfaces, and if all three specify that Bridge 1 is the root, how does the switch choose which interface is its root port?

4. Can the root bridge/switch ports be placed in blocking state?

5. Describe the benefits of Spanning Tree Protocol as used by transparent bridges and switches.

6. When a bridge or switch using Spanning Tree Protocol first initializes, what does it assert should be the tree's root?

7. Name the three reasons why a port is placed in forwarding state as a result of spanning tree.

8. Name the three interface states that Spanning Tree Protocol uses, other than forwarding. Which of these states is transitory?

9. What are the two reasons that a nonroot bridge/switch places a port in forwarding state?

10. Which two 2950 series EXEC commands list information about an interface's spanning-tree state?

This chapter covers the following subjects:

- Review of Virtual LAN Concepts

- Trunking with ISL and 802.1Q

- VLAN Trunking Protocol (VTP)

- VLAN and Trunking Configuration

CHAPTER 3

Virtual LANs and Trunking

The topics of virtual LANs (VLANs) and VLAN trunking are both important for the CCNA exams. They might be even more important in real networking jobs. VLANs allow a switch to separate different ports into different groups (different VLANs), thereby keeping the traffic in each VLAN separate from the other traffic. VLANs allow engineers to build networks that meet their design requirements without having to buy a different switch for each group. VLAN trunking allows each VLAN to span multiple switches, with traffic from multiple VLANs crossing the same Ethernet links. VLANs and VLAN trunking are as much a part of most corporate LANs today as is TCP/IP.

This chapter reviews the basic concepts behind VLANs and then adds more-thorough coverage of VLAN trunking as compared with the *CCNA INTRO Exam Certification Guide*. Also, this chapter explains VLAN Trunking Protocol (VTP), a Cisco-proprietary protocol that helps you reduce errors when you're configuring VLANs. This chapter ends with some switch configuration examples. Please refer to Appendix F for some further details about a few of the topics in this chapter.

"Do I Know This Already?" Quiz

The purpose of the "Do I Know This Already?" quiz is to help you decide if you need to read the entire chapter. If you intend to read the entire chapter, you do not necessarily need to answer these questions now.

The eight-question quiz, derived from the major sections in the "Foundation Topics" section, helps you determine how to spend your limited study time.

Table 3-1 outlines the major topics discussed in this chapter and the "Do I Know This Already?" quiz questions that correspond to those topics.

Table 3-1 *"Do I Know This Already?" Foundation Topics Section-to-Question Mapping*

Foundations Topics Section	Questions Covered in This Section
Review of Virtual LAN Concepts	1 and 2
Trunking with ISL and 802.1Q	3, 4, and 5
VLAN Trunking Protocol (VTP)	6 and 7
VLAN and Trunking Configuration	8

> **CAUTION** The goal of self-assessment is to gauge your mastery of the topics in this chapter. If you don't know the answer to a question or you're only partially sure of the answer, you should mark this question as wrong for purposes of the self-assessment. Giving yourself credit for an answer you guess correctly skews your self-assessment results and might give you a false sense of security.

1. In a LAN, which of the following terms best equates to the term "VLAN"?

    a. Collision domain

    b. Broadcast domain

    c. Subnet domain

    d. Single switch

    e. Trunk

2. Imagine a switch with three configured VLANs. How many IP subnets are required, assuming that all hosts in all VLANs want to use TCP/IP?

    a. 0

    b. 1

    c. 2

    d. 3

    e. You can't tell from the information provided.

3. Which of the following fully encapsulates the original Ethernet frame in a trunking header?

    a. VTP

    b. ISL

    c. 802.1Q

    d. Both ISL and 802.1Q

    e. None of the above

4. Which of the following adds the trunking header for all VLANs except one?

    a. VTP

    b. ISL

    c. 802.1Q

    d. Both ISL and 802.1Q

    e. None of the above

5. Which of the following allows a spanning tree instance per VLAN?

   a. VTP

   b. ISL

   c. 802.1Q

   d. Both ISL and 802.1Q

   e. None of the above

6. Which of the following advertises VLAN information to neighboring switches?

   a. VTP

   b. ISL

   c. 802.1Q

   d. Both ISL and 802.1Q

   e. None of the above

7. Which of the following VTP modes allow VLANs to be created on a switch?

   a. Client

   b. Server

   c. Transparent

   d. Dynamic

   e. None of the above

8. Imagine that you are told that switch 1 is configured with the **auto** parameter for trunking on its Ethernet connection to switch 2. You have to configure switch 2. Which of the following settings for trunking could allow trunking to work?

   a. Trunking turned on

   b. Auto

   c. Desirable

   d. Off

   e. None of the above

The answers to the "Do I Know This Already?" quiz appear in Appendix A. The suggested choices for your next step are as follows:

- **6 or less overall score**—Read the entire chapter. This includes the "Foundation Topics," "Foundation Summary," and "Q&A" sections.

- **7 or 8 overall score**—If you want more review on these topics, skip to the "Foundation Summary" section and then go to the "Q&A" section. Otherwise, move to the next chapter.

Foundation Topics

Whether you have read Chapter 10, "Virtual LANs and Trunking," of the *CCNA INTRO Exam Certification Guide*, or whether you have already passed the INTRO exam, you should have learned the basics of VLANs. Therefore, this chapter just briefly reviews the concepts behind VLANs. You should also already know the basics of VLAN trunking with ISL and IEEE 802.1Q from your study for the INTRO exam. However, because fewer people know about trunking before starting to prepare for CCNA, this chapter describes trunking in detail.

VLAN Trunking Protocol (VTP) provides the only major topic about VLANs that is not on both CCNA exams. VTP is covered in this chapter after trunking. Finally, this chapter closes with a section about VLAN configuration.

Review of Virtual LAN Concepts

VLANs are pretty simple in concept and in practice. The following list hits the high points:

- A *collision domain* is a set of network interface cards (NICs) for which a frame sent by one NIC could result in a collision with a frame sent by any other NIC in the same collision domain.

- A *broadcast domain* is a set of NICs for which a broadcast frame sent by one NIC is received by all other NICs in the same broadcast domain.

- A VLAN is essentially a broadcast domain.

- VLANs are typically created by configuring a switch to place each port in a particular VLAN.

- Layer 2 switches forward frames between devices in the same VLAN; they cannot forward frames between different VLANs.

- A Layer 3 switch, multilayer switch, or router can be used to essentially route packets between VLANs.

- The set of devices in a VLAN typically also is in the same IP subnet; devices in different VLANs are in different subnets.

Figure 3-1 shows a switch with two VLANs. Fred and Dino can send frames to each other, but neither can send frames to Wilma.

Figure 3-1 *Network with Two VLANs Using One Switch*

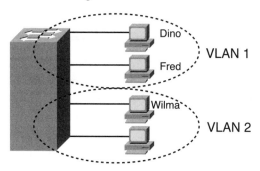

Yes, the concepts behind VLANs are that simple. The use of VLANs does introduce a couple of other concepts you should know. Next you will learn about VLAN trunking, VLAN Trunking Protocol, and some issues related to Layer 3 protocols when using VLANs.

Trunking with ISL and 802.1Q

When using VLANs in networks that have multiple interconnected switches, you need to use VLAN trunking between the switches. With VLAN trunking, the switches tag each frame sent between switches so that the receiving switch knows to what VLAN the frame belongs. Figure 3-2 outlines the basic idea.

Figure 3-2 *VLAN Trunking Between Two Switches*

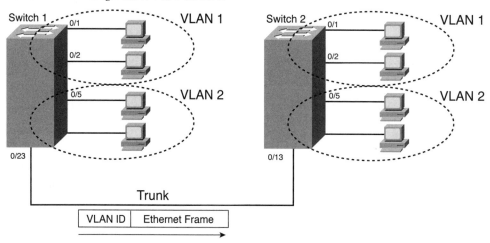

With trunking, you can support multiple VLANs that have members on more than one switch. For instance, when Switch 1 receives a broadcast from a device in VLAN 1, it needs to forward the broadcast to Switch 2. Before sending the frame, Switch1 adds another header to the original Ethernet frame; that new header has the VLAN number in it. When Switch 2 receives the frame, it sees that the frame was from a device in VLAN1, so Switch2 knows that it should only forward the broadcast out its own interfaces in VLAN1.

Cisco switches support two different trunking protocols—Inter-Switch Link (ISL) and IEEE 802.1Q. Both provide basic trunking, as shown in Figure 3-2. They do have some differences, as discussed next.

ISL

Cisco created ISL before the IEEE standardized a trunking protocol. Because ISL is Cisco-proprietary, it can be used only between two Cisco switches. ISL fully encapsulates each original Ethernet frame in an ISL header and trailer. The original Ethernet frame inside the ISL header and trailer remains unchanged. Figure 3-3 shows the framing for ISL.

Figure 3-3 *ISL Header*

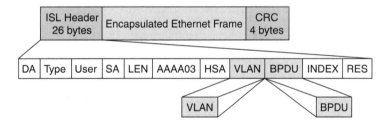

The ISL header includes several fields, but most importantly, the ISL header VLAN field provides a place to encode the VLAN number. By tagging a frame with the correct VLAN number inside the header, the sending switch can ensure that the receiving switch knows to which VLAN the encapsulated frame belongs. Also, the source and destination addresses in the ISL header use MAC addresses of the sending and receiving switch, as opposed to the devices that actually sent the original frame. Other than that, the details of the ISL header are not that important.

802.1Q

The IEEE standardizes many of the protocols relating to LANs today, and VLAN trunking is no exception. After Cisco created ISL, the IEEE completed work on the 802.1Q standard, which defines a different way to do trunking.

802.1Q uses a different style of header than does ISL to tag frames with a VLAN number. In fact, 802.1Q does not actually encapsulate the original frame. Rather, it adds an extra 4-byte header to the original Ethernet header. That additional header includes a field with which to identify the VLAN number. Because the original header has been changed, 802.1Q encapsulation forces a recalculation of the original FCS field in the Ethernet trailer, because the FCS is based on the contents of the entire frame. Figure 3-4 shows the 802.1Q header and framing of the revised Ethernet header.

Figure 3-4 *802.1Q Trunking Header*

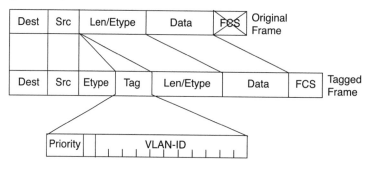

ISL and 802.1Q Compared

Both ISL and 802.1Q provide trunking. The header used by each varies, and only ISL actually encapsulates the original frame, but both allow the use of a 12-bit-long VLAN ID field. So, either works fine, and both support the same number of VLANs because both use a 12-bit VLAN Number field.

ISL and 802.1Q both support a separate instance of spanning tree for each VLAN. ISL supported this feature much earlier than did 802.1Q, so in years past, one of the stated differences between the two trunking protocols was that 802.1Q did not support multiple spanning trees. To appreciate the benefits of multiple spanning trees, examine Figure 3-5, which shows a simple network with two VLANs and three interconnected switches.

Figure 3-5 *ISL Per-VLAN Spanning Tree (PVST)*

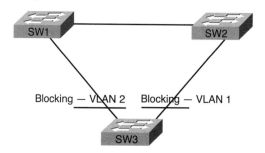

You can tune STP parameters in each VLAN so that when all links are up, different interfaces block in different spanning trees. In the figure, only one of the six switch interfaces connecting the switches needs to block to prevent loops. STP can be configured so that VLAN 1 and VLAN 2 block different interfaces on SW3 in this example. So, SW3 actually uses the available bandwidth on each of its links to the other switches, because traffic in VLAN 1 uses the link to SW1, and traffic in VLAN 2 uses the link to SW2. Of course, if a link fails when you use ISL, both STP instances can converge so that a path is still available.

Cisco provides a variety of STP tools to accommodate multiple spanning trees. ISL uses a Cisco-proprietary feature called Per-VLAN Spanning Tree (PVST+) to support multiple spanning trees. 802.1Q did not originally support multiple spanning trees, but it can by using a couple other protocols. Cisco's proprietary PVST+ allows multiple STP instances over 802.1Q trunks. Also, the IEEE has completed a new specification called 802.1S that adds to the 802.1Q specification, allowing multiple spanning trees. In addition to these protocols, Cisco supports other proprietary variations.

A key difference between ISL and 802.1Q relates to a feature called the *native VLAN*. 802.1Q defines one VLAN on each trunk as the native VLAN; by default, this is VLAN 1. By definition, 802.1Q simply does not encapsulate frames in the native VLAN when sending the frames over the trunk. When the switch on the other side of the link receives a frame in the native VLAN, it notices the lack of an 802.1Q header and knows that the frame is part of the native VLAN.

Native VLANs play a very important role from a practical perspective. Imagine that you have many PCs connected to some switch ports, and those PCs do not understand 802.1Q. You also plan to install IP phones near those PCs. IP phones have a built-in switch so that you can connect the phone to the Ethernet cable from the switch and then connect the phone to a PC. The phone understands 802.1Q, so you can put the phone in one VLAN and the PC in another. You can configure all those ports for 802.1Q, placing the PCs in the native VLAN. They work fine when connected directly to the switch, because the switch does not use any encapsulation for the native VLAN. When you install an IP phone between the switch and the PC, the phone can understand the 802.1Q headers and can send and receive traffic to and from the switch. The phone can just pass the native VLAN traffic between the PC and the switch.

ISL does not use a concept like native VLAN. All frames from all VLANs have an ISL header for transmission across an ISL trunk.

Table 3-2 summarizes the key features and points of comparison between ISL and 802.1Q.

Table 3-2   *ISL and 802.1Q Compared*

Function	ISL	802.1Q
Standards body that defines the protocol	Cisco-proprietary	IEEE
Encapsulates the original frame	Yes	No
Allows multiple spanning trees	Yes, with PVST+	Yes, with PVST+ or 802.1S
Uses a native VLAN	No	Yes

VLAN Trunking Protocol (VTP)

Cisco switches use the proprietary VTP to exchange VLAN configuration information between switches. VTP defines a Layer 2 messaging protocol that allows the switches to exchange VLAN configuration information so that the VLAN configuration stays consistent throughout a network. For instance, if you want to use VLAN 3 and name it "accounting," you can configure that information in one switch, and VTP will distribute that information to the rest of the switches. VTP manages the additions, deletions, and name changes of VLANs across multiple switches, minimizing misconfigurations and configuration inconsistencies that can cause problems, such as duplicate VLAN names or incorrect VLAN-type settings.

VTP makes VLAN configuration easier. However, you have not yet seen how to configure VLANs, so to better appreciate VTP, consider this example: If a network has ten interconnected switches, and parts of VLAN 3 were on all ten switches, you would have to enter the same config command on all ten switches to create the VLAN. With VTP, you would create VLAN 3 on one switch, and the other nine switches would learn about VLAN 3 dynamically.

The VTP process begins with VLAN creation on a switch called a VTP server. The changes are distributed as a broadcast throughout the network. Both VTP clients and servers hear the VTP messages and update their configuration based on those messages. So VTP allows switched network solutions to scale to large sizes by reducing the manual configuration needs in the network.

How VTP Works

VTP floods advertisements throughout the VTP domain every 5 minutes, or whenever there is a change in VLAN configuration. The VTP advertisement includes a configuration revision number, VLAN names and numbers, and information about which switches have ports assigned to each VLAN. By configuring the details on one (or more) VTP server and propagating the information through advertisements, all switches know the names and numbers of all VLANs.

One of the most important components of the VTP advertisements is the *configuration revision number.* Each time a VTP server modifies its VLAN information, it increments the configuration revision number by 1. The VTP server then sends out a VTP advertisement that includes the new configuration revision number. When a switch receives a VTP advertisement with a larger configuration revision number, it updates its VLAN configuration. Figure 3-6 illustrates how VTP operates in a switched network.

Figure 3-6   *VTP Operation*

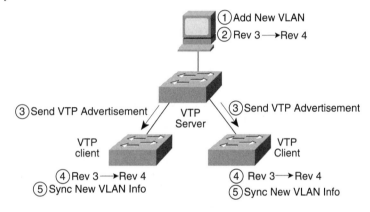

VTP operates in one of three modes:

■   Server mode

■   Client mode

■   Transparent mode

For VTP to exchange information, some switches act as servers, and some act as clients. VTP servers can create, modify, and delete VLANs and other configuration parameters for the entire VTP domain; this information, in turn, is propagated to the VTP clients and servers in that same domain. VTP servers save VLAN configurations in the Catalyst NVRAM, whereas in clients, the VLAN configuration is not stored at all. A VTP client cannot create, change, or delete VLANs, nor can it save VLAN configurations in nonvolatile memory.

So why be a VTP client? Well, if one engineer designs and implements the network, it's a lot more convenient for that person to configure the VLANs in one switch (the VTP server) and have the information propagated to VTP clients.

Interestingly, to avoid using VTP to exchange VLAN information in Cisco switches, you do not "disable" VTP. Instead, you use VTP transparent mode. With VTP transparent mode on all switches in a network, VTP is not used. Alternatively, with VTP transparent mode on just some of the switches in a network, VTP servers and clients can work as they normally do, and the VTP transparent mode switches simply ignore the VTP messages. A switch in transparent mode forwards VTP advertisements received from other switches while ignoring the information in the VTP message.

A switch configured in VTP transparent mode can create, delete, and modify VLANs, but the changes are not transmitted to other switches in the domain; they affect only that switch. Choosing to use transparent mode is typical when a network needs to distribute administrative control of the switches.

Table 3-3 offers a comparative overview of the three VTP modes.

Table 3-3 *VTP Modes*

Function	Server Mode	Client Mode	Transparent Mode
Originates VTP advertisements	Yes	No	No
Processes received advertisements and synchronizes VLAN configuration information with other switches	Yes	Yes	No
Forwards VTP advertisements received in a trunk	Yes	Yes	Yes
Saves VLAN configuration in NVRAM	Yes	No	Yes
Can create, modify, or delete VLANs using configuration commands	Yes	No	Yes

VTP Pruning

By default, a trunk connection carries traffic for all VLANs. Broadcasts (and unknown destination unicasts) in every VLAN are sent to every switch in the network, according to the current STP topology. However, in most networks, a switch does not have interfaces in every VLAN, so the broadcasts for the VLANs in which it has no interfaces simply waste bandwidth.

VTP pruning allows switches to prevent broadcasts and unknown unicasts from flowing to switches that do not have any ports in that VLAN. Figure 3-7 provides an example of VTP pruning.

Figure 3-7   *VTP Pruning*

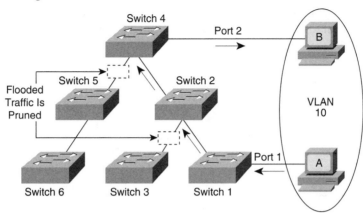

In Figure 3-7, Switches 1 and 4 support ports in VLAN 10. With VTP pruning enabled, when Station A sends a broadcast, the broadcast is flooded only toward any switch with ports assigned to VLAN 10. As a result, broadcast traffic from Station A is not forwarded to Switches 3, 5, and 6, because traffic for VLAN 10 has been pruned by VTP on the links indicated on Switches 2 and 4.

VTP pruning increases the available bandwidth by restricting flooded traffic, which consists of broadcasts and unknown destination unicasts. VTP pruning is one of the two most compelling reasons to use VTP. The other reason is to make VLAN configuration easier and more consistent.

VLAN and Trunking Configuration

You can purchase Cisco switches, install devices with the correct cabling, turn on the switches, and they work. You would never need to configure the switch and it would work fine, even if you interconnected switches—until you needed more than one VLAN. Even the default STP and trunking settings would likely work just fine, but if you want to use VLANs, you need to add some configuration.

In real networks, VLANs are the most likely feature to be configured on a switch. Almost every network uses them, and there is no reasonable dynamic way to assign specific ports to specific VLANs. So you simply need to configure the switch to know which ports are in which VLANs.

As you might expect, you can also configure VTP and trunking. VTP is on by default, and trunking negotiation is attempted on all ports by default. So, although you might not be required to configure either VTP or trunking in a real network you should certainly be ready to configure VTP and trunking for the exams.

Table 3-4 lists and briefly describes the commands covered in this section. Following that, a few examples explain the basics of VLANs, trunking, and VTP configuration.

Table 3-4 *2950 VLAN Command List*

Command	Description
vlan database	EXEC command that puts the user in VLAN configuration mode.
vtp {domain *domain-name* **| password** *password* **| pruning	v2-mode	{server	client	transparent}}**	Defines VTP parameters in VLAN configuration mode.
vlan *vlan-id* [**name** *vlan-name*]	VLAN database configuration command that creates and names a VLAN.
**switchport mode {access	dynamic {auto	desirable}	trunk}**	Interface subcommand that configures the interface for trunking.
switchport trunk {{allowed vlan *vlan-list*}	{**native vlan** *vlan-id*}	{**pruning vlan** *vlan-list*}}	Interface subcommand that refines the list of allowed VLANs, defines the 802.1Q native VLAN, and limits the range of VLANs for which pruning can occur.
switchport access vlan *vlan-id*	Interface subcommand that statically configures the interface into that one VLAN.
show interfaces [*interface-id*	**vlan** *vlan-id*] [switchport	trunk]	Displays trunk status.
show vlan [brief	**id** *vlan-id*	**name** *vlan-name*	*summary*]	EXEC command that lists information about the VLAN.
show vlan [*vlan*]	Displays VLAN information.
show vtp status	Lists VTP configuration and status information.
show spanning-tree vlan *vlan-id*	EXEC command that lists information about the spanning tree for a particular VLAN.

VLAN Configuration for a Single Switch

Cisco 2950 switches use a slightly different configuration mode to configure VLAN and VTP information as compared to the other switch configuration commands. You use VLAN configuration mode, which is reached by using the **vlan database** enable mode EXEC command. So, instead of using the **configure terminal** enable mode command, you enter **vlan database**, after which you are placed in VLAN configuration mode.

In VLAN configuration mode, you can configure VLAN information as well as VTP settings. By default, a 2950 switch uses VTP server mode, so any VLANs you configure are advertised in VTP updates.

Example 3-1 shows a VLAN configuration in a single switch. Figure 3-8 shows the switch that is configured and the VLANs.

Figure 3-8 *Network with One Switch and Three VLANs*

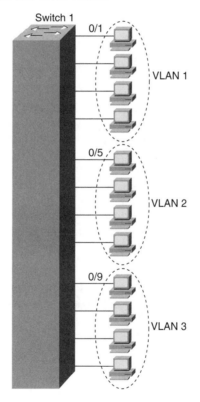

Example 3-1 *Single-Switch VLAN Configuration Matching Figure 3-8*

```
Switch#vlan database
Switch(vlan)#vlan 2 name barney-2
VLAN 2 added:
    Name: barney-2
Switch(vlan)#vlan 3 name wilma-3
VLAN 3 added:
```

continues

Example 3-1 *Single-Switch VLAN Configuration Matching Figure 3-8 (Continued)*

```
      Name: wilma-3
Switch(vlan)#?
VLAN database editing buffer manipulation commands:
  abort  Exit mode without applying the changes
  apply  Apply current changes and bump revision number
  exit   Apply changes, bump revision number, and exit mode
  no     Negate a command or set its defaults
  reset  Abandon current changes and reread current database
  show   Show database information
  vlan   Add, delete, or modify values associated with a single VLAN
  vtp    Perform VTP administrative functions.

Switch(vlan)#exit
APPLY completed.
Exiting....

Switch>enable
Switch#configure terminal
Enter configuration commands, one per line.  End with CNTL/Z.
Switch(config)#interface fastEthernet 0/5
Switch(config-if)#switchport mode access
Switch(config-if)#switchport access vlan 2
Switch(config)#interface fastEthernet 0/6
Switch(config-if)#switchport mode access
Switch(config-if)#switchport access vlan 2
Switch(config)#interface fastEthernet 0/7
Switch(config-if)#switchport mode access
Switch(config-if)#switchport access vlan 2
Switch(config)#interface fastEthernet 0/8
Switch(config-if)#switchport mode access
Switch(config-if)#switchport access vlan 2
Switch(config)#interface range fastEthernet 0/9 - 12
Switch(config-if)#switchport mode access
Switch(config-if)#switchport access vlan 3
Switch(config-if)#^Z

Switch#show vlan brief

VLAN Name                             Status    Ports
---- -------------------------------- --------- -------------------------------
1    default                          active    Fa0/1, Fa0/2, Fa0/3, Fa0/4
                                                Fa0/13, Fa0/14, Fa0/15, Fa0/16
                                                Fa0/18, Fa0/19, Fa0/20, Fa0/21
                                                Fa0/22, Fa0/23, Fa0/24, Gi0/1
                                                Gi0/2
2    barney-2                         active    Fa0/5, Fa0/6, Fa0/7, Fa0/8
3    wilma-3                          active    Fa0/9, Fa0/10, Fa0/11, Fa0/12
```

Example 3-1 *Single-Switch VLAN Configuration Matching Figure 3-8 (Continued)*

```
1002 fddi-default              active
1003 token-ring-default        active
1004 fddinet-default           active
1005 trnet-default             active

Switch#show vlan id 2

VLAN Name                       Status    Ports
---- -------------------------- --------- -------------------------------
2    barney-2                   active    Fa0/5, Fa0/6, Fa0/7, Fa0/8

VLAN Type  SAID     MTU   Parent RingNo BridgeNo Stp  BrdgMode Trans1 Trans2
---- ----- -------- ----- ------ ------ -------- ---- -------- ------ ------
2    enet  100002   1500  -      -      -        -    -        0      0

Remote SPAN VLAN
----------------
Disabled

Primary Secondary Type               Ports
------- --------- ------------------ ------------------------------------
```

In this example, the user starts by creating two new VLANs, barney-2 and wilma-3. Then, interfaces 1 through 4 are placed in VLAN 1, interfaces 5 through 8 in VLAN 2, and interfaces 9 through 12 in VLAN 3, as shown in Figure 3-8. However, the configuration requires the use of VLAN configuration mode as well as the normal configuration mode.

VLAN configuration mode behaves a little differently from configuration mode. First, to enter VLAN configuration mode, you use the **vlan database** EXEC command instead of **configure terminal**. To add VLANs, you use the **vlan** command, as shown in the **vlan 2 name barney-2** and **vlan 3 name Wilma-3** commands.

Interestingly, these two new VLANs are not really created in this example until the **exit** command is used. Before using any configuration added in VLAN configuration mode, you must tell the switch to accept the changes. Notice the highlighted help text shown immediately after the **vlan** commands in the example. It implies that the **exit** and **apply** commands would cause these changes to be accepted, but the **abort** command would cause the changes to be aborted—in other words, not accepted. In the example, the **exit** command is used, both when exiting VLAN configuration mode and when accepting the changes. Notice that the highlighted message following the **exit** command shows that the switch even tells you that the "apply" completed successfully, creating the two VLANs in this case.

After the VLANs are created, configuration mode can be used to assign each interface to the right VLAN. Cisco IOS software assigns each interface to VLAN 1 by default, so no commands are required for interfaces fastethernet 0/1 through 0/4. For the next four ports, the interface subcommand command **switchport access vlan 2** puts each interface into VLAN 2. (Trunk negotiations are disabled on those interfaces by telling the switch that these interfaces are used as access ports, using the **switchport mode access** command.)

Example 3-1 shows the user entering the same commands for interfaces 0/5 through 0/8. The switch IOS lets you configure more than one interface at once, as seen with the **interface range fastEthernet 0/9 - 12** command. This command tells the switch to add the commands that follow to all four interfaces in the range. In this case, each interface is placed in VLAN 3 by the **switchport access vlan 3** command.

After sifting through the configuration, you can see that VLAN configuration doesn't take a lot of commands. In fact, if you had entered just the **switchport access vlan** commands before creating the VLANs in VLAN configuration mode, the switch would have automatically created the VLANs. The VLAN names would have been boring—names such as "VLAN 1" and "VLAN 2," with no Flintstones cartoon characters in the name—but it would have worked.

Finally, the end of Example 3-1 lists a couple of important **show** commands. The **show vlan brief** command gives a quick synopsis of the VLANs and the interfaces in each VLAN. Notice the highlighted portions of the two newly created VLANs. If you want more details about a particular VLAN, you can use the **show vlan** command to list its details, identifying it by name or by VLAN ID. In this case, the **show vlan id 2** command shows information about VLAN 2.

VLAN Trunking Configuration

Example 3-2 shows the same switch as in the previous example, but with a trunk to a second switch added, as shown in Figure 3-9. The new switch is a 2950 series switch. Sw1-2950 is configured as the VTP server, with trunking in a "desirable" state. Sw2-2950 is a VTP client, with trunking in an "auto" state.

Figure 3-9 *Network with Two Switches and Three VLANs*

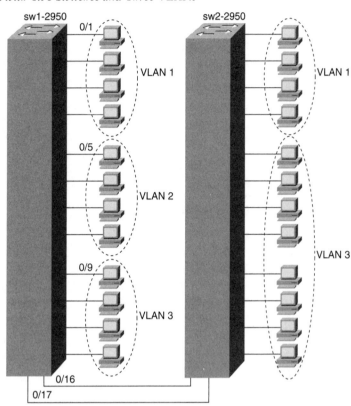

Example 3-2 *Trunking: Configuration and* show *Commands on 2950 Switches 1 and 2*

```
sw1-2950#configure terminal
Enter configuration commands, one per line.  End with CNTL/Z.
sw1-2950(config)#interface fastethernet 0/17
sw1-2950(config-if)#switchport mode dynamic desirable
sw1-2950(config-if)#^Z
sw1-2950#vlan database
sw1-2950(vlan)#vtp domain fred
Changing VTP domain name from NULL to fred
sw1-2950(vlan)#exit
APPLY completed.
Exiting....

sw1-2950#show vtp status
VTP Version                     : 2
Configuration Revision          : 1
Maximum VLANs supported locally : 1005
Number of existing VLANs        : 7
VTP Operating Mode              : Server
VTP Domain Name                 : fred
```

continues

Example 3-2   *Trunking: Configuration and* **show** *Commands on 2950 Switches 1 and 2 (Continued)*

```
VTP Pruning Mode              : Disabled
VTP V2 Mode                   : Disabled
VTP Traps Generation          : Disabled
MD5 digest                    : 0x54 0x80 0xA5 0x82 0x8D 0x8E 0x5F 0x94
Configuration last modified by 0.0.0.0 at 3-1-93 00:31:11
Local updater ID is 10.1.1.10 on interface Vl1 (lowest numbered VLAN interface found)

sw1-2950#show interfaces fastEthernet 0/17 switchport
Name: Fa0/17
Switchport: Enabled
Administrative Mode: dynamic desirable
Operational Mode: trunk
Administrative Trunking Encapsulation: negotiate
Operational Trunking Encapsulation: 802.1Q
Negotiation of Trunking: On
Access Mode VLAN: 1 (default)
Trunking Native Mode VLAN: 1 (default)
Administrative private-vlan host-association: none
Administrative private-vlan mapping: none
Operational private-vlan: none
Trunking VLANs Enabled: ALL
Pruning VLANs Enabled: 2-1001

Protected: false
Unknown unicast blocked: disabled
Unknown multicast blocked: disabled


Voice VLAN: none (Inactive)
Appliance trust: none

sw1-2950#show interfaces fastEthernet 0/17 trunk

Port        Mode         Encapsulation  Status        Native vlan
Fa0/17      desirable    n-isl          trunking      1

Port        Vlans allowed on trunk
Fa0/17      1-4094

Port        Vlans allowed and active in management domain
Fa0/17      1-3

Port        Vlans in spanning tree forwarding state and not pruned
Fa0/17      1-3
!
! Next command from sw2-2950
!
sw2-2950#show vlan
```

Example 3-2 *Trunking: Configuration and* **show** *Commands on 2950 Switches 1 and 2 (Continued)*

```
VLAN Name              Status    Ports
-----------------------------------------
1    default           Enabled   1-12, AUI, fa 0/16, fa 0/17
2    barney-2          Enabled
3    wilma-3           Enabled
1002 fddi-default      Suspended
1003 token-ring-defau  Suspended
1004 fddinet-default   Suspended
1005 trnet-default     Suspended
-----------------------------------------
```

The example begins with interface 0/17 being configured as a trunk. On sw1-2950 the **switchport mode dynamic desirable** command causes the interface to negotiate to form a trunk. It negotiates whether to use trunking at all. sw2-2950 uses a trunk setting of **auto**, so assuming that the link is working, a trunk forms.

The configuration options for trunking commands on Cisco switches can be a little confusing. The most typical mistake is setting both sides to the **dynamic auto** setting. If you set both sides to **auto**, a trunk never forms, and you cannot pass VLAN traffic across the link.

In production networks, you might choose to simply configure the trunks as on, particularly because you know which ports should be trunks. However, **auto** and **desirable** let you configure the trunks remotely, without stopping the flow of traffic.

Table 3-5 summarizes the different trunking options on the 2950 and their meanings.

Table 3-5 *2950 Trunk Configuration Options with the* **switchport mode** *Command*

Option	Description	Trunking Action
access	Disables port trunk mode and does not even attempt to form a trunk on the interface.	Does not trunk.
trunk	Configures the port in permanent trunk mode.	Always tries to trunk.
dynamic desirable	Triggers the port to negotiate the link from nontrunking to trunk mode. The port negotiates to a trunk port if the connected device is in the **trunk, dynamic desirable,** or **dynamic auto** state. Otherwise, the port becomes a nontrunk port.	Trunks to switches set to the **trunk, dynamic desirable,** or **dynamic auto** state.
dynamic auto	Lets a port become a trunk only if the connected device is in the **dynamic desirable** or **trunk** state.	Trunks to switches set to the **trunk** or **dynamic desirable** state.

Next in Example 3-2, VLAN configuration mode is used to set the VTP domain name using the **vtp domain fred** command. sw1-2950 does not need to be configured as a VTP server, because Cisco switches default to be VTP servers. sw2-2950 was already configured to be a VTP client, in VTP domain fred, so in order for VTP to work, sw1-2950 needed to also use VTP domain fred. The **show vtp** command that follows shows that sw1-2950 is a VTP server in domain fred.

To find out if the link between the two interfaces is trunking, you can use either the **show interfaces fastEthernet 0/17 switchport** or **show interfaces fastEthernet 0/17 trunk** command on sw1-2950. As shown in Example 3-2, both commands list the configured setting (**dynamic desirable**), the status (trunking, which means that trunking is working), and the trunking protocol, which is 802.1Q in this case. (2950 switches only support 802.1Q.)

With the trunking protocol working, and with VTP working to distribute VLAN configuration information, sw2-2950 should learn about VLANs 2 and 3. The last command in Example 3-2 is taken from sw2-2950, a 2950 series switch. It shows that sw2-2950 does learn about VLANs barney-2 and wilma-3.

Foundation Summary

The "Foundation Summary" section lists the most important facts from the chapter. Although this section does not list everything that will be on the exam, a well-prepared CCNA candidate should at a minimum know all the details in each Foundation Summary before taking the exam.

Figure 3-10 shows the general idea of a VLAN, showing two different VLANs/broadcast domains.

Figure 3-10   *Network with Two VLANs Using One Switch*

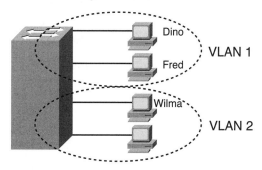

Table 3-6 summarizes the key features and points of comparison between ISL and 802.1Q.

Table 3-6   *ISL and 802.1Q Compared*

Function	ISL	802.1Q
Standards body that defines the protocol	Cisco-proprietary	IEEE
Encapsulates the original frame	Yes	No
Allows multiple spanning trees	Yes, with PVST+	Yes, with PVST+ or 802.1S
Uses a native VLAN	No	Yes

Table 3-7 offers a comparative overview of the three VTP modes.

Table 3-7 *VTP Modes*

Function	Server Mode	Client Mode	Transparent Mode
Originates VTP advertisements	Yes	No	No
Processes received advertisements and synchronizes VLAN configuration information with other switches	Yes	Yes	No
Forwards VTP advertisements received in a trunk	Yes	Yes	Yes
Saves VLAN configuration in NVRAM	Yes	No	Yes
Can create, modify, or delete VLANs using configuration commands	Yes	No	Yes

Table 3-8 summarizes the different trunking options on the 2950 and their meanings.

Table 3-8 *2950 Trunk Configuration Options with the* **switchport mode** *Command*

Option	Description
access	Disables port trunk mode and does not even attempt to form a trunk on the interface.
trunk	Configures the port into permanent trunk mode.
dynamic desirable	Triggers the port to negotiate the link from nontrunking to trunk mode. The port negotiates to a trunk port if the connected device is either in the **trunk, dynamic desirable,** or **dynamic auto** state. Otherwise, the port becomes a nontrunk port.
dynamic auto	Lets a port become a trunk only if the connected device has the state set to **dynamic desirable** or **trunk**.

Q&A

As mentioned in the Introduction, you have two choices for review questions. The following questions give you a bigger challenge than the exam because they are open-ended. By reviewing with this more-difficult question format, you can exercise your memory better and prove your conceptual and factual knowledge of the topics covered in this chapter. The answers to these questions are found in Appendix A.

For more practice with exam-like question formats, including multiple-choice questions and those using a router simulator, use the exam engine on the CD.

1. Define broadcast domain.

2. Define VLAN.

3. If two Cisco LAN switches are connected using Fast Ethernet, what VLAN trunking protocols can be used? If only one VLAN spans both switches, is a VLAN trunking protocol needed?

4. Define VTP.

5. Name the three VTP modes. Which mode does not allow VLANs to be added or modified?

6. What Catalyst 2950 switch command configures 802.1Q trunking on fastethernet port 0/12, so that as long as the switch port on the other end of the trunk is not disabled (off) or configured to not negotiate to become a trunk, the trunk is definitely placed in trunking mode?

7. What type of VTP mode allows a switch to create VLANs and advertise them to other switches?

8. Must all members of the same VLAN be in the same collision domain, the same broadcast domain, or both?

9. What is Cisco's proprietary trunking protocol over Ethernet?

10. Explain the benefits provided by VTP pruning.

11. Consider the phrase "A VLAN is a broadcast domain is an IP subnet." Do you agree or disagree? Why?

12. What fields are added or changed in an Ethernet header when you use 802.1Q? Where is the VLAN ID in those fields?

13. Explain how a switch in VTP transparent mode treats VTP messages received from a VTP server.

14. What command on a 2950 switch creates VLAN 5? What configuration mode is required?

15. What command on a 2950 switch puts an interface into VLAN 5? What configuration mode is required?

16. Describe the basic differences in the processes used by VLAN configuration mode and the normally used configuration mode.

17. Give the correct syntax for the commands that put an interface into the various trunking modes, and identify which commands work when the switch on the other side of the link uses the **auto** option.

18. What 2950 **show** commands list trunk status, both configured and operational?

Cisco Published ICND Exam Topics*
Covered in This Part:

* Always re-check www.cisco.com for the latest posted exam topics

Part II: TCP/IP

This chapter covers the following subjects:

- IP Addressing Review

- Analyzing and Interpreting IP Addresses and Subnets

CHAPTER 4

IP Addressing and Subnetting

In this chapter, you will learn about the concepts and mathematics that let you analyze IP addresses and subnets. IP addressing is the only major topic covered on both CCNA exams. To answer questions on either CCNA exam, you need to understand the structure of IP addresses, list the addresses in the same subnet, list the other subnets of that same network, identify the number of hosts in a subnet, and understand other information about addresses and subnets. This chapter describes the math and processes used to answer these questions.

The material in the "Foundation Topics" section of this chapter is an exact duplicate of the material from Chapter 12, "IP Addressing and Subnetting," of my book *CCNA INTRO Exam Certification Guide*. If you bought both books and you have read Chapter 12 in the other book, the only thing new in this chapter is that some of the questions at the end of the chapter are different. So feel free to review the Q&A questions.

If you need work on IP subnetting and addressing, this chapter is meant for you. It is very thorough, and it is long because of the number of examples and because the text explains how to examine the topic of IP addressing from the same perspectives as the exam. But when you are finished, you should have a thorough understanding, as well as all the skills you need to answer questions well and quickly on either CCNA exam. Please refer to Appendix F for some further details about a few of the topics in this chapter.

"Do I Know This Already?" Quiz

The purpose of the "Do I Know This Already?" quiz is to help you decide if you need to read the entire chapter. If you intend to read the entire chapter, you do not necessarily need to answer these questions now.

The ten-question quiz, derived from the major sections in the "Foundation Topics" section, helps you determine how to spend your limited study time.

Table 4-1 outlines the major topics discussed in this chapter and the "Do I Know This Already?" quiz questions that correspond to those topics.

Table 4-1 *"Do I Know This Already?" Foundation Topics Section-to-Question Mapping*

Foundations Topics Section	Questions Covered in This Section
Analyzing and Interpreting IP Addresses and Subnets	1–10

CAUTION The goal of self-assessment is to gauge your mastery of the topics in this chapter. If you don't know the answer to a question or you're only partially sure of the answer, you should mark this question as wrong for purposes of the self-assessment. Giving yourself credit for an answer you guess correctly skews your self-assessment results and might give you a false sense of security.

1. Which of the following is the result of a Boolean AND between IP address 150.150.4.100 and mask 255.255.192.0?

   a. 1001 0110 1001 0110 0000 0100 0110 0100

   b. 1001 0110 1001 0110 0000 0000 0000 0000

   c. 1001 0110 1001 0110 0000 0100 0000 0000

   d. 1001 0110 0000 0000 0000 0000 0000 0000

2. If mask 255.255.255.128 were used with a Class B network, how many subnets could exist, with how many hosts per subnet, respectively?

   a. a 256 and 256

   b. a 254 and 254

   c. a 62 and 1022

   d. a 1022 and 62

   e. a 510 and 126

   f. a 126 and 510

3. If mask 255.255.255.240 were used with a Class C network, how many subnets could exist, with how many hosts per subnet, respectively?

   a. 16 and 16

   b. 14 and 14

   c. 12 and 12

   d. 8 and 32

   e. 32 and 8

   f. 6 and 30

   g. 30 and 6

4. Which of the following IP addresses are not in the same subnet as 190.4.80.80, mask 255.255.255.0?

   a. 190.4.80.1

   b. 190.4.80.50

   c. 190.4.80.100

   d. 190.4.80.200

   e. 190.4.90.1

   f. 10.1.1.1

5. Which of the following IP addresses is not in the same subnet as 190.4.80.80, mask 255.255.240.0?

   a. 190.4.80.1

   b. 190.4.80.50

   c. 190.4.80.100

   d. 190.4.80.200

   e. 190.4.90.1

   f. 10.1.1.1

6. Which of the following IP addresses are not in the same subnet as 190.4.80.80, mask 255.255.255.128?

   a. 190.4.80.1

   b. 190.4.80.50

   c. 190.4.80.100

   d. 190.4.80.200

   e. 190.4.90.1

   f. 10.1.1.1

7. Which of the following subnet masks lets a Class B network allow subnets to have up to 150 hosts and up to 164 subnets?

   a. 255.0.0.0

   b. 255.255.0.0

   c. 255.255.255.0

   d. 255.255.192.0

   e. 255.255.240.0

   f. 255.255.252.0

   g. 255.255.255.192

   h. 255.255.255.240

8. Which of the following subnet masks let a Class A network allow subnets to have up to 150 hosts and up to 164 subnets?

   a. 255.0.0.0

   b. 255.255.0.0

   c. 255.255.255.0

   d. 255.255.192.0

   e. 255.255.240.0

   f. 255.255.252.0

   g. 255.255.255.192

   h. 255.255.255.240

9. Which of the following are valid subnet numbers in network 180.1.0.0 when using mask 255.255.248.0?

   a. 180.1.2.0

   b. 180.1.4.0

   c. 180.1.8.0

   d. 180.1.16.0

   e. 180.1.32.0

   f. 180.1.40.0

10. Which of the following are valid subnet numbers in network 180.1.0.0 when using mask 255.255.255.0?

   a. 180.1.2.0

   b. 180.1.4.0

   c. 180.1.8.0

   d. 180.1.16.0

   e. 180.1.32.0

   f. 180.1.40.0

The answers to the "Do I Know This Already?" quiz appear in Appendix A. The suggested choices for your next step are as follows:

■ **8 or less overall score**—Read the entire chapter. This includes the "Foundation Topics," "Foundation Summary," and "Q&A" sections.

■ **9 or 10 overall score**—If you want more review on these topics, skip to the "Foundation Summary" section and then go to the "Q&A" section. Otherwise, move to the next chapter.

Foundation Topics

This chapter begins with a brief review of IP addressing and subnetting. Following that, the text takes a thorough look at several types of IP addressing questions and the math you can use to find the answers.

IP Addressing Review

Before we look at the math behind IP addressing, a quick review will be helpful.

Many different Class A, B, and C networks exist. Table 4-2 summarizes the possible network numbers, the total number of each type, and the number of hosts in each Class A, B, and C network.

> **NOTE** In the table, the Valid Network Numbers row shows actual network numbers. There are several reserved cases. For example, network 0.0.0.0 (originally defined for use as a broadcast address) and network 127.0.0.0 (still available for use as the loopback address) are reserved. Networks 128.0.0.0, 191.255.0.0, 192.0.0.0, and 223.255.255.0 also are reserved.

Table 4-2 *List of All Possible Valid Network Numbers*

	Class A	Class B	Class C
First Octet Range	1 to 126	128 to 191	192 to 223
Valid Network Numbers	1.0.0.0 to 126.0.0.0	128.1.0.0 to 191.254.0.0	192.0.1.0 to 223.255.254.0
Number of Networks in This Class	$2^7 - 2$	$2^{14} - 2$	$2^{21} - 2$
Number of Hosts Per Network	$2^{24} - 2$	$2^{16} - 2$	$2^8 - 2$
Size of Network Part of Address (bytes)	1	2	3
Size of Host Part of Address (bytes)	3	2	1

Without subnetting, a different IP network must be used for each physical network. For example, Figure 4-1 shows three IP addresses, each from a different network. One address is in a Class A network, one is in a Class B network, and one is in a Class C network.

Figure 4-1 *Class A, B, and C IP Addresses and Their Formats*

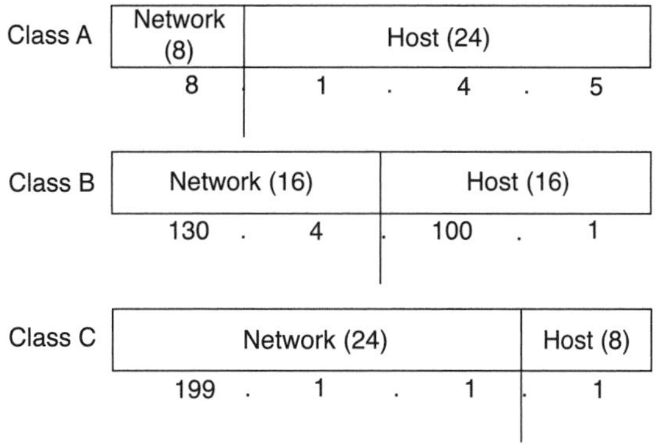

By definition, an IP address that begins with 8 in the first octet is in a Class A network, so the network part of the address is the first byte, or first octet. An address that begins with 130 is in a Class B network. By definition, Class B addresses have a 2-byte network part, as shown. Finally, any address that begins with 199 is in a Class C network, which has a 3-byte network part. Also by definition, a Class A address has a 3-byte host part, Class B has a 2-byte host part, and Class C has a 1-byte host part.

Humans can simply remember the numbers in Table 4-2 and the concepts in Figure 4-1 and then quickly determine the network and host part of an IP address. Computers, however, use a mask to define the size of the network and the host parts of an address. The logic behind the mask results in the same conventions of Class A, B, and C networks that you already know, but the computer can deal with it better as a binary math problem. The mask is a 32-bit binary number, usually written in dotted-decimal format. The purpose of the mask is to define the structure of an IP address. In short, the mask defines the size of the host parts of an IP address, representing the host part of the IP address with binary 0s in the mask. The Class A mask has its last 24 bits as binary 0, which means that the last three octets of the mask are 0s. Table 4-3 summarizes the default masks and reflects the sizes of the two parts of an IP address.

Table 4-3 *Class A, B, and C Networks: Network and Host Parts and Default Masks*

Class of Address	Size of Network Part of Address in Bits	Size of Host Part of Address in Bits	Default Mask for Each Class of Network
A	8	24	255.0.0.0
B	16	16	255.255.0.0
C	24	8	255.255.255.0

IP Subnetting

IP subnetting creates vastly larger numbers of smaller groups of IP addresses compared with simply using Class A, B, and C conventions. The Class A, B, and C rules still exist, but now a single Class A, B, or C network can be subdivided into many smaller groups. Subnetting treats a subdivision of a single Class A, B, or C network as if it were a network itself. By doing so, a single Class A, B, or C network can be subdivided into many nonoverlapping subnets.

Figures 4-2 and 4-3 show the basic differences between a network that does not use subnetting and one that does. First, look at Figure 4-2, which uses six different IP networks.

Figure 4-2 *Network Topology Using Six IP Networks*

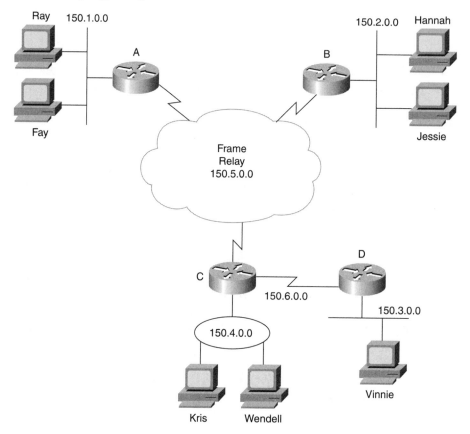

The design shown in Figure 4-2 requires six groups, each of which is a Class B network. The four LANs each use a single Class B network. In other words, the LANs attached to Routers A, B, C, and D are each a separate network. Additionally, the two serial interfaces comprising the point-to-point serial link between Routers C and D use the same network, because these two interfaces are not separated by a router. Finally, the three router interfaces comprising the Frame Relay network with Routers A, B, and C are not separated by an IP router and would comprise the sixth network.

> **NOTE** Other Frame Relay IP addressing options would require one or two more IP network numbers for this physical network.

As in Figure 4-2, the design shown in Figure 4-3 requires six groups. Unlike Figure 4-2, Figure 4-3 uses six subnets, each of which is a subnet of a single Class B network.

Figure 4-3   *Same Network Topology Using One IP Network with Six Subnets*

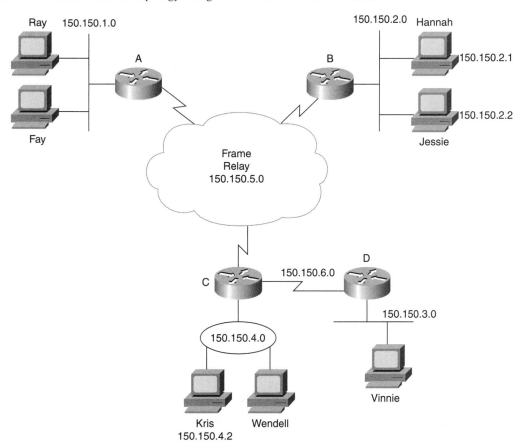

This design subnets Class B network 150.150.0.0. The IP network designer has chosen a mask of 255.255.255.0, the last octet of which implies 8 host bits. Because it is a Class B network, there are 16 network bits. Therefore, there are 8 subnet bits, which happen to be bits 17 through 24—in other words, the third octet.

Note that the network parts (the first two octets in this example) all begin with 150.150, meaning that each of the six subnets is a subnet of Class B network 150.150.0.0.

With subnetting, the third part of an IP address—namely, the subnet—appears in the middle of the address. This field is created by "stealing" or "borrowing" bits from the host part of the address. The size of the network part of the address never shrinks. In other words, Class A, B, and C rules still apply when you define the size of the network part of an address. However, the host part of the address shrinks to make room for the subnet part of the address. Figure 4-4 shows the format of addresses when subnetting is used.

Figure 4-4   *Address Formats When Subnetting Is Used*

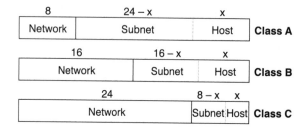

Analyzing and Interpreting IP Addresses and Subnets

You shouldn't be surprised to learn that IP addressing is one of the most important topics on both exams. You need a comfortable, confident understanding of IP addressing and subnetting for success on any Cisco certification. You should be prepared to answer questions about the following:

- An interpretation of an address
- Its network number
- Its subnet number
- The other IP addresses in the same subnet
- The broadcast address
- The other subnets that could be used if the same mask were in use

In other words, you had better know IP addressing and subnetting!

Besides just answering questions on the CCNA exams, network engineers need to understand subnetting very well to do their jobs. Engineers who work with multiple networks must decipher IP addresses quickly, without running off to use a subnet calculator tool. For example, someone with a problem might call and tell you his IP address. After finding out the mask that's used, you enter the **show ip route** command on the router. That command typically lists subnets, so you need to be able to easily figure out the subnet of which the address is a member. And not all networks use nice, easy subnet masks.

No matter how useful this book might be toward helping you with a real networking job, its primary goal is to help you pass the exam. Therefore, the rest of this chapter is geared toward helping you understand how to interpret and analyze IP addresses.

Math Operations Used to Answer Subnetting Questions

Computers, especially routers, do not think about IP addresses in terms of the conventions shown in Table 4-2. They think in terms of 32-bit binary numbers. This is fine, because technically that's what IP addresses are. Also, computers use a mask to define the structure of these binary IP addresses. A full understanding of what this means is not too difficult. However, getting accustomed to doing the binary math in your head can be challenging, particularly if you don't do it every day.

In this section, you will read about two key math operations that will be used throughout the discussion of answering CCNA addressing and subnetting questions. One operation converts IP addresses from decimal to binary and then back to decimal. The other operation performs a binary math operation called a Boolean AND.

Converting IP Addresses from Decimal to Binary and Back Again

If you already know how binary works, how binary-to-decimal and decimal-to-binary conversion work, and how to convert IP addresses from decimal to binary and back, skip to the next section, "The Boolean AND Operation."

IP addresses are 32-bit binary numbers written as a series of decimal numbers separated by periods. To examine an address in its true form, binary, you need to convert from decimal to binary. To put a 32-bit binary number in the decimal form that is needed when configuring a router, you need to convert the 32-bit number back to decimal 8 bits at a time.

One key to the conversion process for IP addresses is remembering these facts:

When you convert from one format to the other, each decimal number represents 8 bits.

When you convert from decimal to binary, each decimal number converts to an 8-bit number.

When you convert from binary to decimal, each set of 8 consecutive bits converts to one decimal number.

Consider the conversion of IP address 150.150.2.1 to binary. The number 150, when converted to its 8-bit binary equivalent, is 10010110. How do you know that? For now, look at the conversion chart in Appendix B, "Binary-to-Decimal Conversion Chart." The next byte, another decimal 150, is converted to 10010110. The third byte, decimal 2, is converted to 00000010. Finally, the fourth byte, decimal 1, is converted to 00000001. The combined series of 8-bit numbers is the 32-bit IP address—in this case, 10010110 10010110 00000010 00000001.

If you start with the binary version of the IP address, you first separate it into four sets of eight digits. Then you convert each set of eight binary digits to its decimal equivalent. For example, writing an IP address as follows is correct, but not very useful:

     10010110100101100000000100000001

To convert this number to a more-convenient decimal form, first separate it into four sets of eight digits:

     10010110 10010110 00000010 00000001

Then look in the conversion chart in Appendix B. You see that the first 8-bit number converts to 150, and so does the second. The third set of 8 bits converts to 2, and the fourth converts to 1, giving you 150.150.2.1.

Using the chart in Appendix B makes this much easier, but you will not have the chart at the exam, of course! So you can do a couple of things. First, you can learn how to do the conversion. The book does not cover it, but the websites referenced at the end of this section can help. The other alternative is to use the chart when studying, and study the examples that show you how to manipulate IP addresses and find the right answers to the test questions without doing any binary math. If that works for you, you do not need to be speedy and proficient at doing binary-to-decimal and decimal-to-binary conversions.

One last important fact: With subnetting, the subnet and host parts of the address might span only part of a byte of the IP address. But when you convert from binary to decimal and decimal to binary, the rule of always converting an 8-bit binary number to a decimal number is always true. However, when thinking about subnetting, you need to ignore byte boundaries and think of IP addresses as 32-bit numbers without specific byte boundaries. This is explained more in the section "Finding the Subnet Number."

Here are some websites that might help you if you want more information:

- For basic information on base 10, base 2 (binary), and conversion practice, visit www.ibilce.unesp.br/courseware/datas/numbers.htm#mark2.
- For a description of the conversion process, try doit.ort.org/course/inforep/135.htm.

- For another description of the conversion process, try www.goshen.edu/compsci/ mis200/decbinary.htm.

- For some free video classes that cover binary, conversion, and subnetting, go to www.learntosubnet.com.

The Boolean AND Operation

George Boole, a mathematician who lived in the 1800s, created a branch of mathematics that came to be called Boolean math after its creator. Boolean math has many applications in computing theory. In fact, you can find subnet numbers given an IP address and subnet mask using a Boolean AND.

A Boolean AND is a math operation performed on a pair of one-digit binary numbers. The result is another one-digit binary number. The actual math is even simpler than those first two sentences! The following list shows the four possible inputs to a Boolean AND, and the result:

- 0 AND 0 yields a 0

- 0 AND 1 yields a 0

- 1 AND 0 yields a 0

- 1 AND 1 yields a 1

In other words, the input to the equation consists of two one-digit binary numbers, and the output of the equation is one single-digit binary number. The only time the result is a binary 1 is when both input numbers are also binary 1; otherwise, the result of a Boolean AND is a 0.

You can perform a Boolean AND on longer binary numbers, but you are really just performing an AND on each pair of numbers. For instance, if you wanted to AND together two four-digit numbers, 0110 and 0011, you would perform an AND on the first digit of each number and write down the answer. Then you would perform an AND on the second digit of each number, and so on, through the four digits. Table 4-4 shows the general idea.

Table 4-4 *Bitwise Boolean AND Between Two Four-Digit Numbers*

	Four-Digit Binary Number	First Digit	Second Digit	Third Digit	Fourth Digit
First Number	0110	0	1	1	0
Second Number	0011	0	0	1	1
Boolean AND Result	0010	0	0	1	0

This table separates the four digits of each original number to make the point more obvious. Look at the "First Digit" column. The first digit of the first number is 0, and the first digit of the second number is also 0. 0 AND 0 yields a binary 0, which is listed as the Boolean AND result in that same column. Similarly, the second digits of the two original numbers are 1 and 0, respectively, so the Boolean AND result in the "Second Digit" column shows a 0. For the third digit, the two original numbers' third digits are 1 and 1, so the AND result this time shows a binary 1. Finally, the fourth digits of the two original numbers are 0 and 1, so the Boolean AND result is 0 for that column.

When you Boolean AND together two longer binary numbers, you perform what is called a *bitwise Boolean AND*. This term simply means that you do what the previous example shows: You AND together the first digits from each of the two original numbers, and then the second digits, and then the third, and so on, until each pair of single-digit binary numbers has been ANDed.

IP subnetting math frequently uses a Boolean AND between two 32-bit binary numbers. The actual operation works just like the example in Table 4-4, except it is longer.

To discover the subnet number in which a particular IP address resides, you perform a bitwise AND between the IP address and the subnet mask. Although humans can sometimes look at an IP address and mask in decimal and derive the subnet number, routers and other computers use a Boolean AND between the IP address and the subnet mask to find the subnet number, so you need to understand this process. In this chapter, you will also read about a process by which you can find the subnet number without using binary conversion or Boolean ANDs.

Table 4-5 shows an example of the derivation of a subnet number.

Table 4-5 *Bitwise Boolean AND Example*

	Decimal	Binary
Address	150.150.2.1	1001 0110 1001 0110 0000 0010 **0000 0001**
Mask	255.255.255.0	1111 1111 1111 1111 1111 1111 **0000 0000**
Result of AND	150.150.2.0	1001 0110 1001 0110 0000 0010 **0000 0000**

First, focus only on the third column of the table. The binary version of the IP address 150.150.2.1 is listed first. The next row shows the 32-bit binary version of the subnet mask (255.255.255.0). The last row shows the results of a bitwise AND of the two numbers. In other words, the first bit in each number is ANDed, and then the second bit in each number, and then the third, and so on, until all 32 bits in the first number have been ANDed with the bit in the same position in the second number.

The resulting 32-bit number is the subnet number in which 150.150.2.1 resides. All you have to do is convert the 32-bit number back to decimal 8 bits at a time. The subnet number in this case is 150.150.2.0.

If you understand the basic idea but would like additional examples to make it more clear, read on. In the next section, you will use Boolean ANDs to answer basic questions about IP subnetting. Also, on the CD, look for the chapter titled "Subnetting Practice: 25 Subnetting Questions." It offers 25 IP addressing practice questions, each with the binary math worked out for performing the Boolean AND.

Prefix Notation

Any Cisco-oriented IP addressing coverage would be incomplete without a discussion of prefix notation.

In this chapter, you will get more and more comfortable using subnet masks. They can be written in decimal form or as a 32-bit binary number. However, a third alternative called *prefix notation* allows a router to display mask information more succinctly.

To understand prefix notation, it is important to know that all subnet masks have some number of consecutive binary 1s, followed by binary 0s. In other words, a subnet mask cannot have 1s and 0s interspersed throughout the mask. The mask always has some number of binary 1s, followed only by binary 0s.

Prefix notation simply denotes the number of binary 1s in a mask, preceded by a /. In other words, for subnet mask 255.255.255.0, whose binary equivalent is 11111111 11111111 11111111 00000000, the equivalent prefix notation is /24, because there are 24 consecutive binary 1s in the mask. When talking about subnets, you can say things like "That subnet uses a *slash 24 prefix*" or "That subnet has a 24-bit prefix" instead of saying something like "That subnet uses a mask of 255.255.255.0."

Prefix notation makes talking about subnet masks a little easier, and it makes the information displayed by the router a little briefer as well. For instance, just try saying "255.255.255.0" a few times, and imagine the network is down while you're saying it, and you'll hear the benefit.

Now that the basic math tools have been covered, the specifics of how to use them to find the right answers to subnetting questions are covered next.

How Many Hosts and How Many Subnets?

You should also know how to figure out how many network, subnet, and host bits are used with that subnetting scheme. From those facts, you can easily figure out how many hosts exist in the subnet and how many subnets you can create in that network using that subnet mask.

You have already learned that Class A, B, and C networks have 8, 16, or 24 bits in their network fields, respectively. Those rules do not change. You've also read that, without subnetting, Class A, B, and C addresses have 24, 16, or 8 bits in their host fields, respectively. With subnetting, the network part of the address does not shrink or change, but the host field shrinks to make room for the subnet field. So the key to answering these types of questions is to figure out how many host bits remain after subnetting. Then you can tell the size of the subnet field. The rest of the answers follow from those two facts.

The following facts tell you how to find the sizes of the network, subnet, and host parts of an IP address:

> The network part of the address is always defined by class rules.

> The host part of the address is always defined by the mask. Binary 0s in the mask mean that the corresponding address bits are part of the host field.

> The subnet part of the address is what's left over in the 32-bit address.

Table 4-6 lists these three key facts along with the first example. If you have forgotten the ranges of values in the first octet for addresses in Class A, B, and C networks, refer to Table 4-2.

Table 4-6 *First Example, with Rules for Learning the Network, Subnet, and Host Part Sizes*

Step	Example	Rules to Remember
Address	8.1.4.5	—
Mask	255.255.0.0	—
Number of Network Bits	8	Always defined by Class A, B, C
Number of Host Bits	16	Always defined as the number of binary 0s in the mask
Number of Subnet Bits	8	32 – (network size + host size)

This example has 8 network bits because the address is in a Class A network, 8.0.0.0. There are 16 host bits because when you convert 255.255.0.0 to binary, there are 16 binary 0s—the last 16 bits in the mask. (If you don't believe me, look at the binary-to-decimal conversion chart in Appendix B. 255 decimal is eight binary 1s, and 0 decimal is eight binary 0s.) The size of the subnet part of the address is what's left over, or 8 bits.

Two other examples with easy-to-convert masks might help your understanding. Consider address 130.4.102.1 with mask 255.255.255.0. First, 130.4.102.1 is in a Class B network, so there are 16 network bits. A subnet mask of 255.255.255.0 has only eight binary 0s, implying 8 host bits, which leaves 8 subnet bits in this case.

As another example, consider 199.1.1.100 with mask 255.255.255.0. This example doesn't even use subnetting! 199.1.1.100 is in a Class C network, which means that there are 24 network bits. The mask has eight binary 0s, yielding 8 host bits, with no bits remaining for the subnet part of the address. In fact, if you remembered that the default mask for Class C networks is 255.255.255.0, you might have already realized that no subnetting was being used in this example.

You probably can calculate the number of host bits easily if the mask uses only decimal 255s and 0s, because it is easy to remember that decimal 255 represents eight binary 1s and decimal 0 represents eight binary 0s. So, for every decimal 0 in the mask, there are 8 host bits. However, when the mask uses decimal values besides 0 and 255, deciphering the number of host bits is more difficult. Examining the subnet masks in binary helps overcome the challenge. Consider the addresses and masks, along with the binary versions of the masks, shown in Table 4-7.

Table 4-7   *Two Examples Using More-Challenging Masks*

Mask in Decimal	Mask in Binary
130.4.102.1, mask 255.255.252.0	1111 1111 1111 1111 1111 1100 0000 0000
199.1.1.100, mask 255.255.255.224	1111 1111 1111 1111 1111 1111 1110 0000

The number of host bits implied by a mask becomes more apparent after you convert the mask to binary. The first mask, 255.255.252.0, has ten binary 0s, implying a 10-bit host field. Because that mask is used with a Class B address (130.4.102.1), implying 16 network bits, there are 6 remaining subnet bits. In the second example, the mask has only five binary 0s, for 5 host bits. Because the mask is used with a Class C address, there are 24 network bits, leaving only 3 subnet bits. The process so far is straightforward:

- The class rules define the network part.
- The mask binary 0s define the host part.
- What's left over defines the size of the subnet part.

The only big problem occurs when the mask is tricky, which is true in the last two examples. When the mask is tricky, you have two alternatives for deciding how many host bits are defined:

Convert the mask to binary using any method of conversion, and count the number of 0s.

Convert the mask to binary after memorizing the nine decimal and binary values shown in Table 4-8. These are the only nine valid decimal values used in a subnet mask. Converting a mask to binary without having to convert from decimal to binary is much faster.

Table 4-8 lists the only valid decimal values in a mask and their binary equivalents. Memorizing these values will help you convert masks between their decimal and binary forms more quickly on the exam.

Table 4-8 *Decimal and Binary Values in a Single Octet of a Valid Subnet Mask*

Decimal	Binary
0	0000 0000
128	1000 0000
192	1100 0000
224	1110 0000
240	1111 0000
248	1111 1000
252	1111 1100
254	1111 1110
255	1111 1111

Binary conversion of a subnet mask without the use of a calculator, PC, or decimal-to-binary conversion chart becomes easy after you memorize this chart. The binary equivalents of 255 and decimal 0 are obvious. The other seven values are not! But notice the values in succession: Each value has an additional binary 1 and one less binary 0. Each successive mask value reduces the number of host bits by 1 and adds 1 to the size of the subnet field. If you simply memorize each decimal value and its binary equivalent, converting masks from decimal to binary will be a breeze. In fact, you could sit down to take the exam, and before starting, go ahead and write down the information in the table so you could easily refer to it during the exam.

This book has not yet told you how to answer questions like this:

> Given an address and mask, how many subnets are there? And how many hosts are there in a single subnet?

Two simple formulas provide the answers. They are based on the information you just learned how to derive:

$$\text{Number of subnets} = 2^{number\text{-}of\text{-}subnet\text{-}bits} - 2$$
$$\text{Number of hosts per subnet} = 2^{number\text{-}of\text{-}host\text{-}bits} - 2$$

These formulas calculate the number of things that can be numbered using a binary number and then subtract 2 for two special cases. IP addressing conventions define that two subnets per network not be used and that two hosts per subnet not be used.

One reserved subnet, the subnet that has all binary 0s in the subnet field, is called the *zero subnet*. The subnet with all binary 1s in the subnet field is called the *broadcast subnet*—and it also is reserved. (In fact, you can use both these subnets on a Cisco router, but it is recommended that you avoid using them. On the exam, the "right" answer is that you do not use them—hence the "minus 2" part of the $2^{number-of-subnet-bits} - 2$ formula.) Actually, the courses upon which CCNA is based now use the term "discouraged" instead of "reserved," meaning that although these two subnets can be used, you should avoid it.

IP addressing conventions also reserve two IP addresses per subnet: the first (all binary 0s in the host field) and last (all binary 1s in the host field) addresses. No tricks exist to make these two addresses usable—they are indeed always reserved.

Table 4-9 summarizes the five examples used so far in this chapter.

Table 4-9 *Five Examples of Addresses/Masks, with the Number of Network, Subnet, and Host Bits*

Address	8.1.4.5/16	130.4.102.1/24	199.1.1.100/24	130.4.102.1/22	199.1.1.100/27
Mask	255.255.0.0	255.255.255.0	255.255.255.0	255.255.252.0	255.255.255.224
Number of Network Bits	8	16	24	16	24
Number of Host Bits	16	8	8	10	5
Number of Subnet Bits	8	8	0	6	3
Number of Hosts Per Subnet	$2^{16} - 2$, or 65,534	$2^8 - 2$, or 254	$2^8 - 2$, or 254	$2^{10} - 2$, or 1022	$2^5 - 2$, or 30
Number of Subnets	$2^8 - 2$, or 254	$2^8 - 2$, or 254	0	$2^6 - 2$, or 62	$2^3 - 2$, or 6

The details of the algorithm used to answer subnetting questions about the number of hosts and subnets are summarized in the following list:

Step 1   Identify the structure of the IP address.

Step 2   Identify the size of the network part of the address based on Class A, B, and C rules.

Step 3   Identify the size of the host part of the address based on the number of binary 0s in the mask. If the mask is tricky, use the chart of typical mask values to convert the mask to binary more quickly.

Step 4   The size of the subnet part is what's "left over"; mathematically, it is 32 – (number of network + host bits).

Step 5 Declare the number of subnets, which is $2^{number-of-subnet-bits} - 2$.

Step 6 Declare the number of hosts per subnet, which is $2^{number-of-host-bits} - 2$.

What Is the Subnet Number, and What Are the IP Addresses in the Subnet?

One of the most common situations you face is after you know an IP address and subnet mask and you must answer questions about them. The question might be straightforward, like "What is the subnet number?", or it might be more subtle, like "Which of the following IP addresses are in the same subnet as the stated address?". In either case, if you can dissect an IP address as described in this chapter, you can answer any variation on this type of question.

In the next several sections, you will learn how to derive the subnet number and the subnet broadcast address. After deriving these two values, you can easily find the range of valid IP addresses in the subnet.

Finding the Subnet Number

Earlier, you learned that computers perform a Boolean AND of the address and mask to find the subnet number. Tables 4-10 through 4-14 show the Boolean AND process for the five examples used in the preceding section.

Table 4-10 *Boolean AND Calculation for the Subnet with Address 8.1.4.5, Mask 255.255.0.0*

Address	8.1.4.5	0000 1000 0000 0001 0000 0100 0000 0101
Mask	255.255.0.0	1111 1111 1111 1111 **0000 0000 0000 0000**
AND Result	8.1.0.0	0000 1000 0000 0001 0000 0000 0000 0000

Table 4-11 *Boolean AND Calculation for the Subnet with Address 130.4.102.1, Mask 255.255.255.0*

Address	130.4.102.1	1000 0010 0000 0100 0110 0110 0000 0001
Mask	255.255.255.0	1111 1111 1111 1111 1111 1111 **0000 0000**
AND Result	130.4.102.0	1000 0010 0000 0100 0110 0110 0000 0000

Table 4-12 *Boolean AND Calculation for the Subnet with Address 199.1.1.100, Mask 255.255.255.0*

Address	199.1.1.100	1100 0111 0000 0001 0000 0001 0110 0100
Mask	255.255.255.0	1111 1111 1111 1111 1111 1111 **0000 0000**
AND Result	199.1.1.0	1100 0111 0000 0001 0000 0001 0000 0000

Table 4-13 *Boolean AND Calculation for the Subnet with Address 130.4.102.1, Mask 255.255.252.0*

Address	130.4.102.1	1000 0010 0000 0100 0110 0110 0000 0001
Mask	255.255.252.0	1111 1111 1111 1111 1111 11**00 0000 0000**
AND Result	130.4.100.0	1000 0010 0000 0100 0110 0100 0000 0000

Table 4-14 *Boolean AND Calculation for the Subnet with Address 199.1.1.100, Mask 255.255.255.224*

Address	199.1.1.100	1100 0111 0000 0001 0000 0001 0110 0100
Mask	255.255.255.224	1111 1111 1111 1111 1111 1111 111**0 0000**
AND Result	199.1.1.96	1100 0111 0000 0001 0000 0001 0110 0000

Although these tables show the answers, they do not show the process. The steps taken to complete the tables are as follows:

Step 1   You start with the decimal address and mask stated in the question.

Step 2   You convert the two numbers to binary, as shown in all five examples.

Step 3   Each bit is ANDed with the bit in the same position in the other number (in other words, a bitwise Boolean AND), giving the result of the Boolean AND.

Step 4   You convert the Boolean AND result back to decimal.

The last step in this process, converting the binary number back to decimal, is the step that causes most of the problems for people new to subnetting. In some cases, the conversion is simple. For instance, in the first example, the subnet mask is 255.255.0.0. Because the mask has only 255s, or 0s in decimal, the boundary between the subnet and host fields is on a byte boundary as well—between the second and third bytes in this case. So the conversion from binary back to decimal for the result of the Boolean AND—0000 1000 0000 0001 0000 0000 0000 0000—typically does not pose a problem.

The confusion typically arises when the boundary between the subnet and host part of the address is in the middle of a byte, which occurs when the subnet mask has a value besides 0 or 255 decimal. For example, with 130.4.102.1, mask 255.255.252.0, the first 6 bits of the third octet comprise the subnet field, and the last 2 bits of the third octet, plus the entire fourth octet, comprise the host field. The problem that some people experience is that they try to convert the 6-bit subnet part from binary to decimal and the 10-bit host part to decimal. However, when converting binary to decimal, to find the dotted decimal IP address you always convert the entire octet—even if part of the octet is in the subnet part of the address and part is in the host part of the address.

So, in this example, the subnet number (130.4.100.0) in binary is 1000 0010 0000 0100 **0110 0100** 0000 0000. The entire third octet is shown in bold, which converts to 100 in decimal. When you convert the whole number, each set of 8 bits is converted to decimal, giving you 130.4.100.0.

Finding the Subnet Broadcast Address

The subnet broadcast address, sometimes called the *directed broadcast address*, can be used to send a packet to every device in a single subnet. However, few tools and protocols use the subnet broadcast address anymore. However, by calculating the subnet broadcast address, you can easily calculate the largest valid IP address in the subnet, which is an important part of answering subnetting questions.

There is a binary math operation to calculate the subnet broadcast address. However, there is a much easier process, especially if you already have the subnet number in binary:

> Change all the host bit values in the subnet number to binary 1s.

You can examine the simple math behind calculating the subnet broadcast address in Tables 4-15 through 4-19. The host parts of the addresses, masks, subnet numbers, and broadcast addresses are in bold.

Table 4-15 *Calculating the Broadcast Address: Address 8.1.4.5, Mask 255.255.0.0*

Address	8.1.4.5	0000 1000 0000 0001 **0000 0100 0000 0101**
Mask	255.255.0.0	1111 1111 1111 1111 **0000 0000 0000 0000**
AND Result	8.1.0.0	0000 1000 0000 0001 **0000 0000 0000 0000**
Broadcast	8.1.255.255	0000 1000 0000 0001 **1111 1111 1111 1111**

Table 4-16 *Calculating the Broadcast Address: Address 130.4.102.1, Mask 255.255.255.0*

Address	130.4.102.1	1000 0010 0000 0100 0110 0110 **0000 0001**
Mask	255.255.255.0	1111 1111 1111 1111 1111 1111 **0000 0000**
AND Result	130.4.102.0	1000 0010 0000 0100 0110 0110 **0000 0000**
Broadcast	130.4.102.255	1000 0010 0000 0100 0110 0110 **1111 1111**

Table 4-17 *Calculating the Broadcast Address: Address 199.1.1.100, Mask 255.255.255.0*

Address	199.1.1.100	1100 0111 0000 0001 0000 0001 **0110 0100**
Mask	255.255.255.0	1111 1111 1111 1111 1111 1111 **0000 0000**
AND Result	199.1.1.0	1100 0111 0000 0001 0000 0001 **0000 0000**
Broadcast	199.1.1.255	1100 0111 0000 0001 0000 0001 **1111 1111**

Table 4-18 *Calculating the Broadcast Address: Address 130.4.102.1, Mask 255.255.252.0*

Address	130.4.102.1	1000 0010 0000 0100 0110 01**10 0000 0001**
Mask	255.255.252.0	1111 1111 1111 1111 1111 11**00 0000 0000**
AND Result	130.4.100.0	1000 0010 0000 0100 0110 01**00 0000 0000**
Broadcast	130.4.103.255	1000 0010 0000 0100 0110 01**11 1111 1111**

Table 4-19 *Calculating the Broadcast Address: Address 199.1.1.100, Mask 255.255.255.224*

Address	199.1.1.100	1100 0111 0000 0001 0000 0001 011**0 0100**
Mask	255.255.255.224	1111 1111 1111 1111 1111 1111 111**0 0000**
AND Result	199.1.1.96	1100 0111 0000 0001 0000 0001 011**0 0000**
Broadcast	199.1.1.127	1100 0111 0000 0001 0000 0001 011**1 1111**

By examining the subnet broadcast addresses in binary, you can see that they are identical to the subnet numbers, except that all host bits have a value of binary 1 instead of binary 0. (Look for the bold digits in the examples.)

> **NOTE** In case you want to know, to derive the broadcast address using Boolean math, start with the subnet number and mask in binary. Invert the mask (change all the 1s to 0s and all the 0s to 1s), and then do a bitwise Boolean OR between the two 32-bit numbers. (An OR yields a 0 when both bits are 0 and yields a 1 in any other case.) The result is the subnet broadcast address.

Finding the Range of Valid IP Addresses in a Subnet

You also need to be able to figure out which IP addresses are in a particular subnet and which are not. You already know how to do the hard part of finding that answer! You know that in any subnet, two numbers are reserved. The two reserved numbers are the subnet number itself and the subnet broadcast address. The subnet number is the numerically smallest number in the subnet, and the broadcast address is the numerically largest number. So the range of valid IP addresses starts with 1 more than the subnet number and ends with the address that is 1 less than the broadcast address. It's that simple!

Here's a formal definition of the "algorithm" to find the first and last IP addresses in a subnet when you know the subnet number and broadcast addresses:

- For the first valid IP address, copy the subnet number, but add 1 to the fourth octet.

- For the last valid IP address, copy the subnet broadcast address, but subtract 1 from the fourth octet.

■ The range of valid IP addresses starts with the first number and ends with the last.

Tables 4-20 through 4-24 summarize the answers for the five examples used in this section.

Table 4-20 *Subnet Chart: 8.1.4.5/255.255.0.0*

Octet	1	2	3	4
Address	8	1	4	5
Mask	255	255	0	0
Subnet Number	8	1	0	0
First Address	8	1	0	1
Broadcast	8	1	255	255
Last Address	8	1	255	254

Table 4-21 *Subnet Chart: 130.4.102.1/255.255.255.0*

Octet	1	2	3	4
Address	130	4	102	1
Mask	255	255	255	0
Subnet Number	130	4	102	0
First Address	130	4	102	1
Broadcast	130	4	102	255
Last Address	130	4	102	254

Table 4-22 *Subnet Chart: 199.1.1.100/255.255.255.0*

Octet	1	2	3	4
Address	199	1	1	100
Mask	255	255	255	0
Subnet Number	199	1	1	0
First Address	199	1	1	1
Broadcast	199	1	1	255
Last Address	199	1	1	254

Table 4-23   *Subnet Chart: 130.4.102.1/255.255.252.0*

Octet	1	2	3	4
Address	130	4	102	1
Mask	255	255	252	0
Subnet Number	130	4	100	0
First Address	130	4	100	1
Broadcast	130	4	103	255
Last Address	130	4	103	254

Table 4-24   *Subnet Chart: 199.1.1.100/255.255.255.224*

Octet	1	2	3	4
Address	199	1	1	100
Mask	255	255	255	224
Subnet Number	199	1	1	96
First Address	199	1	1	97
Broadcast	199	1	1	127
Last Address	199	1	1	126

Finding the Answers Without Using Binary

You can derive the subnet number and broadcast addresses without converting to and from binary or performing Boolean math. Using the binary math required to find the subnet number and broadcast address really does help you understand subnetting to some degree. To get the correct answers faster on the exam, you might want to avoid all the conversions and binary math.

If you can find the subnet number and broadcast address, you can easily find the range of valid addresses in the subnet. The easy math described in this section focuses on helping you find the subnet number and broadcast address.

Easier Math with Easy Masks

Of all the possible subnet masks, three masks, 255.0.0.0, 255.255.0.0, and 255.255.255.0, use only 255s and 0s. I call these "easy" masks because you can find the subnet number and broadcast address easily, without any real math tricks. Perhaps you already know how to find the answers when an easy mask is used. If so, skip to the next section, "Easier Math with Difficult Masks."

Of these three easy masks, 255.0.0.0 does not cause any subnetting. Therefore, this section only worries about how to use the two easy masks that can be used for subnetting— 255.255.0.0 and 255.255.255.0.

The process is simple. To find the subnet number when given an IP address and a mask of 255.255.0.0 or 255.255.255.0, do the following:

Step 1 Copy the first two octets (mask 255.255.0.0) or the first three octets (mask 255.255.255.0) from the original IP address.

Step 2 Write down 0s in the last two octets (mask 255.255.0.0) or the last octet (mask 255.255.255.0).

Yep, it's that easy! Finding the subnet broadcast address is just as easy:

> Do the same thing as you did for finding the subnet, but instead of writing down 0s in the last octet or two, write down 255s.

As soon as you know the subnet number and broadcast address, you can easily find the first and last IP addresses in the subnet using the same simple logic covered earlier:

■ To find the first valid IP address in the subnet, copy the subnet number, but add 1 to the fourth octet.

■ To find the last valid IP address in the subnet, copy the broadcast address, but subtract 1 from the fourth octet.

Easier Math with Difficult Masks

When the subnet mask is not 255.255.0.0 or 255.255.255.0, I consider the mask to be difficult. Why is it difficult? Well, it is difficult only in that most people cannot easily derive the subnet number and broadcast address without using binary math. You can use the same binary processes in exactly the same way whether the mask is easy or difficult. However, these binary processes take time to do when you cannot use a calculator. So a quicker method of finding the same answers can help.

The following process helps you find the subnet number and broadcast address without binary math when the mask is difficult. (You will find 25 more problems with solutions on the CD chapter "Subnetting Practice: 25 Subnetting Questions.") This process uses something I call a *subnet chart*, as shown in Table 4-25.

Table 4-25 *Generic Subnet Chart*

Octet	1	2	3	4
Address				
Mask				
Subnet Number				
First Address				
Broadcast				
Last Address				

With the type of question this shortcut helps you answer, the question supplies the address and subnet mask. You simply record the IP address and mask in the table, putting each octet in a different column.

The unusual part of this shortcut begins when you draw a box around the "interesting" octet in the table. I call a mask octet that's not a 255 or 0 the "interesting" octet because it is the octet that gives everyone heartburn when they first learn subnetting. The box draws attention to the tricky part of the logic used in this shortcut.

For example, consider 130.4.102.1, with mask 255.255.252.0. Because the third octet of the mask is not a 0 or 255, the third octet is where the interesting part of the shortcut takes place. You create a subnet chart, fill in the address and mask, and draw a box around the third octet, as shown in Table 4-26.

Table 4-26 *Subnet Chart: 130.4.102.1/255.255.252.0 After Drawing a Box Around the Interesting Octet*

Octet	1	2	3	4
Address	130	4	102	1
Mask	255	255	252	0
Subnet Number				
First Address				
Broadcast				
Last Address				

Next you complete the chart for everything to the left of the box. To complete the chart, look at the original IP address octets to the left of the box and copy those into the Subnet Number, First Address, Broadcast, and Last Address fields. Note that only octets fully to the left of the box should be copied. The interesting octet, which is inside the box, should not be copied. Table 4-27 shows the same example after this step.

Table 4-27 *Subnet Chart: 130.4.102.1/255.255.252.0 After Copying Octets to the Left*

Octet	1	2	3	4
Address	130	4	102	1
Mask	255	255	252	0
Subnet Number	130	4		
First Address	130	4		
Broadcast	130	4		
Last Address	130	4		

To find the subnet number, you have a couple of steps. The first step is easy. In the subnet number, for any octets fully to the right of the box, write down a 0. That should leave you with one octet of the subnet number missing—the interesting octet.

Next comes the tricky part of this shortcut, which gives you the value of the subnet number in the interesting octet. First you find what I call the "magic number"—256 minus the *mask's interesting octet*. In this case, you have 256 – 252, or a magic number of 4. Then you find the multiple of the magic number that is closest to the *address's interesting octet* but less than or equal to it. In this example, 100 is a multiple of the magic number (4 * 25), and this multiple is less than or equal to 102. The next-higher multiple of the magic number, 104, is, of course, more than 102, so that's not the right number. The multiple of the magic number closest to, but not more than, the address's interesting octet is the subnet's interesting octet value. The following items summarize this important step:

Step 1 Find the magic number, which is 256 minus the value of the *mask's interesting octet*.

Step 2 Find the multiple of the magic number that is closest to, but not greater than, the *address's interesting octet*.

Step 3 Write down that multiple of the magic number as the value of the subnet number's interesting octet.

In this example, simply plug in 100 for the third octet of the subnet number in Table 4-27.

As soon as you know the subnet number, you can easily find the first valid IP address in the subnet:

> To find the first valid IP address in the subnet, copy the subnet number, but add 1 to the fourth octet.

That's all! Table 4-28 shows the same example, but with the subnet number and first valid IP address.

Table 4-28   *Subnet Chart: 130.4.102.1/255.255.252.0 with Subnet and First IP Address*

Octet	1	2	3	4	Comments
Address	130	4	102	1	
Mask	255	255	252	0	
Subnet Number	130	4	100	0	Magic number = 256 – 252 = 4. 4 * 25 = 100, the closest multiple <= 102.
First Address	130	4	100	1	Add 1 to the subnet's last octet.
Broadcast	130	4			
Last Address	130	4			

To review, in Table 4-28, the first two octets of the subnet number and the first valid address were already filled in because they are to the left of the box around the third octet—the interesting octet in this case. In the subnet number, the last octet is 0 because it is to the right of the box. To find the interesting octet value, compare the IP address's interesting octet to find the closest multiple of the magic number that's not larger, which is 100 in this case. To get the first valid address, just add 1 to the last octet of the subnet number, giving you 130.4.100.1.

The final step in the shortcut finds the broadcast address, from which you can easily find the last valid address in the subnet. First, in the broadcast address, write down a decimal 255 for all octets to the right of the line or the box. Do not write down a 255 in the octet inside the box. Remember, the octets to the left of the box in the subnet chart should already be filled in, leaving a single octet with no value—the interesting octet. To fill in the interesting octet of the broadcast address, you again use the magic number. The magic number is 256 minus the mask's interesting octet. In this case, you have 256 – 252, or a magic number of 4. Then you add the magic number to the interesting octet value of the subnet number and subtract 1. The result is the broadcast address's value in the interesting octet. In this case, the value is

100 + 4 (magic number) – 1 = 103.

As soon as you know the broadcast address, you can easily find the last valid IP address in the subnet:

> To find the last valid IP address in the subnet, copy the broadcast address, but subtract 1 from the fourth octet.

To summarize the tricky part of this shortcut algorithm:

> To find the broadcast address's interesting octet value, take the subnet number's interesting octet value, add the magic number, and subtract 1.

Table 4-29 shows the completed answers, with annotations.

Table 4-29 *Subnet Chart: 130.4.102.1/255.255.252.0 Completed*

Octet	1	2	3	4	Comments
Address	130	4	102	1	
Mask	255	255	252	0	
Subnet Number	130	4	100	0	Magic number = 256 − 252 = 4. 4 * 25 = 100, the closest multiple <= 102.
First Address	130	4	100	1	Add 1 to the subnet's last octet.
Broadcast	130	4	103	255	Subnet-interesting-octet, plus the magic number, minus 1 (100 + 4 − 1).
Last Address	130	4	103	254	Subtract 1 from the fourth octet.

The entire process of dissecting IP addresses that use difficult masks is now complete. The following list summarizes the tasks in each step:

Step 1   Create and complete the easy parts of a subnet chart:

   (a)   Create a generic subnet chart.

   (b)   Write down the IP address and subnet mask in the first two rows of the chart.

   (c)   Draw a box around the interesting octet's column.

   (d)   Copy the address octets to the left of the line or the box into the final four rows of the chart.

Step 2   Derive the subnet number and the first valid IP address:

   (a)   Write down 0s in the subnet number for the octets to the right of the box.

   (b)   Find the magic number, which is 256 minus the value of the mask's interesting octet.

(c)   Find the multiple of the magic number that is closest to but not greater than the address's interesting octet.

(d)   Write down that multiple of the magic number as the value of the subnet number's interesting octet.

(e)   To find the first valid IP address in the subnet, copy the subnet number, but add 1 to the fourth octet.

Step 3   Derive the broadcast address and the last valid IP address:

(a)   Write down 255s in the broadcast address octets to the right of the line or the box.

(b)   To find the broadcast address's interesting octet value, take the subnet number's interesting octet value, add the magic number, and subtract 1.

(c)   To find the last valid IP address in the subnet, copy the broadcast address, but subtract 1 from the fourth octet.

Becoming proficient at this shortcut takes some practice. To make sure you have the process down, review the examples in the CD chapter "Subnetting Practice: 25 Subnetting Questions," which has 25 different examples, including the Boolean AND and shortcut methods of finding the subnet number.

Which Subnet Masks Meet the Stated Design Requirements?

This chapter has explained how to answer questions that provide the subnet number. However, some questions do not supply the subnet number, but instead ask you to choose the correct subnet mask given a set of requirements. The most common of these questions reads something like this:

"You are using Class B network X, and you need 200 subnets, with at most 200 hosts per subnet. Which of the following subnet masks can you use?" This is followed by some subnet masks from which you choose the answer.

To find the correct answers to these types of questions, you first need to decide how many subnet bits and host bits you need to meet the requirements. Basically, the number of hosts per subnet is $2^x - 2$, where x is the number of host bits in the address. Likewise, the number of subnets in a network, assuming that the same subnet mask is used all over the network, is also $2^x - 2$, but with x being the number of subnet bits. As soon as you know how many subnet bits and host bits are required, you can figure out what mask or masks meet the stated design goals in the question.

Examples certainly help. The first sample question reads like this:

> "Your network can use Class B network 130.1.0.0. What subnet masks meet the requirement that you plan to allow at most 200 subnets, with at most 200 hosts per subnet?"

First you need to figure out how many subnet bits allow for 200 subnets. You can use the formula $2^x - 2$ and plug in values for x until one of the numbers is at least 200. In this case, x turns out to be 8. In other words, you need at least 8 subnet bits to allow for 200 subnets.

If you do not want to keep plugging values into the $2^x - 2$ formula, you can instead memorize Table 4-30.

Table 4-30 *Maximum Number of Subnets/Hosts*

Number of Bits in the Host or Subnet Field	Maximum Number of Hosts or Subnets ($2^x - 2$)
1	0
2	2
3	6
4	14
5	30
6	62
7	126
8	254
9	510
10	1022
11	2046
12	4094
13	8190
14	16,382

As you can see, if you already have the powers of 2 memorized, you really do not need to memorize the table—just remember the formula.

As for the first sample question, 7 subnet bits is not enough, because that allows for only 126 subnets. You need 8 subnet bits. Similarly, because you need up to 200 hosts per subnet, you need 8 host bits.

Finally, you need to decide what mask(s) to use, knowing that you have a Class B network and that you must have at least 8 subnet bits and 8 host bits. Using the letter N to represent network bits, the letter S to represent subnet bits, and the letter H to represent host bits, the following shows the sizes of the various fields:

NNNNNNNN NNNNNNNN SSSSSSSS HHHHHHHH

All that is left is to derive the actual subnet mask. Because you need 8 bits for the subnet field and 8 for the host field, and the network field takes up 16 bits, you have already allocated all 32 bits of the address structure. Therefore, only one possible subnet mask works. To figure out the mask, you need to write down the 32-bit subnet mask, applying the following fact and subnet masks:

The network and subnet bits in a subnet mask are, by definition, all binary 1s. Similarly, the host bits in a subnet mask are, by definition, all binary 0s.

So, the only valid subnet mask, in binary, is

11111111 11111111 11111111 00000000

When converted to decimal, this is 255.255.255.0.

A second example shows how the requirements stated in the question allow for multiple possible subnet masks:

"Your network can use Class B network 130.1.0.0. What subnet masks meet the requirement that you plan to allow at most 50 subnets, with at most 200 hosts per subnet?"

For this design, you still need at least 8 host bits, but now you only need at least 6 subnet bits. 6 subnet bits allows for $2^6 - 2$, or 62, subnets. Following the same convention as before, but now using an **X** for bits that can be either subnet or host bits, the format of the address structure is as follows:

NNNNNNNN NNNNNNNN SSSSSS**XX** HHHHHHHH

In other words, the addresses have 16 network bits, at least 6 subnet bits, and at least 8 host bits. This example actually allows for three valid subnet masks, whose structure is as follows:

NNNNNNNN NNNNNNNN SSSSSSSS HHHHHHHH – 8 subnet, 8 host
NNNNNNNN NNNNNNNN SSSSSS**S** HHHHHHHH – 7 subnet, 9 host
NNNNNNNN NNNNNNNN SSSSS**HH** HHHHHHHH – 6 subnet, 10 host

So, based on the requirements in the question, three different valid subnet masks meet the requirements:

> 11111111 11111111 11111111 00000000 255.255.255.0
> 11111111 11111111 1111111**0** 00000000 255.255.254.0
> 11111111 11111111 111111**00** 00000000 255.255.252.0

The 2 bits that could be subnet bits or host bits, based on the requirements, are shown in bold.

What Are the Other Subnet Numbers?

The final general type of IP addressing and subnetting question covered in this chapter asks you to list all the subnets of a particular network. You could use a long process that requires you to count in binary and convert many numbers from binary to decimal. However, because most people either learn the shortcut or use a subnet calculator in their jobs, I decided to just show you the shortcut method for this particular type of question.

First, the question needs a better definition—or at least a more-complete one. The question might be better stated like this:

> "If the same subnet mask is used for all subnets of this Class A, B, or C network, what are the valid subnets?"

IP design conventions do not require the engineer to use the same mask for every subnet. Unless specifically stated, the question "What are all the subnets?" probably assumes that the same mask is used for all subnets, unless the question specifically states that different masks can be used on different subnets.

The following easy decimal process lists all the valid subnets given the network number and the only mask used on that network. This three-step process assumes that the size of the subnet part of the address is, at most, 8 bits in length. The same general process can be expanded to work when the size of the subnet part of the address is more than 8 bits, but that expanded process is not described here.

The three-step process uses a chart that I call the *subnet list chart*. I made up the name just for this book. Table 4-31 presents a generic version of the subnet list chart.

Table 4-31 *Three-Step Process Generic Subnet List Chart*

Octet	1	2	3	4
Network Number				
Mask				
Subnet Zero				

Table 4-31 *Three-Step Process Generic Subnet List Chart (Continued)*

Octet	1	2	3	4
First Subnet				
Next Subnet				
Last Subnet				
Broadcast Subnet				

You list the known network number and subnet mask as the first step in the process. If the question gives you an IP address and mask instead of the network number and mask, just write down the network number of which that IP address is a member. (Remember, this three-step process assumes that the subnet part of the addresses is 8 bits or less.)

For the second of the three steps, copy the network number into the Subnet Zero row. *Subnet zero,* or the *zero subnet,* is numerically the first subnet, and it is one of the two reserved subnet numbers in a network. (You can use the zero subnet on a Cisco router if you configure the global configuration command **ip subnet-zero**.) Interestingly, a network's zero subnet has the exact same numeric value as the network itself—which is one of the reasons that it should not be used. For the purposes of answering questions on the exam about the number of valid subnets in a network, consider the zero subnet unusable, unless the question tells you that using it is ok. In real life, do not use the zero subnet if you do not have to.

The third step in the process is covered after Tables 4-32 and 4-33, which list two familiar examples, with the first two steps completed.

Table 4-32 *Subnet List Chart: 130.4.0.0/24*

Octet	1	2	3	4
Network Number	130	4	0	0
Mask	255	255	255	0
Subnet Zero	130	4	0	0

Table 4-33 *Subnet List Chart: 130.4.0.0/22*

Octet	1	2	3	4
Network Number	130	4	0	0
Mask	255	255	252	0
Subnet Zero	130	4	0	0

The last step in this process, Step 3, is repeated many times. This last step uses the magic number, which is 256 minus the mask octet value in the interesting octet. With this process of finding all the subnet numbers, the interesting octet is the octet that contains *all* of the subnet part of the addresses. (Remember, the process assumes 8 or fewer subnet bits!) In both Tables 4-32 and 4-33, the interesting octet is the third octet.

The third and final step in the process to find all the subnet numbers goes like this: Starting with the last completed row in the table, do the following:

a. Because this process assumes 1 byte or less in the subnet part of the addresses, on the next row of the table, copy down the three octets that are not part of the subnet field. Call the octet that is not copied down the "subnet octet" or the "interesting octet."

b. Add the magic number to the previous subnet octet, and write that down as the value of the subnet octet.

c. Repeat the preceding two tasks until the next number you would write down in the subnet octet is 256. (But don't write it down—it's invalid.)

The idea behind the process of finding all the subnets becomes apparent when you review the same two examples used earlier. Table 4-34 lists the example with the easy mask. Note that the magic number is 256 – 255 = 1 in this case, and that the third octet is the interesting subnet octet.

Table 4-34 *Subnet List Chart: 130.4.0.0/255.255.255.0 Completed*

Octet	1	2	3	4
Network Number	130	4	0	0
Mask	255	255	255	0
Subnet Zero	130	4	0	0
First Subnet	130	4	1	0
Next Subnet	130	4	2	0
Next Subnet	130	4	3	0
Next Subnet	130	4	4	0
(Skipping Many Subnets)	130	4	X	0
Last Subnet	130	4	254	0
Broadcast Subnet	130	4	255	0

You might better understand the logic behind how this process works by looking at the first few entries and then the last few entries. The zero subnet is easily found because it's the same number as the network number. The magic number is $256 - 255 = 1$ in this case. Essentially, you increment the third octet (in this case) by the magic number for each successive subnet number.

One row of the table is labeled "Skipping Many Subnets." Rather than make this book even bigger, I left out several entries but included enough that you could see that the subnet number's third octet just gets bigger by 1, in this case, for each successive subnet number.

Looking at the end of the table, the last entry lists 255 in the third octet. 256 decimal is never a valid value in any IP address, and the directions said not to write down a subnet with 256 in it, so the last number in the table is 130.4.255.0. The last subnet is the broadcast subnet, which is the other reserved subnet number. The subnet before the broadcast subnet is the highest, or last, valid subnet number.

With a simple subnet mask, the process of answering this type of question is very simple. In fact, many people might even refer to these subnets using just the third octet. If all subnets of a particular organization were in network 130.4.0.0, with mask 255.255.255.0, you might simply say "subnet 5" when referring to subnet 130.4.5.0.

The process works the same with difficult subnet masks, even though the answers are not as intuitive. Table 4-35 lists the answers for the second example, using a mask of 255.255.252.0. The third octet is again the interesting subnet octet, but this time the magic number is $256 - 252 = 4$.

Table 4-35 *Subnet List Chart: 130.4.0.0/255.255.252.0*

Octet	1	2	3	4
Network Number	130	4	0	0
Mask	255	255	252	0
Subnet Zero	130	4	0	0
First Subnet	130	4	4	0
Next Valid Subnet	130	4	8	0
(Skipping Many Subnets)	130	4	X	0
Last Subnet	130	4	248	0
Broadcast Subnet	130	4	252	0

The first subnet number numerically, the zero subnet, starts the list. By adding the magic number in the interesting octet, you find the rest of the subnet numbers. Like the previous example, to save space in the book, many subnet numbers were skipped.

You probably wouldn't guess that 130.4.252.0 is the broadcast subnet for this latest example. However, adding the magic number 4 to 252 gives you 256 as the next subnet number, which is invalid, so 130.4.252.0 is indeed the broadcast subnet.

The three-step process to find all the subnet numbers of a network is as follows:

Step 1   Write down the network number and subnet mask in the first two rows of the subnet list chart.

Step 2   Write down the network number in the third row. This is the zero subnet, which is one of the two reserved subnets.

Step 3   Do the following two tasks, stopping when the next number you would write down in the interesting column is 256. (But don't write it down— it's invalid.)

        (a)   Copy all three uninteresting octets from the previous line.

        (b)   Add the magic number to the previous interesting octet, and write it down as the value of the interesting octet.

Foundation Summary

The "Foundation Summary" section lists the most important facts from the chapter. Although this section does not list everything that will be on the exam, a well-prepared CCNA candidate should at a minimum know all the details in each Foundation Summary before taking the exam.

The thought process used to answer questions about the number of hosts and subnets in a network, based on a network number and a subnet mask, is summarized in the following list:

Step 1   Identify the structure of the IP address.

Step 2   Identify the size of the network part of the address based on Class A, B, and C rules.

Step 3   Identify the size of the host part of the address based on the number of binary 0s in the mask.

Step 4   The size of the subnet part is what's "left over"; mathematically, it is 32 – (number of network + host bits).

Step 5   Declare the number of subnets, which is $2^{number\text{-}of\text{-}subnet\text{-}bits} - 2$.

Step 6   Declare the number of hosts per subnet, which is $2^{number\text{-}of\text{-}host\text{-}bits} - 2$.

Here's a formal definition of the "algorithm" to find the first and last IP addresses in a subnet when you know the subnet number and broadcast addresses:

- For the first valid IP address, copy the subnet number, but add 1 to the fourth octet.

- For the last valid IP address, copy the broadcast address, but subtract 1 from the fourth octet.

- The range of valid IP addresses starts with the first number and ends with the last.

To find the subnet number, perform a Boolean AND between the address and the subnet mask, as shown in Table 4-36.

Table 4-36 *Bitwise Boolean AND Example*

	Decimal	Binary
Address	150.150.2.1	1001 0110 1001 0110 0000 0010 0000 0001
Mask	255.255.255.0	1111 1111 1111 1111 1111 1111 0000 0000
Result of AND	150.150.2.0	1001 0110 1001 0110 0000 0010 0000 0000

To find the subnet broadcast address, take the subnet number in binary and change all the host bits to binary 1s.

The following three-step process lists all the subnet numbers of a network. This process refers to Table 4-37.

Step 1   Write down the network number and subnet mask in the first two rows of the subnet list chart.

Step 2   Write down the network number in the third row. This is the zero subnet, which is one of the two reserved subnets.

Step 3   Do the following two tasks, stopping when the next number you would write down in the interesting column is 256. (But don't write it down— it's invalid.)

    (a)   Copy all three uninteresting octets from the previous line.

    (b)   Add the magic number to the previous interesting octet, and write it down as the value of the interesting octet.

Table 4-37   *Subnet List Chart*

Octet	1	2	3	4
Network Number				
Mask				
Subnet Zero				
First Subnet				
Next Subnet				
(Skipping Many Subnets)				
Last Subnet				
Broadcast Subnet				

Q&A

As mentioned in the Introduction, you have two choices for review questions. The following questions give you a bigger challenge than the exam because they are open-ended. By reviewing with this more-difficult question format, you can exercise your memory better and prove your conceptual and factual knowledge of the topics covered in this chapter. The answers to these questions are found in appendix A.

If you want more questions and practice with subnetting, you have a couple of options. You can look at the chapter on the CD titled "Subnetting Practice: 25 Subnetting Questions." Also, if you bought the two-book set, and you already own the *CCNA INTRO Exam Certification Guide,* you can look at the questions at the end of Chapter 4, "Fundamentals of WANs," of that book. Chapter 4 of that book repeats what is discussed in this chapter. However, more than half of the questions at the end of that chapter are different from the ones in this chapter, so you can get some more practice.

For more practice with exam-like question formats, including multiple-choice questions and those using a router simulator, use the exam engine on the CD.

1. Name the parts of an IP address.

2. Define subnet mask. What do the bits in the mask whose values are binary 0 tell you about the corresponding IP address(es)?

3. Given the IP address 10.5.118.3 and the mask 255.255.0.0, what is the subnet number?

4. Given the IP address 190.1.42.3 and the mask 255.255.255.0, what is the subnet number?

5. Given the IP address 140.1.1.1 and the mask 255.255.255.248, what is the subnet number?

6. Given the IP address 167.88.99.66 and the mask 255.255.255.192, what is the subnet number?

7. Given the IP address 10.5.118.3 and the mask 255.255.0.0, what is the broadcast address?

8. Given the IP address 190.1.42.3 and the mask 255.255.255.0, what is the broadcast address?

9. Given the IP address 140.1.1.1 and the mask 255.255.255.248, what is the broadcast address?

10. Given the IP address 167.88.99.66 and the mask 255.255.255.192, what is the broadcast address?

11. Given the IP address 10.5.118.3 and the mask 255.255.0.0, what are the assignable IP addresses in this subnet?

12. Given the IP address 190.1.42.3 and the mask 255.255.255.0, what are the assignable IP addresses in this subnet?

13. Given the IP address 140.1.1.1 and the mask 255.255.255.248, what are the assignable IP addresses in this subnet?

14. Given the IP address 167.88.99.66 and the mask 255.255.255.192, what are the assignable IP addresses in this subnet?

15. Given the IP address 10.5.118.3 and the mask 255.255.255.0, what are all the subnet numbers if the same (static) mask is used for all subnets in this network?

16. How many IP addresses can be assigned in each subnet of 10.0.0.0, assuming that a mask of 255.255.255.0 is used? If the same (static) mask is used for all subnets, how many subnets are there?

17. How many IP addresses can be assigned in each subnet of 140.1.0.0, assuming that a mask of 255.255.255.248 is used? If the same (static) mask is used for all subnets, how many subnets are there?

18. You design a network for a customer who wants the same subnet mask on every subnet. The customer will use network 10.0.0.0 and needs 200 subnets, each with 200 hosts maximum. What subnet mask would you use to allow the most growth in subnets? Which mask would work and would allow for the most growth in the number of hosts per subnet?

19. Refer to Figure 4-5. Fred is configured with IP address 10.1.1.1. Router A's Ethernet interface is configured with 10.1.1.100. Router A's serial interface uses 10.1.1.101. Router B's serial interface uses 10.1.1.102. Router B's Ethernet uses 10.1.1.200. The web server uses 10.1.1.201. Mask 255.255.255.192 is used in all cases. Is anything wrong with this network? What is the easiest thing you could do to fix it? You may assume any working interior routing protocol.

Figure 4-5 *Sample Network for Subnetting Questions*

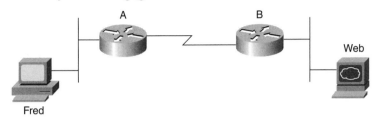

20. Refer to Figure 4-5. Fred is configured with IP address 10.1.1.1, mask 255.255.255.0. Router A's Ethernet is configured with 10.1.1.100, mask 255.255.255.224. Router A's serial interface uses 10.1.1.129, mask 255.255.255.252. Router B's serial interface uses 10.1.1.130, mask 255.255.255.252. Router B's Ethernet uses 10.1.1.200, mask 255.255.255.224. The web server uses 10.1.1.201, mask 255.255.255.224. Is anything wrong with this network? What is the easiest thing you could do to fix it? You may assume any working interior routing protocol.

21. Refer to Figure 4-5. Fred is configured with IP address 10.1.1.1, mask 255.255.255.240. Router A's Ethernet is configured with 10.1.1.2, mask 255.255.255.240. Router A's serial interface uses 10.1.1.129, mask 255.255.255.252. Router B's serial interface uses 10.1.1.130, mask 255.255.255.252. Router B's Ethernet uses 10.1.1.200, mask 255.255.255.128. The web server uses 10.1.1.201, mask 255.255.255.128. Is anything wrong with this network? What is the easiest thing you could do to fix it? You may assume any working interior routing protocol.

This chapter covers the following subjects:

- Configuring and Testing Static Routes

- Distance Vector Concepts

- Configuring RIP and IGRP

CHAPTER 5

RIP, IGRP, and Static Route Concepts and Configuration

Routers forward IP packets based on the destination IP address in the IP packet header. They compare the destination address to the routing table with the hope of finding a matching entry—an entry that tells the router where to forward the packet next. If the router does not match an entry in the routing table, and no default route exists, the router discards the packet. Therefore, having a full and accurate routing table is important.

Chapters 5, 6, "OSPF and EIGRP Concepts and Configuration," and 7, "Advanced Routing Protocol Topics," cover the concepts and configuration required to fill a router's routing table. Cisco expects CCNAs to demonstrate a comfortable understanding of the logic behind the routing of packets and the different but related logic behind routing protocols—the protocols used to discover routes. To fully appreciate the nuances of routing protocols, you need a thorough understanding of routing—the process of forwarding packets. If you bought both my CCNA books, refer to Chapter 5, "Fundamentals of IP," of *CCNA INTRO Exam Certification Guide* for a brief review.

AUTHOR'S NOTE If you happen to not be reading the *INTRO Exam Certification Guide* as well, you may want to refer to appendix D, Comparisons of Dynamic Routing Protocols, for a brief overview of a few other routing protocols. For those of you who are preparing for the CCNA exam and are using the *INTRO Exam Certification Guide* as well, those small details are covered in the other book.

Before diving into routing protocol details, this chapter starts with a short section about how to configure static routes. Thinking through static route configuration can help people new to routing better understand routing and routing protocols. Following that, the text covers the most important topics in this chapter—distance vector concepts, Routing Information Protocol (RIP), and Interior Gateway Routing Protocol (IGRP).

Chapter 6 covers the most basic concepts and configuration of Open Shortest Path First (OSPF) and Enhanced IGRP (EIGRP). Chapter 7 covers several advanced topics related to routing protocols. Please refer to Appendix F for some further details about a few of the topics in this chapter.

"Do I Know This Already?" Quiz

The purpose of the "Do I Know This Already?" quiz is to help you decide if you need to read the entire chapter. If you intend to read the entire chapter, you do not necessarily need to answer these questions now.

The nine-question quiz, derived from the major sections in the "Foundation Topics" section, helps you determine how to spend your limited study time.

Table 5-1 outlines the major topics discussed in this chapter and the "Do I Know This Already?" quiz questions that correspond to those topics.

Table 5-1 *"Do I Know This Already?" Foundation Topics Section-to-Question Mapping*

Foundations Topics Section	Questions Covered in This Section
Configuring and Testing Static Routes	1, 2
Distance Vector Concepts	3, 4, 6
Configuring RIP and IGRP	5, 7, 8, 9

CAUTION   The goal of self-assessment is to gauge your mastery of the topics in this chapter. If you don't know the answer to a question or you're only partially sure of the answer, you should mark this question as wrong for purposes of the self-assessment. Giving yourself credit for an answer you guess correctly skews your self-assessment results and might give you a false sense of security.

1. Which of the following must be true before IOS lists a route as "S" in the output of a **show ip route** command?

    a. The IP address must be configured on an interface.

    b. The router must receive a routing update from a neighboring router.

    c. The **ip route** command must be added to the configuration.

    d. The **ip address** command must use the **special** keyword.

    e. The interface must be **up and up.**

2. Which of the following commands correctly configures a static route?

    a. ip route 10.1.3.0 255.255.255.0 10.1.130.253

    b. ip route 10.1.3.0 serial 0

    c. ip route 10.1.3.0 /24 10.1.130.253

    d. ip route 10.1.3.0 /24 serial 0

3. Which of the following distance vector features prevents routing loops by causing the routing protocol to advertise only a subset of known routes, as opposed to the full routing table?

   a. Distance vector

   b. Link-state

   c. Holddown

   d. Split horizon

   e. Route poisoning

4. Which of the following features prevents routing loops by advertising an infinite metric route when a route fails?

   a. Distance vector

   b. Link-state

   c. Holddown

   d. Split horizon

   e. Route poisoning

5. Router1 has interfaces with addresses 9.1.1.1 and 10.1.1.1. Router 2, connected to Router1 over a serial link, has addresses 10.1.1.2 and 11.1.1.2. Which of the following commands would be part of a complete RIP configuration on Router2, with which Router2 advertises out all interfaces, and about all routes?

   a. router rip

   b. router rip 3

   c. network 9.0.0.0

   d. network 9.1.1.1

   e. network 10.0.0.0

   f. network 10.1.1.1

   g. network 10.1.1.2

   h. network 11.0.0.0

   i. network 11.1.1.2

6. Which of the following situations would cause RIP or IGRP to remove all the routes learned from a particular neighboring router?

   a. Failure to receive a keepalive

   b. It no longer receives updates from that neighbor

   c. Updates received 5 or more seconds after the last update was sent to that neighbor

   d. Updates from that neighbor have the global "route bad" flag

7. Which of the following **network** commands, following a **router rip** command, would cause RIP to send updates out two interfaces whose IP addresses are 10.1.2.1 and 10.1.1.1, mask 255.255.255.0?

    a. network 10.0.0.0

    b. network 10.1.1.0 10.1.2.0

    c. network 10.1.1.1. 10.1.2.1

    d. network 10.1.0.0 255.255.0.0

    e. network 10

    f. You can't do this with only one **network** command.

8. What command(s) list(s) information identifying the neighboring routers that are sending routing information to a particular router?

    a. show ip

    b. show ip protocol

    c. show ip routing-protocols

    d. show ip route

    e. show ip route neighbor

    f. show ip route received

9. What part of the output of the **show ip route** command identifies the metric associated with the route?

    a. The first number in the line describing the route

    b. The last number in the line describing the route

    c. The number after the word "metric" in the line describing the route

    d. The first number in brackets in the line describing the route

    e. The last number in brackets in the line describing the route

The answers to the "Do I Know This Already?" quiz appear in Appendix A. The suggested choices for your next step are as follows:

- **7 or less overall score**—Read the entire chapter. This includes the "Foundation Topics," "Foundation Summary," and "Q&A" sections.

- **8 or 9 overall score**—If you want more review on these topics, skip to the "Foundation Summary" section and then go to the "Q&A" section. Otherwise, move to the next chapter.

Foundation Topics

Configuring and Testing Static Routes

The purpose of configuring static routes, as well as RIP and IGRP, is to add routes to a router's routing table. RIP and IGRP do so automatically. In fact, after you read all the conceptual material in this chapter, the actual RIP and IGRP configuration can be a little anticlimactic. In most networks, all you need are two configuration commands to configure RIP or IGRP. You don't have to understand how they work—they just work. You need to understand both static routing and the distance vector concepts behind RIP and IGRP.

Static routing consists of individual configuration commands that define a route to a router. A router can forward packets only to subnets in its routing table. The router always knows about directly connected routes—routes to subnets off interfaces that have an "up and up" status. By adding static routes, a router can be told how to forward packets to subnets that are not attached to it.

Adding static routes to a router is relatively easy. To see the need, and to see the configuration, look at Example 5-1, which shows two **ping** commands testing IP connectivity from Albuquerque to Yosemite (see Figure 5-1).

Figure 5-1 *Sample Network Used in Static Route Configuration Examples*

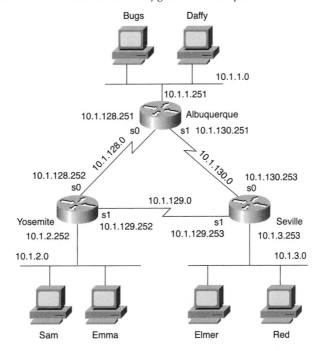

Example 5-1 *Albuquerque Router EXEC Commands with Only Connected Routers*

```
Albuquerque#show ip route
Codes: C - connected, S - static, I - IGRP, R - RIP, M - mobile, B - BGP
       D - EIGRP, EX - EIGRP external, O - OSPF, IA - OSPF inter area
       N1 - OSPF NSSA external type 1, N2 - OSPF NSSA external type 2
       E1 - OSPF external type 1, E2 - OSPF external type 2, E - EGP
       i - IS-IS, L1 - IS-IS level-1, L2 - IS-IS level-2, ia - IS-IS inter area
       * - candidate default, U - per-user static route, o - ODR
       P - periodic downloaded static route

Gateway of last resort is not set

     10.0.0.0/24 is subnetted, 3 subnets

C       10.1.1.0 is directly connected, Ethernet0
C       10.1.130.0 is directly connected, Serial1
C       10.1.128.0 is directly connected, Serial0
Albuquerque#ping 10.1.128.252
Type escape sequence to abort.
Sending 5, 100-byte ICMP Echos to 10.1.128.252, timeout is 2 seconds:
!!!!!
Success rate is 100 percent (5/5), round-trip min/avg/max = 4/4/8 ms

Albuquerque#ping 10.1.2.252
Type escape sequence to abort.
Sending 5, 100-byte ICMP Echos to 10.1.2.252, timeout is 2 seconds:
.....
Success rate is 0 percent (0/5)
```

The **ping** command sends an ICMP echo request packet to the stated destination address. The TCP/IP software at the destination then replies to the ping echo request packet with a similar packet, called an *ICMP echo reply*. The **ping** command sends the first packet and waits on the response. If a response is received, the command displays a "!". If no response is received within the default timeout of 2 seconds, the **ping** command displays a ".". The IOS **ping** command sends 5 of these packets by default.

In Example 5-1, the **ping 10.1.128.252** command works, but the **ping 10.1.2.252** command does not. The first **ping** command works because Albuquerque has a route to the subnet in which 10.1.128.2 resides (subnet 10.1.128.0). However, the **ping** to 10.1.2.252 does not work, because the subnet in which 10.1.2.252 resides, subnet 10.1.2.0, is not connected to Albuquerque, so Albuquerque does not have a route to that subnet. So, none of the five ping packets works, resulting in five periods in the output of the **ping** command.

Configuring Static Routes

One simple solution to the failure of the **ping** command is to enable an IP routing protocol on all three routers. In fact, in a real network, that is the most likely solution. As an alternative, you can configure static routes. Many networks have a few static routes, so you need to configure them occasionally. Example 5-2 shows the **ip route** command on Albuquerque, which adds static routes and makes the failed ping from Example 5-1 work.

Example 5-2 *Static Routes Added to Albuquerque*

```
ip route 10.1.2.0 255.255.255.0 10.1.128.252
ip route 10.1.3.0 255.255.255.0 10.1.130.253
```

The **ip route** commands supply the subnet number and the next-hop IP address. One **ip route** command defines a route to 10.1.2.0 (mask 255.255.255.0), which is located off Yosemite, so the next-hop IP address as configured on Albuquerque is 10.1.128.252, which is Yosemite's Serial0 IP address. Similarly, a route to 10.1.3.0, the subnet off Seville, points to Seville's Serial0 IP address, 10.1.130.253. Note that the next-hop IP address is an IP address in a directly connected subnet—the goal is to define the next router to send the packet to. Now Albuquerque can forward packets to these two subnets.

You can configure static routes in a couple different ways. With point-to-point serial links, you can also configure the outgoing interface instead of the next-hop IP address. For instance, you could have configured **ip route 10.1.2.0 255.255.255.0 serial0** for the first route in Example 5-2.

Unfortunately, adding these two static routes to Albuquerque does not solve all the network's routing problems. The static routes help Albuquerque deliver packets to these two subnets, but the other two routers don't have enough routing information to forward packets back toward Albuquerque. For instance, PC Bugs cannot ping PC Sam in this network. The problem is that although Albuquerque has a route to subnet 10.1.2.0, where Sam resides, Yosemite does not have a route to 10.1.1.0, where Bugs resides. The ping request packet goes from Bugs to Sam correctly, but Sam's ping response packet cannot be routed by the Yosemite router back through Albuquerque to Bugs, so the ping fails.

Extended **ping** Command

In real life, you might not be able to find a user, like Bugs, to ask to test your network by pinging. So you can use the extended **ping** command on a router to test routing in the same way a ping from Bugs to Sam tests routing. Example 5-3 shows Albuquerque with the working **ping 10.1.2.252** command, but with an extended **ping** command that works similarly to a ping from Bugs to Sam—a ping that fails in this case (only the two static routes from Example 5-2 have been added at this point).

Example 5-3 *Albuquerque: Working Ping After Adding Default Routes, Plus Failing Extended* ping *Command*

```
Albuquerque#show ip route
Codes: C - connected, S - static, I - IGRP, R - RIP, M - mobile, B - BGP
       D - EIGRP, EX - EIGRP external, O - OSPF, IA - OSPF inter area
       N1 - OSPF NSSA external type 1, N2 - OSPF NSSA external type 2
       E1 - OSPF external type 1, E2 - OSPF external type 2, E - EGP
       i - IS-IS, L1 - IS-IS level-1, L2 - IS-IS level-2, ia - IS-IS inter area
       * - candidate default, U - per-user static route, o - ODR
       P - periodic downloaded static route

Gateway of last resort is not set

     10.0.0.0/24 is subnetted, 5 subnets
S       10.1.3.0 [1/0] via 10.1.130.253
S       10.1.2.0 [1/0] via 10.1.128.252
C       10.1.1.0 is directly connected, Ethernet0
C       10.1.130.0 is directly connected, Serial1
C       10.1.128.0 is directly connected, Serial0
Albuquerque#ping 10.1.2.252

Type escape sequence to abort.
Sending 5, 100-byte ICMP Echos to 10.1.2.252, timeout is 2 seconds:
!!!!!
Success rate is 100 percent (5/5), round-trip min/avg/max = 4/4/8 ms

Albuquerque#ping
Protocol [ip]:
Target IP address: 10.1.2.252
Repeat count [5]:
Datagram size [100]:
Timeout in seconds [2]:
Extended commands [n]: y
Source address or interface: 10.1.1.251
Type of service [0]:
Set DF bit in IP header? [no]:
Validate reply data? [no]:
Data pattern [0xABCD]:
Loose, Strict, Record, Timestamp, Verbose[none]:
Sweep range of sizes [n]:
Type escape sequence to abort.
Sending 5, 100-byte ICMP Echos to 10.1.2.252, timeout is 2 seconds:
. . . . .
Success rate is 0 percent (0/5)
```

The simple **ping 10.1.2.252** command works for one obvious reason and one not-so-obvious reason. First, Albuquerque can forward a packet to subnet 10.1.2.0 because of the static route. The return packet, sent by Yosemite, is sent to address 10.1.128.251—Albuquerque's Serial0 IP address. Why? Well, the following points are true about the **ping** command on a Cisco router:

- The Cisco **ping** command uses, by default, the output interface's IP address as the packet's source address unless otherwise specified in an extended ping. The first ping in Example 5-3 uses a source of 10.1.128.251, because the route used to send the packet to 10.1.2.252 points out interface Serial0, whose IP address is 10.1.128.251.

- Ping response packets reverse the IP addresses used in the received ping request to which they are responding. So, in this example, Yosemite uses 10.1.128.251 as the destination address and 10.1.2.252 as the source IP address.

Because the **ping** command on Albuquerque uses 10.1.128.251 as the packet's source address, Yosemite can send back a response to 10.1.128.251, because Yosemite happens to have a route to 10.1.128.0.

When you troubleshoot this network, you can use the extended **ping** command to act like you issued a ping from a computer on that subnet, without having to call a user and ask to enter a **ping** command for you on the PC. The extended version of the **ping** command can be used to refine the problem's underlying cause by changing several details of what the **ping** command sends in its request. In fact, when a ping from a router works, but a ping from a host does not, the extended ping could help you re-create the problem without needing to work with the end user on the phone.

For instance, in Example 5-3, the extended **ping** command on Albuquerque sends a packet from 10.1.1.251 (Albuquerque's Ethernet) to 10.1.2.252 (Yosemite's Ethernet). According to the output, no response was received by Albuquerque. Normally, the ping would be sourced from the IP address of the outgoing interface. With the use of the extended ping source address option, the source IP address of the echo packet is set to Albuquerque's Ethernet IP address, 10.1.1.251. Because the ICMP echo generated by the extended ping is sourced from an address in subnet 10.1.1.0, the packet looks more like a packet from an end user in that subnet. Yosemite builds a reply, with destination 10.1.1.251, but it does not have a route to that subnet. So Yosemite cannot send the ping reply packet back to Albuquerque.

To solve this problem, all routers could be configured to use a routing protocol. Alternatively, you could simply define static routes on all the routers in the network.

Distance Vector Concepts

Distance vector logic is pretty simple on the surface. However, the distance vector features that help prevent routing loops can actually be pretty difficult to grasp at first.

Distance vector protocols work by having each router advertise all the routes they know out all their interfaces. Other routers that share the same physical network receive the routing updates and learn the routes. The routers that share a common physical network are generally called *neighbors*. For instance, all routers attached to the same Ethernet are neighbors; the two routers on either end of a point-to-point serial link are also neighbors. If all routers advertise all their routes out all their interfaces, and all their neighbors receive the routing updates, eventually every router will know the routes to all the subnets in the network. It's that simple!

The following list spells out the basic distance vector logic and introduces a few important concepts (which are explained over the next several pages):

- Routers add directly connected subnets to their routing tables, even without a routing protocol.

- Routers send routing updates out their interfaces to advertise the routes that this router already knows. These routes include directly connected routes, as well as routes learned from other routers.

- Routers listen for routing updates from their neighbors so that they can learn new routes.

- The routing information includes the subnet number and a metric. The metric defines how good the route is; lower metric routes are considered better routes.

- When possible, routers use broadcasts or multicasts to send routing updates. By using a broadcast or multicast packet, all neighbors on a LAN can receive the same routing information in a single update.

- If a router learns multiple routes to the same subnet, it chooses the best route based on the metric.

- Routers send periodic updates and expect to receive periodic updates from neighboring routers.

- Failure to receive updates from a neighbor in a timely manner results in the removal of the routes previously learned from that neighbor.

- A router assumes that, for a route advertised by Router X, the next-hop router in that route is Router X.

The following examples explain the concepts in the list in a little more depth. Figure 5-2 demonstrates how Router A's directly connected subnets are advertised to Router B. In this case, Router A advertises two directly connected routes.

Figure 5-2 *Router A Advertising Directly Connected Routes*

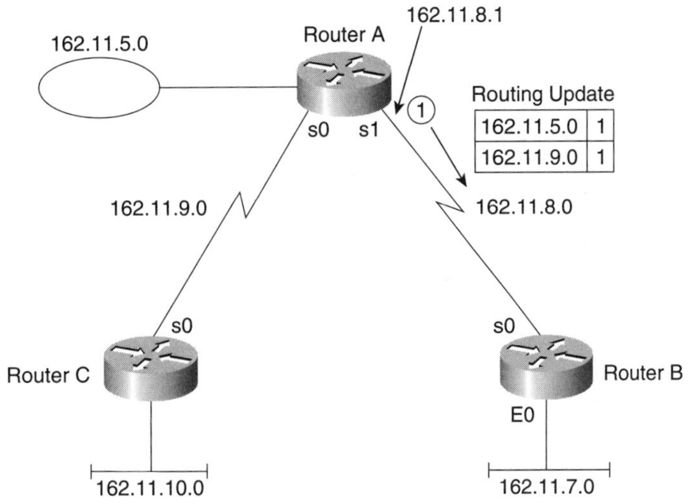

Table 5-2 shows the resulting routing table on Router B.

Table 5-2 *Router B*

Group (Mask Is 255.255.255.0)	Outgoing Interface	Next-Hop Router	Comments
162.11.5.0	S0	162.11.8.1	This is one of two routes learned via the update in the figure.
162.11.7.0	E0	—	This is a directly connected route.
162.11.8.0	S0	—	This is a directly connected route.
162.11.9.0	S0	162.11.8.1	This is one of two routes learned via the update in the figure.

Two interesting facts about what a Cisco IOS software-based Cisco router puts in the routing table become obvious in this example. First, just like for any other directly connected route, the two directly connected routes on Router B do not have an entry in the table's Next-Hop Router field, because packets to those subnets can be sent directly to hosts in those subnets. In other words, there is no need for Router B to forward packets destined for those subnets to another router, because Router B is attached to those subnets. The second interesting fact is that the Next-Hop Router entries for the routes learned from Router A show Router A's IP address as the next router. In other words, a route learned from a neighboring router goes through that router. Router B typically learns Router A's IP address for these routes simply by looking at the routing update's source IP address.

If for some reason Router A stops sending updates to Router B, Router B removes the routes it learned from Router A from the routing table.

The next example gives you some insight into the metric's cumulative effect. A subnet learned via an update from a neighbor is advertised, but with a higher metric. Just like a road sign in Decatur, Ga. might say "Turn here to get to Snellville, 14 miles," another road sign farther away in Atlanta might read "Turn here to get to Snellville, 22 miles." By taking the turn in Atlanta, 8 miles later, you end up in Decatur, looking at the road sign that tells you the next turn to get to Snellville, which is then 14 miles away. This example shows you exactly what happens with RIP, which uses hop count as the metric. Figure 5-3 and Table 5-3 illustrate this concept.

Figure 5-3 *Router A Advertising Routes Learned from Router C*

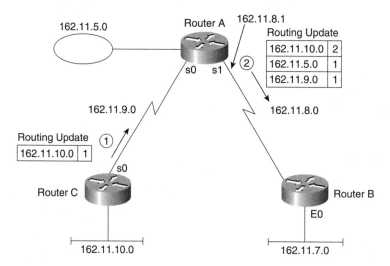

Table 5-3 *Router B Routing Table After Receiving the Update Shown in Figure 5-3*

Group	Outgoing Interface	Next-Hop Router	Metric	Comments
162.11.5.0	S0	162.11.8.1	1	This is the same route that was learned earlier.
162.11.7.0	E0	—	0	This is a directly connected route.
162.11.8.0	S0	—	0	This is a directly connected route.
162.11.9.0	S0	162.11.8.1	1	This one was also learned earlier.
162.11.10.0	S0	162.11.8.1	2	This one was learned from Router A, which learned it from Router C.

Router B believes some subnets are nearer than others, based on the metric. The **show ip route** EXEC command shows connected routes as metric 0, as shown in Table 5-3, because there is no router between Router B and those subnets. Router B uses a metric of 1 for routes directly connected to Router A for two reasons. First, Router A advertises those two routes (162.11.5.0 and 162.11.9.0) with metric 1, so Router B believes those metrics. (Router A, before advertising those two routes, adds 1 to the metric value of its own routes to those subnets.) Conceptually, one router (Router A) separates Router B from those subnets. Because RIP's metric is hop count, a metric of 1 implies that only one router separates Router B from the subnets in question. Similarly, Router B's metric for subnet 162.11.10.0 is 2, because the routing update from Router A advertises the router with a metric of 2. Conceptually, Router B believes that two routers separate it from 162.11.10.0.

The origin of the term distance vector becomes more apparent with this example. The route to 162.11.10.0 that Router B adds to its routing table refers to Router A as the next router because Router B learns the route from Router A. Router B knows nothing about the network topology on the "other side" of Router A. So Router B has a vector (send packets to Router A) and a distance (2) for the route to subnet 10, but no other details! Router B does not know any specific information about Router C.

The next core concept of distance vector routing protocols relates to when to doubt the validity of routing information. Each router sends periodic routing updates. A routing update timer, which is equal on all routers, determines how often the updates are sent. The absence of routing updates for a preset number of routing timer intervals results in the removal of the routes previously learned from the router that has become silent.

You have read about the basic, core concepts for distance vector protocols. The next section provides a deeper look at issues when redundancy exists in the network.

Distance Vector Loop-Avoidance Features

Routing protocols carry out their most important functions when redundancy exists in the network. Most importantly, routing protocols ensure that the currently-best routes are in the routing tables by reacting to network topology changes. Routing protocols also prevent loops.

Distance vector protocols need several mechanisms to prevent loops. Table 5-4 summarizes these issues and lists the solutions, which are explained in the upcoming text.

Table 5-4   *Issues Related to Distance Vector Routing Protocols in Networks with Multiple Paths*

Issue	Solution
Multiple routes to the same subnet have equal metrics	Implementation options involve either using the first route learned or putting multiple routes to the same subnet in the routing table.
Routing loops occur due to updates passing each other over a single link	**Split horizon**—The routing protocol advertises routes out an interface only if they were not learned from updates entering that interface. **Split horizon with poison reverse**—The routing protocol uses split-horizon rules unless a route fails. In that case, the route is advertised out all interfaces, including the interface in which the route was learned, but with an infinite-distance metric.
Routing loops occur because routing information loops through alternative paths	**Route poisoning**—When a route to a subnet fails, the subnet is advertised with an infinite-distance metric. This term specifically applies to routes that are advertised when the route is valid. Poison reverse refers to routes that normally are not advertised because of split horizon but that are advertised with an infinite metric when the route fails.
Counting to infinity	**Hold-down timer**—After finding out that a route to a subnet has failed, a router waits a certain period of time before believing any other routing information about that subnet. **Triggered updates**—When a route fails, an update is sent immediately rather than waiting on the update timer to expire. Used in conjunction with route poisoning, this ensures that all routers know of failed routes before any hold-down timers can expire.

Route Poisoning

Routing loops can occur with distance vector routing protocols when one router advertises that a route is changing from being valid to being invalid. For instance, something as simple as a serial link's going down might cause many routes to become invalid, potentially causing routing loops.

One feature that distance vector protocols use to reduce the chance of loops is called *route poisoning*. Route poisoning begins when a router notices that a connected route is no longer valid. For instance, a router notices that a serial link has failed, changing the link's status from "up and up" to something else, like "down and down." Instead of not advertising that failed route anymore, the routing protocol that uses route poisoning still advertises the route, but with a very large metric—so large that other routers consider the metric infinite and the route invalid. Figure 5-4 shows how route poisoning works with RIP when subnet 162.11.7.0 fails.

Figure 5-4   *Route Poisoning for Subnet 162.11.7.0*

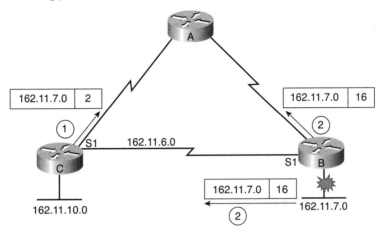

Figure 5-4 shows Router B using route poisoning, but it also provides a good backdrop for
the potential problem. Router B's Ethernet fails, so Router B advertises the route with metric 16.
With RIP, metric 16 is considered an *infinite metric*—a metric for which the route should be
considered invalid. But imagine that Router C sends its next RIP update (Step 1) to Router
A just before receiving the poisoned route (Step 2). If Router B did not use route poisoning,
Router A would believe that the route to subnet 162.11.7.0, through Router C, is valid. By
advertising the infinite metric route to both Routers A and C, Router B ensures that they do
not believe any routes that were based on the idea that Router B could indeed reach subnet
162.11.7.0. As a result, Routers A and C remove their routes to 162.11.7.0.

Split Horizon

Route poisoning does not solve all problems. Even in the simple network shown in Figure 5-4,
loops can still occur without another distance vector routing protocol feature called *split
horizon*. To appreciate split horizon, first consider what happens without it (see Figure 5-5).

Figure 5-5   *Example of the Problem Solved by Split Horizon*

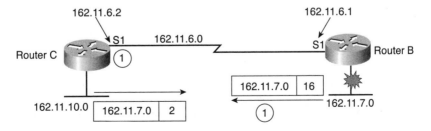

If the RIP updates sent by Routers B and C happen at about the same instant in time, without split horizon, the problem shown in Figure 5-5 can occur. How often do routers send updates to each other at about the same instant? Well, statistically, more often than you might think. The problem occurs the first time Router B advertises an infinite-distance (metric) route to 162.11.7.0, right after the subnet fails. If Router C sends its next update at about the same time, Router C will not yet have heard that the route to subnet 162.11.7.0 has failed. So Router C advertises a metric 2 route to subnet 162.11.7.0, across the serial link to Router B.

After the updates shown in Figure 5-5 are received, Router C has learned that the route has an infinite metric, at the same time that Router B has learned that Router C has a good route (metric 2) to the same subnet. Tables 5-5 and 5-6 show the resulting routing table entries, with a reference to the metric values.

Table 5-5 *Router B Routing Table After Subnet 162.11.7.0 Fails and an Update from Router C Is Received*

Group	Outgoing Interface	Next-Hop Router	Metric	Comments
162.11.6.0	S1	—	0	
162.11.7.0	S1	162.11.6.2	2	The old route failed, but this one is heard from Router C.
162.11.10.0	S1	162.11.6.2	1	

Table 5-6 *Router C Routing Table After Subnet 162.11.7.0 Fails and an Update from Router B Is Received*

Group	Outgoing Interface	Next-Hop Router	Metric	Comments
162.11.6.0	S1	—	0	
162.11.7.0	S1	—	16	The old route was metric 1 through Router B. Now Router B claims that the metric is infinite, so the route must have failed.
162.11.10.0	E0	—	1	

NOTE   In this chapter, the value 16 represents an infinite metric. RIP uses 16 to represent infinite. IGRP uses a delay value of more than 4 billion to imply an infinite-distance route.

Now Router C has an infinite-distance (metric 16 for RIP) route to 162.11.7.0, but Router B has a route to the same subnet, metric 2, pointing through Router C. So Router B now thinks that 162.11.7.0 can be reached through Router C, and Router C thinks that 162.11.7.0 is unreachable.

Because Routers B and C use the same update interval between updates, this process repeats itself with the next routing update. This time, Router B advertises metric 3, and Router C advertises an infinite (bad) metric for subnet 162.11.7.0. This continues until both numbers reach infinity, so this phenomenon is often called *counting to infinity*. Thankfully, each distance vector routing protocol implementation sets a metric value for which the number is considered infinite; otherwise, this process would continue indefinitely.

Split horizon solves the counting-to-infinity problem between two routers. Split horizon can be briefly summarized as follows:

All routes with outgoing interface *x* are not included in updates sent out that same interface *x*.

For example, in Figure 5-6, Router C's route to subnet 162.11.7.0 points out Serial1, so Router C's updates sent out Serial1 do not advertise subnet 162.11.7.0. Therefore, when Routers B and C's updates pass each other, one update shows the route with an infinite metric, and the other says nothing about the route, so the counting-to-infinity problem goes away.

Figure 5-6 *Complete Routing Update with Split Horizon Enabled*

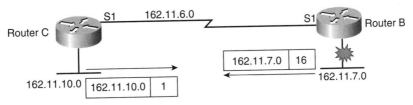

Because of split-horizon rules, Router B does not advertise routes to subnets 162.11.6.0 or 162.11.10.0 in updates it sends to Router C. Similarly, Router C does not advertise routes to subnet 162.11.7.0 in updates sent to Router B. Because Router C does not advertise a route to 162.11.7.0 out its Serial1 interface, the counting-to-infinity problem over the serial link no longer occurs.

Split Horizon with Poison Reverse

So far, you have read about how split horizon and route poisoning work. However, Cisco distance vector routing protocols actually use a variant of split horizon called *split horizon with poison reverse* (or simply *poison reverse*). When the network is stable, it works just like plain old split horizon. When a route fails, the router advertises an infinite-metric route about that subnet out *all* interfaces—including interfaces previously prevented by split horizon. Figure 5-7 shows the pertinent contents of the routing update from Router C, using split horizon with poison reverse.

Figure 5-7 *Split Horizon Enabled with Poison Reverse*

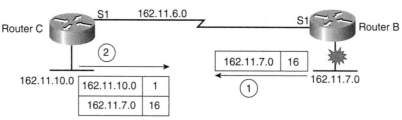

As Figure 5-7 illustrates, after Router C hears of the infinite metric (metric 16 for RIP) route to 162.11.7.0, it then ignores split-horizon rules for that route and advertises the subnet back to Router B with an infinite metric. Using split horizon prevents counting to infinity, and adding poison reverse ensures that all routers know for sure that the route has failed. Both RIP and IGRP use split horizon with poison reverse by default in a Cisco router.

Hold-Down Timer

Split horizon solves the counting-to-infinity problem over a single link. However, counting to infinity can occur in redundant networks (networks with multiple paths) even with split horizon enabled. The hold-down timer defeats the counting-to-infinity problem when networks have multiple paths to many subnets.

Figure 5-8 shows the version of the counting-to-infinity problem that split horizon does not solve but that holddown does solve. Subnet 162.11.7.0 fails again (someone should check the cabling on that Ethernet!), and Router B advertises an infinite-metric route for subnet 162.11.7.0 to both Router A and Router C. However, Router A's update timer expires at the same time as Router B's timer (shown as the circled number 1s in the figure), so the updates sent by Routers A and B occur at the same time. Therefore, Router C hears of an infinite-distance metric to that subnet from Router B, and a metric 2 route from Router A, at about the same time. Router C correctly chooses to use the metric 2 route through Router A. Table 5-7 lists the pertinent information about Router C's routing table entry for subnet 162.11.7.0 after the updates shown in Figure 5-8.

After the updates labeled with a 1 in Figure 5-8, Router C thinks it has a valid route to 162.11.7.0, pointing back to Router A. So, on Router C's next update (the circled 2 in Figure 5-8), it does not advertise subnet 162.11.7.0 out S0 because of split-horizon rules. However, Router C does advertise 162.11.7.0 out Serial1 with metric 3. Now Router B believes it has a valid route, metric 3, to subnet 162.11.7.0. Router B, in its next update (not shown in the figure), also tells Router A that it has a route to 162.11.7.0, this time with metric 4. So counting to infinity occurs even though split horizon is enabled.

Figure 5-8 *Counting to Infinity with a Need for Holddown*

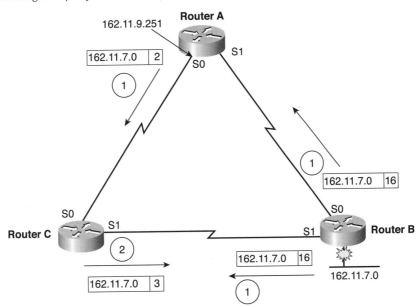

Table 5-7 *Router C Routing Table After the Updates Shown in Step 1 of Figure 5-8 Are Received*

Group	Outgoing Interface	Next-Hop Router	Metric	Comments
162.11.7.0	S0	162.11.9.251	2	Formerly the route pointed directly to Router B. Now the route points through Router A, metric 2.

Distance vector protocols use a hold-down timer to defeat these types of counting-to-infinity problems. The concept is simple—as soon as you see the problem. Holddown is defined as follows:

> When learning that a route has failed, ignore any information about an alternative route to that subnet for a time equal to the hold-down timer.

With holddown enabled, Router C does not believe the metric 2 route learned from Router A in Step 1 of Figure 5-8 for some period of time. During the same time, Router B advertises infinite-metric routes to 162.11.7.0 to Routers A and C, and then Router A starts advertising an infinite-distance route to Router C. In effect, all routers ignore good routing information about that subnet until enough time passes so that everyone has heard the old, bad information. Essentially, the hold-down timer means that the routers just need to exercise a little patience while everyone learns that the route has failed, preventing loops. It is much better to wait a little longer for convergence to prevent the problems caused by looping packets.

Triggered (Flash) Updates

Distance vector protocols typically send updates based on a regular update interval. However, most looping problems occur when a route fails, particularly when some routers have not yet heard the bad news! Therefore, some distance vector protocols send *triggered updates,* also known as *flash updates,* meaning that the router sends a new update as soon as a route fails. This causes the information about the route whose status has changed to be forwarded more quickly and also starts the hold-down timers more quickly on the neighboring routers.

RIP and IGRP

RIP and IGRP have many similarities in their general logic but several differences in the details of their implementation. Table 5-8 outlines some of the differences between RIP and IGRP.

Table 5-8 *RIP and IGRP Feature Comparison*

Feature	RIP (Default)	IGRP (Default)
Update Timer	30 seconds	90 seconds
Metric	Hop count	Function of bandwidth and delay (the default). Can include reliability, load, and MTU.
Hold-Down Timer	180	280
Flash (Triggered) Updates	Yes	Yes
Mask Sent in Update	No	No
Infinite-Metric Value	16	4,294,967,295

The IGRP metric provides a better measurement of how good a route is, as compared with RIP's metric. IGRP's metric is calculated using the bandwidth and delay settings on the interface on which the update was received. When bandwidth and delay are used, the metric is more meaningful than hop count; longer hop routes that go over faster links are considered better routes by IGRP.

RIP uses hop count as its metric. When an update is received, the metric for each subnet in the update signifies the number of routers between the router receiving the update and each subnet. Before sending an update, a router increments by 1 its metric for routes to each subnet.

Finally, the issue of whether the mask is sent is particularly important if variable-length subnet masks (VLSMs) in the same network are desired. You will read more about VLSM in Chapter 7; neither RIP or IGRP support VLSM.

Configuring RIP and IGRP

The key to configuring RIP and IGRP is to master the use of the **network** command. Other than that, configuration is relatively easy. You should also know the more-popular **show** and **debug** commands, which help you examine and troubleshoot routing protocols.

Tables 5-9 and 5-10 summarize the more popular commands used for RIP and IGRP configuration and verification. Two configuration examples follow.

Table 5-9 *IP RIP and IGRP Configuration Commands*

Command	Configuration Mode
router rip	Global
router igrp *as-number*	Global
network *net-number*	Router subcommand
passive-interface [default] {*interface-type interface-number*}	Router subcommand
maximum-paths *number-paths*	Router subcommand
variance *multiplier*	Router subcommand
traffic-share {*balanced*	*min*}	Router subcommand

Table 5-10 *IP RIP and IGRP EXEC Commands*

Command	Description
show ip route [*ip-address* [*mask*] [longer- prefixes]] | [*protocol* [*process-id*]]	Shows the entire routing table, or a subset if parameters are entered.
show ip protocols	Shows routing protocol parameters and current timer values.
debug ip rip	Issues log messages for each RIP update.
debug ip igrp transactions [*ip-address*]	Issues log messages with details of the IGRP updates.
debug ip igrp events [*ip-address*]	Issues log messages for each IGRP packet.
ping [*protocol* | tag] {*host-name* | *system-address*}	Sends and receives ICMP echo messages to verify connectivity.
trace [*protocol*] [*destination*]	Sends a series of ICMP echoes with increasing TTL values to verify the current route to a host.

Basic RIP and IGRP Configuration

Each **network** command enables RIP or IGRP on a set of interfaces. You must understand the subtleties of the **network** command, as explained in this section. However, what "enables" really means in this case is not obvious from the Cisco IOS software documentation. Also, the parameters for the **network** command are not intuitive to many people who are new to Cisco IOS software configuration commands. Therefore, routing protocol configuration, including the **network** command, is a likely topic for tricky questions on the exam.

The **network** command "matches" one or more interfaces on a router. For each interface, the **network** command causes the router to do three things:

- The router broadcasts or multicasts routing updates out an interface.
- The router listens for incoming updates on that same interface.
- The router, when sending an update, includes the subnet off that interface in the routing update.

All you need to know is how to match interfaces using the **network** command. The router matches interfaces with the **network** command by asking this simple question:

> Which of my interfaces have IP addresses with the same network number referenced in this **network** subcommand?

For all interfaces that match the **network** command, the router does the three things just listed.

Examples give you a much better understanding of the **network** command, so examine Figure 5-9 and Example 5-4.

Figure 5-9 *Sample Router with Five Interfaces*

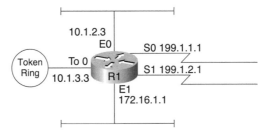

Example 5-4 *Sample Router Configuration with RIP Partially Enabled*

```
interface ethernet 0
ip address 10.1.2.3 255.255.255.0
interface ethernet 1
ip address 172.16.1.1 255.255.255.0
interface tokenring 0
ip address 10.1.3.3 255.255.255.0
interface serial 0
ip address 199.1.1.1 255.255.255.0
interface serial 1
ip address 199.1.2.1 255.255.255.0
!
router rip
network 10.0.0.0
network 199.1.1.0
```

This RIP configuration includes three commands. The **router rip** global command moves the user from global configuration mode to RIP configuration mode. Then two **network** commands appear—and like every RIP **network** command, each configures a different Class A, B, or C network number. So what interfaces were matched, and what did this accomplish? Well, if the goal is to enable RIP on all interfaces, the configuration is incomplete. Table 5-11 summarizes what this configuration accomplishes and what it does not.

Table 5-11 *What Happens with the RIP Configuration Shown in Example 5-4*

Network Command	Interfaces Matched	Actions Taken
network 10.0.0.0	Token0, Ethernet0	Updates are sent out Token0 and Ethernet0. Listen for updates entering Token0 and Ethernet0. Advertise subnets 10.1.3.0 (Token0's subnet) and 10.1.2.0 (Ethernet0's subnet).
network 199.1.1.0	Serial0	Updates are sent out Serial0. Listen for updates entering Serial0. Advertise subnet 199.1.1.0 (Serial0's subnet).

For any interfaces that have IP addresses with the same network number referenced in this **network** subcommand, routing updates are broadcast and listened for, and the connected subnet is advertised. The **network** command requires a network number, not a subnet number, for the parameter. Interestingly, if you enter a subnet number in the command, the Cisco IOS software changes the parameter to the network number in which that subnet resides.

If the goal was to configure RIP for all interfaces, a common mistake was made in this example. No **network** command matches interfaces Serial1 and Ethernet1. Example 5-5 shows the configuration process to add the additional network commands.

Example 5-5 *Completing the RIP Configuration from Example 5-4*

```
R1#configure terminal
R1(config)#router rip
R1(config-router)#network 199.1.2.0
R1(config-router)#network 172.16.0.0
R1(config-router)#CTL-Z
R1#show running-config
! Lines removed for brevity
router rip
 network 10.0.0.0
 network 172.16.0.0
 network 199.1.1.0
 network 199.1.2.0
```

Notice that to add more **network** commands under **router rip**, you first use the **router rip** command to enter RIP configuration mode. The **show running-config** output shows the full RIP configuration as a result of the commands in Examples 5-4 and 5-5.

IGRP Configuration

You configure IGRP just like RIP, except that the **router igrp** command has an additional parameter—the autonomous system (AS) number. The term *autonomous system* refers to a network that is within the control of a single company or organization. The term *AS number* refers to a number assigned to a single company or organization when it registers its connection to the Internet. However, for IGRP, you do not need a registered AS number. All that is needed for IGRP to work is for all the routers to use the same AS number.

In Example 5-6, a complete sample IGRP configuration causes the router to advertise all connected subnets to listen on all interfaces for IGRP updates and to advertise on all interfaces.

Example 5-6 *Sample IGRP Configuration and* **show ip route** *Command Output*

```
interface ethernet 0
ip address 10.1.2.3 255.255.255.0
interface ethernet 1
ip address 172.16.1.1 255.255.255.0
interface tokenring 0
ip address 10.1.3.3 255.255.255.0
interface serial 0
ip address 199.1.1.1 255.255.255.0
```

Example 5-6 *Sample IGRP Configuration and* **show ip route** *Command Output (Continued)*

```
interface serial 1
ip address 199.1.2.1 255.255.255.0
!
router igrp 1
 network 10.0.0.0
 network 199.1.1.0
 network 199.1.2.0
 network 172.16.0.0

Router1#show ip route
Codes: C - connected, S - static, I - IGRP, R - RIP, M - mobile, B - BGP
       D - EIGRP, EX - EIGRP external, O - OSPF, IA - OSPF inter area
       N1 - OSPF NSSA external type 1, N2 - OSPF NSSA external type 2
       E1 - OSPF external type 1, E2 - OSPF external type 2, E - EGP
       i - IS-IS, L1 - IS-IS level-1, L2 - IS-IS level-2, ia - IS-IS inter area
       * - candidate default, U - per-user static route, o - ODR
       P - periodic downloaded static route

Gateway of last resort is not set

     10.0.0.0/24 is subnetted, 3 subnets
C       10.1.3.0 is directly connected, TokenRing0
C       10.1.2.0 is directly connected, Ethernet0
I       10.1.4.0 [100/8539] via 10.1.2.14, 00:00:50, Ethernet0
     172.16.0.0/24 is subnetted, 2 subnets
C       172.16.1.0 is directly connected, Ethernet1
I       172.16.2.0 [100/6244] via 172.16.1.44, 00:00:20, Ethernet1
C     199.1.1.0/24 is directly connected, Serial0
C     199.1.2.0/24 is directly connected, Serial1
```

IGRP configuration begins with the **router igrp 1** global configuration command. Then four consecutive **network** commands match all the interfaces on the router so that IGRP is fully enabled. In fact, these **network** commands are identical to the **network** commands in the complete RIP configuration.

The output of the **show ip route** command in Example 5-6 reflects many of the concepts discussed earlier in this chapter, as well as a few new ones. The router has added some directly connected routes to the routing table, as well as two routes learned with IGRP. First, note that the output begins with a legend describing some codes that identify a route's source. The letter **C** denotes a directly connected route, and the letter **I** denotes a route learned by IGRP. Looking at the actual routes, notice that each line starts with a **C** or an **I**, as appropriate. In this case, IGRP has learned two routes, which are highlighted in the example.

Each route lists the subnet number, the outgoing interface, and possibly the next-hop router's IP address. The next-hop router IP address is preceded by the word "via" in the output. Directly connected routes do not have a next-hop router field, because the packet does not need to be sent to another router, but instead to the destination host.

Finally, the numbers between the brackets mention some very useful information. The first number represents the administrative distance, which is covered later in this chapter. The second number lists the metric associated with this route. For instance, in the route to subnet 10.1.4.0, the administrative distance is 100, and the metric is 8539. Remember, IGRP calculates the metric as a function of bandwidth and delay, so the actual metric value typically is a much larger number than the hop count metric shown in the examples earlier in this chapter.

IGRP Metrics

IGRP uses a composite metric. This metric is calculated as a function of bandwidth, delay, load, reliability, and MTU. By default, only bandwidth and delay are considered; the other parameters are considered only if they are enabled via configuration. Delay and bandwidth are not measured values but are set via the **delay** and **bandwidth** interface subcommands. (The same formula is used to calculate the metric for EIGRP, but with a scaling factor so that the actual metric values are larger, allowing more granularity in the metric.)

The **show ip route** command in Example 5-6 shows the IGRP metric values in brackets. For example, the route to 10.1.4.0 shows the value [100/8539] beside the subnet number. Administrative distance is covered briefly near the end of this chapter. The metric 8539 is a single value, as calculated based on bandwidth and delay. The metric is calculated (by default) as the inverse of the minimum bandwidth, plus the cumulative delay on all links in the route. *In other words, the higher the bandwidth, the lower the metric; the lower the cumulative delay, the lower the metric.*

IGRP uses the value set with the **bandwidth** command on each interface to determine the interface's bandwidth. On LAN interfaces, the **bandwidth** command's default values reflect the correct bandwidth. However, on serial interfaces, the **bandwidth** command defaults to 1544—in other words, T1 speed. (The **bandwidth** command uses units of kbps, so the **bandwidth 1544** command sets the bandwidth to 1544 kbps, or 1.544 Mbps.)

The router cannot figure out the actual physical clock rate and automatically change the **bandwidth** command value for a serial interface. For IGRP to choose the best route, the bandwidth should be configured to the correct value on each interface. For example, Figure 5-10 shows three examples of the same network, with different results for R1's routes based on the routing protocol and the bandwidth settings.

Figure 5-10   *Bandwidth's Effect on Route Choices*

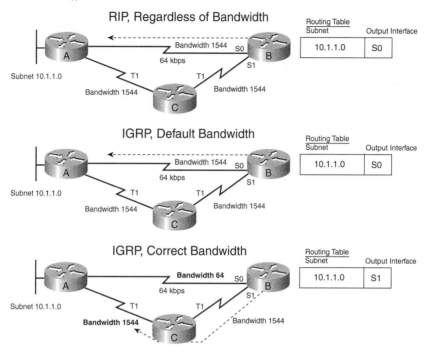

The link between Routers A and B is only a 64-kbps link, but the other two links are T1 links. So the better route from Router B to subnet 10.1.1.0 arguably is through Router C. That route requires an extra hop through a router, but it uses two T1 links instead of one relatively slow 64-kbps link.

RIP uses hop count only for the metric, so regardless of the **bandwidth** command settings, RIP on Router B chooses the route over the slow link directly to Router A. IGRP, with the default **bandwidth** settings in the middle part of the figure, also chooses the route directly through Router A. However, as shown in the bottom part of the figure, after the **bandwidth** commands configure the correct values, IGRP chooses the better route to subnet 10.1.1.0 through Router C.

Examination of RIP and IGRP debug and show Commands

This section on basic RIP and IGRP configuration closes with one more sample network that is first configured with RIP and then is configured with IGRP. Advanced distance vector protocol concepts, such as split horizon and route poisoning, become more obvious when you look at these examples. RIP and IGRP implement split horizon and route poisoning. You can better understand them by examining the upcoming **debug** messages.

First, Figure 5-11 and Example 5-7 show a stable RIP network with split-horizon rules that affect the RIP updates. The numbered arrows in the figure represent routing updates. The comments in Example 5-7 refer to those same numbers to help you correlate the figure and the example. Example 5-7 shows Ethernet 0 on Yosemite being shut down and Yosemite advertising an infinite-distance route to 10.1.2.0. The route is poisoned, as shown in the **debug ip rip** output at the end of the example. Example 5-8 shows the corresponding RIP configuration in Yosemite.

Figure 5-11 *Sample Three-Router Network with Subnet 10.1.2.0 Failing*

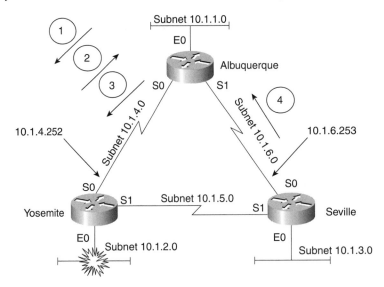

Example 5-7 *RIP Configuration and Debugs on Albuquerque*

```
interface ethernet 0
ip addr 10.1.1.251 255.255.255.0
interface serial 0
ip addr 10.1.4.251 255.255.255.0
interface serial 1
ip addr 10.1.6.251 255.255.255.0
!
router rip
network 10.0.0.0

Albuquerque#debug ip rip
RIP: received v1 update from 10.1.6.253 on Serial1
        10.1.3.0 in 1 hops
        10.1.2.0 in 2 hops
        10.1.5.0 in 1 hops
RIP: sending v1 update to 255.255.255.255 via Serial0 (10.1.4.251)
```

Example 5-7 *RIP Configuration and Debugs on Albuquerque (Continued)*

```
!               (POINT NUMBER 1)
     subnet  10.1.3.0, metric 2
     subnet  10.1.1.0, metric 1
     subnet  10.1.6.0, metric 1
RIP: sending v1 update to 255.255.255.255 via Serial1 (10.1.6.251)
     subnet  10.1.2.0, metric 2
     subnet  10.1.1.0, metric 1
     subnet  10.1.4.0, metric 1
RIP: sending v1 update to 255.255.255.255 via Ethernet0 (10.1.1.251)
     subnet  10.1.3.0, metric 2
     subnet  10.1.2.0, metric 2
     subnet  10.1.6.0, metric 1
     subnet  10.1.5.0, metric 2
     subnet  10.1.4.0, metric 1
RIP: received v1 update from 10.1.4.252 on Serial0
     10.1.3.0 in 2 hops
     10.1.2.0 in 1 hops
     10.1.5.0 in 1 hops
Albuquerque#
(Yosemite E0 shutdown at this time...)

RIP: received v1 update from 10.1.4.252 on Serial0
!               (POINT NUMBER 2)
     10.1.3.0 in 2 hops
     10.1.2.0 in 16 hops (inaccessible)
     10.1.5.0 in 1 hops
RIP: sending v1 update to 255.255.255.255 via Serial0 (10.1.4.251)
!               (POINT NUMBER 3)
     subnet  10.1.3.0, metric 2
     subnet  10.1.2.0, metric 16
     subnet  10.1.1.0, metric 1
     subnet  10.1.6.0, metric 1
RIP: sending v1 update to 255.255.255.255 via Serial1 (10.1.6.251)
     subnet  10.1.2.0, metric 16
     subnet  10.1.1.0, metric 1
     subnet  10.1.4.0, metric 1
RIP: sending v1 update to 255.255.255.255 via Ethernet0 (10.1.1.251)
     subnet  10.1.3.0, metric 2
     subnet  10.1.2.0, metric 16
     subnet  10.1.6.0, metric 1
     subnet  10.1.5.0, metric 2
     subnet  10.1.4.0, metric 1
RIP: received v1 update from 10.1.6.253 on Serial1
!               (POINT NUMBER 4)
     10.1.3.0 in 1 hops
     10.1.2.0 in 16 hops (inaccessible)
     10.1.5.0 in 1 hops
```

Example 5-8 *RIP Configuration on Yosemite*

```
interface ethernet 0
ip addr 10.1.2.252 255.255.255.0
interface serial 0
ip addr 10.1.4.252 255.255.255.0
interface serial 1
ip addr 10.1.5.252 255.255.255.0

router rip
network 10.0.0.0
```

First, examine the configuration on Albuquerque (Example 5-7) and Yosemite (Example 5-8). Because all interfaces on each router are part of network 10.0.0.0, RIP needs only a single **network** command on each router, so the configuration is relatively easy.

For the rest of the explanation, refer to the phrases "POINT NUMBER X" in Example 5-7. The following list describes what happens at each point in the process:

- **POINT NUMBER 1**—Albuquerque sends an update out Serial0, obeying split-horizon rules. Notice that 10.1.2.0, Yosemite's Ethernet subnet, is not in the update sent out Albuquerque's S0 interface.

- **POINT NUMBER 2**—This point begins right after Yosemite's E0 is shut down, simulating a failure. Albuquerque receives an update from Yosemite, entering Albuquerque's S0 interface. The route to 10.1.2.0 has an infinite metric, which in this case is 16.

- **POINT NUMBER 3**—Albuquerque formerly did not mention subnet 10.1.2.0 because of split-horizon rules (point 1). The update at point 3 includes a poisoned route for 10.1.2.0 with metric 16. This is an example of split horizon with poison reverse.

- **POINT NUMBER 4**—Albuquerque receives an update in S1 from Seville. The update includes a metric 16 (infinite) route to 10.1.2.0. Seville does not suspend any split-horizon rules to send this route, because it saw the advertisement of that route earlier, so this is a simple case of route poisoning.

Example 5-9 shows the steps needed to migrate to IGRP. It also lists some **debug** and **show** commands. It shows the configuration added to each of the three routers shown in Figure 5-11 to migrate to IGRP. The logic of the **network** commands works just like with RIP. The output of the **show** and **debug** commands provides some insight into the differences between RIP and IGRP.

NOTE The following configuration commands are used on all three routers.

Example 5-9   *Migrating to IGRP with Sample* show *and* debug *Commands*

```
no router rip
router igrp 5
 network 10.0.0.0

Albuquerque#show ip route
Codes: C - connected, S - static, I - IGRP, R - RIP, M - mobile, B - BGP
       D - EIGRP, EX - EIGRP external, O - OSPF, IA - OSPF inter area
       N1 - OSPF NSSA external type 1, N2 - OSPF NSSA external type 2
       E1 - OSPF external type 1, E2 - OSPF external type 2, E - EGP
       i - IS-IS, L1 - IS-IS level-1, L2 - IS-IS level-2, ia - IS-IS inter area
       * - candidate default, U - per-user static route, o - ODR
       P - periodic downloaded static route


Gateway of last resort is not set


     10.0.0.0/24 is subnetted, 6 subnets
I       10.1.3.0 [100/8539] via 10.1.6.253, 00:00:28, Serial1
I       10.1.2.0 [100/8539] via 10.1.4.252, 00:00:18, Serial0
C       10.1.1.0 is directly connected, Ethernet0
C       10.1.6.0 is directly connected, Serial1
I       10.1.5.0 [100/10476] via 10.1.4.252, 00:00:18, Serial0
                 [100/10476] via 10.1.6.253, 00:00:29, Serial1
C       10.1.4.0 is directly connected, Serial0
Albuquerque#debug ip igrp transactions
IGRP protocol debugging is on
Albuquerque#
07:43:40: IGRP: sending update to 255.255.255.255 via Serial0 (10.1.4.251)
07:43:40:      subnet 10.1.3.0, metric=8539
07:43:40:      subnet 10.1.1.0, metric=688
07:43:40:      subnet 10.1.6.0, metric=8476
07:43:40: IGRP: sending update to 255.255.255.255 via Serial1 (10.1.6.251)
07:43:40:      subnet 10.1.2.0, metric=8539
07:43:40:      subnet 10.1.1.0, metric=688
07:43:40:      subnet 10.1.4.0, metric=8476
07:43:40: IGRP: sending update to 255.255.255.255 via Ethernet0 (10.1.1.251)
07:43:40:      subnet 10.1.3.0, metric=8539
07:43:40:      subnet 10.1.2.0, metric=8539
07:43:40:      subnet 10.1.6.0, metric=8476
07:43:40:      subnet 10.1.5.0, metric=10476
07:43:40:      subnet 10.1.4.0, metric=8476
07:43:59: IGRP: received update from 10.1.6.253 on Serial1
07:43:59:      subnet 10.1.3.0, metric 8539 (neighbor 688)
07:43:59:      subnet 10.1.5.0, metric 10476 (neighbor 8476)
07:44:18: IGRP: received update from 10.1.4.252 on Serial0
07:44:18:      subnet 10.1.2.0, metric 8539 (neighbor 688)
07:44:18:      subnet 10.1.5.0, metric 10476 (neighbor 8476)
Albuquerque#no debug all
```

continues

Example 5-9 *Migrating to IGRP with Sample* show *and* debug *Commands (Continued)*

```
All possible debugging has been turned off
Albuquerque#
Albuquerque#debug ip igrp events
IGRP event debugging is on
Albuquerque#
07:45:00: IGRP: sending update to 255.255.255.255 via Serial0 (10.1.4.251)
07:45:00: IGRP: Update contains 3 interior, 0 system, and 0 exterior routes.
07:45:00: IGRP: Total routes in update: 3
07:45:00: IGRP: sending update to 255.255.255.255 via Serial1 (10.1.6.251)
07:45:00: IGRP: Update contains 3 interior, 0 system, and 0 exterior routes.
07:45:00: IGRP: Total routes in update: 3
07:45:00: IGRP: sending update to 255.255.255.255 via Ethernet0 (10.1.1.251)
07:45:01: IGRP: Update contains 5 interior, 0 system, and 0 exterior routes.
07:45:01: IGRP: Total routes in update: 5
07:45:21: IGRP: received update from 10.1.6.253 on Serial1
07:45:21: IGRP: Update contains 2 interior, 0 system, and 0 exterior routes.
07:45:21: IGRP: Total routes in update: 2
07:45:35: IGRP: received update from 10.1.4.252 on Serial0
07:45:35: IGRP: Update contains 2 interior, 0 system, and 0 exterior routes.
07:45:35: IGRP: Total routes in update: 2
Albuquerque#no debug all
All possible debugging has been turned off
Albuquerque#show ip protocol
Routing Protocol is "igrp 5"
  Sending updates every 90 seconds, next due in 34 seconds
  Invalid after 270 seconds, hold down 280, flushed after 630
  Outgoing update filter list for all interfaces is
  Incoming update filter list for all interfaces is
  Default networks flagged in outgoing updates
  Default networks accepted from incoming updates
  IGRP metric weight K1=1, K2=0, K3=1, K4=0, K5=0
  IGRP maximum hopcount 100
  IGRP maximum metric variance 1
  Redistributing: igrp 5
  Maximum path: 4
  Routing for Networks:
    10.0.0.0
  Routing Information Sources:
    Gateway         Distance       Last Update
    10.1.6.253          100        00:00:23
    10.1.4.252          100        00:00:08
  Distance: (default is 100)
```

You can migrate from RIP to IGRP in this case with only three configuration commands per router. As highlighted in Example 5-9, the **no router rip** command removes all RIP configuration on the router, including any **network** subcommands. The three routers each must use the same IGRP AS number (5 in this case), and because all interfaces on each of the routers are in network 10.0.0.0, only a single **network 10.0.0.0** subcommand is needed.

The **show ip route** command provides the most direct view of what a routing protocol does. First, the legend at the beginning of the **show ip route** command in Example 5-9 defines the letter codes that identify the source of the routing information—such as **C** for connected routes, **R** for RIP, and **I** for IGRP. Each of the Class A, B, and C networks is listed, along with each of that network's subnets. If a static mask is used within that network, the mask is shown only in the line referring to the network. Each routing entry lists the subnet number and the outgoing interface. In most cases, the next-hop router's IP address is also listed.

IGRP learns the same routes that RIP learned, but using different metrics. The output of the **show ip route** command lists six subnets. Also, notice the two routes to 10.1.5.0/24—one through Yosemite and one through Seville. Both routes are included in the routing table, because the default setting for **maximum-paths** is 4, and because the routes have an equal metric. Looking further into the output of the **debug ip igrp transactions** command, you can see the equal-cost routes being advertised. One route is shown in the update received on Serial1; the other route in the update is received on Serial0.

The output of the **debug ip igrp transactions** command shows the details of the routing updates, whereas the **debug ip igrp events** command simply mentions that routing updates have been received.

Finally, the **show ip protocol** command lists several important details about the routing protocol. The update timer is listed, shown with the time remaining until the next routing update is to be sent. Also, the elapsed time since an update was received from each neighboring router is listed at the end of the output. This command also lists each of the neighbors from which routing information was received. If you are in doubt as to whether updates have been received during the recent past and from which routers, the **show ip protocol** command is the place to find out.

Issues When Multiple Routes to the Same Subnet Exist

With redundant links in a network, routers learn about multiple routes to the same subnet. A router might learn one route with one metric and then learn a better route that has a lower metric and replace the old route with the new, better route. Or, the old route might have a better metric. In some cases, the metric might tie, and the router has to decide what to do.

Figure 5-12 outlines an example in which new routes are learned. In the figure, Router B formerly only had a link to Router A; then, a link to Router C was added. Table 5-12 shows Router B's routing table before the serial link between Routers B and C comes up, and Table 5-13 shows Router B's routing table after the link between Routers B and C comes up.

Figure 5-12   *Routers A and C Advertising to Router B*

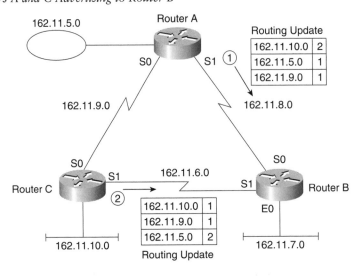

NOTE   The routing updates shown in Figure 5-12 show only the information needed for the point being made in this example. Other routes that would normally be in the routing update have been omitted.

Table 5-12   *Router B Routing Table While Router B Serial1 Is Down*

Group	Outgoing Interface	Next-Hop Router	Metric	Comments
162.11.5.0	S0	162.11.8.1	1	
162.11.7.0	E0	—	0	
162.11.8.0	S0	—	0	
162.11.9.0	S0	162.11.8.1	1	The metric 1 route is learned from Router A.
162.11.10.0	S0	162.11.8.1	2	Currently, the best route is through Router A, because the link to Router C is down.

Table 5-13 *Router B Routing Table After Learning a Second Valid Route to Subnet 162.11.10.0*

Group	Outgoing Interface	Next-Hop Router	Metric	Comments
162.11.5.0	S0	162.11.8.1	1	
162.11.6.0	S1	—	0	This route was added because it is directly connected to S1, which is now up and operational.
162.11.7.0	E0	—	0	
162.11.8.0	S0	—	0	
162.11.9.0	S0	162.11.8.1	1	The metric 1 route was learned from Router A, but Router C also advertises a metric 1 route! Only one route is chosen—the first one that was learned.
162.11.10.0	S1	162.11.6.2	1	A better route replaces the old route. The new route has a smaller metric and points directly out S1 toward Router C.

Router B changes only one route in this case in reaction to the new routing updates from Router C. Router B changes its route to 162.11.10.0 because the metric for the route through Router C (metric 1) is smaller than the one from Router A (metric 2).

Router B adds only one route in this example—the directly connected subnet 162.11.6.0. This route is added not because of this distance vector routing protocol, but because it is a directly connected subnet and that interface is now up.

In this example, Router B does not change its route to subnet 162.11.9.0, even though Router B now learns a metric 1 route to subnet 162.11.9.0 through both Router C and Router A. *In this case, the route that was already in the table is left in the table, which is a reasonable choice.* For Router B to behave as in this example, it needs to configure the **router igrp** or **router rip** subcommand command **maximum-paths 1**, which means that Router B should add at most one route to the same subnet to the routing table. With **maximum-paths** set to 1, the first route that is added to the table stays in the table, and routes learned later, with the same metric, are not added.

By default, Cisco IOS software includes up to four equal-cost routes to the same subnet in the routing table—essentially as if **maximum-paths 4** had been configured. In the last example, if Router B had used the default setting, it would have added a second route to 162.11.9.0, pointing out Serial1 through Router C. You can configure **maximum-paths** as low as 1 or as high as 6.

When RIP places more than one route to the same subnet in the routing table, the router balances the traffic across the various routes. (The details of how Cisco IOS software balances packets is explained in detail in the Cisco Press book *Inside Cisco IOS Software Architectures*.)

The metric formula used for IGRP (and EIGRP) poses an interesting problem when considering equal-metric routes. IGRP can learn more than one route to the same subnet with different metrics; however, the metrics are very unlikely to be equal, because the metric is actually calculated with a mathematical formula. So, with IGRP (and EIGRP), you can tell the routing protocol to think of metrics that are "pretty close" as being equal. To do so, Cisco IOS software uses the **variance** router subcommand to define how different the metrics can be for routes to be considered to have equal metrics.

The **variance** command defines a multiplier; any metrics lower than the product of the lowest metric and the variance are considered equal. For example, if the metric for the better of two routes is 100, and the variance is set to 2, a second route with a metric less than 200 is considered equal-cost and can be added to the routing table (depending on the configuration of maximum-paths). If the **variance** were set to 4 in this example, routes to the same subnet with a metric less than 400 could be added to the routing table.

When IGRP places more than one route to the same subnet in the routing table, the router balances the traffic across the various routes in proportion to the metric values. You can choose to tell the router to use only the lowest-cost route using the **traffic-share min** router IGRP subcommand. This command tells the router that, even if multiple routes to the same subnet are in the routing table, it should use only the route that truly has the smallest metric. So why not just add only the truly lowest metric route to the routing table in the first place? Well, if the other pretty good routes are in the table, and the best one fails, you do not have to wait on IGRP to converge and add a new route to the routing table. Convergence time is practically instantaneous! So you can use the strategy of adding multiple nearly-equal-cost routes using the **variance** command, use the **traffic-share min** command to tell the router to just use the best of these routes, and converge more quickly when that route fails.

Administrative Distance

Many companies and organizations use a single routing protocol. However, in some cases, a company needs to use multiple routing protocols. For instance, if two companies connect their networks so that they can exchange information, they need to exchange some routing information. If one company uses RIP, and the other uses IGRP, on at least one router, both RIP and IGRP must be used. This is just one example, but it is not that unusual to need to run more than one routing protocol in a single router.

Depending on the network topology, two routing protocols might learn routes to the same subnets. When a single routing protocol learns multiple routes to the same subnet, the metric tells it which route is best. However, because different routing protocols use different metrics, the IOS cannot compare the metrics. For instance, RIP might learn a route to subnet 10.1.1.0 with metric 1, and IGRP might learn a route to 10.1.1.0 with metric 8729. There is no basis for comparison between the two metrics.

To decide which route to use, IOS uses a concept called *administrative distance.* Administrative distance is a number that denotes how believable an entire routing protocol is on a single router. The lower the number, the better, or more believable, the routing protocol. For instance, RIP has a default administrative distance of 120, and IGRP defaults to 100, making IGRP more believable than RIP. So, when both routing protocols learn routes to the same subnet, the router adds only the IGRP route to the routing table.

The administrative distance values are configured on a single router and are not exchanged with other routers. Table 5-14 lists the various sources of routing information, along with the default administrative distances.

Table 5-14 *Default Administrative Distances*

Route Type	Administrative Distance
Connected	0
Static	1
EIGRP summary route	5
EBGP	20
EIGRP (internal)	90
IGRP	100
OSPF	110
IS-IS	115
RIP	120
EIGRP (external)	170
iBGP (external)	200

Foundation Summary

The "Foundation Summary" section lists the most important facts from the chapter. Although this section does not list everything that will be on the exam, a well-prepared CCNA candidate should at a minimum know all the details in each Foundation Summary before taking the exam.

All routing protocols have several general goals:

- To dynamically learn and fill the routing table with a route to all subnets in the network.
- If more than one route to a subnet is available, to place the best route in the routing table.
- To notice when routes in the table are no longer valid and to remove them from the routing table.
- If a route is removed from the routing table and another route through another neighboring router is available, to add the route to the routing table. (Many people view this goal and the preceding one as a single goal.)
- To add new routes, or to replace lost routes with the currently-best available route, as quickly as possible. The time between losing the route and finding a working replacement route is called *convergence time*.
- To prevent routing loops.

Table 5-15 summarizes the key routing protocol terms you need to know for the CCNA exam.

Table 5-15 *Routing Protocol Terminology*

Term	Definition
Routing protocol	A protocol whose purpose is to learn the available routes, place the best routes in the routing table, and remove routes when they are no longer valid.
Exterior routing protocol	A routing protocol designed for use between two different organizations. These are typically used between ISPs or between a company and an ISP. For example, a company would run BGP, an exterior routing protocol, between one of its routers and a router inside an ISP.
Interior routing protocol	A routing protocol designed for use within a single organization. For example, an entire company might choose the IGRP routing protocol, which is an interior routing protocol.
Distance vector	The logic behind the behavior of some interior routing protocols, such as RIP and IGRP.
Link state	The logic behind the behavior of some interior routing protocols, such as OSPF.
Balanced hybrid	The logic behind the behavior of EIGRP, which is more like distance vector than link state but is different from these two types of routing protocols.

Table 5-15   *Routing Protocol Terminology (Continued)*

Term	Definition
Dijkstra Shortest Path First (SPF) algorithm	Magic math used by link-state protocols, such as OSPF, when the routing table is calculated.
Diffusing Update Algorithm (DUAL)	The process by which EIGRP routers collectively calculate the routes to place in the routing tables.
Convergence	The time required for routers to react to changes in the network, removing bad routes and adding new, better routes so that the currently-best routes are in all the routers' routing tables.
Metric	The numeric value that describes how good a particular route is. The lower the value, the better the route.

Distance vector protocols need several mechanisms to prevent loops. Table 5-16 summarizes these issues and lists the solutions.

Table 5-16   *Issues Related to Distance Vector Routing Protocols in Networks with Multiple Paths*

Issue	Solution
Multiple routes to the same subnet have equal metrics	Implementation options involve either using the first route learned or putting multiple routes to the same subnet in the routing table.
Routing loops occur because updates pass each other over a single link	**Split horizon**—The routing protocol advertises routes out an interface only if they were not learned from updates entering that interface. **Split horizon with poison reverse**—The routing protocol uses split-horizon rules unless a route fails. In that case, the route is advertised out all interfaces, including the interface in which the route was learned, but with an infinite-distance metric.
Routing loops occur because of routing information looping through alternative paths	**Route poisoning**—When a route to a subnet fails, the subnet is advertised with an infinite-distance metric. This term specifically applies to routes that are advertised when the route is valid, whereas poison reverse refers to routes that are not normally advertised because of split horizon but that are advertised with an infinite metric when the route fails.
Counting to infinity	**Hold-down timer**—After finding out that a route to a subnet has failed, a router waits a certain period of time before believing any other routing information about that subnet. **Triggered updates**—When a route fails, an update is sent immediately rather than waiting on the update timer to expire. Used in conjunction with route poisoning, this ensures that all routers know of failed routes before any hold-down timers can expire.

Table 5-17 outlines some of the key comparison points between RIP and IGRP.

Table 5-17 *RIP and IGRP Feature Comparison*

Feature	RIP (Default)	IGRP (Default)
Update timer	30 seconds	90 seconds
Metric	Hop count	Function of bandwidth and delay (the default). Can include reliability, load, and MTU.
Hold-down timer	180	280
Flash (triggered) updates	Yes	Yes
Mask sent in update	No	No
Infinite-metric value	16	4,294,967,295

Q&A

As mentioned in the introduction, you have two choices for review questions. The following questions give you a bigger challenge than the exam because they are open-ended. By reviewing with this more-difficult question format, you can exercise your memory better and prove your conceptual and factual knowledge of the topics covered in this chapter. The answers to these questions are found in Appendix A.

For more practice with exam-like question formats, including multiple-choice questions and those using a router simulator, use the exam engine on the CD.

1. What type of routing protocol algorithm uses a hold-down timer? What is its purpose?

2. Define what split horizon means to the contents of a routing update. Does this apply to both the distance vector algorithm and the link-state algorithm?

3. What steps would you take to migrate from RIP to IGRP in a router whose current RIP configuration includes only **router rip** followed by a **network 10.0.0.0** command?

4. How does the Cisco IOS software designate a subnet in the routing table as a directly connected network? What about a route learned with IGRP or RIP?

5. Create a configuration for IGRP on a router with these interfaces and addresses: e0 using 10.1.1.1, e1 using 224.1.2.3, s0 using 10.1.2.1, and s1 using 199.1.1.1. Use AS 5.

6. Create a configuration for IGRP on a router with these interfaces and addresses: to0 using 200.1.1.1, e0 using 128.1.3.2, s0 using 192.0.1.1, and s1 using 223.254.254.1.

7. From a router's user mode, without using debugs or privileged mode, how can you determine what routers are sending you routing updates?

8. Imagine that a router has an interface E0 with IP address 168.10.1.1 and E1 with IP address 10.1.1.1. If the commands **router rip** and **network 10.0.0.0**, with no other network commands, are configured in the router, does RIP send updates out Ethernet0?

9. Imagine that a router has an interface E0 with IP address 168.10.1.1 and E1 with IP address 10.1.1.1. If the commands **router igrp 1** and **network 10.0.0.0** are configured in the router, does IGRP advertise 168.10.0.0?

10. If the commands **router igrp 1** and **network 10.0.0.0** are configured in a router that has an Ethernet0 interface with IP address 168.10.1.1, mask 255.255.255.0, does this router have a route to 168.10.1.0?

11. Must IGRP metrics for multiple routes to the same subnet be equal for the multiple routes to be added to the routing table? If not, how close in value do the metrics have to be?

12. When you're using RIP, what configuration command controls the number of equal-cost routes that can be added to the routing table at the same time? What is the maximum number of equal-cost routes to the same destination that can be included in the IP routing table at once?

13. When you're using IGRP, what configuration command controls the number of equal-cost routes that can be added to the routing table at the same time? What is the maximum number of equal-cost routes to the same destination that can be included in the IP routing table at once?

14. Which command lists all the IP routes learned via RIP?

15. Which command or commands list all IP routes in network 172.16.0.0?

16. True or false: Distance vector routing protocols learn routes by transmitting routing updates.

17. Assume that a router is configured to allow only one route in the routing table to each destination network. If more than one route to a particular subnet is learned, and if each route has the same metric value, which route is placed in the routing table if the routing protocol uses distance vector logic?

18. Describe the purpose and meaning of route poisoning.

19. Describe the meaning and purpose of triggered updates.

20. What term describes the underlying logic behind the OSPF routing protocol?

21. Router1 has a serial interface S0 connected via a point-to-point link to Router2. Router2 has an Ethernet interface address of 20.1.21.1, mask 255.255.252.0. Write down the single variation of an **ip route** command on Router1 that defines a static route to reach the subnet off Router2's Ethernet interface.

This chapter covers the following subjects:

- Link-State Routing Protocol and OSPF Concepts

- Balanced Hybrid Routing Protocol and EIGRP Concepts

- OSPF Configuration

- EIGRP Configuration

OSPF and EIGRP Concepts and Configuration

Routing protocols learn routes—the current best routes—and put those subnets in the IP routing table. In the last chapter, you saw how distance vector protocols accomplish that goal. In this chapter, you will read about how two different types of routing protocols, link-state and balanced hybrid, accomplish that same goal.

When people first created distance vector protocols, routers had slow processors connected to slow links (relative to today's technology). For perspective, RFC 1058, published as an Internet standard RFC in June 1988, defined the first version of RIP for IP. The underlying distance vector logic was defined far in advance of the Internet RFC for RIP, mainly in the early 1980s. Therefore, distance vector protocols were designed to advertise just the basic routing information across the network to save bandwidth. These protocols were also designed to use little processing and memory, because the routing devices of the day had, relative to today, only small amounts of memory and processing power.

Link-state and balanced hybrid protocols were developed mainly in the early to mid-1990s, and they were designed under the assumptions of faster links and more processing power in the routers. By sending more information, and requiring the routers to perform more processing, these newer types of routing protocols can gain some important advantages over distance vector protocols—mainly, faster convergence. The goal remains the same—to add the currently-best routes to the routing table—but these protocols use different methods to find and add those routes. This chapter outlines how link-state and balanced hybrid protocols do their work, as well as how to configure the most popular routing protocol of each type—Open Shortest Path First (OSPF) and Enhanced IGRP (EIGRP). Please refer to Appendix F for some further details about a few of the topics in this chapter.

"Do I Know This Already?" Quiz

The purpose of the "Do I Know This Already?" quiz is to help you decide if you need to read the entire chapter. If you intend to read the entire chapter, you do not necessarily need to answer these questions now.

The ten-question quiz, derived from the major sections in the "Foundation Topics" section, helps you determine how to spend your limited study time.

Table 6-1 outlines the major topics discussed in this chapter and the "Do I Know This Already?" quiz questions that correspond to those topics.

Table 6-1   *"Do I Know This Already?" Foundation Topics Section-to-Question Mapping*

Foundations Topics Section	Questions Covered in This Section
Link-State Routing Protocol and OSPF Concepts	3, 5
Balanced Hybrid Routing Protocol and EIGRP Concepts	2, 4, 5
OSPF Configuration	1, 6, 7, 8
EIGRP Configuration	9, 10

CAUTION   The goal of self-assessment is to gauge your mastery of the topics in this chapter. If you don't know the answer to a question or you're only partially sure of the answer, you should mark this question as wrong for purposes of the self-assessment. Giving yourself credit for an answer you guess correctly skews your self-assessment results and might give you a false sense of security.

1. Which of the following affects the calculation of OSPF routes when all possible default values are used?

    a. Bandwidth

    b. Delay

    c. Load

    d. Reliability

    e. MTU

    f. Hop count

2. Which of the following affects the calculation of EIGRP metrics when all possible default values are used?

    a. Bandwidth

    b. Delay

    c. Load

    d. Reliability

    e. MTU

    f. Hop count

3. OSPF runs an algorithm to calculate the currently-best route. Which of the following terms refer to that algorithm?

   a. SPF

   b. DUAL

   c. Feasible successor

   d. Dijkstra

   e. Good old common sense

4. EIGRP uses an algorithm to find routes when no backup route exists. Which of the following terms refers to that algorithm?

   a. SPF

   b. DUAL

   c. Feasible successor

   d. Dijkstra

   e. Good old common sense

5. How do OSPF and EIGRP notice when a neighboring router fails?

   a. The failing router sends a message before failing

   b. The failing router sends a "dying gasp" message

   c. The router notices a lack of routing updates for a period of time

   d. The router notices a lack of Hello messages for a period of time

6. Which of the following network commands, following the command **router ospf 1**, tell this router to start using OSPF on interfaces whose IP addresses are 10.1.1.1, 10.1.100.1, and 10.1.120.1?

   a. network 10.0.0.0 255.0.0.0 area 0

   b. network 10.0.0.0 0.255.255.255 area 0

   c. network 10.0.0.1 255.0.0.255 area 0

   d. network 10.0.0.1 0.255.255.0 area 0

   e. network 10.0.0.0 255.0.0.0

   f. network 10.0.0.0 0.255.255.255

   g. network 10.0.0.1 255.0.0.255

   h. network 10.0.0.1 0.255.255.0

7. Which of the following network commands, following the command **router ospf 1**, tells this router to start using OSPF on interfaces whose IP addresses are 10.1.1.1, 10.1.100.1, and 10.1.120.1?

   a. network 0.0.0.0 255.255.255.255 area 0

   b. network 10.0.0.0 0.255.255.0 area 0

   c. network 10.1.1.0 0.x.1x.0 area 0

   d. network 10.1.1.0 255.0.0.0 area 0

   e. network 10.0.0.0 255.0.0.0 area 0

8. Which of the following commands list the OSPF neighbors off interface serial 0/0?

   a. show ip ospf neighbor

   b. show ip ospf interface

   c. show ip neighbor

   d. show ip interface

   e. show ip ospf neighbor interface serial 0/0

9. In the **show ip route** command, what code designation implies that a route was learned with EIGRP?

   a. E

   b. I

   c. G

   d. R

   e. P

   f. A

   g. B

   h. C

   i. D

10. Which of the following network commands, following the command **router eigrp 1**, tells this router to start using EIGRP on interfaces whose IP addresses are 10.1.1.1, 10.1.100.1, and 10.1.120.1?

   a. network 10.0.0.0

   b. network 10.1.1x.0

   c. network 10.0.0.0 0.255.255.255

   d. network 10.0.0.0 255.255.255.0

The answers to the "Do I Know This Already?" quiz appear in Appendix A. The suggested choices for your next step are as follows:

- **8 or less overall score**—Read the entire chapter. This includes the "Foundation Topics," "Foundation Summary," and "Q&A" sections.

- **9 or 10 overall score**—If you want more review on these topics, skip to the "Foundation Summary" section and then go to the "Q&A" section. Otherwise, move to the next chapter.

Foundation Topics

Link-State Routing Protocol and OSPF Concepts

The ICND exam covers link-state protocol concepts and a single link-state routing protocol—OSPF. In this chapter, you will read about the basics. If you find yourself thinking that there has to be more to OSPF than what is covered here, you're right! If you move on to the CCNP certification, you will need to learn many more details about OSPF and link-state protocols. For CCNA, you just need to know the basics.

Link-state and distance vectors share a common goal—filling the routing tables with the currently-best routes. They differ significantly in how they accomplish this task. The largest difference between the two is that distance vector protocols advertise sparse information. In fact, distance vector protocols know that other routers exist only if the other router broadcasts a routing update to them. When a distance vector protocol in a router receives a routing update, the update says nothing about the routers beyond the neighboring router that sent the update. Conversely, link-state protocols advertise a large amount of topological information about the network, and the routers perform some CPU-intensive computation on the topological data. They even discover their neighbors before exchanging routing information.

Figure 6-1 illustrates what a router might advertise with a link-state protocol. The actual contents of the routing updates are not shown. This is a graphical representation.

The network topology is shown in the upper part of the figure. With a link-state protocol, the whole network topology is described in the routing update, as shown in the lower part of the figure. Rather than Router B's telling Router A what the metric (or cost) for the route should be, Router B tells Router A the metric associated with every link in the network. Router B also tells Router A about all the routers in the network, including which subnets they are attached to and their status. In effect, it is like Router A has been given a map of the network, along with the cost associated with each link. Of course, the map is not literally a drawn map—it is a mathematical model of the network based on the topology information.

The link-state protocol on Router A calculates the lowest-cost route to all subnets based on the topology information, including the route to subnet 10.1.1.0, mask 255.255.255.0. When more than one route to a subnet exists, the link-state routing protocol chooses the path with the lowest metric. Packets traveling to 10.1.1.0 from Router A go through Router C because this route has the lower cost.

Figure 6-1   *Content Advertised to a Neighboring Router: Link State*

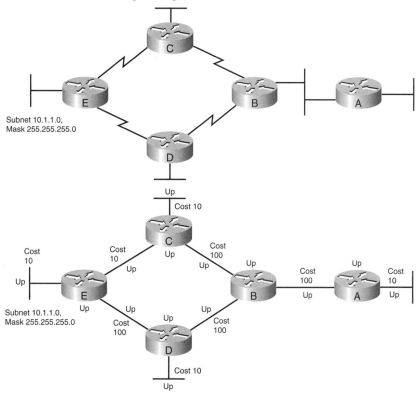

Unlike distance vector protocols, link-state protocols must calculate the metric instead of simply being told the metric in the received routing update. For instance, with distance vector protocols, Router B tells Router A something like "subnet 10.1.1.0, metric 3." With link-state protocols, the topology information learned by a router includes a cost associated with each link in the network. A router totals the cost associated with each link in each route to find the metric associated with the route. For instance, Router A discovers two routes to subnet 10.1.1.10, with a metric of 220 for the route to 10.1.1.0 through Router C and a metric of 310 for the route to 10.1.1.0 through Router D. In both cases, Router A uses Router B as the next hop. Therefore, Router A puts a route to 10.1.1.0 in its routing table, using Router B's interface IP address as the next hop. Similarly, Router B calculates routes to 10.1.1.0 through Router C and Router D and places the better route (through Router C) in Router B's routing table.

The algorithm used to calculate routes with link-state protocols is called the *Shortest Path First (SPF) algorithm*. It is sometimes called the *Dijkstra SPF algorithm*, or simply *Dijkstra* after its inventor. You can look at Figure 6-1 and figure out the two routes and total the metrics to find the lowest-cost route. Routers, however, cannot just look at the figure. In fact, routers really just know the list of routers and subnets and which routers are connected to which subnets. The SPF algorithm processes all that topology information to come up with the best route to each subnet.

Link-state protocols do not just start broadcasting topology information out every interface when the router first boots. Instead, link-state protocols first use a process by which they discover neighbors. (Neighbors can also be statically defined instead of being discovered.) *Neighbors* are other routers, also running the same link-state protocol, that share a common subnet. As soon as routers know that they are neighbors, they can exchange their respective copies of the topology information—called the *topology database*—and then run SPF to calculate new routes.

After a router identifies a neighbor, the routers exchange the information in their topology databases. OSPF sends several types of packets—*link-state updates* (LSUs) and *Database Description* (DD) packets—that contain topology information as well as individual link-state advertisements (LSAs). For instance, a link LSA describes a subnet number and mask, the cost (metric), and other information about the subnet. Also, OSPF uses a reliable protocol to exchange routing information, ensuring that lost LSU packets are retransmitted. So OSPF routers can know with certainty whether a neighbor has yet received all the LSAs when exchanging routing information.

The next several pages cover some of the details of how OSPF and link-state protocols work. The basic process of learning routes for the first time with OSPF goes something like this:

1. Each router discovers its neighbors on each interface. The list of neighbors is kept in a neighbor table.

2. Each router uses a reliable protocol to exchange topology information (LSAs) with its neighbors.

3. Each router places the learned topology information in its topology database.

4. Each router runs the SPF algorithm against its own topology database to calculate the best routes to each subnet in the database.

5. Each router places the best route to each subnet in the IP routing table.

Link-state protocols require more work from the routers, but the work is typically worth the effort. A router running a link-state protocol uses more memory and more processing cycles than do distance vector protocols. The topology updates take many more bytes compared to distance vector routing updates, although because OSPF does not advertise all routes every update interval like distance vector protocols do, the overall number of bytes sent can be smaller with OSPF. A link-state protocol uses a neighbor table and a topology database in addition to adding routes to the routing table. Also, the SPF algorithm must be used to recalculate routes when links go up or down, and the algorithm itself requires memory and processing on each router. However, you can reduce the amount of memory and processing required by following some good design practices, some of which are covered in this section. Also, OSPF converges much more quickly than do distance-vector protocols—and fast convergence is the most important feature of a routing protocol.

OSPF Protocols and Operation

So far, the text has described a wide overview of how link-state protocols work, with a few specific details about OSPF. The next several sections of this chapter take a more detailed look at OSPF operation and protocols. The topics are listed in order with regards to what a router does with OSPF when that router first loads IOS.

Identifying OSPF Routers with a Router ID

The OSPF topology database consists of lists of subnet numbers (called *links*, hence the name *link-state database*). It also contains lists of routers, along with the links (subnets) to which each router is connected. Armed with the knowledge of links and routers, a router can run the SPF algorithm to compute the best routes to all the subnets.

The database entries for subnets can be easily identified with the subnet number and the associated prefix. (Remember, a subnet mask can be represented by a prefix value as well, for instance, /24, to mean the same thing as 255.255.255.0.) To uniquely identify each router in the database, OSPF uses a concept called the *OSPF router ID* (RID). The end goal is to have a way to uniquely identify each router in the database, and to make sure that no two routers have the same RID to avoid confusion. So, OSPF has each router use one of the routers' IP addresses, because the routers should not use duplicate IP addresses.

Of course, routers typically have several interfaces and several IP addresses. A Cisco router uses the following criteria to select its RID:

- The router first looks for the existence of any loopback interfaces that are up. If so, the router picks the highest numeric IP address among the loopback interfaces

- If no loopback is found, the router picks the highest numeric IP address from all its working (up and up) interfaces

NOTE   A loopback interface is a virtual interface that can be configured with the **interface loopback** *interface-number* command, where *interface-number* is an integer. Loopback interfaces are always in an "up and up" state unless administratively placed into a shutdown state. For instance, a simple configuration of the command **interface loopback 0**, followed by **ip address 192.168.200.1 255.255.255.0** would create a loopback interface, and assign it an IP address. Assuming the subnet on the loopback interface is advertised into the internetwork, an engineer can **ping, trace,** and **telnet** to the loopback IP address.

Each router chooses its OSPF RID when OSPF is initialized. Initialization happens during the initial load of IOS. So, if OSPF comes up, and later other interfaces come up that happen to have higher IP addresses, then the OSPF RID does not change until the OSPF process is restarted. (OSPF can be restarted with the **clear ip ospf process** command as well.)

Meeting Neighbors by Saying Hello

Once a router has picked its OSPF RID, and some interfaces come up, the router is ready to meet its OSPF neighbors. OSPF routers can become neighbors if they are connected to the same subnet. To discover other OSPF-speaking routers, a router multicasts OSPF Hello packets out to each interface, and hopes to receive OSPF Hello packets from other routers connected to those interfaces. Figure 6-2 outlines the basic concept.

Figure 6-2 *Link-State Hello Packets*

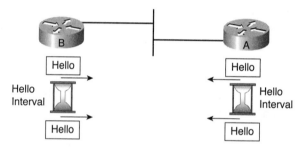

Router A and B both send Hello messages onto the LAN. Soon afterwards, the two routers can begin to exchange topology information with each other, and then run the Dijkstra algorithm in order to fill the routing table with the best routes. The Hello messages themselves have the following features:

- The Hello message follows the IP packet header, with the IP packet protocol type 89.

- Hello packets are sent to multicast IP address 224.0.0.5, which is intended for all OSPF-speaking routers.

- OSPF routers listen for packets sent to IP multicast address 224.0.0.5, in part hoping to receive Hello packets.

Routers learn several important pieces of information from looking at the received Hello packets. The Hello message includes the sending router's RID, Area ID, Hello interval, dead interval, router priority, designated router, backup designated router, and a list of neighbors that the sending router already knows about on the subnet. (More to come on most of these items.)

The list of neighbors is particularly important to the Hello process. For example, when Router A receives a Hello from Router B, Router A needs to somehow tell Router B that Router A got the Hello. To do so, Router A adds Router B's RID to the list of OSPF neighbors inside the next Hello that Router A multicasts onto the network. Likewise, when Router B receives Router A's Hello, Router B's next (and ongoing) Hellos include Router A's RID in the list of neighbors.

Once a router sees its own RID in a received Hello, the router believes that *two-way* communication has been established to that neighbor. The two-way state for a neighbor is important because at that point, more detailed information, such as LSAs, can be exchanged. Also, in some cases on LANs, neighbors might reach the two-way state and stop there—more on that in the section titled "Database Exchange and Becoming Fully Adjacent" coming up in a few pages.

Potential Problems in Becoming a Neighbor

Interestingly, receiving a Hello from a router on the same subnet does not always result in two routers becoming neighbors. It's like meeting a new neighbor in real life—if you happen to disagree about a lot of things, and not get along, you might literally live on the same street, but not really talk all that much. Similarly, with OSPF, routers on the same subnet must agree about several of the parameters exchanged in the Hello; otherwise, the routers simply do not become neighbors. Specifically, the following must match before a pair of routers will become neighbors:

- Subnet mask used on the subnet
- Subnet number (as derived using the subnet mask and each routers' interface IP address)
- Hello Interval
- Dead Interval
- OSPF Area ID

If any one of these parameters differs, the routers do not become neighbors. In short, if troubleshooting OSPF when routers should be neighbors, and they are not, check this list!

Now a quick review of the detailed steps so far—knowing that as of yet, two neighbors have not yet exchanged any routing information:

1. Each router initializes OSPF and picks its RID.

2. Routers discover each other as neighbors using Hello packets.

3. Routers reach a two-way communications state with a neighbor once they see their own RID in the Hello from that neighbor.

The neighbors might finally be ready to exchange topology information—but maybe not. The next step is to elect a *Designated Router* (DR) for LANs, and in some cases, for Frame Relay and ATM WANs.

Reducing OSPF Overhead Using Designated Routers

In some cases, a *Designated Router* (DR) must be elected for the subnet before *Database Description (DD)* packets, containing LSAs, can be exchanged between routers. DRs are always required on a LAN, and sometimes (depending on topology and configuration) required with Frame Relay and ATM. Figure 6-3 shows the classic example, with a DR being required on a LAN, and a DR not being required on a point-to-point serial link.

Figure 6-3   *No DR on a Point-to-Point Link, with a DR on the LAN*

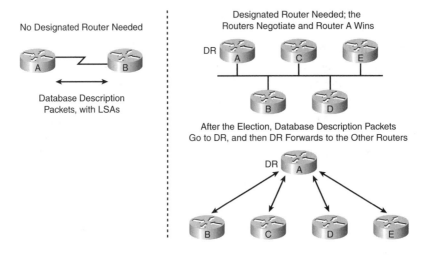

When a DR is not required, neighboring routers can go ahead and start sending routing updates to each other, as shown on the left side of the figure. On the right side, the top figure shows a LAN topology, where a DR election has been held, with Router A winning the election. As a result, all routing updates flow to and from Router A, with Router A essentially distributing the routing updates (topology information in DD and LSU packets) to the other routers.

The DR concept prevents overloading a subnet with too much OSPF traffic when many routers are on a subnet. Of course, lots of routers could be attached to one LAN, which is why a DR is required for routers attached to a LAN. For instance, if 10 routers were attached to the same LAN subnet, and they were allowed to forward OSPF updates to each of the other nine routers, topology updates would flow between 45 different pairs of neighbors—with almost all the information being redundant. With the DR concept, as seen in Figure 6-3 on the right, that same LAN would require routing updates only between the DR and the nine other routers, significantly reducing flooding of OSPF information across the LAN.

A router decides whether it needs to elect a DR, plus some other details of operation, based on an interface's OSPF *network type*. For instance, a point-to-point link has a default OSPF network type of *point-to-point*, which does not require a DR. Similarly, LAN interfaces default to an OSPF network type of *broadcast*, which always requires a DR. For Nonbroadcast Multiaccess (NBMA) networks such as Frame Relay, OSPF allows for the configuration of five different variations of OSPF network types, with some options that require a DR, and with others that do not. (These types can be configured with the **ip ospf network** *type* command.)

Because the DR is so important to the exchange of routing information, the loss of the elected DR could cause delays in convergence. OSPF includes the concept of a *Backup DR* (BDR) on each subnet, so when the DR fails, or loses connectivity to the subnet, the BDR can take over as the DR. (All routers except for the DR and BDR are typically called "DROther" in IOS **show** command output.)

Electing the Designated Router

When a DR is required, the neighboring routers hold an election. To elect a DR, the neighboring routers look at two fields inside the Hello packets they receive, and choose the DR based on the following criteria:

- The router sending the Hello with the *highest OSPF Priority* setting becomes the DR.
- If two or more routers tie with the highest priority setting, the router sending the Hello with the *highest RID* wins.
- While not always the case, typically the router with the second highest priority becomes the BDR.
- A priority setting of 0 means that the router never can become DR.
- The range of priority values that allows a router to be a candidate are 1 through 255.
- If a DR has been elected, and a new router starts sending Hellos onto the same subnet, with a higher priority than the current DR, the new higher-priority router does *not* immediately take over as DR, but rather must wait until the DR and BDR fail.

Database Exchange and Becoming Fully Adjacent

Finally, neighboring routers can begin to exchange routing information with each other using Database Description packets, as well as LSA and LSU packets. First, a quick recap of the steps taken so far:

1. Each router initializes OSPF and picks its RID.
2. Routers discover each other as neighbors using Hello packets.

3. Routers reach a two-way communications state with a neighbor once they see their own RID in the Hello from that neighbor.

4. If the OSPF network type for the interface requires a DR, the DR is elected (as well as the BDR).

At this point, on an interface that does not use a DR, OSPF updates can be sent to all neighbors on that interface. These packets typically use unicast destination IP addresses of each neighbor to which the update is being sent.

On interfaces with an elected DR, the non-DR routers send updates to the DR and BDR, using the 224.0.0.6 multicast address as the destination. This special multicast address means "all OSPF DRs", which means that the DR, and the BDR, will be listening for the packets. Then, the DR relays the updates to all OSPF routers on the subnet, using a destination IP address of 224.0.0.5. Note that the BDR listens for and receives the updates, so it is ready to take over for the DR, but the BDR does not forward the updates to the non-DR routers.

The neighboring routers now exchange their entire topology database with their neighbor. Remember, it is a large amount of information in comparison to the sparse information sent in distance vector updates. Once a router has exchanged its entire link-state database with a neighbor, it transitions into a state called the *Full* state. In normal working operation, the **show ip ospf neighbor** command should list one or more neighbors in a Full state, indicating the expected final resting state of an OSPF neighbor.

> **NOTE** OSPF considers a neighbor in the Full state to be *fully adjacent*. So, while a router might have several neighbors on an interface, only some of them might become *fully adjacent*.

Keep in mind that the Full state is for neighbors with which Link State Updates have been exchanged. On LANs, for instance, non-DR routers never exchange updates with each other, but they do exchange updates with the DR and BDR. As a result, a non-DR router will end up in a Full state with the DR and BDR, and a two-way state with other non-DRs. This concept is shown Example 6-4 later in the chapter.

Once a router has received a full database exchange from a neighbor, it can run the SPF algorithm and update the routing table.

Steady-State Operation

Hello packets serve the same purpose as timed, regular full routing updates serve for distance vector protocols. With distance vector protocols, when a router fails to hear routing updates from a neighbor for some multiple of the update interval, the router believes the silent router has failed. The router then marks all routes it learned from the now-silent router as having an infinite metric.

Similarly, with OSPF, when a router fails to hear Hellos from a neighbor for an interval called the *dead interval,* the router believes the silent router has failed. The dead interval defaults to four times the Hello interval. For instance, on Ethernet interfaces, Cisco routers default to a Hello interval of 10 seconds and a dead interval of 40 seconds. OSPF keeps working until the dead interval expires; after that, the router marks the now-silent router as "down" in its neighbor table. Then the router that stopped receiving the Hellos runs Dijkstra to calculate new routes, based on the fact that one of the network's routers is now out of service. Also, the router floods topology updates to its neighbors to let them know about the failure, with the other routers also running the Dijkstra algorithm again to compute new routes.

Loop Avoidance

The SPF algorithm prevents loops as a natural part of the processing of the topology database with the SPF algorithm. Unlike distance vector protocols, link-state protocols do not need loop-avoidance features such as split horizon, poison reverse, and hold-down timers.

Link-state protocols rely on the rapid dissemination of information about failed routers and subnets to prevent loops. Therefore, when a link or router fails, a router noticing the failure immediately floods the new router or link status to its neighbors, with those routers forwarding the updated status to their neighbors, eventually flooding the new status information to all the routers in the network. (In a way, this feature works like "triggered updates" for distance vector protocols, but this behavior is just a feature of link-state protocols and does not have a specific name.)

Interestingly, the convergence time of most distance vector protocols consists of the time taken by the loop-avoidance features. For instance, the hold-down timer alone accounts for several minutes of convergence time. With link-state protocols, none of the time-consuming loop-avoidance features are needed, which means that link-state protocols can converge very quickly. With proper design, OSPF can converge as quickly as 5 seconds after a router notices a failure in most cases.

Scaling OSPF Through Hierarchical Design

OSPF can be used in some networks with very little thought as to design issues. You just turn on OSPF in all the routers, and it works! However, in large networks, engineers need to think about and plan how to use several OSPF features that allow it to scale well in larger networks. To appreciate the issues behind OSPF scalability, and the need for good design to allow scalability, examine Figure 6-4.

Figure 6-4 *Single-Area OSPF*

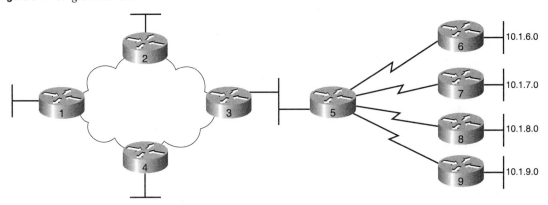

In the network shown in Figure 6-4, the topology database on all nine routers is the same full topology that matches the figure. With a network that size, you can just enable OSPF, and it works fine. But imagine a network with 900 routers instead of only nine, and several thousand subnets. In that size of network, OSPF convergence time might be slow, and the routers might experience memory shortages and processor overloads. The problems can be summarized as follows:

- A larger topology database requires more memory on each router.
- Processing the larger-topology database with the SPF algorithm requires processing power that grows exponentially with the size of the topology database.
- A single interface status change (up to down or down to up) forces every router to run SPF again!

Although there is no exact definition of "large" in this context, in networks with at least 50 routers and at least a few hundred subnets, engineers should use OSPF scalability features to reduce the problems just described. These numbers are gross generalizations. They depend largely on the network design, models of routers, and so on.

OSPF Areas

Using OSPF areas solves many, but not all, of the most common problems with running OSPF in larger networks. OSPF areas break up the network so that routers in one area know less topology information about the subnets in the other area and they do not know about the routers in the other area at all. With smaller-topology databases, routers consume less memory and take less processing time to run SPF.

Figure 6-5 shows the same network as Figure 6-4, but with two OSPF areas, labeled Area 1 and Area 0.

Figure 6-5 *Two-Area OSPF*

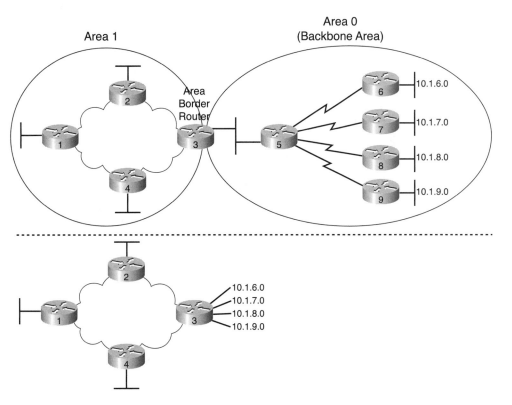

The same topology is shown in the upper part of the figure, but the lower part of the figure shows the topology database on Routers 1, 2, and 4. By placing part of the network in another area, the routers inside Area 1 are shielded from some of the details. Router 3 is known as an OSPF Area Border Router (ABR), because it is on the border between two different areas. Router 3 does not advertise full topology information about the part of the network in Area 0 to Routers 1, 2, and 4. Instead, Router 3 advertises summary information about the subnets in Area 0, effectively making Routers 1, 2, and 4 think the topology looks like the lower part of Figure 6-5. Therefore, Routers 1, 2, and 4 view the world as if it has fewer routers. As a result, the SPF algorithm takes less time, and the topology database takes less memory.

It is very important to note that the summarized information shown in Figure 6-5 does not change the number of subnets known inside Area 1 or Area 0. The summarized information just means that a router inside one area receives routing updates that use fewer bytes, thereby decreasing the amount of memory needed to store the information. Later you will learn about a feature called *route summarization,* in which the number of subnets advertised into another area is reduced as well. The terms are similar, and both happen in Area Border Routers, but the concepts are different.

> **NOTE** Although the perspectives of the routers in Area 1 are shown in Figure 6-5, the same thing happens in reverse—routers in Area 0 do not know the details of Area 1's topology.

Using areas improves all three of the scaling problems that were stated earlier. By making the topology databases smaller, the databases take less memory. With smaller databases, the SPF algorithm takes less time and converges more quickly. Also, although it is not obvious, when links in Area 0 change state, the routers that are totally in Area 1 do not need to run SPF again. So, with areas, many fewer SPF calculations are required in the network's routers.

Notice that the dividing line between areas is not a link, but a router. In Figure 6-5, Router 3 is in both area 1 and Area 0. OSPF uses the term Area Border Router (ABR) to describe a router that sits in both areas. An ABR has the topology database for both areas and runs SPF when links change status in either area. Using areas does not actually reduce memory requirements or the number of SPF calculations for ABRs like Router 3.

Stub Areas

OSPF includes other features to improve how it works in larger networks. The CCNP routing test expects you to know the topics covered in Cisco's Building Scalable Cisco Internetworks (BSCI) course, and you might guess from the course's name that OSPF scalability features are covered in depth. You can also refer to Tom Thomas's *OSPF Network Design Solutions* from Cisco Press, or search on "OSPF Design Guide" at Cisco.com for a great reference document.

When you move on to the CCNP certification, you should pay particular attention to the topic of stub areas. OSPF allows you to define an area as a stub area; as a result, the size of the topology database for routers in that area can be reduced even further. OSPF allows for other variants of areas—called Totally Stubby and Not-So-Stubby areas—that affect the size of the topology database, which in turn affects how fast the SPF algorithm runs. A new OSPF area type, Totally Not-So-Stubby Area (TNSSA), provides yet another type of area. You should be aware of the various types when working with OSPF in a real network.

Summary: Comparing Link-State and OSPF to Distance Vector Protocols

Link-state protocols have a major advantage over distance vector protocols in how fast they converge and in how they prevent loops. With today's networks, a 3-minute wait for a distance vector routing protocol to converge typically is perceived as a network outage. A 10-second convergence time for OSPF might simply be perceived as an irritation. Also, link-state protocols easily prevent loops. In addition, OSPF is publicly defined in RFC 2328, so you can use routers from multiple vendors with some confidence that they will work reasonably well together.

Link-state protocols do have some drawbacks. The biggest negative relates to the planning and design effort that is required for larger networks. Depending on the network's physical topology, OSPF might or might not be a natural fit. For instance, OSPF defines area 0 as the "backbone" area. All nonbackbone areas must connect to each other through the backbone area only, making OSPF designs hierarchical. Many networks work well with a hierarchical OSPF design, but others do not. The other drawbacks are more obvious. Link-state protocols can consume memory and CPU to the point of impacting overall router performance, depending on the network and the OSPF design.

Table 6-2 summarizes some of the key points of comparison between the two types of routing protocols.

Table 6-2 *Comparing Link-State and Distance Vector Protocols*

Feature	Link-State	Distance Vector
Convergence Time	Fast	Slow, mainly because of loop-avoidance features
Loop Avoidance	Built into the protocol	Requires extra features such as split horizon
Memory and CPU Requirements	Can be large; good design can minimize	Low
Requires Design Effort for Larger Networks	Yes	No
Public Standard or Proprietary	OSPF is public	RIP is publicly defined; IGRP is not

Balanced Hybrid Routing Protocol and EIGRP Concepts

Cisco uses the term *balanced hybrid* to describe the category of routing protocols in which EIGRP resides. Cisco supports two distance vector IP routing protocols—RIP and IGRP. It also supports two link-state IP routing protocols—OSPF and Intermediate System-to-Intermediate System (IS-IS). Furthermore, Cisco supports a single balanced hybrid IP routing protocol—EIGRP.

Cisco uses the term balanced hybrid because EIGRP has some features that act like distance vector protocols and some that act like link-state protocols. Cisco also sometimes refers to EIGRP as an advanced distance vector protocol.

EIGRP Features and Comparison with IGRP

EIGRP is an enhanced version of IGRP, so some level of comparison with IGRP is useful. As it turns out, there are more differences than similarities between the two protocols. Table 6-3 summarizes these similarities and differences.

Table 6-3   *EIGRP and IGRP Similarities and Differences*

Similarities	Differences
Both are Cisco proprietary protocols.	EIGRP converges significantly faster than IGRP
They use the same logic for multiple equal-cost paths	EIGRP sends routing information once to a neighbor, and then only sends new or updated information; IGRP repeats the entire routing table every 90 seconds. Therefore, EIGRP has much less overhead than IGRP.
The metrics are practically identical, with EIGRP's formula for calculating the metric simply including a multiplier of 256.	EIGRP can be used to exchange routing information for Novell IPX and Apple Computer AppleTalk Layer 3 protocols, in addition to IP.

Internal processing details differ significantly as well, and will be described in the next few sections of this chapter.

EIGRP Processes and Tables

EIGRP follows three general steps to be able to add routes to the IP routing table. In its basic form, these three steps are similar to OSPF, but with large differences in the underlying detail. The steps are as follows:

1. EIGRP routers discover other EIGRP routers that are attached to the same subnet, and then the routers form a *neighbor relationship* with each other. Each router keeps a list of the neighbors in its *EIGRP neighbor table*.

2. EIGRP then exchanges network topology information with known neighbors, placing the information in the *EIGRP topology table*. (There is no requirement for a DR or BDR concept like OSPF.)

3. EIGRP analyzes the topology information, and puts the lowest-metric routes into the IP routing table.

As a result of these three steps, EIGRP actually works with three tables:

- **The EIGRP neighbor table**—Viewed with the **show ip eigrp neighbor** command
- **The EIGRP topology table**—Viewed with the **show ip eigrp topology** command
- **The IP routing table**—Viewed with the **show ip route** or **show ip route eigrp** commands

EIGRP on a single router could end up creating and updating nine tables due to its support of IP, IPX, and AppleTalk. If configured for all three Layer 3 protocols, EIGRP would have a neighbor table, topology table, and routing table for each of the three Layer 3 protocols. For instance, the **show ipx eigrp topology** command would display EIGRP's topology table used to store information about IPX network numbers, with different information than is shown with the **show ip eigrp topology** command.

The next few sections describe some details about how EIGRP forms neighbor relationships, exchanges routes, and adds entries to the IP routing table.

Neighbors and Sending Topology Information

Figure 6-6 shows the typical sequence used by two EIGRP routers that connect to the same subnet. They discover each other as neighbors, and they reliably exchange full routing information. The process is different from OSPF, but the same goal of reliably ensuring that all neighbors receive all routing information is achieved. EIGRP sends and receives EIGRP hello packets to ensure that the neighbor is still up and working—like OSPF, but with a different Hello packet than OSPF. When link status changes, or new subnets are discovered, reliable routing updates are sent, but only with the new information—again, like OSPF.

Figure 6-6 *Sequence of Events for EIGRP Exchange of Routing Information*

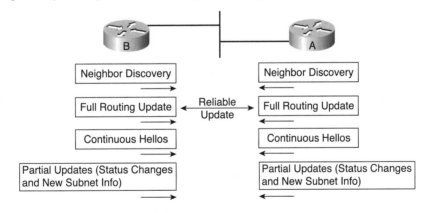

Hello messages are used to perform neighbor discovery, and are continually sent between neighbors to allow neighbors to notice when connectivity has failed. The *Hello interval* defines how often a router should send Hellos, and how often to expect to receive them. The Hello interval can be changed, but it is 5 seconds on LANs and point-to-point WAN links, and 60 seconds on multipoint WANs like Frame Relay, by default.

EIGRP uses EIGRP *update messages* to actually convey topology information to neighbors. These update messages can be sent to multicast IP address 224.0.0.10 if the sending router needs to update multiple routers on the same subnet; otherwise, the updates are sent to the unicast IP address of the particular neighbor. (Hello messages are always sent to the 224.0.0.10 multicast address.)

The update messages are sent using the *Reliable Transport Protocol (RTP)*. The significance of RTP is that, like OSPF, EIGRP will resend routing updates that are lost in transit. By using RTP, EIGRP can better avoid loops.

Updating the Routing Table While Avoiding Loops

Loop avoidance poses one of the most difficult problems with any dynamic routing protocol. Distance vector protocols overcome this problem with a variety of tools, some of which create a large portion of the minutes-long convergence time after a link failure. Link-state protocols overcome this problem by having each router keep a full topology of the network, so that by running a rather involved mathematical model, a router can avoid any loops.

EIGRP avoids loops by keeping some basic topological information but not full information. When a router learns multiple routes to the same subnet, it puts the best route in the routing table. EIGRP keeps some topological information for the same reason as OSPF—so that it can very quickly converge and use a new route without causing a loop. EIGRP keeps its internal algorithms simple by using sparser topology information than OSPF; however, as a result, only some alternate routes can be easily and quickly used without causing loops, and some require more work. Failed routes that have an EIGRP *feasible successor* can be used immediately after the route fails. Failed routes without a feasible successor require EIGRP to use a *Query and Response* process to confirm that no loop exists before an alternate route can be used. Both processes result in fast convergence, typically quicker than 10 seconds, but the query and response process does take slightly longer.

EIGRP Successors and Feasible Successors

Of the other suboptimal routes, some may be used immediately if the currently-best route fails, without fear of having a loop occur. EIGRP runs a simple algorithm to identify which routes could be used immediately after a route failure, without causing a loop. EIGRP then keeps these loop-free backup routes in its topology table and uses them if the currently-best route fails.

Figure 6-7 illustrates how EIGRP figures out which routes can be used after a route fails without causing loops.

Figure 6-7   *Successors and Feasible Successors with EIGRP*

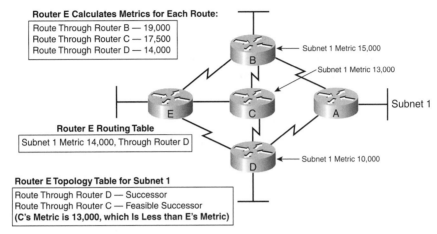

In the figure, Router E learns three routes to Subnet 1, from Routers B, C, and D. After calculating each route's metric based on bandwidth and delay information received in the routing update, Router E finds that the route through Router D has the lowest metric, so Router E adds that route to its routing table, as shown.

EIGRP builds a topology table that includes the currently-best route plus the alternative routes that would not cause loops if they were used when the currently-best route through Router D failed. EIGRP calls the best route (the route with the lowest metric) the *successor*. Any backup routes that could be used without causing a loop are called *feasible successors*. In Figure 6-7, the route through Router C would not cause a loop, so Router E lists the route through Router C as a feasible successor. Router E thinks that using the route through Router B could cause a loop, so that route is not listed as a feasible successor.

EIGRP decides if a route can be a feasible successor if the computed metric for that route on the neighbor is less than its own computed metric. When that neighbor has a lower metric for its route to the subnet in question, that route is said to have met the *feasibility condition*. For example, Router E computes a metric of 14,000 on its best route (through Router D). Router C's computed metric is lower than 14,000 (it's 13,000), so Router E believes that if the existing route failed, it could use the route through Router C and not cause a loop. As a result, Router E adds a route through Router C to the topology table as a feasible successor route. Conversely, Router B's computed metric is 15,000, which is larger than Router E's computed metric of 14,000, so Router E does not consider the route through Router B a feasible successor.

If the route to Subnet 1 through Router D fails, Router E can immediately put the route through Router C into the routing table, without fear of creating a loop. Convergence occurs almost instantly in this case.

The Query and Reply Process

When a route fails and the route has no feasible successor, EIGRP uses a distributed algorithm called Diffusing Update Algorithm (DUAL). DUAL sends queries looking for a loop-free route to the subnet in question. When the new route is found, DUAL adds it to the routing table.

The EIGRP DUAL process simply uses messages to confirm that a route exists, and would not create a loop, before deciding to replace a failed route with an alternate route. For instance, in Figure 6-7, imagine that both routers C and D fail. Router E does not have a feasible successor route to subnet 1, but there is an obvious physically-available path through Router B. In order to use the route, Router E sends EIGRP *query* messages to his working neighbors (in this case, Router B). Router B's route to subnet 1 is still working fine, so Router B replies to Router E with an EIGRP *reply* message, simply stating the details of the working route to subnet 1, and confirming that it is still viable. Router E can then add a new route to subnet 1 to its routing table, without fear of a loop.

Replacing a failed route with a feasible successor takes a very short amount of time, typically less than a second or two. When queries and replies are required, convergence can take slightly longer, but in most networks, convergence can still occur in less than 10 seconds.

EIGRP Summary

EIGRP converges quickly while avoiding loops. EIGRP does not have the same scaling issues as link-state protocols, so no extra design effort is required. EIGRP takes less memory and processing than link-state protocols.

EIGRP converges much more quickly than do distance vector protocols, mainly because EIGRP does not need the loop-avoidance features that slow down distance vector convergence. By sending only partial routing updates, after full routing information has been exchanged, EIGRP reduces overhead on the network.

The only significant disadvantage of EIGRP is that it is a Cisco-proprietary protocol. So, if you want to be prepared to use multiple vendors' routers in a network, you should probably choose an alternative routing protocol. Alternatively, you could use EIGRP in the Cisco routers and OSPF in the others and perform a function called *route redistribution,* in which a router exchanges routes between the two routing protocols inside the router.

Table 6-4 summarizes some of the key comparison points between EIGRP, IGRP, and OSPF.

Table 6-4 *EIGRP Features Compared to OSPF and IGRP*

Feature	EIGRP	IGRP	OSPF
Discovers neighbors before exchanging routing information	Yes	No	Yes
Builds some form of topology table in addition to adding routes to the routing table	Yes	No	Yes
Converges quickly	Yes	No	Yes
Uses metrics based on bandwidth and delay by default	Yes*	Yes	No
Sends full routing information on every routing update cycle	No	Yes	No
Requires distance vector loop-avoidance features	No	Yes	No
Public standard	No	No	Yes
Uses DUAL Algorithm	Yes	No	No

*EIGRP uses the same metric as IGRP, except that EIGRP scales the metric by multiplying by 256.

OSPF Configuration

OSPF includes many configuration options as a result of its complexity. Tables 6-5 and 6-6 summarize the OSPF configuration and troubleshooting commands, respectively.

Table 6-5 *IP OSPF Configuration Commands*

Command	Configuration Mode
router ospf *process-id*	Global
network *ip-address wildcard-mask* **area** *area-id*	Router subcommand
ip ospf cost *interface-cost*	Sets the OSPF cost associated with the interface
bandwidth *bandwidth*	Sets the interface bandwidth, from which OSPF derives the cost based on the formula 10^8 / bandwidth
auto-cost reference bandwidth *number*	Router subcommand that tells OSPF the numerator in the formula used to calculate the OSPF cost based on the interface bandwidth

continues

Table 6-5   *IP OSPF Configuration Commands (Continued)*

Command	Configuration Mode
ip ospf hello *number*	Interface subcommand that sets the OSPF Hello interval, and also resets the Dead interval to 4 times this number
ip ospf network *type*	Interface subcommand that defines the OSPF network type

Table 6-6   *IP OSPF EXEC Commands*

Command	Description
show ip route [*ip-address* [*mask*] [**longer-prefixes**]] | [*protocol* [*process-id*]]	Shows the entire routing table, or a subset if parameters are entered.
show ip protocols	Shows routing protocol parameters and current timer values.
show ip ospf interface	Lists the area in which the interface resides, and neighbors adjacent on this interface.
show ip ospf neighbor	Lists neighbors and current status with neighbors, per interface.
show ip route ospf	Lists routes in the routing table learned by OSPF.
debug ip ospf events	Issues log messages for each OSPF packet.
debug ip ospf packet	Issues log messages describing the contents of all OSPF packets.
debug ip ospf hello	Issues log messages describing Hellos and Hello failures.

This section includes two sample configurations using the same network diagram. The first example shows a configuration with a single OSPF area, and the second example shows multiple areas, along with some **show** commands.

OSPF Single-Area Configuration

When only a single area is used, OSPF configuration differs only slightly from RIP and IGRP configuration. The best way to describe the configuration, and the differences with the configuration of the other routing protocols, is to use an example. Figure 6-8 shows a sample network, and Example 6-1 shows the configuration on Albuquerque.

Figure 6-8 *Sample Network for OSPF Single-Area Configuration*

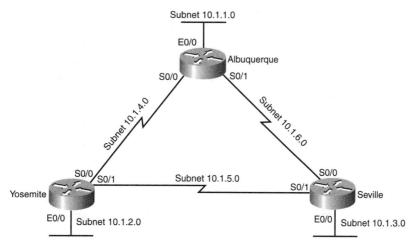

Example 6-1 *OSPF Single-Area Configuration on Albuquerque*

```
interface ethernet 0/0
ip address 10.1.1.1 255.255.255.0
interface serial 0/0
ip address 10.1.4.1 255.255.255.0
interface serial 0/1
ip address 10.1.6.1 255.255.255.0
!
router ospf 1
network 10.0.0.0 0.255.255.255 area 0
```

The configuration correctly enables OSPF on all three interfaces on Albuquerque. First, the **router ospf 1** global command puts the user in OSPF configuration mode. The **router ospf** command has a parameter called the OSPF *process-id*. In some instances, you might want to run multiple OSPF processes in a single router, so the **router** command uses the *process-id* to distinguish between the processes. Although the *process-id* used on the three routers is the same, the actual value is unimportant, and the numbers do not have to match on each router.

The **network** command tells Albuquerque to enable OSPF on all interfaces that match the **network** command and, on those interfaces, to place the interfaces into Area 0. The OSPF **network** command matches interfaces differently than does the **network** command for RIP and IGRP. The OSPF **network** command includes a parameter called the *wildcard mask*. The wildcard mask works just like the wildcard mask used with Cisco access control lists (ACLs), which are covered in more depth in Chapter 12, "IP Access Control List Security."

The wildcard mask represents a 32-bit number. When the mask has a binary 1 in one of the bit positions, that bit is considered a wildcard bit, meaning that the router should not care what binary value is in the corresponding numbers. For that reason, binary 1s in the wildcard mask are called *don't care bits*. If the wildcard mask bit is 0 in a bit position, the corresponding bits in the numbers being compared must match. You can think of these bits as the *do care bits*. So, the router must examine the two numbers and make sure that the values match for the bits that matter—in other words, the do care bits.

For instance, the wildcard mask in Example 6-1 is 0.255.255.255. When converted to binary, this number is 0000 0000 1111 1111 1111 1111 1111 1111—in other words, eight 0s and 24 1s. The **network** command tells Cisco IOS software to compare 10.0.0.0, which is the number in the **network** command, to the IP addresses of each interface on the router. The wildcard mask tells Cisco IOS software to compare only the first octet; the last three octets are wildcards, and anything matches. So, all three interface IP addresses are matched.

Example 6-2 shows an alternative configuration for Albuquerque that also enables OSPF on every interface. In this case, the IP address for each interface is matched with a different **network** command. The wildcard mask of 0.0.0.0 means that all 32 bits must be compared, and they must match—so the **network** commands include the specific IP address of each interface, respectively. Many people prefer this style of configuration in production networks, because it removes any ambiguity as to the interfaces on which OSPF is running.

Example 6-2 *OSPF Single-Area Configuration on Albuquerque Using Three* **network** *Commands*

```
interface ethernet 0/0
ip address 10.1.1.1 255.255.255.0
interface serial 0/0
ip address 10.1.4.1 255.255.255.0
interface serial 0/1
ip address 10.1.6.1 255.255.255.0
!
router ospf 1
network 10.1.1.1 0.0.0.0 area 0
network 10.1.4.1 0.0.0.0 area 0
network 10.1.6.1 0.0.0.0 area 0
```

OSPF Configuration with Multiple Areas

Configuring OSPF with multiple areas is simple once you understand OSPF configuration in a single area. Designing the OSPF network by making good choices as to which subnets should be placed in which areas is the hard part! After the area design is complete, the configuration is easy. For instance, consider Figure 6-9, which shows some subnets in Area 0 and some in Area 1.

Figure 6-9 *Multiarea OSPF Network*

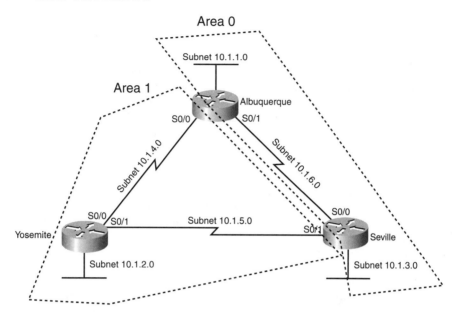

Multiple areas are not needed in such a small network, but two areas are used in this example to show the configuration. Note that Albuquerque and Seville are both ABRs, but Yosemite is totally inside area 1, so it is not an ABR.

Examples 6-3 and 6-4 show the configuration on Albuquerque and Yosemite, along with several **show** commands.

Example 6-3 *OSPF Multiarea Configuration and* **show** *Commands on Albuquerque*

```
!
! Only the OSPF configuration is shown to conserve space
!
router ospf 1
network 10.1.1.1 0.0.0.0 area 0
network 10.1.4.1 0.0.0.0 area 1
network 10.1.6.1 0.0.0.0 area 0
Albuquerque#show ip route
Codes: C - connected, S - static, I - IGRP, R - RIP, M - mobile, B - BGP
       D - EIGRP, EX - EIGRP external, O - OSPF, IA - OSPF inter area
       N1 - OSPF NSSA external type 1, N2 - OSPF NSSA external type 2
       E1 - OSPF external type 1, E2 - OSPF external type 2, E - EGP
       i - IS-IS, L1 - IS-IS level-1, L2 - IS-IS level-2, ia - IS-IS inter area
       * - candidate default, U - per-user static route, o - ODR
       P - periodic downloaded static route
```

continues

Example 6-3 *OSPF Multiarea Configuration and* show *Commands on Albuquerque (Continued)*

```
Gateway of last resort is not set

     10.0.0.0/24 is subnetted, 6 subnets
O       10.1.3.0 [110/65] via 10.1.6.3, 00:01:04, Serial0/1
O       10.1.2.0 [110/65] via 10.1.4.2, 00:00:39, Serial0/0
C       10.1.1.0 is directly connected, Ethernet0/0
C       10.1.6.0 is directly connected, Serial0/1
O       10.1.5.0 [110/128] via 10.1.4.2, 00:00:39, Serial0/0
C       10.1.4.0 is directly connected, Serial0/0

Albuquerque#show ip route ospf
     10.0.0.0/24 is subnetted, 6 subnets
O       10.1.3.0 [110/65] via 10.1.6.3, 00:01:08, Serial0/1
O       10.1.2.0 [110/65] via 10.1.4.2, 00:00:43, Serial0/0
O       10.1.5.0 [110/128] via 10.1.4.2, 00:00:43, Serial0/0
Albuquerque#show ip ospf neighbor

Neighbor ID     Pri   State       Dead Time   Address      Interface
10.1.6.3          1   FULL/   -   00:00:35    10.1.6.3     Serial0/1
10.1.5.2          1   FULL/   -   00:00:37    10.1.4.2     Serial0/0
Albuquerque#show ip ospf interface
Serial0/1 is up, line protocol is up
  Internet Address 10.1.6.1/24, Area 0
  Process ID 1, Router ID 10.1.6.1, Network Type POINT_TO_POINT, Cost: 64
  Transmit Delay is 1 sec, State POINT_TO_POINT,
  Timer intervals configured, Hello 10, Dead 40, Wait 40, Retransmit 5
    Hello due in 00:00:07
  Index 2/3, flood queue length 0
  Next 0x0(0)/0x0(0)
  Last flood scan length is 2, maximum is 2
  Last flood scan time is 0 msec, maximum is 0 msec
  Neighbor Count is 1, Adjacent neighbor count is 1
    Adjacent with neighbor 10.1.6.3
  Suppress hello for 0 neighbor(s)
Ethernet0/0 is up, line protocol is up
  Internet Address 10.1.1.1/24, Area 0
  Process ID 1, Router ID 10.1.6.1, Network Type BROADCAST, Cost: 10
  Transmit Delay is 1 sec, State DR, Priority 1
  Designated Router (ID) 10.1.6.1, Interface address 10.1.1.1
  No backup designated router on this network
  Timer intervals configured, Hello 10, Dead 40, Wait 40, Retransmit 5
    Hello due in 00:00:08
  Index 1/1, flood queue length 0
  Next 0x0(0)/0x0(0)
  Last flood scan length is 0, maximum is 0
  Last flood scan time is 0 msec, maximum is 0 msec
```

Example 6-3 *OSPF Multiarea Configuration and* show *Commands on Albuquerque (Continued)*

```
 Neighbor Count is 0, Adjacent neighbor count is 0
 Suppress hello for 0 neighbor(s)
Serial0/0 is up, line protocol is up
 Internet Address 10.1.4.1/24, Area 1
 Process ID 1, Router ID 10.1.6.1, Network Type POINT_TO_POINT, Cost: 64
 Transmit Delay is 1 sec, State POINT_TO_POINT,
 Timer intervals configured, Hello 10, Dead 40, Wait 40, Retransmit 5
  Hello due in 00:00:01
 Index 1/2, flood queue length 0
 Next 0x0(0)/0x0(0)
 Last flood scan length is 1, maximum is 1
 Last flood scan time is 0 msec, maximum is 0 msec
 Neighbor Count is 1, Adjacent neighbor count is 1
  Adjacent with neighbor 10.1.5.2
 Suppress hello for 0 neighbor(s)
```

Example 6-4 *OSPF Multiarea Configuration and* show *Commands on Yosemite*

```
!
! Only the OSPF configuration is shown to conserve space
!
router ospf 1
network 10.0.0.0 0.255.255.255 area 1
Yosemite#show ip route
Codes: C - connected, S - static, I - IGRP, R - RIP, M - mobile, B - BGP
       D - EIGRP, EX - EIGRP external, O - OSPF, IA - OSPF inter area
       N1 - OSPF NSSA external type 1, N2 - OSPF NSSA external type 2
       E1 - OSPF external type 1, E2 - OSPF external type 2, E - EGP
       i - IS-IS, L1 - IS-IS level-1, L2 - IS-IS level-2, ia - IS-IS inter area
       * - candidate default, U - per-user static route, o - ODR
       P - periodic downloaded static route

Gateway of last resort is not set

     10.0.0.0/24 is subnetted, 6 subnets
IA      10.1.3.0 [110/65] via 10.1.5.1, 00:00:54, Serial0/1
IA      10.1.1.0 [110/65] via 10.1.4.1, 00:00:49, Serial0/0
C       10.1.2.0 is directly connected, Ethernet0/0
C       10.1.5.0 is directly connected, Serial0/1
IA      10.1.6.0 [110/128] via 10.1.4.1, 00:00:38, Serial0/0
C       10.1.4.0 is directly connected, Serial0/0
```

The configuration only needs to show the correct area number on the **network** command matching the appropriate interfaces. For instance, the **network 10.1.4.1 0.0.0.0 area 1** command matches Albuquerque's Serial 0/0 interface IP address, placing that interface in Area 1. The **network 10.1.6.1 0.0.0.0 area 0** and **network 10.1.1.1 0.0.0.0 area 0** commands place Serial 0/1 and Ethernet 0/0, respectively, in Area 0. Unlike Example 6-1, Albuquerque cannot be configured to match all three interfaces with a single **network** command, because one interface (Serial 0/0) is in a different area than the other two interfaces.

The **show ip route ospf** command just lists OSPF-learned routes, as opposed to the entire IP routing table. The **show ip route** command lists all three connected routes, as well as the three OSPF learned routes. Note that Albuquerque's route to 10.1.2.0 has the **O** designation beside it, meaning *intra-area,* because that subnet resides in Area 1, and Albuquerque is part of Area 1 and Area 0.

In Example 6-4, notice that the OSPF configuration in Yosemite requires only a single **network** command. Because all interfaces in Yosemite are in Area 1, and all three interfaces are in network 10.0.0.0, the command can just match all IP addresses in network 10.0.0.0 and put them in Area 1. Also note that the routes learned by Yosemite from the other two routers show up as *interarea (IA) routes,* because those subnets are in Area 0, and Yosemite is in Area 1.

The OSPF topology database includes information about routers and the subnets, or links, to which they are attached. To identify the routers in the neighbor table's topology database, OSPF uses a router ID (RID) for each router. A router's OSPF RID is that router's highest IP address on a physical interface when OSPF starts running. Alternatively, if a loopback interface has been configured, OSPF uses the highest IP address on a loopback interface for the RID, even if that IP address is lower than some physical interface's IP address. Also, you can set the OSPF RID using the **router-id** command in router configuration mode.

> **NOTE**   If you're not familiar with it, a loopback interface is a special virtual interface in a Cisco router. If you create a loopback interface using the **interface loopback** *x* command, where *x* is a number, that loopback interface is up and operational as long as the router IOS is up and working. You can assign an IP address to a loopback interface, you can ping the address, and you can use it for several purposes—including having a loopback interface IP address as the OSPF router ID.

Many commands refer to the OSPF RID, including the **show ip ospf neighbor** command. This command lists all the neighbors, using the neighbors' RIDs to identify them. For instance, in Example 6-3, the first neighbor in the output of the **show ip ospf neighbor** command lists **Router ID 10.1.5.2**, which is Yosemite's RID.

Finally, the **show ip ospf interface** command lists more-detailed information about OSPF operation on each interface. For instance, this command lists the area number, OSPF cost, and any neighbors known on each interface. The timers used on the interface, including the Hello and dead timer, are also listed.

OSPF uses the cost to determine the metric for each route. You can set the cost value on an interface using the **ip ospf cost** x interface subcommand. You can also set the OSPF cost of an interface using the **bandwidth** interface subcommand. If you do not set an interface's cost, IOS defaults to use the formula 10^8 / *bandwidth,* where *bandwidth* is the interface's bandwidth. For instance, Cisco IOS software defaults to a bandwidth of 10,000 (the unit in the **bandwidth** command is kbps, so 10,000 means 10 Mbps) on Ethernet interfaces, so the default cost is 10^8 / 10^7, or 10. Higher-speed serial interfaces default to a bandwidth of 1544, giving a default cost of 10^8 / 1,544,000, which is rounded to 64, as shown in the example. If you change the interface's bandwidth, you change the OSPF cost as well.

You might have noticed that the cost for a Fast Ethernet interface (100 Mbps) is calculated as a cost of 1. For Gigabit interfaces (1000 Mbps), the calculation yields .1, but only integer values can be used, so OSPF uses a cost of 1 for Gigabit interfaces as well. So Cisco lets you change the *reference bandwidth,* which is the value in the numerator of the calculation in the preceding paragraph. For instance, using the router OSPF subcommand **auto-cost reference-bandwidth 1000**, you change the numerator to 1000 Mbps, or 10^9. The calculated cost on a Gigabit interface is then 1, and the cost on a Fast Ethernet is 10.

OSPF Troubleshooting

This section contains two examples, one showing a problem with forming neighbor relationships due to a misconfigured Hello interval, and another showing some information about the DR election process on a LAN. Figure 6-10 depicts the network used for both examples.

Figure 6-10 *LAN with Four Routers, Used in OSPF Troubleshooting Examples*

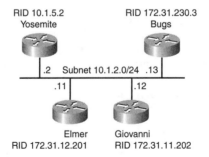

Figure 6-10 shows four routers that will become neighbors in the next two examples. The examples show the network from the perspective of the Yosemite router. Both examples list several commands, with the comments about the commands interspersed in comment lines inside the example.

Example 6-5 lists information in the following sequence:

1. The **show ip ospf neighbor** command confirms that Yosemite has three neighbors on its fa0/0 interface.

2. The **show ip ospf interface fa 0/0** command confirms that the current Hello interval is 10, and the current dead interval is 40.

3. The Hello interval on interface fa0/0 is changed to 4.

4. Yosemite's fa0/0 interface is brought down and back up in order to force Yosemite to attempt to form new neighbor relationships.

5. The **debug ip ospf hello** output shows why Yosemite cannot find any neighbors on that interface anymore.

Example 6-5 *Hello Problems as a Result of Mis-Matched Hello Intervals*

```
Yosemite#show ip ospf neighbor

Neighbor ID     Pri   State        Dead Time   Address      Interface
172.31.11.202    1    FULL/DROTHER 00:00:33    10.1.2.12    FastEthernet0/0
172.31.12.201    1    FULL/BDR     00:00:31    10.1.2.11    FastEthernet0/0
172.31.230.3     1    FULL/DROTHER 00:00:36    10.1.2.13    FastEthernet0/0
!!!!!!!!!!!!!!!!!!!!!!!!!!!!!!!!!!!!!!!!!!!!!!!!!!!!!!!!!!!!!!!!!!!!!!!!!!
! Above, Yosemite has three neighbors over interface Fa0/0.
! Below, Yosemite's Fa0/0 interface has default Hello and Dead
! Intervals of 10 and 40 seconds, respectively.
!!!!!!!!!!!!!!!!!!!!!!!!!!!!!!!!!!!!!!!!!!!!!!!!!!!!!!!!!!!!!!!!!!!!!!!!!!
Yosemite#show ip ospf interface fa 0/0
FastEthernet0/0 is up, line protocol is up
  Internet Address 10.1.2.2/24, Area 0
  Process ID 2, Router ID 10.1.5.2, Network Type BROADCAST, Cost: 1
  Transmit Delay is 1 sec, State BDR, Priority 255
  Designated Router (ID) 172.31.230.3, Interface address 10.1.2.13
  Backup Designated router (ID) 10.1.5.2, Interface address 10.1.2.2
  Timer intervals configured, Hello 10, Dead 40, Wait 40, Retransmit 5
    oob-resync timeout 40
    Hello due in 00:00:00
  Index 1/1, flood queue length 0
  Next 0x0(0)/0x0(0)
  Last flood scan length is 0, maximum is 1
  Last flood scan time is 0 msec, maximum is 4 msec
  Neighbor Count is 3, Adjacent neighbor count is 3
    Adjacent with neighbor 172.31.11.202
    Adjacent with neighbor 172.31.12.201
    Adjacent with neighbor 172.31.230.3  (Designated Router)
  Suppress hello for 0 neighbor(s)
```

Example 6-5 *Hello Problems as a Result of Mis-Matched Hello Intervals (Continued)*

```
Yosemite#configure terminal
Enter configuration commands, one per line.  End with CNTL/Z.
Yosemite(config)#interface fastethernet 0/0
Yosemite(config-if)#ip ospf hello 4
Yosemite(config-if)#^Z


!!!!!!!!!!!!!!!!!!!!!!!!!!!!!!!!!!!!!!!!!!!!!!!!!!!!!!!!!!!!!!!!!!!!!!!!!!!!
! Above, Yosemite's fa0/0 is changed to have a Hello interval of 4.
! Below, the Hello interval has changed, and the Dead interval has
! been reset to 4 times the new Hello interval.
!!!!!!!!!!!!!!!!!!!!!!!!!!!!!!!!!!!!!!!!!!!!!!!!!!!!!!!!!!!!!!!!!!!!!!!!!!!!
Yosemite#show ip ospf interface fast 0/0
FastEthernet0/0 is up, line protocol is up
  Internet Address 10.1.2.2/24, Area 0
  Process ID 2, Router ID 10.1.5.2, Network Type BROADCAST, Cost: 1
  Transmit Delay is 1 sec, State BDR, Priority 255
  Designated Router (ID) 172.31.230.3, Interface address 10.1.2.13
  Backup Designated router (ID) 10.1.5.2, Interface address 10.1.2.2
  Timer intervals configured, Hello 4, Dead 16, Wait 16, Retransmit 5
    oob-resync timeout 40
    Hello due in 00:00:01
  Index 1/1, flood queue length 0
  Next 0x0(0)/0x0(0)
  Last flood scan length is 0, maximum is 1
  Last flood scan time is 0 msec, maximum is 4 msec
  Neighbor Count is 3, Adjacent neighbor count is 3
    Adjacent with neighbor 172.31.11.202
    Adjacent with neighbor 172.31.12.201
    Adjacent with neighbor 172.31.230.3  (Designated Router)
  Suppress hello for 0 neighbor(s)
Yosemite#configure terminal
Enter configuration commands, one per line.  End with CNTL/Z.
Yosemite(config)#interface fast 0/0
Yosemite(config-if)#shutdown
Yosemite(config-if)#no shutdown
Yosemite(config-if)#^Z
!!!!!!!!!!!!!!!!!!!!!!!!!!!!!!!!!!!!!!!!!!!!!!!!!!!!!!!!!!!!!!!!!!!!!!!!!!!!
! Above, Yosemite's fa0/0 interface is brought down and back up.
! Below, Yosemite does not form any neighbor relationships; there
! were three neighbors listed before this change. Debug ip ospf hello
! at the end of the example shows a message stating mismatched Hello
! parameters.
!!!!!!!!!!!!!!!!!!!!!!!!!!!!!!!!!!!!!!!!!!!!!!!!!!!!!!!!!!!!!!!!!!!!!!!!!!!!
Yosemite#show ip ospf neighbor

Yosemite#debug ip ospf hello
OSPF hello events debugging is on
```

continues

Example 6-5   *Hello Problems as a Result of Mis-Matched Hello Intervals (Continued)*

```
Yosemite#
Mar  1 09:48:42.000: OSPF: Rcv hello from 172.31.230.3 area 0 from FastEthernet0/0 10.1.2.13
Mar  1 09:48:42.000: OSPF: Mismatched hello parameters from 10.1.2.13
Mar  1 09:48:42.000: OSPF: Dead R 40 C 16, Hello R 10 C 4  Mask R 255.255.255.0 C 255.255.255.0
Mar  1 09:48:43.034: OSPF: Send hello to 224.0.0.5 area 0 on FastEthernet0/0 from 10.1.2.2
```

Example 6-6 shows an example proving that a when a new router is added to a LAN, even with a higher OSPF priority, it does not take over for the existing DR or BDR. Example 6-6's sequence is as follows:

1.   The **show ip ospf neighbor** and **show ip ospf interface** command confirm that Yosemite is currently not the DR or BDR.

2.   Yosemite's Fa0/0 OSPF priority is changed to 255.

3.   The next couple **show** commands reconfirm that Yosemite is not the current DR or BDR.

4.   Yosemite's fa0/0 is brought down, and back up, forcing Yosemite to re-discover neighbors and re-attempt to become DR.

5.   **show** commands confirm that Yosemite still did not become the DR or BDR.

Example 6-6   *Yosemite Router with Priority 255 Does Not Pre-empt Existing DR*

```
Yosemite#show ip ospf neighbor

Neighbor ID     Pri  State        Dead Time   Address       Interface
172.31.11.202    1   2WAY/DROTHER  00:00:32   10.1.2.12     FastEthernet0/0
172.31.12.201    1   FULL/DR       00:00:30   10.1.2.11     FastEthernet0/0
172.31.230.3     1   FULL/BDR      00:00:35   10.1.2.13     FastEthernet0/0
!!!!!!!!!!!!!!!!!!!!!!!!!!!!!!!!!!!!!!!!!!!!!!!!!!!!!!!!!!!!!!!!!!!!!!!!
! Above, Yosemite has three neighbors on interface fa0/0. Each line
! shows Yosemite's status with each neighbor (2way or full), and what
! kind of router the neighbor is. For instance, the second neighbor
! is the DR, and the third neighbor listed in the BDR.
! Below, Yosemite is confirmed as a non-DR (shown as "DROTHER"), with
! the actual DR and BDR listed. Note that Yomseite's RID is shown as
! well. Also note that the network type is "BROADCAST", which implies
! that a DR and BDR must be elected.
!!!!!!!!!!!!!!!!!!!!!!!!!!!!!!!!!!!!!!!!!!!!!!!!!!!!!!!!!!!!!!!!!!!!!!!!
Yosemite#show ip ospf interface fast 0/0
FastEthernet0/0 is up, line protocol is up
  Internet Address 10.1.2.2/24, Area 0
  Process ID 2, Router ID 10.1.5.2, Network Type BROADCAST, Cost: 1
  Transmit Delay is 1 sec, State DROTHER, Priority 255
  Designated Router (ID) 172.31.12.201, Interface address 10.1.2.11
```

Example 6-6   *Yosemite Router with Priority 255 Does Not Pre-empt Existing DR (Continued)*

```
  Backup Designated router (ID) 172.31.230.3, Interface address 10.1.2.13
  Timer intervals configured, Hello 10, Dead 40, Wait 40, Retransmit 5
    oob-resync timeout 40
    Hello due in 00:00:00
  Index 1/1, flood queue length 0
  Next 0x0(0)/0x0(0)
  Last flood scan length is 1, maximum is 1
Last flood scan time is 0 msec, maximum is 4 msec
  Neighbor Count is 3, Adjacent neighbor count is 2
    Adjacent with neighbor 172.31.12.201  (Designated Router)
    Adjacent with neighbor 172.31.230.3   (Backup Designated Router)
  Suppress hello for 0 neighbor(s)
!!!!!!!!!!!!!!!!!!!!!!!!!!!!!!!!!!!!!!!!!!!!!!!!!!!!!!!!!!!!!!!!!!!!!!!!!!!
! Above, note that the last two highlighted lines show Yosemite
! adjacent with the DR and BDR, but not the "DROTHER" neighbor.
! Yosemite is not a DR or BDR (it is a "DROTHER"), and non-DR
! routers on a LAN do not become fully adjacent with other non-DR
! routers.
! Below, Yosemite is brought down and back up, but the DR and BDR
! do not change, according to the show ip ospf interface command.
!!!!!!!!!!!!!!!!!!!!!!!!!!!!!!!!!!!!!!!!!!!!!!!!!!!!!!!!!!!!!!!!!!!!!!!!!!!
Yosemite#configure terminal
Enter configuration commands, one per line.  End with CNTL/Z.
Yosemite(config)#interface fast 0/0
Yosemite(config-if)#shutdown
Yosemite(config-if)#no shutdown
Yosemite(config-if)#^Z
Yosemite#show ip ospf interface fast 0/0
FastEthernet0/0 is up, line protocol is up
  Internet Address 10.1.2.2/24, Area 0
  Process ID 2, Router ID 10.1.5.2, Network Type BROADCAST, Cost: 1
  Transmit Delay is 1 sec, State DROTHER, Priority 255
  Designated Router (ID) 172.31.12.201, Interface address 10.1.2.11
  Backup Designated router (ID) 172.31.230.3, Interface address 10.1.2.13
! The rest of the lines are omitted for brevity
```

EIGRP Configuration

If you remember how to configure IGRP, EIGRP configuration is painless. You configure
EIGRP exactly like IGRP, except that you use the **eigrp** keyword instead of the **igrp** keyword
in the **router** command.

Tables 6-7 and 6-8 summarize the EIGRP configuration and troubleshooting commands, respectively. After these tables, you will see a short demonstration of EIGRP configuration, along with **show** command output.

Table 6-7 *IP EIGRP Configuration Commands*

Command	Configuration Mode
router eigrp *autonomous-system*	Global
network *network-number* [*wildcard-mask*]	Router subcommand
network *network-number*	Router subcommand
maximum-paths *number-paths*	Router subcommand
variance *multiplier*	Router subcommand
traffic-share {*balanced*	*min*}	Router subcommand

Table 6-8 *IP EIGRP EXEC Commands*

Command	Description
show ip route [*ip-address* [*mask*] [**longer-prefixes**]] | [*protocol* [*process-id*]]	Shows the entire routing table, or a subset if parameters are entered.
show ip protocols	Shows routing protocol parameters and current timer values.
show ip eigrp neighbors	Lists EIGRP neighbors and status.
show ip eigrp topology	Lists the contents of the EIGRP topology table, including successors and feasible successors.
show ip route eigrp	Lists only EIGRP-learned routes from the routing table.
show ip eigrp traffic	Lists traffic statistics about EIGRP.

Example 6-7 shows a sample EIGRP configuration, along with **show** commands, on Albuquerque, in the same network used in the OSPF examples (Figure 6-7). The EIGRP configuration required on Yosemite and Seville matches the two lines of EIGRP configuration on Albuquerque.

Example 6-7 *Sample Router Configuration with EIGRP Partially Enabled*

```
router eigrp 1
network 10.0.0.0
Albuquerque#show ip route
Codes: C - connected, S - static, I - IGRP, R - RIP, M - mobile, B - BGP
       D - EIGRP, EX - EIGRP external, O - OSPF, IA - OSPF inter area
       N1 - OSPF NSSA external type 1, N2 - OSPF NSSA external type 2
       E1 - OSPF external type 1, E2 - OSPF external type 2, E - EGP
```

Example 6-7 *Sample Router Configuration with EIGRP Partially Enabled (Continued)*

```
           i - IS-IS, L1 - IS-IS level-1, L2 - IS-IS level-2, ia - IS-IS inter area
           * - candidate default, U - per-user static route, o - ODR
           P - periodic downloaded static route

Gateway of last resort is not set

     10.0.0.0/24 is subnetted, 6 subnets
D       10.1.3.0 [90/2172416] via 10.1.6.3, 00:00:43, Serial0/1
D       10.1.2.0 [90/2172416] via 10.1.4.2, 00:00:43, Serial0/0
C       10.1.1.0 is directly connected, Ethernet0/0
C       10.1.6.0 is directly connected, Serial0/1
D       10.1.5.0 [90/2681856] via 10.1.6.3, 00:00:45, Serial0/1
                 [90/2681856] via 10.1.4.2, 00:00:45, Serial0/0
C       10.1.4.0 is directly connected, Serial0/0

Albuquerque#show ip route eigrp
     10.0.0.0/24 is subnetted, 6 subnets
D       10.1.3.0 [90/2172416] via 10.1.6.3, 00:00:47, Serial0/1
D       10.1.2.0 [90/2172416] via 10.1.4.2, 00:00:47, Serial0/0
D       10.1.5.0 [90/2681856] via 10.1.6.3, 00:00:49, Serial0/1
                 [90/2681856] via 10.1.4.2, 00:00:49, Serial0/0

Albuquerque#show ip eigrp neighbors
IP-EIGRP neighbors for process 1
H   Address              Interface   Hold Uptime   SRTT   RTO  Q   Seq Type
                                     (sec)         (ms)        Cnt Num
0   10.1.4.2             Se0/0        11 00:00:54   32    200  0   4
1   10.1.6.3             Se0/1        12 00:10:36   20    200  0   24

Albuquerque#show ip eigrp interfaces
IP-EIGRP interfaces for process 1

                    Xmit Queue   Mean   Pacing Time   Multicast    Pending
Interface   Peers   Un/Reliable  SRTT   Un/Reliable   Flow Timer   Routes
Et0/0         0        0/0         0       0/10           0           0
Se0/0         1        0/0        32       0/15          50           0
Se0/1         1        0/0        20       0/15          95           0
```

For EIGRP configuration, all three routers must use the same AS number on the **router eigrp** command. For instance, they all use **router eigrp 1** in this example. The actual number used doesn't really matter, as long as it is the same number on all 3 routers. (The range of valid AS numbers is 1 through 65,535, as is the range of valid Process IDs with the **router ospf** command). The **network 10.0.0.0** command enables EIGRP on all interfaces whose IP addresses are in network 10.0.0.0, which includes all three interfaces on Albuquerque. With the identical two EIGRP configuration statements on the other two routers, EIGRP is enabled on all three interfaces on those routers as well, because those interfaces are also in network 10.0.0.0.

The **show ip route** and **show ip route eigrp** commands both list the EIGRP-learned routes with a **D** beside them. **D** signifies EIGRP. The letter E was already being used for Exterior Gateway Protocol (EGP) when Cisco created EIGRP, so it chose the next-closest letter to denote EIGRP-learned routes.

You can see information about EIGRP neighbors with the **show ip eigrp neighbors** command, and the number of active neighbors (called peers in the command output) with the **show ip eigrp interfaces** command, as seen in the last part of the example. These commands also provide some insight into EIGRP's underlying processes, like the use of RTP for reliable transmission. For instance, the **show ip eigrp neighbors** command lists a "Q Cnt" (short for Queue Count) column, listing the number of packets either waiting to be sent to a neighbor, or packets that have been sent but for which no acknowledgement has been received. The **show ip eigrp interfaces** command lists similar information in the "Xmit Queue Un/Reliable" column, which separates statistics for EIGRP messages that are sent with RTP (reliable) or without (unreliable).

Example 6-8 shows an alternative style of **network** command for EIGRP configuration, along with a detailed look at **show** and **debug** commands related to the feasible successor concept. The beginning of the example shows how to configure EIGRP **network** commands using a wildcard mask, with the same meaning as the wildcard mask used with the OSPF style of **network** command. In the upcoming example, three **network** commands are used on Albuquerque, one matching each of the three interfaces.

After that, Example 6-8 goes on to make the following points (in sequence) about Albuquerque's EIGRP status:

1. Albuquerque is shown to have a single IP route to 10.1.3.0/24, and two equal-cost routes to 10.1.5.0/24.

2. Next, the **show ip eigrp topology** shows information correlating to the ip routing table, with 1 successor route to 10.1.3.0/24, and two successor routes to 10.1.5.0/24.

3. After changing Yosemite's configuration to a higher bandwidth, the results from Albuquerque's **show ip eigrp topology** command reveal a feasible successor route to subnet 10.1.3.0.

4. Finally, Albuquerque's current route to 10.1.3.0 will fail, with **debug** messages showing Albuquerque's fail over to use the feasible successor route.

Example 6-8, with annotations, follows. The details can be a little tricky, but it does shed some light on the internal workings of EIGRP.

Example 6-8   *Using Wildcard Masks with EIGRP Configuration, and Feasible Successor Examination*

```
Albuquerque#router eigrp 1
Albuquerque(config-router)#network 10.1.1.0 0.0.0.255
Albuquerque(config-router)#network 10.1.4.0 0.0.0.255
Albuquerque(config-router)#network 10.1.6.0 0.0.0.255
Albuquerque(config-router)#^z
!!!!!!!!!!!!!!!!!!!!!!!!!!!!!!!!!!!!!!!!!!!!!!!!!!!!!!!!!!!!!!!!!!!!!!!!!
! Above, EIGRP has been changed to use the wildcard mask option. Note
! that a separate network command was used to match each of the three
! interfaces.
! Below, note the single route to subnet 10.1.3.0, and the two
! equal-metric routes to 10.1.5.0.
!!!!!!!!!!!!!!!!!!!!!!!!!!!!!!!!!!!!!!!!!!!!!!!!!!!!!!!!!!!!!!!!!!!!!!!!!
Albuquerque#show ip route
Codes: C - connected, S - static, R - RIP, M - mobile, B - BGP
       D - EIGRP, EX - EIGRP external, O - OSPF, IA - OSPF inter area
       N1 - OSPF NSSA external type 1, N2 - OSPF NSSA external type 2
       E1 - OSPF external type 1, E2 - OSPF external type 2
       i - IS-IS, L1 - IS-IS level-1, L2 - IS-IS level-2, ia - IS-IS inter area
       * - candidate default, U - per-user static route, o - ODR
       P - periodic downloaded static route

Gateway of last resort is not set

     10.0.0.0/24 is subnetted, 6 subnets
D       10.1.3.0 [90/2172416] via 10.1.6.3, 00:00:57, Serial0/1
D       10.1.2.0 [90/2172416] via 10.1.4.2, 00:00:57, Serial0/0
C       10.1.1.0 is directly connected, Ethernet0/0
C       10.1.6.0 is directly connected, Serial0/1
D       10.1.5.0 [90/2681856] via 10.1.4.2, 00:00:57, Serial0/0
                 [90/2681856] via 10.1.6.3, 00:00:57, Serial0/1
C       10.1.4.0 is directly connected, Serial0/0
Albuquerque#show ip eigrp topology
IP-EIGRP Topology Table for AS(1)/ID(10.1.6.1)

Codes: P - Passive, A - Active, U - Update, Q - Query, R - Reply,
       r - reply Status, s - sia Status

P 10.1.3.0/24, 1 successors, FD is 2172416
        via 10.1.6.3 (2172416/28160), Serial0/1
P 10.1.2.0/24, 1 successors, FD is 2172416
        via 10.1.4.2 (2172416/28160), Serial0/0
P 10.1.1.0/24, 1 successors, FD is 281600
        via Connected, Ethernet0/0
P 10.1.6.0/24, 1 successors, FD is 2169856
        via Connected, Serial0/1
P 10.1.5.0/24, 2 successors, FD is 2681856
        via 10.1.4.2 (2681856/2169856), Serial0/0
```

continues

Example 6-8 *Using Wildcard Masks with EIGRP Configuration, and Feasible Successor Examination (Continued)*

```
           via 10.1.6.3 (2681856/2169856), Serial0/1
P 10.1.4.0/24, 1 successors, FD is 2169856
          via Connected, Serial0/0
!!!!!!!!!!!!!!!!!!!!!!!!!!!!!!!!!!!!!!!!!!!!!!!!!!!!!!!!!!!!!!!!!!!!!!!!!!
! Above, the EIGRP topology table shows one successor for the route
! to 10.1.3.0, and two successors for 10.1.5.0, reconfirming that
! EIGRP installs successor routes (not feasible successor routes)
! into the IP routing table.
! Below, the bandwidth of Yosemite's link to Seville (Yosemite's
! S0/1 interface) is changed from 1544 to 2000, which lowers
! Yosemite's metric to 10.1.3.0.
!!!!!!!!!!!!!!!!!!!!!!!!!!!!!!!!!!!!!!!!!!!!!!!!!!!!!!!!!!!!!!!!!!!!!!!!!!
Yosemite(config-if)#bandwidth 2000
!!!!!!!!!!!!!!!!!!!!!!!!!!!!!!!!!!!!!!!!!!!!!!!!!!!!!!!!!!!!!!!!!!!!!!!!!!
! Below, back in Albuquerque, the EIGRP topology table shows a single
! successor route for 10.1.3.0, but two entries listed – the new
! entry is a feasible successor route. The new entry shows a route
! to 10.1.3.0 through 10.1.4.2 (which is Yosemite). See the text
! following this example for more detail.
!!!!!!!!!!!!!!!!!!!!!!!!!!!!!!!!!!!!!!!!!!!!!!!!!!!!!!!!!!!!!!!!!!!!!!!!!!
Albuquerque#show ip eigrp topology
IP-EIGRP Topology Table for AS(1)/ID(10.1.6.1)

Codes: P - Passive, A - Active, U - Update, Q - Query, R - Reply,
       r - reply Status, s - sia Status

P 10.1.3.0/24, 1 successors, FD is 2172416
          via 10.1.6.3 (2172416/28160), Serial0/1
          via 10.1.4.2 (2684416/1794560), Serial0/0
! the rest of the lines omitted for brevity
!!!!!!!!!!!!!!!!!!!!!!!!!!!!!!!!!!!!!!!!!!!!!!!!!!!!!!!!!!!!!!!!!!!!!!!!!!
! The next command is on Yosemite!!
!!!!!!!!!!!!!!!!!!!!!!!!!!!!!!!!!!!!!!!!!!!!!!!!!!!!!!!!!!!!!!!!!!!!!!!!!!
Yosemite#show ip route
Codes: C - connected, S - static, R - RIP, M - mobile, B - BGP
       D - EIGRP, EX - EIGRP external, O - OSPF, IA - OSPF inter area
       N1 - OSPF NSSA external type 1, N2 - OSPF NSSA external type 2
       E1 - OSPF external type 1, E2 - OSPF external type 2
       i - IS-IS, L1 - IS-IS level-1, L2 - IS-IS level-2, ia - IS-IS inter area
       * - candidate default, U - per-user static route, o - ODR
       P - periodic downloaded static route

Gateway of last resort is not set

     10.0.0.0/24 is subnetted, 5 subnets
D       10.1.3.0 [90/1794560] via 10.1.5.3, 00:40:14, Serial0/1
C       10.1.2.0 is directly connected, FastEthernet0/0
D       10.1.1.0 [90/2195456] via 10.1.4.1, 00:42:19, Serial0/0
```

Example 6-8 *Using Wildcard Masks with EIGRP Configuration, and Feasible Successor Examination (Continued)*

```
C       10.1.5.0 is directly connected, Serial0/1
C       10.1.4.0 is directly connected, Serial0/0
!!!!!!!!!!!!!!!!!!!!!!!!!!!!!!!!!!!!!!!!!!!!!!!!!!!!!!!!!!!!!!!!!!!!!!!!!!
! Above, Yosemite's route to 10.1.3.0 lists a metric of 1794560.
! Refer to the notes at the end of the example for more information.
!!!!!!!!!!!!!!!!!!!!!!!!!!!!!!!!!!!!!!!!!!!!!!!!!!!!!!!!!!!!!!!!!!!!!!!!!!
! The next command is on Albuquerque!
!!!!!!!!!!!!!!!!!!!!!!!!!!!!!!!!!!!!!!!!!!!!!!!!!!!!!!!!!!!!!!!!!!!!!!!!!!
! Below, debug eigrp fsm is enabled, and then Seville's link to
! Albuquerque (Seville's S0/0 interface) will be disabled, but not
! shown in the example text. SOME DEBUG MESSAGES are omitted to
! improve readability.
!!!!!!!!!!!!!!!!!!!!!!!!!!!!!!!!!!!!!!!!!!!!!!!!!!!!!!!!!!!!!!!!!!!!!!!!!!
Albuquerque#debug eigrp fsm
EIGRP FSM Events/Actions debugging is on
Albuquerque#
*Mar  1 02:35:31.836: %LINK-3-UPDOWN: Interface Serial0/1, changed state to down
*Mar  1 02:35:31.848: DUAL: rcvupdate: 10.1.6.0/24 via Connected metric 42949672
95/4294967295
*Mar  1 02:35:31.848: DUAL: Find FS for dest 10.1.6.0/24. FD is 2169856, RD is 2
169856
*Mar  1 02:35:31.848: DUAL: 0.0.0.0 metric 4294967295/4294967295 not found D
min is 4294967295
*Mar  1 02:35:31.848: DUAL: Peer total/stub 2/0 template/full-stub 2/0
*Mar  1 02:35:31.848: DUAL: Dest 10.1.6.0/24 entering active state.
*Mar  1 02:35:31.852: DUAL: Set reply-status table. Count is 2.
*Mar  1 02:35:31.852: DUAL: Not doing split horizon
*Mar  1 02:35:31.852: %DUAL-5-NBRCHANGE: IP-EIGRP(0) 1: Neighbor 10.1.6.3 (Serial0/1) is
down: interface down
!!!!!!!!!!!!!!!!!!!!!!!!!!!!!!!!!!!!!!!!!!!!!!!!!!!!!!!!!!!!!!!!!!!!!!!!!!
! The first message following these comments means that EIGRP will
! now start acting on the fact that neighbor 10.1.6.3 is down.
! The second message states that EIGRP is considering route 10.1.3.0.
! The third message means that it is looking for an "FS" (Feasible
! Successor) for this route.
! The next two highlighted messages imply that the old route to
! 10.1.3.0 is removed, and the new successor route (previously the
! feasible successor route) is added to the "RT" (routing table).
!!!!!!!!!!!!!!!!!!!!!!!!!!!!!!!!!!!!!!!!!!!!!!!!!!!!!!!!!!!!!!!!!!!!!!!!!!
*Mar  1 02:35:31.852: DUAL: linkdown: start - 10.1.6.3 via Serial0/1
*Mar  1 02:35:31.852: DUAL: Destination 10.1.3.0/24
*Mar  1 02:35:31.852: DUAL: Find FS for dest 10.1.3.0/24. FD is 2172416, RD is 2172416
*Mar  1 02:35:31.856: DUAL: 10.1.6.3 metric 4294967295/4294967295
*Mar  1 02:35:31.856: DUAL: 10.1.4.2 metric 2684416/1794560 found Dmin is 2684416
*Mar  1 02:35:31.856: DUAL: Removing dest 10.1.3.0/24, nexthop 10.1.6.3
*Mar  1 02:35:31.856: DUAL: RT installed 10.1.3.0/24 via 10.1.4.2
*Mar  1 02:35:31.856: DUAL: Send update about 10.1.3.0/24.  Reason: metric chg
*Mar  1 02:35:31.860: DUAL: Send update about 10.1.3.0/24.  Reason: new if
! Rest of beug messages omitted for brevity
```

Most of the explanations for Example 6-8 are shown inside the example as comments. The output of the **show ip eigrp topology** command, when the feasible successor route to 10.1.3.0 exists, bears a closer look. That's because this command output identifies successor and feasible successor routes, but it is not obvious.

> **NOTE**   Example 6-8 has two **show ip eigrp topology** commands; the one described next is the second occurrence, a little past half-way through the example.

Small portions of three lines of output from the **show ip eigrp topology** command are highlighted. The first of these lines lists "FD is 2172416", which means that the Feasible Distance (FD) is 2,172,416. The *Feasible Distance* is Albuquerque's calculated metric for the route.

Next, look at the two numbers in parentheses in the second highlighted line from the **show ip eigrp topology** command. The first of these is this router's calculated metric for the route. Notice that the first number is 2,172,416, the same as the FD on the previous line. The fact that the first number in parenthesis matches the FD means that the route on this line is the *successor route*—the one that should be currently installed in the routing table. Note that the successor route's next hop address (10.1.6.3) matches next hop address shown for the route to 10.1.3.0/24 in the IP routing table, which confirms that the successor route is the route installed into the IP routing table.

The third line highlighted for this command references the second number in parentheses. (For reference, the highlighted line is "via 10.1.4.2 (2684416/1794560), Serial0/0"). This number (1,794,560 in this case) is the metric for this route *as calculated by the neighbor*. The neighbor on that line of output is 10.1.4.2, or Yosemite. As seen in the **show ip route** command output from Yosemite, which follows the output of the **show ip eigrp topology** command, Yosemite's route to 10.1.3.0 indeed has a metric of 1,794,560.

So, what does all this mean? Well, the requirement for a feasible successor route (in other words, the feasibility condition) is that the next hop neighbor's metric must be smaller than that router's calculated metric for the current best (successor) route. The analysis of the **show ip eigrp topology** command output can be summarized as follows:

■ The route to 10.1.3.0 through 10.1.6.3 (Seville) is the successor route, because the calculated metric (2,172,416), shown as the first of the two numbers in parenthesis, has the same value as the "FD" (feasible distance). FD is by definition the metric of the best route (successor route).

■   The route to 10.1.3.0 through 10.1.4.2 (Yosemite) is a feasible successor route, because
    the neighbor's calculated metric (1,794,560, shown as the second number in parenthesis)
    is lower than the successor route's calculated metric.

IGRP to EIGRP Migration

In the early days of routing, the main options for routing protocol were RIP (Version 1) and
IGRP. IGRP is appreciably better than RIP Version 1, particularly with regards to the metric
and convergence time. As a nice side effect for Cisco stockholders, a choice for IGRP was a
choice to use only Cisco routers.

When Cisco later announced EIGRP, they wanted to make migration simple. If a network is
small enough to allow migration of all routers at one time, the routers could simply be
configured with the new EIGRP configuration, the old IGRP configuration deleted, and the
process was complete. However, most medium to large networks might want to migrate a
subset of the routers to EIGRP, and migrate other routers later, just due to the size of the
project. To make migration simple, Cisco created a feature of EIGRP called *automatic
redistribution*. Figure 6-11 depicts the idea, and shows the configurations required on all
three routers in order to enable automatic redistribution.

Figure 6-11   *Example Automatic Redistribution Between IGRP and EIGRP*

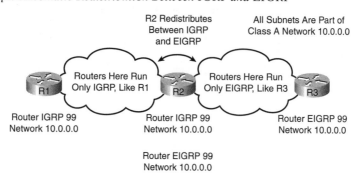

When using any other pair of IP routing protocols in different parts of an internetwork, a
more detailed manual configuration of a feature called *Route Redistribution* is required.
However, with IGRP and EIGRP, R2's routes learned with IGRP are automatically advertised
with EIGRP, and visa versa. The only requirement is that both IGRP and EIGRP be
configured on the same router at the border between the two routing protocols, and that they
both use the same AS number (AS numbers range between 1 and 65,535).

Foundation Summary

The "Foundation Summary" section lists the most important facts from the chapter. Although this section does not list everything that will be on the exam, a well-prepared CCNA candidate should at a minimum know all the details in each Foundation Summary before taking the exam.

The basic process of learning routes for the first time with OSPF goes something like this:

1. Each router discovers its neighbors on each interface. The list of neighbors is kept in a neighbor table.

2. Each router uses a reliable protocol to exchange topology information (LSAs) with its neighbors.

3. Each router places the learned topology information in its topology database.

4. Each router runs the SPF algorithm against its own topology database to calculate the best routes to each subnet in the database.

5. Each router places the best route to each subnet in the IP routing table.

Figure 6-12 shows a network with multiple areas, along with the perspective of the topology for routers inside Area 1.

Figure 6-12   *Two-Area OSPF*

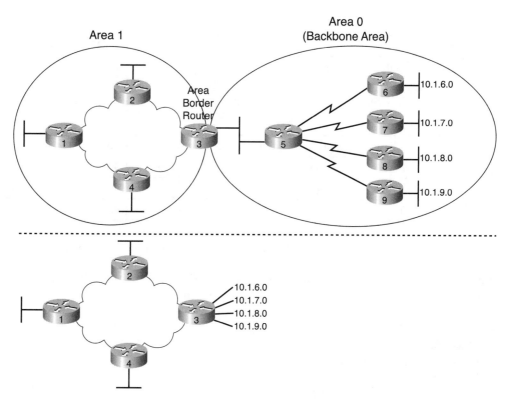

Table 6-9 summarizes some of the key points of comparison between the two types of routing protocols.

Table 6-9   *Comparing Link-State and Distance Vector Protocols*

Feature	Link State	Distance Vector
Convergence Time	Fast	Slow, mainly because of loop-avoidance features
Loop Avoidance	Built into the protocol	Requires extra features such as split horizon
Memory and CPU Requirements	Can be large; good design can minimize	Low
Requires Design Effort for Larger Networks	Yes	No
Public Standard or Proprietary	OSPF is public	RIP is publicly defined; IGRP is not

Table 6-10 summarizes some of the key comparison points between EIGRP, IGRP, and OSPF.

Table 6-10 *EIGRP Features Compared to OSPF and IGRP*

Feature	EIGRP	IGRP	OSPF
Discovers neighbors before exchanging routing information	Yes	No	Yes
Builds some form of topology table in addition to adding routes to the routing table	Yes	No	Yes
Converges quickly	Yes	No	Yes
Uses metrics based on bandwidth and delay by default	Yes*	Yes	No
Sends full routing information on every routing update cycle	No	Yes	No
Requires distance vector loop-avoidance features	No	Yes	No
Public standard	No	No	Yes

*EIGRP uses the same metric as IGRP, except that EIGRP scales the metric by multiplying by 256.

Example 6-9 shows two alternative OSPF configurations for a router. All interfaces are in Area 0.

Example 6-9 *OSPF Single-Area Configuration Alternatives*

```
interface ethernet 0/0
ip address 10.1.1.1 255.255.255.0
interface serial 0/0
ip address 10.1.4.1 255.255.255.0
interface serial 0/1
ip address 10.1.6.1 255.255.255.0
!
router ospf 1
network 10.0.0.0 0.255.255.255 area 0
!
! Alternately:
!
router ospf 1
network 10.1.1.1 0.0.0.0 area 0
network 10.1.4.1 0.0.0.0 area 0
network 10.1.6.1 0.0.0.0 area 0
```

The wildcard mask represents a 32-bit number. When the mask has a binary 1 in one of the bit positions, that bit is considered a wildcard bit, meaning that the router should not care what binary value is in the corresponding numbers. For that reason, binary 1s in the wildcard mask are called *don't care bits*. If the wildcard mask bit is 0 in a bit position, the corresponding bits in the numbers being compared must match. You can think of these bits as the *do care bits*. The router must examine the two numbers and make sure that the values match for the bits that matter—in other words, the do care bits.

For instance, the first wildcard mask in Example 6-8 is 0.255.255.255. When converted to binary, this number is 0000 0000 1111 1111 1111 1111 1111 1111—in other words, eight 0s and 24 1s. The **network** command tells the IOS to compare 10.0.0.0, which is the number in the **network** command, to the IP addresses of each interface on the router. The wildcard mask tells IOS to compare only the first octet; the last three octets are wildcards, and anything matches. So, all three interface IP addresses are matched.

With the wildcard mask of 0.0.0.0, entire numbers must be compared—hence the specific **network** commands referring to the specific IP addresses of the interfaces in the alternative configuration.

Q&A

As mentioned in the Introduction, you have two choices for review questions. The following questions give you a bigger challenge than the exam because they are open-ended. By reviewing with this more-difficult question format, you can exercise your memory better and prove your conceptual and factual knowledge of the topics covered in this chapter. The answers to these questions are found in Appendix A.

For more practice with exam-like question formats, including multiple-choice questions and those using a router simulator, use the exam engine on the CD.

1. Create a minimal configuration enabling IP on each interface on a 2600 series router (two serial, one Ethernet). The Network Information Center (NIC) assigns you network 192.168.1.0. Your boss says that you need, at most, 60 hosts per LAN subnet. You also have point-to-point links attached to the serial interfaces. When choosing the IP address values and subnet numbers, you decide to start with the lowest numerical values. Assume that point-to-point serial links will be attached to this router and that EIGRP is the routing protocol.

2. Write down the steps you would take to migrate from RIP to OSPF in a router whose current RIP configuration includes only **router rip** followed by a **network 10.0.0.0** command. Assume a single OSPF area, and use as few **network** commands as possible.

3. Create a configuration for EIGRP on a router with these interfaces and addresses: e0 using 10.1.1.1, e1 using 224.1.2.3, s0 using 10.1.2.1, and s1 using 199.1.1.1. Use AS number 5.

4. Create a configuration for EIGRP on a router with these interfaces and addresses: e0 using 200.1.1.1, e1 using 128.1.3.2, s0 using 192.0.1.1, and s1 using 223.254.254.1.

5. From a router's user mode, without using debugs or privileged mode, how can you determine what routers are sending you EIGRP routing updates?

6. If the command **router eigrp 1**, followed by **network 10.0.0.0**, with no other network commands, is configured in a router that has an Ethernet0 interface with IP address 168.10.1.1, does EIGRP send updates out Ethernet0?

7. If the command **router ospf 1**, followed by **network 10.0.0.0 0.255.255.255 area 0**, with no other network commands, is configured in a router that has an Ethernet0 interface with IP address 10.10.1.1, does OSPF send updates out Ethernet0?

8. If the commands **router eigrp 1** and **network 10.0.0.0** are configured in a router that has an Ethernet0 interface with IP address 168.10.1.1, mask 255.255.255.0, does this router have a route to 168.10.1.0?

9. Which command lists all IP routes learned via OSPF?

10. Compare and contrast the type of information exchanged in routing updates sent by distance vector routing protocols versus link-state protocols.

11. Define balanced hybrid and give an example of a balanced hybrid protocol.

12. Describe how balanced hybrid protocols differ from distance vector protocols in terms of how a router notices that a neighboring router has failed.

13. List the distance vector loop-avoidance features used by OSPF, such as split horizon.

14. List two OSPF features that help decrease the size of the OSPF topology database.

15. Assume that you must choose between OSPF and EIGRP for a routing protocol in a new network you are building. List and explain the most compelling reason to choose OSPF and the most compelling reason to choose EIGRP.

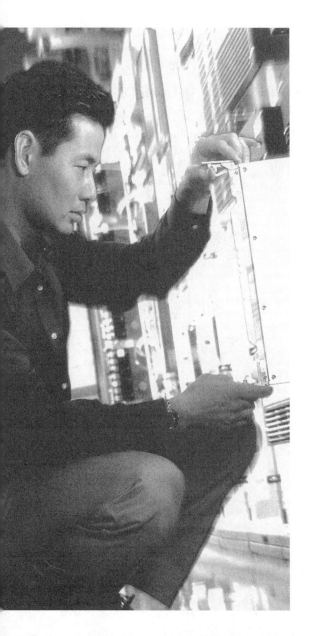

This chapter covers the following subjects:

- Route Summarization and Variable-Length Subnet Masks

- Classless Routing Protocols and Classless Routing

CHAPTER 7

Advanced Routing Protocol Topics

In Chapters 5 and 6, you read about the concepts and configuration of the four interior routing protocols covered on the ICND exam—RIP, IGRP, EIGRP, and OSPF. Those chapters focused on the details specific to each routing protocol.

This chapter covers several topics related to designing a network's IP subnetting scheme, with considerations for the routing protocol's capabilities. For instance, you must consider whether the routing protocol will support variable-length subnet masking (VLSM). If the routing protocol does not support VLSM, you need to pick a single subnet mask for the entire network—and as a result, you might waste a lot of IP addresses in each subnet.

This chapter describes several concepts related to IP subnetting design. VLSM is covered in the first section, along with route summarization. Route summarization requires VLSM support in the routing protocol, so these two topics are covered in the same section. The second section describes classful and classless routing protocols. These terms are used in many different ways, and this section clears up their meanings.

"Do I Know This Already?" Quiz

The purpose of the "Do I Know This Already?" quiz is to help you decide if you need to read the entire chapter. If you intend to read the entire chapter, you do not necessarily need to answer these questions now.

The eight-question quiz, derived from the major sections in the "Foundation Topics" section, helps you determine how to spend your limited study time.

Table 7-1 outlines the major topics discussed in this chapter and the "Do I Know This Already?" quiz questions that correspond to those topics.

Table 7-1 *"Do I Know This Already?" Foundation Topics Section-to-Question Mapping*

Foundations Topics Section	Questions Covered in This Section
Route Summarization and Variable-Length Subnet Masks	1–4, 8
Classless Routing Protocols and Classless Routing	5–7

> **CAUTION** The goal of self-assessment is to gauge your mastery of the topics in this chapter. If you don't know the answer to a question or you're only partially sure of the answer, you should mark this question as wrong for purposes of the self-assessment. Giving yourself credit for an answer you guess correctly skews your self-assessment results and might give you a false sense of security.

1. Which of the following summarized subnets is the smallest summary route that includes subnets 10.1.55.0, 10.1.56.0, and 10.1.57.0, mask 255.255.255.0?

   a. 10.0.0.0 255.255.255.0

   b. 10.1.0.0 255.255.0.0

   c. 10.1.55.0 255.255.255.0

   d. 10.1.48.0 255.255.240.0

   e. 10.1.32.0 255.255.224.0

2. Which of the following summarized subnets is not a valid summary that includes subnets 10.1.55.0, 10.1.56.0, and 10.1.57.0, mask 255.255.255.0?

   a. 10.0.0.0 255.0.0.0

   b. 10.1.0.0 255.255.0.0

   c. 10.1.55.0 255.255.255.0

   d. 10.1.48.0 255.255.240.0

   e. 10.1.32.0 255.255.224.0

3. What does the acronym VLSM stand for?

   a. Variable-length subnet mask

   b. Very long subnet mask

   c. Vociferous longitudinal subnet mask

   d. Vector-length subnet mask

   e. Vector loop subnet mask

4. Imagine a router that lists three routes to subnets in network 10.0.0.0. Assume that VLSM is in use. How many times does the **show ip route** command list mask/prefix information about routes in network 10.0.0.0?

    a. 1

    b. 2

    c. 3

    d. 4

    e. 5

5. Which routing protocol(s) perform(s) autosummarization by default?

    a. RIP-1

    b. IGRP

    c. EIGRP

    d. OSPF

6. Which of the following routing protocols are classless?

    a. RIP-1

    b. IGRP

    c. EIGRP

    d. OSPF

7. Which of the following is affected by whether a router is performing classful or classless routing?

    a. When to use a default route

    b. When to use masks in routing updates

    c. When to convert a packet's destination IP address to a network number

    d. When to perform queuing based on the classification of a packet into a particular queue

8. Which of the following routing protocols support route summarization?

   a. RIP-1

   b. IGRP

   c. EIGRP

   d. OSPF

The answers to the "Do I Know This Already?" quiz appear in Appendix A. The suggested choices for your next step are as follows:

■ **6 or less overall score**—Read the entire chapter. This includes the "Foundation Topics," "Foundation Summary," and "Q&A" sections.

■ **7 or 8 overall score**—If you want more review on these topics, skip to the "Foundation Summary" section and then go to the "Q&A" section. Otherwise, move to the next chapter.

Foundation Topics

Route Summarization and Variable-Length Subnet Masks

Small networks might have only a few dozen routes in their routers' routing tables. The larger the network, the larger the number of routes. In fact, Internet routers have more than 100,000 routes in some cases.

When larger IP networks are created, the routing table might become too large. As routing tables grow, they consume more memory in a router. Also, each router can take more time to route a packet, because the router has to match a route in the routing table, and searching a larger table generally takes more time. And with a large routing table, it takes more time to troubleshoot problems, because the engineers working on the network need to sift through more information.

Therefore, reducing the size of the IP routing tables has some advantages. *Route summarization* reduces the size of routing tables while maintaining routes to all the destinations in the network. Summarization also improves convergence time, because the router that summarizes the route no longer has to announce any changes to the status of the individual subnets. By advertising only that the whole summary route is either up or down, the routers that have the summary route do not have to reconverge every time one of the component subnets goes up or down.

The routing protocol must support *variable-length subnet masks (VLSMs)* when the network uses route summarization.

VLSM means that, in a single Class A, B, or C network, more than one subnet mask value is used. If the same mask is used throughout the same network, many subnets might have far more IP addresses than will ever be used. VLSM allows some subnets to be smaller and some to be larger, which reduces wasted IP addresses. This also allows the network to grow, without the need to reserve another registered network number with the Network Information Center (NIC).

VLSM can save a significant number of IP addresses, even just by using two different masks. For instance, many networks use a mask of 255.255.255.252 on point-to-point serial links because it allows only two valid IP addresses (you need only two IP addresses on a point-to-point serial link). Then, on LAN subnets, the network uses a mask that allows larger subnets, such as 255.255.255.0. The network uses VLSM because two different masks are used in the same Class A, B, or C network.

This section starts by describing route summarization concepts, followed by VLSM. At the end of this section, you will read about some tips for finding the answers to summarization questions on the ICND exam.

Route Summarization Concepts

Engineers use route summarization to reduce the size of the routing tables in the network. Route summarization causes some number of more-specific routes to be replaced with a single route that includes all the IP addresses covered by the subnets in the original routes.

Summary routes, which replace multiple routes, must be configured by a network engineer. Although the configuration command does not look exactly like a **static route** command, the same basic information is configured—but now the routing protocol advertises just the summary route, as opposed to the original routes.

Route summarization works much better when the network was designed with route summarization in mind. Figure 7-1 shows a network for which route summarization was planned.

Figure 7-1 *Network with Route Summarization Planned*

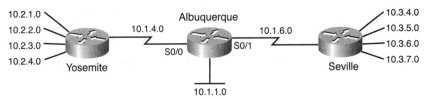

Mask: 255.255.255.0 in All Cases

In this network, the engineer planned his choices of subnet numbers relative to his goal of using route summarization. All subnets off the main site (Albuquerque), including WAN links, start with 10.1. All LAN subnets off Yosemite start with 10.2, and likewise, all LAN subnets off Seville start with 10.3.

Albuquerque's routing table, without summarization, shows four routes to subnets that begin with 10.2, all pointing out its serial 0/0 interface to Yosemite. Similarly, Albuquerque shows four routes to subnets that begin with 10.3, all pointing out its serial 0/1 interface to Seville. Therefore, summarization can be used to make Albuquerque replace the four routes to 10.2 subnets with one route, and likewise for the four routes to 10.3 subnets. First, examine the routing table on Albuquerque shown in Example 7-1, with EIGRP as the routing protocol.

Example 7-1 *Albuquerque Routing Table Before Route Summarization*

```
Albuquerque#show ip route
Codes: C - connected, S - static, I - IGRP, R - RIP, M - mobile, B - BGP
       D - EIGRP, EX - EIGRP external, O - OSPF, IA - OSPF inter area
       N1 - OSPF NSSA external type 1, N2 - OSPF NSSA external type 2
       E1 - OSPF external type 1, E2 - OSPF external type 2, E - EGP
       i - IS-IS, L1 - IS-IS level-1, L2 - IS-IS level-2, ia - IS-IS inter area
       * - candidate default, U - per-user static route, o - ODR
       P - periodic downloaded static route

Gateway of last resort is not set

     10.0.0.0/24 is subnetted, 11 subnets
D       10.2.1.0 [90/2172416] via 10.1.4.2, 00:02:18, Serial0/0
D       10.2.2.0 [90/2297856] via 10.1.4.2, 00:02:07, Serial0/0
C       10.1.1.0 is directly connected, Ethernet0/0
D       10.2.3.0 [90/2297856] via 10.1.4.2, 00:02:02, Serial0/0
D       10.3.5.0 [90/2297856] via 10.1.6.3, 00:00:39, Serial0/1
D       10.2.4.0 [90/2297856] via 10.1.4.2, 00:01:57, Serial0/0
D       10.3.4.0 [90/2172416] via 10.1.6.3, 00:00:46, Serial0/1
C       10.1.6.0 is directly connected, Serial0/1
D       10.3.7.0 [90/2297856] via 10.1.6.3, 00:00:28, Serial0/1
D       10.3.6.0 [90/2297856] via 10.1.6.3, 00:00:33, Serial0/1
C       10.1.4.0 is directly connected, Serial0/0
```

Albuquerque's routing table shows 11 subnets, all with mask 255.255.255.0, as shown in Figure 7-1. The network engineer knows that his network plan ensures that all subnets added off Yosemite start with 10.2, and all new subnets off Seville start with 10.3. More importantly, the engineer will never put subnets that begin with 10.2 somewhere other than at the Yosemite site and will never put 10.3 subnets anywhere except off Seville. Therefore, the routes off Yosemite and Seville can be summarized. Examples 7-2, 7-3, and 7-4 show the routing tables on Albuquerque, Yosemite, and Seville, along with the route summarization configuration on Yosemite and Seville.

Example 7-2 *Albuquerque Routing Table After Route Summarization*

```
Albuquerque#show ip route
Codes: C - connected, S - static, I - IGRP, R - RIP, M - mobile, B - BGP
       D - EIGRP, EX - EIGRP external, O - OSPF, IA - OSPF inter area
       N1 - OSPF NSSA external type 1, N2 - OSPF NSSA external type 2
       E1 - OSPF external type 1, E2 - OSPF external type 2, E - EGP
       i - IS-IS, L1 - IS-IS level-1, L2 - IS-IS level-2, ia - IS-IS inter area
       * - candidate default, U - per-user static route, o - ODR
       P - periodic downloaded static route

Gateway of last resort is not set
```

Example 7-2 *Albuquerque Routing Table After Route Summarization (Continued)*

```
      10.0.0.0/8 is variably subnetted, 5 subnets, 2 masks
D        10.2.0.0/16 [90/2172416] via 10.1.4.2, 00:05:59, Serial0/0
D        10.3.0.0/16 [90/2172416] via 10.1.6.3, 00:05:40, Serial0/1
C        10.1.1.0/24 is directly connected, Ethernet0/0
C        10.1.6.0/24 is directly connected, Serial0/1
C        10.1.4.0/24 is directly connected, Serial0/0
```

Example 7-3 *Yosemite Configuration and Routing Table After Route Summarization*

```
Yosemite#configure terminal
Enter configuration commands, one per line.  End with CNTL/Z.
Yosemite(config)#interface serial 0/0
Yosemite(config-if)#ip summary-address eigrp 1 10.2.0.0 255.255.0.0
Yosemite(config-if)#^Z


Yosemite#show ip route
Codes: C - connected, S - static, I - IGRP, R - RIP, M - mobile, B - BGP
        D - EIGRP, EX - EIGRP external, O - OSPF, IA - OSPF inter area
        N1 - OSPF NSSA external type 1, N2 - OSPF NSSA external type 2
        E1 - OSPF external type 1, E2 - OSPF external type 2, E - EGP
        i - IS-IS, L1 - IS-IS level-1, L2 - IS-IS level-2, ia - IS-IS inter area
        * - candidate default, U - per-user static route, o - ODR
        P - periodic downloaded static route

Gateway of last resort is not set

      10.0.0.0/8 is variably subnetted, 9 subnets, 2 masks
D        10.2.0.0/16 is a summary, 00:04:57, Null0
D        10.3.0.0/16 [90/2684416] via 10.1.4.1, 00:04:30, Serial0/0
C        10.2.1.0/24 is directly connected, FastEthernet0/0
D        10.1.1.0/24 [90/2195456] via 10.1.4.1, 00:04:52, Serial0/0
C        10.2.2.0/24 is directly connected, Loopback2
C        10.2.3.0/24 is directly connected, Loopback3
C        10.2.4.0/24 is directly connected, Loopback4
D        10.1.6.0/24 [90/2681856] via 10.1.4.1, 00:04:53, Serial0/0
C        10.1.4.0/24 is directly connected, Serial0/0
```

Example 7-4 *Seville Configuration and Routing Table After Route Summarization*

```
Seville#configure terminal
Enter configuration commands, one per line.  End with CNTL/Z.
Seville(config)#interface serial 0/0
Seville(config-if)#ip summary-address eigrp 1 10.3.0.0 255.255.0.0
Seville(config-if)#^Z
Seville#show ip route
Codes: C - connected, S - static, I - IGRP, R - RIP, M - mobile, B - BGP
```

Example 7-4   *Seville Configuration and Routing Table After Route Summarization (Continued)*

```
            D - EIGRP, EX - EIGRP external, O - OSPF, IA - OSPF inter area
            N1 - OSPF NSSA external type 1, N2 - OSPF NSSA external type 2
            E1 - OSPF external type 1, E2 - OSPF external type 2, E - EGP
            i - IS-IS, L1 - IS-IS level-1, L2 - IS-IS level-2, ia - IS-IS inter area
            * - candidate default, U - per-user static route, o - ODR
            P - periodic downloaded static route

Gateway of last resort is not set

     10.0.0.0/8 is variably subnetted, 9 subnets, 2 masks
D       10.2.0.0/16 [90/2684416] via 10.1.6.1, 00:00:36, Serial0/0
D       10.3.0.0/16 is a summary, 00:00:38, Null0
D       10.1.1.0/24 [90/2195456] via 10.1.6.1, 00:00:36, Serial0/0
C       10.3.5.0/24 is directly connected, Loopback5
C       10.3.4.0/24 is directly connected, FastEthernet0/0
C       10.1.6.0/24 is directly connected, Serial0/0
C       10.3.7.0/24 is directly connected, Loopback7
D       10.1.4.0/24 [90/2681856] via 10.1.6.1, 00:00:36, Serial0/0
C       10.3.6.0/24 is directly connected, Loopback6
```

Route summarization configuration differs with different routing protocols; EIGRP is used in this example. The summary routes for EIGRP are created by the **ip summary-address** interface subcommands on Yosemite and Seville in this case. Each command defines a new summarized route and tells EIGRP to only advertise the summary out this interface and not to advertise any routes contained in the larger summary. For instance, Yosemite defines a summary route to 10.2.0.0, mask 255.255.0.0, which defines a route to all hosts whose IP addresses begin with 10.2. In effect, this command causes Yosemite and Seville to advertise routes 10.2.0.0 255.255.0.0 and 10.3.0.0 255.255.0.0, respectively, and not to advertise their original four LAN subnets.

Notice that Albuquerque's routing table now contains a route to 10.2.0.0 255.255.0.0 (the mask is listed in prefix notation as /16). None of the original four subnets that begin with 10.2 show up in Albuquerque's routing table. The same thing occurs for route 10.3.0.0/16.

Also notice the highlighted section in Example 7-2 (Albuquerque) that says "variably subnetted". This phrase means that more than one subnet mask is used in the network. Because of the summarization, Albuquerque knows some /24 routes and some /16 routes in network 10.0.0.0. So Albuquerque must use a routing protocol that supports VLSM for this to work. As it turns out, EIGRP supports VLSM.

The routing tables on Yosemite and Seville look a little different from Albuquerque. Focusing on Yosemite, notice that the four 10.2 routes show up because they are directly connected subnets. Yosemite does not see the four 10.3 routes. Instead, it sees a summary route, because Albuquerque now advertises the 10.3.0.0/16 summarized route only.

The most interesting part of the routing tables is Yosemite's route to 10.2.0.0/16, with the outgoing interface set to **null0**. Routes pointing out the null0 interface mean that packets matching this route are discarded. EIGRP added this route, with interface null0, as a result of the **ip summary-address** command. The logic works like this:

> Yosemite needs this route because now it might receive packets destined for other 10.2 addresses besides the four existing 10.2 subnets. If a packet destined for one of the 4 existing 10.2.x subnets arrives, Yosemite has a correct, more specific route to match the packet. If a packet whose destination starts with 10.2 arrives, but it is not in one of those 4 subnets, the null route matches the packet, causing Yosemite to discard the packet—as it should.

The routing table on Seville is similar to Yosemite's in terms of the table entries and why they are in the table.

VLSM

VLSM occurs when more than one mask is used in a single Class A, B, or C network. Although route summarization causes more than one mask to be used, requiring support for VLSM, you can also simply design a network to use multiple subnet masks. By using VLSM, you can reduce the number of wasted IP addresses in each subnet, allow for more subnets, and avoid having to obtain another registered IP network number from the NIC.

Figure 7-2 depicts the same familiar network, but this time without summarization and with two different subnet masks used in network 10.0.0.0.

Figure 7-2 *VLSM in Network 10.0.0.0: Masks 255.255.255.0 and 255.255.255.252*

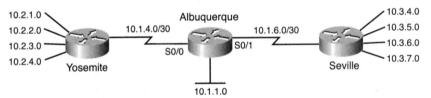

This figure shows a typical choice of using a /30 prefix (mask 255.255.255.252) on point-to-point serial links, with some other mask (255.255.255.0 in this example) on the LAN subnets. The only real requirements for VLSM are that the subnets do not overlap and that the routing protocol supports VLSM. Subnets overlap when the range of IP addresses in one subnet includes some addresses in the range of valid addresses in another subnet. When using a single mask in a single Class A, B, or C network, you can usually avoid overlapping subnets easily. However, with VLSM, you can more easily overlook cases in which you assign subnets that overlap.

Example 7-5 lists the routing table on Albuquerque again, this time with the masks shown in Figure 7-2 and with summarization still configured on Yosemite and Seville.

Example 7-5 *Albuquerque Routing Table with Two Separate Masks Configured on Interfaces, Plus Route Summarization*

```
Albuquerque#show ip route
Codes: C - connected, S - static, I - IGRP, R - RIP, M - mobile, B - BGP
       D - EIGRP, EX - EIGRP external, O - OSPF, IA - OSPF inter area
       N1 - OSPF NSSA external type 1, N2 - OSPF NSSA external type 2
       E1 - OSPF external type 1, E2 - OSPF external type 2, E - EGP
       i - IS-IS, L1 - IS-IS level-1, L2 - IS-IS level-2, ia - IS-IS inter area
       * - candidate default, U - per-user static route, o - ODR
       P - periodic downloaded static route

Gateway of last resort is not set

     10.0.0.0/8 is variably subnetted, 5 subnets, 3 masks
D       10.2.0.0/16 [90/2172416] via 10.1.4.2, 00:00:34, Serial0/0
D       10.3.0.0/16 [90/2172416] via 10.1.6.2, 00:00:56, Serial0/1
C       10.1.1.0/24 is directly connected, Ethernet0/0
C       10.1.6.0/30 is directly connected, Serial0/1
C       10.1.4.0/30 is directly connected, Serial0/0
```

Albuquerque uses VLSM with three masks now. Albuquerque knows the /24 and /30 prefixes (masks 255.255.255.0 and 255.255.255.252, respectively) from the configuration of the connected interfaces. Albuquerque learns about the 255.255.0.0 mask from the summarized routes advertised by Yosemite and Seville.

Regardless of how Albuquerque learns about these routes, to share these routes with other routers, it must use a routing protocol that supports VLSM. For a routing protocol to support VLSM, it must advertise not only the subnet number, but also the subnet mask, when advertising routes. Also, because VLSM support is required to support route summarization, the same routing protocols that support VLSM also support summarization. Table 7-2 lists the routing protocols and their support (or nonsupport) of VLSM.

Table 7-2 *Interior IP Routing Protocol VLSM Support*

Routing Protocol	VLSM Support	Sends Mask/Prefix in Routing Updates	Route Summarization Support
RIP-1	No	No	No
IGRP	No	No	No
RIP-2	Yes	Yes	Yes
EIGRP	Yes	Yes	Yes
OSPF	Yes	Yes	Yes

Route Summarization Strategies

As mentioned earlier, route summarization works best when the network engineer plans his choice of subnet numbers anticipating route summarization. For instance, the earlier examples assumed a well-thought-out plan. The only place where subnets beginning with 10.2 were added was at the Yosemite router. That convention allowed for the creation of a summary route for all addresses beginning with 10.2 by having Yosemite advertise a route describing subnet 10.2.0.0, mask 255.255.0.0.

Some summarized routes combine many routes into one route, but that might not be the "best" summarization. "Best" generally implies, in this case, that the summary should include all the subnets specified in the question and a few other IP addresses that do not exist. For instance, in the earlier summarization example, four subnets (10.2.1.0, 10.2.2.0, 10.2.3.0, and 10.2.4.0, all with mask 255.255.255.0) were summarized into 10.2.0.0, all with mask 255.255.0.0. However, this summary includes a lot of IP addresses that are not in those four subnets. Does the summary work given that network's design goals? Sure. However, instead of just defining a summary that encompasses all routes, you might want to list the "tightest," "most concise," or "best" summary—the summary that includes all the subnets but as few extra subnets (the ones that have not been assigned yet) as possible. This section describes a strategy for finding those concise summaries.

The following list describes a generalized process by which you can summarize a group of subnets into one summary route:

Step 1   Find the parts of the subnet numbers that are identical, moving left to right. (For our purposes, consider this first part the "in common" part.)

Step 2   The summary route's subnet number has the same value in the "in common" part of the summarized subnets and binary 0s in the second part.

Step 3   The subnet mask for the summary route has binary 1s in the "in common" part and binary 0s in the rest of the mask.

Step 4   Check your work by calculating the range of valid IP addresses implied by the new summary route, comparing the range to the summarized subnets. The new summary should encompass all IP addresses in the summarized subnets.

For instance, the earlier example used 10.2 to begin all subnets off Yosemite. Therefore, the "in common" part is the first two octets. By examining the network diagram, and knowing the convention of placing only subnets beginning with 10.2 off Yosemite, you know that there are no subnets beginning with 10.2 somewhere else in the network. In Step 2, because the "in common" part is the first two octets, the subnet number is 10.2.0.0. In Step 3, again, because the "in common" part is the first two octets, the mask is 255.255.0.0—two octets of binary 1s and two octets of binary 0s.

Although this simple example might be interesting, the process (so far) still has two problems:

- Most summaries force you to notice "in common" parts of subnets that do not use octet boundaries, so you have to look at the numbers in binary.
- To find the "best," "most concise," or "tightest" summary, you almost always need to use summaries that use a more difficult mask.

By looking at the subnet numbers in binary, you will more easily discover the bits in common among all the subnet numbers. By using the longest number of bits "in common," you will find the best summary.

Sample "Best" Summary on Seville

Seville has subnets 10.3.4.0, 10.3.5.0, 10.3.6.0, and 10.3.7.0, all with mask 255.255.255.0. You start the process by writing down all the subnet numbers in binary:

```
0000 1010 0000 0011 0000 01 00 0000 0000 - 10.3.4.0
0000 1010 0000 0011 0000 01 01 0000 0000 - 10.3.5.0
0000 1010 0000 0011 0000 01 10 0000 0000 - 10.3.6.0
0000 1010 0000 0011 0000 01 11 0000 0000 - 10.3.7.0
```

Even before looking at the numbers in binary, you can guess that the first two octets are identical in all four subnets. So, at least the first 16 bits, going from left to right, are identical among all four subnets. This means that the "in common" part is at least 16 bits long. Further examination shows that the first 6 bits of the third octet are also identical, but the seventh bit in the third octet has some different values. So the "in common" part of these four subnets is the first 22 bits.

Step 2 says to create a subnet number for the summary by taking the same value for the "in common" part and binary 0s for the rest. In this case:

```
0000 1010 0000 0011 0000 01 00 0000 0000 - 10.3.4.0
```

Step 3 creates the mask by using binary 1s for the "in common" part and binary 0s for the rest. The "in common" part in this example is the first 22 bits:

```
1111 1111 1111 1111 1111 11 00 0000 0000 - 255.255.252.0
```

So, the summary route uses subnet 10.3.4.0, mask 255.255.252.0.

Step 4 suggests a method to check your work. The summary route should include all the IP addresses in the summarized routes. In this case, the range of addresses starts with 10.3.4.0. The first valid IP address is 10.3.4.1, the final valid IP address is 10.3.7.254, and the broadcast address is 10.3.7.255. In this case, the summary route includes all the IP addresses in the four routes it summarizes and no extraneous IP addresses.

Sample "Best" Summary on Yosemite

The four subnets on Yosemite cannot be summarized quite as efficiently as those on Seville. On Seville, the summary route itself covers the same set of IP addresses as the four subnets. As you will see, the best summary route at Yosemite includes twice as many addresses in the summary as there are in the original four subnets.

Yosemite has subnets 10.2.1.0, 10.2.2.0, 10.2.3.0, and 10.2.4.0, all with mask 255.255.255.0. The process starts with writing down all the subnet numbers in binary:

```
0000 1010 0000 0010 0000 0|001 0000 0000 - 10.2.1.0
0000 1010 0000 0010 0000 0|010 0000 0000 - 10.2.2.0
0000 1010 0000 0010 0000 0|011 0000 0000 - 10.2.3.0
0000 1010 0000 0010 0000 0|100 0000 0000 - 10.2.4.0
```

In this example, only the first 5 bits of the third octet are identical. So, the first 21 bits of the four subnet numbers are "in common."

Step 2 says to create a subnet number for the summary by taking the same value for the "in common" part and binary 0s for the rest. In this case:

```
0000 1010 0000 0011 0000 0|000 0000 0000 - 10.2.0.0
```

Step 3 creates the mask by using binary 1s for the "in common" part and binary 0s for the rest. The "in common" part in this example is the first 21 bits:

```
1111 1111 1111 1111 1111 1|000 0000 0000 - 255.255.248.0
```

So, the best summary is 10.2.0.0, mask 255.255.248.0.

Step 4 suggests a method to check your work. The summary route should define a superset of the IP addresses in the summarized routes. In this case, the range of addresses starts with 10.2.0.0. The first valid IP address is 10.2.0.1, the final valid IP address is 10.2.7.254, and the broadcast address is 10.2.7.255. In this case, the summary route summarizes a larger set of addresses than just the four subnets.

Classless Routing Protocols and Classless Routing

Cisco documents occasionally mention the terms *classless* and *classful* when referring to topics related to routing and addressing. The root word, *class,* refers to the Class A, B, and C network classes defined by IP addressing. The terms classless and classful can be applied to several topics related to routing and addressing. This section covers the basic meaning of the terms and their application.

Classless and Classful Routing Protocols

Some routing protocols must consider the Class A, B, or C network number that a subnet resides in when performing some of its tasks. Other routing protocols can ignore Class A, B, and C rules altogether. Routing protocols that must consider class rules are called *classful routing protocols;* those that do not need to consider class rules are called *classless routing protocols.*

You can easily remember which routing protocols fall into each category because of one fact:

> Classful routing protocols do not transmit the mask information along with the subnet number, whereas classless routing protocols do transmit mask information.

You might recall that routing protocols that support VLSM do so because they send mask information along with the routing information. Table 7-3 lists the routing protocols and whether they transmit mask information, support VLSM, and are classless or classful.

Table 7-3   *Interior IP Routing Protocol: Classless or Classful?*

Routing Protocol	Classless	Sends Mask/Prefix in Routing Updates	VLSM Support	Route Summarization Support
RIP-1	No	No	No	No
IGRP	No	No	No	No
RIP-2	Yes	Yes	Yes	Yes
EIGRP	Yes	Yes	Yes	Yes
OSPF	Yes	Yes	Yes	Yes

Classless routing protocols have an advantage over classful routing protocols because of their support of advanced features such as VLSM and summarization. Also, classless routing protocols overcome a few design issues only seen with classful routing protocols, as covered in the next short section.

Autosummarization

As covered earlier in this chapter, routers generally perform routing more quickly if the routing table size can be made shorter. Route summarization helps shorten the routing table while retaining all the needed routes in the network.

Because classful routing protocols do not advertise subnet mask information, the routing updates simply have numbers in them representing the subnet numbers, but no accompanying mask. A router receiving a routing update with a classful routing protocol looks at the subnet number in the update and "guesses" the correct mask. For instance, with Cisco routers, if R1 and R2 have connected networks of the same single Class A, B, or C network, and if R2 receives an update from R1, R2 assumes that the routes described in R1's update use the same mask that R2 uses. In other words, the classful routing protocols expect a static-length subnet mask (SLSM) throughout the network, because they can then reasonably assume that the mask configured for their own interfaces is the same mask used throughout the network.

When a router has interfaces in more than one Class A, B, or C network, it advertises a single route for an entire Class A, B, or C network into the other network. This feature is called *autosummarization*. It can be characterized as follows:

> When advertised on an interface whose IP address is not in network X, routes related to subnets in network X are summarized and advertised as one route. That route is for the entire Class A, B, or C network X.

In other words, if R3 has interfaces in networks 10.0.0.0 and 11.0.0.0, when R3 advertises routing updates out interfaces with IP addresses that start with 11, the updates advertise a single route for network 10.0.0.0. Similarly, R3 advertises a single route to 11.0.0.0 out its interfaces whose IP addresses start with 10.

RIP and IGRP perform autosummarization by default. It cannot be disabled—it is simply a feature of classful routing protocols. (For RIP-2 and EIGRP, autosummarization can be enabled or disabled.)

As usual, an example makes the concept much clearer. Consider Figure 7-3, which shows two networks in use: 10.0.0.0 and 172.16.0.0. Seville has four (connected) routes to subnets of network 10.0.0.0. Example 7-6 shows the output of the **show ip route** command on Albuquerque, as well as RIP-1 **debug ip rip** output.

Figure 7-3 *Autosummarization*

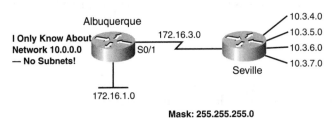

Example 7-6 *Albuquerque Routes and RIP Debugs*

```
Albuquerque#show ip route
Codes: C - connected, S - static, I - IGRP, R - RIP, M - mobile, B - BGP
       D - EIGRP, EX - EIGRP external, O - OSPF, IA - OSPF inter area
       N1 - OSPF NSSA external type 1, N2 - OSPF NSSA external type 2
       E1 - OSPF external type 1, E2 - OSPF external type 2, E - EGP
       i - IS-IS, L1 - IS-IS level-1, L2 - IS-IS level-2, ia - IS-IS inter area
       * - candidate default, U - per-user static route, o - ODR
       P - periodic downloaded static route

Gateway of last resort is not set

     172.16.0.0/24 is subnetted, 2 subnets
C       172.16.1.0 is directly connected, Ethernet0/0
C       172.16.3.0 is directly connected, Serial0/1
R    10.0.0.0/8 [120/1] via 172.16.3.3, 00:00:28, Serial0/1

Albuquerque#debug ip rip
RIP protocol debugging is on

00:05:36: RIP: received v1 update from 172.16.3.3 on Serial0/1
00:05:36:      10.0.0.0 in 1 hops
```

As shown in Example 7-6, Albuquerque's received update on Serial0/1 from Seville advertises only the entire Class A network 10.0.0.0 because autosummarization is enabled on Seville (by default). The Albuquerque IP routing table lists just one route to network 10.0.0.0.

This example also points out another feature of how classful routing protocols make assumptions. Albuquerque does not have any interfaces in network 10.0.0.0. So, when Albuquerque receives the routing update, it assumes that the mask used with 10.0.0.0 is 255.0.0.0—the default mask for a Class A network. In other words, classful routing protocols expect autosummarization to occur.

Autosummarization does not cause any problems—as long as network 10.0.0.0 is contiguous. Consider Figure 7-4, in which Yosemite also has subnets of network 10.0.0.0 but has no connectivity to Seville other than through Albuquerque.

Figure 7-4 *Autosummarization Pitfalls*

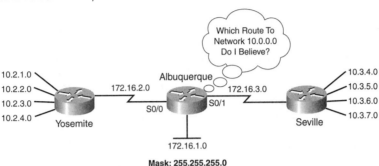

Mask: 255.255.255.0

IP subnet design traditionally has not allowed discontiguous networks. A *contiguous network* is a single Class A, B, or C network for which all routes to subnets of that network pass through only other subnets of that same single network. *Discontiguous networks* refers to the concept that, in a single Class A, B, or C network, there is at least one case in which the only routes to one subnet pass through subnets of a different network. An easy analogy for residents of the U.S. is the term contiguous 48, referring to the 48 states besides Alaska and Hawaii. To drive to Alaska from the contiguous 48, for example, you must drive through another country (Canada, for the geographically impaired!), so Alaska is not contiguous with the 48 states. In other words, it is discontiguous.

Figure 7-4 shows the discontiguous network 10.0.0.0. Simply put, classful routing protocols do not support a design with discontiguous networks, but classless routing protocols do support discontiguous networks. Example 7-7 shows the network shown in Figure 7-4, with classful RIP causing confused routing at Albuquerque.

Example 7-7 *Albuquerque Routing Table: Classful Routing Protocol Not Allowing Discontiguous Network*

```
Albuquerque#show ip route
Codes: C - connected, S - static, I - IGRP, R - RIP, M - mobile, B - BGP
       D - EIGRP, EX - EIGRP external, O - OSPF, IA - OSPF inter area
       N1 - OSPF NSSA external type 1, N2 - OSPF NSSA external type 2
       E1 - OSPF external type 1, E2 - OSPF external type 2, E - EGP
       i - IS-IS, L1 - IS-IS level-1, L2 - IS-IS level-2, ia - IS-IS inter area
       * - candidate default, U - per-user static route, o - ODR
       P - periodic downloaded static route

Gateway of last resort is not set

     172.16.0.0/24 is subnetted, 3 subnets
C       172.16.1.0 is directly connected, Ethernet0/0
C       172.16.2.0 is directly connected, Serial0/0
C       172.16.3.0 is directly connected, Serial0/1
R    10.0.0.0/8 [120/1] via 172.16.3.3, 00:00:13, Serial0/1
                 [120/1] via 172.16.2.2, 00:00:04, Serial0/0
```

As shown in Example 7-7, Albuquerque now has two routes to network 10.0.0.0. Instead of sending packets destined for Yosemite's subnets out serial 0/0, Albuquerque sends some packets out S0/1 to Seville! Albuquerque simply balances the packets across the two routes, because as far as Albuquerque can tell, the two routes are simply equal-cost routes to the same destination—the entire network 10.0.0.0. So, applications would cease to function correctly in this network.

Migrating to use a classless routing protocol with autosummarization disabled takes care of this problem. Example 7-8 shows the same network, this time with EIGRP configured and no autosummarization.

Example 7-8 *Albuquerque Routing Table: Classless Routing Protocol Allowing Discontiguous Network*

```
Albuquerque#show ip route
Codes: C - connected, S - static, I - IGRP, R - RIP, M - mobile, B - BGP
       D - EIGRP, EX - EIGRP external, O - OSPF, IA - OSPF inter area
       N1 - OSPF NSSA external type 1, N2 - OSPF NSSA external type 2
       E1 - OSPF external type 1, E2 - OSPF external type 2, E - EGP
       i - IS-IS, L1 - IS-IS level-1, L2 - IS-IS level-2, ia - IS-IS inter area
       * - candidate default, U - per-user static route, o - ODR
       P - periodic downloaded static route

Gateway of last resort is not set

     172.16.0.0/24 is subnetted, 3 subnets
C       172.16.1.0 is directly connected, Ethernet0/0
C       172.16.2.0 is directly connected, Serial0/0
C       172.16.3.0 is directly connected, Serial0/1
     10.0.0.0/24 is subnetted, 8 subnets
D       10.2.1.0/24 [90/2172416] via 172.16.2.2, 00:00:01, Serial0/0
D       10.2.2.0/24 [90/2297856] via 172.16.2.2, 00:00:01, Serial0/0
D       10.2.3.0/24 [90/2297856] via 172.16.2.2, 00:00:01, Serial0/0
D       10.2.4.0/24 [90/2297856] via 172.16.2.2, 00:00:01, Serial0/0
D       10.3.5.0/24 [90/2297856] via 172.16.3.3, 00:00:29, Serial0/1
D       10.3.4.0/24 [90/2172416] via 172.16.3.3, 00:00:29, Serial0/1
D       10.3.7.0/24 [90/2297856] via 172.16.3.3, 00:00:29, Serial0/1
D       10.3.6.0/24 [90/2297856] via 172.16.3.3, 00:00:29, Serial0/1
```

Notice that Albuquerque knows the four LAN subnets off Yosemite, as well as the four LAN subnets off Seville. Because EIGRP is classless, it can transmit the mask with the routes. Interestingly, EIGRP performs autosummarization by default, but in this configuration, EIGRP autosummarization is disabled. Had autosummarization still been enabled, this network design would have the same problem with the discontiguous network 10.0.0.0, as shown in Example 7-7.

Classful and Classless Routing

IP routing—the actual process of forwarding IP packets—can be considered either classful or classless. As mentioned in the preceding section, routing protocols also are considered either classful or classless. Classless routing protocols ignore Class A, B, and C rules, because they have much better information—the actual subnet masks sent with routing updates.

Similarly, IP routing is classless when the process of forwarding packets ignores class rules, and it is classful when routing must consider class rules when making a decision. However, the concepts behind classless and classful routing are totally independent of the routing protocol used and how it is configured. In fact, a router can use only static routes, and the concepts of classless and classful routing would still apply.

The choice of whether a router uses classful or classless routing determines how that router uses its default route. So, to fully understand what classless and classful routing really mean, you must first understand a little more about default routes. When a router needs to route a packet, and there is no route matching that packet's destination in the routing table, the router discards the packet. Routers that have a default route can consider that packets that do not match a more specific route at least match the default route, so the packet is forwarded according to the default route, as opposed to being discarded. To appreciate the meaning of the terms classless routing and classful routing, you must first take a closer look at default routes in Cisco routers.

Default Routes

Default routes work best when only one path exists to a part of the network. In Figure 7-5, R1, R2, and R3 are connected to the rest of the network only through R1's Token Ring interface. All three routers can forward packets to the rest of the network as long as the packets get to R1, which forwards them to Dist1.

Figure 7-5 *Sample Network Using a Default Route*

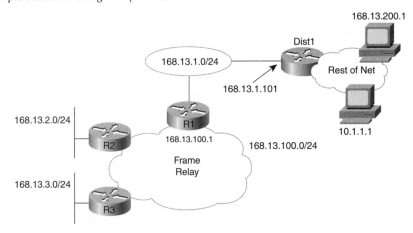

By coding a default route on R1 that points to router Dist1 in Figure 7-5, and by having R1 advertise the default to R2 and R3, default routing can be accomplished. (Chapter 5, "RIP, IGRP, and Static Route Concepts and Configuration," covers the basics of how to configure static routes.) R1, R2, and R3 should not need specific routes to the subnets to the right of router Dist1. Examples 7-9 and 7-10, along with Figure 7-5, show an example of a default route on R1.

Example 7-9 *R1 Static Default Route Configuration and Routing Table*

```
R1(config)#ip route 0.0.0.0 0.0.0.0 168.13.1.101
R1#show ip route
Codes: C - connected, S - static, I - IGRP, R - RIP, M - mobile, B - BGP
       D - EIGRP, EX - EIGRP external, O - OSPF, IA - OSPF inter area
       N1 - OSPF NSSA external type 1, N2 - OSPF NSSA external type 2
       E1 - OSPF external type 1, E2 - OSPF external type 2, E - EGP
       i - IS-IS, L1 - IS-IS level-1, L2 - IS-IS level-2, ia - IS-IS inter area
       * - candidate default, U - per-user static route, o - ODR
       P - periodic downloaded static route

Gateway of last resort is 168.13.1.101 to network 0.0.0.0

     168.13.0.0/24 is subnetted, 4 subnets
C       168.13.1.0 is directly connected, TokenRing0
R       168.13.3.0 [120/1] via 168.13.100.3, 00:00:05, Serial0.1
R       168.13.2.0 [120/1] via 168.13.100.2, 00:00:21, Serial0.1
C       168.13.100.0 is directly connected, Serial0.1
S*   0.0.0.0/0 [1/0] via 168.13.1.101
R1#
```

Example 7-10 *R3: Nuances of the Successful Use of the Static Route on R1*

```
R3#show ip route
Codes: C - connected, S - static, I - IGRP, R - RIP, M - mobile, B - BGP
       D - EIGRP, EX - EIGRP external, O - OSPF, IA - OSPF inter area
       N1 - OSPF NSSA external type 1, N2 - OSPF NSSA external type 2
       E1 - OSPF external type 1, E2 - OSPF external type 2, E - EGP
       i - IS-IS, L1 - IS-IS level-1, L2 - IS-IS level-2, ia - IS-IS inter area
       * - candidate default, U - per-user static route, o - ODR
       P - periodic downloaded static route

Gateway of last resort is 168.13.100.1 to network 0.0.0.0

     168.13.0.0/24 is subnetted, 4 subnets
R       168.13.1.0 [120/1] via 168.13.100.1, 00:00:13, Serial0.1
C       168.13.3.0 is directly connected, Ethernet0
R       168.13.2.0 [120/1] via 168.13.100.2, 00:00:06, Serial0.1
C       168.13.100.0 is directly connected, Serial0.1
```

R1 defines the default route with a static **ip route** command, with destination 0.0.0.0, mask 0.0.0.0. This route matches all destinations by convention. R1 advertises this default route to R2 and R3, as shown in the output of the **show ip route** command on R3 in Example 7-10.

Different routing protocols advertise default routes in a couple of different ways. As an example, this chapter covers how RIP handles the default in this network. R1 lists a static route to 0.0.0.0, mask 0.0.0.0, with next hop 168.13.1.101—essentially, the same information that was entered in the **ip route 0.0.0.0 0.0.0.0 168.13.1.101** global configuration command. RIP advertises this default to R2 and R3, which, instead of listing 0.0.0.0 as a network in their routing tables, list the phrase that begins "Gateway of last resort". When no other route is matched, the gateway of last resort can be used to forward the packet. In other words, it is the default route.

Another style of configuration for the default route uses the **ip default-network** command. This command is used most typically when you want to reach other Class A, B, or C networks by default but all the subnets of your own network are expected to be in your own routing tables. For example, imagine that the cloud next to Dist1 in Figure 7-5 has subnets of network 10.0.0.0 in it as well as other networks. (Dist1 could be an ISP router.) Dist1 already advertises a route to network 10.0.0.0 to R1, so R1 decides to use the same routing information for that route as its default route. To do that instead of using the **ip route 0.0.0.0 0.0.0.0 168.13.1.101** command, the **ip default-network 10.0.0.0** command is used on R1. R1 uses its route to network 10.0.0.0 as its default and advertises this route as a default route to other routers. Examples 7-11 and 7-12 show several details about R1 and R3.

Example 7-11 *R1's Use of the* ip default-network *Command*

```
R1#configure terminal
R1(config)#ip default-network 10.0.0.0
R1(config)#exit
R1#show ip route
Codes: C - connected, S - static, I - IGRP, R - RIP, M - mobile, B - BGP
       D - EIGRP, EX - EIGRP external, O - OSPF, IA - OSPF inter area
       N1 - OSPF NSSA external type 1, N2 - OSPF NSSA external type 2
       E1 - OSPF external type 1, E2 - OSPF external type 2, E - EGP
       i - IS-IS, L1 - IS-IS level-1, L2 - IS-IS level-2, ia - IS-IS inter area
       * - candidate default, U - per-user static route, o - ODR
       P - periodic downloaded static route

Gateway of last resort is 168.13.1.101 to network 10.0.0.0

     168.13.0.0/24 is subnetted, 5 subnets
R       168.13.200.0 [120/1] via 168.13.1.101, 00:00:12, TokenRing0
C       168.13.1.0 is directly connected, TokenRing0
R       168.13.3.0 [120/1] via 168.13.100.3, 00:00:00, Serial0.1
R       168.13.2.0 [120/1] via 168.13.100.2, 00:00:00, Serial0.1
C       168.13.100.0 is directly connected, Serial0.1
R*   10.0.0.0/8 [120/1] via 168.13.1.101, 00:00:12, TokenRing0
R1#
```

Example 7-12   *R3 Routing Table and* trace *Command Samples*

```
R3#show ip route
Codes: C - connected, S - static, I - IGRP, R - RIP, M - mobile, B - BGP
       D - EIGRP, EX - EIGRP external, O - OSPF, IA - OSPF inter area
       N1 - OSPF NSSA external type 1, N2 - OSPF NSSA external type 2
       E1 - OSPF external type 1, E2 - OSPF external type 2, E - EGP
       i - IS-IS, L1 - IS-IS level-1, L2 - IS-IS level-2, ia - IS-IS inter area
       * - candidate default, U - per-user static route, o - ODR
       P - periodic downloaded static route

Gateway of last resort is 168.13.100.1 to network 0.0.0.0

     168.13.0.0/24 is subnetted, 5 subnets
R       168.13.200.0 [120/2] via 168.13.100.1, 00:00:26, Serial0.1
R       168.13.1.0 [120/1] via 168.13.100.1, 00:00:26, Serial0.1
C       168.13.3.0 is directly connected, Ethernet0
R       168.13.2.0 [120/1] via 168.13.100.2, 00:00:18, Serial0.1
C       168.13.100.0 is directly connected, Serial0.1
R    10.0.0.0/8 [120/2] via 168.13.100.1, 00:00:26, Serial0.1
R*   0.0.0.0/0 [120/2] via 168.13.100.1, 00:00:26, Serial0.1
R3#trace 168.13.222.2

Type escape sequence to abort.
Tracing the route to 168.13.222.2

  1 168.13.100.1 68 msec 56 msec 52 msec
  2 168.13.1.101 52 msec 56 msec 52 msec
R3#trace 10.1.1.1

Type escape sequence to abort.
Tracing the route to 10.1.1.1

  1 168.13.100.1 68 msec 56 msec 52 msec
  2 168.13.1.101 48 msec 56 msec 52 msec
R3#
```

Both R1 and R3 have default routes, but they are shown differently in their respective routing tables. R1 shows a route to network 10.0.0.0 with an *, meaning that it is a candidate to be the default route. In R3, 0.0.0.0 shows up in the routing table as the candidate default route. R3 shows this information differently because RIP advertises default routes using network number 0.0.0.0. If IGRP or EIGRP were in use, there would be no route to 0.0.0.0 on R3, and network 10.0.0.0 would be the candidate default route. That's because IGRP and EIGRP would flag 10.0.0.0 as a candidate default route in their routing updates rather than advertise the special case of 0.0.0.0. The RIP protocol simply uses a different convention for how to advertise a default route.

Regardless of how the default route shows up—whether it's a gateway of last resort, a route to 0.0.0.0, or a route to some other network with an * beside it in the routing table—it is used according to the rules of classless or classful routing, depending on which is enabled on that router.

Classless Routing

Even if there is a default route in the routing table, it might not be used. Again consider the network shown in Figure 7-5, with the same default route. As shown in Example 7-13, on R3, a ping of 10.1.1.1 works when the default route is used. However, a ping of 168.13.200.1, which would seemingly need to use the default route as well, fails.

Example 7-13 *Classful Routing Causes One Ping to Fail*

```
R3#show ip route
Codes: C - connected, S - static, I - IGRP, R - RIP, M - mobile, B - BGP
       D - EIGRP, EX - EIGRP external, O - OSPF, IA - OSPF inter area
       N1 - OSPF NSSA external type 1, N2 - OSPF NSSA external type 2
       E1 - OSPF external type 1, E2 - OSPF external type 2, E - EGP
       i - IS-IS, L1 - IS-IS level-1, L2 - IS-IS level-2, ia - IS-IS inter area
       * - candidate default, U - per-user static route, o - ODR
       P - periodic downloaded static route

Gateway of last resort is 168.13.100.1 to network 0.0.0.0

     168.13.0.0/24 is subnetted, 4 subnets
R       168.13.1.0 [120/1] via 168.13.100.1, 00:00:13, Serial0.1
C       168.13.3.0 is directly connected, Ethernet0
R       168.13.2.0 [120/1] via 168.13.100.2, 00:00:06, Serial0.1
C       168.13.100.0 is directly connected, Serial0.1
R3#ping 10.1.1.1

Type escape sequence to abort.
Sending 5, 100-byte ICMP Echos to 10.1.1.1, timeout is 2 seconds:
!!!!!
Success rate is 100 percent (5/5), round-trip min/avg/max = 84/89/114 ms
R3#
R3#ping 168.13.200.1

Type escape sequence to abort.
Sending 5, 100-byte ICMP Echos to 168.13.200.1, timeout is 2 seconds:
...
Success rate is 0 percent (0/5)
```

So the **ping 10.1.1.1** command on R3 works, just as it should. However, the **ping 168.13.200.1** command does not work. Why?

Cisco IOS software uses either classful or classless routing logic when "matching" between a destination IP address and the routing table's routes. The key to knowing why one ping works, and another does not, is based on what Cisco IOS software thinks is a "match" of the routing table. With classful routing, the router first matches the Class A, B, or C network number in which a destination resides. If the Class A, B, or C network is found, Cisco IOS software then looks for the specific subnet number. If it isn't found, the packet is discarded, as is the case with the ICMP echoes sent with the **ping 168.13.200.1** command. However, with classful routing, if the packet does not match a Class A, B, or C network in the routing table, and a default route exists, the default route is indeed used—which is why R3 can forward the ICMP echoes sent by the successful **ping 10.1.1.1** command.

In short, with classful routing, the only time the default route is used is when a packet's destination Class A, B, or C network number is not in the routing table. With classless routing, the default is used whenever the packet does not match a more specific route in the routing table.

You can toggle between classful and classless routing with the **ip classless** and **no ip classless** global configuration commands. With classless routing, Cisco IOS software looks for the best match, ignoring class rules. If a default route exists, with classless routing, the packet always at least matches the default route. If a more specific route matches the packet's destination, that route is used. If not, the default route is used, regardless of whether the Class A, B, or C network that destination resides in is in the routing table.

Example 7-14 shows R3 changed to use classless routing, and the successful ping.

Example 7-14   *Classless Routing Allows Ping 168.13.200.1 to Now Succeed*

```
R3#conf t
Enter configuration commands, one per line.  End with CNTL/Z.
R3(config)#ip classless
R3(config)#^Z
R3#ping 168.13.200.1

Type escape sequence to abort.
Sending 5, 100-byte ICMP Echos to 168.13.200.1, timeout is 2 seconds:
!!!!!
Success rate is 100 percent (5/5), round-trip min/avg/max = 80/88/112 ms
R3#
```

The following lists close out this section with a more explicit description of what happens with classful routing that causes the ping in Example 7-13 to fail and what causes the ping in Example 7-14, using classless routing, to succeed.

The classful logic of Example 7-13 works like this:

1. I need to send a packet to 168.13.200.1.

2. I match Class B network 168.13.0.0 because I am using classful routing; there is a match.

3. I do not match a specific subnet of network 168.13.0.0 that contains 168.13.200.1.

4. Because I matched network 168.13.0.0, I cannot use the default route in this case, so I discard the packet.

The classless logic of Example 7-14 works like this:

1. I need to send a packet to 168.13.200.1.

2. I do not match a specific route that contains 168.13.200.1.

3. I use the default route only if there is not a more specific match. Because there is no match, I use the default route.

Foundation Summary

The "Foundation Summary" section lists the most important facts from the chapter. Although this section does not list everything that will be on the exam, a well-prepared CCNA candidate should at a minimum know all the details in each Foundation Summary before taking the exam.

- **Route summarization**—Route summarization reduces the size of the network's routing tables by causing a number of more specific routes to be replaced with a single route that includes all the IP addresses covered by the subnets in the original routes.

- **Variable-length subnet masking**—VLSM occurs when more than one mask is used in a single Class A, B, or C network. Although route summarization causes more than one mask to be used, requiring support for VLSM, you can also simply design a network to use multiple subnet masks.

Table 7-4 lists the routing protocols and their support (or nonsupport) of VLSM.

Table 7-4 *Interior IP Routing Protocol VLSM Support*

Routing Protocol	VLSM Support	Sends Mask/Prefix in Routing Updates	Route Summarization Support
RIP-1	No	No	No
IGRP	No	No	No
RIP-2	Yes	Yes	Yes
EIGRP	Yes	Yes	Yes
OSPF	Yes	Yes	Yes

The following list describes a generalized process by which you can summarize a group of subnets into one summary route. This process attempts to find the "best" summary that includes all subnets, as opposed to finding all summary routes that include all subnets:

Step 1   Find the longest part of the subnet numbers that are identical, moving left to right. (For our purposes, consider this first part the "in common" part.)

Step 2   The summary route's subnet number has the same value in the "in common" part of the summarized subnets and binary 0s in the second part.

Step 3   The subnet mask for the summary route has binary 1s in the "in common" part and binary 0s in the rest of the mask.

Step 4   Check your work by calculating the range of valid IP addresses implied by the new summary route, comparing the range to the summarized subnets. The new summary should encompass all IP addresses in the summarized subnets.

Table 7-5 lists the routing protocols, whether they transmit mask information, support VLSM, and are classless or classful.

Table 7-5 *Interior IP Routing Protocol: Classless or Classful?*

Routing Protocol	Classless	Sends Mask/Prefix in Routing Updates	VLSM Support	Route Summarization Support
RIP-1	No	No	No	No
IGRP	No	No	No	No
RIP-2	Yes	Yes	Yes	Yes
EIGRP	Yes	Yes	Yes	Yes
OSPF	Yes	Yes	Yes	Yes

- **Classless and classful routing protocols**—With classful routing protocols, the routing protocol must consider class rules; classless routing protocols do not. Specifically, classful routing protocols must automatically summarize routing information at network boundaries, meaning that they cannot support discontiguous networks. Classful routing protocols also cannot support VLSM. Classless routing protocols can support discontiguous networks, and support VLSM.

- **Classless and classful routing**—With classful routing, the only time the default route is used is when a packet's destination Class A, B, or C network number is not in the routing table. With classless routing, the default is used whenever the packet does not match a more specific route in the routing table.

Q&A

As mentioned in the Introduction, you have two choices for review questions. The following questions give you a bigger challenge than the exam because they are open-ended. By reviewing with this more-difficult question format, you can exercise your memory better and prove your conceptual and factual knowledge of the topics covered in this chapter. The answers to these questions are found in Appendix A.

For more practice with exam-like question formats, including multiple-choice questions and those using a router simulator, use the exam engine on the CD.

1. Name the two commands typically used to create a default route for a router.

2. Assume that subnets of network 10.0.0.0 are in the IP routing table in a router but that no other network and subnets are known, except that there is also a default route (0.0.0.0) in the routing table. A packet destined for 192.1.1.1 arrives at the router. What configuration command determines whether the default route is used in this case?

3. Assume that subnets of network 10.0.0.0 are in the IP routing table in a router but that no other network and its subnets are known, except that there is also a default route (0.0.0.0) in the routing table. A packet destined for 10.1.1.1 arrives at the router, but no known subnet of network 10 matches this destination address. What configuration command determines whether the default route is used in this case?

4. What feature supported by EIGRP allows it to support VLSM?

5. List the interior IP routing protocols that have autosummarization enabled by default. Which of these protocols allow autosummarization to be disabled using a configuration command?

6. Which interior IP routing protocols support route summarization?

7. Assume that several subnets of network 172.16.0.0 exist in a router's routing table. What must be true about these routes for the output of the **show ip route** command to list mask information only on the line that lists network 172.16.0.0 but that doesn't show mask information on each route for each subnet?

8. Router A and Router B are connected via a point-to-point serial link. Router A's interfaces use IP address 172.16.1.1, mask 255.255.255.0 and address 172.16.2.1, mask 255.255.255.0. Router B's interfaces use address 172.16.2.2, mask 255.255.255.0 and address 10.1.1.1, mask 255.255.254.0. Is VLSM in use? Explain your answer.

9. What is the smallest summarized route that summarizes the subnets 10.1.63.0, 10.1.64.0, 10.1.70.0, and 10.1.71.0, all with mask 255.255.255.0?

10.   What is the smallest summarized route that summarizes the subnets 10.5.111.0, 10.5.112.0, 10.5.113.0, and 10.5.114.0, all with mask 255.255.255.0?

11.   What is the smallest summarized route that summarizes the subnets 10.5.110.32, 10.5.110.48, and 10.5.110.64, all with mask 255.255.255.248?

12.   Of the routing protocols RIP-1, IGRP, EIGRP, and OSPF, which are classless?

13.   Of the routing protocols RIP-1, IGRP, EIGRP, and OSPF, which support VLSM?

14.   Of the routing protocols RIP-1, IGRP, EIGRP, and OSPF, which advertise mask information along with subnet numbers?

15.   Of the terms classful routing, classful routing protocol, classless routing, and classless routing protocol, which describe a feature that affects when a router uses the default route?

16.   What allows for the successful use of a discontiguous Class A, B, or C IP network— classful routing, classful routing protocol, classless routing, or classless routing protocol?

17.   Compare and contrast route summarization and autosummarization.

18.   Of the routing protocols RIP-1, IGRP, EIGRP, and OSPF, which use autosummarization by default and also cannot have autosummarization disabled?

19.   What command switches a router from classless routing to classful routing?

This chapter covers the following subjects:

- Scaling the IP Address Space for the Internet

- Miscellaneous TCP/IP Topics

CHAPTER 8

Advanced TCP/IP Topics

TCP/IP is undoubtedly the most important protocol suite in the networking world today. In the last few chapters, the coverage of TCP/IP has focused on issues related to routing protocols. However, other TCP/IP topics are important for the ICND exam as well. This chapter covers a variety of TCP/IP topics, some related and some totally unrelated—but all important.

This chapter starts by covering several topics related to improving IP addressing scalability. Classless Interdomain Routing (CIDR) reduces the size of Internet routing tables, much like route summarization, but specifically for routes in the Internet. Private addressing used with Network Address Translation (NAT) reduces the need for each company to have its own entire Class A, B, and C registered networks when connecting to the Internet, thereby delaying the day when the world runs out of registered IP addresses.

The second section of this chapter covers several unrelated topics, including ICMP, secondary IP addresses, FTP and TFTP, fragmentation, and routing between VLANs.

If you're studying for the CCNA exam, the single-exam method of getting your CCNA certification, you might be using both of my books, following the reading plan outlined in the Introduction to both books. If so, review your reading plan, and note that after this chapter, you should go back to CCNA INTRO Exam Certification Guide and pick up with Chapter 15, "Remote Access Technologies."

"Do I Know This Already?" Quiz

The purpose of the "Do I Know This Already?" quiz is to help you decide if you need to read the entire chapter. If you intend to read the entire chapter, you do not necessarily need to answer these questions now.

The 14-question quiz, derived from the major sections in the "Foundation Topics" section, helps you determine how to spend your limited study time.

Table 8-1 outlines the major topics discussed in this chapter and the "Do I Know This Already?" quiz questions that correspond to those topics.

Table 8-1 *"Do I Know This Already?" Foundation Topics Section-to-Question Mapping*

Foundations Topics Section	Questions Covered in This Section
Scaling the IP Address Space for the Internet	1–8
Miscellaneous TCP/IP Topics	9–14

CAUTION The goal of self-assessment is to gauge your mastery of the topics in this chapter. If you don't know the answer to a question or you're only partially sure of the answer, you should mark this question as wrong for purposes of the self-assessment. Giving yourself credit for an answer you guess correctly skews your self-assessment results and might give you a false sense of security.

1. What does CIDR stand for?

    a. Classful IP Default Routing

    b. Classful IP D-class Routing

    c. Classful Interdomain Routing

    d. Classless IP Default Routing

    e. Classless IP D-class Routing

    f. Classless Interdomain Routing

2. Which of the following summarized subnets are valid routes according to the main purpose of CIDR?

    a. 10.0.0.0 255.255.255.0

    b. 10.1.0.0 255.255.0.0

    c. 200.1.1.0 255.255.255.0

    d. 200.1.0.0 255.255.0.0

3. Which of the following are not private addresses according to RFC 1918?

    a. 172.31.1.1

    b. 172.33.1.1

    c. 10.255.1.1

    d. 10.1.255.1

    e. 191.168.1.1

4. With static NAT, performing translation for inside addresses only, what causes NAT table entries to be created?

   a. The first packet from the inside network to the outside network

   b. The first packet from the outside network to the inside network

   c. Configuration using the **ip nat inside source** command

   d. Configuration using the **ip nat outside source** command

5. With dynamic NAT, performing translation for inside addresses only, what causes NAT table entries to be created?

   a. The first packet from the inside network to the outside network

   b. The first packet from the outside network to the inside network

   c. Configuration using the **ip nat inside source** command

   d. Configuration using the **ip nat outside source** command

6. Which of the following commands identifies the inside local IP addresses when using dynamic NAT to translate only the source addresses of packets from a private network number?

   a. **ip nat inside source list 1 pool barney**

   b. **ip nat pool barney 200.1.1.1 200.1.1.254 netmask 255.255.255.0**

   c. **ip nat inside**

   d. **ip nat inside 200.1.1.1 200.1.1.2**

   e. None of the above

7. Which of the following commands identifies the outside local IP addresses when using dynamic NAT to translate only the source addresses of packets from a private network number?

   a. **ip nat inside source list 1 pool barney**

   b. **ip nat pool barney 200.1.1.1 200.1.1.254 netmask 255.255.255.0**

   c. **ip nat inside**

   d. **ip nat inside 200.1.1.1 200.1.1.2**

   e. None of the above

8. Imagine that an Ethernet interface on a router has already been configured with IP address 10.1.1.1, mask 255.255.255.0. Which of the following commands adds a secondary IP address to the interface?

   a. ip address 10.1.1.2 255.255.255.0

   b. ip address 10.1.1.254 255.255.255.0

   c. ip address 10.1.2.1 255.255.255.0

   d. secondary ip address 10.1.2.1 255.255.255.0

   e. ip secondary address 10.1.2.1 255.255.255.0

   f. ip secondary 10.1.2.1 255.255.255.0

   g. ip address 10.1.2.1 255.255.255.0 secondary

9. Which of the following file transfer protocols, defined in various Internet RFCs, provides the most features?

   a. FTP

   b. TFTP

   c. FTPO

   d. BFTP

10. Imagine that Fred is a PC attached to an Ethernet, and that its default router, R1, is attached to the same Ethernet. R1 has a point-to-point serial link to R2, which has an Ethernet attached, to which PC Barney is attached. The MTU of each Ethernet has the default value. What must be true for R1 to fragment packets sent from Fred to Barney?

   a. The serial link's MTU must be less than 1500.

   b. The serial link's MTU must be less than 1518.

   c. The serial link's MTU must be less than 1526.

   d. R1 must have the **fragment on** command configured on the serial interface.

11. Router1 has a FastEthernet interface 0/0 with IP address 10.1.1.1. The interface is connected to a switch. This connection is then migrated to ISL. Which of the following commands could be useful to configure Router1 for ISL?

    a. interface fastethernet 0/0.4

    b. isl enable

    c. isl enable 4

    d. trunking enable

    e. trunking enable 4

    f. encapsulation isl

    g. encapsulation isl 4

12. What is the meaning of "." in the output of a **ping** command?

    a. The ping worked.

    b. The ping did not work because an echo request could not be sent.

    c. The ping did not work because an echo reply was not received.

    d. The ping did not work because an ICMP message was returned implying that the lifetime was exceeded.

    e. The ping did not work because an ICMP message was returned implying that there was no route to the subnet.

13. What is the meaning of "U" in the output of a **ping** command?

    a. The ping worked.

    b. The ping did not work because an echo request could not be sent.

    c. The ping did not work because an echo reply was not received.

    d. The ping did not work because an ICMP message was returned implying that the lifetime was exceeded.

    e. The ping did not work because an ICMP message was returned implying that there was no route to the subnet.

14. What ICMP message code(s) does the **trace** command rely on?

    a. Host Unreachable

    b. Subnet Unreachable

    c. Time to Live Exceeded

    d. Can't Fragment

The answers to the "Do I Know This Already?" quiz appear in Appendix A. The suggested choices for your next step are as follows:

- **11 or less overall score**—Read the entire chapter. This includes the "Foundation Topics," "Foundation Summary," and "Q&A" sections.

- **12, 13, or 14 overall score**—If you want more review on these topics, skip to the "Foundation Summary" section and then go to the "Q&A" section. Otherwise, move to the next chapter.

Foundation Topics

Scaling the IP Address Space for the Internet

The original design for the Internet required every organization to ask for, and receive, one or more registered IP network numbers. The people administering the program ensured that none of the IP networks were reused. As long as every organization used only IP addresses inside its own registered network numbers, IP addresses would never be duplicated, and IP routing could work well.

Connecting to the Internet using only a registered network number, or several registered network numbers, worked very well for a while. In the early to mid-1990s, it became apparent that the Internet was growing so fast that all IP network numbers would be assigned by the mid-1990s! Concern arose that the available networks would be completely assigned, and some organizations would not be able to connect to the Internet.

One solution to the IP network scalability problem was to increase the size of the IP address. This one fact was the most compelling reason for the advent of IP Version 6 (IPv6). (This book discusses Version 4 [IPv4]. Version 5 was defined for experimental reasons and was never deployed.) IPv6 calls for a much larger address structure so that the convention of all organizations using unique groupings (networks) of IP addresses would still be reasonable. The numbers of IPv6-style networks would reach into the trillions and beyond. That solution is still technically viable and possibly one day will be used, because IPv6 is still evolving in the marketplace. (The same kind of problem has even happened with telephone numbers in North America. The U.S. Federal Communications Commission (FCC) has been working toward moving from ten-digit phone numbers to 12-digit phone numbers for the last few years.)

Three other IP functions have been used to reduce the need for IPv4 registered network numbers. Network Address Translation (NAT), along with a feature called *private addressing,* allows organizations to use unregistered IP network numbers internally and still communicate well with the Internet. Classless Interdomain Routing (CIDR) allows Internet service providers (ISPs) to reduce the wasting of IP addresses by assigning a company a subset of a network number rather than the entire network. CIDR also can allow ISPs to summarize routes such that multiple Class A, B, or C networks match a single route, which helps reduce the size of Internet routing tables.

CIDR

CIDR is a convention defined in RFC 1817 (www.ietf.org/rfc/rfc1817.txt) that calls for aggregating multiple network numbers into a single routing entity. CIDR was created to help the scalability of Internet routers. Imagine a router in the Internet with a route to every Class A, B, and C network on the planet! There are more than 2 million Class C networks alone! By aggregating the routes, fewer routes would need to exist in the routing table.

Figure 8-1 shows a typical case of how CIDR might be used to consolidate routes to multiple Class C networks into a single route.

Figure 8-1 *Typical Use of CIDR*

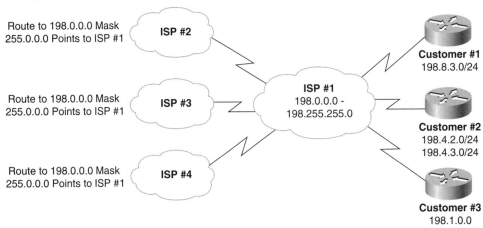

Imagine that ISP #1 owns Class C networks 198.0.0.0 through 198.255.255.0 (these might look funny, but they are valid Class C network numbers). Without CIDR, all other ISPs' routing tables would have a separate route to each of the 2^{16} Class C networks that begin with 198. With CIDR, as shown in the figure, the other ISPs' routers have a single route to 198.0.0.0/8—in other words, a route to all hosts whose IP address begins with 198. More than two million Class C networks alone exist, but CIDR has helped Internet routers reduce their routing tables to a more manageable size—in the range of 120,000 routes by mid-2003.

By using a routing protocol that exchanges the mask as well as the subnet/network number, a *classless* view of the number can be attained. In other words, treat the grouping as a math problem, ignoring the Class A, B, and C rules. For instance, 198.0.0.0/8 (198.0.0.0, mask 255.0.0.0) defines a set of addresses whose first 8 bits are equal to decimal 198. ISP #1 advertises this route to the other ISPs, who need a route only to 198.0.0.0/8. In its routers, ISP #1 knows which Class C networks are at which customer sites. This is how CIDR gives Internet routers a much more scalable routing table—by reducing the number of entries in the tables.

For CIDR to work as shown in Figure 8-1, ISPs need to be in control of consecutive network numbers. Today, IP networks are allocated by administrative authorities for various regions of the world. The regions in turn allocate consecutive ranges of network numbers to particular ISPs in those regions. This allows summarization of multiple networks into a single route, as shown in Figure 8-1.

CIDR also helps reduce the chance of our running out of IP addresses for new companies connecting to the Internet. Furthermore, CIDR allows an ISP to allocate a subset of a Class A, B, or C network to a single customer. For instance, imagine that ISP #1's Customer #1 needs only ten IP addresses and that Customer #3 needs 25 IP addresses. ISP #1 does something like this: It assigns IP subnet 198.8.3.16/28, with assignable addresses 198.8.3.17 to 198.8.3.30, to Customer #1. For Customer #3, ISP #1 suggests 198.8.3.32/27, with 30 assignable addresses (198.8.3.33 to 198.8.3.62). (Feel free to check the math with the IP addressing algorithms discussed in Chapter 4, "IP Addressing and Subnetting.")

CIDR helps prevent the wasting of IP addresses, thereby reducing the need for registered IP network numbers. Instead of two customers consuming two whole Class C networks, each consumes a small portion of a single Class C network. At the same time, CIDR, along with the intelligent administration of consecutive network numbers to each ISP, allows the Internet routing table to support a much smaller routing table in Internet routers than would otherwise be required.

Private Addressing

Some computers will never be connected to the Internet. These computers' IP addresses could be duplicates of registered IP addresses in the Internet. When designing the IP addressing convention for such a network, an organization could pick and use any network number(s) it wanted, and all would be well. For instance, you can buy a few routers, connect them in your office, and configure IP addresses in network 1.0.0.0, and it would work. The IP addresses you use might be duplicates of real IP addresses in the Internet, but if all you want to do is learn on the lab in your office, everything will be fine.

When building a private network that will have no Internet connectivity, you can use IP network numbers called *private internets,* as defined in RFC 1918, "Address Allocation for Private Internets" (www.ietf.org/rfc/rfc1918.txt). This RFC defines a set of networks that will never be assigned to any organization as a registered network number. Instead of using someone else's registered network numbers, you can use numbers in a range that are not used by anyone else in the public Internet. Table 8-2 shows the private address space defined by RFC 1918.

Table 8-2 *RFC 1918 Private Address Space*

Range of IP Addresses	Class of Networks	Number of Networks
10.0.0.0 to 10.255.255.255	A	1
172.16.0.0 to 172.31.255.255	B	16
192.168.0.0 to 192.168.255.255	C	256

In other words, any organization can use these network numbers. However, no organization is allowed to advertise these networks using a routing protocol on the Internet.

You might be wondering why you would bother to reserve special private network numbers when it doesn't matter if the addresses are duplicates. Well, as it turns out, you can use private addressing in a network, and use the Internet at the same time, as long as you use Network Address Translation (NAT).

Network Address Translation

NAT, defined in RFC 1631, allows a host that does not have a valid registered IP address to communicate with other hosts through the Internet. The hosts might be using private addresses or addresses assigned to another organization. In either case, NAT allows these addresses that are not Internet-ready to continue to be used and still allows communication with hosts across the Internet.

NAT achieves its goal by using a valid registered IP address to represent the private address to the rest of the Internet. The NAT function changes the private IP addresses to publicly registered IP addresses inside each IP packet, as shown in Figure 8-2.

Figure 8-2 *NAT IP Address Swapping: Private Addressing*

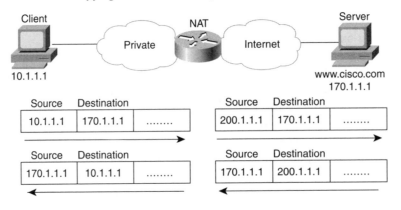

Notice that the router, performing NAT, changes the packet's source IP address when leaving the private organization and the destination address in each packet forwarded back into the private network. (Network 200.1.1.0 is registered in Figure 8-2.) The NAT feature, configured in the router labeled NAT, performs the translation.

Cisco IOS software supports several variations of NAT. The next few pages cover the concepts behind several of these variations. The section after that covers the configuration related to each option.

Static NAT

Static NAT works just like the example shown in Figure 8-2, but with the IP addresses statically mapped to each other. To help you understand the implications of static NAT, and to explain several key terms, Figure 8-3 shows a similar example with more information.

Figure 8-3 *Static NAT Showing Inside Local and Global Addresses*

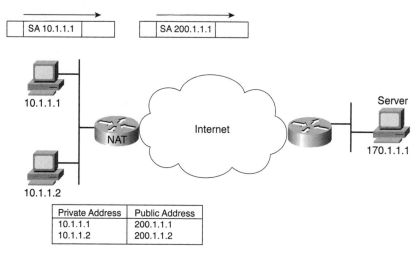

First, the concepts. The company's ISP has assigned it registered network 200.1.1.0. Therefore, the NAT router must make the private IP addresses look like they are in network 200.1.1.0. To do so, the NAT router changes the source IP addresses in the packets going left to right in the figure.

In this example, the NAT router changes the source address ("SA" in the figure) of 10.1.1.1 to 200.1.1.1. With static NAT, the NAT router simply configures a one-to-one mapping between the private address and the registered address that is used on its behalf. The NAT router has statically configured a mapping between private address 10.1.1.1 and public, registered address 200.1.1.1.

Supporting two IP hosts in the private network requires a second static one-to-one mapping using a second IP address in the public address range. For instance, to support 10.1.1.2, the router statically maps 10.1.1.2 to 200.1.1.2. Because the enterprise has a single registered Class C network, it can support at most 254 private IP addresses with NAT.

The terminology used with NAT, particularly with configuration, can be a little confusing. Notice in Figure 8-3 that the NAT table lists the private IP addresses as "private" and the public, registered addresses from network 200.1.1.0 as "public." Cisco uses the term *inside local* for the private IP addresses in this example and *inside global* for the public IP addresses.

In Cisco terminology, the enterprise network that uses private addresses, and therefore that needs NAT, is the "inside" part of the network. The Internet side of the NAT function is the "outside" part of the network. A host that needs NAT (such as 10.1.1.1 in the example) has the IP address it uses inside the network, and it needs an IP address to represent it in the outside network. So, because the host essentially needs two different addresses to represent it, you need two terms. Cisco calls the private IP address used in the "inside" network the inside local address and the address used to represent the host to the rest of the Internet the inside global address. (Although Cisco doesn't use these exact terms, sometimes substituting "private" for "local" and "public" for "global" makes a little more sense to many people. Just keep all terms in mind for the exam.)

Figure 8-4 repeats the same example, with some of the terminology shown.

Figure 8-4 *Static NAT Terminology*

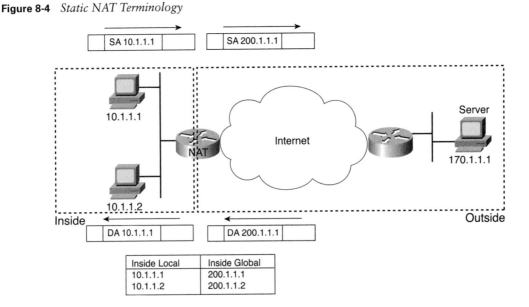

Most typical NAT features change only the IP address of "inside" hosts. Therefore, the current NAT table shown in Figure 8-4 shows the inside local and corresponding inside global registered addresses. However, the outside host IP address can also be changed with NAT. When that occurs, the terms *outside local* and *outside global* are used to denote the IP address used to represent that host in the inside network and the outside network, respectively. An example later in this section explains more about translating outside addresses. Table 8-3 summarizes the terminology and meanings.

Table 8-3 *NAT Addressing Terms*

Term	Meaning
Inside local	In a typical NAT design, the term "inside" refers to an address used for a host inside an enterprise. An inside local is the actual IP address assigned to a host in the private enterprise network. A more descriptive term might be "inside private," because when using RFC 1918 addresses in an enterprise, the inside local represents the host inside the enterprise, and it is a private RFC 1918 address.
Inside global	In a typical NAT design, the term "inside" refers to an address used for a host inside an enterprise. NAT uses an inside global address to represent the inside host as the packet is sent through the outside network, typically the Internet. A NAT router changes the source IP address of a packet sent by an inside host from an inside local address to an inside global address as the packet goes from the inside to the outside network. A more descriptive term might be "inside public," because when using RFC 1918 addresses in an enterprise, the inside global represents the inside host with a public IP address that can be used for routing in the public Internet.
Outside global	In a typical NAT design, the term "outside" refers to an address used for a host outside an enterprise—in other words, in the Internet. An outside global is the actual IP address assigned to a host that resides in the outside network, typically the Internet. A more descriptive term might be "outside public," because the outside global represents the outside host with a public IP address that can be used for routing in the public Internet.
Outside local	In a typical NAT design, the term "outside" refers to an address used for a host outside an enterprise—in other words, in the Internet. NAT uses an outside local address to represent the outside host as the packet is sent through the private enterprise network (inside network). A NAT router changes a packet's destination IP address, sent from an inside host to the outside global address, as the packet goes from the inside to the outside network. A more descriptive term might be "outside private," because when using RFC 1918 addresses in an enterprise, the outside local represents the outside host with a private IP address from RFC 1918.

Dynamic NAT

Dynamic NAT has some similarities and differences compared to static NAT. Like static NAT, the NAT router creates a one-to-one mapping between an inside local and inside global address and changes the IP addresses in packets as they exit and enter the inside network. However, the mapping of an inside local address to an inside global address happens dynamically.

Dynamic NAT sets up a pool of possible inside global addresses and defines criteria for the set of inside local IP addresses whose traffic should be translated with NAT. For instance, in Figure 8-5, a pool of five inside global IP addresses has been established—200.1.1.1 through 200.1.1.5. NAT has also been configured to translate any inside local addresses that start with 10.1.1.

Figure 8-5 *Dynamic NAT*

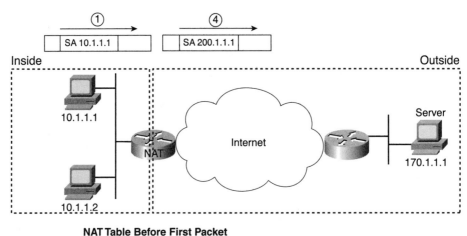

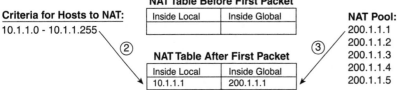

The numbers 1, 2, 3, and 4 in the figure refer to a sequence of events:

1. Host 10.1.1.1 sends its first packet to the server at 170.1.1.1.

2. As the packet enters the NAT router, the router applies some matching logic to decide if the packet should have NAT applied. Because the logic has been configured to NAT inside local addresses that start with 10.1.1, the router adds an entry in the NAT table for 10.1.1.1 as an inside local address.

3. The NAT router needs to allocate an IP address from the pool of valid inside global addresses. It picks the first one available (200.1.1.1 in this case) and adds it to the NAT table to complete the entry.

4. The NAT router translates the source IP address and forwards the packet.

The dynamic entry stays in the table as long as traffic flows occasionally. You can configure a timeout value that defines how long the router should wait, having not translated any packets with that address, before removing the dynamic entry. You can also manually clear the dynamic entries from the table using the **clear ip nat translation** * command.

NAT can be configured with more IP addresses in the inside local address list than in the inside global address pool. In the next section, you will learn about a feature called Port Address Translation (PAT), which allows all flows from the inside hosts to be supported by NAT, even when the inside global pool is smaller than the number of inside local addresses. However, without PAT, NAT can concurrently support only the number of hosts defined in the NAT pool.

When the number of registered public IP addresses is defined in the inside global address pool, as shown in Figure 8-5, the router allocates addresses from the pool until all are allocated. If a new packet arrives, and it needs a NAT entry, but all the pooled IP addresses are in use, the router simply discards the packet. The user must try again until a NAT entry times out, at which point the NAT function works for the next host that sends a packet. Essentially, the inside global pool of addresses needs to be as large as the maximum number of concurrent hosts that need to use the Internet at the same time—unless you use PAT.

Overloading NAT with Port Address Translation (PAT)

Some networks need to have most, if not all, IP hosts reach the Internet. If that network uses private IP addresses, the NAT router needs a very large set of registered IP addresses. With static NAT, for each private IP host that needs Internet access, you need a publicly registered IP address—completely defeating the advantage of using NAT. Dynamic NAT lessens the problem to some degree, but you might imagine that a large percentage of the IP hosts in a network will need Internet access throughout that company's normal business hours—once again requiring a large number of registered IP addresses.

Overloading allows NAT to scale to support many clients with only a few public IP addresses. The key to understanding how overloading works is to recall how ports are used in TCP/IP. Figure 8-6 details an example that helps make the logic behind overloading more obvious.

Figure 8-6   *Three TCP Connections: From Three Different Hosts, and from One Host*

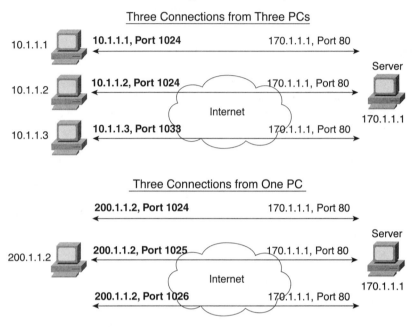

The top part of the figure shows a network with three different hosts connecting to a web server using TCP. The bottom half of the figure shows the same network later in the day, with three TCP connections from the same client. All six connections connect to the server IP address (170.1.1.1) and port (80, the well-known port for web services). In each case, the server differentiates between the various connections because their combined IP address and port numbers are unique.

NAT takes advantage of the fact that the server really doesn't care if it has one connection each to three different hosts or three connections to a single host IP address. So, to support lots of inside local IP addresses with only a few inside global, publicly registered IP addresses, NAT overload uses Port Address Translation (PAT). Instead of just translating the IP address, it also translates the port number. Figure 8-7 outlines the logic.

When NAT creates the dynamic mapping, it selects not only an inside global IP address but also a unique port number to use with that address. The NAT router keeps a NAT table entry for every unique combination of inside local IP address and port, with translation to the inside global address and a unique port number associated with the inside global address. And because the port number field has 16 bits, NAT overload can use more than 65,000 port numbers, allowing it to scale well without needing very many registered IP addresses—in many cases, needing only one.

Figure 8-7 *NAT Overload Using PAT*

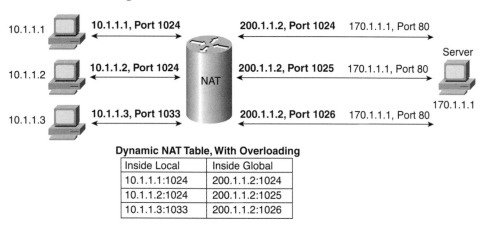

Dynamic NAT Table, With Overloading

Inside Local	Inside Global
10.1.1.1:1024	200.1.1.2:1024
10.1.1.2:1024	200.1.1.2:1025
10.1.1.3:1033	200.1.1.2:1026

Translating Overlapping Addresses

NAT also can be used when the private organization is not using private addressing but instead is using a network number registered to another company.

> **NOTE** A client company of mine once did just that. The company was using a network number registered to Cabletron, which the company saw used in a presentation by an ex-Cabletron employee who was working at 3COM. The 3COM employee explained IP addressing using the Cabletron registered network number because he was accustomed to it. My client liked the design and took him at his word—literally.

If one company inappropriately uses a network number that is registered appropriately to a different company, and they both connect to the Internet, NAT can be used to solve the problem. NAT translates both the source and the destination IP addresses in this case.

For example, consider Figure 8-8, in which Company A uses a network that is registered to Cisco (170.1.0.0).

With an overlapping address space, a client in Company A cannot send a packet to the legitimate IP host 170.1.1.1—or, if it did, the packet would never get to the real 170.1.1.1. Why? The routing tables inside the company (on the left) probably have a route matching 170.1.1.1 in its routing table. For host 170.1.1.10 in the figure, it is in the subnet in which the "private" 170.1.1.1 would reside, so host 170.1.1.10 would not even try to forward packets destined for 170.1.1.1 to a router. Instead, it would forward them directly to host 170.1.1.1, assuming it was on the same LAN!

Figure 8-8 *NAT IP Address Swapping: Unregistered Networks*

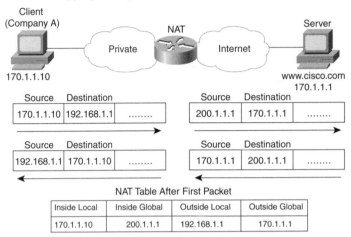

NAT can solve this problem, but both the source and the destination addresses must be changed as the packet passes through the NAT router. In Figure 8-8, notice that the original packet sent by the client has a destination address of 192.168.1.1. That address, called the outside local address, represents the registered IP address 170.1.1.1 on the left side of the network. "Outside" means that the address represents the host that physically sits in the "outside" part of the network. "Local" means that this address represents the host on the private side of the network.

As the packet passes through the NAT router (left to right), the source address is changed, just like in the previous example. However, the destination address is also changed—in this case, to 170.1.1.1. The destination address is also called the outside global address at this point, because it represents a host that is always physically on the outside network, and the address is the global, publicly registered IP address that can be routed through the Internet.

The NAT configuration includes a static mapping between the real IP address (outside global), 170.1.1.1, and the private IP address (outside local) used to represent it inside the private network—192.168.1.1.

Because the client initiates a connection to the server on the right, the NAT router not only must translate addresses, but it also must modify DNS responses. The client, for instance, performs a DNS request for www.cisco.com. When the DNS reply comes back (right to left) past the NAT router, NAT changes the DNS reply so that the client in the company thinks that www.cisco.com's IP address is 192.168.1.1.

Today, given a choice, companies tend to simply use private addressing to avoid the need to translate both IP addresses in each packet. Also, the NAT router needs a static entry for every server in the overlapped network number—a potentially painstaking task. By using private addresses, you can use NAT to connect the network to the Internet, reduce the number of registered IP addresses needed, and have to perform only the NAT function for the private address in each packet.

Table 8-4 summarizes the use of NAT terminology in Figure 8-8.

Table 8-4 *NAT Addressing Terms as Used in Figure 8-8*

Term	Value in Figure 8-8
Inside local	170.1.1.10
Inside global	200.1.1.1
Outside global	170.1.1.1
Outside local	192.168.1.1

NAT Configuration

In this section, you will read about how to configure several variations of NAT, along with the **show** and **debug** commands used to troubleshoot NAT. Table 8-5 lists the NAT configuration commands. Table 8-6 lists the EXEC commands related to NAT.

Table 8-5 *NAT Configuration Commands*

Command	Configuration Mode
ip nat {**inside**	**outside**}	Interface subcommand
ip nat inside source {**list** {*access-list-number*	*access-list-name*}	**route-map** *name*} {**interface** *type number*	**pool** *pool-name*} [**overload**]	Global command
ip nat inside destination list {*access-list-number*	*access-list-name*} **pool** *pool-name*	Global command
ip nat outside source {**list** {*access-list-number*	*access-list-name*}	**route-map** *name*} **pool** *pool-name* [**add-route**]	Global command
ip nat pool *name start-ip end-ip* {**netmask** *netmask*	**prefix-length** *prefix-length*} [**type rotary**]	Global command
ip nat inside source {**list** {*access-list-number*	*access-list-name*}	**route-map** *name*} {**interface** *type number*	**pool** *pool-name*} [**overload**]	Global command

Table 8-6 *NAT EXEC Commands*

Command	Description
show ip nat statistics	Lists counters for packets and NAT table entries, as well as basic configuration information.
show ip nat translations [**verbose**]	Displays the NAT table.
clear ip nat translation {*****	[**inside** *global-ip local-ip*] [**outside** *local-ip global-ip*]}	Clears all or some of the dynamic entries in the NAT table, depending on which parameters are used.
clear ip nat translation *protocol* **inside** *global-ip global-port local-ip local-port* [**outside** *local-ip global-ip*]	Clears some of the dynamic entries in the NAT table, depending on which parameters are used.
debug ip nat	Issues a log message describing each packet whose IP address is translated with NAT.

Static NAT Configuration

Static NAT configuration, as compared to the other variations of NAT, requires the fewest configuration steps. Each static mapping between a local (private) address and a global (public) address must be configured. Then, each interface needs to be identified as either an inside or outside interface.

Figure 8-9 shows the familiar network used in the description of static NAT earlier in this chapter.

Figure 8-9 *NAT IP Address Swapping: Private Networks*

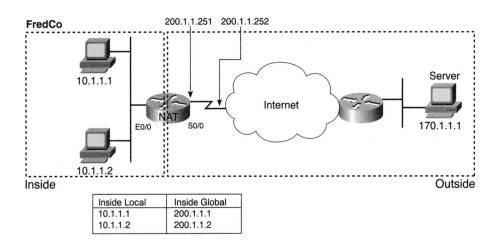

Inside Local	Inside Global
10.1.1.1	200.1.1.1
10.1.1.2	200.1.1.2

In Figure 8-9, you can see that FredCo has obtained Class C network 200.1.1.0 as a registered network number. That entire network, with mask 255.255.255.0, is configured on the serial link between FredCo and the Internet. With a point-to-point serial link, only two of the 254 valid IP addresses in that network are consumed, leaving 252 addresses for use with static NAT. Example 8-1 lists the NAT configuration, using 200.1.1.1 and 200.1.1.2 for the two static NAT mappings.

Example 8-1 *Static NAT Configuration*

```
NAT# show running-config
!
! Lines omitted for brevity
!
interface Ethernet0/0
 ip address 10.1.1.3 255.255.255.0
 ip nat inside
```

Example 8-1 *Static NAT Configuration (Continued)*

```
!
interface Serial0/0
 ip address 200.1.1.251 255.255.255.0
 ip nat outside
!
ip nat inside source static 10.1.1.2 200.1.1.2
ip nat inside source static 10.1.1.1 200.1.1.1

NAT# show ip nat translations
Pro Inside global      Inside local      Outside local      Outside global
--- 200.1.1.1          10.1.1.1          ---                ---
--- 200.1.1.2          10.1.1.2          ---                ---

NAT# show ip nat statistics
Total active translations: 2 (2 static, 0 dynamic; 0 extended)
Outside interfaces:
  Serial0/0
Inside interfaces:
  Ethernet0/0
Hits: 100  Misses: 0
Expired translations: 0
Dynamic mappings:
```

The static mappings are created using the **ip nat inside source static** command. The **inside** keyword means that NAT translates addresses for hosts on the inside part of the network. The **source** keyword means that NAT translates the source IP address of packets coming into its inside interfaces. **static** means that the parameters define a static entry, which should never be removed from the NAT table due to timeout. Because the design calls for two hosts, 10.1.1.1 and 10.1.1.2, to have Internet access, two **ip nat inside** commands are needed.

After creating the static NAT entries, the router needs to know which interfaces are "inside" and which are "outside." The **ip nat inside** and **ip nat outside** interface subcommands identify each interface appropriately.

A couple of **show** commands list the most important information about NAT. The **show ip nat translations** command lists the two static NAT entries created in the configuration. The **show ip nat statistics** command lists statistics, listing things such as the number of currently active translation table entries. The statistics also include the number of hits, which increments for every packet for which NAT must translate addresses.

Dynamic NAT Configuration

As you might imagine, dynamic NAT configuration differs in some ways from static NAT, but it has some similarities as well. Dynamic NAT still requires that each interface be identified as either an inside or outside interface. However, the static mapping is no longer required. Dynamic NAT uses the **ip nat inside** command to identify which inside local (private) IP addresses need to have their addresses translated. With the **ip nat pool command**, dynamic NAT defines the set of IP addresses used as inside global (public) addresses.

The next example uses the same network topology as the previous example (see Figure 8-9). In this case, the same two inside local addresses, 10.1.1.1 and 10.1.1.2, need translation. The same inside global addresses used in the static mappings in the previous example, 200.1.1.1 and 200.1.1.2, are instead placed in a pool of dynamically assignable inside global addresses. Example 8-2 shows the configuration, as well as some **show** commands.

Example 8-2 *Dynamic NAT Configuration*

```
NAT# show running-config
!
! Lines omitted for brevity
!
interface Ethernet0/0
 ip address 10.1.1.3 255.255.255.0
 ip nat inside
!
interface Serial0/0
 ip address 200.1.1.251 255.255.255.0
 ip nat outside
!
ip nat pool fred 200.1.1.1 200.1.1.2 netmask 255.255.255.252
ip nat inside source list 1 pool fred
!
access-list 1 permit 10.1.1.2
access-list 1 permit 10.1.1.1
!
NAT# show ip nat translations

NAT# show ip nat statistics
Total active translations: 0 (0 static, 0 dynamic; 0 extended)
Outside interfaces:
  Serial0/0
Inside interfaces:
  Ethernet0/0
Hits: 0  Misses: 0
Expired translations: 0
Dynamic mappings:
-- Inside Source
access-list 1 pool fred refcount 0
```

Example 8-2   *Dynamic NAT Configuration (Continued)*

```
  pool fred: netmask 255.255.255.252
     start 200.1.1.1 end 200.1.1.2
     type generic, total addresses 2, allocated 0 (0%), misses 0
  !
  ! Telnet from 10.1.1.1 to 170.1.1.1 happened next; not shown
  !
  NAT# show ip nat statistics
  Total active translations: 1 (0 static, 1 dynamic; 0 extended)
  Outside interfaces:
    Serial0/0
  Inside interfaces:
    Ethernet0/0
  Hits: 69  Misses: 1
  Expired translations: 0
  Dynamic mappings:
  -- Inside Source
  access-list 1 pool fred refcount 1
   pool fred: netmask 255.255.255.252
      start 200.1.1.1 end 200.1.1.2
      type generic, total addresses 2, allocated 1 (50%), misses 0
  NAT# show ip nat translations
  Pro Inside global     Inside local     Outside local     Outside global
  --- 200.1.1.1         10.1.1.1         ---               ---
  NAT# clear ip nat translation *


  !
  ! telnet from 10.1.1.2 to 170.1.1.1 happened next; not shown
  !
  NAT# show ip nat translations
  Pro Inside global     Inside local     Outside local     Outside global
  --- 200.1.1.1         10.1.1.2         ---               ---
  !
  ! Telnet from 10.1.1.1 to 170.1.1.1 happened next; not shown
  !

  NAT# debug ip nat
  IP NAT debugging is on

  01:25:44: NAT: s=10.1.1.1->200.1.1.2, d=170.1.1.1 [45119]
  01:25:44: NAT: s=170.1.1.1, d=200.1.1.2->10.1.1.1 [8228]
  01:25:56: NAT: s=10.1.1.1->200.1.1.2, d=170.1.1.1 [45120]
  01:25:56: NAT: s=170.1.1.1, d=200.1.1.2->10.1.1.1 [0]
```

The configuration for dynamic NAT includes a pool of inside global addresses, as well as an IP access list to define the inside local addresses for which NAT is performed. The **ip nat pool** command lists the first and last numbers in a range of inside global addresses. For instance, if the pool needed ten addresses, the command might have listed 200.1.1.1 and 200.1.1.10. This command also lists a subnet mask, but it has no real effect, because the first and last IP addresses are listed.

Like static NAT, dynamic NAT uses the **ip nat inside source** command. Unlike static NAT, the dynamic NAT version of this command refers to the name of the NAT pool it wants to use for inside global addresses—in this case, fred. It also refers to an IP Access Control List (ACL), which defines the matching logic for inside local IP addresses. The command **ip nat inside source list 1 pool fred** maps between hosts matched by ACL 1 and the pool called fred, which was created by the **ip nat pool fred** command.

> **NOTE**   Chapter 12, "IP Access Control List Security," covers the details of how IP ACLs work. For now, just know that ACL 1 in this example matches packets whose source IP addresses are either 10.1.1.1 or 10.1.1.2 and does not match any other packets.

Example 8-2 contains several **show** commands. Several instances of **show** command output change based on what has happened on the two client host computers. Comments describe what has been done on the two hosts that causes a change in the output of the **show** commands.

First, the **show ip nat translations** and **show ip nat statistics** commands display either nothing or minimal configuration information. Because neither host 10.1.1.1 nor 10.1.1.2 has sent any packets, NAT has not created any dynamic entries in the NAT table or translated addresses in any packets.

After the Telnet from 10.1.1.1 to 170.1.1.1, the statistics show that a dynamic NAT entry has been added. The NAT table shows a single entry, mapping 10.1.1.1 to 200.1.1.1. The NAT table entry times out after a period of inactivity. However, to force the entry out of the table, the **clear ip nat translation** command can be used. As shown in Table 8-6, this command has several variations. Example 8-2 uses the brute-force option—**clear ip nat translation ***. With this command, all dynamic NAT entries are removed.

After clearing the NAT entry, host 10.1.1.2 Telnets to 170.1.1.1. The **show ip nat translations** command now shows a mapping between 10.1.1.2 and 200.1.1.1. Because 200.1.1.1 is no longer allocated in the NAT table, the NAT router can allocate it for the next NAT request.

Finally, at the end of Example 8-2, you see the output from the **debug ip nat** command. This command causes the router to issue a message every time a packet has its address translated for NAT. You generate the output results by entering a few lines from the Telnet connection from 10.1.1.2 to 170.1.1.1. Notice that the output implies a translation from 10.1.1.2 to 200.1.1.1, but it does not imply any translation of the outside address.

NAT Overload Configuration (PAT Configuration)

NAT overload, as mentioned earlier, allows NAT to use a single IP address to support many inside local IP addresses. By essentially translating the private IP address and port number to a single inside global address, but with a unique port number, NAT can support many private hosts with only a single public, global address.

Figure 8-10 shows the same familiar network, with a few changes. In this case, the ISP has given FredCo a subset of network 200.1.1.0—CIDR subnet 200.1.1.248/30. In other words, FredCo has two usable addresses—200.1.1.249 and 200.1.1.250. These addresses are used on either end of the serial link between FredCo and its ISP. The NAT feature on FredCo's router translates all NAT addresses to its serial IP address, 200.1.1.249.

Figure 8-10   *NAT Overload and PAT*

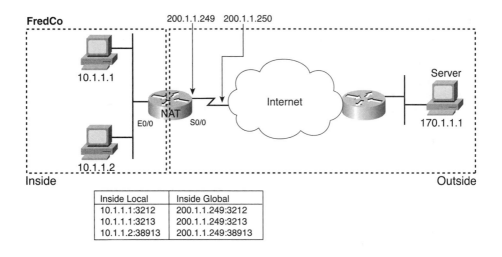

Registered Subnet: 200.1.1.248, Mask 255.255.255.252

Inside Local	Inside Global
10.1.1.1:3212	200.1.1.249:3212
10.1.1.1:3213	200.1.1.249:3213
10.1.1.2:38913	200.1.1.249:38913

In Example 8-3, which shows the NAT overload configuration, NAT translates using inside global address 200.1.1.249 only. So the NAT pool is not required. In the example, as implied in Figure 8-10, host 10.1.1.1 creates two Telnet connections, and host 10.1.1.2 creates one

Telnet connection, causing three dynamic NAT entries, each using inside global address 200.1.1.249, but each with a unique port number.

Example 8-3 *NAT Overload Configuration*

```
NAT# show running-config
!
! Lines Omitted for Brevity
!
interface Ethernet0/0
 ip address 10.1.1.3 255.255.255.0
 ip nat inside
!
interface Serial0/0
 ip address 200.1.1.249 255.255.255.252
 ip nat outside
!
ip nat inside source list 1 interface Serial0/0 overload
!
access-list 1 permit 10.1.1.2
access-list 1 permit 10.1.1.1
!

NAT# show ip nat translations
Pro Inside global      Inside local      Outside local      Outside global
tcp 200.1.1.249:3212   10.1.1.1:3212     170.1.1.1:23       170.1.1.1:23
tcp 200.1.1.249:3213   10.1.1.1:3213     170.1.1.1:23       170.1.1.1:23
tcp 200.1.1.249:38913  10.1.1.2:38913    170.1.1.1:23       170.1.1.1:23
NAT# show ip nat statistics
Total active translations: 3 (0 static, 3 dynamic; 3 extended)
Outside interfaces:
  Serial0/0
Inside interfaces:
  Ethernet0/0
Hits: 103  Misses: 3
Expired translations: 0
Dynamic mappings:
-- Inside Source
access-list 1 interface Serial0/0 refcount 3
```

The **ip nat inside source list 1 interface serial 0/0 overload** command has several parameters, but if you understand the dynamic NAT configuration, the new parameters shouldn't be too hard to grasp. The **list 1** parameter means the same thing as it does for dynamic NAT: Inside local IP addresses matching ACL 1 have their addresses translated. The **interface serial 0/0** parameter means that the only inside global IP address available is the IP address of the NAT router's interface serial 0/0. Finally, the **overload** parameter means that overload is enabled. Without this parameter, the router does not perform overload, just dynamic NAT.

As you can see in the output of **show ip nat translations,** three translations have been added to the NAT table. Before this command, host 10.1.1.1 creates two Telnet connections to 170.1.1.1, and host 10.1.1.2 creates a single Telnet connection. Three entries are created—one for each unique combination of inside local IP address and port.

Miscellaneous TCP/IP Topics

The TCP/IP protocol has a large variety of component protocols, such as IP, ARP, TCP, and UDP. In fact, this chapter is the fifth chapter in this book (and the eighth between my two CCNA books) that is either entirely or mostly devoted to TCP/IP topics. As you wind down your reading about TCP/IP topics, a small number of important, but unrelated, topics still need to be covered. These topics are discussed in this final section.

Internet Control Message Protocol (ICMP)

TCP/IP includes ICMP, a protocol designed to help manage and control the operation of a TCP/IP network. The ICMP protocol provides a wide variety of information about a network's health and operational status. *Control Message* is the most descriptive part of the name. ICMP helps control and manage IP's work and therefore is considered part of TCP/IP's network layer. Because ICMP helps control IP, it can provide useful troubleshooting information. In fact, the ICMP messages sit inside an IP packet, with no transport layer header at all—so it is truly an extension of the TCP/IP network layer.

RFC 792 defines ICMP. The following excerpt from RFC 792 describes the protocol well:

Occasionally a gateway (router) or destination host will communicate with a source host, for example, to report an error in datagram processing. For such purposes, this protocol, the Internet Control Message Protocol (ICMP), is used. ICMP uses the basic support of IP as if it were a higher level protocol; however, ICMP is actually an integral part of IP and must be implemented by every IP module.

ICMP uses messages to accomplish its tasks. Many of these messages are used in even the smallest IP network. Table 8-7 lists several ICMP messages. They are described in more detail following Table 8-7.

Table 8-7   *ICMP Message Types*

Message	Description
Destination Unreachable	Tells the source host that there is a problem delivering a packet.
Time Exceeded	The time that it takes a packet to be delivered has expired, so the packet has been discarded.
Redirect	The router sending this message has received a packet for which another router has a better route. The message tells the sender to use the better route.
Echo	Used by the **ping** command to verify connectivity.

ICMP Echo Request and Echo Reply

The ICMP Echo Request and Echo Reply messages are sent and received by the **ping** command. In fact, when people say they sent a ping packet, they really mean that they sent an ICMP Echo Request. These two messages are self-explanatory. The Echo Request simply means that the host to which it is addressed should reply to the packet. The Echo Reply is the ICMP message type that should be used in the reply. The Echo Request includes some data that can be specified by the **ping** command; whatever data is sent in the Echo Request is sent back in the Echo Reply.

The **ping** command itself supplies many creative ways to use Echo Requests and Replies. For instance, the **ping** command lets you specify the length as well as the source and destination addresses, and it also lets you set other fields in the IP header. Chapter 5, "RIP, IGRP, and Static Route Concepts and Configuration," shows an example of the extended **ping** command that lists the various options.

Destination Unreachable ICMP Message

The ICMP Destination Unreachable message is sent when a message cannot be delivered completely to the application at the destination host. Because packet delivery can fail for many reasons, there are five separate unreachable functions (codes) using this single ICMP unreachable message. All five code types pertain directly to an IP, TCP, or UDP feature. The network shown in Figure 8-11 helps you understand them.

Figure 8-11 *Sample Network for Discussing ICMP Unreachable Codes*

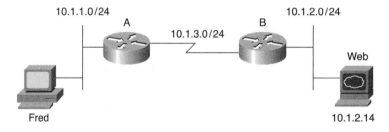

Assume that Fred is trying to connect to the web server, called Web. (Web uses HTTP, which in turn uses TCP as the transport layer protocol.) Three of the ICMP unreachable codes can possibly be used by Routers A and B. The other two codes are used by the web server. These ICMP codes are sent to Fred as a result of the packet originally sent by Fred.

Table 8-8 summarizes the more common ICMP unreachable codes. After the table, the text explains how each ICMP code might be needed for the network in Figure 8-11.

Table 8-8   *ICMP Unreachable Codes*

Unreachable Code	When It Is Used	What It Typically Is Sent By
Network unreachable	There is no match in a routing table for the packet's destination.	Router
Host unreachable	The packet can be routed to a router connected to the destination subnet, but the host is not responding.	Router
Can't fragment	The packet has the Don't Fragment bit set, and a router must fragment to forward the packet.	Router
Protocol unreachable	The packet is delivered to the destination host, but the transport layer protocol is not available on that host.	Endpoint host
Port unreachable	The packet is delivered to the destination host, but the destination port has not been opened by an application.	Endpoint host

The following list explains each code in Table 8-8 in greater detail using the network in Figure 8-11 as an example:

- **Network unreachable**—Router A uses this code if it does not have a route telling it where to forward the packet. In this case, Router A needs a route to subnet 10.1.2.0. Router A sends Fred the ICMP Destination Unreachable message with the code "network unreachable" in response to Fred's packet destined for 10.1.2.14.

- **Host unreachable**—This code implies that the single destination host is unavailable. If Router A has a route to 10.1.2.0, the packet is delivered to Router B. However, if the web server is down, Router B does not get an ARP reply from the web. Router B sends Fred the ICMP Destination Unreachable message with the code "host unreachable" in response to Fred's packet destined for 10.1.2.14.

- **Can't fragment**—This code is the last of the three ICMP unreachable codes that a router might send. Fragmentation defines the process in which a router needs to forward a packet, but the outgoing interface allows only packets that are smaller than the forwarded packet. The router can break the packet into pieces. However, if Router A or B needs to fragment the packet, but the Do Not Fragment bit is set in the IP header, the router discards the packet. Router A or B sends Fred the ICMP Destination Unreachable message with the code "can't fragment" in response to Fred's packet destined for 10.1.2.14.

■ **Protocol unreachable**—If the packet successfully arrives at the web server, two other unreachable codes are possible. One implies that the protocol above IP, typically TCP or UDP, is not running on that host. This is highly unlikely, because most operating systems that use TCP/IP use a single software package that provides IP, TCP, and UDP functions. But if the host receives the IP packet and TCP or UDP is unavailable, the web server host sends Fred the ICMP Destination Unreachable message with the code "protocol unreachable" in response to Fred's packet destined for 10.1.2.14.

■ **Port unreachable**—The final code field value is more likely today. If the server is up but the web server software is not running, the packet can get to the server but cannot be delivered to the web server software. The web server host sends Fred the ICMP Destination Unreachable message with the code "port unreachable" in response to Fred's packet destined for 10.1.2.14.

One key to troubleshooting with the **ping** command is understanding the various codes the command uses to signify the various responses it can receive. Table 8-9 lists the various codes that the Cisco IOS software **ping** command can supply.

Table 8-9 *Codes That the* ping *Command Receives in Response to Its ICMP Echo Request*

ping Command Code	Description
!	ICMP Echo Reply received
.	Nothing was received before the **ping** command timed out
U	ICMP unreachable (destination) received
N	ICMP unreachable (network) received
P	ICMP unreachable (port) received
Q	ICMP source quench received
M	ICMP Can't Fragment message received
?	Unknown packet received

Time Exceeded ICMP Message

The ICMP Time Exceeded message notifies a host when a packet it sent has been discarded because it was "out of time." Packets are not actually timed, but to prevent them from being forwarded forever when there is a routing loop, each IP header uses a Time to Live (TTL) field. Routers decrement TTL by 1 every time they forward a packet; if a router decrements TTL to 0, it throws away the packet. This prevents packets from rotating forever. Figure 8-12 shows the basic process.

Figure 8-12   *TTL Decremented to 0*

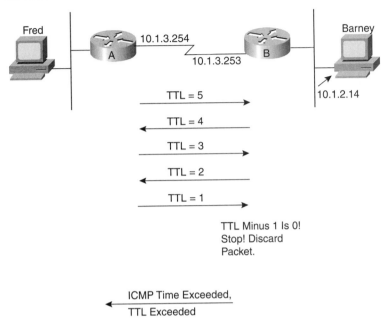

As you can see in the figure, the router that discards the packet also sends an ICMP Time Exceeded message, with a Code field of "time exceeded" to the host that sent the packet. That way, the sender knows that the packet was not delivered. Getting a Time Exceeded message can also help you when you troubleshoot a network. Hopefully, you do not get too many of these; otherwise, you have routing problems.

The IOS **trace** command uses the Time Exceeded message and the IP TTL field to its advantage. By purposefully sending IP packets (with a UDP transport layer) with the TTL set to 1, an ICMP Time Exceeded message is returned by the first router in the route. That's because that router decrements TTL to 0, causing it to discard the packet, and also sends the Time Exceeded message. The **trace** command learns the first router's IP address by receiving the Time Exceeded message from that router. (The **trace** command actually sends three successive packets with TTL = 1.) The **trace** command then sends another set of three IP packets, this time with TTL = 2. These messages make it through the first router but are discarded by the second router because the TTL is decremented to 0. The original packets sent by the host **trace** command use a destination UDP port number that is very unlikely to be used so that the destination host will return a Port Unreachable message. The ICMP Port Unreachable message signifies that the packets reached the true destination host without having time exceeded, so the **trace** command knows that the packets are getting to the true endpoint. Figure 8-13 outlines this process. Router A uses the **trace** command to try to find the route to Barney. Example 8-4 shows this **trace** command on Router A, with **debug** messages from Router B, showing the three resulting Time Exceeded messages.

Figure 8-13 *Cisco IOS Software* **trace** *Command: Messages Generated*

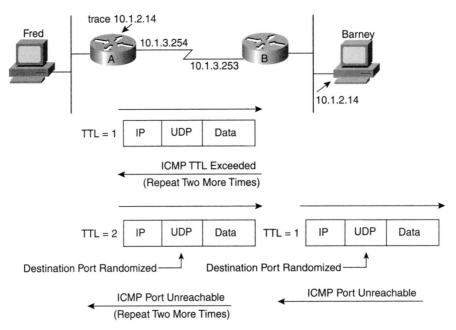

Example 8-4 *ICMP* **debug** *on Router B When Running the* **trace** *Command on Router A*

```
RouterA#trace 10.1.2.14

Type escape sequence to abort.
Tracing the route to 10.1.2.14

  1 10.1.3.253 8 msec 4 msec 4 msec
  2 10.1.2.14 12 msec 8 msec 4 msec
RouterA#
!
! Moving to Router B now
!
RouterB#debug ip icmp
RouterB#
ICMP: time exceeded (time to live) sent to 10.1.3.254 (dest was 10.1.2.14)
ICMP: time exceeded (time to live) sent to 10.1.3.254 (dest was 10.1.2.14)
ICMP: time exceeded (time to live) sent to 10.1.3.254 (dest was 10.1.2.14)
```

Redirect ICMP Message

ICMP Redirect messages provide a very important element in routed IP networks. Many hosts are preconfigured with a default router IP address. When sending packets destined for subnets other than the one to which they are directly connected, these hosts send the packets to their default router. If there is a better local router to which the host should send the packets, an ICMP redirect can be used to tell the host to send the packets to this different router.

For example, in Figure 8-14, the PC uses Router B as its default router. However, Router A's route to subnet 10.1.4.0 is a better route. (Assume the use of mask 255.255.255.0 in each subnet in Figure 8-14.) The PC sends a packet to Router B (Step 1 in Figure 8-14). Router B then forwards the packet based on its own routing table (Step 2); that route points through Router A, which has a better route. Finally, Router B sends the ICMP redirect message to the PC (Step 3), telling it to forward future packets destined for 10.1.4.0 to Router A instead. Ironically, the host can ignore the redirect and keep sending the packets to Router B, but in this example, the PC believes the redirect message, sending its next packet (Step 4) directly to Router A.

Figure 8-14 *ICMP Redirect*

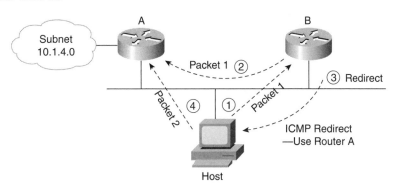

In summary, ICMP defines several message types and several subtypes. RFC 792 is a short and straightforward RFC to read if you want more information.

Secondary IP Addressing

Imagine that you planned your IP addressing scheme for a network. Later, a particular subnet grows, and you have used all the valid IP addresses in the subnet. What should you do? You could change the mask used on that subnet, making the existing subnet larger. However, changing the mask could cause several problems. For instance, if 10.1.4.0/24 is running out of addresses, and you make a change to mask 255.255.254.0 (9 host bits, 23 network/subnet bits), the new subnet includes addresses 10.1.4.0 to 10.1.5.255. If you have already assigned subnet 10.1.5.0/24, with assignable addresses 10.1.5.1 through 10.1.5.254, you would create an overlap, which is not allowed.

You could change all the IP addresses in the constrained network, replacing the original addresses with addresses from a new, larger subnet. However, this solution requires administrative effort to change the IP addresses.

Both of these solutions imply a strategy of using different masks in different parts of the network. Use of these different masks is called variable-length subnet masking (VLSM), which brings up another set of complex routing protocol issues.

The router needs to have more than one IP address on the interface attached to that medium. Secondary addressing provides yet another solution to the problem of running out of addresses in a subnet. Secondary addressing uses multiple networks or subnets on the same data link. The concept is simple: By using more than one subnet on the same medium you increase the number of available IP addresses. For example, Figure 8-15 has subnet 10.1.2.0/ 24; assume that it has all IP addresses assigned. Assuming secondary addressing to be the chosen solution, subnet 10.1.7.0/24 also could be used on the same Ethernet. Example 8-5 shows the configuration for secondary IP addressing on Yosemite.

Figure 8-15 *TCP/IP Network with Secondary Addresses*

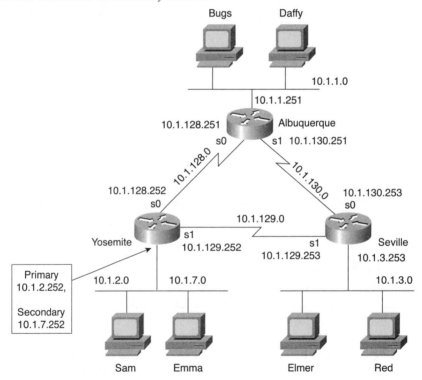

Example 8-5 *Secondary IP Addressing Configuration and the* **show ip route** *Command on Yosemite*

```
! Excerpt from show running-config follows...
Hostname Yosemite
ip domain-lookup
ip name-server 10.1.1.100 10.1.2.100
interface ethernet 0
ip address 10.1.7.252  255.255.255.0 secondary
ip address 10.1.2.252  255.255.255.0
interface serial 0
ip address 10.1.128.252  255.255.255.0
interface serial 1
ip address 10.1.129.252  255.255.255.0

Yosemite# show ip route
Codes: C - connected, S - static, I - IGRP, R - RIP, M - mobile, B - BGP
       D - EIGRP, EX - EIGRP external, O - OSPF, IA - OSPF inter area
       N1 - OSPF NSSA external type 1, N2 - OSPF NSSA external type 2
       E1 - OSPF external type 1, E2 - OSPF external type 2, E - EGP
       i - IS-IS, L1 - IS-IS level-1, L2 - IS-IS level-2, ia - IS-IS inter area
       * - candidate default, U - per-user static route, o - ODR
       P - periodic downloaded static route

Gateway of last resort is not set

     10.0.0.0/24 is subnetted, 4 subnets
C       10.1.2.0 is directly connected, Ethernet0
C       10.1.7.0 is directly connected, Ethernet0
C       10.1.129.0 is directly connected, Serial1
C       10.1.128.0 is directly connected, Serial0
Yosemite#
```

The router has routes to subnets 10.1.2.0/24 and 10.1.7.0/24, so it can forward packets to each subnet. The router also can receive packets from hosts in one subnet and can forward them to the other subnet using the same interface.

FTP and TFTP

File Transfer Protocol (FTP) and Trivial File Transfer Protocol (TFTP) are two popularly used file transfer protocols in a typical IP network. Most end users use FTP, but Cisco router and switch administrators often use TFTP. Which is "better" depends partially on what is being done. A more important question might be, "Which is supported on the devices that need to transfer the file?" Given the choice today, most end users choose FTP because it has more robust features. However, Cisco IOS software did not originally support FTP for moving files in and out of the router, so many people continue to use TFTP out of habit.

FTP

FTP is a TCP-based application that has many options and features, including the capability to change directories, list files using wildcard characters, transfer multiple files with a single command, and use a variety of character sets or file formats. More important in this context is the basic operation of FTP. Figures 8-16 and 8-17 show a typical FTP connection—or, better stated, connections.

Figure 8-16 *FTP Control Connection*

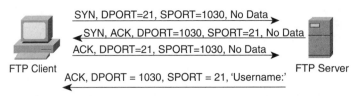

The connection shown in Figure 8-16 is called an *FTP control connection*. When a user (FTP client) asks to connect to an FTP server, a TCP connection is established to the FTP server's well-known port (21). The connection is established like any other TCP connection. The user typically is required to enter a username and password, which the server uses to authenticate the files available to that user for read and write permissions. This security is based on the file security on the server's platform. All the commands used to control the transfer of a file are sent across this connection—hence the name *FTP control connection*.

At this point, the user has a variety of commands available to enable settings for transfer, change directories, list files, and so forth. However, whenever a **get** or **put** command is entered (or **mget** or **mput**—m is for multiple) or the equivalent button is clicked on the user interface, a file is transferred. The data is transferred over a separate FTP data connection. Figure 8-17 outlines the FTP data connection process.

Figure 8-17 *FTP Data Connection*

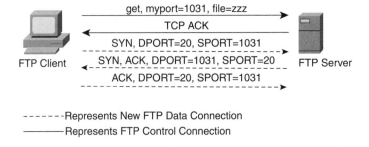

As shown in Figure 8-17, another TCP connection is established for the actual data transfer, this time to well-known port 20. Using this convention, a file can be transferred without getting in the way of the control connection. If many files are to be transferred rather than making a single control/data connection for each file, the control connection is made once. The environment is defined using the control connection, and these settings affect the functioning of the data connection. For example, the default directory to use in future transfers can be defined using commands on the control connection as well as the type of data (binary or ASCII). You might choose to use binary when transferring text files between computers that might use slightly different ASCII character sets but use binary to transfer executable files. The control connection stays up until the user breaks it or the connection times out. While the control connection is up, a separate data connection is established for each file transfer.

An additional step helps prevent hackers from breaking in and transferring files, as shown in Figure 8-17. Rather than just creating a new connection, the client tells the server, with an application layer message over the control connection, which port number will be used for the new data connection. The server does not transfer the file (zzz in this case) over any other data connection except the one to the correct socket—the one with the client's IP address, TCP, and the port number declared to the server (1031 in this case).

TFTP

Trivial File Transfer Protocol (TFTP) performs basic file transfer with a small set of features. One of the reasons that such an application is needed, even when the more robust FTP is available, is that TFTP takes little memory to load and little time to program. With the advent of extremely low-cost memory and processing, such advantages seem trivial. Practically speaking, if you intend to frequently transfer files from your PC, you probably will use FTP. However, Cisco has supported TFTP for a much longer time, and many people still use it.

TFTP uses User Datagram Protocol (UDP), so there is no connection establishment and no error recovery by the transport layer. However, TFTP uses application layer recovery by embedding a small header between the UDP header and the data. This header includes codes—for example, read, write, and acknowledgment—along with a numbering scheme that numbers 512-byte blocks of data. The TFTP application uses these block numbers to acknowledge receipt and resend the data. TFTP sends one block and waits on an acknowledgment before sending another block.

Table 8-10 summarizes some features of TFTP and FTP.

Table 8-10 *Comparison of FTP and TFTP*

FTP	TFTP
Uses TCP	Uses UDP
Uses robust control commands	Uses simple control commands
Sends data over a TCP connection separate from control commands	Uses no connections because of UDP
Requires more memory and programming effort	Requires less memory and programming effort

MTU and Fragmentation

TCP/IP defines a maximum length for an IP packet. The term used to describe that maximum length is *maximum transmission unit (MTU)*.

The MTU varies based on configuration and the interface's characteristics. By default, a computer calculates an interface's MTU based on the maximum size of the data portion of the data-link frame (where the packet is placed). For instance, the default MTU value on Ethernet interfaces is 1500.

Routers, like any IP host, cannot forward a packet out an interface if the packet is longer than the MTU. If a router's interface MTU is smaller than a packet that must be forwarded, the router fragments the packet into smaller packets. Fragmentation is the process of breaking the packet into smaller packets, each of which is less than or equal to the MTU value.

Figure 8-18 shows an example of fragmentation in a network where the MTU on the serial link has been lowered to 1000 bytes via configuration.

Figure 8-18 *IP Fragmentation*

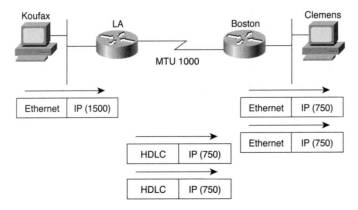

As Figure 8-18 illustrates, Koufax sends a 1500-byte packet toward Router LA. LA removes the Ethernet header but cannot forward the packet as is, because it is 1500 bytes and the HDLC link supports an MTU of only 1000. So LA fragments the original packet into two packets, each 750 bytes in length. (The router does the math required to figure out the minimum number of fragments [2 in this case] and breaks the original packet into equal-length packets. Because of this, any other routers the packets might go through are less likely to need to perform fragmentation.) After forwarding the two packets, Boston receives the packets and forwards them without reassembling them. Reassembly is done by the endpoint host, which in this case is Clemens.

The IP header contains fields useful for reassembling the fragments into the original packet. The IP header includes an ID value that is the same in each fragmented packet, as well as an offset value that defines which part of the original packet is held in each fragment. Fragmented packets arriving out of order can be identified as a part of the same original packet and can be reassembled in the correct order using the offset field in each fragment.

Two configuration commands can be used to change the IP MTU size on an interface: the **mtu** interface subcommand and the **ip mtu** interface subcommand. The **mtu** command sets the MTU for all Layer 3 protocols; unless there is a need to vary the setting per Layer 3 protocol, this command is preferred. If a different setting is desired for IP, the **ip mtu** command sets the value used for IP. If both are configured on an interface, the IP MTU setting takes precedence on that interface. However, if the **mtu** command is configured after **ip mtu** is configured, the **ip mtu** value is reset to the same value as that of the **mtu** command. Care must be taken when changing these values.

ISL and 802.1Q Configuration on Routers

As discussed in Chapter 3, "Virtual LANs and Trunking," VLAN trunking can be used between two switches and between a switch and a router. Trunking between a switch and a router reduces the number of router interfaces needed to route between the various VLANs. Instead of a single physical interface on the router for each VLAN on the switch, one physical interface can be used, and the router can still route packets between the various VLANs.

Figure 8-19 shows a router with a single Fast Ethernet interface and a single connection to a switch. Either ISL or 802.1Q trunking can be used, with only small differences in the configuration for each. For frames that contain packets that the router routes between the two virtual LANs (VLANs), the incoming frame is tagged by the switch with one VLAN ID, and the outgoing frame is tagged by the router with the other VLAN ID. Example 8-6 shows the router configuration required to support ISL encapsulation and forwarding between these VLANs.

Figure 8-19 *Router Forwarding Between VLANs*

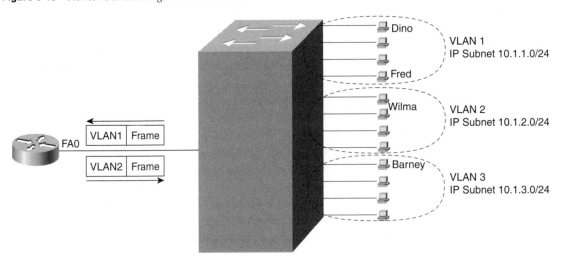

Example 8-6 *Router Configuration for the ISL Encapsulation Shown in Figure 8-19*

```
interface fastethernet 0.1
ip address 10.1.1.1 255.255.255.0
encapsulation isl 1
!
interface fastethernet 0.2
ip address 10.1.2.1 255.255.255.0
encapsulation isl 2
!
interface fastethernet 0.3
ip address 10.1.3.1 255.255.255.0
encapsulation isl 3
```

Example 8-6 shows the configuration for three subinterfaces of the FastEthernet interface on the router. Each is assigned an IP address because the interface is actually a part of three VLANs, implying three IP subnets. So, instead of three physical interfaces, each attached to a different subnet and broadcast domain, there is one physical router interface with three logical subinterfaces, each attached to a different subnet and broadcast domain. The **encapsulation** command numbers the VLANs, which must match the configuration for VLAN IDs in the switch.

This example uses subinterface numbers that match the VLAN ID on each subinterface. There is no requirement that the numbers match, but most people choose to make them match, just to make the configuration more obvious. In other words, the VLAN IDs may be 1, 2, and 3, but the subinterface numbers could have been 4, 5 and 6, because the subinterface numbers are just used internally by the router.

Example 8-7 shows the same network, but this time with 802.1Q used instead of ISL. IEEE 802.1Q has a concept called the native VLAN, which is a special VLAN on each trunk for which no 802.1Q headers are added to the frames. By default, VLAN 1 is the native VLAN. Example 8-7 shows the difference in configuration.

Example 8-7   *Router Configuration for the 802.1Q Encapsulation Shown in Figure 8-19*

```
interface fastethernet 0
ip address 10.1.1.1 255.255.255.0
!
interface fastethernet 0.2
ip address 10.1.2.1 255.255.255.0
encapsulation dot1q 2
!
interface fastethernet 0.3
ip address 10.1.3.1 255.255.255.0
encapsulation dot1q 3
```

The router IP address in the subnet of the 802.1Q native VLAN is configured on the physical interface instead of the subinterface. Note that the keyword for the **encapsulation** is **dot1q**. Also note that for the native VLAN, VLAN 1 in this case, the **encapsulation** command should not be used, or the router will encapsulate frames in an 802.1Q header. The rest of the configuration is identical to ISL. Also, there is no need to match the subinterface numbers and VLAN numbers. It's just a good practice to help you keep track of things.

Foundation Summary

The "Foundation Summary" section lists the most important facts from the chapter. Although this section does not list everything that will be on the exam, a well-prepared CCNA candidate should at a minimum know all the details in each Foundation Summary before taking the exam.

Table 8-11 shows the private address space defined by RFC 1918.

Table 8-11   *RFC 1918 Private Address Space*

Range of IP Addresses	Class of Networks	Number of Networks
10.0.0.0 to 10.255.255.255	A	1
172.16.0.0 to 172.31.255.255	B	16
192.168.0.0 to 192.168.255.255	C	256

Figure 8-20 and Table 8-12 outline some of the terminology used with NAT.

Figure 8-20   *Static NAT Terminology*

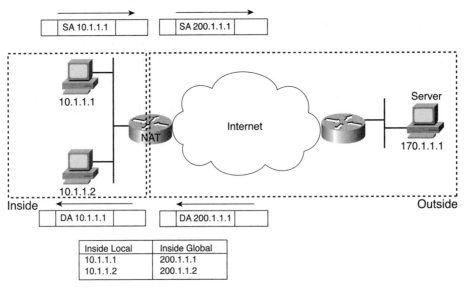

Table 8-12 *NAT Addressing Terms*

Term	Description
Inside local	In a typical NAT design, the term "inside" refers to an address used for a host inside an enterprise. An inside local is the actual IP address assigned to a host in the private enterprise network. A more descriptive term might be "inside private," because when using RFC 1918 addresses in an enterprise, the inside local represents the host inside the enterprise, and it is a private RFC 1918 address.
Inside global	In a typical NAT design, the term "inside" refers to an address used for a host inside an enterprise. NAT uses an inside global address to represent the inside host as the packet is sent through the outside network, typically the Internet. A NAT router changes the source IP address of a packet sent by an inside host from an inside local address to an inside global address as the packet goes from the inside to the outside network. A more descriptive term might be "inside public," because when using RFC 1918 addresses in an enterprise, the inside global represents the inside host with a public IP address that can be used for routing in the public Internet.
Outside global	In a typical NAT design, the term "outside" refers to an address used for a host outside an enterprise—in other words, in the Internet. An outside global is the actual IP address assigned to a host that resides in the outside network, typically the Internet. A more descriptive term might be "outside public," because the outside global represents the outside host with a public IP address that can be used for routing in the public Internet.
Outside local	In a typical NAT design, the term "outside" refers to an address used for a host outside an enterprise—in other words, in the Internet. NAT uses an outside local address to represent the outside host as the packet is sent through the private enterprise network (inside network). A NAT router changes a packet's destination IP address, sent from an inside host to the outside global address, as the packet goes from the inside to the outside network. A more descriptive term might be "outside private," because when using RFC 1918 addresses in an enterprise, the outside local represents the outside host with a private IP address from RFC 1918.

Example 8-8 shows a typical NAT configuration, as well as some **show** commands.

Example 8-8 *Dynamic NAT Configuration*

```
NAT# show running-config
!
! Lines omitted for Brevity
!
interface Ethernet0/0
 ip address 10.1.1.3 255.255.255.0
 ip nat inside
!
```

continues

Example 8-8 *Dynamic NAT Configuration (Continued)*

```
interface Serial0/0
 ip address 200.1.1.251 255.255.255.0
 ip nat outside
!
ip nat pool fred 200.1.1.1 200.1.1.2 netmask 255.255.255.252
ip nat inside source list 1 pool fred
!
access-list 1 permit 10.1.1.2
access-list 1 permit 10.1.1.1
!
NAT# show ip nat translations

NAT# show ip nat statistics
Total active translations: 0 (0 static, 0 dynamic; 0 extended)
Outside interfaces:
  Serial0/0
Inside interfaces:
  Ethernet0/0
Hits: 0  Misses: 0
Expired translations: 0
Dynamic mappings:
-- Inside Source
access-list 1 pool fred refcount 0
 pool fred: netmask 255.255.255.252
    start 200.1.1.1 end 200.1.1.2
    type generic, total addresses 2, allocated 0 (0%), misses 0
!
! Telnet from 10.1.1.1 to 170.1.1.1 happened next; not shown
!
NAT# show ip nat statistics
Total active translations: 1 (0 static, 1 dynamic; 0 extended)
Outside interfaces:
  Serial0/0
Inside interfaces:
  Ethernet0/0
Hits: 69  Misses: 1
Expired translations: 0
Dynamic mappings:
-- Inside Source
access-list 1 pool fred refcount 1
 pool fred: netmask 255.255.255.252
    start 200.1.1.1 end 200.1.1.2
    type generic, total addresses 2, allocated 1 (50%), misses 0
NAT# show ip nat translations
Pro Inside global     Inside local      Outside local     Outside global
--- 200.1.1.1         10.1.1.1          ---               ---
```

The Destination Unreachable, Time Exceeded, Redirect, and Echo messages are described in Table 8-13.

Table 8-13   *ICMP Message Types*

Message	Purpose
Destination Unreachable	Tells the source host that there is a problem delivering a packet.
Time Exceeded	The time it takes a packet to be delivered has expired, so the packet has been discarded.
Redirect	The router sending this message has received a packet for which another router has a better route. The message tells the sender to use the better route.
Echo	Used by the **ping** command to verify connectivity.

Table 8-14 summarizes some features of TFTP and FTP.

Table 8-14   *Comparison of FTP and TFTP*

FTP	TFTP
Uses TCP	Uses UDP
Uses robust control commands	Uses simple control commands
Sends data over a TCP connection separate from control commands	Uses no connections because of UDP
Requires more memory and programming effort	Requires less memory and programming effort

Example 8-9 shows the router configuration required to support ISL encapsulation and forwarding between three VLANs.

Example 8-9   *Router Configuration for ISL Encapsulation*

```
interface fastethernet 0.1
ip address 10.1.1.1 255.255.255.0
encapsulation isl 1
!
interface fastethernet 0.2
ip address 10.1.2.1 255.255.255.0
encapsulation isl 2
!
interface fastethernet 0.3
ip address 10.1.3.1 255.255.255.0
encapsulation isl 3
```

Q&A

As mentioned in the Introduction, you have two choices for review questions. The following questions give you a bigger challenge than the exam because they are open-ended. By reviewing with this more-difficult question format, you can exercise your memory better and prove your conceptual and factual knowledge of the topics covered in this chapter. The answers to these questions are found in Appendix A.

For more practice with exam-like question formats, including multiple-choice questions and those using a router simulator, use the exam engine on the CD.

1. Define private addressing as defined in RFC 1918.

2. List the range of private networks defined in RFC 1918.

3. Does CIDR affect the size of Internet routing tables? If so, what does it do to those routing tables?

4. Define NAT and explain the basics of its operation.

5. Define the term inside local address in relation to NAT. Use Figure 8-21 to describe the answer.

Figure 8-21 *Network for Use in Answering NAT Questions*

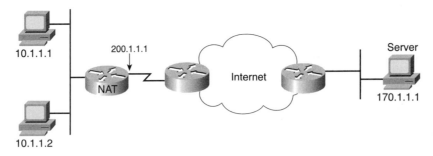

6. Define the term inside global address in relation to NAT. Use Figure 8-21 to describe the answer.

7. Create a configuration for NAT overload to a single IP address for the router shown in Figure 8-21.

8. Create a configuration for static NAT, mapping host 10.1.1.1 to 200.1.1.11, for the router shown in Figure 8-21.

9. Which requires more lines of source code, FTP or TFTP? Explain your answer.

10. Does FTP or TFTP perform error recovery? If so, describe the basics of how this occurs.

11. Describe the process used by IP routers to perform fragmentation and reassembly of packets.

12. How many Class B-style networks are reserved by RFC 1918 private addressing?

13. Describe why ARP requests use an Ethernet broadcast address instead of an Ethernet unicast address.

14. Imagine that host 10.1.1.1 in Figure 8-21 sends a packet to the server at 170.1.1.1 and that the NAT router also happens to fragment the packet. Inside the context of this network, explain how reassembly of the fragments into the original packet occurs.

15. Imagine that R1 has an interface, FastEthernet 0/0, that uses ISL trunking to a switch. R1 needs to route between VLAN 1 and VLAN 2. Create a valid router configuration.

16. Describe how NAT overload manages to support more than one inside local IP address using a single inside global address.

Cisco Published ICND Exam Topics*
Covered in This Part:

4   Design a simple internetwork using Cisco products

6   Choose WAN protocols to meet design requirements

14 Implement simple WAN protocols

15 Utilize the OSI model as a guide for systematic network troubleshooting

19 Troubleshoot a device as part of a working network

21 Perform simple WAN troubleshooting

26 Evaluate key characteristics of HDLC, PPP, Frame Relay, DDR, and ISDN technologies

* Always re-check www.cisco.com for the latest posted exam topics

Part III: Wide-Area Networks

This chapter covers the following subjects:

- Review of WAN Basics

- Data-Link Protocols for Point-to-Point Leased Lines

- Authentication Over WAN Links

CHAPTER 9

Point-to-Point Leased Line Implementation

This chapter covers the details of point-to-point WAN links. It starts with a review of the basics and provides background information that gives you the right perspective for Chapters 10, "ISDN and Dial-on-Demand Routing," and 11, "Frame Relay." This chapter also includes deeper coverage of HDLC and PPP, plus CHAP configuration.

Perhaps you are using both this book and CCNA INTRO Exam Certification Guide to prepare to pass the CCNA exam—the single-exam method of getting your CCNA certification. If you are using the reading plan suggested in the Introduction to both books, be aware that this chapter is the first WAN chapter in this book. After this chapter, you should read Chapters 10 and 11 before moving on to the final chapters in each book. Refer to this book's Introduction for details.

"Do I Know This Already?" Quiz

The purpose of the "Do I Know This Already?" quiz is to help you decide if you need to read the entire chapter. If you intend to read the entire chapter, you do not necessarily need to answer these questions now.

The eight-question quiz, derived from the major sections in the "Foundation Topics" section, helps you determine how to spend your limited study time.

Table 9-1 outlines the major topics discussed in this chapter and the "Do I Know This Already?" quiz questions that correspond to those topics.

Table 9-1 *Do I Know This Already?" Foundation Topics Section-to-Question Mapping*

Foundations Topics Section	Questions Covered in This Section
Review of WAN Basics	1, 2
Data-Link Protocols for Point-to-Point Leased Lines	3, 7, 8
Authentication Over WAN Links	4, 5, 6

> **CAUTION** The goal of self-assessment is to gauge your mastery of the topics in this chapter. If you don't know the answer to a question or you're only partially sure of the answer, you should mark this question as wrong for purposes of the self-assessment. Giving yourself credit for an answer you guess correctly skews your self-assessment results and might give you a false sense of security.

1. Which of the following types of WAN connections allow the direct use of PPP as the encapsulation type on the interface?

    a. Circuit switching

    b. Packet switching

    c. Leased lines

    d. LAN switching

2. Which of the following commands are required on the router connected to a DTE cable to make the serial link between two routers work when the two routers are connected in a lab using a DTE and DCE cable and no CSU/DSUs?

    a. clock rate 56000

    b. clockrate 56000

    c. bandwidth 56000

    d. band width 56000

    e. None of the above

3. Which of the following commands make a serial interface revert to the default data-link protocol if it is currently configured with PPP?

    a. wan default

    b. default

    c. encapsulation ppp

    d. encapsulation frame-relay

    e. encapsulation hdlc

    f. no encapsulation

    g. no encapsulation ppp

    h. no encapsulation hdlc

    i. no encapsulation frame-relay

4. Which of the following authentication protocols authenticates a device on the other end of a link without sending any password information in clear text?

   a. MD5

   b. PAP

   c. CHAP

   d. DES

   e. Triple DES

5. Imagine that two routers, R1 and R2, have a leased line between them. Each router had its configuration erased and was then reloaded. R1 was then configured with the following commands:

```
interface s0/0
encapsulation ppp
ppp authentication chap
```

Which of the following configuration commands can complete the configuration on R1 so that CHAP can work correctly? Assume that R2 has been configured correctly and that the password is fred.

   a. No other configuration is needed.

   b. **ppp chap** (global command)

   c. **user R1 password fred**

   d. **user R2 password fred**

   e. **ppp chap password fred**

6. Which of the following is a reason to avoid using link compression?

   a. Reduction in the cumulative number of bytes sent on a link

   b. Reduction in queuing delay

   c. Reduction in available router CPU cycles for other tasks

   d. Reduction in serialization delay

7. Which of the following does PPP use as part of how it notices when a link has been looped, causing packets sent by a router to be returned to that router?

   a. LQM

   b. Magic number

   c. Type field

   d. MD5 hash

8. Which of the following are protocols defined as part of PPP?

   a. HDLC

   b. LCP

   c. LAPD

   d. IPCP

The answers to the "Do I Know This Already?" quiz appear in Appendix A. The suggested choices for your next step are as follows:

- **6 or less overall score**—Read the entire chapter. This includes the "Foundation Topics," "Foundation Summary," and "Q&A" sections.

- **7 or 8 overall score**—If you want more review on these topics, skip to the "Foundation Summary" section and then go to the "Q&A" section. Otherwise, move to the next chapter.

Foundation Topics

Review of WAN Basics

Networking professionals need to know about many WAN options when designing networks. In this part of the book, you will read about the three main categories of WAN options:

- Leased point-to-point lines
- Dial lines (also called *circuit-switched lines*)
- Packet-switched networks

This chapter covers the details of leased lines. Before we get into those details, you should have a basic understanding of all three general options for WAN connectivity.

Table 9-2 gives the basic definitions for the three types of WAN services, as first covered in Chapter 4 of CCNA INTRO Exam Certification Guide.

Table 9-2   *Definitions of Leased Line, Circuit Switching, and Packet Switching*

Term	Description
Leased line	A dedicated, always-on circuit between two endpoints. The service provider just passes a constant rate bit stream; it does not interpret or make decisions based on the bits sent over the circuit. Generally is more expensive than packet switching today.
Circuit switching/dial	Provides dedicated bandwidth between two points, but only for the duration of the call. Typically used as a cheaper alternative to leased lines, particularly when connectivity is not needed all the time. Also is useful for backup when a leased line or packet-switched service fails.
Packet switching	Provides virtual circuits between pairs of sites, with contracted traffic rates for each VC. Each site's physical connectivity consists of a leased line from the site to a device in the provider's network. Generally cheaper than leased lines.

This chapter covers a few topics that relate to how routers use both leased lines and "dial" or circuit-switched lines. HDLC and PPP can be used on either type of line, because both these data-link protocols are designed for a point-to-point environment. Chapter 10 covers many of the details of circuit switching, including detailed coverage of ISDN. Chapter 11 covers Frame Relay, which can be called a packet-switching service, or sometimes a frame-switching service, because its logic relates mostly to OSI Layer 2.

Physical Components of Point-to-Point Leased Lines

Many options for WAN connectivity are available, including synchronous point-to-point serial links. These synchronous point-to-point links include a cable from a service provider, with the service including the capability to send and receive bits across that cable at a predetermined speed. The physical connection includes a CSU/DSU on each end of the link, as shown in Figure 9-1.

Figure 9-1 *Physical Components of a Point-to-Point Serial Link*

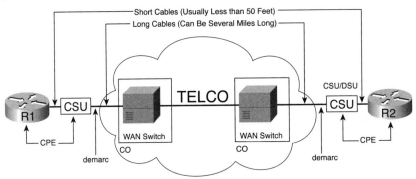

The physical details of WAN links are covered in Chapter 4, "Fundamentals of WANs," of CCNA INTRO Exam Certification Guide. After the CSU/DSUs are configured and the lines are installed, only a small amount of configuration is required on the routers. To get the two routers working so that they can ping each other across the link, you actually only need to configure IP addresses on each router and do a **no shutdown** command on each interface.

In some cases, two routers are physically close to each other, but they still need a point-to-point WAN link. For instance, if you are studying for a Cisco certification exam, and you want to have some WAN links, you do not need to lease a point-to-point circuit from the phone company. You can instead do a cabling "trick," connecting a DCE cable to a DTE cable to create a point-to-point WAN link, as described in Chapter 4 of CCNA INTRO Exam Certification Guide. Figure 9-2 shows the basic idea behind the cabling with the DCE and DTE cables, which allows the two routers to send and receive bits without a pair of CSU/DSUs and a leased line.

Figure 9-2 *Back-to-Back Serial Cabling*

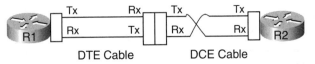

To get the serial link in Figures 9-1 and 9-2 working, the router configuration is simple. Example 9-1 lists the configuration on R1 and R2.

Example 9-1   *Minimal Configuration for IP on a Point-to-Point Link*

```
R1                                   R2

interface serial 1                   interface serial 1
ip address 10.1.1.1 255.255.255.0    ip address 10.1.1.2 255.255.255.0
no shutdown                          no shutdown
                                     clock rate 56000
```

Note that the IP addresses must be in the same subnet, because the two routers' interfaces are not separated by some other IP router. In many cases, the **no shutdown** command is unneeded. However, when a Cisco router comes up, and the physical WAN link is not working, the router might place a **shutdown** command on the interface configuration. So the **no shutdown** interface subcommand would be needed to put the interface in service.

The **clock rate** command sets the clock rate on interfaces when a DCE cable has been used, as in Figure 9-2. In Example 9-1, the **clock rate 56000** command sets the clock rate to 56,000 bps. If external CSU/DSUs were used, as in Figure 9-1, as is typical when you use an actual leased line from a provider, this command is unneeded. In fact, the router wouldn't let you add the command to the configuration if a DTE cable was connected to the interface!

Data-Link Protocols for Point-to-Point Leased Lines

The more interesting part of point-to-point WANs relates to the choices of different data link layer protocols and how each protocol behaves differently. WAN data-link protocols used on point-to-point serial links provide the basic function of data delivery across that one link. The two most popular WAN data-link protocols are High-Level Data Link Control (HDLC) and PPP. Each of these WAN protocols has the following functions in common:

- HDLC and PPP provide for the delivery of data across a single point-to-point serial link.
- HDLC and PPP deliver data on synchronous serial links; PPP also supports asynchronous serial links.

Each synchronous serial data-link protocol uses the concept of *framing*. Each data-link protocol defines the beginning and end of the frame, the information and format of a header and trailer, and the location of the packet between the header and trailer. In other words, synchronous WAN data-link protocols are frame-oriented, just like LAN data-link protocols.

Synchronous WAN links require the CSU/DSUs on each end of the link to operate at the exact same speed. Essentially, the CSU/DSUs on each side of the WAN link agree to use a certain clock rate, or speed, to send and receive bits. It is expensive to build CSU/DSUs that can truly operate at exactly the same speed, so after they agree to a particular speed, both CSU/DSUs try to operate at that speed. Then one CSU/DSU watches for small differences in clock rates between itself and the other CSU/DSU and makes small adjustments. (The CSU/DSU that does not adjust its clock is called the *clock source.*) This process works almost like the scenes in spy novels in which the spies synchronize their watches; in this case, the watches or clocks are synchronized automatically several times per minute.

Synchronous CSU/DSUs adjust their clocks by noticing when the electrical signal received on the physical line changes. When the routers send data frames across the link, plenty of signal transitions are made, because the transitions are typically used to imply either a 1 or a 0. However, if no traffic were sent across the link, there would be no transitions in the electrical signal, and clock synchronization would be lost. So synchronous data-link protocols send frames continuously, even sending idle frames when there is no end-user data to be sent over the link. By always at least sending frames with no data in them, the routers ensure that there are plenty of electrical signal transitions on the line, allowing the clock adjustments required for synchronization. So HDLC and PPP define idle frames, called *Receiver Ready*, implying that the sender has nothing to send other than idle frames to allow for continued synchronization.

Unlike asynchronous links, in which no bits are sent during idle times, synchronous data links define idle frames. These frames do nothing more than provide plenty of signal transitions so that clocks can be adjusted on the receiving end, consequently maintaining synchronization.

HDLC and PPP Compared

The next few pages compare and contrast several key features of HDLC and PPP. These features, including how each protocol supports each feature, are summarized at the end of the section in Table 9-3. These three features are used to compare the two protocols:

■ Whether the protocol supports synchronous communications, asynchronous communications, or both.

■ Whether the protocol provides error recovery.

■ Whether an architected Protocol Type field exists. In other words, the protocol specifications define a field in the header that identifies the type of packet contained in the data portion of the frame.

First, a few words about the criteria used to compare these WAN protocols might prove helpful. Synchronous protocols allow more throughput over a serial link than asynchronous protocols. However, asynchronous protocols require less-expensive hardware, because there is no need to watch transitions and adjust the clock rate. For links between routers, synchronous links are typically desired and used. When you use a PC with a modem to dial up an Internet provider, you use an asynchronous link. All the protocols covered in this section support synchronous links, because that is what routers typically use between each other.

Another comparison criteria is error recovery. Do not confuse error recovery with error detection. Almost all data-link protocols, PPP and HDLC included, perform error detection. All the data-link protocols described here use a field in the trailer, usually called the frame check sequence (FCS), that verifies whether bit errors occurred during transmission of the frame. If so, the frame is discarded. Error recovery is the process that causes retransmission of the lost or errored frame(s). Error recovery can be performed by the data-link protocol or a higher-layer protocol, or it might not be performed at all. Regardless, all WAN data-link protocols perform error detection, which involves noticing the error and discarding the frame.

Finally, the people who created these protocols might or might not have defined a Protocol Type field. As described in more detail in Chapter 3, "Data Link Layer Fundamentals: Ethernet LANs," from CCNA INTRO Exam Certification Guide, each data-link protocol that supports multiple network layer protocols needs a method of defining the type of packet encapsulated in the data-link frame. If such a field is part of the protocol specification, it is considered architected—in other words, specified in the protocol. If the protocol specification does not include a Protocol Type field, Cisco might add some other header information to create a Protocol Type field.

Figure 9-3 shows the framing details of HDLC and PPP, showing the proprietary HDLC Protocol field and the standardized PPP Protocol field.

Figure 9-3   *PPP and HDLC Framing*

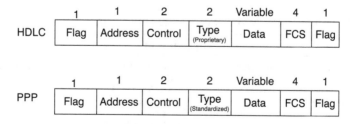

Table 9-3 lists the important comparison points between HDLC and PPP.

Table 9-3   *Point-to-Point Data-Link Protocol Attributes*

Protocol	Error Recovery	Architected Type Field	Other Attributes
HDLC	No	No	HDLC serves as Cisco's default on serial links. Cisco uses a Proprietary Type field to support multiprotocol traffic. Supports synchronous links only.
PPP	Supported but not enabled by default	Yes	PPP was meant for multiprotocol interoperability from its inception, unlike HDLC. PPP also supports asynchronous communication.

HDLC and PPP Configuration

HDLC and PPP configuration is straightforward. You just need to be sure to configure the same WAN data-link protocol on each end of the serial link. Otherwise, the routers will misinterpret the incoming frames, because each WAN data-link protocol uses a different frame format. Other than configuring some optional features, that's all you need to do!

Tables 9-4 and 9-5 summarize the configuration commands and EXEC commands used for HDLC and PPP configuration. Most of the commands relate to the optional features.

Table 9-4   *PPP and HDLC Configuration Commands*

Command	Configuration Mode
encapsulation {hdlc | ppp}	Interface subcommand
compress [predictor | stac | mppc [ignore-pfc]]	Interface subcommand

Table 9-5   *Point-to-Point-Related* **show** *and* **debug** *Commands*

Command	Description
show interfaces [*type number*]	Lists statistics and details of interface configuration, including the encapsulation type.
show compress	Lists compression ratios.
show processes [cpu]	Lists processor and task utilization. Is useful for watching for increased utilization because of compression.

Example 9-2 shows the configuration for PPP, followed by the changed configuration for a migration to HDLC. Assume that Router A and Router B have a serial link attached to their serial 1 ports.

Example 9-2   *Configuration for PPP and HDLC*

```
Router A-Mars                        Router B-Seville

interface serial 1                   interface serial 1
encapsulation ppp                    encapsulation ppp
.                                    .
. later, changed to...               . later, changed to...
.                                    .
interface serial 1                   interface serial 1
encapsulation hdlc                   encapsulation hdlc
```

Changing serial encapsulations in configuration mode is tricky compared to some other configuration commands in a Cisco router. In Example 9-2, converting back to HDLC (the default) is accomplished with the **encapsulation hdlc** command, but it can also be accomplished with the command **no encapsulation ppp**, because that causes the router to revert back to the default encapsulation, which is HDLC. Additionally, any other interface subcommands that are pertinent only to PPP, but not HDLC, are also removed when the **encapsulation hdlc** command is used.

PPP-Specific Features

PPP was defined much later than the original HDLC specifications. As a result, the creators of PPP included many additional features that had not been seen in WAN data-link protocols up to that time. As a result, PPP has become the most popular and feature-rich WAN data link layer protocol.

PPP-unique features fall into two main categories:

- Those needed regardless of the Layer 3 protocol sent across the link
- Those specific to each Layer 3 protocol

PPP uses a protocol that focuses on the features that apply regardless of the Layer 3 protocol used and another protocol to support each Layer 3 protocol supported on the link. The PPP Link Control Protocol (LCP) provides the core features for PPP. For features related to a specific Layer 3 protocol, PPP uses a series of PPP control protocols, such as IP Control Protocol (IPCP). For example, IPCP provides for IP address assignment; this feature is used extensively with Internet dialup connections today.

PPP uses one LCP per link and one Control Protocol for each Layer 3 protocol defined on the link. If a router is configured for IPX, AppleTalk, and IP on a PPP serial link, the router configured for PPP encapsulation automatically tries to bring up the appropriate control protocols for each Layer 3 protocol (for example, IPCP). Cisco routers also use a PPP CP for supporting CDP traffic, called *CDPCP*.

LCP provides a variety of optional features for PPP. You should at least be aware of the concepts behind these features. They are summarized in Table 9-6.

Table 9-6 *PPP LCP Features*

Function	LCP Feature	Description
Error detection	Link Quality Monitoring (LQM)	PPP can take down a link based on the percentage of errors on the link. LQM exchanges statistics about lost packets versus sent packets in each direction. When compared to packets and bytes sent, this yields a percentage of errored traffic. The percentage of loss that causes a link to be taken down is enabled and defined by a configuration setting.
Looped link detection	Magic number	Using different magic numbers, routers send messages to each other. If you receive your own magic number, the link is looped. A configuration setting determines whether the link should be taken down when looped.
Multilink support	Multilink PPP	Fragments of packets are load-balanced across multiple links.
Authentication	PAP and CHAP	Exchanges names and passwords so that each device can verify the identity of the device on the other end of the link.

The next few pages discuss how two of these features work. Chapter 10 covers Multilink PPP (MLP) support.

Looped Link Detection

Error detection and looped link detection are two key features of PPP. Looped link detection allows for faster convergence when a link fails because it is looped. What does "looped" mean? Well, to test a circuit, the phone company might loop the circuit. The technician can sit at his desk and, using commands, cause the phone company's switch to loop the circuit. This means that the phone company takes the bits you send in and sends them right back to you.

The routers cannot send bits to each other while the link is looped, of course. However, the router might not notice that the link is looped, because the router is receiving something! PPP helps the router recognize a looped link quickly so that it can bring the interface down and possibly use an alternative route.

In some cases, routing protocol convergence can be sped up by LCP recognition of the loop. If the router can immediately notice that the link is looped, it can put the interface in a "down and down" status, and the routing protocols can change their routing updates based on the fact that the link is down. If a router does not notice that the link has been looped, the routing protocol must wait for timeouts—things such as not hearing from the router on the other end of the link for some period of time.

LCP notices looped links quickly using a feature called *magic numbers*. When using PPP, the router sends PPP LCP messages instead of Cisco-proprietary keepalives across the link; these messages include a magic number, which is different on each router. If a line is looped, the router receives an LCP message with its own magic number instead of getting a message with the other router's magic number. A router receiving its own magic number knows that the frame it sent has been looped back. If configured to do so, the router can take down the interface, which speeds convergence.

Enhanced Error Detection

Just like many other data-link protocols, PPP uses an FCS field in the PPP trailer to determine if an individual frame has an error. If a frame is received in error, it is discarded. However, PPP monitors the frequency with which frames are received in error, and it can be configured to take down an interface if too many errors occur.

PPP LCP analyzes the error rates on a link using a PPP feature called Link Quality Monitoring (LQM). LCP at each end of the link sends messages describing the number of correctly received packets and bytes. The router that sent the packets compares this number to the number of packets and bytes it sent, and it calculates percentage loss. The router can be configured to take down the link after a configured error rate has been exceeded.

The only time this feature helps is when you have redundant routes in the network. By taking down a link that has many errors, you can cause packets to use an alternative path that might not have as many errors.

Authentication Over WAN Links

Security issues in a WAN can differ compared to security in a LAN. In a LAN, most devices can be under the control of the organization owning the devices. Traffic between devices in the same building might not ever leave the confines of the office space used by that company. However, with WANs, by definition, the traffic leaves one location and travels through some other network owned by the service provider and back into another site.

The term *authentication* refers to a set of security functions that help one device ensure that it is communicating with the correct other device. For instance, if R1 and R2 are supposed to be communicating over a serial link, R1 might want R2 to somehow prove that it really is R2. Authentication provides a way to prove one's identity.

WAN authentication is most often needed when dial lines are used. However, the configuration of the authentication features remains the same whether a leased line or dial line is used. This section covers the basics of two authentication methods. Chapter 10, which covers ISDN and dial concepts, briefly mentions cases in which authentication should be used.

PAP and CHAP Authentication

Password Authentication Protocol (PAP) and *Challenge Handshake Authentication Protocol (CHAP)* authenticate the endpoints on either end of a point-to-point serial link. CHAP is the preferred method today because the identifying codes flowing over the link are created using a Message Digest 5 (MD5) one-way hash, which is more secure than the clear-text passwords sent by PAP.

Both PAP and CHAP require the exchange of messages between devices. When a dialed line is used, the dialed-to router expects to receive a username and password from the dialing router with both PAP and CHAP. With a leased line, one router starts the process, and the other responds. Whether leased line or dial, with PAP, the username and password are sent in the first message. With CHAP, the protocol begins with a message called a *challenge*, which asks the other router to send its username and password. Figure 9-4 outlines the different processes in the case where the links are dialed. The process works the same when the link uses a leased line.

PAP flows are much less secure than CHAP because PAP sends the host name and password in clear text in the message. These can be read easily if someone places a tracing tool in the circuit. CHAP instead uses a one-way hash algorithm, with input to the algorithm being a password and a shared random number. The CHAP challenge states the random number; both routers are preconfigured with the password. The challenged router runs the hash algorithm using the just-learned random number and the secret password and sends the results back to the router that sent the challenge. The router that sent the challenge runs the same algorithm using the random number (sent across the link) and the password (not sent across the link). If the results match, the passwords must match.

The most interesting part of the process is that at no time does the password itself ever cross the link. With the random number, the hash value is different every time. So even if someone sees the calculated hash value using a trace tool, the value is meaningless as a way to break in next time. CHAP authentication is difficult to break, even with a tracing tool on the WAN link.

Figure 9-4 *PAP and CHAP Messages*

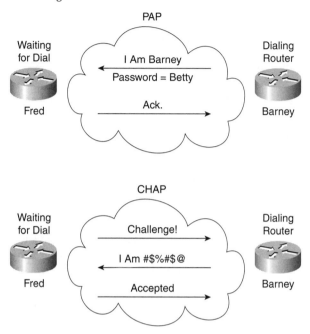

Example 9-3 shows the CHAP configuration for Figure 9-4.

Example 9-3 *CHAP Configuration Example*

```
Router Fred                              Router Barney

username Barney password Bedrock         username Fred password Bedrock
!                                        !
interface serial 0                       interface serial 0
encapsulation ppp                        encapsulation ppp
ppp authentication chap                  ppp authentication chap
.                                        .
```

Notice that each router refers to the other router's host name; each router uses its own host name in CHAP flows unless overridden by configuration. Each side configures the same password. When Router Barney receives a challenge from Router Fred, Router Barney sends the calculated hash value based on the password and the random number. Fred computes the same hash value using the same random number and password, comparing the calculated value with what Barney sends back to perform authentication. CHAP authentication is completed if the two values match.

Foundation Summary

The "Foundation Summary" section lists the most important facts from the chapter. Although this section does not list everything that will be on the exam, a well-prepared CCNA candidate should at a minimum know all the details in each Foundation Summary before taking the exam.

Table 9-7 gives the basic definitions of the three types of WAN services.

Table 9-7 *Definitions of Leased Line, Circuit Switching, and Packet Switching*

Term	Description
Leased line	A dedicated, always-on circuit between two endpoints. The service provider just passes a constant rate bit stream; it does not interpret or make decisions based on the bits sent over the circuit. Generally is more expensive than packet switching today.
Circuit switching/dial	Provides dedicated bandwidth between two points, but only for the duration of the call. Typically used as a cheaper alternative to leased lines, particularly when connectivity is not needed all the time. Also is useful for backup when a leased line or packet-switched service fails.
Packet switching	Provides virtual circuits between pairs of sites, with contracted traffic rates for each VC. Each site's physical connectivity consists of a leased line from the site to a device in the provider's network. Generally cheaper than leased lines.

The physical connection for leased lines includes a CSU/DSU on each end of the link, as shown in Figure 9-5.

Figure 9-5 *Physical Components of a Point-to-Point Serial Link*

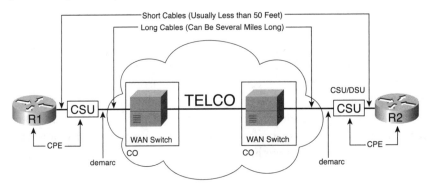

Table 9-8 lists the important comparison points between HDLC and PPP.

Table 9-8   *Point-to-Point Data-Link Protocol Attributes*

Protocol	Error Recovery	Architected Type Field	Other Attributes
HDLC	No	No	HDLC serves as Cisco's default on serial links. Cisco uses a Proprietary Type field to support multiprotocol traffic. Supports synchronous links only.
PPP	Supported but not enabled by default	Yes	PPP was meant for multiprotocol interoperability from its inception, unlike HDLC. PPP also supports asynchronous communication.

Figure 9-6 outlines the different PAP and CHAP flows.

Figure 9-6 *PAP and CHAP Messages*

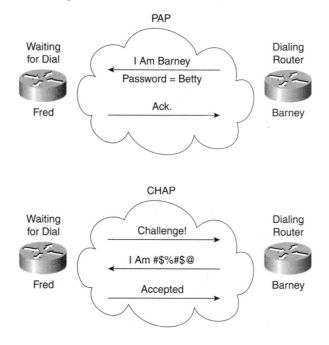

Q&A

As mentioned in the Introduction, you have two choices for review questions. The following questions give you a bigger challenge than the exam because they are open-ended. By reviewing with this more-difficult question format, you can exercise your memory better and prove your conceptual and factual knowledge of the topics covered in this chapter. The answers to these questions are found in Appendix A.

For more practice with exam-like question formats, including multiple-choice questions and those using a router simulator, use the exam engine on the CD.

1. Define the terms DCE and DTE in the context of the physical layer and a point-to-point serial link.

2. Identify the command used to set the clock rate on an interface in which a DCE cable has been inserted. Compare and contrast the two styles of the command that may be entered in configuration mode versus which style shows up in the configuration.

3. Name one WAN data-link protocol used on point-to-point leased lines that defines a method of announcing the interface's IP addresses to other devices attached to the WAN.

4. Can PPP dynamically assign IP addresses? If so, is this feature always enabled?

5. Create a configuration to enable PPP on serial 0 for IP. Make up IP Layer 3 addresses as needed.

6. Define the terms PAP and CHAP. Which one sends passwords in clear-text format?

7. CHAP configuration uses names and passwords. Given Routers A and B, describe what names and passwords must match in the respective CHAP configurations.

8. What field has Cisco added to the HDLC header, making it proprietary?

9. List the types of packet switching mentioned in this chapter. Identify the one for which all traffic is segmented into smaller pieces.

10. Two-wire leased circuits are seldom used today, and certainly not between two routers. What problem was solved with the advent of four-wire leased circuits versus two-wire?

11. Define "synchronous" in relation to leased lines.

12. Create a CHAP configuration between two routers. Make up specific details as needed.

This chapter covers the following subjects:

- ISDN Protocols and Design

- ISDN Configuration and Dial-on-Demand Routing

CHAPTER 10

ISDN and Dial-on-Demand Routing

Most of the time, sites that use routers need some sort of permanent, always-on WAN connectivity to other sites in the network. However, that permanent connectivity might fail, so these routers might want to use some sort of dial (circuit-switched) technology to be able to send and receive packets while the failed leased line or packet-switched service is being repaired. Also, for sites that truly need only occasional WAN connectivity, dialed circuits, for which a service provider charges a small fee per call and per minute, might actually be cheaper than using a leased line or packet-switched service. So, although they aren't the typical choice for WAN connectivity for everyday use, dialed links are still popular.

Of all the circuit-switched "dial" options that have emerged over the years, ISDN is probably the most popular choice for connectivity between routers. ISDN uses digital signals, which allows for faster speeds than analog lines. ISDN has grown to be commonly available in many countries and cities, so it is a viable option for many companies worldwide.

This chapter covers the basics of ISDN technology, along with the related router configuration. In particular, the Cisco IOS software feature called dial-on-demand routing (DDR), which allows you to essentially define when the dialed connection should be brought up and taken down, is covered in detail. Please refer to Appendix F for some further details about a few of the topics in this chapter.

"Do I Know This Already?" Quiz

The purpose of the "Do I Know This Already?" quiz is to help you decide if you need to read the entire chapter. If you intend to read the entire chapter, you do not necessarily need to answer these questions now.

The ten-question quiz, derived from the major sections in the "Foundation Topics" section, helps you determine how to spend your limited study time.

Table 10-1 outlines the major topics discussed in this chapter and the "Do I Know This Already?" quiz questions that correspond to those topics.

Table 10-1 *"Do I Know This Already?" Foundation Topics Section-to-Question Mapping*

Foundations Topics Section	Questions Covered in This Section
ISDN Protocols and Design	1–5
ISDN Configuration and Dial-on-Demand Routing	6–10

CAUTION The goal of self-assessment is to gauge your mastery of the topics in this chapter. If you don't know the answer to a question or you're only partially sure of the answer, you should mark this question as wrong for purposes of the self-assessment. Giving yourself credit for an answer you guess correctly skews your self-assessment results and might give you a false sense of security.

1. How fast do the D channels run on a BRI and PRI, respectively?

    a. 8 kbps and 8 kbps

    b. 8 kbps and 16 kbps

    c. 8 kbps and 64 kbps

    d. 16 kbps and 16 kbps

    e. 16 kbps and 64 kbps

    f. 64 kbps and 64 kbps

    g. None of the above

2. Which of the following protocols defines call setup signaling for ISDN?

    a. I.411

    b. I.319

    c. Q.911

    d. Q.921

    e. Q.931

    f. Q.941

    g. None of the above

3. Which of the following reference points are used by ISDN BRI interfaces in a Cisco router?

    a. R

    b. R/S

    c. S/T

    d. U

    e. V

4. Which of the following PRI function groups is appropriate for use with a PC with a simple serial interface?

    a. TA

    b. NT1

    c. NT2

    d. SBus

    e. None of the above

5. Which of the following encoding formats could be used on a PRI in North America?

    a. AMI

    b. B8ZS

    c. SF

    d. ESF

    e. 10B8N

    f. None of the above

6. Assume that a router has an IP ACL numbered 109 that permits traffic going to IP address 10.1.1.1. Which of the following commands correctly refers to the ACL, causing traffic sent to IP address 10.1.1.1 to be considered "interesting"?

   a. dialer acl 109

   b. dialer list 109

   c. dialer-list 1 protocol ip 10.1.1.1

   d. dialer list 1 protocol ip 10.1.1.1

   e. dialer-list 1 protocol ip list 109

   f. dialer list 1 protocol ip list 109

   g. dialer-list 1 list 109

   h. dialer list 1 list 109

   i. None of the above

7. Which of the following could be necessary in a configuration that uses DDR and ISDN BRI interfaces?

   a. Switch type

   b. Encoding

   c. Framing

   d. SPIDs

   e. Identification of DS0 channels used

   f. Polarity

   g. None of the above

8. Which of the following could be necessary in a configuration that uses DDR and ISDN PRI interfaces in North America?

   a. Switch type

   b. Encoding

   c. Framing

   d. SPIDs

   e. Identification of DS0 channels used

   f. Polarity

   g. None of the above

9. When you configure DDR using the style of DDR configuration called dialer profiles, which of the following commands are useful on the dialer interface?

   a. dialer-group

   b. dialer-list

   c. encapsulation ppp

   d. All of the above

   e. None of the above

10. Which of the following interface subcommands enables multilink PPP?

   a. ppp multilink

   b. encapsulation ppp multilink

   c. enable mlp

   d. mlp on

   e. None of the above

The answers to the "Do I Know This Already?" quiz appear in Appendix A. The suggested choices for your next step are as follows:

■ **8 or less overall score**—Read the entire chapter. This includes the "Foundation Topics," "Foundation Summary," and "Q&A" sections.

■ **9 or 10 overall score**—If you want more review on these topics, skip to the "Foundation Summary" section and then go to the "Q&A" section. Otherwise, move to the next chapter.

Foundation Topics

ISDN Protocols and Design

Integrated Services Digital Network (ISDN) provides switched (dialed) digital WAN services in increments of 64 kbps. Before ISDN, most dial services used the same analog lines that were connected to phones. Before ISDN was created, data rates using modems and analog phone lines typically did not exceed 9600 bits per second. The phone companies of the world created ISDN as a key building block for digital services of the future. They wanted to have a dialed digital service that not only allowed faster transmission rates but that also was pervasive as a simple analog line used for voice. Today, you could argue that the collective phone companies of the world were ultimately successful with these goals, but not totally successful: ISDN availability is widespread, but you can still find places where it is simply not available.

ISDN was created more than 20 years ago, and it began being widely deployed in the U.S. by the early 1990s. Competing technologies might eventually overtake the need for ISDN. As covered in Chapter 15, "Remote Access Technologies," of *CCNA INTRO Exam Certification Guide*, for Internet access, ISDN has been usurped by competing technologies such as DSL, cable modems, and simply faster analog modems. ISDN remains a popular option for temporary connectivity between routers.

This chapter begins with some perspectives on when to use ISDN, followed by the technical details of the ISDN specifications. After that, you will read about how to configure ISDN.

Typical Uses of ISDN

One key reason to use dialed connections of any kind, including ISDN, might be to send and receive data for only short periods of time. "Occasional" connections might be used by a site for which instant access to data is not needed, but for which access is needed a few times per day. For example, a store might send in sales and resupply information overnight.

Routers frequently use ISDN to create a backup link when their primary leased line or Frame Relay connection is lost. Although the leased line or Frame Relay access link might seldom fail, when it does, a remote site might be completely cut off from the rest of the network. Depending on the network's business goals, long outages might not be acceptable, so ISDN could be used to dial back to the main site.

Figure 10-1 shows some typical network topologies when you're using ISDN. These scenarios can be described as follows:

- Case 1 shows dial-on-demand routing. Logic is configured in the routers to trigger the dial when the user sends traffic that needs to get to another site.

- Case 2 shows a typical telecommuting environment.

- Case 3 shows a typical dial-backup topology. The leased line fails, so an ISDN call is established between the same two routers.

- Case 4 shows where an ISDN BRI can be used to dial directly to another router to replace a Frame Relay access link or a failed virtual circuit (VC).

Figure 10-1 *Typical Occasional Connections Between Routers*

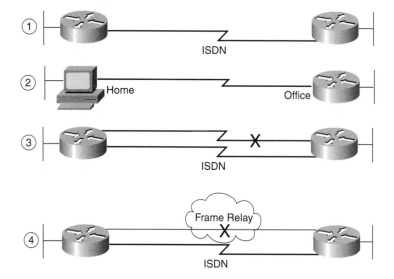

ISDN Channels

ISDN includes two types of interfaces: Basic Rate Interface (BRI) and Primary Rate Interface (PRI). Both BRI and PRI provide multiple digital bearer channels (B channels), over which temporary connections can be made and data can be sent. Because both BRI and PRI have multiple B channels, a single BRI or PRI line can have concurrent digital dial circuits to multiple sites, or multiple circuits to the same remote router to increase available bandwidth to that site.

B channels are used to transport data. B channels are called bearer channels because they bear or carry the data. B channels operate at speeds of up to 64 kbps, although the speed might be lower depending on the service provider.

ISDN signals new data calls using the D channel. When a router creates a B channel call to another device using a BRI or PRI, it sends the phone number it wants to connect to inside a message sent across the D channel. The phone company's switch receives the message and sets up the circuit. Signaling a new call over the D channel is effectively the same thing as picking up the phone and dialing a number to create a voice call.

The different types of ISDN lines are often described with a phrase that implies the number of each type of channel. For instance, BRIs are referred to as 2B+D, meaning two B channels and one D channel. PRIs based on T1 framing, as in the U.S., are referred to as 23B+D, and PRIs based on E1 framing are referred to as 30B+D. Table 10-2 lists the number of channels for each type of ISDN line and the terminology used to describe them.

Table 10-2 *BRI and PRI B and D Channels*

Type of Interface	Number of Bearer (B) Channels	Number of Signaling Channels	Descriptive Term
BRI	2	1 (16 kbps)	2B+D
PRI (T1)	23	1 (64 kbps)	23B+D
PRI (E1)	30	1 (64 kbps)	30B+D

ISDN Protocols

The characterizations of several key protocols made by the Cisco ICND course are important for the exam. Table 10-3 is directly quoted from the ICND course. Be sure to learn the information in the Issue column. Knowing what each series of specifications is about is useful.

Table 10-3 *ISDN Protocols*

Issue	Protocol	Key Examples
Telephone network and ISDN	E-series	E.163—International telephone numbering plan E.164—International ISDN addressing
ISDN concepts, aspects, and interfaces	I-series	I.100 series—Concepts, structures, and terminology I.400 series—User-Network Interface (UNI)
Switching and signaling	Q-series	Q.921—Link Access Procedure on the D channel (LAPD) Q.931—ISDN network layer

The OSI layers correlating to the different ISDN specifications are also mentioned in the ICND course. It's also useful to memorize the specifications listed in Table 10-4, as well as which OSI layer each specification matches.

Table 10-4 *ISDN I-Series and Q-Series Mentioned in ICND: OSI Layer Comparison*

Layer as Compared to OSI	I-Series	Equivalent Q-Series Specification	Description
1	ITU-T I.430 ITU-T I.431	—	Defines connectors, encoding, framing, and reference points.
2	ITU-T I.440 ITU-T I.441	ITU-T Q.920 ITU-T Q.921	Defines the LAPD protocol used on the D channel to encapsulate signaling requests.
3	ITU-T I.450 ITU-T I.451	ITU-T Q.930 ITU-T Q.931	Defines signaling messages, such as call setup and teardown messages.

NOTE A tool to help you remember the specifications and layers is that the second digit in the Q-series numbers matches the OSI layer. For example, in ITU-T Q.920, the second digit, 2, corresponds to OSI Layer 2. In the I-series, the second digit of the specification numbers is 2 more than the corresponding OSI layer. For example, I.430, with its second digit of 3, defines OSI Layer 1 equivalent functions.

Now that you have at least seen the names and numbers behind some of the ISDN protocols, you can concentrate on the more important protocols. The first of these is LAPD, defined in Q.921, which is used as a data-link protocol across an ISDN D channel. Essentially, a router with an ISDN interface needs to send and receive signaling messages to and from the local ISDN switch to which it is connected. LAPD provides the data-link protocol that allows delivery of messages across that D channel to the local switch. Note that LAPD does not define the signaling messages. It just provides a data-link protocol that can be used to send the signaling messages.

The call setup and teardown messages themselves are defined by the Q.931 protocol. So, the local switch can receive a Q.931 call setup request from a router over the LAPD-controlled D channel, and it should react to that Q.931 message by setting up a circuit over the public network, as shown in Figure 10-2.

Figure 10-2   *LAPD and PPP on D and B Channels*

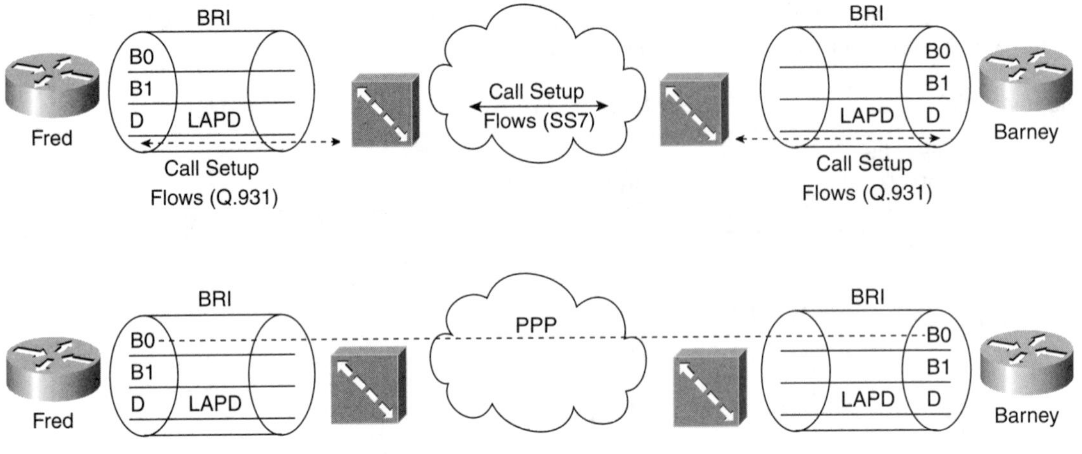

The service provider can use anything it wants to set up the call inside its network, but between each local switch and the routers, ISDN Q.931 messages are used for signaling. Typically, Signaling System 7 (SS7) is used between the two switches—the same protocol used inside phone company networks to set up circuits for phone calls.

As soon as the call is established, a 64-kbps circuit exists between a B channel on each of the two routers shown in Figure 10-2. The routers can use HDLC, but they typically use PPP as the data-link protocol on the B channel from end to end. As on leased lines, the switches in the phone company do not interpret the bits sent inside this circuit.

The D channel remains up all the time so that new signaling messages can be sent and received. Because the signals are sent outside the channel used for data, this is called *out-of-band signaling.*

An ISDN switch often requires some form of authentication with the device connecting to it. Switches use a free-form decimal value, called the service profile identifier (SPID), to perform authentication. In short, before any Q.931 call setup messages are accepted, the switch asks for the configured SPID values. If the values match what is configured in the switch, call setup flows are accepted. When you order new ISDN lines, the provider gives you some paperwork. If the paperwork includes SPIDs, you simply need to configure that number in the ISDN configuration for that line.

ISDN BRI Function Groups and Reference Points

When the ITU first began work on ISDN protocols, it took a very realistic approach to the technology. Any technology that interfaces with devices located at the customer site—which is exactly what ISDN was designed to do—will be accepted more quickly by some people, and in some geographies, and more slowly by other people. Therefore, the ITU defined several different options as to what equipment might be used at the customer site while still ultimately using an ISDN line. By doing so, ISDN could grow and give customers many migration options.

The ISDN specifications identify the various functions that must be performed to support customer premises equipment (CPE). ISDN uses the term *function group* to refer to a set of functions that a piece of hardware or software must perform. Because the ITU wanted several options for the customer, it defined several different function groups. Because the function groups might be implemented by separate products, possibly even from different vendors, the ITU needed to explicitly define the interfaces between the devices that perform each function. Therefore, ISDN uses the term *reference point* to refer to this interface between two function groups.

Many people get confused about the ISDN terms reference point and function group. One key reason for the confusion is that only some function groups—and therefore some reference points—are used in a single topology. Another reason is that if you just work with ISDN on routers, you do not typically need to think about some of the function groups and reference points. Also, most people who work with ISDN every day do not even use the terms function group and reference point. In an effort to clear up these two topics, consider the following inexact but more-familiar definitions of the two:

- **Function group**—A set of functions implemented by a device and software
- **Reference point**—The interface between two function groups, including cabling details

Most people understand concepts better if they can visualize or actually implement a network. A cabling diagram is helpful for examining the reference points and function groups. Figure 10-3 shows the cabling diagram for several examples.

Routers A and B represent typical cabling with a Cisco router, using ISDN, in North America. Router A is ordered with an ISDN BRI U interface; the U implies that it uses the U reference point, referring to the I.430 reference point for the interface between the customer premises and the telco in North America. No other device needs to be installed; the line supplied by the telco is simply plugged into the router's BRI interface.

Router B uses a BRI card with an S/T interface, implying that it must be cabled to a function group NT1 device in North America. An NT1 function group device must be connected to the telco line through a U reference point in North America. When using a router BRI card with an S/T reference point, the router must be cabled to an external NT1, which in turn is plugged into the line from the telco (the U interface).

Figure 10-3 *ISDN Function Groups and Reference Points*

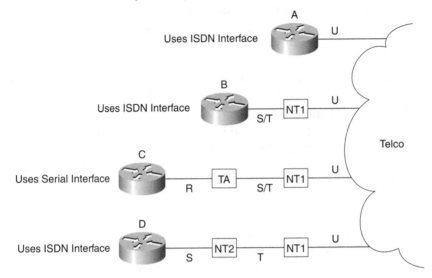

Both Router A and Router B use an ISDN BRI card, but they have different reference points. The list price of the BRI-U card is typically several hundred dollars higher than a BRI-S/T card, because the BRI-U essentially contains the NT1 function group on the card, making an external NT1 unnecessary.

A router can connect to an ISDN service with a simple serial interface, as shown with Router C in Figure 10-3. Router C must implement an ISDN function group called TE2 (Terminal Equipment 2) and connect directly to a device called a terminal adapter using the R reference point.

Fun, isn't it? The real goal of ISDN is to allow various migration paths. Imagine that you already own a router at a remote site, and the router does not support ISDN interfaces. You could buy an external ISDN TA and NT1, and use ISDN, for a lot less money than buying a new router with an ISDN BRI-U card. For another site, you might deploy a new router, so you buy a router with a BRI-U card, and you can avoid worrying about all the external devices. In either case, the ITU tried to provide options to the public and to the service providers selling ISDN to the public—with the unfortunate side effect of requiring CCNA candidates to memorize a lot of details!

Table 10-5 summarizes the types shown in Figure 10-3. Tables 10-6 and 10-7 summarize the formal definitions.

Table 10-5 *Function Groups and Reference Point Summary*

Router	Function Group(s)	Connected to Which Reference Point(s)	Type of Interface Used in the Router
A	TE1, NT1	U	ISDN card, U interface
B	TE1	S/T (combined S and T)	ISDN card, S/T interface
C	TE2	R	Serial interface (no ISDN hardware/software in the router)
D	TE1	S	ISDN card, S/T interface

Table 10-6 *Definitions for the Function Groups Shown in Figure 10-3*

Function Group	What the Acronym Stands For	Description
TE1	Terminal Equipment 1	ISDN-capable four-wire cable. Understands signaling and 2B+D. Uses an S reference point.
TE2	Terminal Equipment 2	Equipment that does not understand ISDN protocols and specifications (no ISDN awareness). Uses an R reference point, typically an RS-232 or V.35 cable, to connect to a TA.
TA	Terminal adapter	Equipment that uses R and S reference points. Can be thought of as the TE1 function group on behalf of a TE2.
NT1	Network Termination Type 1	CPE equipment in North America. Connects with a U reference point (two-wire) to the telco. Connects with T or S reference points to other CPE.
NT2	Network Termination Type 2	Equipment that uses a T reference point to the telco outside North America or to an NT1 inside North America. Uses an S reference point to connect to other CPE.
NT1/NT2	—	A combined NT1 and NT2 in the same device. This is relatively common in North America.

Table 10-7 *Definitions for the Reference Points Shown in Figure 10-3*

Reference Point	What It Connects Between
R	TE2 and TA
S	TE1 or TA and NT2
T	NT2 and NT1
U	NT1 and the telco
S/T	TE1 or TA, connected to an NT1, when no NT2 is used. Alternatively, the connection from a TE1 or TA to a combined NT1/NT2.

For the home PC user, marketing jargon can get in the way of learning the true ISDN terminology. Figure 10-4 outlines the problem.

Figure 10-4 *Home ISDN User and Reference Points*

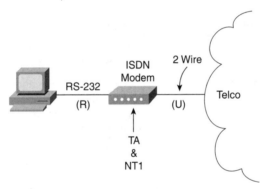

Popularly used ISDN terminology for home-based consumers sometimes muddles the terminology from the ISDN specifications. The home user orders the ISDN service, and the telco offers to sell the user one of several "ISDN modems." What is actually received is a single device that includes a TA and an NT1. A PC uses a serial port to connect to the TA, which uses reference point R to connect to the PC and reference point U to connect to the BRI line itself. However, the terms reference point, TA, and NT1 are almost never used by providers—hence the confusion with the official terminology covered here.

ISDN PRI Function Groups and Reference Points

The ITU planned for multiple implementation options with BRI because BRI would typically be installed when connecting to consumers. PRI was seen as a service for businesses, mainly because of the larger anticipated costs and a PRI's larger number of B channels. So the ITU did not define function groups and reference points for ISDN PRI!

BRI and PRI Encoding and Framing

The physical layer always includes some specifications about encoding and framing. Without those specifications, the devices attached to the network would not know how to send and receive bits across the medium. In some cases, you can just ignore those details. Unless you are building hardware for a networking vendor, you seldom think about those details. However, to configure an ISDN PRI, you need to know something about encoding and framing at Layer 1, because you need to pick between two options for each when configuring a PRI on a Cisco router.

In some parts of the world, the telco bases its networks on T1 services, and other parts of the world use E1 services. In fact, the Cisco router hardware used for PRIs consists mostly of chips and software used by T1 and E1 lines. When configuring these cards, you need to know what to configure for the encoding and framing options. If you code a value different from what the telco uses, the line will not work.

PRI Encoding

For any physical layer specification, the line encoding defines which energy levels sent over the cable mean a 1 and which energy levels mean a 0. For instance, an early and simple encoding scheme simply used a +5 volt signal to mean a binary 1 and a −5 volt signal to mean a binary 0. Today, encoding schemes vary greatly from one Layer 1 technology to another. Some consider a signal of a different frequency to mean a 1 or 0. Others examine amplitude (signal strength), look for phase shifts in the signal, or look for more than one of these differences in electrical signals.

ISDN PRI in North America is based on a digital T1 circuit. T1 circuits use two different encoding schemes—Alternate Mark Inversion (AMI) and Binary 8 with Zero Substitution (B8ZS). You will configure one or the other for a PRI; all you need to do is make the router configuration match what the telco is using. For PRI circuits in Europe, Australia, and other parts of the world that use E1s, the only choice for line coding is High-Density Bipolar 3 (HDB3).

PRI Framing

PRI lines send and receive a serial stream of bits. So how does a PRI interface know which bits are part of the D channel, or the first B channel, or the second, or the third, and so on? In a word—framing.

Framing, at ISDN's physical layer, defines how a device can decide which bits are part of each channel. As is true of encoding, PRI framing is based on the underlying T1 or E1 specifications. The two T1 framing options define 24 different 64-kbps DS0 channels, plus an 8-kbps management channel used by the telco, which gives you a total speed of 1.544 Mbps. That's true regardless of which of the two framing methods are used on the T1. With E1s, framing defines 32 64-kbps channels, for a total of 2.048 Mbps, regardless of the type of framing used.

The two options for framing on T1s are to use either Extended Super Frame (ESF) or the older option—Super Frame (SF). In most cases today, new T1s use ESF. For PRIs in Europe and Australia, based on E1s, the line uses CRC-4 framing or the original line framing defined for E1s. You simply need to tell the router whether to enable CRC-4 or not.

As soon as the framing details are known, the PRI can assign some channels as B channels and one channel as the D channel. For PRIs based on T1s, the first 23 DS0 channels are the B channels, and the last DS0 channel is the D channel, giving you 23B+D. The E1-based PRI uses channel 0 for framing, channel 16 for the D-channel, and the rest (1-15 and 17-31) as B-channels.

Table 10-8 summarizes the key concepts behind framing and encoding, along with the options for each with T1 and E1 circuits.

Table 10-8   *Definitions for Encoding and Framing*

Term	Description	Examples
Encoding	Electrical signals sent over a medium that mean either a binary 0 or 1.	B8ZS and AMI (T1), HDB3 (E1)
Framing	The use of a standard for how to interpret a serial bit stream to identify the individual component channels of that bit stream.	SF and ESF (T1), CRC4 (E1)

BRI Framing and Encoding

ISDN BRI uses a single encoding scheme and a single option for framing. Because of this, there are no configuration options for either framing or encoding in a router.

ISDN Configuration and Dial-on-Demand Routing

This section covers ISDN configuration and the related DDR configuration that causes Cisco IOS software to use the BRI interface. You must understand DDR configuration and concepts for the ISDN configuration topics to make sense. ISDN configuration can be very brief. In spite of the noise surrounding all the protocols and terminology, you can configure just a few ISDN options in a router. However, the DDR configuration to tell the router when to dial and when to tear down the call can become quite involved.

This section first covers DDR configuration when using BRI interfaces, and then it covers the ISDN configuration for both BRI and PRI. After that, a different style of DDR configuration, DDR dialer profiles, is discussed. A feature called multilink PPP (MLP), which allows multiple B channels to be connected to the same remote site, closes the chapter.

Tables 10-9 and 10-10 summarize the commands used throughout this section.

Table 10-9 *ISDN Configuration Commands*

Command	Description	Configuration Mode
isdn switch-type *switch-type*	Defines to the router the type of ISDN switch to which the ISDN line is connected at the central office.	Global or interface
isdn spid1 *spid*	Defines the first SPID.	Interface
isdn spid2 *spid*	Defines the second SPID.	Interface
isdn caller *phone-number* [**callback**]	Defines a valid number for incoming calls when using call screening.	Interface
dialer-list *dialer-group* **protocol** *protocol-name* {**permit** I **deny** I **list** *access-list-number* I *access-group*}	Defines the types of traffic that are considered interesting.	Global
dialer-group *n*	Enables a dialer list on this interface.	Interface
dialer string *string*	The dial string used when dialing only one site.	Interface
dialer map *protocol next-hop-address* [**name** *host-name*] [**spc**] [**speed 56** I **speed 64**] [**broadcast**] [*dial-string*[:*isdn-subaddress*]]	The dial string to reach the next hop. The **map** command is used when dialing more than one site. This also is the name used for authentication. The **broadcast** option ensures that copies of broadcasts go to this next-hop address.	Interface
dialer idle-timeout *seconds* [**inbound** I **either**]	Defines how long to wait with no interesting traffic before terminating a dial.	Interface
dialer fast-idle *seconds*	If all lines are in use, and new interesting traffic arrives for which another line must be dialed, no dial can occur. **fast-idle** defines how long to wait to time out the existing dialed lines when this occurs, allowing for a quicker timeout than the normal idle timeout.	Interface
controller t1 *int-number*	Selects the channelized T1 interface to be used as a PRI.	Global

continues

Table 10-9 *ISDN Configuration Commands (Continued)*

pri-group timeslots *range*	Defines which of the DS0 channels will be used in this PRI.	Controller interface subcommand
framing "sf" | "esf"	Defines the type of framing used on T1-based PRI.	Controller interface subcommand
linecode "ami" | "b8zs"	Defines the type of encoding on T1-based PRI.	Controller interface subcommand

Table 10-10 *ISDN-Related EXEC Commands*

Command	Description
show interfaces bri *number* [:B *channel*]	Includes a reference to the access lists enabled on the interface.
show controllers bri *number*	Shows Layer 1 statistics and status for B and D channels.
show isdn {active | history | memory | status | timers}	Shows various ISDN status information.
show interfaces bri *number*[[:bchannel] | [first] [last]] [accounting]	Displays interface information about the D channel or the B channel(s).
show dialer interface bri *number*	Lists DDR parameters on the BRI interface. Shows whether a number is currently dialed by indicating the current status. Also shows previous attempts to dial and whether they were successful.
debug isdn q921	Lists ISDN Layer 2 messages.
debug isdn q931	Lists ISDN Layer 3 messages (call setup/teardown).
debug dialer {events | packets | map}	Lists information when a packet is directed out a dial interface, specifying whether the packet is interesting.

DDR Legacy Concepts and Configuration

You can configure DDR in several ways, including *Legacy DDR* and *DDR dialer profiles*. The main difference between the two is that Legacy DDR associates dial details with a physical interface, whereas DDR dialer profiles disassociate the dial configuration from a physical interface, allowing a great deal of flexibility. The concepts behind Legacy DDR apply to DDR dialer profiles as well, but Legacy DDR configuration is a little less detailed. Legacy DDR is covered first. Dialer profiles are covered later in this chapter. (Another very useful DDR feature, called *dialer watch,* is very interesting and useful if you have a requirement for DDR.)

DDR can be used to cause the router to dial or to receive a dialed call on asynchronous serial interfaces, synchronous serial interfaces, and ISDN BRI and PRI interfaces. All examples in this chapter use ISDN.

The following list identifies the four key concepts behind Legacy DDR configuration. The first two concepts are not actually related to the dial process, but they relate to the process of choosing when to dial and when not to dial. The other two concepts relate to dialing, or signaling.

The term *signaling* is used in ISDN to describe the processes of call setup and teardown. Many people say "dial" or "dialing" instead of signaling, but it means the same thing.

Here are the four key concepts behind how Legacy DDR works:

1. Route packets out the interface to be dialed.

2. Determine the subset of the packets that trigger the dialing process.

3. Dial (signal).

4. Determine when the connection is terminated.

DDR Step 1: Routing Packets Out the Interface to Be Dialed

Figure 10-5 provides the backdrop for these discussions. In these discussions, the SanFrancisco router dials into the main site in LosAngeles.

Figure 10-5   *Sample DDR Network*

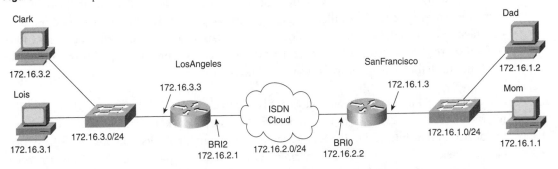

The router must choose when to dial. The first step in this process relates to the following fact:

DDR does not dial until some traffic is directed (routed) out the dial interface.

The router needs to route packets so that they are queued to go out the dial interface. Cisco's design for DDR defines that the router receives some user-generated traffic and, through normal routing processes, decides to route the traffic out the interface to be dialed. The router (SanFrancisco) can receive a packet that must be routed out BRI0; routing the packet out BRI0 triggers the Cisco IOS software, causing the dial to occur.

Of course, routing protocols cannot learn routes over a BRI line that is not normally up! In Figure 10-5, for example, SanFrancisco has no routes to 172.16.3.0/24 learned via a routing protocol, because no B channel call has been placed yet. Therefore, static routes must be configured on SanFrancisco, pointing to subnets in LosAngeles. Then, packets are routed out the interface, which can trigger a dial of a B channel to LosAngeles.

All routable protocols can be configured to trigger the dial by routing packets of that type out the interface. Because IP is so popular, it is used in the upcoming examples.

To begin the process of building a DDR configuration, IP routes are added to the configuration so that packets can be directed out BRI0 on SanFrancisco, as shown in Example 10-1. This static route points out interface BRI0, because SanFrancisco's BRI0 interface is in the same subnet as 172.16.2.1.

Example 10-1 *Defining a Static Route to Send Packets Out the ISDN BRI Interface*

```
! SanFrancisco static routes
ip route 172.16.3.0 255.255.255.0 172.16.2.1
```

DDR Step 2: Determining the Subset of the Packets That Trigger the Dialing Process

Together, Steps 1 and 2 of Legacy DDR logic determine when to dial a circuit. These combined steps are typically called *triggering the dial*. In Step 1, a packet is routed out an interface to be dialed, but that alone does not necessarily cause the dial to occur. The Cisco IOS software allows Step 2 to define a subset of the packets routed in Step 1 to actually cause the route to dial. The logic flow is shown in Figure 10-6.

The choice in Step 2 is simply put like this: "Is this packet, which is being routed out this dial interface, worthy of causing the dial to occur?" Cisco calls packets that are worthy of causing the device to dial *interesting packets*. Cisco does not name packets that are not worthy of causing the dial; in effect, they are "boring." Only interesting packets cause the dial to occur, but when the circuit is up, both interesting and boring traffic can flow across the link.

The network engineer has control over what causes the dial, meaning that he or she also controls when the router spends the company's money. Providers typically charge a base fee for the ISDN line, plus incremental charges per minute of use for a B channel.

Figure 10-6 *DDR Logic for Triggering the Dial*

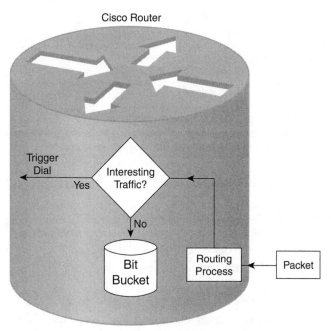

Two different methods can be used to define interesting packets. In the first method, *interesting* is defined as all packets of one or more Layer 3 protocols (for example, all IP packets). In that case, any user in SanFrancisco can send a packet to any host in 172.16.3.0/24 and trigger the dial connection. That might be exactly what is desired, or it might not be. The second method allows you to define packets as interesting if they are permitted by an access list. IP access control lists (ACLs), covered in Chapter 12, "IP Access Control List Security," create matching logic to match packets. ACLs consider the packets either permitted or denied. With DDR, if the access list permits the packet, it is considered interesting.

Example 10-2 shows additional configuration on SanFrancisco, with two alternatives. One shows all IP packets being considered interesting, and the other shows all packets to the Web server Lois (refer to Figure 10-5) considered interesting.

Example 10-2 *Defining Interesting Packets to Activate the Circuit from SanFrancisco to LosAngeles*

```
ip route 172.16.3.0 255.255.255.0 172.16.2.1
!
access-list 101 permit tcp any host 172.16.3.1 eq 80
!
dialer-list 1 protocol ip permit
!
dialer-list 2 protocol ip list 101
```

continues

Example 10-2 *Defining Interesting Packets to Activate the Circuit from SanFrancisco to LosAngeles (Continued)*

```
!
interface bri 0
 encapsulation ppp
 ip address 172.16.2.2 255.255.255.0
!Use this one if all IP is considered interesting ...
 dialer-group 1
!
! OR use next statement to trigger for web to server Lois
! Note: If you typed the next command, it would replace the dialer-group 1
! command; only one dialer-group is allowed per interface!
!
 dialer-group 2
```

The **dialer-group** interface subcommand enables the logic that determines what is interesting. It refers to a **dialer-list,** which can refer to either an entire protocol suite (as seen in **dialer-list 1**) or an access list (as seen in **dialer-list 2**). With **dialer-group 1** under interface BRI0, any IP traffic that tries to exit the interface is considered interesting and causes a dial to occur.

The other dialer list in the example, **dialer-list 2,** refers to IP access list number 101. If the access list matches a packet that has been routed out interface BRI0, the router dials. If the ACL matching logic does not match the packet, the dial does not occur. This allows you to choose specific subsets of IP traffic that cause the dial to occur. (Chapter 12 has more information on Cisco ACLs.)

DDR Step 3: Dialing (Signaling)

Before the router can dial, or signal, to set up a call, it needs to know the phone number of the other router. With the network shown in Figure 10-5, the configuration is straightforward. The command is **dialer string** *string,* where *string* is the phone number. Example 10-3 completes the DDR configuration associated with Figure 10-5 that allows the dial to occur.

Example 10-3 *SanFrancisco Configuration: Dialing Can Now Occur*

```
ip route 172.16.3.0 255.255.255.0 172.16.2.1
!
access-list 101 permit tcp any host 172.16.3.1 eq 80
!
dialer-list 2 protocol ip list 101
!
interface bri 0
 ip address 172.16.2.2 255.255.255.0
 encapsulation ppp
 dialer string 14045551234
 dialer-group 2
```

The only new command added here is **dialer string,** which shows the phone number that is to be used to signal a connection. The signaling occurs on the BRI's D channel using Q.931 signaling.

With only one site to dial, you can simply configure a single dial string. However, with multiple remote sites, the router needs to know each site's phone number.

For example, Figure 10-7 adds a third site, GothamCity, to the network. Example 10-4 adds a configuration to San Francisco so that an FTP connection from Mom or Dad to the FTP server running on Commissioner (near GothamCity) is considered interesting traffic for causing dial connections to GothamCity.

Figure 10-7   *Mapping Between the Next Hop and the Dial String*

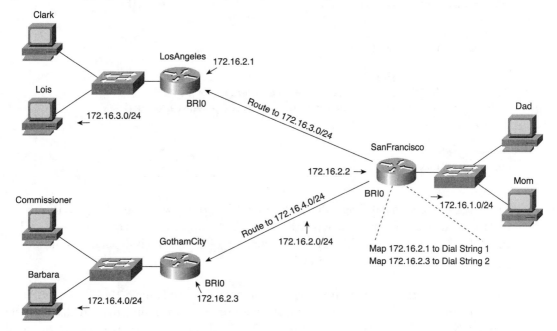

SanFrancisco now must know two phone numbers, as well as when to dial each number. DDR links the number to be dialed to the route that was used to route the packet out the interface. Because the static routes direct the router to send the packet to either 172.16.2.1 (LosAngeles) or 172.16.2.3 (GothamCity), all that is needed is a mapping between these next-hop addresses and their respective ISDN telephone numbers. The **dialer map** command does exactly that.

Example 10-4 shows the mostly complete configuration. CHAP configuration has been added in this step as well.

Example 10-4 *SanFrancisco Configuration: Two Dial-To Sites with a Dialer Map in Use*

```
ip route 172.16.3.0 255.255.255.0 172.16.2.1
ip route 172.16.4.0 255.255.255.0 172.16.2.3
! Added usernames for CHAP support!
username LosAngeles password Clark
username GothamCity password Bruce
!
access-list 101 permit tcp any host 172.16.3.1 eq 80
! Added next statement to make The Client's FTP connection interesting!
access-list 101 permit tcp any host 172.16.4.1 eq 21
!
dialer-list 2 protocol ip list 101
!
interface bri 0
 ip address 172.16.2.2 255.255.255.0
 encapsulation ppp
 ppp authentication chap
 dialer map ip 172.16.2.1 broadcast name LosAngeles 14045551234
 dialer map ip 172.16.2.3 broadcast name GothamCity 19999999999
 dialer-group 2
!
router igrp 6
network 172.16.0.0
```

The **dialer map** commands imply that if the interesting packet were routed to 172.16.2.1, the dial to LosAngeles would occur. Similarly, if an interesting packet were routed to 172.16.2.3, the dial to GothamCity would occur. The definition of *interesting* is expanded to include packets to the FTP server in GothamCity.

Two other important configuration elements are included in Example 10-4. First, CHAP authentication is configured. PAP or CHAP is required if you're dialing to more than one site with ISDN—and PAP and CHAP require PPP. Notice that the usernames and password used with the two remote routers are shown near the top of the configuration. Because SanFrancisco gets CHAP challenges from two different remote sites, it must somehow know which router is sending the CHAP request. So, the username that SanFrancisco expects from the other router is based on the *name* parameter in the **dialer map** command.

You should also note the importance of the **broadcast** keyword on the **dialer map** commands. Just as with any other point-to-point serial link, there is no true data-link broadcast. If a broadcast must be sent on the interface after the circuit has been created, you must use the **broadcast** keyword to tell the interface to forward the packet across the link.

The dialed link acts just like a leased line while it is up. If a particular Layer 3 protocol is enabled on the link, it can be routed across the link. Transparent (encapsulated) bridging can be used just like any other point-to-point link. Routing updates, IPX SAPs, AppleTalk ZIP, and other broadcasts are sent across the link if the **broadcast** keyword is coded.

Although you might not have read Chapter 12 yet, you should note that the ACLs used to define which packets are interesting and which are not do not actually filter any packets. All packets that the router routes out the interface are forwarded—interesting and boring traffic alike. For instance, when the dial connection to LosAngeles is up, not only do packets to the web server flow, but all other packets flow as well. You will read about the additional commands required for filtering traffic with an access list in Chapter 12.

DDR Step 4: Determining When the Connection Is Terminated

The decision to take down the link is the most interesting part about what happens while the link is up. Although any type of packet can be routed across the link, only interesting packets are considered worthy of keeping the link up and spending more money. The router keeps an idle timer, which counts the time since the last interesting packet went across the link. If no interesting traffic happens for the number of seconds defined by the idle timer, the router brings the link down.

Two idle timers can be set. With the **dialer idle-timeout** *seconds* command, the idle time is set. However, if the router wants to dial other sites based on receiving interesting traffic for those sites, and all the B channels are in use, another shorter idle timer can be used. The **dialer fast-idle** *seconds* command lets you configure a typically lower number than the idle timer so that when other sites need to be dialed, the link that is currently up can be brought down more quickly.

ISDN BRI Configuration

This configuration section so far has shown no ISDN-specific configuration commands, other than to refer to the BRI interfaces themselves. In this section, you will learn about the two items you might configure to support BRI. These commands will be used in the context of the same example that has been used throughout this chapter so that the resulting configuration shows a complete, working ISDN DDR configuration.

Examples 10-5 and 10-6 show the completed ISDN DDR configuration for the sample network, including the ISDN-specific configuration. The text following these two examples describes the ISDN commands shown.

Example 10-5 *Completed SanFrancisco Configuration*

```
ip route 172.16.3.0 255.255.255.0 172.16.2.1
ip route 172.16.4.0 255.255.255.0 172.16.2.3
! Added usernames for CHAP support!
username LosAngeles password Clark
```

continues

Example 10-5 *Completed SanFrancisco Configuration (Continued)*

```
username GothamCity password Bruce
!
isdn switch-type basic-ni1
!
access-list 101 permit tcp any host 172.16.3.1 eq 80
access-list 101 permit tcp any host 172.16.4.1 eq 21
!
dialer-list 2 protocol ip list 101
!
interface bri 0
 ip address 172.16.2.2 255.255.255.0
 encapsulation ppp
 ppp authentication chap
 isdn spid1 555555111101
 isdn spid2 555555222202
 dialer idle-timeout 300
 dialer fast-idle 120
 dialer map ip 172.16.2.1 broadcast name LosAngeles 14045551234
 dialer map ip 172.16.2.3 broadcast speed 56 name GothamCity 19999999999
 dialer-group 2
!
router igrp 6
network 172.16.0.0
```

Example 10-6 *LosAngeles Configuration: Receive Only*

```
username SanFrancisco password Clark
!
interface bri 0
ip address 172.16.2.1 255.255.255.0
 encapsulation ppp
 ppp authentication chap
 isdn switch-type basic-ni1
!
router igrp 6
network 172.16.0.0
```

IOS expects you to define the type of ISDN switch to which the router is connected. You can do so with the **isdn switch-type** command, either as a global command or with an interface subcommand. When you have multiple ISDN lines, you can use the global command to cover all interfaces.

Table 10-11 lists the types of switches.

Table 10-11 *ISDN Switch Types*

Type of Switch	Where It Is Typically Found
basic-net3	Australia, Europe, UK
vn3	France
ntt	Japan
basic-5ess	North America
basic-dms100	North America
basic-ni1	North America

You might need to configure the Service Profile Identifier (SPID) for one or both B channels, depending on the switch's expectations. When the telco switch has configured SPIDs, it might not allow the BRI line to work unless the router announces the correct SPID values to the switch. SPIDs, when used, provide a basic authentication feature. If your service provider tells you it uses SPIDs, you should configure them, or signaling will not work.

Example 10-5 shows the commands used to configure the SPIDs. The **isdn spid1** and **isdn spid2** commands define the SPIDs for the first and second B channels, respectively.

To actually configure the ISDN BRI details, you simply configure the switch type, and SPIDs, if needed. The hard part typically is configuring the DDR commands. Table 10-12 summarizes the commands needed to configure ISDN BRI, beyond what is needed for Legacy DDR configuration.

Table 10-12 *Summary of the New Configuration Needed for ISDN BRI Beyond Legacy DDR Configuration*

Command	Description	Configuration Mode
isdn spid1 *spid* **isdn spid2** *spid*	Configures SPIDs as necessary.	Physical interface
isdn switch-type *type*	Configures the ISDN switch type.	Global or physical interface

Summary of Legacy DDR Configuration

You have finally made it through enough details to see a completed working configuration for Legacy DDR using the ISDN BRI interfaces. Before moving on to the other topics in this chapter, a brief review might help. Table 10-13 summarizes the commands needed to configure Legacy DDR, with some explanation of each function.

Table 10-13 *Summary Legacy DDR Configuration Commands*

Command	Description
ip route	Global command that configures static routes that route traffic out an ISDN interface.
username *name* password *secret*	Global command that configures CHAP usernames and passwords.
access-list	Global command that creates ACLs if you need to define a subset of traffic as "interesting."
dialer-list *number* protocol ip [list *acl-number*]	Global command that creates a dialer list that either makes all IP traffic interesting or references the ACL to make a subset interesting.
interface bri *int-number*	Global command that selects ISDN BRI to use for DDR.
encapsulation ppp ppp authentication chap	Interface subcommands that configure PPP and enable CHAP.
isdn spid1 *value* isdn spid2 *value*	Interface subcommands that set ISDN SPID values if needed.
dialer idle-timeout *time* dialer fast-idle *time*	Interface subcommands that set idle timeout values.
dialer-group *number*	Interface subcommand that references the dialer list to define what is interesting.
dialer string *number* dialer map ip *next-hop-ip number*	Interface subcommands that define dial numbers for one site or many.

ISDN and DDR show and debug Commands

To examine the status of ISDN, you can use ISDN **show** and **debug** commands. Example 10-7 also includes some sample output that matches the completed example shown in this chapter.

Example 10-7 *SanFrancisco DDR Commands*

```
!
! This next command occurred before the physical interface even came up.
!
SanFrancisco# show interfaces bri 0:1
BRI0:1 is down, line protocol is down
  Hardware is BRI
```

Example 10-7 *SanFrancisco DDR Commands (Continued)*

```
        MTU 1500 bytes, BW 64 Kbit, DLY 20000 usec, rely 255/255, load 1/255
        Encapsulation PPP, loopback not set, keepalive set (10 sec)
        LCP Closed
        Open:
        Last input 00:00:05, output 00:00:05, output hang never
        Last clearing of "show interface" counters never
        Input queue: 0/75/0 (size/max/drops); Total output drops: 0
        Queuing strategy: weighted fair
        Output queue: 0/1000/64/0 (size/max total/threshold/drops)
           Conversations  0/1/256 (active/max active/max total)
           Reserved Conversations 0/0 (allocated/max allocated)
        5 minute input rate 0 bits/sec, 0 packets/sec
        5 minute output rate 0 bits/sec, 0 packets/sec
           44 packets input, 1986 bytes, 0 no buffer
           Received 0 broadcasts, 0 runts, 0 giants, 0 throttles
           0 input errors, 0 CRC, 0 frame, 0 overrun, 0 ignored, 0 abort
           49 packets output, 2359 bytes, 0 underruns
           0 output errors, 0 collisions, 7 interface resets
           0 output buffer failures, 0 output buffers swapped out
           11 carrier transitions
           DCD=up  DSR=up  DTR=up  RTS=up  CTS=up
!
! This next command was done when the call was up. Look for the "dial reason" in
! the output.
!
SanFrancisco# show dialer interface bri 0
BRI0 - dialer type = ISDN
Dial String      Successes     Failures    Last called    Last status
0 incoming call(s) have been screened.
BRI0: B channel 1
Idle timer (300 secs), Fast idle timer (120 secs)
Wait for carrier (30 secs), Re-enable (15 secs)
Dialer state is data link layer up
Dial reason: ip (s=172.16.1.1, d=172.16.3.1)
Time until disconnect 18 secs
Current call connected 00:14:00
Connected to 14045551234 (LosAngeles)
BRI0: B channel 2
Idle timer (300 secs), Fast idle timer (120 secs)
Wait for carrier (30 secs), Re-enable (15 secs)
Dialer state is idle
!
! This command was performed when the dial was up, showing an active call.
!
SanFrancisco# show isdn active
------------------------------------------------------------------------
                         ISDN ACTIVE CALLS
```

continues

Example 10-7 *SanFrancisco DDR Commands (Continued)*

```
-----------------------------------------------------------------------------
History Table MaxLength = 320 entries
History Retain Timer = 15 Minutes
-----------------------------------------------------------------------------
Call Calling    Called       Duration Remote   Time until  Recorded Charges
Type Number     Number       Seconds  Name     Disconnect  Units/Currency
-----------------------------------------------------------------------------
Out             14045551234  Active(847) LosAngeles   11      u
-----------------------------------------------------------------------------
!
! This next command shows an active "Layer 3" call, meaning that the Q.931
! signaling has created a call.
!
SanFrancisco# show isdn status
The current ISDN Switchtype = ntt
ISDN BRI0 interface
    Layer 1 Status:
        ACTIVE
    Layer 2 Status:
        TEI = 64, State = MULTIPLE_FRAME_ESTABLISHED
    Layer 3 Status:
        1 Active Layer 3 Call(s)
    Activated dsl 0 CCBs = 1
        CCB:callid=8003, callref=0, sapi=0, ces=1, B-chan=1
    Number of active calls = 1
    Number of available B channels = 1
    Total Allocated ISDN CCBs = 1
!
! The debug was turned on while the call was down, and then the call was made,
! so the debug output would show the Q.931 signaling to set up the call.
!
SanFrancisco# debug isdn q931
ISDN q931 protocol debugging is on
TX -> SETUP pd = 8 callref = 0x04
 Bearer Capability i = 0x8890
 Channel ID i = 0x83
 Called Party Number i = 0x80, '14045551234'
SanFrancisco#no debug all
All possible debugging has been turned off
!
! This next debug command was also done before the call was established so that
! when the call was set up, the output would show some useful information. In
! this case, the "interesting" traffic that causes the call is shown.
!
SanFrancisco# debug dialer events
Dialer event debugging is on
Dialing cause: BRI0: ip (s=172.16.1.1, d=172.16.3.1)
```

Example 10-7 *SanFrancisco DDR Commands (Continued)*

```
SanFrancisco#no debug all
All possible debugging has been turned off
SanFrancisco# debug dialer packets
Dialer packet debugging is on
BRI0: ip (s=172.16.1.1, d=172.16.3.1) 444 bytes, interesting (ip PERMIT)
```

Example 10-7 shows a lot of different commands, some at different points in the process of dialing a B channel call from SanFrancisco to LosAngeles. Be sure to look at the comments in the example for some more details about what is happening at each point in the example.

The second command in Example 10-7, **show dialer interface bri 0**, lists the current timer values and call setup reason. The call has been up for 14 minutes, and 18 seconds are left before the 300-second inactivity timer will expire and take the connection down. The **show isdn active** command indicates that a single active call exists to LosAngeles, with only 11 seconds left until disconnect. (This command is entered just a few seconds after the previous **show dialer interface** command.) The **show isdn status** command lists the switch type (ntt) and indicates that one call is active, which leaves one inactive B channel. It is also a very useful command for basic ISDN troubleshooting, because it displays Layer 1, 2, and 3 status for ISDN.

Remembering the general idea behind the **debug** command output is also useful so that the right options can be enabled quickly. The **debug isdn q921** command (not shown) lists details of the LAPD protocol between the router and the ISDN switch. The **debug isdn q931** command lists output for call setup and disconnect. For instance, Example 10-7 shows output typical of what happens on SanFrancisco when a call to LosAngeles is made.

The **debug dialer events** and **debug dialer packets** commands provide similar information when a packet is a candidate for causing the dial to occur—in other words, when a packet is routed out the dial interface.

The coverage of ISDN BRI and Legacy DDR is now complete. In the next few sections, you will read about how to configure PRI, how to configure DDR using dialer profiles, and how to configure multilink PPP.

ISDN PRI Configuration

To configure ISDN BRI, you need to configure only the switch type, plus the SPIDs if the service provider needs to have them configured. Most of the configuration relates to DDR, which causes the ISDN BRI to be used.

With PRI, you have only a few things to configure as well. Other than the same familiar DDR and interface configuration, you mainly need to configure the following:

- Configure the type of ISDN switch to which this router is connected.

- Configure the T1 or E1 encoding and framing options (controller configuration mode).

- Configure the T1 or E1 channel range for the DS0 channels used on this PRI (controller configuration mode).

- Configure any interface settings (for example, PPP encapsulation and IP address) on the interface representing the D channel.

The configuration itself does not require a lot of extra effort as compared with ISDN BRI. The only truly new things are the T1 or E1 controller and the new way to identify the D channel on the PRI interface.

Configuring a T1 or E1 Controller

When you add a physical interface to a Cisco router, the router recognizes a new serial interface with a new unique number. With PRIs, IOS calls the interface a *serial interface*. For instance, a PRI interface might simply be known as "interface serial 1/0."

Along with the interface, any channelized T1 or E1 interface in a router, including a PRI, also has a separate configuration mode associated with each physical interface. *Controller configuration mode* allows you to configure physical layer parameters—the encoding, framing, and T1 or E1 channels that are in use. By separating these Layer 1 configuration details from the serial interface, the configuration on the serial interface looks like it would on any other dial interface, and with the PRI-specific configuration sitting under the controller.

The things you configure under the controller can typically be learned simply by looking at the paperwork from where you ordered the PRI. Your service provider will tell you what encoding and framing to configure on the router. Also, in almost every case, you will use all 24 DS0 channels in the PRI—23 B channels and the D channel.

To configure these options, you must first enter controller configuration mode. Example 10-8 shows the basics.

Example 10-8 *PRI Controller Configuration Example*

```
SanFrancisco(config)#controller t1 1/0
SanFrancisco(config-controller)#framing esf
SanFrancisco(config-controller)#linecode b8zs
SanFrancisco(config-controller)#pri-group timeslots 1-24
```

In this example, the PRI interface is installed as interface serial 1/0. To configure the PRI's Layer 1 details, you use the **controller t1 1/0** command to enter controller configuration mode for that interface. The rest of the commands are somewhat self-explanatory. You should note that the controller numbers the channels 1 through 24, unlike other PRI references inside IOS that number them 0 through 23. Channel 24 is the D channel.

Full PRI Configuration

The only other thing you need to configure for PRI is the switch type, plus all the other things you need to configure DDR—an IP address, PPP, dialer groups, and so on. Example 10-9 shows a completed configuration on SanFrancisco, with the BRI replaced with a PRI.

Example 10-9   *PRI Controller Configuration Example: Completed Configuration on SanFrancisco*

```
Controller t1 1/0
 framing esf
 linecode b8zs
 pri-group timeslots 1-24
!
ip route 172.16.3.0 255.255.255.0 172.16.2.1
ip route 172.16.4.0 255.255.255.0 172.16.2.3
!
username LosAngeles password Clark
username GothamCity password Bruce
!
isdn switch-type basic-ni1
!
access-list 101 permit tcp any host 172.16.3.1 eq 80
access-list 101 permit tcp any host 172.16.4.1 eq 21
!
dialer-list 2 protocol ip list 101
!
interface serial 1/0:23
 ip address 172.16.2.2 255.255.255.0
 encapsulation ppp
 ppp authentication chap
 dialer idle-timeout 300
 dialer fast-idle 120
 dialer map ip 172.16.2.1 broadcast name LosAngeles 14045551234
 dialer map ip 172.16.2.3 broadcast speed 56 name GothamCity 19999999999
 dialer-group 2
!
router igrp 6
network 172.16.0.0
```

There are a couple of very important things to notice about this example. First, the highlighted commands are those added specifically for PRI. The rest are exactly like the ones in the complete configuration for DDR using BRI in Example 10-4. Also note that no SPIDs are listed under the interface, because PRIs do not use SPIDs.

The most unusual part of the configuration introduces the concept of actually identifying the D channel in the **interface** command. Notice the command **interface serial 1/0:23**. The :*x* notation, where *x* identifies one of the channels inside the PRI, tells the IOS which of the 24 channels you want to configure. The DDR interface subcommands should be configured on the D channel, which is channel 23 according to the command! The **interface** command numbers the channels from 0 through 23, with the D channel as the last channel, so the :23 at the end correctly tells IOS that you are configuring details for the 24th channel—the D channel. (You do not need to configure anything on the B channels specifically for PRI, but you will see specific B channels listed in the output of **show** and **debug** commands.)

So, to actually configure the ISDN PRI details, you simply configure the ISDN switch type, ignore SPIDs completely, and configure the details needed under the controller. Table 10-14 summarizes the commands needed to configure ISDN PRI beyond what is needed for Legacy DDR configuration.

Table 10-14 *Summary of the New Configuration Needed for ISDN PRI Beyond Legacy DDR Configuration*

Command	Description	Configuration Mode
isdn switch-type *type*	Configures the ISDN switch type.	Global or physical interface
linecode "ami" | "b8zs" | "hdb3"	Configures encoding for the T1/E1 circuit.	Controller configuration
framing "sf" | "esf" | "crc4"	Configures framing for the T1/E1 circuit.	Controller configuration
pri-group timeslots *starting_channel - ending_channel*	Configures the DS0 channels used on this PRI.	Controller configuration

DDR Configuration with Dialer Profiles

The configuration for Legacy DDR requires a route to point packets out a particular physical interface. As soon as the packets are routed out the interface, DDR logic can decide if the packet is interesting. If it is interesting, DDR logic causes the dial to occur.

With Legacy DDR, there is no way to support a single set of remote sites through configuration using multiple different BRIs or PRIs in a single router. When you have multiple BRIs or PRIs, Legacy DDR allows you to dial only one set of sites using one interface and another set of sites with the other, as shown in Figure 10-8.

Figure 10-8   *Legacy DDR with Two BRIs and Eight Remote Sites*

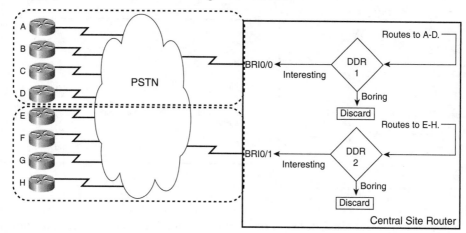

Figure 10-8 shows the logic that can be configured using Legacy DDR. The routes to four sites point out BRI0/0, and the routes to four other sites (E through H) point out BRI0/1. DDR uses a different dialer group on the two BRI interfaces, as noted in the diamonds with "DDR 1" (dialer group 1) and "DDR 2" (dialer group 2).

The problem with Legacy DDR in this case is that it cannot be configured to dial all eight sites using any available B channel on either BRI. Even if you configured two routes for each of the eight remote sites, one pointing out BRI0/0 and one out BRI0/1, Legacy DDR would still be confused as to which of the two BRI interfaces to use to dial a remote site. The root of the problem is that, with Legacy DDR, the static routes used by DDR can direct packets out a single physical BRI interface so that only a single BRI can be used to reach an individual remote site.

Dialer profiles overcome this problem with Legacy DDR using a slightly different style of DDR configuration. Dialer profiles pool the physical interfaces so that the router simply uses an available B channel on any of the BRIs or PRIs in the pool. Dialer profile configuration allows the Central Site router to dial any of the eight remote routers using either of the BRIs, as shown in Figure 10-9.

Figure 10-9   *Dialer Profiles: Pooling Multiple BRIs to Reach Eight Remote Sites*

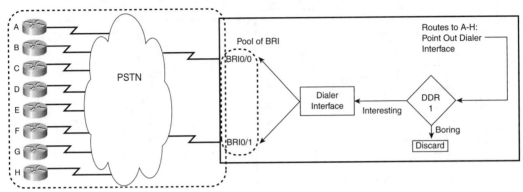

DDR dialer profiles are a different style of configuration for DDR. This style of configuration moves most of the DDR interface configuration to a virtual interface called a *dialer interface*. Each physical BRI or PRI interface can be included in a pool of available physical ISDN interfaces. DDR logic relies on the routing of packets out the dialer interface. If a packet is interesting, DDR picks an interface from the pool over which to place the actual call.

The configuration for dialer profiles looks very similar to Legacy DDR configuration. Table 10-15 summarizes the differences.

Table 10-15   *Summary of the New Configuration Needed for Dialer Profiles Versus Legacy DDR*

Command	Description	Configuration Mode
interface dialer *x*	Creates the virtual dialer interface.	Global
dialer pool-member *x*	Groups the physical ISDN interfaces into a dialer pool.	Physical interface
dialer pool *x*	Tells the dialer interface which dialer pool to use.	Dialer interface
encapsulation ppp ppp authentication chap	Configures PPP and authentication on the physical interfaces.	Physical interface and dialer interface
isdn spid1 *spid* isdn spid2 *spid*	Configures SPIDs as necessary.	Physical interface
isdn switch-type *type*	Configures the ISDN switch type.	Global or physical interface

The same familiar configuration from the SanFrancisco router, used with legacy DDR, has now been updated to use dialer profiles. With dialer profiles, you create a dialer interface for each remote site to which you want to connect. In this case, with two remote sites, two dialer interfaces are needed. Because there is only one remote site associated with each dialer interface, the **dialer string** command is used instead of the **dialer map** command. Also, it requires a separate subnet for each of the dialer interfaces, much like having a separate subnet for each point-to-point link. In effect, it's like setting up a virtual point-to-point interface between the San Fran router and each remote site.

Example 10-10 shows the complete configuration, with the new parts highlighted. The example only shows configuration for connecting to two sites.

Example 10-10 *SanFrancisco Configuration Migrated to Use Dialer Profiles and Two BRIs*

```
ip route 172.16.3.0 255.255.255.0 172.16.2.1
ip route 172.16.4.0 255.255.255.0 172.16.21.3
! Added usernames for CHAP support!
username LosAngeles password Clark
username GothamCity password Bruce
!
isdn switch-type basic-ni1
!
access-list 101 permit tcp any host 172.16.3.1 eq 80
access-list 102 permit tcp any host 172.16.4.1 eq 21
!
dialer-list 1 protocol ip list 101
dialer-list 2 protocol ip list 102
!
interface dialer 1
 ip address 172.16.2.2 255.255.255.0
 encapsulation ppp
 ppp authentication chap
 dialer idle-timeout 300
 dialer fast-idle 120
 dialer remote-name LosAngeles
 dialer string 172.16.2.1 14045551234
 dialer-group 1
 dialer pool 3
!
interface dialer 2
 description this dialer interface uses a different subnet - 172.16.21.0
 ip address 172.16.21.2 255.255.255.0
 encapsulation ppp
 ppp authentication chap
 dialer idle-timeout 300
 dialer fast-idle 120
 dialer remote-name GothamCity
 dialer string 172.16.21.3 199999999901 class slow
 dialer-group 2
```

continues

Example 10-10 *SanFrancisco Configuration Migrated to Use Dialer Profiles and Two BRIs (Continued)*

```
dialer pool 3
!
map-class dialer slow
 isdn speed 56
!
interface bri0
 encapsulation ppp
 ppp authentication chap
 isdn spid1 555555111101
 isdn spid2 555555222202
 dialer pool-member 3
!
interface bri1
 encapsulation ppp
 ppp authentication chap
 isdn spid1 555555333301
 isdn spid2 555555444402
 dialer pool-member 3
!
router igrp 6
network 172.16.0.0
```

The following paragraphs take you through the configuration from top to bottom. First, the **ip route** commands are slightly different than the earlier examples. Each route points to a different next-hop router IP address, and the addresses are in different subnets. That's because a different subnet is used between SanFrancisco and each remote site.

Next, you see several items that are unchanged in both syntax and how they are used. The CHAP usernames and password come next, followed by the global **isdn switch-type** command. These work just as they always have. Likewise, the **access-list** commands define the same logic as in Example 10-5, however, with two remote sites, the ACL logic is in two different ACLs. ACL 101 for interesting traffic to LosAngeles, and ACL 102 for interesting traffic for Gotham City. To use the different ACLs, a different **dialer-list** command is used for each remote site, with **dialer-list 1** referring to ACL 101, and **dialer-list 2** referring to ACL 102.

The **interface dialer 1** command comes next. This creates the virtual dialer interface which contains the commands and logic for dialing a single site, namely LosAngeles. Of particular interest, note that the **dialer-string** command is used to identify the phone number used. The name of the remote router was configured as a paramter in the dialer-map command; with dialer profiles, it is configured using the **dialer remote-name** command. Otherwise, the configuration under the dialer interface resembles the configuration under the BRI interfaces in Example 10-5.

Interface dialer 2 configures the details of the connection to the Gotham City router. The details are basically the same as the first dialer interface except that for Gotham City, a 56 kbps B-channel is requested. To do so, the **dialer string 172.16.21.3 199999999901 class slow** command is used. This command refers to map-class **slow**, which defines the speed as 56 kbps.

The dialer interfaces are logical, not physical, so they cannot place an actual call. When the dialer-list logic on a dialer interface notices that a call should be made, it looks for the **dialer pool** command under the dialer interface. In this case, the **dialer pool 3** command tells this router to look for all interfaces in dialer pool 3 and chooses an available interface for making the call.

Finally, the two BRI interfaces come next. Each has their respective SPIDs configured. Also, each is placed in the same pool with the **dialer pool-member 3** command. So both interfaces are available to the dialer interface for use to dial remote sites.

Figure 10-10   *Dialer Profiles: Pooling Multiple BRIs*

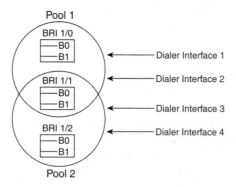

As Figure 10-10 illustrates, dialer profiles allow great flexibility. You can put the same physical interface into multiple pools, enabling better usage of the interfaces and connected lines. You can use separate logic as defined on different dialer interfaces. In fact, you can use IP addresses in different IP subnets on different dialer interfaces, giving you much greater control over your network design and IP addressing choices. So, whether you just want to allow a router to use multiple interfaces to dial the same set of sites, or if you want to do something more complex, dialer profiles help give you the necessary functionality.

Multilink PPP

Multilink PPP allows multiple links between a router and some other device over which traffic is balanced. The need for this function is straightforward; some of the motivations for using it can be subtle. Figure 10-11 illustrates the most obvious need for multilink PPP.

Figure 10-11 *Multilink PPP for a Dial-In Device*

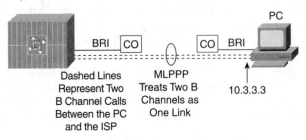

For faster service, the PC dials two B channels instead of one. To use both channels at the same time, and to get the most out of the extra available bandwidth, MLP can be used. MLP breaks each packet into fragments, sends some fragments across each of the two links, and reassembles them at the other end of the link. With two dialed circuits, it breaks each packet into two equal-sized packets. The net result is that the links are used approximately the same percentage.

Multilink PPP is also useful between routers. For example, in Figure 10-12, videoconferencing between Atlanta and Nashville uses six B channels between two routers.

Figure 10-12 *Multilink B Channels Between Routers*

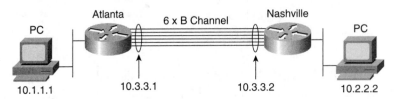

In this example, if multilink PPP is used, the links have almost identical usage. However, the 384 KB needed for the videoconference is available.

Now consider the alternative to MLP—six parallel links without multilink PPP. Six routes to subnet 10.2.2.0/24 would exist in Router A's routing table, assuming that Router A uses the **ip maximum-paths 6** command. Presumably, some traffic would use each of the six routes in the routing table.

The problem with not using MLP in this case relates to the default internal switching method in a Cisco router, called *fast switching*. Fast switching balances across equal-cost routes by sending all packets to the same IP address over the same link. The result is that router Atlanta sends some packets over one link and some over the other, but the balancing is unpredictable. More importantly, all packets to the videoconference system's single IP address in Nashville use the same link, effectively limiting the videoconference to 64 kbps. MLP solves this problem.

With MLP, the router treats the multiple links as a single link, with one route in the routing table, and lets MLP balance the traffic. Example 10-11 shows a sample multilink PPP configuration. The Atlanta and Nashville routers use two B channels of the same BRI.

Example 10-11 *Multilink PPP Configuration for Atlanta*

```
username Nashville password Robert
interface bri 0
ip addr 10.3.3.1 255.255.255.0
encapsulation ppp
dialer idle-timeout 300
dialer load-threshold 25 either
dialer map 10.3.3.2 name Nashville 16155551234
dialer-group 1
ppp authentication chap
ppp multilink
```

MLP requires just a few additional commands compared to typical DDR and ISDN configuration. The two key commands are **ppp multilink** and **dialer load-threshold**. The **ppp multilink** command enables multilink PPP. The router can dynamically sense when two links are actually parallel links to the same other device based on some hidden PPP flows, so the command does not have to explicitly identify which links are working together with MLP.

The **dialer load-threshold** command tells the router to dial another B channel if the utilization average on the currently used links is more than 10 percent for either inbound or outbound utilization. Although it isn't necessarily required for MLP, this command is useful so that you can simply add more B channel calls when the load requires it; MLP then ensures that the additional bandwidth is used. (Note: the load percentage is calculated as $x/255$, with x being the configured load value.)

Table 10-16 summarizes the additional commands used with MLP in dial environments.

Table 10-16 *Summary of the New Configuration Needed for MLP Versus Legacy DDR*

Command	Description	Configuration Mode
ppp multilink	Enables MLP.	Interface
dialer load-threshold *load* [outbound | inbound | either]	Tells the router when to dial additional calls to the same location based on load.	Interface

ISDN and DDR Configuration Summary

ISDN and DDR configuration can be overwhelming. They include a lot of different commands, and most people simply do not get to practice ISDN in a lab. You should be ready to interpret configurations and recognize the commands for each feature.

Legacy DDR configuration includes the most commands. You need static routes to send packets out the dial interfaces. You need dialer groups, sometimes referring to ACLs, to define what traffic causes a dial to occur. In other words, you define the "interesting" traffic. You then define the phone numbers to dial, either with the **dialer string** command when you want to dial a single site, or with the **dialer map** command when you want to dial multiple different sites. Finally, you might change the default settings for both idle timers.

For BRIs, you only need to worry about configuring the ISDN switch type and, in some cases, the ISDN SPIDs. For PRIs, you configure the switch type, and you never configure SPIDs. You also need to configure the encoding, framing, and list of channels inside the PRI that will be used. These are the commands that are configured under the **controller** configuration mode.

With dialer profiles, you essentially pool multiple physical interfaces and create a dialer interface. The DDR configuration causes packets to be routed out the dialer interface. If a dial needs to be made, the dialer interface picks one of the physical ISDN interfaces that has an available B channel to dial the line.

Finally, MLP allows you to efficiently use multiple parallel B channels connected between two devices. To configure it, you use the **ppp multilink** command.

Foundation Summary

The "Foundation Summary" section lists the most important facts from the chapter. Although this section does not list everything that will be on the exam, a well-prepared CCNA candidate should at a minimum know all the details in each Foundation Summary before taking the exam.

Table 10-17 lists the number of channels for BRI and PRI.

Table 10-17 *BRI and PRI B and D Channels*

Type of Interface	Number of Bearer (B) Channels	Number of Signaling Channels
BRI	2	1 (16 kbps)
PRI (T1)	23	1 (64 kbps)
PRI (E1)	30	1 (64 kbps)

The OSI layers correlating to the different ISDN specifications are also mentioned in the ICND course. It's also useful to memorize the specifications listed in Table 10-18, as well as which OSI layer each specification matches.

Table 10-18 *ISDN I-Series and Q-Series Mentioned in ICND: OSI Layer Comparison*

Layer as Compared to OSI	I-Series	Equivalent Q-Series Specification	Description
1	ITU-T I.430 ITU-T I.431	—	Defines connectors, encoding, framing, and reference points.
2	ITU-T I.440 ITU-T I.441	ITU-T Q.920 ITU-T Q.921	Defines the LAPD protocol used on the D channel to encapsulate signaling requests.
3	ITU-T I.450 ITU-T I.451	ITU-T Q.930 ITU-T Q.931	Defines signaling messages, such as call setup and teardown messages.

Figure 10-13 shows the cabling diagram for several examples of ISDN BRI function groups and reference points.

Figure 10-13 *ISDN Function Groups and Reference Points*

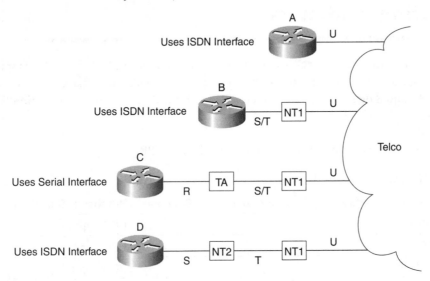

The four key concepts behind Legacy DDR are as follows:

1. Route packets out the interface to be dialed.

2. Determine the subset of the packets that trigger the dialing process.

3. Dial (signal).

4. Determine when the connection is terminated.

Table 10-19 summarizes the commands needed to configure Legacy DDR, with some explanation of each function.

Table 10-19 *Summary Legacy DDR Configuration Commands*

Command	Description
ip route	Global command that configures static routes that route traffic out an ISDN interface.
username *name* password *secret*	Global command that configures CHAP usernames and passwords.
access-list	Global command that creates ACLs if you need to define a subset of traffic as "interesting."
dialer-list *number* protocol ip [list *acl-number*]	Global command that creates a dialer list that either makes all IP traffic interesting or references the ACL to make a subset interesting.

Table 10-19 *Summary Legacy DDR Configuration Commands (Continued)*

Command	Description
interface bri *int-number*	Global command that selects ISDN BRI to use for DDR.
encapsulation ppp ppp authentication chap	Interface subcommands that configure PPP and enable CHAP.
isdn spid1 *value* isdn spid2 *value*	Interface subcommands that set ISDN SPID values if needed.
dialer idle-timeout *time* dialer fast-idle *time*	Interface subcommands that set idle timeout values.
dialer-group *number*	Interface subcommand that references the dialer list to define what is interesting.
dialer string *number* dialer map ip *next-hop-ip number*	Interface subcommands that define dial numbers for one site or many.

Table 10-20 summarizes the configuration details for ISDN BRI.

Table 10-20 *Summary of the New Configuration Needed for ISDN BRI Beyond Legacy DDR Configuration*

Command	Description	Configuration Mode
isdn spid1 *spid* isdn spid2 *spid*	Configures SPIDs as necessary.	Physical interface
isdn switch-type *type*	Configures the ISDN switch type.	Global or physical interface

Table 10-21 summarizes the configuration details for ISDN PRI.

Table 10-21 *Summary of the New Configuration Needed for ISDN PRI Beyond Legacy DDR Configuration*

Command	Description	Configuration Mode
isdn switch-type *type*	Configures the ISDN switch type.	Global or physical interface
linecode ami | b8zs | hdb3	Configures encoding for the T1/E1 circuit.	Controller configuration

Table 10-21 *Summary of the New Configuration Needed for ISDN PRI Beyond Legacy DDR Configuration (Continued)*

Command	Description	Configuration Mode
framing sf | esf | crc4	Configures framing for the T1/E1 circuit.	Controller configuration
pri-group timeslots *starting_channel - ending_channel*	Configures the DS0 channels used on this PRI.	Controller configuration

The configuration for dialer profiles is very similar to Legacy DDR configuration. The differences are summarized in Table 10-22.

Table 10-22 *Summary of the New Configuration Needed for Dialer Profiles Versus Legacy DDR*

Command	Description	Configuration Mode
interface dialer *x*	Creates the virtual dialer interface.	Global
dialer pool-member *x*	Groups the physical ISDN interfaces into a dialer pool.	Physical interface
dialer pool *x*	Tells the dialer interface which dialer pool to use.	Dialer interface
encapsulation ppp ppp authentication chap	Configures PPP and authentication on the physical interfaces.	Physical interface and dialer interface
isdn spid1 *spid* isdn spid2 *spid*	Configures SPIDs as necessary.	Physical interface
isdn switch-type *type*	Configures the ISDN switch type.	Global or physical interface

The additional commands used with MLP in dial environments are summarized in Table 10-23.

Table 10-23 *Summary of the New Configuration Needed for MLP Versus Legacy DDR*

Command	Description	Configuration Mode
ppp multilink	Enables MLP.	Interface
dialer load-threshold *load* [outbound | inbound | either]	Tells the router when to dial additional calls to the same location based on load.	Interface

Q&A

As mentioned in the Introduction, you have two choices for review questions. The following questions give you a bigger challenge than the exam because they are open-ended. By reviewing with this more-difficult question format, you can exercise your memory better and prove your conceptual and factual knowledge of the topics covered in this chapter. The answers to these questions are found in Appendix A.

For more practice with exam-like question formats, including multiple-choice questions and those using a router simulator, use the exam engine on the CD.

1. What does LAPD stand for? Is it used as the Layer 2 protocol on dialed ISDN bearer channels? If not, what is?

2. What do ISDN, BRI, and PRI stand for?

3. Define function group. List two examples of function groups.

4. Define the term reference point. Give two examples of reference points.

5. How many bearer channels are in a BRI? What about a PRI in North America? What about a PRI in Europe?

6. True or false: ISDN defines protocols that can be functionally equivalent to OSI Layers 1, 2, and 3. Explain your answer.

7. What reference points do ISDN BRI interfaces on Cisco routers use?

8. Is LAPD used on ISDN channels? If so, which ones?

9. What standards body defines ISDN protocols?

10. What ISDN functions do standards ITU-T Q.920 and Q.930 define? Does either standard correlate to an OSI layer?

11. What ISDN functions does standard ITU-T I.430 define? Does it correlate to an OSI layer?

12. What does SPID stand for? What does it mean?

13. Define TE1, TE2, and TA. Which implies that one of the other two must be in use?

14. How many B channels are there on a PRI in countries where the PRI is based on a T1? On an E1?

15. What reference point is used between the customer premises and the phone company in North America? What about in Europe?

16. What problem does multilink PPP solve when multiple B channels have circuits set up between a pair of routers?

17. What is the syntax of an **interface** command used to configure the encapsulation, IP address, and DDR parameters on a PRI in North America? What is the significance of entering a colon and a number after entering the interface number?

18. What data-link (OSI Layer 2) protocols are valid on an ISDN B channel?

19. Define MLPPP. Describe the typical home or small office use of MLPPP.

20. Configure ISDN interface BRI1, assuming that it is attached to a DMS-100 ISDN switch and that it uses only one SPID of 404555121201.

21. Describe the decision process performed by the Cisco IOS software to attempt to dial a connection using Legacy DDR.

22. If packets from 10.1.1.0/24 are "interesting" in relation to DDR configuration, such that packets from 10.1.1.0/24 cause a DDR connection out interface BRI0, list the configuration commands that make the Cisco IOS software think that those packets are interesting on BRI0. (If you have not yet studied access lists, you might simply note what kind of packets you would match with an access list, rather than writing down the full syntax.)

23. Router R1 has two BRI interfaces. Configure a dialer profile such that R1 can dial any of six different remote routers using any of the B channels on either BRI. Assume that all traffic is interesting. You may ignore the static route commands needed to send the packets out the correct interface. Do not use any SPIDs, and do not use CHAP. For other parameters not listed, you can make up values.

This chapter covers the following subjects:

- Frame Relay Protocols

- Frame Relay Configuration

CHAPTER 11

Frame Relay

Frame Relay is the most popular WAN technology used today, so it's no surprise that Frame Relay is an important topic on the ICND exam. This chapter reviews the details of how Frame Relay accomplishes its goal of delivering frames to multiple WAN-connected sites.

Frame Relay most closely compares to the OSI data link layer (Layer 2). If you remember that the word "frame" describes the data link layer protocol data unit (PDU), it will be easy to remember that Frame Relay relates to OSI Layer 2. Like other data-link protocols, Frame Relay can be used to deliver packets (Layer 3 PDUs) between routers. Frame Relay protocol headers and trailers are simply used to let a packet traverse the Frame Relay network, just like Ethernet headers and trailers are used to help a packet traverse an Ethernet segment.

This chapter describes the Frame Relay protocol details, along with the associated configuration. Please refer to Appendix F for some further details about a few of the topics in this chapter.

"Do I Know This Already?" Quiz

The purpose of the "Do I Know This Already?" quiz is to help you decide if you need to read the entire chapter. If you intend to read the entire chapter, you do not necessarily need to answer these questions now.

The ten-question quiz, derived from the major sections in the "Foundation Topics" section, helps you determine how to spend your limited study time.

Table 11-1 outlines the major topics discussed in this chapter and the "Do I Know This Already?" quiz questions that correspond to those topics.

Table 11-1 *"Do I Know This Already?" Foundation Topics Section-to-Question Mapping*

Foundations Topics Section	Questions Covered in This Section
Frame Relay Concepts	1–6
Frame Relay Configuration	7–10

> **CAUTION** The goal of self-assessment is to gauge your mastery of the topics in this chapter. If you don't know the answer to a question or you're only partially sure of the answer, you should mark this question as wrong for purposes of the self-assessment. Giving yourself credit for an answer you guess correctly skews your self-assessment results and might give you a false sense of security.

1. Which of the following defines a protocol used between the Frame Relay DTE and the Frame Relay switch in the service provider's network?

   a. VC

   b. CIR

   c. LMI

   d. Q.921

   e. DLCI

   f. FRF.5

   g. Encapsulation

   h. None of the above

2. Which of the following defines a protocol or feature that matters to what the provider might do inside its network but that is transparent to the DTE/router using the Frame Relay service?

   a. VC

   b. CIR

   c. LMI

   d. DLCI

   e. Q.921

   f. FRF.5

g. Encapsulation

h. None of the above

3. What does DLCI stand for?

   a. Data Link Connection Identifier

   b. Data Link Connection Indicator

   c. Data Link Circuit Identifier

   d. Data Link Circuit Indicator

   e. None of the above

4. Imagine two Cisco routers, R1 and R2, using a Frame Relay service. R1 connects to a switch that uses LMI type ANSI T1.617, and R2 connects to a switch that uses ITU Q.933a. What can R1 and R2 configure for the LMIs to work correctly?

   a. ANSI and ITU

   b. T1617 and q933

   c. ANSI and q933

   d. T1617 and ITU

   e. This won't work with two different types.

   f. No configuration is needed.

5. FredCo has five sites, with routers connected to the same Frame Relay network. Virtual circuits (VCs) have been defined between each pair of routers. What is the fewest subnets that FredCo could use on the Frame Relay network?

   a. 1

   b. 2

   c. 3

   d. 4

   e. 5

   f. 6

   g. 7

   h. 8

   i. 9

   j. 10

6. BarneyCo has five sites, with routers connected to the same Frame Relay network. VCs have been defined between each pair of routers. Barney, the president of the company, will fire anyone who configures Frame Relay without using point-to-point subinterfaces. What is the fewest subnets that BarneyCo could use on the Frame Relay network?

   a. 1

   b. 4

   c. 8

   d. 10

   e. 12

   f. 15

7. BettyCo has five sites, with routers connected to the same Frame Relay network. VCs have been defined between each pair of routers. Betty, the president of the company, will fire anyone who configures anything that could just as easily be left as a default. Which of the following configuration commands, configured for the Frame Relay network, would get the engineer fired?

   a. ip address

   b. encapsulation

   c. lmi-type

   d. frame-relay map

   e. inverse-arp

8. WilmaCo has some routers connected to a Frame Relay network. R1 is a router at a remote site, with a single VC back to WilmaCo's headquarters. The R1 configuration currently looks like this:

   ```
   interface serial 0/0
    ip address 10.1.1.1 255.255.255.0
    encapsulation frame-relay
   ```

   Wilma, the president, has heard that point-to-point subinterfaces are cool, and she wants you to change the configuration to use a point-to-point subinterface. Which of the following commands do you need to use to migrate the configuration?

   a. no ip address

   b. interface-dlci

   c. no encapsulation

   d. encapsulation frame-relay

   e. frame-relay interface-dlci

9. WilmaCo has another network, with a main site router that has ten VCs connecting to the ten remote sites. Wilma now thinks that multipoint subinterfaces are even cooler than point-to-point. The current main site router's configuration looks like this:

```
interface serial 0/0
  ip address 172.16.1.1 255.255.255.0
  encapsulation frame-relay
```

Wilma wants you to change the configuration to use a multipoint subinterface. Which of the following do you need to use to migrate the configuration? (Note: DLCIs 101 through 110 are used for the ten VCs.)

  a. interface-dlci 101 110

  b. interface dlci 101-110

  c. Ten different **interface-dlci** commands

  d. frame-relay interface-dlci 101 110

  e. frame-relay interface dlci 101-110

  f. Ten different **frame-relay interface-dlci** commands

10. Which of the following commands lists the information learned by Inverse ARP?

  a. show ip arp

  b. show arp

  c. show inverse arp

  d. show frame-relay inverse-arp

  e. show map

  f. show frame-relay map

The answers to the "Do I Know This Already?" quiz appear in Appendix A. The suggested choices for your next step are as follows:

- **8 or less overall score**—Read the entire chapter. This includes the "Foundation Topics," "Foundation Summary," and "Q&A" sections.

- **9 or 10 overall score**—If you want more review on these topics, skip to the "Foundation Summary" section and then go to the "Q&A" section. Otherwise, move to the next chapter.

Foundation Topics

Frame Relay Protocols

If you're using both books, in Chapter 4, "Fundamentals of WANs," of CCNA INTRO Exam Certification Guide, you read about the basics of Frame Relay. This chapter begins with a brief review of those concepts, and then it dives into the details of Frame Relay protocols and concepts. This chapter ends with coverage of Frame Relay configuration.

Frame Relay networks provide more features and benefits than simple point-to-point WAN links, but to do that, Frame Relay protocols are more detailed. For example, Frame Relay networks are multiaccess networks, which means that more than two devices can attach to the network, similar to LANs. Unlike LANs, you cannot send a data link layer broadcast over Frame Relay. Therefore, Frame Relay networks are called *nonbroadcast multiaccess* (*NBMA*) networks. Also, because Frame Relay is multiaccess, it requires the use of an address that identifies to which remote router each frame is addressed.

Figure 11-1 outlines the basic physical topology and related terminology in a Frame Relay network.

Figure 11-1 *Frame Relay Components*

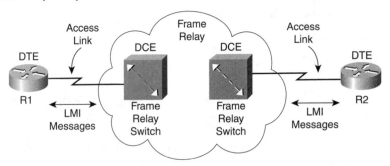

Figure 11-1 shows the most basic components of a Frame Relay network. A leased line is installed between the router and a nearby Frame Relay switch; this link is called the *access link*. To ensure that the link is working, the device outside the Frame Relay network, called the *data terminal equipment* (*DTE*), exchanges regular messages with the Frame Relay switch. These keepalive messages, along with other messages, are defined by the Frame Relay *Local Management Interface* (*LMI*) protocol. The routers are considered DTE, and the Frame Relay switches are *data communications equipment* (*DCE*).

Whereas Figure 11-1 shows the physical connectivity at each connection to the Frame Relay network, Figure 11-2 shows the logical, or virtual, end-to-end connectivity associated with a virtual circuit (VC).

Figure 11-2   *Frame Relay PVC Concepts*

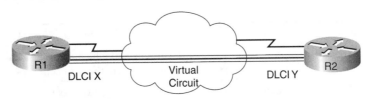

The logical communications path between each pair of DTEs is a VC. The trio of parallel lines in the figure represents a single VC; this book uses a different line style to make sure you notice the line easily. Typically, the service provider preconfigures all the required details of a VC; predefined VCs are called permanent virtual circuits (PVCs).

Routers use the data-link connection identifier (DLCI) as the Frame Relay address, which identifies the VC over which the frame should travel. So, in Figure 11-2, when R1 needs to forward a packet to R2, it encapsulates the Layer 3 packet into a Frame Relay header and trailer and then sends the frame. The Frame Relay header includes the correct DLCI so that the provider's Frame Relay switches correctly forward the frame to R2.

Table 11-2 lists the components shown in Figures 11-1 and 11-2 and some associated terms. After the tables, the most important features of Frame Relay are described in further detail.

Table 11-2   *Frame Relay Terms and Concepts*

Term	Description
Virtual circuit (VC)	A logical concept that represents the path that frames travel between DTEs. VCs are particularly useful when comparing Frame Relay to leased physical circuits.
Permanent virtual circuit (PVC)	A predefined VC. A PVC can be equated to a leased line in concept.
Switched virtual circuit (SVC)	A VC that is set up dynamically when needed. An SVC can be equated to a dial connection in concept.
Data terminal equipment (DTE)	DTEs are connected to a Frame Relay service from a telecommunications company and typically reside at sites used by the company buying the Frame Relay service.

continues

Table 11-2   *Frame Relay Terms and Concepts (Continued)*

Term	Description
Data communications equipment (DCE)	Frame Relay switches are DCE devices. DCEs are also known as data circuit-terminating equipment. DCEs are typically in the service provider's network.
Access link	The leased line between the DTE and DCE.
Access rate (AR)	The speed at which the access link is clocked. This choice affects the connection's price.
Data-link connection identifier (DLCI)	A Frame Relay address used in Frame Relay headers to identify the VC.
Nonbroadcast multiaccess (NBMA)	A network in which broadcasts are not supported, but more than two devices can be connected.
Local Management Interface (LMI)	The protocol used between a DCE and DTE to manage the connection. Signaling messages for SVCs, PVC status messages, and keepalives are all LMI messages.

Frame Relay Standards

The definitions for Frame Relay are contained in documents from the International Telecommunications Union (ITU) and the American National Standards Institute (ANSI). The Frame Relay Forum (www.frforum.com), a vendor consortium, also defines several Frame Relay specifications, many of which predate the original ITU and ANSI specifications, with the ITU and ANSI picking up many of the forum's standards. Table 11-3 lists the most important of these specifications.

Table 11-3   *Frame Relay Protocol Specifications*

What the Specification Defines	ITU Document	ANSI Document
Data-link specifications, including LAPF header/trailer	Q.922 Annex A (Q.922-A)	T1.618
PVC management, LMI	Q.933 Annex A (Q.933-A)	T1.617 Annex D (T1.617-D)
SVC signaling	Q.933	T1.617
Multiprotocol encapsulation (originated in RFC 1490/2427)	Q.933 Annex E (Q.933-E)	T1.617 Annex F (T1.617-F)

Virtual Circuits

Frame Relay provides significant advantages over simply using point-to-point leased lines. The primary advantage has to do with virtual circuits. Consider Figure 11-3, which is a typical Frame Relay network with three sites.

Figure 11-3 *Typical Frame Relay Network with Three Sites*

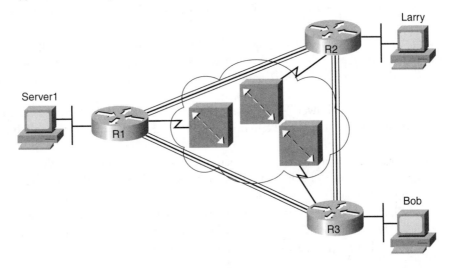

A virtual circuit defines a logical path between two Frame Relay DTEs. The term *virtual circuit* describes the concept well. It acts like a point-to-point circuit, providing the ability to send data between two endpoints over a WAN. There is no physical circuit directly between the two endpoints, so it's virtual. For example, R1 terminates two VCs—one whose other endpoint is R2, and one whose other endpoint is R3. R1 can send traffic directly to either of the other two routers by sending it over the appropriate VC. R1 has only one physical access link to the Frame Relay network.

VCs share the access link and the Frame Relay network. For example, both VCs terminating at R1 use the same access link. In fact, many customers share the same Frame Relay network. Originally, people with leased-line networks were reluctant to migrate to Frame Relay, because they would be competing with other customers for the provider's capacity inside the cloud. To address these fears, Frame Relay is designed with the concept of a committed information rate (CIR). Each VC has a CIR, which is a guarantee by the provider that a particular VC gets at least that much bandwidth. So you can migrate from a leased line to Frame Relay, getting a CIR of at least as much bandwidth as you previously had with your leased line.

Interestingly, even with a three-site network, it's probably less expensive to use Frame Relay than to use point-to-point links. Imagine an organization with 100 sites that needs any-to-any connectivity. How many leased lines are required? 4950! And besides that, the organization would need 99 serial interfaces per router if it used point-to-point leased lines. With Frame Relay, an organization could have 100 access links to local Frame Relay switches, one per router, and have 4950 VCs running over them. That requires a lot fewer actual physical links, and you would need only one serial interface on each router!

Service providers can build their Frame Relay networks more cost-effectively than for leased lines. As you would expect, that makes it less expensive to the Frame Relay customer as well. For connecting many WAN sites, Frame Relay is simply more cost-effective than leased lines.

Two types of VCs are allowed—permanent (PVC) and switched (SVC). PVCs are predefined by the provider; SVCs are created dynamically. PVCs are by far the more popular of the two.

When the Frame Relay network is engineered, the design might not include a PVC between each pair of sites. Figure 11-3 includes PVCs between each pair of sites, which is called a full-mesh Frame Relay network. When not all pairs have a direct PVC, it is called a partial-mesh network. Figure 11-4 shows the same network as Figure 11-3, but this time with a partial mesh and only two PVCs. This is typical when R1 is at the main site and R2 and R3 are at remote offices that rarely need to communicate directly.

Figure 11-4 *Typical Partial-Mesh Frame Relay Network*

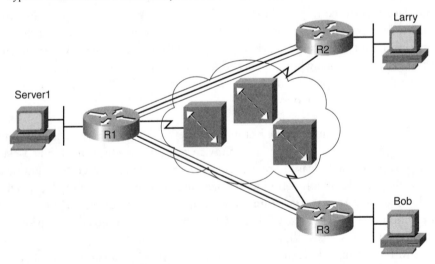

The partial mesh has some advantages and disadvantages when compared to a full mesh. The primary advantage is that partial mesh is cheaper, because the provider charges per VC. The downside is that traffic from R2's site to R3's site must go to R1 first and then be forwarded. If that's a small amount of traffic, it's a small price to pay. If it's a lot of traffic, a full mesh is probably worth the extra money.

One conceptual hurdle with PVCs is that there is typically a single access link across which multiple PVCs flow. For example, consider Figure 11-4 from R1's perspective. Server1 sends a packet to Larry. It comes across the Ethernet. R1 gets it and matches Larry's routing table, which tells him to send the packet out Serial0, which is R1's access link. He encapsulates the packet in a Frame Relay header and trailer and then sends it. Which PVC does it use? The Frame Relay switch should forward it to R2, but why does it?

Frame Relay uses an address to differentiate one PVC from another. This address is called a data-link connection identifier (DLCI). The name is descriptive: The address is for an OSI Layer 2 (data link) protocol, and it identifies a VC, which is sometimes called a *virtual connection*. So, in this example, R1 uses the DLCI that identifies the PVC to R2, so the provider forwards the frame correctly over the PVC to R2. To send frames to R3, R1 uses the DLCI that identifies the VC for R3. DLCIs and how they work are covered in more detail later in this chapter.

LMI and Encapsulation Types

When you're first learning about Frame Relay, it's often easy to confuse the LMI and the encapsulation used with Frame Relay. The LMI is a definition of the messages used between the DTE (for example, a router) and the DCE (for example, the Frame Relay switch owned by the service provider). The encapsulation defines the headers used by a DTE to communicate some information to the DTE on the other end of a VC. The switch and its connected router care about using the same LMI; the switch does not care about the encapsulation. The endpoint routers (DTEs) do care about the encapsulation.

The most important LMI message relating to topics on the exam is the LMI status inquiry message. Status messages perform two key functions:

■ Perform a keepalive function between the DTE and DCE. If the access link has a problem, the absence of keepalive messages implies that the link is down.

■ Signal whether a PVC is active or inactive. Even though each PVC is predefined, its status can change. An access link might be up, but one or more VCs could be down. The router needs to know which VCs are up and which are down. It learns that information from the switch using LMI status messages.

Three LMI protocol options are available in Cisco IOS software: Cisco, ITU, and ANSI. Each LMI option is slightly different and therefore is incompatible with the other two. As long as both the DTE and DCE on each end of an access link use the same LMI standard, LMI works fine.

The differences between LMI types are subtle. For example, the Cisco LMI calls for the use of DLCI 1023, whereas ANSI T1.617-D and ITU Q.933-A specify DLCI 0. Some of the messages have different fields in their headers. The DTE simply needs to know which of the three LMIs to use so that it can use the same one as the local switch.

Configuring the LMI type is easy. Today's most popular option is to use the default LMI setting, which uses the LMI autosense feature, in which the router simply figures out which LMI type the switch is using. So you can simply let the router autosense the LMI and never bother coding the LMI type. If you choose to configure the LMI type, it disables the autosense feature.

Table 11-4 outlines the three LMI types, their origin, and the keyword used in the Cisco IOS software **frame-relay lmi-type** interface subcommand.

Table 11-4   *Frame Relay LMI Types*

Name	Document	IOS LMI-Type Parameter
Cisco	Proprietary	cisco
ANSI	T1.617 Annex D	ansi
ITU	Q.933 Annex A	q933a

A Frame Relay-connected router encapsulates each Layer 3 packet inside a Frame Relay header and trailer before it is sent out an access link. The header and trailer are defined by the Link Access Procedure Frame Bearer Services (LAPF) specification, ITU Q.922-A. The sparse LAPF framing provides error detection with an FCS in the trailer, as well as the DLCI, DE, FECN, and BECN fields in the header (which are discussed later). Figure 11-5 diagrams the frame.

Figure 11-5   *LAPF Header*

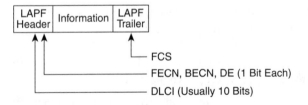

However, the LAPF header and trailer do not provide all the fields typically needed by routers. In particular, Figure 11-5 does not show a Protocol Type field. As discussed in Chapters 3, "Virtual LANs and Trunking," and 4, "IP Addressing and Subnetting," a field in the data-link header must define the type of packet that follows the data-link header. If Frame Relay is using only the LAPF header, DTEs (including routers) cannot support multiprotocol traffic, because there is no way to identify the type of protocol in the Information field.

Two solutions were created to compensate for the lack of a Protocol Type field in the standard Frame Relay header:

- Cisco and three other companies created an additional header, which comes between the LAPF header and the Layer 3 packet shown in Figure 11-5. It includes a 2-byte Protocol Type field, with values matching the same field used for HDLC by Cisco.

- RFC 1490 (which was later superceded by RFC 2427—you should know both numbers), "Multiprotocol Interconnect over Frame Relay," defined the second solution. RFC 1490 was written to ensure multivendor interoperability between Frame Relay DTEs. This RFC defines a similar header, also placed between the LAPF header and Layer 3 packet, and includes a Protocol Type field as well as many other options. ITU and ANSI later incorporated RFC 1490 headers into their Q.933 Annex E and T1.617 Annex F specifications, respectively.

Figure 11-6 outlines these two alternatives.

Figure 11-6 *Cisco and RFC 1490/2427 Encapsulation*

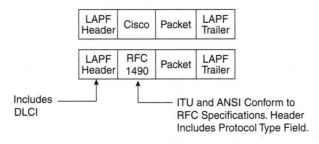

DTEs use and react to the fields specified by these two types of encapsulation, but Frame Relay switches ignore these fields. *Because the frames flow from DTE to DTE, both DTEs must agree to the encapsulation used. The switches don't care.* However, each VC can use a different encapsulation. In the configuration, the encapsulation created by Cisco is called **cisco**, and the other one is called **ietf**.

DLCI Addressing Details

So far, you know some basic information about Frame Relay. First, the routers (DTEs) connect to the Frame Relay switches (DCEs) over an access link, which is a leased line between the router and the switch. The logical path between a pair of DTEs is called a virtual circuit (VC). Most networks use permanent virtual circuits (PVCs) instead of switched virtual circuits (SVCs), and the data-link connection identifier (DLCI) addresses or identifies each individual PVC. The LMI protocol manages the access link, and the LMI type must match between the router and the local switch. Finally, the routers on either end of each VC must agree on the style of encapsulation used. Both encapsulation types include a Protocol Type field, which identifies the header that follows the Frame Relay header.

DLCIs can be both simple and confusing. It was just stated that the DLCI identifies a VC, so when multiple VCs use the same access link, the Frame Relay switches know how to forward the frames to the correct remote sites. You could know just that, look at the configuration examples later in this chapter, and probably learn to create new configurations. However, a closer look at DLCIs shows how they really work. This is important for actually understanding the configurations you create. If you want to get a deeper understanding, read on. If you prefer to get the basics right now and fill in more details later, you might want to jump ahead to the "Frame Relay Configuration" section.

Frame Relay addressing and switching define how to deliver frames across a Frame Relay network. Because a router uses a single access link that has many VCs connecting it to many routers, there must be something to identify each of the remote routers—in other words, an address. The DLCI is the Frame Relay address.

DLCIs work slightly differently from the other data-link addresses covered on the CCNA exams. This difference is mainly because of the use of the DLCI and the fact that *the header has a single DLCI field, not both Source and Destination DLCI fields.*

A few characteristics of DLCIs are important to understand before getting into their use. Frame Relay DLCIs are locally significant; this means that the addresses need to be unique only on the local access link. A popular analogy that explains local addressing is that there can be only a single street address of 2000 Pennsylvania Avenue, Washington, DC, but there can be a 2000 Pennsylvania Avenue in every town in the United States. Likewise, DLCIs must be unique on each access link, but the same DLCI numbers can be used on every access link in your network. For example, in Figure 11-7, notice that DLCI 40 is used on two access links to describe two different PVCs. No conflict exists, because DLCI 40 is used on two different access links.

Local addressing, which is the common term for the fact that DLCIs are locally significant, is a fact. It is how Frame Relay works. Simply put, a single access link cannot use the same DLCI to represent multiple VCs on the same access link. Otherwise, the Frame Relay switch would not know how to forward frames correctly. For instance, in Figure 11-7, Router A must use different DLCI values for the PVCs on its local access link (41 and 42 in this instance).

Figure 11-7 *Frame Relay Addressing with Router A Sending to Routers B and C*

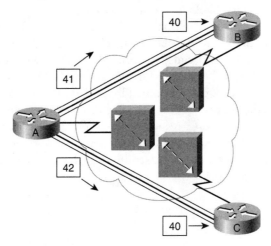

Most people get confused about DLCIs the first time they think about the local significance of DLCIs and the existence of only a single DLCI field in the Frame Relay header. Global addressing solves this problem by making DLCI addressing look like LAN addressing in concept. Global addressing is simply a way of choosing DLCI numbers when planning a Frame Relay network so that working with DLCIs is much easier. Because local addressing is a fact, global addressing does not change these rules. Global addressing just makes DLCI assignment more obvious—as soon as you get used to it.

Here's how global addressing works: The service provider hands out a planning spreadsheet and a diagram. Figure 11-8 is an example of such a diagram, with the global DLCIs shown.

Figure 11-8 *Frame Relay Global DLCIs*

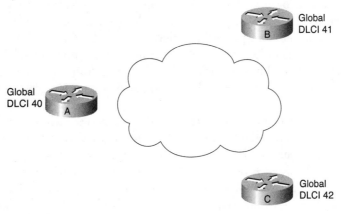

Global addressing is planned as shown in Figure 11-8, with the DLCIs placed in Frame Relay frames as shown in Figure 11-9. For example, Router A uses DLCI 41 when sending a frame to Router B, because Router B's global DLCI is 41. Likewise, Router A uses DLCI 42 when sending frames over the VC to Router C. The nice thing is that global addressing is much more logical to most people, because it works like a LAN, with a single MAC address for each device. On a LAN, if the MAC addresses are MAC-A, MAC-B, and MAC-C for the three routers, Router A uses destination address MAC-B when sending frames to Router B and MAC-C as the destination to reach Router C. Likewise, with global DLCIs 40, 41, and 42 used for Routers A, B, and C, respectively, the same concept applies. Because DLCIs address VCs, the logic is something like this when Router A sends a frame to Router B: "Hey, local switch! When you get this frame, send it over the VC that we agreed to number with DLCI 41." Figure 11-9 outlines this example.

Figure 11-9 *Frame Relay Global Addressing from the Sender's Perspective*

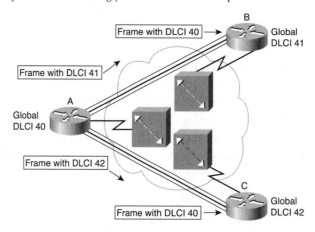

Router A sends frames with DLCI 41, and they reach the local switch. The local switch sees the DLCI field and forwards the frame through the Frame Relay network until it reaches the switch connected to Router B. Then Router B's local switch forwards the frame out the access link to Router B. The same process happens between Router A and Router C when Router A uses DLCI 42. The beauty of global addressing is that you think of each router as having an address, like LAN addressing. If you want to send a frame to someone, you put his or her DLCI in the header, and the network delivers the frame to the correct DTE.

The final key to global addressing is that the Frame Relay switches actually change the DLCI value before delivering the frame. Did you notice that Figure 11-9 shows a different DLCI value as the frames are received by Routers B and C? For example, Router A sends a frame to Router B, and Router A puts DLCI 41 in the frame. The last switch changes the field to DLCI 40 before forwarding it to Router B. The result is that when Routers B and C receive their frames, the DLCI value is actually the sender's DLCI. Why? Well, when Router B receives the frame, because the DLCI is 40, it knows that the frame came in on the PVC between itself and Router A. In general, the following are true:

- The sender treats the DLCI field as a destination address, using the destination's global DLCI in the header.
- The receiver thinks of the DLCI field as the source address, because it contains the global DLCI of the frame's sender.

Figure 11-9 describes what happens in a typical Frame Relay network. Service providers supply a planning spreadsheet and diagrams with global DLCIs listed. Table 11-5 gives you an organized view of what DLCIs are used in Figure 11-9.

Table 11-5 *DLCI Swapping in the Frame Relay Cloud of Figure 11-9*

Frame Sent by Router	With DLCI Field	Is Delivered to Router	With DLCI Field
A	41	B	40
A	42	C	40
B	40	A	41
C	40	A	42

Global addressing makes DLCI addressing more intuitive to most people. It also makes router configuration more straightforward and lets you add new sites more conveniently. For instance, examine Figure 11-10, which adds Routers D and E to Figure 11-9's network. The service provider simply states that global DLCIs 43 and 44 are used for these two routers. If these two routers also have only one PVC to Router A, all the DLCI planning is complete. You know that Router D and Router E use DLCI 40 to reach Router A and that Router A uses DLCI 43 to reach Router D and DLCI 44 to reach Router E.

Figure 11-10 *Adding Frame Relay Sites: Global Addressing*

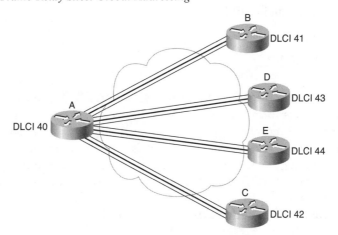

The remaining examples in this chapter use global addressing in any planning diagrams unless otherwise stated. One practical way to determine whether the diagram lists the local DLCIs or the global DLCI convention is this: If two VCs terminate at the same DTE, and a single DLCI is shown, it probably represents the global DLCI convention. If one DLCI is shown per VC, local DLCI addressing is depicted.

Network Layer Concerns with Frame Relay

Most of the important Frame Relay concepts have been covered. First, the routers (DTEs) connect to the Frame Relay switches (DCEs) over an access link, which is a leased line between the router and the switch. The LMI protocol is used to manage the access link, and the LMI type must match between the router and the local switch. The routers agree to the style of encapsulation used. The single DLCI field in the Frame Relay header identifies the VC used to deliver the frame. The DLCI is used like a destination address when the frame is being sent and like a source address as the frame is received. The switches actually swap the DLCI in transit.

Frame Relay networks have both similarities and differences as compared to LAN and point-to-point WAN links. These differences introduce some additional considerations for passing Layer 3 packets across a Frame Relay network. You need to concern yourself with a couple of key issues relating to Layer 3 flows over Frame Relay:

- Choices for Layer 3 addresses on Frame Relay interfaces
- Broadcast handling

The following sections cover these issues in depth.

Layer 3 Addressing with Frame Relay

Cisco's Frame Relay implementation defines three different options for assigning subnets and IP addresses on Frame Relay interfaces:

- One subnet containing all Frame Relay DTEs
- One subnet per VC
- A hybrid of the first two options

Frame Relay Layer 3 Addressing: One Subnet Containing All Frame Relay DTEs

Figure 11-11 shows the first alternative, which is to use a single subnet for the Frame Relay network. The figure shows a fully meshed Frame Relay network because the single-subnet option is typically used when a full mesh of VCs exists. In a full mesh, each router has a VC to every other router, meaning that each router can send frames directly to every other router—which more closely equates to how a LAN works. So, a single subnet can be used for all the routers' Frame Relay interfaces, as configured on the routers' serial interfaces. Table 11-6 summarizes the addresses used in Figure 11-11.

Figure 11-11 *Full Mesh with IP Addresses*

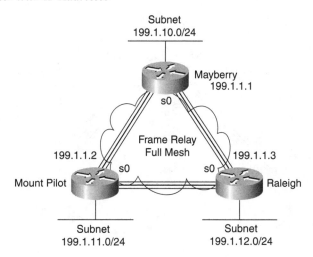

Table 11-6 *IP Addresses with No Subinterfaces*

Router	IP Address of Frame Relay Interface
Mayberry	199.1.1.1
Mount Pilot	199.1.1.2
Raleigh	199.1.1.3

The single-subnet alternative is straightforward, and it conserves your IP address space. It also looks like what you are used to with LANs, which makes it easier to conceptualize. Unfortunately, most companies build partial-mesh Frame Relay networks, and the single-subnet option has some deficiencies when the network is a partial mesh.

Frame Relay Layer 3 Addressing: One Subnet Per VC

The second IP addressing alternative, the single-subnet-per-VC alternative, works better with a partially meshed Frame Relay network, as shown in Figure 11-12. Boston cannot forward frames directly to Charlotte, because no VC is defined between the two. This is a more typical Frame Relay network, because most organizations with many sites tend to group applications on servers at a few centralized locations, and most of the traffic is between each remote site and those servers.

Figure 11-12 *Partial Mesh with IP Addresses*

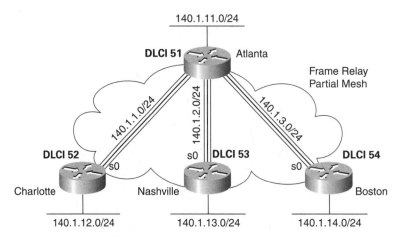

The single-subnet-per-VC alternative matches the logic behind a set of point-to-point links. Using multiple subnets instead of one larger subnet wastes some IP addresses, but it overcomes some issues with distance vector routing protocols.

Table 11-7 shows the IP addresses for the partially meshed Frame Relay network shown in Figure 11-12.

Table 11-7 *IP Addresses with Point-to-Point Subinterfaces*

Router	Subnet	IP Address
Atlanta	140.1.1.0	140.1.1.1
Charlotte	140.1.1.0	140.1.1.2
Atlanta	140.1.2.0	140.1.2.1
Nashville	140.1.2.0	140.1.2.3
Atlanta	140.1.3.0	140.1.3.1
Boston	140.1.3.0	140.1.3.4

Cisco IOS software has a configuration feature called *subinterfaces* that creates a logical subdivision of a physical interface. Subinterfaces allow the Atlanta router to have three IP addresses associated with its Serial0 physical interface by configuring three separate subinterfaces. A router can treat each subinterface, and the VC associated with it, as if it were a point-to-point serial link. Each of the three subinterfaces of Serial0 on Atlanta would be assigned a different IP address from Table 11-7. (Sample configurations appear in the next section.)

> **NOTE**   The example uses IP address prefixes of /24 to keep the math simple. In
> production networks, point-to-point subinterfaces typically use a prefix of /30 (mask
> 255.255.255.252), because that allows for only two valid IP addresses—the exact number
> needed on a point-to-point subinterface. Of course, using different masks in the same
> network means your routing protocol must also support VLSM.

Frame Relay Layer 3 Addressing: Hybrid Approach

The third alternative of Layer 3 addressing is a hybrid of the first two alternatives. Consider
Figure 11-13, which shows a trio of routers with VCs between each of them, as well as two
other VCs to remote sites.

Figure 11-13   *Hybrid of Full and Partial Mesh*

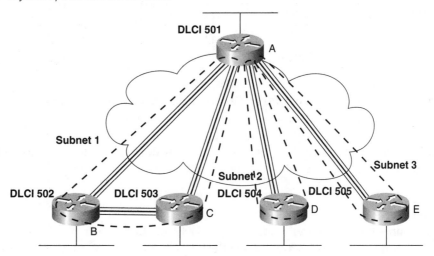

Two options exist for Layer 3 addressing in this case. The first is to treat each VC as a
separate Layer 3 group. In this case, five subnets are needed for the Frame Relay network.
However, Routers A, B, and C create a smaller full mesh between each other. This allows
Routers A, B, and C to use one subnet. The other two VCs—one between Routers A and D
and one between Routers A and E—are treated as two separate Layer 3 groups. The result is
a total of three subnets.

To accomplish either style of Layer 3 addressing in this third and final case, subinterfaces are
used. Point-to-point subinterfaces are used when a single VC is considered to be all that is in
the group—for instance, between Routers A and D and between Routers A and E. Multipoint
subinterfaces are used when more than two routers are considered to be in the same group—
for instance, with Routers A, B, and C.

Multipoint subinterfaces logically terminate more than one VC. In fact, the name "multipoint" implies the function, because more than one remote site can be reached via a VC associated with a multipoint subinterface.

Table 11-8 summarizes the addresses and subinterfaces that are used in Figure 11-13.

Table 11-8 *IP Addresses with Point-to-Point and Multipoint Subinterfaces*

Router	Subnet	IP Address	Subinterface Type
A	140.1.1.0/24	140.1.1.1	Multipoint
B	140.1.1.0/24	140.1.1.2	Multipoint
C	140.1.1.0/24	140.1.1.3	Multipoint
A	140.1.2.0/24	140.1.2.1	Point-to-point
D	140.1.2.0/24	140.1.2.4	Point-to-point
A	140.1.3.0/24	140.1.3.1	Point-to-point
E	140.1.3.0/24	140.1.3.5	Point-to-point

What will you see in a real network? Most of the time, point-to-point subinterfaces are used, with a single subnet per PVC.

The later section "Frame Relay Configuration" provides full configurations for all three cases illustrated in Figures 11-11, 11-12, and 11-13.

Broadcast Handling

After contending with Layer 3 addressing over Frame Relay, the next consideration is how to deal with Layer 3 broadcasts. Frame Relay can send copies of a broadcast over all VCs, but there is no equivalent to LAN broadcasts. In other words, no capability exists for a Frame Relay DTE to send a single frame into the Frame Relay network and have that frame replicated and delivered across multiple VCs to multiple destinations. However, routers need to send broadcasts for several features to work. In particular, routing protocol updates are often broadcasts.

The solution to the Frame Relay broadcast dilemma has two parts. First, Cisco IOS software sends copies of the broadcasts across each VC, assuming that you have configured the router to forward these necessary broadcasts. If there are only a few VCs, this is not a big problem. However, if hundreds of VCs terminate in one router, for each broadcast, hundreds of copies could be sent.

As the second part of the solution, the router tries to minimize the impact of the first part of the solution. The router places these broadcasts in a different output queue than the one for user traffic so that the user does not experience a large spike in delay each time a broadcast is replicated and sent over every VC. Cisco IOS software can also be configured to limit the amount of bandwidth that is used for these replicated broadcasts.

Although such scalability issues are more likely to appear on the CCNP Routing exam, a short example shows the significance of broadcast overhead. If a router knows 1000 routes, uses RIP, and has 50 VCs, 1.072 MB of RIP updates is sent every 30 seconds. That averages out to 285 kbps. (The math is as follows: 536-byte RIP packets, with 25 routes in each packet, for 40 packets per update, with copies sent over 50 VCs. 536 * 40 * 50 = 1.072 MB per update interval. 1.072 * 8 / 30 seconds = 285 kbps.) That's a lot of overhead!

Knowing how to tell the router to forward these broadcasts to each VC is covered in the section "Frame Relay Configuration." The issues that relate to dealing with the volume of these updates are more likely a topic for the CCNP and CCIE exams.

Frame Relay Service Interworking

Inside a service provider's Frame Relay network, the provider can use any kind of gear it wants to create the Frame Relay network. One large vendor many years ago built its Frame Relay network with a bunch of Cisco routers! But today, most well-established Frame Relay networks use Asynchronous Transfer Mode (ATM) in the core of their Frame Relay networks.

ATM works similarly to Frame Relay, but it has many features that make it much more robust than Frame Relay. For instance, ATM uses virtual connections (VCs), which provide the same function as Frame Relay VCs. However, ATM differs in that it segments all frames into 53-byte-long cells before transmitting them across the ATM network, and it reassembles them at the other side of the network. ATM also has significantly better quality of service (QoS) features, which lets the service provider better control the use of its core networks.

Service providers can use ATM to build the core of their Frame Relay networks. This concept is depicted in Figure 11-14.

The Frame Relay Forum and other standards bodies use the term *service interworking* to refer to the use of ATM between the two Frame Relay switches. In Figure 11-14, you see that the two routers use Frame Relay to communicate with the provider. You normally think of the internals of the Frame Relay network as being hidden from the customer. Often, inside the service provider network, ATM is used between the Frame Relay switches at the edges of the network.

Figure 11-14 *FRF.5 Service Interworking*

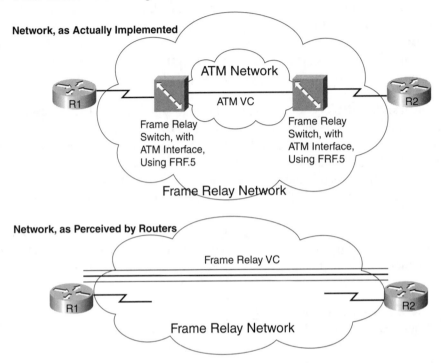

The Frame Relay Forum defined a specification about how Frame Relay switches interoperate using ATM in a Frame Relay Forum document called *FRF.5*. FRF.5 defines how a Frame Relay switch can convert from a Frame Relay VC to an ATM VC and back to a Frame Relay VC. The end result is totally transparent to the two routers.

A second variation of service interworking was defined by the Frame Relay Forum in document FRF.8. FRF.8 service interworking defines how two routers communicate when one router is connected to a Frame Relay network and the other is connected to an ATM network. ATM services can be used for WAN connectivity, much like Frame Relay. So, with FRF.8, a service provider can sell VCs to its customers, with some endpoints connected via Frame Relay and some with ATM. FRF.8 defines how to convert between the ATM and Frame Relay sides of the networks, as shown in Figure 11-15.

For the exam, you should remember the basic idea behind service interworking, and the two types—FRF.5 and FRF.8.

Figure 11-15 *FRF.8 Service Interworking*

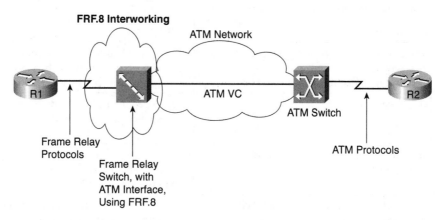

Frame Relay Configuration

Basic configuration of Frame Relay in a Cisco router is relatively straightforward, partly because Cisco IOS software uses good default values. Of course, you still need to know the optional parameters that are described in this section and the methods of changing the default values. The configuration examples start with a configuration with all the default settings and then begin adding optional features.

There is no substitute for hands-on experience! However, in lieu of hands-on experience, this section lists commands, provides examples, and points out tricky features. Tables 11-9 and 11-10 summarize the more popular commands used for Frame Relay configuration and verification. Several configuration examples follow. If you are interested in other references as well, the Cisco IOS software documentation is an excellent reference for additional IP commands.

Table 11-9 *Frame Relay Configuration Commands*

Command	Description
encapsulation frame-relay [ietf | cisco]	Interface configuration mode command that defines the Frame Relay encapsulation that is used rather than HDLC, PPP, and so on.
frame-relay lmi-type {ansi | q933a | cisco}	Interface configuration mode command that defines the type of LMI messages sent to the switch.
bandwidth *num*	Interface configuration mode command that sets the router's perceived interface speed. Bandwidth is used by some routing protocols to influence the metric and is used in link utilization calculations seen with the **show interfaces** command.

continues

Table 11-9   *Frame Relay Configuration Commands (Continued)*

Command	Description
frame-relay map {*protocol protocol-address dlci*} payload-compression frf9 stac caim [*element-number*] [broadcast] [ietf | cisco]	Interface configuration mode command that statically defines a mapping between a network layer address and a DLCI.
keepalive *sec*	Interface configuration mode command that defines whether and how often LMI status inquiry messages are sent and expected.
interface serial *number.sub* [point-to-point | multipoint]	Global configuration mode command that creates a subinterface or references a previously created subinterface.
frame-relay interface-dlci *dlci* [ietf | cisco] [voice-cir *cir*] [ppp *virtual-template-name*]	Subinterface configuration mode command that links or correlates a DLCI to the subinterface.

Table 11-10   *Frame Relay-Related EXEC Commands*

Command	Description
show interfaces [*type number*]	Shows the physical interface status.
show frame-relay pvc [interface *interface*][*dlci*]	Lists information about the PVC status.
show frame-relay lmi [*type number*]	Lists LMI status information.

A network engineer might plan the Frame Relay configuration based on several factors. When the service is ordered, the service provider specifies the LMI type that will be used. The engineer chooses the endpoints of the VCs, including whether to use a full mesh or partial mesh. Based on the location of the VCs, the engineer then decides which IP addressing option to use: single subnet, single subnet per VC, or a combination of the two. Finally, the encapsulation type is chosen—totally without input from the provider, because only the routers on the ends of each VC need to agree on the encapsulation type. Because Frame Relay switches do not care about the encapsulation type, nor do they care about IP addressing, the only details that have to be discussed with the carrier are the VCs and the LMI type, along with the CIR and burst sizes.

Three examples of Layer 3 addressing were given earlier in this chapter, with the networks diagrammed in Figures 11-11, 11-12, and 11-13. The configurations matching those networks and addresses are shown next.

A Fully-Meshed Network with One IP Subnet

In this first example, the configuration uses all default values, and it does not use subinterfaces. The Frame Relay configuration is listed under the physical interfaces. Examples 11-1, 11-2, and 11-3 show the configuration for the network shown in Figure 11-16.

Figure 11-16   *Full Mesh with IP Addresses*

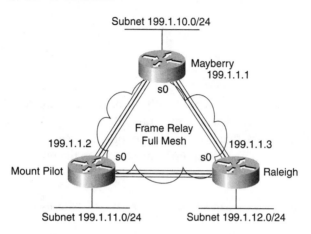

Example 11-1   *Mayberry Configuration*

```
interface serial0
encapsulation frame-relay
ip address  199.1.1.1  255.255.255.0
!
interface ethernet 0
ip address  199.1.10.1  255.255.255.0
!
router igrp 1
network 199.1.1.0
network 199.1.10.0
```

Example 11-2   *Mount Pilot Configuration*

```
interface serial0
encapsulation frame-relay
ip address  199.1.1.2  255.255.255.0
!
interface ethernet 0
ip address  199.1.11.2   255.255.255.0
!
router igrp 1
network 199.1.1.0
network 199.1.11.0
```

Example 11-3   *Raleigh Configuration*

```
interface serial0
encapsulation frame-relay
ip address  199.1.1.3  255.255.255.0
!
interface ethernet 0
ip address  199.1.12.3   255.255.255.0
!
router igrp 1
network 199.1.1.0
network 199.1.12.0
```

The configuration is simple in comparison with the protocol concepts. The **encapsulation frame-relay** command tells the routers to use Frame Relay data-link protocols instead of the default, which is HDLC. Note that the IP addresses on the three routers' serial interfaces are all in the same subnet. When you configure Frame Relay on the physical interfaces, all three routers must be in the same subnet.

Yes, Frame Relay configuration can be that easy, because IOS uses some very good choices for default settings:

■ The LMI type is automatically sensed.

■ The encapsulation is Cisco instead of IETF.

■ PVC DLCIs are learned via LMI status messages.

■ Inverse ARP is enabled (by default) and is triggered when the status message declaring that the VCs are up is received. (Inverse ARP is covered in the next section.)

In some cases, the default values are inappropriate. For example, you must use IETF encapsulation if one router is not a Cisco router. For the purpose of showing an alternative configuration, suppose that the following requirements were added:

■ The Raleigh router requires IETF encapsulation on both VCs.

■ Mayberry's LMI type should be ANSI, and LMI autosense should not be used.

Examples 11-4 and 11-5 show the changes that would be made to Mayberry and Raleigh.

Example 11-4   *Mayberry Configuration with New Requirements*

```
interface serial0
 encapsulation frame-relay
 frame-relay lmi-type ansi
 frame-relay interface-dlci 53 ietf
 ip address 199.1.1.1  255.255.255.0
! rest of configuration unchanged from Example 11-1.
```

Example 11-5 *Raleigh Configuration with New Requirements*

```
interface serial0
 encapsulation frame-relay ietf
 ip address  199.1.1.3  255.255.255.0
!
! rest of configuration unchanged from Example 11-3.
```

These configurations differ from the previous ones in two ways: Raleigh changed its encapsulation for both its PVCs with the **ietf** keyword on the **encapsulation** command. This keyword applies to all VCs on the interface. However, Mayberry cannot change its encapsulation in the same way, because only one of the two VCs terminating in Mayberry needs to use IETF encapsulation—the other needs to use Cisco encapsulation. So Mayberry is forced to code the **frame-relay interface-dlci** command, referencing the DLCI for the VC to Raleigh, with the **ietf** keyword. With that command, you can change the encapsulation setting per-VC, as opposed to the configuration on Raleigh, which changes the encapsulation for all VCs.

The LMI configuration in Mayberry would be fine without any changes, because autosense would recognize ANSI. However, by coding the **frame-relay lmi-type ansi** command, Mayberry must use ANSI, because this command not only sets the LMI type, it also disables autonegotiation of the LMI type.

Mount Pilot needs to configure a **frame-relay interface-dlci** command with the **ietf** keyword for its VC to Raleigh, just like Mayberry. This change is not shown in the examples.

Frame Relay Address Mapping

Figure 11-16 does not even bother listing the DLCIs used for the VCs. The configurations work as stated, and frankly, if you never knew the DLCIs, this network would work! However, for the exam, and for real networking jobs, you need to understand an important concept related to Frame Relay—namely, Frame Relay address mapping. Figure 11-17 shows the same network, this time with Global DLCI values shown.

Frame Relay "mapping" creates a correlation between a Layer 3 address and its corresponding Layer 2 address. For example, the IP Address Resolution Protocol (ARP) cache used on LANs is an example of Layer 3-to-Layer 2 address mapping. With IP ARP, you know the IP address of another device on the same LAN, but not the MAC address; when the ARP completes, you know another device's LAN (Layer 2) address. Similarly, routers that use Frame Relay need a mapping between a router's Layer 3 address and the DLCI used to reach that other router.

Figure 11-17 *Full Mesh with IP Addresses*

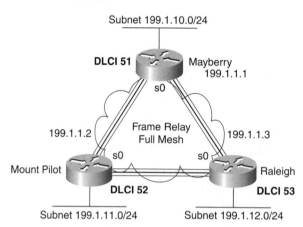

This section discusses the basics of why mapping is needed for LAN connections and Frame Relay, with a focus on Frame Relay. Here's a more general definition of mapping:

> The information that correlates to the next-hop router's Layer 3 address, and the Layer 2 address used to reach it, is called mapping. Mapping is needed on multiaccess networks.

Thinking about routing helps make the need for mapping more apparent. Imagine that a host on the Mayberry Ethernet sends an IP packet to a host on the Mount Pilot Ethernet. The packet arrives at the Mayberry router over the LAN, and Mayberry discards the Ethernet header and trailer. Mayberry looks at the routing table, which lists a route to 199.1.11.0, outgoing interface Serial0, and next-hop router 199.1.1.2, which is Mount Pilot's Frame Relay IP address.

The next decision that the router must make to complete the process points out the need for mapping: What DLCI should Mayberry put in the Frame Relay header? We configured no DLCIs. However, it would work as configured! To see the answer, consider Example 11-6, which shows some important commands that can be used to see how Mayberry makes the right choice for the DLCI.

Example 11-6 show *Commands on Mayberry, Showing the Need for Mapping*

```
Mayberry#show ip route
Codes: C - connected, S - static, I - IGRP, R - RIP, M - mobile, B - BGP
       D - EIGRP, EX - EIGRP external, O - OSPF, IA - OSPF inter area
       N1 - OSPF NSSA external type 1, N2 - OSPF NSSA external type 2
       E1 - OSPF external type 1, E2 - OSPF external type 2, E - EGP
       i - IS-IS, L1 - IS-IS level-1, L2 - IS-IS level-2, ia - IS-IS inter area
       * - candidate default, U - per-user static route, o - ODR
```

Example 11-6 show *Commands on Mayberry, Showing the Need for Mapping (Continued)*

```
        P - periodic downloaded static route

Gateway of last resort is not set

I    199.1.11.0/24 [100/8576] via 199.1.1.2, 00:00:26, Serial0
C    199.1.10.0/24 is directly connected, Ethernet0
I    199.1.12.0/24 [100/8539] via 199.1.1.3, 00:01:04, Serial0
C    199.1.1.0/24 is directly connected, Serial0
C    192.68.1.0/24 is directly connected, Ethernet0
C    192.168.1.0/24 is directly connected, Ethernet0


Mayberry#show frame-relay pvc
PVC Statistics for interface Serial0 (Frame Relay DTE)


                Active      Inactive     Deleted       Static
    Local         2            0            0            0
    Switched      0            0            0            0
    Unused        0            0            0            0

DLCI = 52, DLCI USAGE = LOCAL, PVC STATUS = ACTIVE, INTERFACE = Serial0

    input pkts 46           output pkts 22          in bytes 2946
    out bytes 1794          dropped pkts 0          in FECN pkts 0
    in BECN pkts 0          out FECN pkts 0         out BECN pkts 0
    in DE pkts 0            out DE pkts 0
    out bcast pkts 21       out bcast bytes 1730
    pvc create time 00:23:07, last time pvc status changed 00:21:38


DLCI = 53, DLCI USAGE = LOCAL, PVC STATUS = ACTIVE, INTERFACE = Serial0

    input pkts 39           output pkts 18          in bytes 2564
    out bytes 1584          dropped pkts 0          in FECN pkts 0
    in BECN pkts 0          out FECN pkts 0         out BECN pkts 0
    in DE pkts 0            out DE pkts 0
    out bcast pkts 18       out bcast bytes 1584
    pvc create time 00:23:08, last time pvc status changed 00:21:20


Mayberry#show frame-relay map
Serial0 (up): ip 199.1.1.2 dlci 52(0x34,0xC40), dynamic,
              broadcast,, status defined, active
Serial0 (up): ip 199.1.1.3 dlci 53(0x35,0xC50), dynamic,
              broadcast,, status defined, active
```

All the information needed for Mayberry to pick DLCI 52 is in the command output. The route to 199.1.11.0 points out Serial0 to 199.1.1.2 as the next-hop address. The **show frame-relay pvc** command lists two DLCIs, 52 and 53, and both are active. How does Mayberry know the DLCIs? Well, the LMI status messages tell Mayberry about the VCs, the associated DLCIs, and the status (active).

Which DLCI should Mayberry use to forward the packet? The **show frame-relay map** command output holds the answer. Notice the highlighted phrase **ip 199.1.1.2 dlci 52** in the output. Somehow, Mayberry has mapped 199.1.1.2, which is the next-hop address in the route, to the correct DLCI, which is 52. So, Mayberry knows to use DLCI 52 to reach next-hop IP address 199.1.1.2.

Mayberry can use two methods to build the mapping shown in Example 11-6. One uses a statically configured mapping, and the other uses a dynamic process called *Inverse ARP*.

Inverse ARP dynamically creates a mapping between the Layer 3 address (for example, the IP address) and the Layer 2 address (the DLCI). The end result of Inverse ARP is the same as IP ARP on a LAN: The router builds a mapping between a neighboring Layer 3 address and the corresponding Layer 2 address. However, the process used by Inverse ARP differs for ARP on a LAN. After the VC is up, each router announces its network layer address by sending an Inverse ARP message over that VC. This works as shown in Figure 11-18.

Figure 11-18 *Inverse ARP Process*

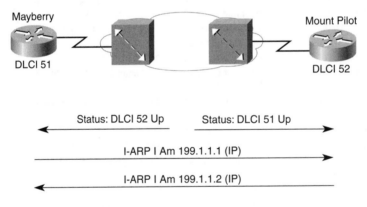

As shown in Figure 11-18, Inverse ARP announces its Layer 3 addresses as soon as the LMI signals that the PVCs are up. Inverse ARP starts by learning the DLCI data link layer address (via LMI messages), and then it announces its own Layer 3 addresses that use that VC.

Inverse ARP is enabled by default in Cisco IOS software Release 11.2 and later.

In Example 11-6, Mayberry shows two different entries in the **show frame-relay map** command output. Mayberry uses Inverse ARP to learn that DLCI 52 is mapped to next-hop IP address 199.1.1.2 and that DLCI 53 is mapped to next-hop IP address 199.1.1.3. Interestingly, Mayberry learns this information by receiving an Inverse ARP from Mount Pilot and Raleigh, respectively—another case of learning by listening, a great lesson for real life!

Table 11-11 summarizes what occurs with Inverse ARP in the network shown in Figure 11-17.

Table 11-11   *Inverse ARP Messages for Figure 11-17*

Sending Router	DLCI When the Frame Is Sent	Receiving Router	DLCI When the Frame Is Received	Information in the Inverse ARP Message
Mayberry	52	Mount Pilot	51	I am 199.1.1.1.
Mayberry	53	Raleigh	51	I am 199.1.1.1.
Mount Pilot	51	Mayberry	52	I am 199.1.1.2.
Mount Pilot	53	Raleigh	52	I am 199.1.1.2.
Raleigh	51	Mayberry	53	I am 199.1.1.3.
Raleigh	52	Mount Pilot	53	I am 199.1.1.3.

To understand Inverse ARP, focus on the last two columns of Table 11-11. Each router receives some Inverse ARP "announcements." The Inverse ARP message contains the sender's Layer 3 address, and the Frame Relay header, of course, has a DLCI in it. These two values are placed in the Inverse ARP cache on the receiving router. For example, in the third row, Mayberry receives an Inverse ARP. The DLCI is 52, and the IP address is 199.1.1.2. This is added to the Frame Relay map table in Mayberry, which is shown in the highlighted part of the **show frame-relay map** command in Example 11-6.

You can statically configure the same mapping information instead of using Inverse ARP. In a production network, you probably would just go ahead and use Inverse ARP. For the exam, you need to know how to configure the static map commands. Example 11-7 lists the static Frame Relay map for the three routers shown in Figure 11-11, along with the configuration used to disable Inverse ARP.

Example 11-7 frame-relay map *Commands*

```
Mayberry
interface serial 0
no frame-relay inverse-arp
frame-relay map ip 199.1.1.2 52 broadcast
frame-relay map ip 199.1.1.3 53 broadcast
Mount Pilot
interface serial 0
no frame-relay inverse-arp
frame-relay map ip 199.1.1.1 51 broadcast
frame-relay map ip 199.1.1.3 53 broadcast
Raleigh
interface serial 0
no frame-relay inverse-arp
frame-relay map ip 199.1.1.1 51 broadcast
frame-relay map ip 199.1.1.2 52 broadcast
```

The **frame-relay map** command entry for Mayberry, referencing 199.1.1.2, is used for packets in Mayberry going to Mount Pilot. When Mayberry creates a Frame Relay header, expecting it to be delivered to Mount Pilot, Mayberry must use DLCI 52. Mayberry's **map** statement correlates Mount Pilot's IP address, 199.1.1.2, to the DLCI used to reach Mount Pilot—namely, DLCI 52. Likewise, a packet sent back from Mount Pilot to Mayberry causes Mount Pilot to use its **map** statement to refer to Mayberry's IP address of 199.1.1.1. Mapping is needed for each next-hop Layer 3 address for each Layer 3 protocol being routed. Even with a network this small, the configuration process can be laborious.

A Partially-Meshed Network with One IP Subnet Per VC

The second sample network, based on the environment shown in Figure 11-19, uses point-to-point subinterfaces. Examples 11-8 through 11-11 show the configuration for this network. The command prompts are included in the first example because they change when you configure subinterfaces.

Figure 11-19 *Partial Mesh with IP Addresses*

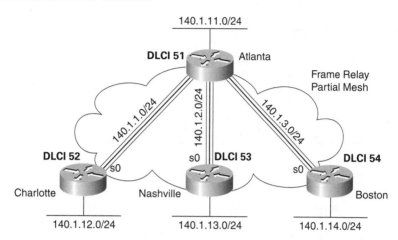

Example 11-8 *Atlanta Configuration*

```
Atlanta(config)#interface serial0
Atlanta(config-if)#encapsulation frame-relay

Atlanta(config-if)#interface serial 0.1 point-to-point
Atlanta(config-subif)#ip address 140.1.1.1  255.255.255.0
Atlanta(config-subif)#frame-relay interface-dlci 52

Atlanta(config-fr-dlci)#interface serial 0.2 point-to-point
Atlanta(config-subif)#ip address 140.1.2.1 255.255.255.0
Atlanta(config-subif)#frame-relay interface-dlci 53

Atlanta(config-fr-dlci)#interface serial 0.3 point-to-point
Atlanta(config-subif)#ip address 140.1.3.1 255.255.255.0
Atlanta(config-subif)#frame-relay interface-dlci 54

Atlanta(config-fr-dlci)#interface ethernet 0
Atlanta(config-if)#ip address 140.1.11.1 255.255.255.0
```

Example 11-9 *Charlotte Configuration*

```
interface serial0
encapsulation frame-relay
!
interface serial 0.1 point-to-point
ip address 140.1.1.2  255.255.255.0
frame-relay interface-dlci 51
!
interface ethernet 0
ip address 140.1.12.2 255.255.255.0
```

Example 11-10 *Nashville Configuration*

```
interface serial0
encapsulation frame-relay
!
interface serial 0.2 point-to-point
ip address 140.1.2.3 255.255.255.0
frame-relay interface-dlci 51
!
interface ethernet 0
ip address 140.1.13.3 255.255.255.0
```

Example 11-11 *Boston Configuration*

```
interface serial0
encapsulation frame-relay
!
interface serial 0.3 point-to-point
ip address 140.1.3.4 255.255.255.0
frame-relay interface-dlci 51
!
interface ethernet 0
ip address 140.1.14.4  255.255.255.0
```

Again, defaults abound in this configuration, but some defaults are different than when you're configuring on the main interface, as in the preceding example. The LMI type is autosensed, and Cisco encapsulation is used, which is just like the fully-meshed example. However, Inverse ARP is disabled on each point-to-point subinterface by default. As you will see, Inverse ARP is not needed with point-to-point subinterfaces.

Two new commands create the configuration required with point-to-point subinterfaces. First, the **interface serial 0.1 point-to-point** command creates logical subinterface number 1 under physical interface Serial0. The **frame-relay interface-dlci** subinterface subcommand then tells the router which single DLCI is associated with that subinterface.

An example of how the **interface-dlci** command works can help. Consider router Atlanta in Figure 11-19. Atlanta receives LMI messages on Serial0 stating that three PVCs, with DLCIs 52, 53, and 54, are up. Which PVC goes with which subinterface? Cisco IOS software needs to associate the correct PVC with the correct subinterface. This is accomplished with the **frame-relay interface-dlci** command.

The subinterface numbers do not have to match on the router on the other end of the PVC, nor does the DLCI number. In this example, I just numbered them to be easier to remember! In real life, it is useful to encode some information about your network numbering scheme into the subinterface number. One client I worked with encoded part of the carrier's circuit ID in the subinterface number so that the operations staff could find the correct information to tell the Telco when troubleshooting the link. Many sites use the DLCI as the subinterface number. Of course, useful troubleshooting information, such as the DLCI, the name of the router on the other end of the VC, and so on, could be configured as text with the **description** command as well. In any case, there are no requirements for matching subinterface numbers. Here, all I did was match the subinterface number to the third octet of the IP address.

Example 11-12 shows the output from the most popular Cisco IOS software Frame Relay EXEC commands for monitoring Frame Relay, as issued on router Atlanta.

Example 11-12 *Output from EXEC Commands on Atlanta*

```
Atlanta#show frame-relay pvc

PVC Statistics for interface Serial0 (Frame Relay DTE)

                Active      Inactive      Deleted       Static
  Local           3           0             0             0
  Switched        0           0             0             0
  Unused          0           0             0             0
DLCI = 52, DLCI USAGE = LOCAL, PVC STATUS = ACTIVE, INTERFACE = Serial0.1

  input pkts 843          output pkts 876          in bytes 122723
  out bytes 134431        dropped pkts 0           in FECN pkts 0
  in BECN pkts 0          out FECN pkts 0          out BECN pkts 0
  in DE pkts 0            out DE pkts 0
  out bcast pkts 876       out bcast bytes 134431
  pvc create time 05:20:10, last time pvc status changed 05:19:31
  --More--
DLCI = 53, DLCI USAGE = LOCAL, PVC STATUS = ACTIVE, INTERFACE = Serial0.2

  input pkts 0            output pkts 875          in bytes 0
  out bytes 142417        dropped pkts 0           in FECN pkts 0
  in BECN pkts 0          out FECN pkts 0          out BECN pkts 0
  in DE pkts 0            out DE pkts 0
  out bcast pkts 875       out bcast bytes 142417
  pvc create time 05:19:51, last time pvc status changed 04:55:41
  --More--
DLCI = 54, DLCI USAGE = LOCAL, PVC STATUS = ACTIVE, INTERFACE = Serial0.3

  input pkts 10           output pkts 877          in bytes 1274
  out bytes 142069        dropped pkts 0           in FECN pkts 0
  in BECN pkts 0          out FECN pkts 0          out BECN pkts 0
```

continues

Example 11-12 *Output from EXEC Commands on Atlanta (Continued)*

```
    in DE pkts 0              out DE pkts 0
    out bcast pkts 877        out bcast bytes 142069
    pvc create time 05:19:52, last time pvc status changed 05:17:42

Atlanta#show frame-relay map
Serial0.3 (up): point-to-point dlci, dlci 54(0x36,0xC60), broadcast
          status defined, active
Serial0.2 (up): point-to-point dlci, dlci 53(0x35,0xC50), broadcast
          status defined, active
Serial0.1 (up): point-to-point dlci, dlci 52(0x34,0xC40), broadcast
          status defined, active

Atlanta#debug frame-relay lmi
Frame Relay LMI debugging is on
Displaying all Frame Relay LMI data

Serial0(out): StEnq, myseq 163, yourseen 161, DTE up
datagramstart = 0x45AED8, datagramsize = 13
FR encap = 0xFCF10309
00 75 01 01 01 03 02 A3 A1

Serial0(in): Status, myseq 163
RT IE 1, length 1, type 1
KA IE 3, length 2, yourseq 162, myseq 163
```

The **show frame-relay pvc** command lists useful management information. For instance, the packet counters for each VC, plus the counters for FECN and BECN, can be particularly useful. Likewise, comparing the packets/bytes sent on one router versus the counters of what is received on the router on the other end of the VC is also quite useful, because it reflects the number of packets/bytes lost inside the Frame Relay cloud. Also, the PVC status is a great place to start when troubleshooting. In addition, an SNMP manager can better gather all this information with this command.

The **show frame-relay map** command lists mapping information. With the earlier example of a fully-meshed network, in which the configuration did not use any subinterfaces, a Layer 3 address was listed with each DLCI. In this example, a DLCI is listed in each entry, but no mention of corresponding Layer 3 addresses is made. The whole point of mapping is to correlate a Layer 3 address to a Layer 2 address, but there is no Layer 3 address in the **show frame-relay map** command output! The reason is that the information is stored somewhere else. Subinterfaces require the use of the **frame-relay interface-dlci** configuration command. Because these subinterfaces are point-to-point, when a route points out a single subinterface, the DLCI to use to send frames is implied by the configuration. Mapping via Inverse ARP or static **frame-relay map** statements is needed only when more than two VCs terminate on the interface or subinterface, because those are the only instances in which confusion about which DLCI to use might occur.

The **debug frame-relay lmi** output lists information for the sending and receiving LMI inquiries. The switch sends the status message, and the DTE (router) sends the status inquiry. The default setting with Cisco IOS software is to send, and to expect to receive, these status messages. The Cisco IOS software **no keepalive** command is used to disable the use of LMI status messages. Unlike other interfaces, Cisco keepalive messages do not flow from router to router over Frame Relay. Instead, they are simply used to detect whether the router has connectivity to its local Frame Relay switch.

A Partially-Meshed Network with Some Fully-Meshed Parts

You can also choose to use multipoint subinterfaces for a Frame Relay configuration. This last sample network, based on the network shown in Figure 11-20, uses both multipoint and point-to-point subinterfaces. Examples 11-13 through 11-17 show the configuration for this network. Table 11-12 summarizes the addresses and subinterfaces used.

Figure 11-20 *Hybrid of Full and Partial Mesh*

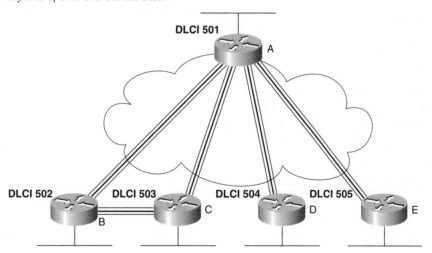

Example 11-13   *Router A Configuration*

```
hostname RouterA
!
interface serial0
encapsulation frame-relay
!
interface serial 0.1 multipoint
ip address 140.1.1.1  255.255.255.0
frame-relay interface-dlci 502
frame-relay interface-dlci 503
!
interface serial 0.2 point-to-point
ip address 140.1.2.1 255.255.255.0
frame-relay interface-dlci 504
!
interface serial 0.3 point-to-point
ip address 140.1.3.1 255.255.255.0
frame-relay interface-dlci 505
!
interface ethernet 0
ip address 140.1.11.1 255.255.255.0
```

Example 11-14   *Router B Configuration*

```
hostname RouterB
!
interface serial0
encapsulation frame-relay
!
interface serial 0.1 multipoint
ip address 140.1.1.2  255.255.255.0
frame-relay interface-dlci 501
frame-relay interface-dlci 503
!
interface ethernet 0
ip address 140.1.12.2 255.255.255.0
```

Example 11-15   *Router C Configuration*

```
hostname RouterC
!
interface serial0
encapsulation frame-relay
!
interface serial 0.1 multipoint
ip address 140.1.1.3  255.255.255.0
frame-relay interface-dlci 501
frame-relay interface-dlci 502
```

Example 11-15 *Router C Configuration (Continued)*

```
!
interface ethernet 0
ip address 140.1.13.3 255.255.255.0
```

Example 11-16 *Router D Configuration*

```
hostname RouterD
!
interface serial0
encapsulation frame-relay
!
interface serial 0.1 point-to-point
ip address 140.1.2.4  255.255.255.0
frame-relay interface-dlci 501
!
interface ethernet 0
ip address 140.1.14.4 255.255.255.0
```

Example 11-17 *Router E Configuration*

```
hostname RouterE
!
interface serial0
encapsulation frame-relay
!
interface serial 0.1 point-to-point
ip address 140.1.3.5 255.255.255.0
frame-relay interface-dlci 501
!
interface ethernet 0
ip address 140.1.15.5 255.255.255.0
```

Table 11-12 *IP Addresses with Point-to-Point and Multipoint Subinterfaces*

Router	Subnet	IP Address	Subinterface Type
A	140.1.1.0/24	140.1.1.1	Multipoint
B	140.1.1.0/24	140.1.1.2	Multipoint
C	140.1.1.0/24	140.1.1.3	Multipoint
A	140.1.2.0/24	140.1.2.1	Point-to-point
D	140.1.2.0/24	140.1.2.4	Point-to-point
A	140.1.3.0/24	140.1.3.1	Point-to-point
E	140.1.3.0/24	140.1.3.5	Point-to-point

Multipoint subinterfaces work best when you have a full mesh between a set of routers. On Routers A, B, and C, a multipoint subinterface is used for the configuration referencing the other two routers, because you can think of these three routers as forming a fully meshed subset of the network.

The term multipoint simply means that there is more than one VC, so you can send and receive to and from more than one VC on the subinterface. Like point-to-point subinterfaces, multipoint subinterfaces use the **frame-relay interface-dlci** command. Notice that there are two commands for each multipoint subinterface in this case, because each of the two PVCs associated with this subinterface must be identified as being used with that subinterface.

Router A is the only router using both multipoint and point-to-point subinterfaces. On Router A's multipoint Serial0.1 interface, DLCIs for Router B and Router C are listed. On Router A's other two subinterfaces, which are point-to-point, only a single DLCI needs to be listed. In fact, only one **frame-relay interface-dlci** command is allowed on a point-to-point subinterface, because only one VC is allowed. Otherwise, the configurations between the two types are similar.

No mapping statements are required for the configurations shown in Examples 11-13 through 11-17 because Inverse ARP is enabled on the multipoint subinterfaces by default. No mapping is ever needed for the point-to-point subinterface, because the only DLCI associated with the interface is statically configured with the **frame-relay interface-dlci** command.

Example 11-18 lists another **show frame-relay map** command, showing the mapping information learned by Inverse ARP for the multipoint subinterface. Notice that the output now includes the Layer 3 addresses! The reason is that the routes might point out a multipoint interface, but because more than one DLCI is associated with the interface, the router needs mapping information to identify the correct DLCI.

Example 11-18 *Frame Relay Maps and Inverse ARP on Router C*

```
RouterC#show frame-relay map
Serial0.1 (up): ip 140.1.1.1 dlci 501(0x1F5,0x7C50), dynamic,
            broadcast,, status defined, active
Serial0.1 (up): ip 140.1.1.2 dlci 502(0x1F6,0x7C60), dynamic,
            broadcast,, status defined, active


RouterC#debug frame-relay events
Frame Relay events debugging is on

RouterC#configure terminal
Enter configuration commands, one per line.  End with Ctrl-Z.
```

Example 11-18 *Frame Relay Maps and Inverse ARP on Router C (Continued)*

```
RouterC(config)#interface serial 0.1
RouterC(config-subif)#no shutdown
RouterC(config-subif)#^Z
RouterC#

Serial0.1: FR ARP input
Serial0.1: FR ARP input
Serial0.1: FR ARP input
datagramstart = 0xE42E58, datagramsize = 30
FR encap = 0x7C510300
80 00 00 00 08 06 00 0F 08 00 02 04 00 09 00 00
8C 01 01 01 7C 51 8C 01 01 03

datagramstart = 0xE420E8, datagramsize = 30
FR encap = 0x7C610300
80 00 00 00 08 06 00 0F 08 00 02 04 00 09 00 00
8C 01 01 02 7C 61 8C 01 01 03
```

The messages about Inverse ARP in the **debug frame-relay events** output are not so obvious.
One easy exercise is to search for the hex version of the IP addresses in the output. These
addresses are highlighted in Example 11-18. For example, the first 3 bytes of 140.1.1.0 are
8C 01 01 in hexadecimal. This field starts on the left side of the output, so it is easy to
recognize.

Foundation Summary

The "Foundation Summary" section lists the most important facts from the chapter. Although this section does not list everything that will be on the exam, a well-prepared CCNA candidate should at a minimum know all the details in each Foundation Summary before taking the exam.

Figure 11-21 outlines the basic physical topology and related terminology in a Frame Relay network.

Figure 11-21 *Frame Relay Components*

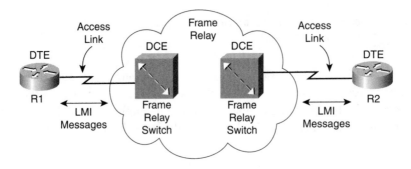

Figure 11-22 depicts a typical partially-meshed Frame Relay network.

Figure 11-22 *Typical Partial-Mesh Frame Relay Network*

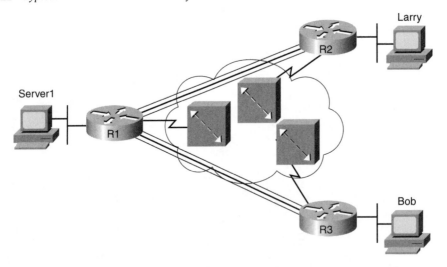

Table 11-13 outlines the three LMI types, their origin, and the keyword used in the Cisco **frame-relay lmi-type** interface subcommand.

Table 11-13 *Frame Relay LMI Types*

Name	Document	IOS LMI-Type Parameter
Cisco	Proprietary	cisco
ANSI	T1.617 Annex D	ansi
ITU	Q.933 Annex A	q933a

Figure 11-23 outlines the two Frame Relay encapsulation options on Cisco routers.

Figure 11-23 *Cisco and RFC 1490/2427 Encapsulation*

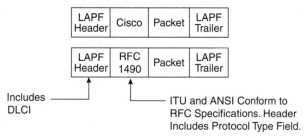

Cisco's Frame Relay implementation defines three different options for assigning subnets and IP addresses on Frame Relay interfaces:

- One subnet containing all Frame Relay DTEs
- One subnet per VC
- A hybrid of the first two options

Cisco IOS software uses some very good choices for default Frame Relay settings:

- The LMI type is automatically sensed.
- The encapsulation is Cisco instead of IETF.
- PVC DLCIs are learned via LMI status messages.
- Inverse ARP is enabled (by default) and is triggered when the status message declaring that the VCs are up is received.

Figure 11-24 outlines how Inverse ARP works.

Figure 11-24 *Inverse ARP Process*

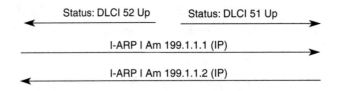

Q&A

As mentioned in the Introduction, you have two choices for review questions. The following questions give you a bigger challenge than the exam because they are open-ended. By reviewing with this more-difficult question format, you can exercise your memory better and prove your conceptual and factual knowledge of the topics covered in this chapter. The answers to these questions are found in Appendix A.

For more practice with exam-like question formats, including multiple-choice questions and those using a router simulator, use the exam engine on the CD.

1. What two WAN data-link protocols define a method of announcing the interface's Layer 3 addresses to other devices attached to the WAN?

2. Explain the purpose of Inverse ARP, as well as how it uses Frame Relay broadcasts.

3. Would a Frame Relay switch connected to a router behave differently if the IETF option were deleted from the **encapsulation frame-relay ietf** command on that attached router? Would a router on the other end of the VC behave any differently if the same change were made?

4. What does NBMA stand for? Does it apply to X.25 networks or Frame Relay networks?

5. Which layer or layers of OSI are most closely related to the functions of Frame Relay? Why?

6. When Inverse ARP is used by default, what additional configuration is needed to get IGRP routing updates to flow over each VC, assuming IGRP has already been configured correctly?

7. Define the attributes of a partial-mesh and full-mesh Frame Relay network.

8. What key pieces of information are required in the **frame-relay map** statement?

9. Create a configuration for Router1 that has Frame Relay VCs to Router2 and Router3 (DLCIs 202 and 203, respectively) on Router1's Serial1 interface. Use any IP addresses you like. Assume that the network is not fully meshed.

10. What **show** command tells you when a PVC became active? How does the router know what time the PVC became active?

11. What **show** command lists Frame Relay information about mapping? In what instances does the information displayed include the Layer 3 addresses of other routers?

12. True or false: The **no keepalive** command on a Frame Relay serial interface causes no further Cisco-proprietary keepalive messages to be sent to the Frame Relay switch.

13. What **debug** option shows Inverse ARP messages?

14. True or false: The Frame Relay **map** configuration command allows more than one Layer 3 protocol address mapping on the same configuration command.

15. What is the name of the field that identifies, or addresses, a Frame Relay virtual circuit?

16. Describe the difference between FRF.5 and FRF.8 service interworking.

Cisco Published ICND Exam Topics*
Covered in This Part:

* Always re-check www.cisco.com for the latest posted exam topics

Part IV: Network Security

This chapter covers the following subjects:

- Standard IP Access Control Lists

- Extended IP Access Control Lists

- Miscellaneous ACL Topics

CHAPTER 12

IP Access Control List Security

Network security is one of the hottest topics in networking today. Although security has always been important, the evolution of the Internet has created more security exposures. In years past, most companies were not permanently connected to a global network—a network through which others could attempt to illegally access their networks. Today, because most companies connect to the Internet, many companies receive significant income through their network-based facilities—facts that increase the exposure and increase the impact when security is breached.

Cisco routers can be used as part of a good overall security strategy. The most important tool in Cisco IOS software used as part of that strategy are Access Control Lists (ACLs). ACLs define rules that can be used to prevent some packets from flowing through the network. Whether you simply prevent anyone not in the accounting department from accessing the payroll server, or whether you are trying to stop Internet hackers from bringing your e-commerce web server to its knees, IOS ACLs can be a key security tool that is part of a larger security strategy.

If you're studying for the ICND exam, this chapter is the last chapter before you begin the review process. If you're using both this book and *CCNA INTRO Exam Certification Guide* to get your CCNA certification by passing just one exam (the CCNA exam), after finishing this chapter you should go back to *CCNA INTRO Exam Certification Guide* and read Chapter 16, "Final Preparation." As always, refer to the Introduction in this book for a suggested reading plan if you're using both books to study for the combined exam.

"Do I Know This Already?" Quiz

The purpose of the "Do I Know This Already?" quiz is to help you decide if you need to read the entire chapter. If you intend to read the entire chapter, you do not necessarily need to answer these questions now.

The eight-question quiz, derived from the major sections in the "Foundation Topics" section, helps you determine how to spend your limited study time.

Table 12-1 outlines the major topics discussed in this chapter and the "Do I Know This Already?" quiz questions that correspond to those topics.

Table 12-1 *"Do I Know This Already?" Foundation Topics Section-to-Question Mapping*

Foundations Topics Section	Questions Covered in This Section
Standard IP Access Control Lists	1, 4, 5
Extended IP Access Control Lists	2, 6, 7
Miscellaneous ACL Topics	3, 8

> **CAUTION** The goal of self-assessment is to gauge your mastery of the topics in this chapter. If you don't know the answer to a question or you're only partially sure of the answer, you should mark this question as wrong for purposes of the self-assessment. Giving yourself credit for an answer you guess correctly skews your self-assessment results and might give you a false sense of security.

1. Barney is a host with IP address 10.1.1.1 in subnet 10.1.1.0/24. Which of the following are things that a standard IP ACL could be configured to do?

   a. Match the exact source IP address

   b. Match IP addresses 10.1.1.1 through 10.1.1.4 with one **access-list** command without matching other IP addresses

   c. Match all IP addresses in Barney's subnet with one **access-list** command without matching other IP addresses

   d. Match only the packet's destination IP address

2. Which of the following fields cannot be compared based on an extended IP ACL?

   a. Protocol

   b. Source IP address

   c. Destination IP address

   d. TOS byte

   e. URL

   f. Filename for FTP transfers

   g. All of the above

   h. None of the above

3. Which of the following fields can be compared using a named IP ACL but not a numbered extended IP ACL?

   a. Protocol

   b. Source IP address

   c. Destination IP address

   d. TOS byte

   e. URL

   f. Filename for FTP transfers

   g. All of the above

   h. None of the above

4. Which of the following wildcard masks is most useful for matching all IP packets in subnet 10.1.128.0, mask 255.255.255.0?

   a. 0.0.0.0

   b. 0.0.0.31

   c. 0.0.0.240

   d. 0.0.0.255

   e. 0.0.15.0

   f. 0.0.248.255

   g. 0.0.255.255

   h. 0.255.255.255

   i. 255.255.255.255

5. Which of the following wildcard masks is most useful for matching all IP packets in subnet 10.1.128.0, mask 255.255.240.0?

   a. 0.0.0.0

   b. 0.0.0.31

   c. 0.0.0.240

   d. 0.0.0.255

   e. 0.0.15.255

   f. 0.0.248.255

   g. 0.0.255.255

   h. 0.255.255.255

   i. 255.255.255.255

6. Which of the following **access-list** commands permits traffic that matches packets going to a web server from 10.1.1.1 for all web servers whose IP addresses begin with 172.16.5?

   a. access-list 101 permit tcp host 10.1.1.1 172.16.5.0 0.0.0.255 eq www

   b. access-list 1951 permit ip host 10.1.1.1 172.16.5.0 0.0.0.255 eq www

   c. access-list 2523 permit ip host 10.1.1.1 eq www 172.16.5.0 0.0.0.255

   d. access-list 2523 permit tcp host 10.1.1.1 eq www 172.16.5.0 0.0.0.255

   e. access-list 2523 permit tcp host 10.1.1.1 172.16.5.0 0.0.0.255 eq www

7. Which of the following **access-list** commands permits traffic that matches packets going to a web client from all web servers whose IP addresses begin with 172.16.5?

   a. access-list 101 permit tcp host 10.1.1.1 172.16.5.0 0.0.0.255 eq www

   b. access-list 1951 permit ip host 10.1.1.1 172.16.5.0 0.0.0.255 eq www

   c. access-list 2523 permit tcp any eq www 172.16.5.0 0.0.0.255

   d. access-list 2523 permit tcp 172.16.5.0 0.0.0.255 eq www 172.16.5.0 0.0.0.255

   e. access-list 2523 permit tcp 172.16.5.0 0.0.0.255 eq www any

8. What general guideline should be followed when placing IP ACLs, at least according to the ICND course on which CCNA is based?

   a. Perform all filtering on output if at all possible.

   b. Put more-general statements early in the ACL.

   c. Filter packets as close to the source as possible.

   d. Order the ACL commands based on the source IP addresses, lowest to highest, to improve performance.

The answers to the "Do I Know This Already?" quiz appear in Appendix A. The suggested choices for your next step are as follows:

■ **6 or less overall score**—Read the entire chapter. This includes the "Foundation Topics," "Foundation Summary," and "Q&A" sections.

■ **7 or 8 overall score**—If you want more review on these topics, skip to the "Foundation Summary" section and then go to the "Q&A" section. Otherwise, move to the next chapter.

Foundation Topics

Standard IP Access Control Lists

IP access control lists (ACLs) cause a router to discard some packets based on criteria defined by the network engineer. The goal of these filters is to prevent unwanted traffic in the network—whether to prevent hackers from penetrating the network or just to prevent employees from using systems they should not be using. Access lists should simply be part of an organization's security policy.

By the way, IP access lists can also be used to filter routing updates, to match packets for prioritization, to match packets for VPN tunneling, and to match packets for implementing quality of service features. So you will see ACLs in most of the other Cisco certification exams as you move on in your career.

This chapter covers two main categories of IOS IP ACLs—standard and extended. Standard ACLs use simpler logic, and extended ACLs use more-complex logic. The first section of this chapter covers standard IP ACLs, followed by a section on extended IP ACLs. Several sections related to both types of ACLs close the chapter.

IP Standard ACL Concepts

As soon as you know what needs to be filtered, the next step is to decide where to filter the traffic. Figure 12-1 serves as an example. In this case, imagine that Bob is not allowed to access Server1, but Larry is.

Figure 12-1 *Locations Where Access List Logic Can Be Applied in the Network*

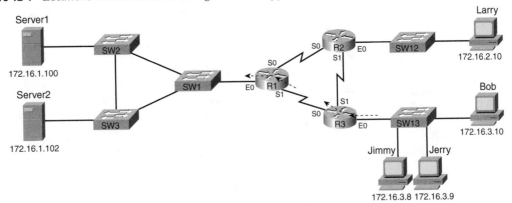

Filtering logic could be configured on any of the three routers and on any of their interfaces. The dotted arrowed lines in the figure show the most appropriate points at which to apply the filtering logic in an ACL. Because Bob's traffic is the only traffic that needs to be filtered, and the goal is to stop access to Server1, the access list could be applied at either R1 or R3. And because Bob's attempted traffic to Server1 would not need to go through R2, R2 would not be a good place to put the access list logic. For the sake of discussion, assume that R1 should have the access list applied.

Cisco IOS software applies the filtering logic of an ACL either as a packet enters an interface or as it exits the interface. In other words, IOS associates an ACL with an interface, and specifically for traffic either entering or exiting the interface. After you have chosen the router on which you want to place the access list, you must choose the interface on which to apply the access logic, as well as whether to apply the logic for inbound or outbound packets.

For instance, imagine that you want to filter Bob's packets sent to Server1. Figure 12-2 shows the options for filtering the packet.

Figure 12-2 *Internal Processing in R1 in Relation to Where R1 Can Filter Packets*

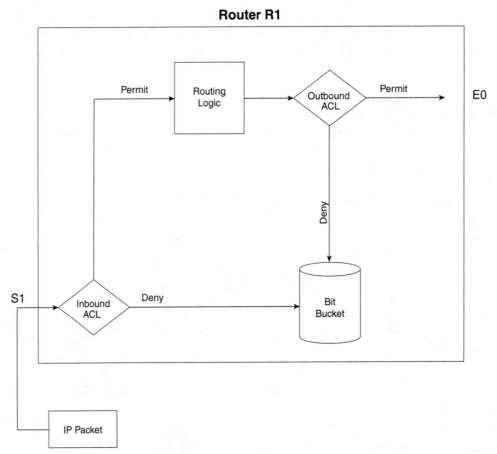

Filtering logic can be applied to packets entering S1 or to packets exiting E0 on R1 to match the packet sent by Bob to Server1. In general, you can filter packets by creating and enabling access lists for both incoming and outgoing packets on each interface. Here are some key features of Cisco access lists:

- Packets can be filtered as they enter an interface, before the routing decision.
- Packets can be filtered before they exit an interface, after the routing decision.
- *Deny* is the term used in Cisco IOS software to imply that the packet will be filtered.
- *Permit* is the term used in Cisco IOS software to imply that the packet will not be filtered.
- The filtering logic is configured in the access list.
- At the end of every access list is an implied "deny all traffic" statement. Therefore, if a packet does not match any of your access list statements, it is blocked.

For example, you might create an access list in R1 and enable it on R1's S1 interface. The access list would look for packets that came from Bob. Therefore, the access list would need to be enabled for inbound packets, because in this network, packets from Bob enter S1, and packets to Bob exit S1.

Access lists have two major steps in their logic: matching and action. Matching logic examines each packet and determines whether it matches the **access-list** statement. For instance, Bob's IP address would be used to match packets sent from Bob.

IP ACLs tell the router to take one of two actions when a statement is matched: deny or permit. Deny means to discard the packet, and permit implies that the packet should continue on its way.

So the access list for preventing Bob's traffic to the server might go something like this:

> Look for packets with Bob's source IP address and Server1's destination IP address. When you see them, discard them. If you see any other packets, do not discard them.

Not surprisingly, IP ACLs can get a lot more difficult than that in real life. Even a short list of matching criteria can create complicated access lists on a variety of interfaces in a variety of routers. I've even heard of a couple of large networks with a few full-time people who do nothing but plan and implement access lists!

Cisco calls its packet-filtering features "Access Control Lists" in part because the logic is created with multiple configuration commands that are considered to be in the same list. When an access list has multiple entries, IOS searches the list sequentially until the first statement is matched. The matched statement determines the action to be taken. The two diamond shapes in Figure 12-2 represent the application of access list logic.

The logic that IOS uses with a multiple-entry ACL can be summarized as follows:

1. The matching parameters of the **access-list** statement are compared to the packet.

2. If a match is made, the action defined in this **access-list** statement (permit or deny) is performed.

3. If a match is not made in Step 2, repeat Steps 1 and 2 using each successive statement in the ACL until a match is made.

4. If no match is made with an entry in the access list, the deny action is performed.

Wildcard Masks

IOS IP ACLs match packets by looking at the IP, TCP, and UDP headers in the packet. Extended access lists can check source and destination IP addresses, as well as source and destination port numbers, along with several other fields. However, standard IP access lists can examine only the source IP address.

Regardless of whether you use standard or extended IP ACLs, you can tell the router to match based on the entire IP address or just a part of the IP address. For instance, if you wanted to stop Bob from sending packets to Server1, you would look at the entire IP address of Bob and Server1 in the access list. But what if the criteria were to stop all hosts in Bob's subnet from getting to Server1? Because all hosts in Bob's subnet have the same numbers in their first three octets, the access list could just check the first three octets of the address to match all packets with a single **access-list** command.

Cisco *wildcard masks* define the portion of the IP address that should be examined. When defining the ACL statements, as you'll see in the next section of this chapter, you can define a wildcard mask along with the IP address. The wildcard mask tells the router which part of the IP address in the configuration statement must be compared with the packet header.

For example, suppose that one mask implies that the whole packet should be checked and another implies that only the first three octets of the address need to be examined. (You might choose to do that to match all IP hosts in the same subnet when using a subnet mask of 255.255.255.0.) To perform this matching, Cisco access lists use wildcard masks.

Wildcard masks look similar to subnet masks, but they are not the same. Wildcard masks represent a 32-bit number, as do subnet masks. However, the wildcard mask's 0 bits tell the router that those corresponding bits in the address must be compared when performing the matching logic. The binary 1s in the wildcard mask tell the router that those bits do not need to be compared. In fact, many people call these bits the "don't care" bits.

To get a sense of the idea behind a wildcard mask, Table 12-2 lists some of the more popular wildcard masks, along with their meanings.

Table 12-2 *Sample Access List Wildcard Masks*

Wildcard Mask	Binary Version of the Mask	Description
0.0.0.0	00000000.00000000.00000000.00000000	The entire IP address must match.
0.0.0.255	00000000.00000000.00000000.11111111	Just the first 24 bits must match.
0.0.255.255	00000000.00000000.11111111.11111111	Just the first 16 bits must match.
0.255.255.255	00000000.11111111.11111111.11111111	Just the first 8 bits must match.
255.255.255.255	11111111.11111111.11111111.11111111	Don't even bother to compare; it's automatically considered to match (all 32 bits are "don't care" bits).
0.0.15.255	00000000.00000000.00001111.11111111	Just the first 20 bits must match.
0.0.3.255	00000000.00000000.00000011.11111111	Just the first 22 bits must match.

The first several examples show typical uses of the wildcard mask. As you can see, it is not a subnet mask. A wildcard of 0.0.0.0 means that the entire IP address must be examined, and be equal, to be considered a match. 0.0.0.255 means that the last octet automatically matches, but the first three must be examined, and so on. More generally, the wildcard mask means the following:

> Bit positions of binary 0 mean that the access list compares the corresponding bit position in the IP address and makes sure it is equal to the same bit position in the address configured in the **access-list** statement. Bit positions of binary 1 are "don't care" bits—those bit positions are immediately considered to be a match.

The next two rows of Table 12-2 show two reasonable, but not obvious, wildcard masks. 0.0.15.255 in binary is 20 0s followed by 12 1s. This means that the first 20 bits must match.

Similarly, 0.0.3.255 means that the first 22 bits must be examined to find out if they match. Why are these useful? If the subnet mask is 255.255.240.0, and you want to match all hosts in the same subnet, the 0.0.15.255 wildcard means that all network and subnet bits must be matched, and all host bits are automatically considered to match. Likewise, if you want to filter all hosts in a subnet that uses subnet mask 255.255.252.0, the wildcard mask 0.0.3.255 matches the network and subnet bits. In general, if you want a wildcard mask that helps you match all hosts in a subnet, invert the subnet mask, and you have the correct wildcard mask.

> **NOTE**   In real jobs, you might want to match all the hosts in a single subnet. If you already know the subnet mask, and you want to use a wildcard mask that matches the same set of addresses, you can easily find the wildcard mask with a math trick. One octet at a time, in decimal, subtract the subnet mask from 255.255.255.255. The result is the "right" wildcard mask. For instance, a subnet mask of 255.255.255.0 subtracted from 255.255.255.255 gives you 0.0.0.255 as a wildcard mask. This mask checks only the first 24 bits, which in this case are the network and subnet parts of the address. Similarly, if the subnet mask is 255.255.240.0, subtracting from 255.255.255.255 gives you 0.0.15.255. This is the same wildcard mask as one of the examples mentioned in Table 12-2.

Standard IP Access List Configuration

Before diving into the configuration, here's a quick review of how standard IP ACLs work:

> If statement 1 is matched, carry out the action defined in that statement. If it isn't matched, examine the next statement. If it matches, carry out the action it defines. Continue looping through the list until a statement is matched or until the last statement in the list is not matched. If none of the statements is matched, the packet is discarded.

A standard access list is used to match a packet and then take the directed action. Each standard ACL can match all, or only part, of the packet's source IP address. The only two actions taken when an **access-list** statement is matched are to either deny (discard) or permit (forward) the packet.

Table 12-3 lists the configuration commands related to standard IP access lists. Table 12-4 lists the related EXEC commands. Several examples follow these lists of commands.

Table 12-3   *Standard IP Access List Configuration Commands*

Command	Configuration Mode and Description
access-list *access-list-number* {**deny**	**permit**} *source* [*source-wildcard*] [**log**]	Global command for standard numbered access lists. Use a number between 1 and 99 or 1300 and 1999, inclusive.
access-list *access-list-number* **remark** *text*	Defines a remark that helps you remember what the ACL is supposed to do.

Table 12-3 *Standard IP Access List Configuration Commands (Continued)*

Command	Configuration Mode and Description
ip access-group {*number* | *name* [in | out]}	Interface subcommand to enable access lists.
access-class *number* | *name* [in | out]	Line subcommand to enable either standard or extended access lists.

Table 12-4 *Standard IP Access List EXEC Commands*

Command	Description
show ip interface [*type number*]	Includes a reference to the access lists enabled on the interface.
show access-lists [*access-list-number* | *access-list-name*]	Shows details of configured access lists for all protocols.
show ip access-list [*access-list-number* | *access-list-name*]	Shows IP access lists.

Example 12-1 attempts to stop Bob's traffic to Server1. As shown in Figure 12-1, Bob is not allowed to access Server1. In Example 12-1, the configuration enables an ACL for all packets going out R1's Ethernet0 interface. The ACL matches the source address in the packet— Bob's IP address. Example 12-1 shows the configuration on R1.

Example 12-1 *Standard Access List on R1 Stopping Bob from Reaching Server1*

```
interface Ethernet0
ip address 172.16.1.1 255.255.255.0
ip access-group 1 out

access-list 1 remark stop all traffic whose source IP is Bob
access-list 1 deny 172.16.3.10 0.0.0.0
access-list 1 permit 0.0.0.0 255.255.255.255
```

First, focus on the basic syntax of the commands. Standard IP access lists use a number in the range of 1 to 99 or 1300 to 1999. I used number 1 versus the other available numbers for no particular reason. (There is absolutely no difference in using one number or another, as long as it is in the correct range. In other words, list 1 is no better or worse than list 99.) The **access-list** commands, under which the matching and action logic are defined, are global configuration commands. To enable the ACL on an interface and define the direction of packets to which the ACL is applied, the **ip access-group** command is used. In this case, it enables the logic for ACL 1 on Ethernet0 for packets going out the interface.

ACL 1 keeps packets sent by Bob from exiting R1's Ethernet interface, based on the matching logic of the **access-list 1 deny 172.16.3.10 0.0.0.0** command. The wildcard mask of 0.0.0.0 means "match all 32 bits," so only packets whose IP address exactly matches 172.16.3.10 match this statement and are discarded. The **access-list 1 permit 0.0.0.0 255.255.255.255** command, the last statement in the list, matches all packets, because the wildcard mask of 255.255.255.255 means "don't care" about all 32 bits. In other words, the statement matches all IP source addresses. These packets are permitted.

The list stops Bob from getting packets to Server1, but it also stops Bob from getting packets to Server2. With the topology shown in Figure 12-1, you cannot use a standard ACL and deny Bob access to Server 1 while permitting access to Server2. You need to use an extended ACL, as discussed in the next section.

Interestingly, IOS changes the configuration shown in Example 12-1. The output of the **show running-config** command in Example 12-2 shows what IOS actually places in the configuration file.

Example 12-2 *Revised Standard Access List Stopping Bob from Reaching Server1*

```
interface Ethernet0
ip address 172.16.1.1 255.255.255.0
ip access-group 1 out

access-list 1 remark stop all traffic whose source IP is Bob
access-list 1 deny host 172.16.3.10
access-list 1 permit any
```

The commands in Example 12-1 are changed based on three factors. Cisco IOS allows both an older style and newer style of configuration for some parameters. Example 12-1 shows the older style, and the router changes to the equivalent newer-style configuration in Example 12-2. First, the use of a wildcard mask of 0.0.0.0 does indeed mean that the router should match that specific host IP address. The newer-style configuration uses the **host** keyword in *front* of the specific IP address. The other change to the newer-style configuration involves the use of wildcard mask 255.255.255.255 to mean "match anything." The newer-style configuration uses the keyword **any** to replace wildcard mask 255.255.255.255. **any** simply means that any IP address is matched.

Standard IP ACL: Example 2

The second standard IP ACL exposes more ACL issues. Figure 12-3 and Examples 12-3 and 12-4 show a basic use of standard IP access lists, with two typical oversights in the first attempt at a complete solution. The criteria for the access lists are as follows:

■ Sam is not allowed access to Bugs or Daffy.

■ Hosts on the Seville Ethernet are not allowed access to hosts on the Yosemite Ethernet.

■ All other combinations are allowed.

Figure 12-3   *Network Diagram for Standard Access List Example*

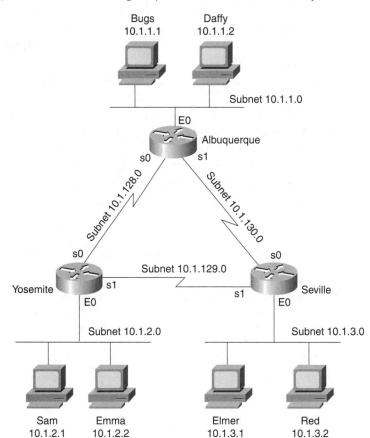

Example 12-3   *Yosemite Configuration for Standard Access List Example*

```
interface serial 0
ip access-group 3 out
!
access-list 3 deny host 10.1.2.1
access-list 3 permit any
```

Example 12-4   *Seville Configuration for Standard Access List Example*

```
interface serial 1
ip access-group 4 out
!
access-list 4 deny 10.1.3.0    0.0.0.255
access-list 4 permit any
```

At first glance, these two access lists seem to perform the desired function. ACL 3, enabled for packets exiting Yosemite's S0 interface, takes care of criterion 1, because ACL 3 matches Sam's IP address exactly. ACL 4 in Seville, enabled for packets exiting its S1 interface, takes care of criterion 2, because ACL 4 matches all packets coming from subnet 10.1.3.0/24. Both routers meet criterion 3: A wildcard **permit any** is used at the end of each access list to override the default, which is to discard all other packets. So all the criteria appear to be met.

However, when one of the WAN links fails, some holes can appear in the ACLs. For example, if the link from Albuquerque to Yosemite fails, Yosemite learns a route to 10.1.1.0/24 through Seville. Packets from Sam, forwarded by Yosemite and destined for hosts in Albuquerque, leave Yosemite's serial 1 interface without being filtered. So criterion 1 is no longer met. Similarly, if the link from Seville to Yosemite fails, Seville routes packets through Albuquerque, routing around the access list enabled on Seville, so criterion 2 is no longer met.

Example 12-5 illustrates an alternative solution—one that works even when some of the links fail.

Example 12-5   *Yosemite Configuration for Standard Access List Example: Alternative Solution to Examples 12-3 and 12-4*

```
interface serial 0
ip access-group 3 out
!
interface serial 1
ip access-group 3 out
!
interface ethernet 0
ip access-group 4 out
!
access-list 3 remark meets criteria 1
access-list 3 deny host 10.1.2.1
access-list 3 permit any
!
access-list 4 remark meets criteria 2
access-list 4 deny 10.1.3.0 0.0.0.255
access-list 4 permit any
```

The configuration in Example 12-5 solves the problem from Examples 12-3 and 12-4. ACL 3 checks for Sam's source IP address, and it is enabled on both serial links for outbound traffic. So, of the traffic that is rerouted because of a WAN link failure, the packets from SAM are still filtered. To meet criterion 2, Yosemite filters packets as they exit its Ethernet interface. Therefore, regardless of which of the two WAN links the packets enter, packets from Seville's subnet are not forwarded to Yosemite's Ethernet.

Extended IP Access Control Lists

Extended IP access lists have both similarities and differences compared to standard IP ACLs. Just like standard lists, you enable extended access lists on interfaces for packets either entering or exiting the interface. IOS searches the list sequentially. The first statement matched stops the search through the list and defines the action to be taken. All these features are true of standard access lists as well.

The one key difference between the two is the variety of fields in the packet that can be compared for matching by extended access lists. A single ACL statement can examine multiple parts of the packet headers, requiring that all the parameters be matched correctly in order to match that one ACL statement. That matching logic is what makes extended access lists both much more useful and much more complex than standard IP ACLs.

This section starts with coverage of the extended IP ACL concepts that differ from standard ACLs—namely, the matching logic. Following that, the configuration details are covered.

Extended IP ACL Concepts

Extended access lists create powerful matching logic by examining many parts of a packet. Figure 12-4 shows several of the fields in the packet headers that can be matched.

Figure 12-4 *Extended Access List Matching Options*

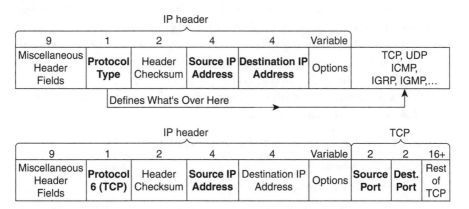

The top set of headers shows the IP protocol type, which identifies what header follows the IP header. You can specify all IP packets, or those with TCP headers, UDP headers, ICMP, and so on, by checking the Protocol field. You can also check both the source and destination IP addresses, as shown. The lower part of the figure shows an example with a TCP header following the IP header, pointing out the location of the TCP source and destination port numbers. These port numbers identify the application. For instance, web uses port 80 by default. If you specify a protocol of TCP or UDP, you can also check the port numbers.

Table 12-5 summarizes the different fields that can be matched with an extended IP ACL, as compared with standard IP ACLs.

Table 12-5 *Standard and Extended IP Access Lists: Matching*

Type of Access List	What Can Be Matched
Both Standard and Extended ACLs	Source IP address
	Portions of the source IP address using a wildcard mask
Only Extended ACLs	Destination IP address
	Portions of the destination IP address using a wildcard mask
	Protocol type (TCP, UDP, ICMP, IGRP, IGMP, and others)
	Source port
	Destination port
	All TCP flows except the first
	IP TOS
	IP precedence

Knowing what to look for is just half the battle. IOS checks all the matching information configured in a single **access-list** command. Everything must match for that single command to be considered a match and for the defined action to be taken. The options start with the protocol type (IP, TCP, UDP, and others), followed by the source IP address, source port, destination IP address, and destination port number. (Remember that the port numbers can be referenced only if the protocol type is configured as TCP or UDP.) Table 12-6 lists several sample **access-list** commands, with several options configured and some explanations. Only the matching options are shown in bold.

Table 12-6 *Extended* **access-list** *Commands and Logic Explanations*

access-list Statement	What It Matches
access-list 101 deny **ip any host 10.1.1.1**	Any IP packet, any source IP address, with a destination IP address of 10.1.1.1.
access-list 101 deny **tcp any gt 1023 host 10.1.1.1 eq 23**	Packets with a TCP header, any source IP address, with a source port greater than (**gt**) 1023. The packet must have a destination IP address of 10.1.1.1 and a destination port of 23.

Table 12-6 *Extended* **access-list** *Commands and Logic Explanations (Continued)*

access-list Statement	What It Matches
access-list 101 deny **tcp any host 10.1.1.1 eq 23**	The same as the preceding example, but any source port matches, because that parameter is omitted in this case.
access-list 101 deny **tcp any host 10.1.1.1 eq telnet**	The same as the preceding example. The **telnet** keyword is used instead of port 23.
access-list 101 deny **udp 1.0.0.0 0.255.255.255 lt 1023 any**	A packet with a source in network 1.0.0.0, using UDP with a source port less than (**lt**) 1023, with any destination IP address.

The sequence of the parameters in the command affects exactly what the IOS ACL logic examines in the packet when trying to make a match. When configuring an ACL to check port numbers, the parameter in the **access-list** command checks the *source* port number when the parameter is placed immediately after the source IP address. Likewise, the parameter in the **access-list** command checks the destination port number when the parameter is placed immediately after the destination IP address. For example, the command **access-list 101 deny tcp any eq telnet any** matches all packets that use TCP and whose source TCP port is 23 (Telnet). The ACL statement matches packets whose source port equals 23 because the **eq telnet** parameter follows the source IP address, not the destination IP address. For similar reasons, the command **access-list 101 deny tcp any any eq telnet** matches all packets that use TCP and whose destination TCP port is 23 (Telnet). Depending on where you enable an extended ACL, and for which direction, you might need to check for the source or destination port number.

Extended IP ACL Configuration

Table 12-7 lists the configuration commands associated with creating extended IP access lists. Table 12-8 lists the associated EXEC commands. Several examples follow these lists of commands.

Table 12-7 *Extended IP Access List Configuration Commands*

Command	Configuration Mode and Description
access-list *access-list-number* {**deny** | **permit**} *protocol source source-wildcard destination destination-wildcard* [**log** | **log-input**]	Global command for extended numbered access lists. Use a number between 100 and 199 or 2000 and 2699, inclusive.

continues

Table 12-7 *Extended IP Access List Configuration Commands (Continued)*

Command	Configuration Mode and Description
access-list *access-list-number* {**deny**	**permit**} **tcp** *source source-wildcard* [*operator* [*port*]] *destination destination-wildcard* [*operator* [*port*]] [**established**] [**log**	**log-input**]	A version of the **access-list** command with TCP-specific parameters.
access-list *access-list-number* **remark** *text*	Defines a remark that helps you remember what the ACL is supposed to do.
ip access-group {*number*	*name* [**in**	**out**]}	Interface subcommand to enable access lists.
access-class *number*	*name* [**in**	**out**]	Line subcommand for standard or extended access lists.

Table 12-8 *Extended IP Access List EXEC Commands*

Command	Description
show ip interface [*type number*]	Includes a reference to the access lists enabled on the interface.
show access-lists [*access-list-number*	*access-list-name*]	Shows the details of configured access lists for all protocols.
show ip access-list [*access-list-number*	*access-list-name*]	Shows IP access lists.

Extended IP Access Lists: Example 1

This example focuses on understanding the basic syntax. In this case, Bob is denied access to all FTP servers on R1's Ethernet, and Larry is denied access to Server1's web server. Figure 12-5 is a reminder of the network topology. Example 12-6 shows the configuration on R1.

Figure 12-5 *Network Diagram for Extended Access List Example 1*

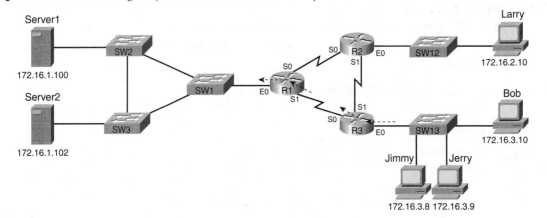

Example 12-6 *R1's Extended Access List: Example 1*

```
interface Serial0
ip address 172.16.12.1 255.255.255.0
ip access-group 101 in

interface Serial1
ip address 172.16.13.1 255.255.255.0
ip access-group 101 in

access-list 101 remark Stop Bob to FTP servers, and Larry to Server1 web
access-list 101 deny tcp host 172.16.3.10 172.16.1.0 0.0.0.255 eq ftp
access-list 101 deny tcp host 172.16.2.10 host 172.16.1.100 eq http
access-list 101 permit ip any any
```

Focusing on the syntax for a moment, there are several new items to review. First, the access list number for extended access lists falls in the range of 100 to 199 or 2000 to 2699. Following the **permit** or **deny** action, the *protocol parameter* defines whether you want to check for all IP packets or just those with TCP or UDP headers. When you check for TCP or UDP port numbers, you must specify the TCP or UDP protocol.

You can check for specific port numbers or ranges. The **eq** parameter means "equals," as shown in the example. It implies that you are checking the port numbers—in this case, the destination port numbers. You can use the numeric values—or, for the more popular options, a more obvious text version is valid. (If you were to enter **eq 80**, the config would show **eq http**.)

In Example 12-6, the first ACL statement prevents Bob's access to FTP servers in subnet 172.16.1.0. The second statement prevents Larry's access to web services on Server1. The final statement permits all other traffic.

In this first extended ACL example, the access lists could have been placed on R2 and R3. As you will read near the end of this chapter, Cisco makes some specific recommendations about where to locate IP ACLs. With extended IP ACLs, Cisco suggests that you locate them as close to the source of the packet as possible. Therefore, Example 12-7 achieves the same goal as Example 12-6 of stopping Bob's access to FTP servers at the main site, and it does so with an ACL on R3.

Example 12-7 *R3's Extended Access List Stopping Bob from Reaching FTP Servers Near R1*

```
interface Ethernet0
ip address 172.16.3.1 255.255.255.0
ip access-group 101 in

access-list 101 remark deny Bob to FTP servers in subnet 172.16.1.0/24
access-list 101 deny tcp host 172.16.3.10 172.16.1.0 0.0.0.255 eq ftp
access-list 101 permit ip any any
```

ACL 101 looks a lot like ACL 101 from Example 12-6, but this time, the ACL does not bother checking for the criteria to match Larry's traffic, because Larry's traffic will never enter R3's Ethernet 0 interface. Because the ACL has been placed on R3, near Bob, it watches for packets Bob sends that enter its Ethernet0 interface. Because of the ACL, Bob's FTP traffic to 172.16.1.0/24 is denied, with all other traffic entering R3's E0 interface making it into the network. Example 12-7 does not show any logic for stopping Larry's traffic.

Extended IP Access Lists: Example 2

Example 12-8, based on the network shown in Figure 12-6, shows another example of how to use extended IP access lists. This example uses the same criteria and network topology as the second standard IP ACL example, as repeated here:

- Sam is not allowed access to Bugs or Daffy.

- Hosts on the Seville Ethernet are not allowed access to hosts on the Yosemite Ethernet.

- All other combinations are allowed.

Figure 12-6 *Network Diagram for Extended Access List Example 2*

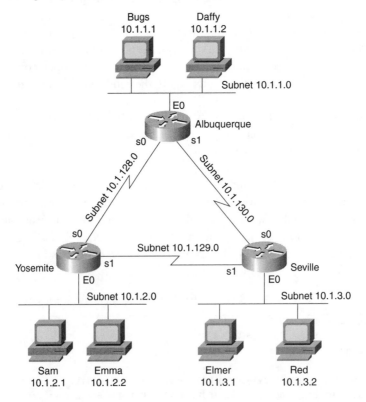

Example 12-8 *Yosemite Configuration for Extended Access List Example 2*

```
interface ethernet 0
ip access-group 110 in

!
access-list 110 deny ip host 10.1.2.1 10.1.1.0 0.0.0.255
access-list 110 deny ip 10.1.2.0 0.0.0.255 10.1.3.0 0.0.0.255
access-list 110 permit ip any any
```

This configuration solves the problem with few statements while keeping to Cisco's design guideline of placing extended ACLs as close to the source of the traffic as possible. The ACL filters packets that enter Yosemite's E0 interface, which is the first router interface the packets sent by Sam touch. The issue of having packets "routed around" access lists on serial interfaces is taken care of with the placement on Yosemite's only Ethernet interface. Also, the filtering mandated by the second requirement (to disallow Seville's LAN hosts from accessing Yosemite's) is met by the second **access-list** statement. Stopping packet flow from Yosemite's LAN subnet to Seville's LAN subnet stops effective communication between the two subnets. Alternatively, the opposite logic could have been configured at Seville.

Miscellaneous ACL Topics

This short section covers a couple of small topics, including named access lists, filtering Telnet traffic, and some general implementation guidelines for ACLs.

Named IP Access Lists

Named ACLs can be used to match the same packets, with the same parameters, you can match with standard and extended IP ACLs. Named IP ACLs do have some differences, however, some of which make them easier to work with. The most obvious difference is that IOS identifies named ACLs using names you make up, as opposed to numbers—and you have a better chance of remembering names. Named ACLs also have another key feature that numbered ACLs do not: You can delete individual lines in a named IP access list. With numbered ACLs, if you enter **no access-list 101** and then enter the rest of the command, you don't just delete that single line—you delete the whole list! With named ACLs, you can enter a command that removes individual lines in an ACL. Other than that, the only differences are the changes in the configuration syntax.

The configuration syntax is very similar between named and numbered IP access lists. The items that can be matched with a numbered standard IP access list are identical to the items that can be matched with a named standard IP access list. Likewise, the items are identical with both numbered and named extended IP access lists.

Two important configuration differences exist between numbered and named access lists. One key difference is that named access lists use a global command that places the user in a named IP access list submode, under which the matching and permit/deny logic is configured. The other key difference is that when a named matching statement is deleted, only that one statement is deleted. With numbered lists, the deletion of any statement in the list deletes all the statements in the list. (This feature is demonstrated in more detail in an upcoming example.)

Example 12-9 shows an example that uses named IP ACLs. It shows the changing command prompt in configuration mode, showing that the user has been placed in ACL configuration mode. It also lists the pertinent parts of the output of a **show running-configuration** command. It ends with an example of how you can delete individual lines in a named ACL.

Example 12-9 *Named Access List Configuration*

```
conf t
Enter configuration commands, one per line.  End with Ctrl-Z.
Router(config)#ip access-list extended barney
Router(config-ext-nacl)#permit tcp host 10.1.1.2 eq www any
Router(config-ext-nacl)#deny udp host 10.1.1.1 10.1.2.0 0.0.0.255
Router(config-ext-nacl)#deny ip 10.1.3.0 0.0.0.255 10.1.2.0 0.0.0.255
! The next statement is purposefully wrong so that the process of changing
! the list can be seen.
Router(config-ext-nacl)#deny ip 10.1.2.0 0.0.0.255 10.2.3.0 0.0.0.255

Router(config-ext-nacl)#deny ip host 10.1.1.130 host 10.1.3.2
Router(config-ext-nacl)#deny ip host 10.1.1.28 host 10.1.3.2
Router(config-ext-nacl)#permit ip any any
Router(config-ext-nacl)#interface serial1
Router(config-if)#ip access-group barney out
Router(config-if)#^Z
Router#show running-config
Building configuration...

Current configuration:

.
. (unimportant statements omitted)
.
interface serial 1
 ip access-group barney out
!
```

Example 12-9   *Named Access List Configuration (Continued)*

```
ip access-list extended barney
 permit tcp host 10.1.1.2 eq www any
 deny   udp host 10.1.1.1 10.1.2.0 0.0.0.255
 deny   ip 10.1.3.0 0.0.0.255 10.1.2.0 0.0.0.255
 deny   ip 10.1.2.0 0.0.0.255 10.2.3.0 0.0.0.255
 deny   ip host 10.1.1.130 host 10.1.3.2
 deny   ip host 10.1.1.28 host 10.1.3.2
 permit ip any any
Router#conf t
Enter configuration commands, one per line.  End with Ctrl-Z.
Router(config)#ip access-list extended barney
Router(config-ext-nacl)#no deny ip 10.1.2.0 0.0.0.255 10.2.3.0 0.0.0.255
Router(config-ext-nacl)#^Z
Router#show access-list

Extended IP access list barney
    permit tcp host 10.1.1.2 eq www any
    deny   udp host 10.1.1.1 10.1.2.0 0.0.0.255
    deny   ip 10.1.3.0 0.0.0.255 10.1.2.0 0.0.0.255
    deny   ip host 10.1.1.130 host 10.1.3.2
    deny   ip host 10.1.1.28 host 10.1.3.2
    permit ip any any
```

Example 12-9 begins with the creation of an ACL named Barney. The **ip access-list extended barney** command creates the ACL, naming it barney and placing the user in ACL configuration mode. This command also tells the IOS that barney is an extended ACL. Next, seven different **permit** and **deny** statements define the matching logic and action to be taken upon a match. The **permit** and **deny** commands use the exact same syntax that the numbered **access-list** commands use, starting with the **deny** and **permit** keywords. In this example, a comment is added just before the command that is deleted later in the example.

The **show running-config** command output lists the named ACL configuration before the single entry is deleted. Next, the **no deny ip...** command deletes a single entry from the ACL. Notice that the output of the **show running-config** command still lists the ACL, with six **permit** and **deny** commands instead of seven.

Controlling Telnet Access with ACLs

Access into and out of the virtual terminal line (vty) ports of the Cisco IOS software can be controlled by IP access lists. IOS uses vtys to represent a user who has Telnetted to a router, as well as for Telnet sessions a user of a router has created to other devices. You can use ACLs to limit the IP hosts that can Telnet into the router, and you can also limit the hosts to which a user of the router can Telnet.

For instance, imagine that only hosts in subnet 10.1.1.0/24 are supposed to be able to Telnet into any of the Cisco routers in a network. In such a case, the configuration shown in Example 12-10 could be used on each router to deny access from IP addresses not in that subnet.

Example 12-10 *vty Access Control Using the* access-class *Command*

```
line vty 0 4
 login
 password cisco
 access-class 3 in
!
! Next command is a global command
 access-list 3 permit 10.1.1.0 0.0.0.255
```

The **access-class** command refers to the matching logic in **access-list 3**. The keyword **in** refers to Telnet connections into this router—in other words, people Telnetting into this router. As configured, ACL 3 checks the source IP address of packets for incoming Telnet connections.

If the command **access-class 3 out** had been used, it would have checked for not only outgoing Telnets, but also the packets' destination IP address. Conceptually, checking the source IP address, which by definition must be one of the interface IP addresses in that router, would not really make any sense for the function desired. For filtering outgoing Telnet sessions, it makes the most sense to filter based on the destination IP address. So, the use of the **access-class 3 out** command, particularly the **out** keyword, is one of those rare cases in which a standard IP ACL actually looks at the destination IP address and not the source.

ACL Implementation Considerations

In production IP networks, IP ACL creation, troubleshooting, and updates can consume a large amount of time and effort. I have met people over the years who work in large IP networks whose jobs were nothing but figuring out what to do with IP ACLs in Cisco routers! The ICND exam does not have many questions about things to watch for when you implement IP ACLs in live networks, but it does cover a few small items, which are discussed in this final section of the chapter.

Cisco makes the following general recommendations, as mentioned in the ICND course, upon which CCNA is partly based:

- Create your ACLs using a text editor outside the router, and copy and paste the configurations into the router.

- Place extended ACLs as close to the source of the packet as possible to discard the packets quickly.

- Place standard ACLs as close to the packet's destination as possible, because standard ACLs often discard packets that you do not want discarded when they are placed close to the source.

- Place more-specific statements early in the ACL.

- Disable an ACL from its interface (using the **no ip access-group** command) before making changes to it.

The first suggestion states that you should create the ACLs outside the router using an editor. That way, if you make mistakes when typing, you can fix them in the editor. Why the big deal for ACLs? Well, with numbered ACLs, to delete a single line, you have to delete the whole ACL and reenter all the commands—in order. Also, even if you create the ACL correctly, you might later want to add a line to it—in the middle of the list! If you do, with numbered ACLs, you have to delete the whole list and then reenter all the lines in order. Having the ACLs stored somewhere outside the routers makes your life easier.

The second and third points deal with the concept of where to locate your ACLs. If you are going to filter a packet, filtering closer to the packet's source means that the packet takes up less bandwidth in the network, which seems to be more efficient—and it is. Therefore, Cisco suggests locating extended ACLs as close to the source as possible.

However, Cisco also suggests, at least in the CCNA-related courses, to locate standard ACLs close to the destination. Why not close to the source of the packets? Well, because standard ACLs look only at the source IP address, they tend to filter more than you want filtered when placed close to the source. For instance, imagine that Fred and Barney are separated by four routers. If you filter Barney's traffic sent to Fred on the first router, Barney can't reach any hosts near the other three routers. So the Cisco ICND course makes a blanket recommendation to locate standard ACLs closer to the destination to avoid filtering traffic you don't mean to filter.

By placing more-specific matching parameters early in each list, you are less likely to make mistakes in the ACL. For instance, imagine that you have a statement that permits all traffic from 10.1.1.1 to 10.2.2.2, destined for port 80 (the web), and another statement that denies all other packets sourced in subnet 10.1.1.0/24. Both statements would match packets sent by host 10.1.1.1 to a web server at 10.2.2.2, but you probably meant to match the more-specific statement (permit) first. In general, placing the more-specific statements first tends to ensure that you don't miss anything.

Finally, Cisco recommends that you disable the ACLs on the interfaces before you change the statements in the list. Thankfully, if you have an IP ACL enabled on an interface with the **ip access-group** command, and you delete the entire ACL, IOS does not filter any packets. (That was not always the case in earlier IOS versions!) Even so, as soon as you add a command to the ACL, the IOS starts filtering packets. Suppose you have ACL 101 enabled on S0 for output packets. You delete list 101 so that all packets are allowed through. Then you enter a single **access-list 101** command. As soon as you press Enter, the list exists, and the router filters all packets exiting S0 based on the one-line list. If you want to enter a long ACL, you might temporarily filter packets you don't want to filter! Therefore, the better way is to disable the list from the interface, make the changes to the list, and then reenable it on the interface.

Foundation Summary

The "Foundation Summary" section lists the most important facts from the chapter. Although this section does not list everything that will be on the exam, a well-prepared CCNA candidate should at a minimum know all the details in each Foundation Summary before taking the exam.

Figure 12-7 shows the basic logic behind where an ACL can perform its filtering logic inside a router.

Figure 12-7 *Locations Where Access List Logic Can Be Applied on Router R1*

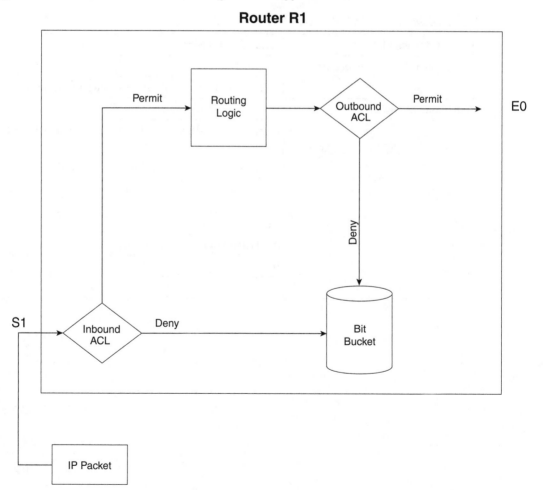

The logic that Cisco IOS software uses with a multiple-entry ACL can be summarized as follows:

1. The matching parameters of the **access-list** statement are compared to the packet.

2. If a match is made, the action defined in this **access-list** statement (permit or deny) is performed.

3. If a match is not made in Step 2, repeat Steps 1 and 2 using each successive statement in the ACL until a match is made.

4. If no match is made with an entry in the access list, the deny action is performed.

Table 12-9 summarizes the different fields that can be matched with an extended IP ACL, as compared with standard IP ACLs.

Table 12-9 *Standard and Extended IP Access Lists: Matching*

Type of Access List	What Can Be Matched
Both Standard and Extended ACLs	Source IP address
	Portions of the source IP address using a wildcard mask
Only Extended ACLs	Destination IP address
	Portions of the destination IP address using a wildcard mask
	Protocol type (TCP, UDP, ICMP, IGRP, IGMP, and others)
	Source port
	Destination port
	All TCP flows except the first
	IP TOS
	IP precedence

Table 12-10 lists several sample **access-list** commands, with several options configured and some explanations.

Table 12-10 *Extended* access-list *Commands and Logic Explanations*

access-list Statement	What It Matches
access-list 101 deny **ip any host 10.1.1.1**	Any IP packet, any source IP address, with a destination IP address of 10.1.1.1.
access-list 101 deny **tcp any gt 1023 host 10.1.1.1 eq 23**	Packets with a TCP header, any source IP address, with a source port greater than (**gt**) 1023. The packet must have a destination IP address of 10.1.1.1 and a destination port of 23.
access-list 101 deny **tcp any host 10.1.1.1 eq 23**	The same as the preceding example, but any source port matches, because that parameter is omitted in this case.
access-list 101 deny **tcp any host 10.1.1.1 eq telnet**	The same as the preceding example. The **telnet** keyword is used instead of port 23.
access-list 101 deny **udp 1.0.0.0 0.255.255.255 lt 1023 any**	A packet with a source in network 1.0.0.0, using UDP with a source port less than (**lt**) 1023, with any destination IP address.

Figure 12-8 and Example 12-11 demonstrate a sample configuration of a numbered extended IP ACL. In this case, Bob is denied access to all FTP servers on R1's Ethernet, and Larry is denied access to Server1's web server.

Figure 12-8 *Network Diagram for Extended Access List*

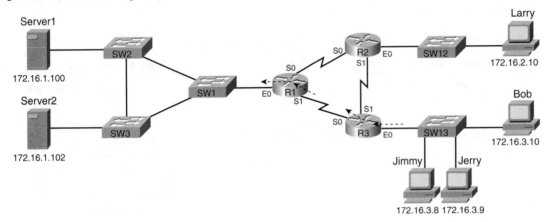

Example 12-11 *R1's Extended Access List*

```
interface Serial0
ip address 172.16.12.1 255.255.255.0
ip access-group 101 in

interface Serial1
ip address 172.16.13.1 255.255.255.0
ip access-group 101 in

access-list 101 remark Stop Bob to FTP servers, and Larry to Server1 web
access-list 101 deny tcp host 172.16.3.10 172.16.1.0 0.0.0.255 eq ftp
access-list 101 deny tcp host 172.16.2.10 host 172.16.1.100 eq http
access-list 101 permit ip any any
```

Cisco makes the following general recommendations, as mentioned in the ICND course:

- Create your ACLs using a text editor outside the router, and copy and paste the configurations into the router.

- Place extended ACLs as close to the source of the packet as possible to discard the packets quickly.

- Place standard ACLs as close to the destination of the packet as possible, because standard ACLs often discard packets that you do not want discarded when placed close to the source.

- Place more-specific statements early in the ACL.

- Disable ACLs from their interfaces (using the **no ip access-group** command) before making changes to the ACL.

Q&A

As mentioned in the Introduction, you have two choices for review questions. The following questions give you a bigger challenge than the exam because they are open-ended. By reviewing with this more-difficult question format, you can exercise your memory better and prove your conceptual and factual knowledge of the topics covered in this chapter. The answers to these questions are found in Appendix A.

For more practice with exam-like question formats, including multiple-choice questions and those using a router simulator, use the exam engine on the CD.

1. Configure a numbered IP access list that stops packets from subnet 134.141.7.0 255.255.255.0 from exiting serial 0 on a router. Allow all other packets.

2. Configure an IP access list that allows only packets from subnet 193.7.6.0 255.255.255.0, going to hosts in network 128.1.0.0 and using a web server in 128.1.0.0, to enter serial 0 on a router.

3. How would a user who does not have the enable password find out what access lists have been configured and where they are enabled?

4. Configure and enable an IP access list that stops packets from subnet 10.3.4.0/24 from exiting serial interface S0 and that stops packets from 134.141.5.4 from entering S0. Permit all other traffic.

5. Configure and enable an IP access list that allows packets from subnet 10.3.4.0/24, to any web server, to exit serial interface S0. Also allow packets from 134.141.5.4 going to all TCP-based servers using a well-known port to enter serial 0. Deny all other traffic.

6. Can standard IP access lists be used to check the source IP address when enabled with the **ip access-group 1 in** command, and can they check the destination IP addresses when using the **ip access-group 1 out** command?

7. True or false: If all IP **access-list** statements in a particular list define the deny action, the default action is to permit all other packets.

8. How many IP access lists of either type can be active on an interface at the same time?

For questions 9 through 11, assume that all parts of the network shown in Figure 12-9 are up and working. IGRP is the IP routing protocol in use. Answer the questions following Example 12-12, which contains an additional configuration in the Mayberry router.

Figure 12-9 *Network Diagram for Questions 10 Through 12*

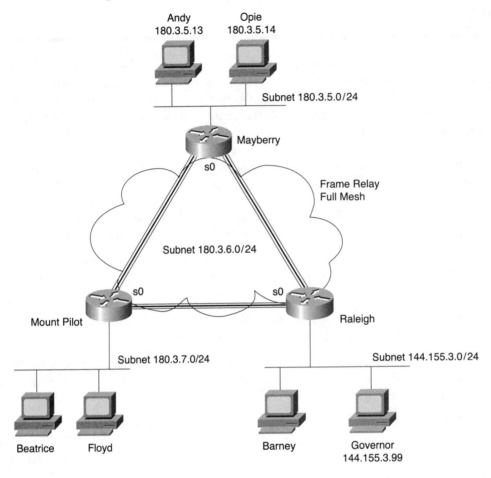

Example 12-12 *Access List at Mayberry*

```
access-list 44 permit 180.3.5.13 0.0.0.0
!
interface serial 0
ip access-group 44 out
```

9. Describe the types of packets that this filter discards, and specify at what point they are discarded.

10. Does the access list shown in Example 12-12 stop packets from getting to web server Governor? Why or why not?

11. Referring to Figure 12-9, create and enable access lists so that access to web server Governor is allowed from hosts at any site and so that no other access to hosts in Raleigh is allowed.

12. Name all the items that a standard IP access list can examine to make a match.

13. Name six items that an extended IP access list can examine to make a match.

14. True or false: When you use extended IP access lists to restrict vty access, the matching logic is a best match of the list rather than a first match in the list.

15. In a standard numbered IP access list with three statements, a **no** version of the first statement is issued in configuration mode. Immediately following, another access list configuration command is added for the same access list. How many statements are in the list now, and in what position is the newly added statement?

16. In a standard named IP access list with three statements, a **no** version of the first statement is issued in configuration mode. Immediately following, another access list configuration command is added for the same access list. How many statements are in the list now, and in what position is the newly added statement?

17. Name all the items that a named standard IP access list can examine to make a match.

18. Configure a named IP access list that stops packets from subnet 134.141.7.0 255.255.255.0 from exiting serial 0 on a router. Allow all other packets.

19. Configure a named IP access list that allows only packets from subnet 193.7.6.0 255.255.255.0, going to hosts in network 128.1.0.0 and using a web server in 128.1.0.0, to enter serial 0 on a router.

20. List the types of IP access lists (numbered standard, numbered extended, named standard, named extended) that can be enabled to prevent Telnet access into a router. What commands would be used to enable this function, assuming that **access-list 2** was already configured to match the right packets?

21. What command lists the IP extended access lists enabled on serial 1 without showing other interfaces?

22. Name six items that a named extended IP access list can examine to make a match.

Part V: Final Preparation

Final Preparation

You have made it through most of the book, and you probably have scheduled your ICND or CCNA exam or have at least thought about when you want to take it. Congratulations for getting this far! You will soon have finished the first step toward building your networking career resume.

This chapter provides some tips on your final preparation for the exam. It also provides a sample scenario that helps you pull together many hands-on skills in a single review section.

Suggestions for Final Preparation

Everyone has their own study habits, and you should know what works well for you. However, here are a few suggestions of some things you can try in the week or two before you take the exam:

- Reread the "Foundation Summary" sections of each chapter.

- When reviewing tables and definitions, cover up portions of summary tables with a piece of paper, forcing yourself to try to remember the details, instead of just glancing at them.

- Answer all the book's questions again. Strive to master these questions so that you can answer them quickly.

- If you are still slow in answering subnetting questions, practice until you can find the subnet number and broadcast address within 1 minute when the mask is "hard." You can use the CD-only Appendix A for more practice.

- Before using the CD for general questions, use the mode that lets you perform a simulated exam. This helps you prepare for the exam experience.

- Repeat answering all the questions on the CD until you can answer most of them almost automatically.

- Using a real set of routers and switches, or using a simulation product (such as NetSim, which is included on the accompanying CD), practice these basic skills:

    — Accessing a switch and router

    — Configuring basic administrative settings (passwords, host names, IP addresses)

    — Practice configuring IP, static routes, and RIP

    — Refer to Appendix C for a list of labs from this book that can be performed using the NetSim simulator that is included on the accompanying CD.

Preparing for the Exam Experience

If the CCNA exam will be your first experience with a proctored computer-based exam for Cisco certification, don't be alarmed. It's not terribly different from using the exam software on the CD that comes with this book. However, you should go into the exam day with the following in mind:

- You typically need two forms of ID, at least one of which is a picture ID. Driver's license, passport, and military ID are all valid.

- The testing center is probably just an extra room inside the offices of a company that does something else as its primary business. Training companies often also are testing centers. The proctor often has other responsibilities besides monitoring the exams. The proctor seldom enters the testing room other than to bring in another person who has an exam scheduled. So don't worry about someone staring at you and making you nervous! However, most testing centers have video cameras for monitoring. So just because you can't see them doesn't mean they aren't watching!

- You need to turn off all electronic devices you bring with you—phone, pager, and secret decoder ring! I typically just leave them in the car. You might be asked to leave your pager or phone at the front desk.

- You cannot bring any of your own paper into the room. The proctor will give you something to write on—either paper or a dry-erase board and marker. In either case, you should return these to the proctor when you are done.

- You will take the exam using a PC. The proctor will start the software for you; all you have to do is follow the instructions. You do not have to start the exam the instant you sit down; you typically are allowed to take a four- or five-question practice test. The practice exam asks you questions in different formats about an unrelated topic to help you get used to the interface. Cisco often adds an optional survey before the exam as well, just to gather demographic information about who is taking the exam. If you've never taken a Cisco exam, take the extra few minutes to take the practice test, just to get completely comfortable with the environment.

■   You can write on your scratch paper before the exam begins if you like. For instance, some people like to write down all the valid subnet masks, the corresponding prefixes, and possibly even the binary equivalents for the decimal numbers used in subnet masks. I've heard of some people writing down hard-to-memorize information that they were cramming for in the lobby of the testing center! Personally, I do not find it helpful to write down the hard-to-memorize things right before the exam begins, but for some people, it does help. Many people find it helpful to write down the subnetting information just mentioned.

■   The exam engine does not let you go back and change an earlier answer. So read each question and answer thoroughly. As soon as you move on to the next question, you can't go back!

■   Some questions require that you drag and drop the answers into the correct slots in an answer area. Exam question writers like to use this type of question for lists or sequences in particular. As with all the questions, you can answer and then change your answer as long as you have not moved on to the next question. For drag-and-drop questions, you might benefit from moving the answers you are confident about into the (presumably) correct place and then fitting the others in. Often this helps you complete the answers correctly. Just don't forget that as soon as you move on to the next question, you can't go back!

■   For simulated lab questions, you should go back and confirm that any new configurations are working. For instance, if the question asks you to configure RIP, but you do not see any routes when you use a **show ip route** command, you have not finished the question correctly. The simulator used on the exam works so that the **show** commands reflect what should happen. Many of the simulated lab questions require that you configure something, but it is also helpful if you know the pertinent **show** commands to verify the correct operation. Also, just for good measure, save your configuration unless the question tells you not to.

That's a long list, but hopefully it will help you prepare for taking the exam. The most important tip is to simply relax. For most people, a good night's rest is better than a night full of cramming.

The following list gives you a short reminder of the things you might want to keep in mind as you prepare to walk through the door of the testing center:

■   Bring two pens.

■   Bring two IDs, one with a picture.

■   Turn off your electronic devices before going to the exam room.

■   Relax!

Final Lab Scenarios

The current CCNA exams include simulated lab questions. The best way to prepare for these is to work with live networks using Cisco routers and switches. You should also make sure to do all the questions in the testing engine on the accompanying CD, as it contains a large number of simulated lab questions. You can also use the NetSim network simulator on the CD, or rent time via online labs.

Regardless of how much time and effort you spend with hands-on practice, the following lab scenario can help you with your final preparation if you simply read through the scenarios. Throughout this book, the portions that covered how to do something on a switch or router focused on the specific topics covered in that chapter. The scenarios in this chapter touch on many of the topics in this book that are in some way related to configuration or operating a router or switch. You can use these scenarios as part of your final exam preparation strategy.

If you have enough time, review all the parts of each scenario, and try to perform all the tasks outlined in Parts A, B, and C. However, if you have limited time, you might want to review the problem statements and then the answers for each of the three parts. At least you will get a good review of some of the more important commands that could be on the exam.

If you are reading this chapter as your final review before taking the exam, let me take this opportunity to wish you success. Hopefully you will be relaxed and confident for your exam—and hopefully this book has helped you build your knowledge and confidence.

Scenario 1

Scenario 1 uses a Frame Relay network with three routers and a full mesh of virtual circuits. Some planning exercises begin the scenario (Part A), followed by configuration (Part B). Finally, a series of questions, some based on **show** and **debug** command output, finish the scenario (Part C).

Scenario 1, Part A: Planning

Your job is to deploy a new network with three sites, as shown in Figure 13-1. The decision to use Frame Relay has already been made, and the products have been chosen. For Part A of this scenario, perform the following task:

■ Subnet planning has been completed. Before implementation, you are responsible for providing a list for the local LAN administrators defining the IP addresses they can assign to hosts. Using Table 13-1, derive the subnet numbers and broadcast addresses, and define the range of valid IP addresses. A static mask of 255.255.255.192 is used on all subnets.

Figure 13-1   *Scenario 1 Network Diagram*

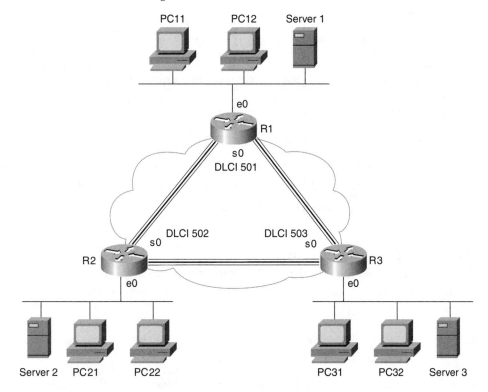

Table 13-1   *Scenario 1, Part A: IP Subnet Planning Chart, Mask 255.255.255.192*

Router Interface	IP Address	Subnet Number	Subnet Broadcast Address	Range of Valid Addresses
R1 E0	168.11.11.101			
R2 E0	168.11.12.102			
R3 E0	168.11.13.103			
R1 S0	168.11.123.201			
R2 S0	168.11.123.202			
R3 S0	168.11.123.203			

Solutions to Scenario 1, Part A: Planning

For Part A, you need to derive the subnet numbers and broadcast addresses, so the assignable addresses in each subnet become obvious. One important point is that the three Frame Relay interfaces are in the same subnet, which is a clue that subinterfaces are not used and that the

Frame Relay interfaces are treated as a single network. Table 13-2 provides the answers to this question.

Table 13-2 *Scenario 1, Part A: IP Subnet Network Planning Chart*

Router Interface	IP Address	Subnet Number	Subnet Broadcast Address	Range of Valid Addresses
R1 E0	168.11.11.101	168.11.11.64	168.11.11.127	65 to 126 in last octet
R2 E0	168.11.12.102	168.11.12.64	168.11.12.127	65 to 126 in last octet
R3 E0	168.11.13.103	168.11.13.64	168.11.13.127	65 to 126 in last octet
R1 S0	168.11.123.201	168.11.123.192	168.11.123.255	193 to 254 in last octet
R2 S0	168.11.123.202	168.11.123.192	168.11.123.255	193 to 254 in last octet
R3 S0	168.11.123.203	168.11.123.192	168.11.123.255	193 to 254 in last octet

Scenario 1, Part B: Configuration

The next step in your job is to deploy the network designed in Scenario 1, Part A. Use the solutions to Scenario 1, Part A to help you identify IP addresses to be used. Perform the following tasks:

Step 1   Configure IP to be routed. Use IP IGRP as the routing protocol. Use IGRP autonomous system number 1.

Step 2   Configure Frame Relay without the use of subinterfaces. R1's attached switch uses LMI type ANSI. Cisco encapsulation should be used for all routers.

Step 3   Assume that, after you installed the network, you were forced to disable IP IGRP on R2. Define the required IP static routes to allow hosts on all three Ethernets to communicate. (This is unlikely to happen in real life; it's just an excuse to review IP static routes!)

Step 4   Assume that, after you installed the network, you were forced to disable Inverse ARP on R2. Define static mappings as necessary for all hosts to communicate.

Solutions to Scenario 1, Part B: Configuration

Examples 13-1, 13-2, and 13-3 show the configurations for Tasks 1 and 2.

Example 13-1 *R1 Configuration*

```
interface serial0
encapsulation frame-relay
ip address  168.11.123.201  255.255.255.192
```

Example 13-1   *R1 Configuration (Continued)*

```
!
interface ethernet 0
ip address 168.11.11.101  255.255.255.192
!
router igrp 1
network 168.11.0.0
```

Example 13-2   *R2 Configuration*

```
interface serial0
encapsulation frame-relay
ip address  168.11.123.202 255.255.255.192
!
interface ethernet 0
ip address 168.11.12.102  255.255.255.192
!
router igrp 1
network 168.11.0.0
```

Example 13-3   *R3 Configuration*

```
interface serial0
encapsulation frame-relay
ip address 168.11.123.203  255.255.255.192
!
interface ethernet 0
ip address 168.11.13.103  255.255.255.192
!
router igrp 1
network 168.11.0.0
```

For Task 3 in Scenario 1, Part B, static routes need to be defined in all three routers. R2 needs routes to the two LAN-based subnets at the other sites. Likewise, R1 and R3 need routes to 168.11.12.64 (Ethernet off R2). Example 13-4 lists the routes in all three routers.

Example 13-4   *Static Routes*

```
R1(config)#ip route 168.11.12.64 255.255.255.192 168.11.123.202

R2(config)#ip route 168.11.11.64 255.255.255.192 168.11.123.201
```

continues

Example 13-4 *Static Routes (Continued)*

```
R2(config)#ip route 168.11.13.64 255.255.255.192 168.11.123.203

R3(config)#ip route 168.11.12.64 255.255.255.192 168.11.123.202
```

Finally, Task 4 requests that static **frame-relay map** commands be configured. The **map** commands are necessary for each routed protocol. Also, the **broadcast** keyword is needed so that packets that would normally be broadcast, such as routing updates, will be sent as unicasts across each VC for each protocol. Example 13-5 lists the additional commands.

Example 13-5 frame-relay map *Commands*

```
R1(config)#frame-relay map ip 168.11.123.202 502 broadcast

R2(config)#frame-relay map ip 168.11.123.201 501 broadcast
R2(config)#frame-relay map ip 168.11.123.203 503 broadcast

R3(config)#frame-relay map ip 168.11.123.202 502 broadcast
```

Scenario 1, Part C: Verification and Questions

The CCNA exams test your memory of the kinds of information you can find in the output of various **show** commands. Using Examples 13-6, 13-7, and 13-8 as references, answer the questions following the examples.

> **NOTE** In the network from which these commands were captured, several administrative settings not mentioned in the scenario were configured. For example, the enable password was configured. Any **show running-config** commands in the examples might have other unrelated configurations.

Example 13-6 *Scenario 1, Part C: R1* **show** *and* **debug** *Output*

```
R1#show ip interface brief
Interface          IP-Address       OK? Method Status                 Protocol
Serial0            168.11.123.201   YES NVRAM  up                     up
Serial1            unassigned       YES unset  administratively down  down
Ethernet0          168.11.11.101    YES NVRAM  up                     up

R1#debug ip igrp transactions
IGRP protocol debugging is on
R1#
IGRP: sending update to 255.255.255.255 via Serial0 (168.11.123.201)
      subnet 168.11.123.192, metric=180571
      subnet 168.11.11.64, metric=688
      subnet 168.11.13.64, metric=180634
      subnet 168.11.12.64, metric=180634
IGRP: sending update to 255.255.255.255 via Ethernet0 (168.11.11.101)
```

Example 13-6 *Scenario 1, Part C: R1* **show** *and* **debug** *Output (Continued)*

```
        subnet 168.11.123.192, metric=180571
        subnet 168.11.13.64, metric=180634
        subnet 168.11.12.64, metric=180634
IGRP: received update from 168.11.123.202 on Serial0
        subnet 168.11.123.192, metric 182571 (neighbor 180571)
        subnet 168.11.11.64, metric 182634 (neighbor 180634)
        subnet 168.11.13. 64, metric 182634 (neighbor 180634)
        subnet 168.11.12. 64, metric 180634 (neighbor 688)
IGRP: received update from 168.11.123.203 on Serial0
        subnet 168.11.123.192, metric 182571 (neighbor 8476)
        subnet 168.11.11. 64, metric 182634 (neighbor 8539)
        subnet 168.11.13. 64, metric 180634 (neighbor 688)
        subnet 168.11.12. 64, metric 182634 (neighbor 8539)
IGRP: sending update to 255.255.255.255 via Serial0 (168.11.123.201)
        subnet 168.11.123.192, metric=180571
        subnet 168.11.11. 64, metric=688
        subnet 168.11.13. 64, metric=180634
        subnet 168.11.12. 64, metric=180634
IGRP: sending update to 255.255.255.255 via Ethernet0 (168.11.11.101)
        subnet 168.11.123.192, metric=180571
        subnet 168.11.13. 64, metric=180634
        subnet 168.11.12. 64, metric=180634
R1#undebug all
All possible debugging has been turned off
```

Example 13-7 *Scenario 1, Part C: R2* **show** *and* **debug** *Output*

```
R2#show interface
Serial0 is up, line protocol is up
  Hardware is HD64570
  Internet address is 168.11.123.202/26
    MTU 1500 bytes, BW 56 Kbit, DLY 20000 usec,
      reliability 255/255, txload 1/255, rxload 1/255
  Encapsulation FRAME-RELAY, loopback not set, keepalive set (10 sec)
  LMI enq sent  1657, LMI stat recvd 1651, LMI upd recvd 0, DTE LMI up
  LMI enq recvd 0, LMI stat sent  0, LMI upd sent  0
  LMI DLCI 0  LMI type is ANSI Annex D  frame relay DTE
  Broadcast queue 0/64, broadcasts sent/dropped 979/0, interface broadcasts 490
  Last input 00:00:01, output 00:00:01, output hang never
  Last clearing of "show interface" counters never
  Queuing strategy: fifo
  Output queue 0/40, 0 drops; input queue 0/75, 0 drops
  5 minute input rate 0 bits/sec, 0 packets/sec
  5 minute output rate 0 bits/sec, 0 packets/sec
     4479 packets input, 165584 bytes, 0 no buffer
     Received 1 broadcasts, 0 runts, 0 giants, 0 throttles
     0 input errors, 0 CRC, 0 frame, 0 overrun, 0 ignored, 0 abort
     4304 packets output, 154785 bytes, 0 underruns
```

continues

Example 13-7 *Scenario 1, Part C: R2* **show** *and* **debug** *Output (Continued)*

```
      0 output errors, 0 collisions, 4 interface resets
      0 output buffer failures, 0 output buffers swapped out
      12 carrier transitions
     DCD=up  DSR=up  DTR=up  RTS=up  CTS=up
Serial1 is administratively down, line protocol is down
  Hardware is HD64570
  MTU 1500 bytes, BW 1544 Kbit, DLY 20000 usec, rely 255/255, load 1/255
  Encapsulation PPP, loopback not set, keepalive set (10 sec)
  LCP Closed
  Closed: CDPCP, LLC2
  Last input never, output never, output hang never
  Last clearing of "show interface" counters never
    Input queue: 0/75/0/0 (size/max/drops/flushes); Total output drops: 0
  Queueing strategy: weighted fair
  Output queue: 0/1000/64/0 (size/max total/threshold/drops)
     Conversations  0/1/256 (active/max active/max total)
     Reserved Conversations 0/0 (allocated/max allocated)
     Available Bandwidth 1158 kilobits/sec
  5 minute input rate 0 bits/sec, 0 packets/sec
  5 minute output rate 0 bits/sec, 0 packets/sec
     0 packets input, 0 bytes, 0 no buffer
     Received 0 broadcasts, 0 runts, 0 giants, 0 throttles
     0 input errors, 0 CRC, 0 frame, 0 overrun, 0 ignored, 0 abort
     0 packets output, 0 bytes, 0 underruns
     0 output errors, 0 collisions, 5 interface resets
     0 output buffer failures, 0 output buffers swapped out
     0 carrier transitions
     DCD=down  DSR=down  DTR=down  RTS=down  CTS=down
Ethernet0 is up, line protocol is up
  Hardware is MCI Ethernet, address is 0000.0c89.b170 (bia 0000.0c89.b170)
  Internet address is 168.11.12.102/26, subnet mask is 255.255.255.192
    MTU 1500 bytes, BW 10000 Kbit, DLY 1000 usec,
       reliability 255/255, txload 1/255, rxload 1/255
  Encapsulation ARPA, loopback not set, keepalive set (10 sec)
  ARP type: ARPA, ARP Timeout 4:00:00
  Last input 00:00:04, output 00:00:04, output hang never
  Last clearing of "show interface" counters never
  Queuing strategy: fifo
  Output queue 0/40, 0 drops; input queue 0/75, 0 drops
  5 minute input rate 0 bits/sec, 0 packets/sec
  5 minute output rate 0 bits/sec, 0 packets/sec
     6519 packets input, 319041 bytes, 0 no buffer
     Received 5544 broadcasts, 0 runts, 0 giants, 0 throttles
     0 input errors, 0 CRC, 0 frame, 0 overrun, 0 ignored, 0 abort
     2055 packets output, 192707 bytes, 0 underruns
     0 output errors, 0 collisions, 2 interface resets
     0 output buffer failures, 0 output buffers swapped out
     6 transitions
```

Example 13-7   *Scenario 1, Part C: R2* **show** *and* **debug** *Output (Continued)*

```
R2#show ip protocol
Routing Protocol is "igrp 1"
  Sending updates every 90 seconds, next due in 6 seconds
  Invalid after 270 seconds, hold down 280, flushed after 630
  Outgoing update filter list for all interfaces is not set
  Incoming update filter list for all interfaces is not set
  Default networks flagged in outgoing updates
  Default networks accepted from incoming updates
  IGRP metric weight K1=1, K2=0, K3=1, K4=0, K5=0
  IGRP maximum hopcount 100
  IGRP maximum metric variance 1
  Redistributing: igrp 1
  Automatic network summarization is in effect
    maximum path: 4
  Routing for Networks:
    168.11.0.0
  Routing Information Sources:
    Gateway          Distance      Last Update
    168.11.123.201        100      00:00:02
    168.11.123.203        100      00:00:09
  Distance: (default is 100)


R2#show frame-relay pvc

PVC Statistics for interface Serial0 (Frame Relay DTE)

DLCI = 501, DLCI USAGE = LOCAL, PVC STATUS = ACTIVE, INTERFACE = Serial0

  input pkts 780          output pkts 529          in bytes 39602
  out bytes 29260         dropped pkts 0           in FECN pkts 0
  in BECN pkts 0          out FECN pkts 0          out BECN pkts 0
  in DE pkts 0            out DE pkts 0
  out bcast pkts 525        out bcast bytes 28924
  pvc create time 04:36:40, last time pvc status changed 04:34:54
DLCI = 503, DLCI USAGE = LOCAL, PVC STATUS = ACTIVE, INTERFACE = Serial0

  input pkts 481          output pkts 493          in bytes 30896
  out bytes 34392         dropped pkts 0           in FECN pkts 0
  in BECN pkts 0          out FECN pkts 0          out BECN pkts 0
  in DE pkts 0            out DE pkts 0
  out bcast pkts 493        out bcast bytes 34392
  pvc create time 04:36:41, last time pvc status changed 04:34:55

R2#show frame-relay map
Serial0 (up): ip 168.11.123.201 dlci 501(0x1F5,0x7C50), dynamic,
              broadcast,, status defined, active
Serial0 (up): ip 168.11.123.203 dlci 503(0x1F7,0x7C70), dynamic,
              broadcast,, status defined, active
```

Example 13-8 *Scenario 1, Part C: R3* show *and* debug *Output*

```
R3#show running-config
Building configuration...

Current configuration : 912 bytes
!
version 12.2
service timestamps debug uptime
service timestamps log uptime
no service password-encryption
!
hostname R3
!
enable secret 5 $1$J3Fz$QaEYNIiI2aMu.3Ar.q0Xm.
!
ip subnet-zero
no ip domain-lookup
!

ipx routing 0200.cccc.cccc
!
interface Serial0
 ip address 168.11.123.203 255.255.255.192
 encapsulation frame-relay
 no fair-queue
 frame-relay interface-dlci 501
 frame-relay interface-dlci 502
!
interface Serial1
 no ip address
 encapsulation ppp
 shutdown
 clockrate 56000
!
interface Ethernet0
 ip address 168.11.13.103 255.255.255.192
!
router igrp 1
 network 168.11.0.0
!
ip classless
no ip http server
!
!
line con 0
 password cisco
 login
line aux 0
```

Example 13-8 *Scenario 1, Part C: R3* **show** *and* **debug** *Output (Continued)*

```
line vty 0 4
 password cisco
 login
!
end

R3#show ip arp
Protocol  Address          Age (min)  Hardware Addr   Type    Interface
Internet  168.11.13.103        -      0000.0c89.b1b0  SNAP    Ethernet0

R3#show ip route
Codes: C - connected, S - static, I - IGRP, R - RIP, M - mobile, B - BGP
       D - EIGRP, EX - EIGRP external, O - OSPF, IA - OSPF inter area
       N1 - OSPF NSSA external type 1, N2 - OSPF NSSA external type 2
       E1 - OSPF external type 1, E2 - OSPF external type 2, E - EGP
       i - IS-IS, L1 - IS-IS level-1, L2 - IS-IS level-2, ia - IS-IS inter area
       * - candidate default, U - per-user static route, o - ODR
       P - periodic downloaded static route

Gateway of last resort is not set

     168.11.0.0/26 is subnetted, 4 subnets
C       168.11.123.192 is directly connected, Serial0
I       168.11.11.64 [100/8539] via 168.11.123.201, 00:00:06, Serial0
C       168.11.13. 64 is directly connected, Ethernet0
I       168.11.12. 64 [100/8539] via 168.11.123.202, 00:00:46, Serial0

R3#ping 168.11.11.80

Type escape sequence to abort.
Sending 5, 100-byte ICMP Echos to 168.11.11.80, timeout is 2 seconds:
!!!!!
Success rate is 100 percent (5/5), round-trip min/avg/max = 76/76/76 ms

R3#trace 168.11.11.80

Type escape sequence to abort.
Tracing the route to 168.11.11.80

  1 168.11.123.201 44 msec 44 msec 44 msec
  2 168.11.11.250 44 msec *  40 msec

R3#show frame-relay map
Serial0 (up): ip 168.11.123.201 dlci 501(0x1F5,0x7C50), dynamic,
              broadcast,, status defined, active
Serial0 (up): ip 168.11.123.202 dlci 502(0x1F6,0x7C60), dynamic,
              broadcast,, status defined, active
```

continues

Example 13-8 *Scenario 1, Part C: R3 **show** and **debug** Output (Continued)*

```
R3#show frame-relay lmi

LMI Statistics for interface Serial0 (Frame Relay DTE) LMI TYPE = CISCO
  Invalid Unnumbered info 0        Invalid Prot Disc 0
  Invalid dummy Call Ref 0         Invalid Msg Type 0
  Invalid Status Message 0         Invalid Lock Shift 0
  Invalid Information ID 0          Invalid Report IE Len 0
  Invalid Report Request 0         Invalid Keep IE Len 0
  Num Status Enq. Sent 1677        Num Status msgs Rcvd 1677
  Num Update Status Rcvd 0         Num Status Timeouts 0
```

Using Examples 13-6, 13-7, and 13-8 as references, answer the following questions:

1. What command tells you how much time must elapse before the next IP IGRP update is sent by a router?

2. What command shows you a summary of the IP addresses on that router?

3. What **show** command identifies which routes were learned with IP IGRP?

4. Describe the contents of an IP IGRP update from R1 to R3. What **debug** command options provide the details of what is in the IGRP update?

5. In this network, if setup mode were used to configure the IP addresses on the interface, how would the subnet mask information be entered?

6. If a routing loop occurs so that IP packets destined for 168.11.12.66 are routed between routers continually, what stops the packets from rotating forever? Are any notification messages sent when the routers notice what is happening? If so, what is the message?

7. Describe how R2 learns that R1's IP address is 168.11.123.201.

8. What does NBMA stand for?

9. When does IGRP use split-horizon rules on interfaces with Frame Relay encapsulation?

10. What effect does the **no keepalive** interface subcommand have on Frame Relay interfaces?

11. If just the VC between R1 and R3 needed to use encapsulation of **ietf,** what configuration changes would be needed?

12. What command lists the total number of Status Enquiry messages received on a Frame Relay interface?

Solutions to Scenario 1, Part C: Verification and Questions

The answers to the questions for Scenario 1, Part C are as follows:

1. The **show ip protocol** command gives this information (refer to Example 13-7).

2. The **show ip interface brief** command gives this information (refer to Example 13-6).

3. The **show ip route** command identifies the routing protocol used to learn each route via the first item in each route listed in the routing tables. For instance, the **show ip route** command in Example 13-8 lists **I** as the first entry for two routes, which means that IGRP learned each route, according to the legend at the beginning of the command output.

4. The **debug ip igrp transaction** command provides debug output with details of the IGRP updates. The output immediately follows the "IGRP: sending update to 255.255.255.255 via Serial0 (168.11.123.201)" message in Example 13-6. Notice that all four routes are advertised, because split horizon is disabled on the serial interface when no subinterfaces are used.

5. Enter the mask information as the number of subnet bits rather than simply entering the mask. In this network, mask 255.255.255.192 implies 6 host bits. A Class B network is used, which implies 16 network bits, leaving 10 subnet bits.

6. Each router decrements the Time To Live (TTL) field in the IP header. After the number is decremented to 0, the router discards the packet. That router also sends an ICMP TTL-exceeded message to the host that originally sent the packet.

7. R1 uses Inverse ARP to announce its IP and IPX addresses on the serial interface used for Frame Relay. The Inverse ARP message is sent over the VC between the two routers. R2 learns based on receiving the message.

8. NBMA stands for nonbroadcast multiaccess.

9. IGRP disables split horizon only on physical interfaces; it is enabled for either type of subinterface.

10. LMI keepalive messages, which flow between the router and the switch, are no longer sent. No keepalive messages pass from router to router.

11. The **frame-relay interface-dlci** command could be changed on Router1 and Router3 to include the keyword **ietf** at the end of the command—for example, **frame-relay interface-dlci 501 ietf** on R3.

12. The **show frame-relay lmi** command lists this information (refer to Example 13-8).

Scenario 2

Part A of the final review scenario begins with some planning guidelines that include planning IP addresses and the location of IP standard access lists. After you complete Part A, Part B of Scenario 2 asks you to configure the three routers to implement the planned design and a few other features. Finally, in Part C of Scenario 2, some errors have been introduced into the network, and you are asked to examine router command output to find them. Part C also lists some questions relating to the user interface and protocol specifications.

Scenario 2, Part A: Planning

Your job is to deploy a new network with three sites, as shown in Figure 13-2. The decision to use Frame Relay has already been made, and the products have been chosen. To complete Part A, perform the following tasks:

1. Plan the IP addressing and subnets used in this network. Class B network 170.1.0.0 has been assigned by the Network Information Center (NIC). The maximum number of hosts per subnet is 300. Assign IP addresses to the PCs as well. Use Tables 13-3 and 13-4 to record your answers.

2. Plan the location and logic of IP access lists to filter for the following criteria:

   — Access to servers in PC11 and PC12 is allowed for web and FTP clients from anywhere else.

   — All other traffic to or from PC11 and PC12 is not allowed.

   — No IP traffic between the Ethernets off R2 and R3 is allowed.

   — All other IP traffic between any sites is allowed.

3. After choosing your subnet numbers, calculate the broadcast addresses and the range of valid IP addresses in each subnet. Use Table 13-5 if convenient.

Figure 13-2   *Scenario 13-2 Network Diagram*

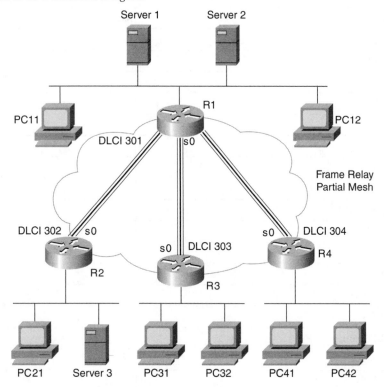

Table 13-3   *Scenario 2, Part A: IP Subnet Planning Chart*

Geographic Location of Subnet/Network	Subnet Mask	Subnet Number
Ethernet off R1		
Ethernet off R2		
Ethernet off R3		
Ethernet off R4		
Virtual circuit between R1 and R2		
Virtual circuit between R1 and R3		
Virtual circuit between R1 and R4		
Server 1 internal		
Server 2 internal		
Server 3 internal		

Table 13-4 *Scenario 2, Part A: IP Address Planning Chart*

Host	Address
PC11	
PC12	
PC21	
PC31	
PC32	
PC41	
PC42	
R1-E0	
R1-S0-sub ____	
R1-S0-sub ____	
R1-S0-sub ____	
R2-E0	
R2-S0-sub ____	
R3-E0	
R3-S0-sub ____	
R4-E0	
R4-S0-sub ____	
Server 1	
Server 2	
Server 3	

Table 13-5 *Scenario 2, Part A: Subnets, Broadcast Addresses, and Range of Valid Addresses*

Subnet Number	Subnet Broadcast Address	Range of Valid Addresses

Solutions to Scenario 2, Part A: Planning

The IP subnet design includes the use of mask 255.255.254.0. The same mask is used throughout the network. Therefore, at least 9 host bits are needed, because at least one subnet contains 300 hosts (see Table 13-6).

Table 13-6   *Scenario 2, Part A: Completed IP Subnet Planning Chart*

Geographic Location of Subnet/Network	Subnet Mask	Subnet Number
Ethernet off R1	255.255.254.0	170.1.2.0
Ethernet off R2	255.255.254.0	170.1.4.0
Ethernet off R3	255.255.254.0	170.1.6.0
Ethernet off R4	255.255.254.0	170.1.8.0
Virtual circuit between R1 and R2	255.255.254.0	170.1.10.0
Virtual circuit between R1 and R3	255.255.254.0	170.1.12.0
Virtual circuit between R1 and R4	255.255.254.0	170.1.14.0

The choice of IP addresses can conform to any standard you like, as long as the addresses are in the correct subnets. Refer to Table 13-8 for the list of valid addresses for the subnets chosen. Table 13-7 uses a convention in which the numbers reflect the number of the PC. For the routers, the convention uses addresses in the second half of the range of addresses in each subnet. This convention is simply a reminder of the addresses that are valid in this subnetting scheme.

Table 13-7   *Scenario 2, Part A: Completed IP Address Planning Chart*

Host	Address
PC11	170.1.2.11
PC12	170.1.2.12
PC21	170.1.4.21
PC31	170.1.6.31
PC32	170.1.6.32
PC41	170.1.8.41
PC42	170.1.8.42
R1-E0	170.1.3.1
R1-S0-sub 2	170.1.10.1
R1-S0-sub 3	170.1.12.1

continues

Table 13-7 *Scenario 2, Part A: Completed IP Address Planning Chart (Continued)*

Host	Address
R1-S0-sub 4	170.1.14.1
R2-E0	170.1.5.2
R2-S0-sub 2	170.1.10.2
R3-E0	170.1.7.3
R3-S0-sub 3	170.1.12.3
R4-E0	170.1.9.4
R4-S0-sub 4	170.1.14.4
Server 1	170.1.2.101
Server 2	170.1.2.102
Server 3	170.1.4.103

The IP access lists can effectively be placed in several places. Stopping packets in one of the two directions succeeds in stopping users from connecting to the servers. For the first set of criteria, an access list stopping packets from entering the serial interface of R1, thus stopping packets destined for PC11 and PC12, suffices. For the second criteria to disallow traffic between Site 2 and Site 3, the access lists are also placed in R1. The access lists stop the packets earlier in their life if they are placed in R2 and R3, but the traffic is minimal, because no true application traffic will ever be successfully generated between IP hosts at Sites 2 and 3.

The design shown here calls for all filtered packets to be filtered via access lists enabled on subinterfaces on R1's S0 interface. Other options are valid as well. Remember, the strategy outlined in the Cisco ICND course suggests that denying packets as close to the source as possible when using extended access lists is the best option.

Table 13-8 shows the answers, which include the subnet numbers, their corresponding broadcast addresses, and the range of valid assignable IP addresses.

Table 13-8 *Scenario 2, Part A: Completed IP Subnet Planning Chart*

Subnet Number	Subnet Broadcast Address	Range of Valid Addresses (Last 2 Bytes)
170.1.2.0	170.1.3.255	2.1 through 3.254
170.1.4.0	170.1.5.255	4.1 through 5.254
170.1.6.0	170.1.7.255	6.1 through 7.254
170.1.8.0	170.1.9.255	8.1 through 9.254
170.1.10.0	170.1.11.255	10.1 through 11.254
170.1.12.0	170.1.13.255	12.1 through 13.254
170.1.14.0	170.1.15.255	14.1 through 15.254

Scenario 2, Part B: Configuration

The next step is to deploy the network designed in Part A. Use the solutions to Scenario 2, Part A to help identify the IP addresses, access lists, and encapsulations to be used. For Part B, perform the following tasks:

Step 1   Configure IP to be routed. Use IP IGRP as the routing protocol. Use IGRP autonomous system number 1.

Step 2   Configure Frame Relay using point-to-point subinterfaces. R1's attached Frame Relay switch uses LMI type ANSI. Cisco encapsulation should be used for all routers, except for the VC between R1 and R4.

Solutions to Scenario 2, Part B: Configuration

Examples 13-9 through 13-12 show the configurations for Tasks 1, 2, and 3 for Part B of Scenario 2.

Example 13-9   *R1 Configuration*

```
interface serial0
encapsulation frame-relay
interface serial 0.2 point-to-point
 ip address  170.1.10.1  255.255.254.0
 frame-relay interface-dlci 302
 ip access-group 102 in
!
interface serial 0.3 point-to-point
 ip address  170.1.12.1  255.255.254.0
 frame-relay interface-dlci 303
 ip access-group 103 in
!
interface serial 0.4 point-to-point
 ip address  170.1.14.1  255.255.254.0
 frame-relay interface-dlci 304 ietf
 ip access-group 104 in
!
interface ethernet 0
  ip address  170.1.3.1  255.255.254.0
!
router igrp 1
  network 170.1.0.0
!
access-list 102 permit tcp any host 170.1.2.11 eq ftp
access-list 102 permit tcp any host 170.1.2.11 eq www
access-list 102 permit tcp any host 170.1.2.12 eq ftp
access-list 102 permit tcp any host 170.1.2.12 eq www
access-list 102 deny ip any host 170.1.2.11
access-list 102 deny ip any host 170.1.2.12
```

continues

Example 13-9 *R1 Configuration (Continued)*

```
access-list 102 deny ip 170.1.4.0 0.0.1.255 170.1.6.0 0.0.1.255
access-list 102 permit ip any any

access-list 103 permit tcp any host 170.1.2.11 eq ftp
access-list 103 permit tcp any host 170.1.2.11 eq www
access-list 103 permit tcp any host 170.1.2.12 eq ftp
access-list 103 permit tcp any host 170.1.2.12 eq www
access-list 103 deny ip any host 170.1.2.11
access-list 103 deny ip any host 170.1.2.12
access-list 103 deny ip 170.1.6.0 0.0.1.255 170.1.4.0 0.0.1.255
access-list 103 permit ip any any

access-list 104 permit tcp any host 170.1.2.11 eq ftp
access-list 104 permit tcp any host 170.1.2.11 eq www
access-list 104 permit tcp any host 170.1.2.12 eq ftp
access-list 104 permit tcp any host 170.1.2.12 eq www
access-list 104 deny ip any host 170.1.2.11
access-list 104 deny ip any host 170.1.2.12
access-list 104 permit ip any any
```

Example 13-10 *R2 Configuration*

```
interface serial0
encapsulation frame-relay
interface serial 0.1 point-to-point
 ip address  170.1.10.2  255.255.254.0
 frame-relay interface-dlci 301
!
interface ethernet 0
ip address  170.1.5.2  255.255.254.0
!
router igrp 1
network 170.1.0.0
!
```

Example 13-11 *R3 Configuration*

```
interface serial0
encapsulation frame-relay
interface serial 0.1 point-to-point
 ip address  170.1.12.3  255.255.254.0
 frame-relay interface-dlci 301
!
interface ethernet 0
ip address  170.1.7.3  255.255.254.0
!
router igrp 1
network 170.1.0.0
```

Example 13-12 *R4 Configuration*

```
interface serial0
  encapsulation frame-relay ietf
interface serial 0.1 point-to-point
  ip address  170.1.14.4  255.255.254.0
  frame-relay interface-dlci 301
!
interface ethernet 0
  ip address  170.1.9.4  255.255.254.0
!
router igrp 1
  network 170.1.0.0
```

Three different access lists are shown on R1. List 102 is used for packets entering subinterface 2. List 103 is used for packets entering subinterface 3, and list 104 is used for packets entering subinterface 4. Lists 102 and 103 check for packets between Sites 2 and 3, and they also check for packets to PC11 and PC12. The mask used to check all hosts in subnets 170.1.4.0 and 170.1.6.0 is rather tricky. The mask represents 23 binary 0s and nine binary 1s, meaning that the first 23 bits of the number in the access list must match the first 23 bits in the source or destination address in the packet. This matches all hosts in each subnet, because there are 23 combined network and subnet bits.

The Frame Relay configuration is relatively straightforward. The LMI type is autosensed. The encapsulation of **ietf** between R1 and R4 is configured in two ways. First, R1 uses the **ietf** keyword on the **frame-relay interface-dlci** command. On R4, the **encapsulation** command lists the **ietf** option, implying **ietf** encapsulation for all VCs on this serial interface.

Scenario 2, Part C: Verification and Questions

The CCNA exam tests your memory of the kinds of information you can find in the output of various **show** commands. Using Examples 13-13 through 13-16 as references, answer the questions following the examples.

Example 13-13 *Scenario 2, Part C: R1* **show** *and* **debug** *Output*

```
R1#show ip interface brief
Interface          IP-Address      OK? Method Status                 Protocol
Serial0            unassigned      YES unset  up                     up
Serial0.2          170.1.10.1      YES NVRAM  up                     up
Serial0.3          170.1.12.1      YES NVRAM  up                     up
Serial0.4          170.1.14.1      YES NVRAM  up                     up
Serial1            unassigned      YES unset  administratively down  down
Ethernet0          170.1.3.1       YES NVRAM  up                     up

R1#show cdp neighbor detail
```

continues

Example 13-13 *Scenario 2, Part C: R1* **show** *and* **debug** *Output (Continued)*

```
- - - - - - - - - - - - - - - - - - - - - - - -
Device ID: R2
Entry address(es):
  IP address: 170.1.10.2
Platform: cisco 2500,  Capabilities: Router
Interface: Serial0.2,  Port ID (outgoing port): Serial0.1
Holdtime : 132 sec
Version :
Cisco Internetwork Operating System Software
 IOS (tm) 2500 Software (C2500-DS-L), Version 12.2(1), RELEASE SOFTWARE (fc2)
 Copyright  1986-2001 by cisco Systems, Inc.
 Compiled Fri 27-Apr-01 14:43 by cmong


 advertisement version: 2


- - - - - - - - - - - - - - - - - - - - - - - -
Device ID: R3
Entry address(es):
  IP address: 170.1.12.3
Platform: Cisco 2500,  Capabilities: Router
Interface: Serial0.3,  Port ID (outgoing port): Serial0.1
Holdtime : 148 sec

Version :
Cisco Internetwork Operating System Software
 IOS (tm) 2500 Software (C2500-DS-L), Version 12.2(1), RELEASE SOFTWARE (fc2)
 Copyright  1986-2001 by cisco Systems, Inc.
 Compiled Fri 27-Apr-01 14:43 by cmong


 advertisement version: 2


- - - - - - - - - - - - - - - - - - - - - - - -
Device ID: R4
Entry address(es):
  IP address: 170.1.14.4
Platform: Cisco 2500,  Capabilities: Router
Interface: Serial0.4,  Port ID (outgoing port): Serial0.1
Holdtime : 149 sec

Version :
Cisco Internetwork Operating System Software
 IOS (tm) 2500 Software (C2500-DS-L), Version 12.2(1), RELEASE SOFTWARE (fc2)
 Copyright  1986-2001 by cisco Systems, Inc.
 Compiled Fri 27-Apr-01 14:43 by cmong


 advertisement version: 2
```

Example 13-13 *Scenario 2, Part C: R1* show *and* debug *Output (Continued)*

```
R1#
R1#debug ip igrp transactions
IGRP protocol debugging is on
R1#
IGRP: received update from 170.1.14.4 on Serial0.4
      subnet 170.1.8.0, metric 8539 (neighbor 688)
IGRP: sending update to 255.255.255.255 via Serial0.2 (170.1.10.1)
      subnet 170.1.8.0, metric=8539
      subnet 170.1.14.0, metric=8476
      subnet 170.1.12.0, metric=8476
      subnet 170.1.2.0, metric=688
      subnet 170.1.6.0, metric=8539
IGRP: sending update to 255.255.255.255 via Serial0.3 (170.1.12.1)
      subnet 170.1.10.0, metric=8476
      subnet 170.1.8.0, metric=8539
      subnet 170.1.14.0, metric=8476
      subnet 170.1.2.0, metric=688
      subnet 170.1.4.0, metric=8539
IGRP: sending update to 255.255.255.255 via Serial0.4 (170.1.14.1)
      subnet 170.1.10.0, metric=8476
      subnet 170.1.12.0, metric=8476
      subnet 170.1.2.0, metric=688
      subnet 170.1.6.0, metric=8539
      subnet 170.1.4.0, metric=8539
IGRP: sending update to 255.255.255.255 via Ethernet0 (170.1.3.1)
      subnet 170.1.10.0, metric=8476
      subnet 170.1.8.0, metric=8539
      subnet 170.1.14.0, metric=8476
      subnet 170.1.12.0, metric=8476
      subnet 170.1.6.0, metric=8539
      subnet 170.1.4.0, metric=8539
IGRP: received update from 170.1.10.2 on Serial0.2
      subnet 170.1.4.0, metric 8539 (neighbor 688)
IGRP: received update from 170.1.12.3 on Serial0.3
      subnet 170.1.6.0, metric 8539 (neighbor 688)
R1#
R1#undebug all
All possible debugging has been turned off
```

Example 13-14 *Scenario 2, Part C: R2* show *and* debug *Output*

```
R2#show interfaces
Serial0 is up, line protocol is up
  Hardware is HD64570
  MTU 1500 bytes, BW 56 Kbit, DLY 20000 usec,
      reliability 255/255, txload 1/255, rxload 1/255
  Encapsulation FRAME-RELAY, loopback not set, keepalive set (10 sec)
```

continues

Example 13-14 *Scenario 2, Part C: R2* **show** *and* **debug** *Output (Continued)*

```
    LMI enq sent   144, LMI stat recvd 138, LMI upd recvd 0, DTE LMI up
    LMI enq recvd 0, LMI stat sent  0, LMI upd sent  0
    LMI DLCI 0  LMI type is ANSI Annex D  frame relay DTE
    Broadcast queue 0/64, broadcasts sent/dropped 73/0, interface broadcasts 48
    Last input 00:00:04, output 00:00:04, output hang never
    Last clearing of "show interface" counters never
      Input queue: 0/75/0/0 (size/max/drops/flushes); Total output drops: 0
      Queueing strategy: weighted fair
      Output queue: 0/1000/64/0 (size/max total/threshold/drops)
         Conversations  0/0/256 (active/max active/max total)
         Reserved Conversations 0/0 (allocated/max allocated)
         Available Bandwidth 42 kilobits/sec
    5 minute input rate 0 bits/sec, 0 packets/sec
    5 minute output rate 0 bits/sec, 0 packets/sec
       232 packets input, 17750 bytes, 0 no buffer
       Received 1 broadcasts, 0 runts, 0 giants, 0 throttles
       0 input errors, 0 CRC, 0 frame, 0 overrun, 0 ignored, 0 abort
       225 packets output, 12563 bytes, 0 underruns
       0 output errors, 0 collisions, 4 interface resets
       0 output buffer failures, 0 output buffers swapped out
       12 carrier transitions
       DCD=up  DSR=up  DTR=up  RTS=up  CTS=up
  --More--
Serial0.1 is up, line protocol is up
  Hardware is HD64570
  Internet address is 170.1.10.2/23
  MTU 1500 bytes, BW 1544 Kbit, DLY 20000 usec,
      reliability 255/255, txload 1/255, rxload 1/255
  Encapsulation FRAME-RELAY
  --More--
Serial1 is administratively down, line protocol is down
  Hardware is HD64570
    MTU 1500 bytes, BW 1544 Kbit, DLY 20000 usec,
      reliability 255/255, txload 1/255, rxload 1/255
  Encapsulation PPP, loopback not set, keepalive set (10 sec)
  LCP Closed
  Closed: CDPCP, LLC2
  Last input never, output never, output hang never
  Last clearing of "show interface" counters never
     Input queue: 0/75/0/0 (size/max/drops/flushes); Total output drops: 0
       Queueing strategy: weighted fair
     Output queue: 0/1000/64/0 (size/max total/threshold/drops)
      Conversations  0/1/256 (active/max active/max total)
      Reserved Conversations 0/0 (allocated/max allocated)
      Available Bandwidth 1158 kilobits/sec
    5 minute input rate 0 bits/sec, 0 packets/sec
    5 minute output rate 0 bits/sec, 0 packets/sec
```

Example 13-14 *Scenario 2, Part C: R2* **show** *and* **debug** *Output (Continued)*

```
        0 packets input, 0 bytes, 0 no buffer
        Received 0 broadcasts, 0 runts, 0 giants, 0 throttles
        0 input errors, 0 CRC, 0 frame, 0 overrun, 0 ignored, 0 abort
        0 packets output, 0 bytes, 0 underruns
        0 output errors, 0 collisions, 5 interface resets
        0 output buffer failures, 0 output buffers swapped out
        0 carrier transitions
        DCD=down  DSR=down  DTR=down  RTS=down  CTS=down
  --More--
Ethernet0 is up, line protocol is up
  Hardware is TMS380, address is 0000.0c89.b170 (bia 0000.0c89.b170)
  Internet address is 170.1.5.2/23
    MTU 1500 bytes, BW 10000 Kbit, DLY 1000 usec,
        reliability 255/255, txload 1/255, rxload 1/255
  Encapsulation ARPA, loopback not set, keepalive set (10 sec)
  ARP type: ARPA, ARP Timeout 4:00:00
  Last input 00:00:00, output 00:00:01, output hang never
  Last clearing of "show interface" counters never
  Queuing strategy: fifo
Output queue 0/40, 0 drops; input queue 0/75, 0 drops
  5 minute input rate 0 bits/sec, 0 packets/sec
  5 minute output rate 0 bits/sec, 0 packets/sec
      583 packets input, 28577 bytes, 0 no buffer
      Received 486 broadcasts, 0 runts, 0 giants, 0 throttles
      0 input errors, 0 CRC, 0 frame, 0 overrun, 0 ignored, 0 abort
      260 packets output, 31560 bytes, 0 underruns
      0 output errors, 0 collisions, 2 interface resets
      0 output buffer failures, 0 output buffers swapped out
      6 transitions


R2#show frame-relay pvc

PVC Statistics for interface Serial0 (Frame Relay DTE)

DLCI = 301, DLCI USAGE = LOCAL, PVC STATUS = ACTIVE, INTERFACE = Serial0.1

  input pkts 102            output pkts 82          in bytes 16624
  out bytes 11394           dropped pkts 0          in FECN pkts 0
  in BECN pkts 0            out FECN pkts 0         out BECN pkts 0
  in DE pkts 0              out DE pkts 0
  out bcast pkts 76          out bcast bytes 10806
  pvc create time 00:25:09, last time pvc status changed 00:23:15


R2#show frame-relay lmi

LMI Statistics for interface Serial0 (Frame Relay DTE) LMI TYPE = ANSI
  Invalid Unnumbered info 0          Invalid Prot Disc 0
```

continues

Example 13-14 *Scenario 2, Part C: R2* **show** *and* **debug** *Output (Continued)*

```
Invalid dummy Call Ref 0         Invalid Msg Type 0
Invalid Status Message 0         Invalid Lock Shift 0
Invalid Information ID 0         Invalid Report IE Len 0
Invalid Report Request 0        Invalid Keep IE Len 0
Num Status Enq. Sent 151        Num Status msgs Rcvd 145
Num Update Status Rcvd 0        Num Status Timeouts 7
```

Example 13-15 *Scenario 2, Part C: R3* **show** *and* **debug** *Output*

```
R3#show ip arp
Protocol  Address         Age (min)  Hardware Addr   Type    Interface
Internet  170.1.7.3            -      0000.0c89.b1b0  SNAP    Ethernet0

R3#show ip route
Codes: C - connected, S - static, I - IGRP, R - RIP, M - mobile, B - BGP
       D - EIGRP, EX - EIGRP external, O - OSPF, IA - OSPF inter area
       N1 - OSPF NSSA external type 1, N2 - OSPF NSSA external type 2
       E1 - OSPF external type 1, E2 - OSPF external type 2, E - EGP
       i - IS-IS, L1 - IS-IS level-1, L2 - IS-IS level-2, ia - IS-IS inter area
       * - candidate default, U - per-user static route, o - ODR
       P - periodic downloaded static route

Gateway of last resort is not set

     170.1.0.0/23 is subnetted, 7 subnets
I       170.1.10.0 [100/10476] via 170.1.12.1, 00:00:57, Serial0.1
I       170.1.8.0 [100/10539] via 170.1.12.1, 00:00:57, Serial0.1
I       170.1.14.0 [100/10476] via 170.1.12.1, 00:00:57, Serial0.1
C       170.1.12.0 is directly connected, Serial0.1
I       170.1.2.0 [100/8539] via 170.1.12.1, 00:00:57, Serial0.1
C       170.1.6.0 is directly connected, Ethernet0
I       170.1.4.0 [100/10539] via 170.1.12.1, 00:00:57, Serial0.1

R3#trace 170.1.9.4

Type escape sequence to abort.
Tracing the route to 170.1.9.4

  1 170.1.12.1 40 msec 40 msec 44 msec
  2 170.1.14.4 80 msec *  80 msec

R3#trace 170.1.5.2

Type escape sequence to abort.
Tracing the route to 170.1.5.2

  1 170.1.12.1 40 msec 40 msec 40 msec
```

Example 13-15 *Scenario 2, Part C: R3* **show** *and* **debug** *Output (Continued)*

```
 2 170.1.10.2 72 msec *  72 msec

R3#ping 170.1.5.2

Type escape sequence to abort.
Sending 5, 100-byte ICMP Echos to 170.1.5.2, timeout is 2 seconds:
!!!!!
Success rate is 100 percent (5/5), round-trip min/avg/max = 136/136/140 ms

R3#ping
Protocol [ip]:
Target IP address: 170.1.5.2
Repeat count [5]:
Datagram size [100]:
Timeout in seconds [2]:
Extended commands [n]: y
Source address or interface: 170.1.7.3
Type of service [0]:
Set DF bit in IP header? [no]:
Validate reply data? [no]:
Data pattern [0xABCD]:
Loose, Strict, Record, Timestamp, Verbose[none]:
Sweep range of sizes [n]:
Type escape sequence to abort.
Sending 5, 100-byte ICMP Echos to 170.1.5.2, timeout is 2 seconds:
UUUUU
Success rate is 0 percent (0/5)

R3#show frame-relay lmi

LMI Statistics for interface Serial0 (Frame Relay DTE) LMI TYPE = CISCO
  Invalid Unnumbered info 0        Invalid Prot Disc 0
  Invalid dummy Call Ref 0         Invalid Msg Type 0
  Invalid Status Message 0         Invalid Lock Shift 0
  Invalid Information ID 0         Invalid Report IE Len 0
  Invalid Report Request 0         Invalid Keep IE Len 0
  Num Status Enq. Sent 172         Num Status msgs Rcvd 172
  Num Update Status Rcvd 0         Num Status Timeouts 0

R3#show frame-relay map
Serial0.1 (up): point-to-point dlci, dlci 301(0x12D,0x48D0), broadcast
          status defined, active
```

Example 13-16 *Scenario 2, Part C: R4* show *and* debug *Output*

```
R4#show ip interface brief
Interface            IP-Address    OK? Method Status                 Protocol
Serial0              unassigned    YES unset  up                     up
Serial0.1            170.1.14.4    YES NVRAM  up                     up
Serial1              unassigned    YES unset  administratively down  down
Ethernet0            170.1.9.4     YES NVRAM  up                     up


R4#show cdp neighbor detail
-------------------------
Device ID: R1
Entry address(es):
  IP address: 170.1.14.1
Platform: Cisco 2500,  Capabilities: Router
Interface: Serial0.1,  Port ID (outgoing port): Serial0.4
Holdtime : 178 sec


Version :
Cisco Internetwork Operating System Software
IOS (tm) 2500 Software (C2500-DS-L), Version 12.2(1), RELEASE SOFTWARE (fc2)
Copyright  1986-2001 by cisco Systems, Inc.
Compiled Fri 27-Apr-01 14:43 by cmong


advertisement version: 2


R4#show frame-relay pvc

PVC Statistics for interface Serial0 (Frame Relay DTE)


DLCI = 301, DLCI USAGE = LOCAL, PVC STATUS = ACTIVE, INTERFACE = Serial0.1

  input pkts 85          output pkts 63         in bytes 14086
  out bytes 8464         dropped pkts 0         in FECN pkts 0
  in BECN pkts 0         out FECN pkts 0        out BECN pkts 0
  in DE pkts 0           out DE pkts 0
  out bcast pkts 53       out bcast bytes 7614
  pvc create time 00:18:40, last time pvc status changed 00:18:40
```

Using Examples 13-13 through 13-16 as references, answer the following questions:

1. The ping of 170.1.5.2 (R2's E0 interface) from R3 was successful (refer to Example 13-15). Why was it successful if the access lists in R1 are enabled as shown in its configuration?

2. What **show** commands can be executed on R4 to display R1's IP addresses?

3. What command lists the IP subnet numbers to which R2 is connected?

4. What commands list the routing metrics used for IP subnets?

5. If you do not know the enable password, how can you see what access lists are used?

6. What does ICMP stand for?

7. Describe how R2 learns that R1's IP address is 170.1.10.1.

8. What does DLCI stand for? How big can a DLCI be?

9. What additional configuration is needed on R3 to get routing updates to flow over the VC to R1?

10. What **show** command lists Frame Relay PVCs and the IP addresses on the other end of the PVC in this network?

11. What **show** command lists the status of the VC between R1 and R2?

12. What do ISDN, BRI, and PRI stand for?

13. Give examples of two ISDN reference points.

Solutions to Scenario 2, Part C: Verification and Questions

The answers to the questions for Scenario 2, Part C are as follows:

1. The **ping** command uses the outgoing interface's IP address as the source address in the packet, which in this case is 170.1.12.3. Access lists 102 and 103 check the source and destination IP addresses, looking for the subnets on the Ethernet segments. Therefore, the packet is not matched. If you look further in Example 13-15 to see the extended **ping** with source IP address 170.1.7.3 (R3's E0 IP address), you see that it fails. This is because the extended **ping** calls for the use of 170.1.7.3 as the source IP address.

2. The **show ip route** command (refer to Example 13-15) lists the IP addresses of the neighboring routers. Because only point-to-point subinterfaces are in use, the **show frame-relay map** command (refer to Example 13-15) does not show details of the neighboring routers' Layer 3 addresses. The **show cdp neighbor detail** command (refer to Example 13-16) also shows information about IP addresses.

3. The **show ip route** command lists these numbers (refer to Example 13-15). Routes with a C in the left column signify connected subnets.

4. The **show ip route** command lists the metric values (refer to Example 13-15). The metric value for each IP subnet is the second of the two numbers in brackets.

5. Use the **show access-lists** command.

6. ICMP stands for Internet Control Message Protocol.

7. The Inverse ARP process is not used when the subinterface is a point-to-point subinterface. Therefore, R2 can learn of R1's IP and IPX addresses only with CDP, or by looking at the source addresses of the IPX RIP and IP IGRP routing updates.

8. DLCI stands for data-link connection identifier. Lengths between 10 and 14 bits are defined. A 10-bit number is the most typically implemented size.

9. No other configuration is necessary; this is a trick question. This is the kind of misdirection you might see on the exam. Read the questions slowly, and read them twice.

10. The **show frame-relay pvc** command lists the PVCs. When multipoint subinterfaces are used, or when no subinterfaces are used for Frame Relay configuration, the **show frame-relay map** command lists the IP addresses. The **show ip route** command, or the **show cdp neighbor detail** command, can be used to see the addresses in either case.

11. The **show frame-relay pvc** command displays the status.

12. ISDN stands for Integrated Services Digital Network. BRI stands for Basic Rate Interface. PRI stands for Primary Rate Interface.

13. A reference point is an interface between function groups. R, S, T, and U are the reference points. S and T are combined in many cases and together are called the S/T reference point.

Part VI: Appendixes

Answers to the "Do I Know This Already?" Quizzes and Q&A Questions

Chapter 1

"Do I Know This Already?" Quiz

1. Which of the following statements describes part of the process of how a switch decides to forward a frame destined for a unicast MAC address?

   Answer: A

2. Which of the following statements describes part of the process of how a LAN switch decides to forward a frame destined for a broadcast MAC address?

   Answer: C

3. Which of the following statements best describes what a switch does with a frame destined for an unknown unicast address?

   Answer: A

4. Which of the following comparisons does a switch make when deciding whether to add a new MAC address to its bridging table?

   Answer: B

5. In which of the following CLI modes could you configure the duplex setting for interface fastethernet 0/5?

   Answer: E. The duplex command is an interface subcommand.

6. In which of the following CLI modes could you issue a command to erase the switch's initial configuration?

   Answer: B. The erase command is an EXEC command, so it cannot be issued from any configuration mode. User mode does not allow the use of the erase command.

7. What type of switch memory is used to store the configuration used by the switch when the switch first comes up?

   Answer: D. IOS loads the configuration from NVRAM into RAM during the boot sequence.

8. What command copies the configuration from RAM into NVRAM?

   Answer: F. The first parameter identifies the source of the configuration, and the last parameter identifies the destination.

9. You configure the **enable secret** command, followed by the **enable password** command, from the console. You log out of the switch and log back in at the console. Which command defines the password you had to enter to access privileged mode again from the console?

   Answer: B. When both are configured, the enable secret password takes precedence over the enable password.

10. What command is used on a switch to set the switch's IP address for in-band management to 10.1.1.1, subnet mask 255.255.255.0?

    Answer: A. Interestingly, the syntax matches the syntax of the same command in router IOS.

11. Imagine a 2950 switch with a PC plugged into interface fastethernet 0/1 and a router plugged into interface fastethernet 0/2. The PC needs to use TCP/IP to communicate through the router with other TCP/IP hosts. In what configuration mode could you enter the switch's IP address?

    Answer: G. First of all, the switch does not need an IP address for the PC to use TCP/IP to send packets through the switch to the router. Those details in the question were put there to help make sure you really know the answer. The ip address command is added to interface vlan 1, so the command is used in interface configuration mode for interface vlan 1.

12. What interface subcommand tells the switch to take an interface out of service?

    Answer: C. The shutdown command takes the interface out of service, and the no shutdown command puts it in service again.

Q&A

1. Describe how a switch decides whether it should forward a frame, and tell how it chooses the output interface.

   Answer: The switch examines the frame's destination MAC address and looks for the address in its bridge (or address) table. If it's found, the matching entry tells the switch which output interface to use to forward the frame. If it isn't found, the switch forwards the frame out all the other interfaces (except for interfaces blocked by spanning tree and the interface in which the frame was received). The switch table is built by examining incoming frames' source MAC addresses.

2. How does a switch build its address table?

   Answer: The switch listens for incoming frames and examines the source MAC address. If it isn't in the table, the source address is added, along with the port (interface) on which the frame entered the switch. The switch also marks an entry for freshness so that entries can be removed after a period of disuse. This reduces table size and allows for easier table changes in case a spanning tree change forces more-significant changes in the switch (address) table.

3. What configuration command causes the switch to require a password from a user at the console? What configuration mode context must you be in? (That is, what command(s) must you enter before this command after entering configuration mode?) List the commands in the order you must enter them while in config mode.

   Answer:

   line console 0
   login

   The line console 0 command is a context-setting command; it adds no information to the configuration. It can be entered from any part of configuration mode. The login command, which follows the line console 0 command, tells IOS that a password prompt is desired at the console.

4. What configuration command is used to tell the switch the password that is required at the console? What configuration mode context must you be in? (That is, what command(s) must you enter before this command after entering configuration mode?) List the commands in the order in which you must enter them while in config mode.

   Answer:

   line console 0
   password *xxxxxxx*

   The password command tells IOS the value that should be entered when a user wants access from the console. This value is requested by IOS because of the login command. The password *xxxxxxx* must be entered while in console configuration mode, which you reach by entering line console 0.

5. What command sets the password that is required after you enter the **enable** command? Is that password encrypted by default?

   Answer: enable password or enable secret. The password in the enable command is not encrypted by default. The enable secret password is encrypted using MD5.

6. Is the password required at the console the same one that is required when Telnet is used to access a switch?

   Answer: No. The Telnet ("virtual terminal") password is not the same password, although many installations use the same value.

7. Name two commands used to view the configuration to be used at the 2950 switch's next reload. Which one is the more-recent addition to IOS?

   Answer: show config and show startup-config. show startup-config is the newer one and hopefully is easier to remember.

8. Name two commands used to view the configuration that is currently used in a 2950 switch. Which one is the more-recent addition to IOS?

   Answer: write terminal and show running-config. show running-config is the newer command and hopefully is easier to remember.

Chapter 2

"Do I Know This Already?" Quiz

1. Which of the following are the port states when STP has completed convergence?

   Answer: A, B

2. Which of the following are transitory port states used only during the process of STP convergence?

   Answer: C, D

3. Which of the following bridge IDs would win election as root, assuming that the switches with these bridge IDs were in the same network?

   Answer: C

4. Which of the following facts determines how often a root bridge or switch sends a BPDU message?

   Answer: B

5. What feature causes an interface to be placed in forwarding state as soon as the interface is physically active?

   Answer: E

6. What feature combines multiple parallel Ethernet links between two switches so that traffic is balanced across the links, and so that STP treats all links as one link?

   Answer: F

7. What name represents the improved STP standard that lowers convergence time?

   Answer: B, D

8. Which of the following RSTP port roles have the same name as a similar role in STP?

   Answer: B, D

9. On a 2950 switch, what command lets you change the value of the bridge ID without having to configure a specific value for any part of the bridge ID?

   Answer: B

10. What command lists spanning-tree status information on 2950 series switches?

    Answer: A

Q&A

1. What routing protocol does a transparent bridge use to learn about Layer 3 address groupings?

   Answer: None. Bridges do not use routing protocols. Transparent bridges do not care about Layer 3 address groupings. Devices on either side of a transparent bridge are in the same Layer 3 group—in other words, the same IP subnet.

2. What settings does a bridge or switch examine to determine which should be elected as root of the spanning tree?

   Answer: The bridge priority is examined first (the lowest wins). In case of a tie, the lowest MAC address wins. The priority is prepended to the bridge ID in the actual BPDU message so that the combined fields can be compared easily.

3. If a switch hears three different hello BPDUs from three different neighbors on three different interfaces, and if all three specify that Bridge 1 is the root, how does the switch choose which interface is its root port?

   Answer: The root port is the port on which the BPDU with the lowest-cost value is received. The root port is placed in forwarding state on each bridge and switch.

4. Can the root bridge/switch ports be placed in blocking state?

   Answer: The root bridge's ports are always in forwarding state because they always have cost 0 to the root, which ensures that they are always the designated bridges on their respective LAN segments.

5. Describe the benefits of Spanning Tree Protocol as used by transparent bridges and switches.

   Answer: Physically redundant paths in the network are allowed to exist and be used when other paths fail. Also, loops in the bridged network are avoided. Loops are particularly bad because bridging uses LAN headers, which do not provide a mechanism to mark a frame so that its lifetime can be limited; in other words, the frame can loop forever.

6. When a bridge or switch using Spanning Tree Protocol first initializes, what does it assert should be the tree's root?

   Answer: Each bridge/switch begins by sending BPDUs claiming itself as the root bridge.

7. Name the three reasons why a port is placed in forwarding state as a result of spanning tree.

    Answer: First, all ports on the root bridge are placed in forwarding state. Second, one port on each bridge is considered its root port, which is placed in forwarding state. Finally, on each LAN segment, one bridge is considered the designated bridge on that LAN; that designated bridge's interface on the LAN is placed in forwarding state.

8. Name the three interface states that Spanning Tree Protocol uses, other than forwarding. Which of these states is transitory?

    Answer: Blocking, listening, and learning. Blocking is the only stable state; the other two are transitory between blocking and forwarding. Table 2-2 summarizes the states and their features.

9. What are the two reasons that a nonroot bridge/switch places a port in forwarding state?

    Answer: If the port is the designated bridge on its LAN segment, the port is placed in forwarding state. Also, if the port is the root port, it is placed in forwarding state. Otherwise, the port is placed in blocking state.

10. Which two 2950 series EXEC commands list information about an interface's spanning-tree state?

    Answer: The show spanning-tree command lists details of the current spanning tree for all VLANs, including port status. show spanning-tree interface x/y lists the details just for interface x/y.

Chapter 3

"Do I Know This Already?" Quiz

1. In a LAN, which of the following terms best equates to the term "VLAN"?

    Answer: B. By definition, a VLAN includes all devices in the same LAN broadcast domain.

2. Imagine a switch with three configured VLANs. How many IP subnets are required, assuming that all hosts in all VLANs want to use TCP/IP?

    Answer: D. The hosts in each VLAN must be in different subnets.

3. Which of the following fully encapsulates the original Ethernet frame in a trunking header?

   Answer: B. ISL fully encapsulates the original frame, whereas 802.1q simply adds an additional header inside the original Ethernet frame.

4. Which of the following adds the trunking header for all VLANs except one?

   Answer: C. 802.1q treats one VLAN as the "native" VLAN. It does not add the trunking header for frames in the native VLAN.

5. Which of the following allows a spanning tree instance per VLAN?

   Answer: D

6. Which of the following advertises VLAN information to neighboring switches?

   Answer: A. The primary feature of VTP is to distribute VLAN configuration information.

7. Which of the following VTP modes allow VLANs to be created on a switch?

   Answer: B, C

8. Imagine that you are told that switch 1 is configured with the **auto** parameter for trunking on its Ethernet connection to switch 2. You have to configure switch 2. Which of the following settings for trunking could allow trunking to work?

   Answer: A, C. Auto means that a switch waits for the switch on the other end of the trunk to attempt trunking first. With auto set on both ends of the trunk, trunking would never work.

Q&A

1. Define broadcast domain.

   Answer: A broadcast domain is a set of Ethernet devices for which a broadcast sent by any one of them should be received by all others in the group. Unlike routers, bridges and switches do not stop the flow of broadcasts. Two segments separated by a router would each be in a different broadcast domain. A switch can create multiple broadcast domains by creating multiple VLANs, but a router must be used to route packets between the VLANs.

2. Define VLAN.

   Answer: A virtual LAN is the process of treating one subset of a switch's interfaces as one broadcast domain. Broadcasts from one VLAN are not forwarded to other VLANs; unicasts between VLANs must use a router. Advanced methods, such as Layer 3 switching, can be used to allow the LAN switch to forward traffic between VLANs without each individual frame's being routed by a router. However, for the depth of CCNA, such detail is not needed.

3. If two Cisco LAN switches are connected using Fast Ethernet, what VLAN trunking protocols can be used? If only one VLAN spans both switches, is a VLAN trunking protocol needed?

   Answer: ISL and 802.1q are the trunking protocols that Cisco uses over Fast Ethernet. If only one VLAN spans the two switches, a trunking protocol is not needed. Trunking or tagging protocols are used to tag a frame as being in a particular VLAN; if only one VLAN is used, tagging is unnecessary.

4. Define VTP.

   Answer: VLAN Trunking Protocol transmits configuration information about VLANs between interconnected switches. VTP helps prevent misconfiguration, eases switch administration, and reduces broadcast overhead through the use of VTP pruning.

5. Name the three VTP modes. Which mode does not allow VLANs to be added or modified?

   Answer: Server and client modes are used to actively participate in VTP; transparent mode is used to simply stay out of the way of servers and clients while not participating in VTP. Switches in client mode cannot change or add VLANs.

6. What Catalyst 2950 switch command configures 802.1Q trunking on fastethernet port 0/12 so that as long as the switch port on the other end of the trunk is not disabled (off) or configured to not negotiate to become a trunk, the trunk is definitely placed in trunking mode?

   Answer: The switchport mode dynamic desirable interface subcommand tells this switch to be in trunking mode as long as the switch on the other end of the trunk is configured for trunk, auto, or desirable. If the other switch has configured the trunk as an access port, the interface does not use trunking.

7. What type of VTP mode allows a switch to create VLANs and advertise them to other switches?

   Answer: Only VTP servers can create and advertise VLANs with VTP.

8. Must all members of the same VLAN be in the same collision domain, the same broadcast domain, or both?

   Answer: By definition, members of the same VLAN are all part of the same broadcast domain. They might all be in the same collision domain, but only if all devices in the VLAN are connected to hubs.

9. What is Cisco's proprietary trunking protocol over Ethernet?

   Answer: Inter-Switch Link (ISL)

10. Explain the benefits provided by VTP pruning.

    Answer: VTP pruning reduces network overhead by preventing broadcasts and unknown unicast frames in a VLAN from being sent to switches that have no interfaces in that VLAN.

11. Consider the phrase "A VLAN is a broadcast domain is an IP subnet." Do you agree or disagree? Why?

    Answer: From one perspective, this statement is false, because an IP subnet is a Layer 3 protocol concept, and broadcast domain and VLAN are Layer 2 concepts. However, the devices in one broadcast domain comprise the same set of devices that would be in the same VLAN and in the same IP subnet.

12. What fields are added or changed in an Ethernet header when you use 802.1q? Where is the VLAN ID in those fields?

    Answer: A new 4-byte 802.1q header that includes the VLAN ID is added after the source MAC address field. The original FCS field in the Ethernet trailer is modified, because the value must be recalculated as a result of changing the header.

13. Explain how a switch in VTP transparent mode treats VTP messages received from a VTP server.

    Answer: A switch in VTP transparent mode receives the VTP messages and forwards them as broadcasts. However, the switch ignores the contents of the messages, so it does not learn any VLAN information from the messages.

14. What command on a 2950 switch creates VLAN 5? What configuration mode is required?

    In VLAN database configuration mode, the vlan 5 name newvlan5 command would create the new vlan, and give it a name.

15. What command on a 2950 switch puts an interface into VLAN 5? What configuration mode is required?

Answer: **In interface configuration mode for that interface, the command switchport access vlan 5 assigns the interface to VLAN 5.**

16. Describe the basic differences in the processes used by VLAN configuration mode and the normally used configuration mode.

Answer: **In VLAN configuration mode, the commands do not take immediate effect. You must exit configuration mode or use the apply command to cause the configuration to be accepted.**

17. Give the correct syntax for the commands that put an interface into the various trunking modes, and identify which commands work when the switch on the other side of the link uses the **auto** option.

Answer:

switchport mode dynamic desirable
switchport mode dynamic auto
switchport mode trunk
switchport mode access

The first and third commands work with auto set on the other side of the link.

18. What 2950 **show** commands list trunk status, both configured and operational?

Answer:

show interfaces fastethernet 0/x switchport
show interfaces fastethernet 0/x trunk

Chapter 4

"Do I Know This Already?" Quiz

1. Which of the following is the result of a Boolean AND between IP address 150.150.4.100 and mask 255.255.192.0?

   Answer: B

2. If mask 255.255.255.128 were used with a Class B network, how many subnets could exist, with how many hosts per subnet, respectively?

   Answer: E. Class B networks imply 16 network bits, and the mask implies 7 host bits (7 binary 0s in the mask), leaving 9 subnet bits. $2^9 - 2$ yields 510 subnets, and $2^7 - 2$ yields 126 hosts per subnet.

3. If mask 255.255.255.240 were used with a Class C network, how many subnets could exist, with how many hosts per subnet, respectively?

   Answer: B. Class C networks imply 24 network bits, and the mask implies 4 host bits (4 binary 0s in the mask), leaving 4 subnet bits. $2^4 - 2$ yields 14 subnets, and $2^4 - 2$ yields 14 hosts per subnet.

4. Which of the following IP addresses are not in the same subnet as 190.4.80.80, mask 255.255.255.0?

   Answer: E, F. 190.4.80.80, mask 255.255.255.0, is in subnet 190.4.80.0, broadcast address 190.4.80.255, with a range of valid addresses between 190.4.80.1 and 190.4.80.254.

5. Which of the following IP addresses is not in the same subnet as 190.4.80.80, mask 255.255.240.0?

   Answer: F. 190.4.80.80, mask 255.255.240.0, is in subnet 190.4.80.0, broadcast address 190.4.95.255, with a range of valid addresses between 190.4.80.1 and 190.4.95.254.

6. Which of the following IP addresses are not in the same subnet as 190.4.80.80, mask 255.255.255.128?

   Answer: D, E, F. 190.4.80.80, mask 255.255.255.128, is in subnet 190.4.80.0, broadcast address 190.4.80.127, with a range of valid addresses between 190.4.80.1 and 190.4.80.126.

7. Which of the following subnet masks lets a Class B network allow subnets to have up to 150 hosts and up to 164 subnets?

    Answer: C. You need 8 bits to number up to 150 hosts, because $2^7 - 2$ is less than 150, but $2^8 - 2$ is greater than 150. Similarly, you need 8 subnet bits as well. The only valid Class B subnet mask with 8 hosts and 8 subnet bits is 255.255.255.0.

8. Which of the following subnet masks let a Class A network allow subnets to have up to 150 hosts and up to 164 subnets?

    Answer: B, C, D, E, F. You need 8 host bits and 8 subnet bits. Because the mask is used with a Class A network, any mask with the entire second octet as part of the subnet field and with the entire fourth octet as part of the host field meets the requirement.

9. Which of the following are valid subnet numbers in network 180.1.0.0 when using mask 255.255.248.0?

    Answer: C, D, E, F. In this case, the subnet numbers begin with 180.1.0.0 (subnet zero) and then go to 180.1.8.0, 180.1.16.0, 180.1.24.0, and so on, increasing by 8 in the third octet, up to 180.1.240.0 (the last valid subnet) and 180.1.248.0 (the broadcast subnet).

10. Which of the following are valid subnet numbers in network 180.1.0.0 when using mask 255.255.255.0?

    Answer: A, B, C, D, E, F. In this case, the subnet numbers begin with 180.1.0.0 (subnet zero) and then go to 180.1.1.0, 180.1.2.0, 180.1.3.0, and so on, increasing by 1 in the third octet, up to 180.1.254.0 (the last valid subnet) and 180.1.255.0 (the broadcast subnet).

Q&A

1. Name the parts of an IP address.

    Answer: Network, subnet, and host are the three parts of an IP address. However, many people commonly treat the network and subnet parts as a single part, leaving only two parts, the subnet and host. On the exam, the multiple-choice format should provide extra clues as to which terminology is used.

2. Define subnet mask. What do the bits in the mask whose values are binary 0 tell you about the corresponding IP address(es)?

    Answer: A subnet mask defines the number of host bits in an address. The bits of value 0 define which bits in the address are host bits. The mask is an important ingredient in the formula to dissect an IP address. Along with knowledge of the number of network bits implied for Class A, B, and C networks, the mask provides a clear definition of the size of the network, subnet, and host parts of an address.

3. Given the IP address 10.5.118.3 and the mask 255.255.0.0, what is the subnet number?

Answer: The subnet number is 10.5.0.0. The binary algorithm math is shown in the following table.

Address	10.5.118.3	0000 1010 **0000 0101** 0111 0110 0000 0011
Mask	255.255.0.0	1111 1111 **1111 1111** 0000 0000 0000 0000
Result	10.5.0.0	0000 1010 **0000 0101** 0000 0000 0000 0000

4. Given the IP address 190.1.42.3 and the mask 255.255.255.0, what is the subnet number?

Answer: The subnet number is 190.1.42.0. The binary algorithm math is shown in the following table.

Address	190.1.42.3	1011 1110 0000 0001 **0010 1010** 0000 0011
Mask	255.255.255.0	1111 1111 1111 1111 **1111 1111** 0000 0000
Result	190.1.42.0	1011 1110 0000 0001 **0010 1010** 0000 0000

5. Given the IP address 140.1.1.1 and the mask 255.255.255.248, what is the subnet number?

Answer: The subnet number is 140.1.1.0. The following subnet chart helps you learn how to calculate the subnet number without binary math. The magic number is 256 – 248 = 8.

Octet	1	2	3	4	Comments
Address	140	1	1	1	
Mask	255	255	255	248	The interesting octet is the fourth octet.
Subnet Number	140	1	1	0	0 is the closest multiple of the magic number not greater than 1.
First Address	140	1	1	1	Add 1 to the last octet.
Broadcast	140	1	1	7	Subnet + magic number – 1.
Last Address	140	1	1	6	Subtract 1 from the broadcast.

6. Given the IP address 167.88.99.66 and the mask 255.255.255.192, what is the subnet number?

    Answer: The subnet number is 167.88.99.64. The following subnet chart helps you learn how to calculate the subnet number without binary math. The magic number is 256 – 192 = 64.

Octet	1	2	3	4	Comments
Address	167	88	99	66	
Mask	255	255	255	192	The interesting octet is the fourth octet.
Subnet Number	167	88	99	64	64 is the closest multiple of the magic number that is not greater than 66.
First Address	167	88	99	65	Add 1 to the last octet.
Broadcast	167	88	99	127	Subnet + magic number – 1.
Last Address	167	88	99	126	Subtract 1 from the broadcast.

7. Given the IP address 10.5.118.3 and the mask 255.255.0.0, what is the broadcast address?

    Answer: The broadcast address is 10.5.255.255. The binary algorithm math is shown in the following table.

Address	10.5.118.3	0000 1010 0000 0101 0111 0110 0000 0011
Mask	255.255.0.0	1111 1111 1111 1111 0000 0000 0000 0000
Result	10.5.0.0	0000 1010 0000 0101 0000 0000 0000 0000
Broadcast Address	10.5.255.255	0000 1010 0000 0101 **1111 1111 1111 1111**

8. Given the IP address 190.1.42.3 and the mask 255.255.255.0, what is the broadcast address?

    Answer: The broadcast address is 190.1.42.255. The binary algorithm math is shown in the following table.

Address	190.1.42.3	1011 1110 0000 0001 0010 1010 0000 0011
Mask	255.255.255.0	1111 1111 1111 1111 1111 1111 0000 0000
Result	190.1.42.0	1011 1110 0000 0001 0010 1010 0000 0000
Broadcast Address	190.1.42.255	1011 1110 0000 0001 0010 1010 **1111 1111**

9. Given the IP address 140.1.1.1 and the mask 255.255.255.248, what is the broadcast address?

   Answer: The broadcast address is 140.1.1.7. The binary algorithm math is shown in the following table.

Address	140.1.1.1	1000 1100 0000 0001 0000 0001 0000 0001
Mask	255.255.255.248	1111 1111 1111 1111 1111 1111 1111 1000
Result	140.1.1.0	1000 1100 0000 0001 0000 0001 0000 0000
Broadcast Address	140.1.1.7	1000 1100 0000 0001 0000 0001 0000 **0111**

10. Given the IP address 167.88.99.66 and the mask 255.255.255.192, what is the broadcast address?

    Answer: The broadcast address is 167.88.99.127. The binary algorithm math is shown in the following table.

Address	167.88.99.66	1010 0111 0101 1000 0110 0011 0100 0010
Mask	255.255.255.192	1111 1111 1111 1111 1111 1111 1100 0000
Result	167.88.99.64	1010 0111 0101 1000 0110 0011 0100 0000
Broadcast Address	167.88.99.127	1010 0111 0101 1000 0110 0011 01**11 1111**

11. Given the IP address 10.5.118.3 and the mask 255.255.0.0, what are the assignable IP addresses in this subnet?

    Answer: The subnet number is 10.5.0.0, and the subnet broadcast address is 10.5.255.255. The assignable addresses are all the addresses between the subnet and broadcast addresses—namely, 10.5.0.1 to 10.5.255.254.

12. Given the IP address 190.1.42.3 and the mask 255.255.255.0, what are the assignable IP addresses in this subnet?

    Answer: The subnet number is 190.1.42.0, and the subnet broadcast address is 190.1.42.255. The assignable addresses are all the addresses between the subnet and broadcast addresses—namely, 190.1.42.1 to 190.1.42.254.

13. Given the IP address 140.1.1.1 and the mask 255.255.255.248, what are the assignable IP addresses in this subnet?

    Answer: The subnet number is 140.1.1.0, and the subnet broadcast address is 140.1.1.7. The assignable addresses are all the addresses between the subnet and broadcast addresses—namely, 140.1.1.1 to 140.1.1.6.

14. Given the IP address 167.88.99.66 and the mask 255.255.255.192, what are the assignable IP addresses in this subnet?

Answer: The subnet number is 167.88.99.64, and the subnet broadcast address is 167.88.99.127. The assignable addresses are all the addresses between the subnet and broadcast addresses—namely, 167.88.99.65 to 167.88.99.126.

15. Given the IP address 10.5.118.3 and the mask 255.255.255.0, what are all the subnet numbers if the same (static) mask is used for all subnets in this network?

Answer: The numbers are 10.0.1.0, 10.0.2.0, 10.0.3.0, and so on, up to 10.255.254.0. The Class A network number is 10.0.0.0. The mask implies that the entire second and third octets, and only those octets, comprise the subnet field. The first subnet number, called the zero subnet (10.0.0.0), and the last subnet number, called the broadcast subnet (10.255.255.0), are reserved.

16. How many IP addresses can be assigned in each subnet of 10.0.0.0, assuming that a mask of 255.255.255.0 is used? If the same (static) mask is used for all subnets, how many subnets are there?

Answer: There are $2^{number-of-host-bits}$, or 2^8, hosts per subnet, minus two special cases. The number of subnets is $2^{number-of-subnet-bits}$, or 2^{16}, minus two special cases.

Network and Mask	Number of Network Bits	Number of Host Bits	Number of Subnet Bits	Number of Hosts Per Subnet	Number of Subnets
10.0.0.0, 255.255.255.0	8	8	16	254	65,534

17. How many IP addresses can be assigned in each subnet of 140.1.0.0, assuming that a mask of 255.255.255.248 is used? If the same (static) mask is used for all subnets, how many subnets are there?

Answer: There are $2^{number-of-host-bits}$, or 2^3, hosts per subnet, minus two special cases. The number of subnets is $2^{number-of-subnet-bits}$, or 2^{13}, minus two special cases.

Network and Mask	Number of Network Bits	Number of Host Bits	Number of Subnet Bits	Number of Hosts Per Subnet	Number of Subnets
140.1.0.0	16	3	13	6	8190

18. You design a network for a customer who wants the same subnet mask on every subnet. The customer will use network 10.0.0.0 and needs 200 subnets, each with 200 hosts maximum. What subnet mask would you use to allow the most growth in subnets? Which mask would work and would allow for the most growth in the number of hosts per subnet?

    Answer: Network 10.0.0.0 is a Class A network, so you have 24 host bits with no subnetting. To number 200 subnets, you need at least 8 subnet bits, because 2^8 is 256. Likewise, to number 200 hosts per subnet, you need 8 host bits. So, you need to pick a mask with at least 8 subnet bits and 8 host bits. 255.255.0.0 is a mask with 8 subnet bits and 16 host bits. That would allow for the 200 subnets and 200 hosts while allowing the number of hosts per subnet to grow to $2^{16} - 2$—quite a large number. Similarly, a mask of 255.255.255.0 gives you 16 subnet bits, allowing $2^{16} - 2$ subnets, each with $2^8 - 2$ hosts per subnet.

19. Refer to Figure A-1. Fred is configured with IP address 10.1.1.1. Router A's Ethernet interface is configured with 10.1.1.100. Router A's serial interface uses 10.1.1.101. Router B's serial interface uses 10.1.1.102. Router B's Ethernet uses 10.1.1.200. The web server uses 10.1.1.201. Mask 255.255.255.192 is used in all cases. Is anything wrong with this network? What is the easiest thing you could do to fix it? You may assume any working interior routing protocol.

Figure A-1 *Sample Network for Subnetting Questions*

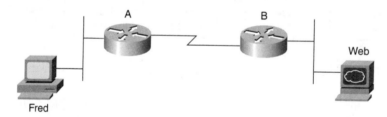

Answer: Router A's Ethernet interface and Fred's Ethernet interface should be in the same subnet, but they are not. Fred's configuration implies a subnet with IP addresses ranging from 10.1.1.1 to 10.1.1.62; Router A's Ethernet configuration implies a subnet with addresses between 10.1.1.65 and 10.1.1.126. Also, Router A's two interfaces must be in different subnets; as configured, they are in the same subnet. So the solution is to change Router A's Ethernet IP address to something between 10.1.1.2 and 10.1.1.62, putting it in the same subnet as Fred.

20.   Refer to Figure A-1. Fred is configured with IP address 10.1.1.1, mask 255.255.255.0. Router A's Ethernet is configured with 10.1.1.100, mask 255.255.255.224. Router A's serial interface uses 10.1.1.129, mask 255.255.255.252. Router B's serial interface uses 10.1.1.130, mask 255.255.255.252. Router B's Ethernet uses 10.1.1.200, mask 255.255.255.224. The web server uses 10.1.1.201, mask 255.255.255.224. Is anything wrong with this network? What is the easiest thing you could do to fix it? You may assume any working interior routing protocol.

Answer: Fred's configuration implies a subnet with a range of addresses from 10.1.1.1 to 10.1.1.254, so he thinks that Router A's Ethernet interface is in the same subnet. However, Router A's configuration implies a subnet with addresses from 10.1.1.97 to 10.1.1.126, so Router A does not think Fred is on the same subnet as Router A's Ethernet. Several options exist for fixing the problem. You could change the mask used by Fred and Router A's Ethernet to 255.255.255.128, which makes them both reside in the same subnet.

21.   Refer to Figure A-1. Fred is configured with IP address 10.1.1.1, mask 255.255.255.240. Router A's Ethernet is configured with 10.1.1.2, mask 255.255.255.240. Router A's serial interface uses 10.1.1.129, mask 255.255.255.252. Router B's serial interface uses 10.1.1.130, mask 255.255.255.252. Router B's Ethernet uses 10.1.1.200, mask 255.255.255.128. The web server uses 10.1.1.201, mask 255.255.255.128. Is anything wrong with this network? What is the easiest thing you could do to fix it? You may assume any working interior routing protocol.

Answer: Router B's configuration implies a subnet with a range of addresses from 10.1.1.129 to 10.1.1.130 on the serial link and from 10.1.1.129 to 10.1.1.254 on the Ethernet. So the subnets overlap. One solution is to configure Router B and the web server's masks to 255.255.255.192, which changes the subnet so that the valid addresses are between 10.1.1.193 and 10.1.1.254.

Chapter 5

"Do I Know This Already?" Quiz

1. Which of the following must be true before IOS lists a route as "S" in the output of a **show ip route** command?

   Answer: C. The "S" designation implies that the route is a static route. Static routes are created with the ip route command.

2. Which of the following commands correctly configures a static route?

   Answer: A

3. Which of the following distance vector features prevents routing loops by causing the routing protocol to advertise only a subset of known routes, as opposed to the full routing table?

   Answer: D. Split horizon causes a router to not advertise routes out an interface if the route would cause packets to be sent out that same interface.

4. Which of the following features prevents routing loops by advertising an infinite metric route when a route fails?

   Answer: E. Route poisoning means advertising the failed route with an "infinite" metric, as opposed to simply ceasing to advertise the route. Poison reverse is route poisoning by advertising a route that previously was not advertised because of split horizon.

5. Router1 has interfaces with addresses 9.1.1.1 and 10.1.1.1. Router 2, connected to Router1 over a serial link, has addresses 10.1.1.2 and 11.1.1.2. Which of the following commands would be part of a complete RIP configuration on Router2, with which Router2 advertises out all interfaces, and about all routes?

   Answer: A, E, H. A router only needs network commands matching its own interfaces.

6. Which of the following situations would cause RIP or IGRP to remove all the routes learned from a particular neighboring router?

   Answer: B. Distance vector protocols rely on the regular receipt of routing updates from their neighbors to continue believing that the routes through that neighbor are still valid.

7. Which of the following **network** commands, following a **router rip** command, would cause RIP to send updates out two interfaces whose IP addresses are 10.1.2.1 and 10.1.1.1, mask 255.255.255.0?

   Answer: A. The network command has a Class A, B, or C network number as the parameter. The router enables RIP on all interfaces in that network.

8. What command(s) list(s) information identifying the neighboring routers that are sending routing information to a particular router?

Answer: B, D

9. What part of the output of the **show ip route** command identifies the metric associated with the route?

Answer: E. The first number in brackets is the administrative distance, and the second number is the metric.

Q&A

1. What type of routing protocol algorithm uses a hold-down timer? What is its purpose?

Answer: Distance vector. Holddown helps prevent counting-to-infinity problems. After learning that a route has failed, a router waits for a hold-down timer before believing any new information about the route.

2. Define what split horizon means to the contents of a routing update. Does this apply to both the distance vector algorithm and the link-state algorithm?

Answer: Routing updates sent out an interface do not contain routing information about subnets learned from updates entering the same interface. Split horizon is used only by distance vector routing protocols.

3. What steps would you take to migrate from RIP to IGRP in a router whose current RIP configuration includes only **router rip** followed by a **network 10.0.0.0** command?

Answer: Issue the following commands in configuration mode:
```
router igrp 5
network 10.0.0.0
no router rip
```

If RIP still were configured, IGRP's routes would be chosen over RIP. The Cisco IOS software considers IGRP a better source of routing information by default, as defined in the administrative distance setting (the defaults are 120 for RIP and 100 for IGRP).

4. How does the Cisco IOS software designate a subnet in the routing table as a directly connected network? What about a route learned with IGRP or RIP?

Answer: The show ip route command lists routes with a designator on the left side of the command output. C represents connected routes, I is used for IGRP, and R represents routes derived from RIP.

5. Create a configuration for IGRP on a router with these interfaces and addresses: e0 using 10.1.1.1, e1 using 224.1.2.3, s0 using 10.1.2.1, and s1 using 199.1.1.1. Use AS 5.

   Answer:
   ```
   router igrp 5
   network 10.0.0.0
   network 199.1.1.0
   ```

   If you noticed that 224.1.2.3 is not a valid Class A, B, or C address, you get full credit. A new address is needed for Ethernet1, with a matching network command.

6. Create a configuration for IGRP on a router with these interfaces and addresses: to0 using 200.1.1.1, e0 using 128.1.3.2, s0 using 192.0.1.1, and s1 using 223.254.254.1.

   Answer:
   ```
   router igrp 1
   network 200.1.1.0
   network 128.1.0.0
   network 192.0.1.0
   network 223.254.254.0
   ```

   Because four different networks are used, four network commands are required. If you noticed that this question does not specify the process ID (1 in this example) but configured one, you get full credit. A few of these network numbers are used in examples; memorize the range of valid Class A, B, and C network numbers.

7. From a router's user mode, without using debugs or privileged mode, how can you determine what routers are sending you routing updates?

   Answer: The show ip protocol command output lists the routing sources—the IP addresses of routers sending updates to this router. Knowing how to determine a fact without looking at the configuration will better prepare you for the exam. Also, the show ip route command lists next-hop router IP addresses. The next-hop routers listed identify the routers that are sending routing updates.

8. Imagine that a router has an interface E0 with IP address 168.10.1.1 and E1 with IP address 10.1.1.1. If the commands **router rip** and **network 10.0.0.0**, with no other network commands, are configured in the router, does RIP send updates out Ethernet0?

   Answer: No. There must be a network statement for network 168.10.0.0 before RIP advertises out that interface. The network command simply selects the connected interfaces on which to send and receive updates.

9. Imagine that a router has an interface E0 with IP address 168.10.1.1 and E1 with IP address 10.1.1.1. If the commands **router igrp 1** and **network 10.0.0.0** are configured in the router, does IGRP advertise 168.10.0.0?

   Answer: No. There must be a network statement for network 168.10.0.0 before IGRP advertises that directly connected subnet.

10. If the commands **router igrp 1** and **network 10.0.0.0** are configured in a router that has an Ethernet0 interface with IP address 168.10.1.1, mask 255.255.255.0, does this router have a route to 168.10.1.0?

Answer: Yes. The route is in the routing table because it is a directly connected subnet, not because of any action by IGRP.

11. Must IGRP metrics for multiple routes to the same subnet be equal for the multiple routes to be added to the routing table? If not, how close in value do the metrics have to be?

Answer: IGRP (and EIGRP) use a concept called variance, which represents how close the metrics to the same subnet must be before they are considered equal. The variance router subcommand is used to set the value.

12. When you're using RIP, what configuration command controls the number of equal-cost routes that can be added to the routing table at the same time? What is the maximum number of equal-cost routes to the same destination that can be included in the IP routing table at once?

Answer: The maximum-paths x router subcommand is used in RIP configuration mode to set the number. The maximum is 6, and the default is 4.

13. When you're using IGRP, what configuration command controls the number of equal-cost routes that can be added to the routing table at the same time? What is the maximum number of equal-cost routes to the same destination that can be included in the IP routing table at once?

Answer: The maximum-paths x router subcommand is used in IGRP configuration mode to set the number. The maximum is 6, and the default is 4.

14. Which command lists all the IP routes learned via RIP?

Answer: The show ip route rip command lists only RIP-learned routes.

15. Which command or commands list all IP routes in network 172.16.0.0?

Answer: show ip route 172.16.0.0 lists all the routes in 172.16.0.0. Also, the show ip route list 1 command lists routes in network 172.16.0.0 assuming that the access-list 1 permit 172.16.0.0 0.0.255.255 configuration command also exists.

16. True or false: Distance vector routing protocols learn routes by transmitting routing updates.

Answer: False. Routes are learned by receiving routing updates from neighboring routers.

17. Assume that a router is configured to allow only one route in the routing table to each destination network. If more than one route to a particular subnet is learned, and if each route has the same metric value, which route is placed in the routing table if the routing protocol uses distance vector logic?

    Answer: In this scenario, the first route learned is placed in the table. If that route is removed later, the next routing update received after the original route has been removed is added to the routing table.

18. Describe the purpose and meaning of route poisoning.

    Answer: Route poisoning is the distance vector routing protocol feature in which a newly bad route is advertised with an infinite metric. Routers receiving this routing information then can mark the route as a bad route immediately. The purpose is to prevent routing loops.

19. Describe the meaning and purpose of triggered updates.

    Answer: A triggered update is the routing protocol feature in which an update is sent immediately when new routing information is learned rather than waiting on a timer to complete before sending another routing update.

20. What term describes the underlying logic behind the OSPF routing protocol?

    Answer: Link state

21. Router1 has a serial interface S0 connected via a point-to-point link to Router2. Router2 has an Ethernet interface address of 20.1.21.1, mask 255.255.252.0. Write down the single variation of the **ip route** command for which you now have enough information to configure a complete, syntactically correct command.

    Answer: You must use the ip route 20.1.20.0 255.255.252.0 serial0 command instead of ip route 20.1.20.0 255.255.252.0 next-hop. Both work, but because you do not know Router2's IP address on the serial link, you do not have enough information to configure the command in the style that refers to the next-hop IP address.

Chapter 6

"Do I Know This Already?" Quiz

1. Which of the following affects the calculation of OSPF routes when all possible default values are used?

   Answer: A. OSPF calculates metrics based on the cost associated with each interface. OSPF, by default, calculates interface cost based on the bandwidth setting.

2. Which of the following affects the calculation of EIGRP metrics when all possible default values are used?

Answer: A, B. Like IGRP, EIGRP by default uses bandwidth and delay when calculating its metrics.

3. OSPF runs an algorithm to calculate the currently-best route. Which of the following terms refer to that algorithm?

Answer: A, D. OSPF uses the SPF algorithm, conceived by a mathematician named Dijkstra.

4. EIGRP uses an algorithm to find routes when no backup route exists. Which of the following terms refers to that algorithm?

Answer: B. A feasible successor route is considered a backup route. If one does not exist, EIGRP uses the DUAL algorithm to find any possible routes and to ensure that no loops exist when using that route.

5. How do OSPF and EIGRP notice when a neighboring router fails?

Answer: D. OSPF and EIGRP both use Hello messages, but they use Hello messages unique to that routing protocol.

6. Which of the following network commands, following the command **router ospf 1**, tell this router to start using OSPF on interfaces whose IP addresses are 10.1.1.1, 10.1.100.1, and 10.1.120.1?

Answer: B, D. Answer D works because the wildcard mask matches all IP addresses that start with 10 and end with 1. Answer B also works, because it matches all interfaces in Class A network 10.0.0.0.

7. Which of the following network commands, following the command **router ospf 1**, tells this router to start using OSPF on interfaces whose IP addresses are 10.1.1.1, 10.1.100.1, and 10.1.120.1?

Answer: A

8. Which of the following commands list the OSPF neighbors off interface serial 0/0?

Answer: A, B, E

9. In the **show ip route** command, what code designation implies that a route was learned with EIGRP?

Answer: I

10.   Which of the following network commands, following the command **router eigrp 1**, tells this router to start using EIGRP on interfaces whose IP addresses are 10.1.1.1, 10.1.100.1, and 10.1.120.1?

Answer: A

Q&A

1.   Create a minimal configuration enabling IP on each interface on a 2600 series router (two serial, one Ethernet). The Network Information Center (NIC) assigns you network 192.168.1.0. Your boss says that you need, at most, 60 hosts per LAN subnet. You also have point-to-point links attached to the serial interfaces. When choosing the IP address values and subnet numbers, you decide to start with the lowest numerical values. Assume that point-to-point serial links will be attached to this router and that EIGRP is the routing protocol.

```
interface ethernet 0/0
ip address 192.168.1.65 255.255.255.192
interface serial 0/0
ip address 192.168.1.129 255.255.255.252
interface serial 0/1
ip address 192.168.1.133 255.255.255.252

router eigrp 1
network 192.168.1.0
```

Answer: Several correct answers are possible. Be sure to use a mask of 255.255.255.252 on the serial links and 255.255.255.192 on the LAN interface. Also be sure to configure EIGRP just like the answer shown here, although you can use a number other than 1 for the autonomous system number. Also, this solution avoids using the zero subnet.

2.   Write down the steps you would take to migrate from RIP to OSPF in a router whose current RIP configuration includes only **router rip** followed by a **network 10.0.0.0** command. Assume a single OSPF area, and use as few **network** commands as possible.

Answer: Issue the following commands in configuration mode:

```
router ospf 5
network 10.0.0.0 0.255.255.255 area 0
no router rip
```

3.   Create a configuration for EIGRP on a router with these interfaces and addresses: e0 using 10.1.1.1, e1 using 224.1.2.3, s0 using 10.1.2.1, and s1 using 199.1.1.1. Use AS 5.

```
router eigrp 5
network 10.0.0.0
network 199.1.1.0
```

Answer: If you noticed that 224.1.2.3 is not a valid Class A, B, or C address, you get full credit. A new address is needed for Ethernet1, with a matching network command.

4. Create a configuration for EIGRP on a router with these interfaces and addresses: e0 using 200.1.1.1, e1 using 128.1.3.2, s0 using 192.0.1.1, and s1 using 223.254.254.1.

```
router eigrp 1
network 200.1.1.0
network 128.1.0.0
network 192.0.1.0
network 223.254.254.0
```

Answer: Because four different networks are used, four network commands are required. If you noticed that this question does not specify the AS number (1 in this example) but configures one, you get full credit. A few of these network numbers are used in examples; memorize the range of valid Class A, B, and C network numbers.

5. From a router's user mode, without using debugs or privileged mode, how can you determine what routers are sending you EIGRP routing updates?

Answer: The show ip protocol command output lists the routing sources—the IP addresses of routers sending updates to this router. Knowing how to determine a fact without looking at the configuration will better prepare you for the exam. Also, the show ip route command lists next-hop router IP addresses. The next-hop routers listed identify the routers that are sending routing updates. The show ip eigrp neighbor and show ip ospf interface commands also list neighbors that by definition send routing updates.

6. If the command **router eigrp 1,** followed by **network 10.0.0.0,** with no other network commands, is configured in a router that has an Ethernet0 interface with IP address 168.10.1.1, does EIGRP send updates out Ethernet0?

Answer: No. There must be a network statement for network 168.10.0.0 before EIGRP advertises out that interface. The network command simply selects the connected interfaces on which to send and receive updates.

7. If the command **router ospf 1,** followed by **network 10.0.0.0 0.255.255.255 area 0,** with no other network commands, is configured in a router that has an Ethernet0 interface with IP address 10.10.1.1, does OSPF send updates out Ethernet0?

Answer: Not necessarily. OSPF must discover other OSPF neighbors on the interface before it advertises routing information (LSAs.)

8. If the commands **router eigrp 1** and **network 10.0.0.0** are configured in a router that has an Ethernet0 interface with IP address 168.10.1.1, mask 255.255.255.0, does this router have a route to 168.10.1.0?

Answer: Yes. The route is in the routing table because it is a directly connected subnet, not because of any action by EIGRP.

9. Which command lists all IP routes learned via OSPF?

   Answer: The show ip route ospf command lists only OSPF-learned routes.

10. Compare and contrast the type of information exchanged in routing updates sent by distance vector routing protocols versus link-state protocols.

    Answer: Distance vector protocols advertise subnets and their associated metric values. Link-state protocols advertise information about routers and subnets, or links, in the network, along with metric information for the links. Link-state protocols describe the full topology in the network. As a result, link-state routing information is much more detailed than distance vector protocols.

11. Define balanced hybrid, and give an example of a balanced hybrid protocol.

    Answer: Cisco uses the term balanced hybrid to describe a class of routing protocols that have some distance vector characteristics and some link-state characteristics. Currently, only EIGRP falls into this category.

12. Describe how balanced hybrid protocols differ from distance vector protocols in terms of how a router notices that a neighboring router has failed.

    Answer: Distance vector routing protocols rely on regular full routing updates from each neighboring router. If a router fails to receive those updates for a period of time, the router that fails to receive the updates assumes that the other router has failed. Balanced hybrid protocols do not send full updates regularly; instead, they send periodic Hello messages. If Hello messages are not received for some timeout period, the router that is no longer receiving the updates assumes that the other router has failed.

13. List the distance vector loop-avoidance features used by OSPF, such as split horizon.

    Answer: OSPF, as a link-state routing protocol, does not need to use any of the distance vector loop-avoidance features. Loop avoidance is effectively built into the routing protocol.

14. List two OSPF features that help decrease the size of the OSPF topology database.

    Answer: If you use multiple OSPF areas, the size of the database in routers that are not ABRs decreases. Also, by using some stub area type, you can reduce the size of the topology database even further.

15. Assume that you must choose between OSPF and EIGRP for a routing protocol in a new network you are building. List and explain the most compelling reason to choose OSPF and the most compelling reason to choose EIGRP.

Answer: OSPF converges fast, like EIGRP, but it is an open standard, unlike EIGRP. Therefore, OSPF would more easily allow routers from multiple vendors to be used. EIGRP converges quickly, like OSPF, but requires little or no engineering design, whereas OSPF requires significant engineering design effort in larger networks.

Chapter 7

"Do I Know This Already?" Quiz

1. Which of the following summarized subnets is the smallest summary route that includes subnets 10.1.55.0, 10.1.56.0, and 10.1.57.0, mask 255.255.255.0?

   Answer: D

2. Which of the following summarized subnets is not a valid summary that includes subnets 10.1.55.0, 10.1.56.0, and 10.1.57.0, mask 255.255.255.0?

   Answer: C. You can check your answer by deriving the range of valid IP addresses for each subnet shown, as compared with the range of valid IP addresses in the three subnets stated in the question.

3. What does the acronym VLSM stand for?

   Answer: A

4. Imagine a router that lists three routes to subnets in network 10.0.0.0. Assume that VLSM is in use. How many times does the **show ip route** command list mask/prefix information about routes in network 10.0.0.0?

   Answer: C. When VLSM is used, the mask information is listed beside each route, because each route can have a different mask associated with it.

5. Which routing protocol(s) perform(s) autosummarization by default?

   Answer: A, B, C. Of these routing protocols, only EIGRP allows autosummarization to be disabled.

6. Which of the following routing protocols are classless?

   Answer: C, D

7. Which of the following is affected by whether a router is performing classful or classless routing?

   Answer: A. Classless routing always matches a default route if one exists. Classful routing matches a default route only if the destination Class A, B, or C network is not in the routing table.

8. Which of the following routing protocols support route summarization?

   Answer: C, D. RIP-1 and IGRP perform autosummarization. If you chose A and B as well, but you know that they support only autosummarization, give yourself credit for a right answer!

Q&A

1. Name the two commands typically used to create a default route for a router.

   Answer: The ip default-network command and the ip route 0.0.0.0 0.0.0.0 commands accomplish the goal of having the router use a known route as the default for packets that are not matched in the routing table. The ip route 0.0.0.0 0.0.0.0 command uses the fact that network 0.0.0.0 is used by Cisco IOS software to represent the default network.

2. Assume that subnets of network 10.0.0.0 are in the IP routing table in a router but that no other network and subnets are known, except that there is also a default route (0.0.0.0) in the routing table. A packet destined for 192.1.1.1 arrives at the router. What configuration command determines whether the default route is used in this case?

   Answer: The packet is routed using the default route, regardless of other configuration commands. In this scenario, in which the Class A, B, or C network is known, there is no match for the destination in the known subnets, and a default exists, so the default must be used.

3. Assume that subnets of network 10.0.0.0 are in the IP routing table in a router but that no other network and its subnets are known, except that there is also a default route (0.0.0.0) in the routing table. A packet destined for 10.1.1.1 arrives at the router, but no known subnet of network 10 matches this destination address. What configuration command determines whether the default route is used in this case?

   Answer: If the command ip classless is configured, the packet is routed using the default route. If no ip classless is configured, the packet is discarded.

4. What feature supported by EIGRP allows it to support VLSM?

   Answer: The association and transmission of mask information with each route allows VLSM support with any routing protocol.

5. List the interior IP routing protocols that have autosummarization enabled by default. Which of these protocols allow autosummarization to be disabled using a configuration command?

   Answer: RIP-1, IGRP, EIGRP, and RIP-2 all have autosummarization enabled by default. EIGRP and RIP-2 can disable this feature.

6. Which interior IP routing protocols support route summarization?

   Answer: EIGRP, OSPF, IS-IS, and RIP-2 support route summarization. (Give yourself credit on this question if you included OSPF and EIGRP.)

7. Assume that several subnets of network 172.16.0.0 exist in a router's routing table. What must be true about these routes for the output of the **show ip route** command to list mask information only on the line that lists network 172.16.0.0 but that doesn't show mask information on each route for each subnet?

   Answer: If all the subnets of 172.16.0.0 use the same mask, the output of the show ip route command lists only the mask in the heading line for the network. If VLSM were in use, each route for each subnet would reflect the mask used in that case.

8. Router A and Router B are connected via a point-to-point serial link. Router A's interfaces use IP address 172.16.1.1, mask 255.255.255.0 and address 172.16.2.1, mask 255.255.255.0. Router B's interfaces use address 172.16.2.2, mask 255.255.255.0 and address 10.1.1.1, mask 255.255.254.0. Is VLSM in use? Explain your answer.

   Answer: Although two different masks are used, VLSM is not used. VLSM implies that two different masks are in use in the same Class A, B, or C network. In this example, only one mask is used for each classful network.

9. What is the smallest summarized route that summarizes the subnets 10.1.63.0, 10.1.64.0, 10.1.70.0, and 10.1.71.0, all with mask 255.255.255.0?

   Answer: Only the first 17 bits of these subnet numbers are in common. Therefore, the smallest summary is 10.1.0.0, mask 255.255.128.0.

10. What is the smallest summarized route that summarizes the subnets 10.5.111.0, 10.5.112.0, 10.5.113.0, and 10.5.114.0, all with mask 255.255.255.0?

    Answer: The first 19 bits of these subnet numbers are in common. Therefore, the smallest summary is 10.5.96.0, mask 255.255.224.0.

11. What is the smallest summarized route that summarizes the subnets 10.5.110.32, 10.5.110.48, and 10.5.110.64, all with mask 255.255.255.248?

    Answer: The first 25 bits of these subnet numbers are in common. Therefore, the smallest summary is 10.5.110.0, mask 255.255.255.128.

12. Of the routing protocols RIP-1, IGRP, EIGRP, and OSPF, which are classless?

    Answer: EIGRP and OSPF

13. Of the routing protocols RIP-1, IGRP, EIGRP, and OSPF, which support VLSM?

    Answer: EIGRP and OSPF

14. Of the routing protocols RIP-1, IGRP, EIGRP, and OSPF, which advertise mask information along with subnet numbers?

    Answer: EIGRP and OSPF

15. Of the terms classful routing, classful routing protocol, classless routing, and classless routing protocol, which describe a feature that affects when a router uses the default route?

    Answer: Classful routing and classless routing define rules by which a router chooses whether to use the default route.

16. What allows for the successful use of a discontiguous Class A, B, or C IP network—classful routing, classful routing protocol, classless routing, or classless routing protocol?

    Answer: Whether a routing protocol is or is not classless defines whether it can support discontiguous networks. Only a classless routing protocol supports discontiguous networks.

17. Compare and contrast route summarization and autosummarization.

    Answer: Route summarization allows an engineer to choose a summary route to configure, advertising the summary as opposed to the more specific routes. Autosummarization summarizes only a Class A, B, or C network number, and only at the boundary between that network and another network.

18. Of the routing protocols RIP-1, IGRP, EIGRP, and OSPF, which use autosummarization by default and also cannot have autosummarization disabled?

    Answer: RIP-1 and IGRP

19.   What command switches a router from classless routing to classful routing?

Answer: The no ip classless global configuration command disables classless routing, thereby enabling classful routing.

Chapter 8

"Do I Know This Already?" Quiz

1.   What does CIDR stand for?

Answer: F

2.   Which of the following summarized subnets are valid routes according to the main purpose of CIDR?

Answer: D. CIDR's original intent was to allow the summarization of multiple Class A, B, and C networks to reduce the size of Internet routing tables. Only answer D summarizes multiple networks.

3.   Which of the following are not private addresses according to RFC 1918?

Answer: B, E. RFC 1918 identifies private network numbers. It includes Class A network 10.0.0.0, Class B networks 172.16.0.0 through 172.31.0.0, and 192.168.0.0 through 192.168.255.0.

4.   With static NAT, performing translation for inside addresses only, what causes NAT table entries to be created?

Answer: C. With static NAT, the entries are statically configured. Because the question mentions translation for inside addresses, the inside keyword is needed on the command.

5.   With dynamic NAT, performing translation for inside addresses only, what causes NAT table entries to be created?

Answer: A. With dynamic NAT, the entries are created as a result of the first packet flow from the inside network.

6.   Which of the following commands identifies the inside local IP addresses when using dynamic NAT to translate only the source addresses of packets from a private network number?

Answer: A. The list 1 parameter references an IP ACL, which matches packets, identifying the inside local addresses.

7. Which of the following commands identifies the outside local IP addresses when using dynamic NAT to translate only the source addresses of packets from a private network number?

   Answer: E. The outside local IP address is not changed when only the source address of packets from a private network are translated.

8. Imagine that an Ethernet interface on a router has already been configured with IP address 10.1.1.1, mask 255.255.255.0. Which of the following commands adds a secondary IP address to the interface?

   Answer: G. The ip address command is used, but with the secondary keyword at the end. Without the secondary keyword, the IP address would replace the original IP address.

9. Which of the following file transfer protocols, defined in various Internet RFCs, provides the most features?

   Answer: A. Only FTP and TFTP are file transfer protocols defined in RFCs. FTP is easily the more feature-filled protocol, as compared to TFTP.

10. Imagine that Fred is a PC attached to an Ethernet, and that its default router, R1, is attached to the same Ethernet. R1 has a point-to-point serial link to R2, which has an Ethernet attached, to which PC Barney is attached. The MTU of each Ethernet has the default value. What must be true for R1 to fragment packets sent from Fred to Barney?

    Answer: A. Ethernet interfaces default to an MTU of 1500. So the serial link would need an MTU lower than 1500 to cause fragmentation. Otherwise, R1 would never receive an IP packet from Fred that needed to be fragmented.

11. Router1 has a FastEthernet interface 0/0 with IP address 10.1.1.1. The interface is connected to a switch. This connection is then migrated to ISL. Which of the following commands could be useful to configure Router1 for ISL?

    Answer: A, G

12. What is the meaning of "." in the output of a ping command?

    Answer: C. The "." implies that the ping command sent the request, and waited, but did not receive a reply.

13. What is the meaning of "U" in the output of a **ping** command?

Answer: E. The "U" designation implies that the ping command received an ICMP unreachable message, which might mean that the router had no route to the subnet to which the packet was sent.

14. What ICMP message code(s) does the **trace** command rely on?

Answer: C. The trace command sends packets with TTL = 1, and then TTL = 2, and so on. By receiving TTL Exceeded messages from the various routers in the route, the trace command can identify the routers.

Q&A

1. Define private addressing as defined in RFC 1918.

Answer: Some hosts will never need to communicate with other hosts across the Internet. For such hosts, assigning IP addresses from registered networks wastes IP addresses. To conserve IP addresses, a set of network numbers, called private addresses, has been reserved and can be used in these cases to help conserve IP addresses for use over the Internet.

2. List the range of private networks defined in RFC 1918.

Answer: Class A network 10.0.0.0, Class B networks 172.16.0.0 to 172.31.0.0, and Class C networks 192.168.0.0 to 192.168.255.0.

3. Does CIDR affect the size of Internet routing tables? If so, what does it do to those routing tables?

Answer: CIDR allows ISPs to summarize multiple Class A, B, or C networks, typically Class C networks, into summary routes. It shortens the length of the IP routing table, improving Internet routing performance.

4. Define NAT and explain the basics of its operation.

Answer: Network Address Translation is a mechanism for allowing hosts with private addresses or addresses that conflict with IP addresses from a registered network to communicate with hosts over the Internet. The basic operation involves the NAT router's changing the IP addresses in packets to and from these hosts so that only legitimately registered IP addresses are used in flows through the Internet.

5. Define the term inside local address in relation to NAT. Use Figure A-2 to describe the answer.

Figure A-2   *Network for Use in Answering NAT Questions*

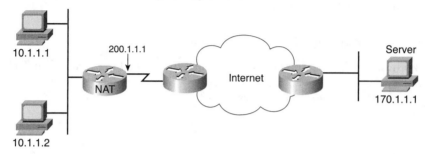

Answer: The inside network is the enterprise network on the left in Figure A-2. The private IP addresses reside in this network. Inside local refers to the IP address actually assigned to the computer. For instance, 10.1.1.1 is an inside local address in this figure.

6. Define the term inside global address in relation to NAT. Use Figure A-2 to describe the answer.

Answer: The inside network is the enterprise network on the left in Figure A-2. The inside global address is the address in the public Internet that represents the inside local address. 200.1.1.1 would be a likely candidate for an inside global IP address in this example.

7. Create a configuration for NAT overload to a single IP address for the router shown in Figure A-2.

Answer:

```
interface Ethernet0/0
 ip address 10.1.1.3 255.255.255.0
 ip nat inside
!
interface Serial0/0
 ip address 200.1.1.1 255.255.255.252
 ip nat outside
!
ip nat inside source list 1 interface Serial0/0 overload
!
access-list 1 permit 10.1.1.2
access-list 1 permit 10.1.1.1
```

8. Create a configuration for static NAT, mapping host 10.1.1.1 to 200.1.1.11, for the router shown in Figure A-2.

   Answer:

   ```
   interface Ethernet0/0
    ip address 10.1.1.3 255.255.255.0
    ip nat inside
   !
   interface Serial0/0
    ip address 200.1.1.1 255.255.255.252
    ip nat outside
   !
   ip nat inside source static 10.1.1.1 200.1.1.11
   ```

9. Which requires more lines of source code, FTP or TFTP? Explain your answer.

   Answer: FTP requires more code. TFTP was designed to be simple (that is, trivial). The small amount of memory needed to load its code is one of its advantages. FTP is much more robust, with many more features and code.

10. Does FTP or TFTP perform error recovery? If so, describe the basics of how this occurs.

    Answer: Both FTP and TFTP perform error recovery. FTP relies on TCP, whereas TFTP performs application layer recovery one block of data at a time.

11. Describe the process used by IP routers to perform fragmentation and reassembly of packets.

    Answer: When a packet must be forwarded, but the packet is larger than the maximum transmission unit (MTU) size for the outgoing interface, the router fragments the packet as long as the Don't Fragment bit is not set in the packet header. No IP router reassembles the fragments; fragments are reassembled at the final destination host.

12. How many Class B-style networks are reserved by RFC 1918 private addressing?

    Answer: Sixteen Class B networks are reserved for use as private networks in RFC 1918—networks 172.16.0.0 to 172.31.0.0.

13. Describe why ARP requests use an Ethernet broadcast address instead of an Ethernet unicast address.

    Answer: Hosts use ARP when they need to learn the MAC address of another IP host. Because the host does not know the MAC address, it would be impossible to use an Ethernet unicast, because the host would not know the right MAC address to put in the destination address field in the Ethernet frame.

14. Imagine that host 10.1.1.1 in Figure 8-21 sends a packet to the server at 170.1.1.1 and that the NAT router also happens to fragment the packet. Inside the context of this network, explain how reassembly of the fragments into the original packet occurs.

    Answer: The endpoint host for which the packets are destined always reassembles the fragments. In this case, host 170.1.1.1 reassembles the packet.

15. Imagine that R1 has an interface, FastEthernet 0/0, that uses ISL trunking to a switch. R1 needs to route between VLAN 1 and VLAN 2. Create a valid router configuration.

    Answer:
    ```
    interface fastethernet 0/0.1
    ip address 10.1.1.1 255.255.255.0
    encapsulation isl 1
    !
    interface fastethernet 0/0.2
    ip address 10.1.2.1 255.255.255.0
    encapsulation isl 2
    ```

16. Describe how NAT overload manages to support more than one inside local IP address using a single inside global address.

    Answer: NAT overload uses Port Address Translation (PAT) to essentially translate both the source address and port numbers for incoming inside packets. By allocating unique port numbers to be used with a single inside global IP address, NAT overload can make multiple sockets on multiple inside hosts appear to be multiple sockets, but from a single host, on the public part of the network.

Chapter 9

"Do I Know This Already?" Quiz

1. Which of the following types of WAN connections allow the direct use of PPP as the encapsulation type on the interface?

   Answer: A, C

2. Which of the following commands are required on the router connected to a DTE cable to make the serial link between two routers work when the two routers are connected in a lab using a DTE and DCE cable and no CSU/DSUs?

   Answer: E. None of these commands is needed at the DTE. The clock rate 56000 command, or one like it, is needed on the router with a DCE cable.

3. Which of the following commands make a serial interface revert to the default data-link protocol if it is currently configured with PPP?

   Answer: E, G. HDLC is the default setting.

4. Which of the following authentication protocols authenticates a device on the other end of a link without sending any password information in clear text?

   Answer: C. Of these answers, only PAP and CHAP are authentication protocols. PAP sends the password in clear text.

5. Imagine that two routers, R1 and R2, have a leased line between them. Each router had its configuration erased and was then reloaded. R1 was then configured with the following commands:

   ```
   interface s0/0
   encapsulation ppp
   ppp authentication chap
   ```

   Which of the following configuration commands can complete the configuration on R1 so that CHAP can work correctly? Assume that R2 has been configured correctly and that the password is fred.

   Answer: D. R1 needs to know the password associated with the router on the other end of the link—namely, R2.

6. Which of the following is a reason to avoid using link compression?

   Answer: C. "Reducing" available CPU cycles is an odd way to say that compression uses CPU in the router, which is one reason to choose not to perform compression.

7. Which of the following does PPP use as part of how it notices when a link has been looped, causing packets sent by a router to be returned to that router?

   Answer: B

8. Which of the following are protocols defined as part of PPP?

   Answer: B, D

Q&A

1. Define the terms DCE and DTE in the context of the physical layer and a point-to-point serial link.

   Answer: At the physical layer, DTE refers to the device that looks for clocking from the device on the other end of the cable on a link. The DCE supplies that clocking. For example, the computer is typically the DTE, and the modem or CSU/DSU is the DCE. At the data link layer, both X.25 and Frame Relay define a logical DTE and DCE. In this case, the customer premises equipment (CPE), such as a router and CSU/DSU, is the logical DTE, and the service provider equipment (the Frame Relay switch and CSU/DSU) is the DCE.

2. Identify the command used to set the clock rate on an interface in which a DCE cable has been inserted. Compare and contrast the two styles of the command that may be entered in configuration mode versus which style shows up in the configuration.

   Answer: The clock rate command and the clockrate command both set the rate at which an interface clocks over a serial DCE cable. When you ask for help while in interface configuration mode, the clock rate command is shown, but help does not list the clockrate command. However, after you issue the command, a show running-config lists the clockrate command under the interface, regardless of which of the two commands was entered in configuration mode.

3. Name one WAN data-link protocol used on point-to-point leased lines that defines a method of announcing the interface's IP addresses to other devices attached to the WAN.

   Answer: PPP uses an IP Control Protocol (IPCP) to announce, and sometimes assign, IP addresses to each end of the link.

4. Can PPP dynamically assign IP addresses? If so, is this feature always enabled?

   Answer: PPP's IPCP protocol can assign an IP address to the device on the other end of the link. This process is not required and is not performed by default. PPP usually does address assignment for dial access, such as when a user dials an Internet service provider.

5. Create a configuration to enable PPP on serial 0 for IP. Make up IP Layer 3 addresses as needed.

   ```
   interface serial 0
   ip addr 1.1.1.1 255.255.255.0
   encapsulation ppp
   ```

   Answer: encapsulation ppp is all that is needed for PPP.

6. Define the terms PAP and CHAP. Which one sends passwords in clear-text format?

   Answer: PAP stands for Password Authentication Protocol. CHAP stands for Challenge Handshake Authentication Protocol. PAP sends passwords as simple text, whereas CHAP uses MD5 hashing to protect the password contents.

7. CHAP configuration uses names and passwords. Given Routers A and B, describe what names and passwords must match in the respective CHAP configurations.

   Answer: Router A has name B and a corresponding password configured. Router B has name A and the same password configured. The names used are the host names of the routers unless the CHAP name is configured.

8. What field has Cisco added to the HDLC header, making it proprietary?

Answer: A Protocol Type field has been added to allow support for multiprotocol traffic. HDLC was not originally designed to allow for multiprotocol support.

9. List the types of packet switching mentioned in this chapter. Identify the one for which all traffic is segmented into smaller pieces.

Answer: Frame Relay, X.25, and ATM were all mentioned as packet switching services. ATM, also called cell switching, segments all traffic into 53-byte cells before transmission and reassembles the cells into the original frame after they are through the WAN.

10. Two-wire leased circuits are seldom used today, and certainly not between two routers. What problem was solved with the advent of four-wire leased circuits versus two-wire?

Answer: Two-wire leased lines could be used as each single pair, for transmission in only one direction at a time. With a four-wire circuit, each pair could be used for transmission in a different direction, allowing full-duplex data transmission.

11. Define synchronous in relation to leased lines.

Answer: The imposition of time ordering on a bit stream. Practically speaking, a device tries to use the same speed as another device on the other end of a serial link. However, by examining transitions between voltage states on the link, the device can notice slight variations in the speed on each end and can adjust its speed accordingly.

12. Create a CHAP configuration between two routers. Make up specific details as needed.

Answer: Your configuration will probably be a little different from the one shown here. To be correct, you need the username global commands that refer to the other router's host name, with correct case and the same password on each side. PPP must be enabled on each serial link, and ppp authentication chap must be on each interface.

```
Router Fred                          Router Barney

username Barney password Bedrock     username Fred password Bedrock
!                                    !
interface serial 0                   interface serial 0
encapsulation ppp                    encapsulation ppp
ppp authentication chap              ppp authentication chap
.                                    .
```

Chapter 10

"Do I Know This Already?" Quiz

1. How fast do the D channels run on a BRI and PRI, respectively?

   Answer: E

2. Which of the following protocols defines call setup signaling for ISDN?

   Answer: E

3. Which of the following reference points are used by ISDN BRI interfaces in a Cisco router?

   Answer: C, D. The router can use a serial interface with the R reference point, but the question asks about ISDN interfaces in the router.

4. Which of the following PRI function groups is appropriate for use with a PC with a simple serial interface?

   Answer: E. BRIs support different reference points and function groups, but PRIs do not.

5. Which of the following encoding formats could be used on a PRI in North America?

   Answer: A, B. In North America, PRIs are based on T1 circuits, which support either AMI or B8ZS encoding.

6. Assume that a router has an IP ACL numbered 109 that permits traffic going to IP address 10.1.1.1. Which of the following commands correctly refers to the ACL, causing traffic sent to IP address 10.1.1.1 to be considered "interesting"?

   Answer: E. The dialer-list global command first refers to all IP traffic and then can optionally refer to an IP ACL to further refine the set of IP traffic that DDR considers "interesting."

7. Which of the following could be necessary in a configuration that uses DDR and ISDN BRI interfaces?

   Answer: A, D. ISDN configuration requires the switch type in most cases. SPIDs are needed only when the service provider's switches expect to use the SPIDs as a basic authentication mechanism. Because there is only one option each for BRI encoding and framing, you never need to configure them.

8. Which of the following could be necessary in a configuration that uses DDR and ISDN PRI interfaces in North America?

Answer: A, B, C, E. ISDN configuration requires the switch type in most cases. For PRI, you have two choices for encoding and framing. You also need to tell the router which DS0 channels will be used in the PRI.

9. When you configure DDR using the style of DDR configuration called dialer profiles, which of the following commands are useful on the dialer interface?

Answer: D. The encapsulation must be on the physical interfaces as well, but it is also needed on the dialer interface.

10. Which of the following interface subcommands enables multilink PPP?

Answer: A

Q&A

1. What does LAPD stand for? Is it used as the Layer 2 protocol on dialed ISDN bearer channels? If not, what is?

Answer: LAPD stands for Link Access Procedure on the D channel. LAPD is used not on bearer channels but on the signaling channel. PPP is typically used on bearer channels.

2. What do ISDN, BRI, and PRI stand for?

Answer: ISDN stands for Integrated Services Digital Network. BRI stands for Basic Rate Interface. PRI stands for Primary Rate Interface.

3. Define function group. List two examples of function groups.

Answer: A function group is a set of ISDN functions that a device implements. NT1, NT2, TE1, TE2, and TA are all function groups.

4. Define the term reference point. Give two examples of reference points.

Answer: A reference point is an interface between function groups. R, S, T, and U are reference points. S and T are combined in many cases and are then called the S/T reference point. Reference points refer to cabling, which implies the number of wires used. In particular, the S and T points use a four-wire interface, and the U interface uses a two-wire cable.

5. How many bearer channels are in a BRI? What about a PRI in North America? What about a PRI in Europe?

   Answer: BRI uses two bearer channels and one signaling channel (2B+D). PRI uses 23B+D in North America and 30B+D in Europe. The signaling channel on BRI is a 16-kbps channel; on PRI, it is a 64-kbps channel.

6. True or false: ISDN defines protocols that can be functionally equivalent to OSI Layers 1, 2, and 3. Explain your answer.

   Answer: True. Reference points in part define the physical interfaces. Used on the signaling channel, LAPD is a data-link protocol. SPIDs define a logical addressing structure and are roughly equivalent to OSI Layer 3.

7. What reference points do ISDN BRI interfaces on Cisco routers use?

   Answer: A BRI interface with an S/T reference point, or a BRI with a U reference point, can be bought from Cisco. With an S/T interface, an external NT1, NT2, or NT1/NT2 device is required. With the U interface, no external device is required.

8. Is LAPD used on ISDN channels? If so, which ones?

   Answer: LAPD is used only on ISDN D channels to deliver signaling messages to the local ISDN switch. Many people don't understand the function of LAPD, thinking it is used on the B channels after the dial is complete. The encapsulation chosen in the router configuration determines the data-link protocol on the bearer channels. Cisco routers do not have an option to turn off LAPD on the signaling channel.

9. What standards body defines ISDN protocols?

   Answer: The International Telecommunications Union (ITU) defines ISDN protocols. This group was formerly called CCITT.

10. What ISDN functions do standards ITU-T Q.920 and Q.930 define? Does either standard correlate to an OSI layer?

    Answer: Q.920 defines ISDN data-link specifications, such as LAPD; Q.930 defines Layer 3 functions, such as call setup messages. I.440 and I.450 are equivalent to Q.920 and Q.930, respectively.

11. What ISDN functions does standard ITU-T I.430 define? Does it correlate to an OSI layer?

    Answer: I.430 defines ISDN BRI physical layer specifications. It is similar to OSI Layer 1. I.430 has no Q-series equivalent specification.

12. What does SPID stand for? What does it mean?

Answer: SPID stands for service profile identifier. An optional feature, it is used for basic authentication between the telco switch and the device on the other end of the line, such as a router.

13. Define TE1, TE2, and TA. Which implies that one of the other two must be in use?

Answer: TE1 stands for Terminal Equipment 1. TE2 stands for Terminal Equipment 2. TA stands for terminal adapter. A TE2 device requires a TA. A TE2 uses the R reference point. An S reference point is needed to perform ISDN signaling. It is provided in that case by the TA.

14. How many B channels are there on a PRI in countries where the PRI is based on a T1? On an E1?

Answer: There are 23 B channels on a PRI in countries where the PRI is based on a T1. There are 30 B channels on a PRI in countries where the PRI is based on an E1.

15. What reference point is used between the customer premises and the phone company in North America? What about in Europe?

Answer: The U interface is used in North America. Elsewhere, the T interface is used. The NT1 function, the dividing point between the T and U reference points, is implemented in telco equipment outside North America.

16. What problem does multilink PPP solve when multiple B channels have circuits set up between a pair of routers?

Answer: MLP balances the traffic across multiple links efficiently, distributing the traffic evenly across the multiple links. Without MLP, the routers would let the routing process balance the traffic, which typically does not result in even balancing across the links.

17. What is the syntax of an **interface** command used to configure the encapsulation, IP address, and DDR parameters on a PRI in North America? What is the significance of entering a colon and a number after entering the interface number?

Answer: The interface serial 0/0:23 command places you in interface configuration mode for a PRI's D channel. The D channel is where you place the interface configuration commands for DDR. The :23 identifies the last DS0 channel in the PRI. The numbering of the channels in the interface command starts at 0, so the 24th channel is number 23.

18. What data-link (OSI Layer 2) protocols are valid on an ISDN B channel?

Answer: HDLC, PPP, and LAPB are all valid options. PPP is the preferred choice, however. If you're using DDR to more than one site, PAP or CHAP authentication is required. If it is used, PPP must also be used. PPP also provides automatic IP address assignment, which is convenient for PC dial-in.

19. Define MLPPP. Describe the typical home or small office use of MLPPP.

Answer: MLPPP stands for Multilink Point-to-Point Protocol. It is used to treat multiple B channels as a single link, because MLPPP fragments packets and sends different fragments across the multiple links to balance the traffic. MLPPP is very useful for sharing two B channels in a home or small office. so that you can increase and use the available bandwidth.

20. Configure ISDN interface BRI1, assuming that it is attached to a DMS-100 ISDN switch and that it uses only one SPID of 404555121201.

Answer:

```
isdn switch-type basic-dms100
interface bri1
  isdn spid1 404555121201
```
The switch-type command is required. SPIDs are required with only some switches.

21. Describe the decision process performed by the Cisco IOS software to attempt to dial a connection using Legacy DDR.

Answer: First, some traffic must be routed out the interface to be dialed; this is typically accomplished by adding static routes pointing out the interface. Then, "interesting" traffic must be defined; any packets routed out the interface that are considered interesting cause the interface to be dialed.

22. If packets from 10.1.1.0/24 are "interesting" in relation to DDR configuration, such that packets from 10.1.1.0/24 cause a DDR connection out interface BRI0, list the configuration commands that make the Cisco IOS software think that those packets are interesting on BRI0. (If you have not yet studied access lists, you may simply note what kind of packets you would match with an access list, rather than writing down the full syntax.)

Answer: The following access list defines the packets from 10.1.1.0/24. The dialer-list command defines the use of access-list 1 to decide what is interesting. The dialer-group command enables that logic on interface BRI0.

```
access-list 1 permit 10.1.1.0 0.0.0.255
!
dialer-list 2 protocol ip list 1
!
interface bri 0
 dialer-group 2
```

23. Router R1 has two BRI interfaces. Configure a dialer profile such that R1 can dial any of six different remote routers using any of the B channels on either BRI. Assume that all traffic is interesting. You may ignore the static route commands needed to send the packets out the correct interface. Do not use any SPIDs, and do not use CHAP. For other parameters not listed, you can make up values.

Answer:

```
dialer-list 2 protocol ip permit
!
interface dialer 0
 encapsulation ppp
dialer map ip 172.16.2.1 broadcast 15551111111
dialer map ip 172.16.2.2 broadcast 15552222222
dialer map ip 172.16.2.3 broadcast 15553333333
dialer map ip 172.16.2.4 broadcast 15554444444
dialer map ip 172.16.2.5 broadcast 15555555555
dialer map ip 172.16.2.6 broadcast 15556666666
dialer-group 2
dialer pool 3
!
interface bri0
encapsulation ppp
dialer pool-member 3
!
interface bri1
encapsulation ppp
dialer pool-member 3
```

Chapter 11

"Do I Know This Already?" Quiz

1. Which of the following defines a protocol used between the Frame Relay DTE and the Frame Relay switch in the service provider's network?

   Answer: C. The LMI manages the link between the DTE and the switch, including noticing when a VC comes up or goes down.

2. Which of the following defines a protocol or feature that matters to what the provider might do inside its network but that is transparent to the DTE/router using the Frame Relay service?

   Answer: F. FRF.5 service interworking defines how a provider can use an ATM network between the Frame Relay switches. The routers outside the Frame Relay cloud cannot tell, and do not care, if FRF.5 is used or not.

3. What does DLCI stand for?

   Answer: A

4. Imagine two Cisco routers, R1 and R2, using a Frame Relay service. R1 connects to a switch that uses LMI type ANSI T1.617, and R2 connects to a switch that uses ITU Q.933a. What can R1 and R2 configure for the LMIs to work correctly?

    Answer: C, F. The correct keywords are in answer C. However, the routers autodetect the LMI type by default, so not bothering to configure the LMI also works.

5. FredCo has five sites, with routers connected to the same Frame Relay network. Virtual circuits (VCs) have been defined between each pair of routers. What is the fewest subnets that FredCo could use on the Frame Relay network?

    Answer: A. A single subnet can be used in any Frame Relay topology, but with a full mesh, a single subnet can be used with no tricky issues related to routing protocols.

6. BarneyCo has five sites, with routers connected to the same Frame Relay network. VCs have been defined between each pair of routers. Barney, the president of the company, will fire anyone who configures Frame Relay without using point-to-point subinterfaces. What is the fewest subnets that BarneyCo could use on the Frame Relay network?

    Answer: D. BarneyCo has a total of ten VCs. With all of them configured on point-to-point subinterfaces, you need ten subnets, because you need one subnet per VC.

7. BettyCo has five sites, with routers connected to the same Frame Relay network. VCs have been defined between each pair of routers. Betty, the president of the company, will fire anyone who configures anything that could just as easily be left as a default. Which of the following configuration commands, configured for the Frame Relay network, would get the engineer fired?

    Answer: C, D, E. The lmi-type defaults to autodetect, which works fine. inverse-arp is on by default on the physical interface, so there is no need to turn it on (answer E), and there is no need for static maps (answer D).

8. WilmaCo has some routers connected to a Frame Relay network. R1 is a router at a remote site, with a single VC back to WilmaCo's headquarters. The R1 configuration currently looks like this:

    ```
    interface serial 0/0
     ip address 10.1.1.1 255.255.255.0
     encapsulation frame-relay
    ```

    Wilma, the president, has heard that point-to-point subinterfaces are cool, and she wants you to change the configuration to use a point-to-point subinterface. Which of the following commands do you need to use to migrate the configuration?

    Answer: A, E. The IP address moves to the subinterface, so it needs to be removed from the serial interface first (answer A). The encapsulation stays on the physical interface. The frame-relay interface-dlci command must be used on the subinterface so that the router knows which DLCI goes with which subinterface—even if only one DLCI exists.

9. WilmaCo has another network, with a main site router that has ten VCs connecting to the ten remote sites. Wilma now thinks that multipoint subinterfaces are even cooler than point-to-point. The current main site router's configuration looks like this:

```
interface serial 0/0
  ip address 172.16.1.1 255.255.255.0
  encapsulation frame-relay
```

Wilma wants you to change the configuration to use a multipoint subinterface. Which of the following do you need to use to migrate the configuration? (Note: DLCIs 101 through 110 are used for the ten VCs.)

Answer: F. You can code DLCI only on a frame-relay interface-dlci command, and you need one for each VC under the multipoint interface.

10. Which of the following commands lists the information learned by Inverse ARP?

Answer: F

Q&A

1. What two WAN data-link protocols define a method of announcing the interface's Layer 3 addresses to other devices attached to the WAN?

Answer: PPP and Frame Relay. PPP uses control protocols specific to each Layer 3 protocol supported. Frame Relay uses Inverse ARP.

2. Explain the purpose of Inverse ARP, as well as how it uses Frame Relay broadcasts.

Answer: A router discovers the Layer 3 address(es) of a router on the other end of a VC when that other router sends an Inverse ARP message. The message is not a broadcast.

3. Would a Frame Relay switch connected to a router behave differently if the IETF option were deleted from the **encapsulation frame-relay ietf** command on that attached router? Would a router on the other end of the VC behave any differently if the same change were made?

Answer: The switch does not behave differently. The other router, however, must also use IETF encapsulation. Otherwise, the routers will not look at the correct fields to learn the packet type.

4. What does NBMA stand for? Does it apply to X.25 networks or Frame Relay networks?

Answer: NBMA stands for nonbroadcast multiaccess. X.25 and Frame Relay are NBMA networks. Multiaccess really means that more than two devices are connected to the data link, because many other devices may be reached by a single device. For instance, Router1 might have a PVC to Router2 and Router3, making it multiaccess.

5. Which layer or layers of OSI are most closely related to the functions of Frame Relay? Why?

   Answer: OSI Layers 1 and 2 are most closely related to the functions of Frame Relay. Frame Relay refers to well-known physical layer specifications. Frame Relay defines headers for delivery across the Frame Relay cloud, but it provides no addressing structure to allow VCs among many different Frame Relay networks. Thus, it is not considered to match OSI Layer 3 functions. With the advent of Frame Relay SVCs, it could be argued that Frame Relay performs some Layer 3-like functions.

6. When Inverse ARP is used by default, what additional configuration is needed to get IGRP routing updates to flow over each VC, assuming IGRP has already been configured correctly?

   Answer: No additional configuration is required. The forwarding of broadcasts as unicasts can be enabled on each VC and protocol for which Inverse ARP is received.

7. Define the attributes of a partial-mesh and full-mesh Frame Relay network.

   Answer: In a partial-mesh network, not all DTEs are directly connected with a VC. In a full-mesh network, all DTEs are directly connected with a VC.

8. What key pieces of information are required in the **frame-relay map** statement?

   Answer: The pieces of information required are the Layer 3 protocol, the next-hop router's Layer 3 address, the DLCI to reach that router, and whether to forward broadcasts. Frame Relay maps are not required if Inverse ARP is in use.

9. Create a configuration for Router1 that has Frame Relay VCs to Router2 and Router3 (DLCIs 202 and 203, respectively) on Router1's Serial1 interface. Use any IP addresses you like. Assume that the network is not fully meshed.

   Answer:
   ```
   interface serial 1
   encapsulation frame-relay
   interface serial 1.1 point-to-point
   ip address 168.10.1.1 255.255.255.0
   frame-relay interface-dlci 202
   interface serial 1.2 point-to-point
   ip address 168.10.2.1 255.255.255.0
   frame-relay interface-dlci 203
   ```

   This is not the only valid configuration given the problem statement. However, because there is not a full mesh, point-to-point subinterfaces are the best choice. Cisco encapsulation is used by default. The LMI type is autosensed.

10. What **show** command tells you when a PVC became active? How does the router know what time the PVC became active?

    Answer: The show frame-relay pvc command lists the time since the PVC came up. You can subtract this time from the current time to derive the time at which the VC came up. The router learns about when PVCs come up and go down from LMI messages.

11. What **show** command lists Frame Relay information about mapping? In what instances does the information displayed include the Layer 3 addresses of other routers?

    Answer: show frame-relay map lists Frame Relay information about mapping. The mapping information includes Layer 3 addresses when multipoint subinterfaces are used or when no subinterfaces are used. The two cases in which the neighboring routers' Layer 3 addresses are shown are the two cases in which Frame Relay acts like a multiaccess network. With point-to-point subinterfaces, the logic works like a point-to-point link, in which the next router's Layer 3 address is unimportant to the routing process.

12. True or false: The **no keepalive** command on a Frame Relay serial interface causes no further Cisco-proprietary keepalive messages to be sent to the Frame Relay switch.

    Answer: False. This command stops LMI status inquiry messages from being sent. They are defined in Frame Relay Forum standards. Cisco sends proprietary keepalive messages on point-to-point serial and LAN interfaces.

13. What **debug** option shows Inverse ARP messages?

    Answer: debug frame-relay events shows Inverse ARP messages, as shown in Example 11-18.

14. True or false: The Frame Relay **map** configuration command allows more than one Layer 3 protocol address mapping on the same configuration command.

    Answer: False. The syntax allows only a single network layer protocol and address to be configured.

15. What is the name of the field that identifies, or addresses, a Frame Relay virtual circuit?

    Answer: The data-link connection identifier (DLCI) is used to identify a VC. The number may be different on either side of the VC.

16. Describe the difference between FRF.5 and FRF.8 service interworking.

    Answer: FRF.5 defines how Frame Relay switches can use an ATM VC between each other inside a service provider's network. FRF.8 defines how two DTEs, like routers, can communicate with one router using a Frame Relay VC and the other router using an ATM VC. With FRF.5, the endpoint DTEs both connect to a Frame Relay cloud. With FRF.8, one DTE is directly connected to an ATM network.

Chapter 12

"Do I Know This Already?" Quiz

1. Barney is a host with IP address 10.1.1.1 in subnet 10.1.1.0/24. Which of the following are things that a standard IP ACL could be configured to do?

   Answer: A, C. Standard ACLs check the source IP address. Option B is not possible with a single command. You would need multiple commands to match that set of IP addresses.

2. Which of the following fields cannot be compared based on an extended IP ACL?

   Answer: E, F. Named extended ACLs can look for the same fields.

3. Which of the following fields can be compared using a named IP ACL but not a numbered extended IP ACL?

   Answer: H. Named extended IP ACLs can match the exact same set of fields, as can numbered extended IP ACLs.

4. Which of the following wildcard masks is most useful for matching all IP packets in subnet 10.1.128.0, mask 255.255.255.0?

   Answer: D. 0.0.0.255 matches all packets that have the same first three octets. This is useful when you want to match a subnet in which the subnet part comprises the first three octets, as in this case.

5. Which of the following wildcard masks is most useful for matching all IP packets in subnet 10.1.128.0, mask 255.255.240.0?

   Answer: E. 0.0.15.255 matches all packets with the same first 20 bits. This is useful when you want to match a subnet in which the subnet part comprises the first 20 bits, as in this case.

6. Which of the following **access-list** commands permit traffic that matches packets going to a web server from 10.1.1.1 for all web servers whose IP addresses begin with 172.16.5?

   Answer: A, E. The correct range of ACL numbers for extended IP access lists is 100 to 199 and 2000 to 2699.

7. Which of the following **access-list** commands permits traffic that matches packets going to a web client from all web servers whose IP addresses begin with 172.16.5?

    Answer: E. Because the packet is going toward a web client, you need to check for the web server's port number as a source port. The client IP address range is not specified in the question, but the servers are, so the source address beginning with 172.16.5 is the correct answer.

8. What general guideline should be followed when placing IP ACLs, at least according to the ICND course on which CCNA is based?

    Answer: C. Cisco makes this suggestion mainly for extended IP ACLs.

Q&A

1. Configure a numbered IP access list that stops packets from subnet 134.141.7.0 255.255.255.0 from exiting serial 0 on a router. Allow all other packets.

    ```
    access-list 4 deny 134.141.7.0 0.0.0.255
    access-list 4 permit any
    interface serial 0
    ip access-group 4 out
    ```

    Answer: The first access-list statement denies packets from that subnet. The other statement is needed because the default action to deny packets is not explicitly matched in an access-list statement.

2. Configure an IP access list that allows only packets from subnet 193.7.6.0 255.255.255.0, going to hosts in network 128.1.0.0 and using a web server in 128.1.0.0, to enter serial 0 on a router.

    ```
    access-list 105 permit tcp 193.7.6.0 0.0.0.255
      128.1.0.0 0.0.255.255 eq www
    !
    interface serial 0
    ip access-group 105 in
    ```

    Answer: A deny all is implied at the end of the list.

3. How would a user who does not have the enable password find out what access lists have been configured and where they are enabled?

    Answer: The show access-list command lists all access lists. The show ip interfaces command identify interfaces on which the access lists are enabled.

4. Configure and enable an IP access list that stops packets from subnet 10.3.4.0/24 from exiting serial interface S0 and that stops packets from 134.141.5.4 from entering S0. Permit all other traffic.

```
access-list 1 deny 10.3.4.0 0.0.0.255
access-list 1 permit any
access-list 2 deny host 134.141.5.4
access-list 2 permit any
interface serial 0
ip access-group 1 out
ip access-group 2 in
```

5. Configure and enable an IP access list that allows packets from subnet 10.3.4.0/24, to any web server, to exit serial interface S0. Also allow packets from 134.141.5.4 going to all TCP-based servers using a well-known port to enter serial 0. Deny all other traffic.

```
access-list 101 permit tcp 10.3.4.0 0.0.0.255 any eq www
access-list 102 permit tcp host 134.141.5.4 any lt 1023
interface serial 0
ip access-group 101 out
ip access-group 102 in
```

Answer: Two extended access lists are required. List 101 permits packets in the first of the two criteria, in which packets exiting S0 are examined. List 102 permits packets for the second criterion, in which packets entering S0 are examined.

6. Can standard IP access lists be used to check the source IP address when enabled with the **ip access-group 1 in** command, and can they check the destination IP addresses when using the **ip access-group 1 out** command?

Answer: No. Standard IP access lists check only the source IP address, regardless of whether the packets are checked when inbound or outbound.

7. True or false: If all IP **access-list** statements in a particular list define the deny action, the default action is to permit all other packets.

Answer: False. The default action at the end of any IP access list is to deny all other packets.

8. How many IP access lists of either type can be active on an interface at the same time?

Answer: Only one IP access list per interface, per direction, can be active. In other words, one inbound and one outbound are allowed, but no more.

For questions 9 through 11, assume that all parts of the network shown in Figure A-3 are up and working. IGRP is the IP routing protocol in use. Answer the questions following Example A-1, which contains an additional configuration in the Mayberry router.

Figure A-3   *Network Diagram for Questions 9 Through 11*

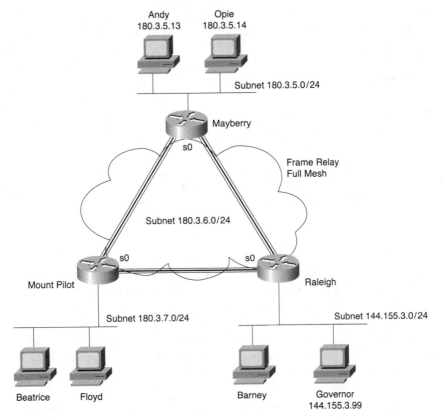

Example A-1   *Access List at Mayberry*

```
access-list 44 permit 180.3.5.13 0.0.0.0
!
interface serial 0
ip access-group 44 out
```

9. Describe the types of packets that this filter discards, and specify at what point they are discarded.

   Answer: Only packets coming from Andy exit Mayberry's serial 0 interface. Packets originating inside the Mayberry router—such as a ping command issued from Mayberry—work because the Cisco IOS software does not filter packets originating in that router. Opie is still out of luck—he'll never get (a packet) out of Mayberry!

10. Does the access list shown in Example A-1 stop packets from getting to web server Governor? Why or why not?

    Answer: Packets from Andy can get to web server Governor. Packets from Mount Pilot can be delivered to Governor if the route points directly from Mount Pilot to Raleigh so that the packets do not pass through Mayberry. Therefore, the access list, as coded, stops only hosts other than Andy on the Mayberry Ethernet from reaching web server Governor.

11. Referring to Figure A-3, create and enable access lists so that access to web server Governor is allowed from hosts at any site and so that no other access to hosts in Raleigh is allowed.

    ```
    ! this access list is enabled on the Raleigh router
    access-list 130 permit tcp 180.3.5.0  0.0.0.255 host 144.155.3.99 eq www
    access-list 130 permit tcp 180.3.7.0  0.0.0.255 host 144.155.3.99 eq www
    !
    interface serial 0
    ip access-group 130 in
    ```

    Answer: This access list performs the function and also filters IGRP updates. That is part of the danger of inbound access lists. With outbound lists, the router does not filter packets originating in that router. With inbound access lists, all packets entering the interface are examined and can be filtered. An IGRP protocol type is allowed in the extended access-list command; therefore, this problem can be easily solved by matching IGRP updates. The command access-list 130 permit igrp any any performs the needed matching of IGRP updates, permitting those packets. (This command needs to appear before any statements in list 130 that might match IGRP updates.)

12. Name all the items that a standard IP access list can examine to make a match.

    Answer:

    Source IP address

    Subset of the entire source address (using a mask)

13. Name all the items that an extended IP access list can examine to make a match.

    Answer:

    Protocol type

    Source port

    Source IP address

    Subset of the entire source address (using a mask)

    Destination port

    Destination IP address

    Subset of the entire destination address (using a mask)

14. True or false: When you use extended IP access lists to restrict vty access, the matching logic is a best match of the list rather than a first match in the list.

    Answer: False. Access list logic is always a first match for any application of the list.

15. In a standard numbered IP access list with three statements, a **no** version of the first statement is issued in configuration mode. Immediately following, another access list configuration command is added for the same access list. How many statements are in the list now, and in what position is the newly added statement?

    Answer: Only one statement remains in the list: the newly added statement. The no access-list *x* command deletes the entire access list, even if you enter all the parameters in an individual command when issuing the no version of the command.

16. In a standard named IP access list with three statements, a **no** version of the first statement is issued in configuration mode. Immediately following, another access list configuration command is added for the same access list. How many statements are in the list now, and in what position is the newly added statement?

    Answer: Three statements remain in the list, with the newly added statement at the end of the list. The no deny | permit... command deletes only that single named access list subcommand in named lists. However, when the command is added again, it cannot be placed anywhere except at the end of the list.

17. Name all the items that a named standard IP access list can examine to make a match.

    Answer:

    Source IP address

    Subset of the entire source address (using a mask)

    Named standard IP access lists match the same items that numbered IP access lists match.

18. Configure a named IP access list that stops packets from subnet 134.141.7.0 255.255.255.0 from exiting serial 0 on a router. Allow all other packets.

```
ip access-list standard fred
 deny 134.141.7.0 0.0.0.255
 permit any
!
interface serial 0
ip access-group fred out
```

Answer: The first access-list statement denies packets from that subnet. The other statement is needed because the default action to deny packets is not explicitly matched in an access-list statement.

19. Configure a named IP access list that allows only packets from subnet 193.7.6.0 255.255.255.0, going to hosts in network 128.1.0.0 and using a web server in 128.1.0.0, to enter serial 0 on a router.

```
ip access-list extended barney
 permit tcp 193.7.6.0 0.0.0.255 128.1.0.0 0.0.255.255 eq www
!
interface serial 0
ip access-group barney in
```

Answer: A deny all is implied at the end of the list.

20. List the types of IP access lists (numbered standard, numbered extended, named standard, named extended) that can be enabled to prevent Telnet access into a router. What commands would be used to enable this function, assuming that **access-list 2** was already configured to match the right packets?

Answer: Any type of IP access list can be enabled to prevent vty access. The command line vty 0 4, followed by ip access-class 2 in, enables the feature using access list 2. Because ACLs used for preventing Telnet access into a router check only the source IP address, there is no need for an extended ACL in this case, anyway.

21. What command lists the IP extended access lists enabled on serial 1 without showing other interfaces?

Answer: The show ip interface serial 1 command lists the names and numbers of the IP access lists enabled on serial 1.

22. Name all the items that a named extended IP access list can examine to make a match.

Answer:

Protocol type

Source port

Source IP address

Subset of the entire source address (using a mask)

Destination port

Destination IP address

Subset of the entire destination address (using a mask)

These are the same things that can be matched with a numbered extended IP access list.

Decimal to Binary Conversion Table

Decimal Value	Binary Value	Decimal Value	Binary Value
0	0000 0000	23	0001 0111
1	0000 0001	24	0001 1000
2	0000 0010	25	0001 1001
3	0000 0011	26	0001 1010
4	0000 0100	27	0001 1011
5	0000 0101	28	0001 1100
6	0000 0110	29	0001 1101
7	0000 0111	30	0001 1110
8	0000 1000	31	0001 1111
9	0000 1001	32	0010 0000
10	0000 1010	33	0010 0001
11	0000 1011	34	0010 0010
12	0000 1100	35	0010 0011
13	0000 1101	36	0010 0100
14	0000 1110	37	0010 0101
15	0000 1111	38	0010 0110
16	0001 0000	39	0010 0111
17	0001 0001	40	0010 1000
18	0001 0010	41	0010 1001
19	0001 0011	42	0010 1010
20	0001 0100	43	0010 1011
21	0001 0101	44	0010 1100
22	0001 0110	45	0010 1101

continues

Decimal Value	Binary Value	Decimal Value	Binary Value
46	0010 1110	76	0100 1100
47	0010 1111	77	0100 1101
48	0011 0000	78	0100 1110
49	0011 0001	79	0100 1111
50	0011 0010	80	0101 0000
51	0011 0011	81	0101 0001
52	0011 0100	82	0101 0010
53	0011 0101	83	0101 0011
54	0011 0110	84	0101 0100
55	0011 0111	85	0101 0101
56	0011 1000	86	0101 0110
57	0011 1001	87	0101 0111
58	0011 1010	88	0101 1000
59	0011 1011	89	0101 1001
60	0011 1100	90	0101 1010
61	0011 1101	91	0101 1011
62	0011 1110	92	0101 1100
63	0011 1111	93	0101 1101
64	0100 0000	94	0101 1110
65	0100 0001	95	0101 1111
66	0100 0010	96	0110 0000
67	0100 0011	97	0110 0001
68	0100 0100	98	0110 0010
69	0100 0101	99	0110 0011
70	0100 0110	100	0110 0100
71	0100 0111	101	0110 0101
72	0100 1000	102	0110 0110
73	0100 1001	103	0110 0111
74	0100 1010	104	0110 1000
75	0100 1011	105	0110 1001

Decimal Value	Binary Value	Decimal Value	Binary Value
106	0110 1010	136	1000 1000
107	0110 1011	137	1000 1001
108	0110 1100	138	1000 1010
109	0110 1101	139	1000 1011
110	0110 1110	140	1000 1100
111	0110 1111	141	1000 1101
112	0111 0000	142	1000 1110
113	0111 0001	143	1000 1111
114	0111 0010	144	1001 0000
115	0111 0011	145	1001 0001
116	0111 0100	146	1001 0010
117	0111 0101	147	1001 0011
118	0111 0110	148	1001 0100
119	0111 0111	149	1001 0101
120	0111 1000	150	1001 0110
121	0111 1001	151	1001 0111
122	0111 1010	152	1001 1000
123	0111 1011	153	1001 1001
124	0111 1100	154	1001 1010
125	0111 1101	155	1001 1011
126	0111 1110	156	1001 1100
127	0111 1111	157	1001 1101
128	1000 0000	158	1001 1110
129	1000 0001	159	1001 1111
130	1000 0010	160	1010 0000
131	1000 0011	161	1010 0001
132	1000 0100	162	1010 0010
133	1000 0101	163	1010 0011
134	1000 0110	164	1010 0100
135	1000 0111	165	1010 0101

continues

Decimal Value	Binary Value	Decimal Value	Binary Value
166	1010 0110	196	1100 0100
167	1010 0111	197	1100 0101
168	1010 1000	198	1100 0110
169	1010 1001	199	1100 0111
170	1010 1010	200	1100 1000
171	1010 1011	201	1100 1001
172	1010 1100	202	1100 1010
173	1010 1101	203	1100 1011
174	1010 1110	204	1100 1100
175	1010 1111	205	1100 1101
176	1011 0000	206	1100 1110
177	1011 0001	207	1100 1111
178	1011 0010	208	1101 0000
179	1011 0011	209	1101 0001
180	1011 0100	210	1101 0010
181	1011 0101	211	1101 0011
182	1011 0110	212	1101 0100
183	1011 0111	213	1101 0101
184	1011 1000	214	1101 0110
185	1011 1001	215	1101 0111
186	1011 1010	216	1101 1000
187	1011 1011	217	1101 1001
188	1011 1100	218	1101 1010
189	1011 1101	219	1101 1011
190	1011 1110	220	1101 1100
191	1011 1111	221	1101 1101
192	1100 0000	222	1101 1110
193	1100 0001	223	1101 1111
194	1100 0010	224	1110 0000
195	1100 0011	225	1110 0001

Decimal Value	Binary Value	Decimal Value	Binary Value
226	1110 0010		
227	1110 0011		
228	1110 0100		
229	1110 0101		
230	1110 0110		
231	1110 0111		
232	1110 1000		
233	1110 1001		
234	1110 1010		
235	1110 1011		
236	1110 1100		
237	1110 1101		
238	1110 1110		
239	1110 1111		
240	1111 0000		
241	1111 0001		
242	1111 0010		
243	1111 0011		
244	1111 0100		
245	1111 0101		
246	1111 0110		
247	1111 0111		
248	1111 1000		
249	1111 1001		
250	1111 1010		
251	1111 1011		
252	1111 1100		
253	1111 1101		
254	1111 1110		
255	1111 1111		

Using the Simulation Software for the Hands-on Exercises

One of the most important skills required for passing the INTRO, ICND, and CCNA exams is the ability to configure Cisco routers and switches with confidence. In fact, one of the reasons that this book is relatively long is the effort put into explaining the commands, the output of **show** commands, and how the commands work together. Many CCNA candidates simply do not get a lot of hands-on experience, so this book is designed to help those who do not have real gear.

Another way to practice and develop hands-on skills is to use a simulator. A company called Boson Software, Inc. (www.boson.com) produces a network simulation product called the Boson NetSim™. The full NetSim product, available over the Internet from Boson, contains a large number of lab exercises and support for a large number of devices. You can even design your own network topology from scratch! It is a very impressive product.

The CD-ROM included with this book has a version of NetSim built specifically for this book. This version of NetSim includes support for several lab exercises and lab scenarios that were written just for this book. Although the software lets you work through these exercises, it is a limited-feature demo version of the actual NetSim software, which requires paid registration for full functionality. The full-feature version of NetSim includes a large set of other labs, including labs appropriate for the CCNP exams. You can also build a network topology with the full version of the product, so you can try any of the examples in this book or to just experiment with networks.

This short appendix explains the following:

- How to get to the NetSim user interface on the CD-ROM
- What hands-on exercises in the book can be performed using this special edition of NetSim

Accessing NetSim from the CD

Accessing NetSim from the CD is relatively simple. Put the CD in the CD drive, and the software on the CD starts. (If it doesn't, run the command **autorun.exe** that is on the CD's root directory.) After logging in, select the Hands-on Practice Exercises and NetSim Demo Software link in the main menu. Another menu opens that allows you to view the CD-only appendixes of labs and to start the NetSim software.

NetSim lets you pick which lab topology to load. You pick a lab topology, and you next see the NetSim user interface.

You can think of what you see next as a real lab, with real routers and switches. The cabling topology and interface numbers match the labs and scenarios in this book. So you can access the devices and start entering commands!

The NetSim software includes the NetSim user guide, which helps you figure out how to navigate and use the NetSim product. (Just select "help" and "User guide" from NetSim.) However, the user manual does not tell you anything about the hands-on exercises you can do with this special version of NetSim! You can always just experiment using NetSim, trying all the commands you can think of, but remember that this is a limited-use version of the software, so not all commands are enabled. If you want some instructions on good things to try to do with the simulator, read the next section. It lists all the labs and scenarios in this book that can be performed using NetSim!

Hands-on Exercises Available with NetSim

This book includes three main types of exercises that can be duplicated using real gear or the special NetSim network simulator—scenarios, labs, and basic configuration exercises. You can improve your hands-on skills whether you perform these exercises using real gear, perform them using NetSim, or just read through the exercises.

Scenarios

In this Cisco Press Exam Certification Guide series, scenarios include some form of a problem statement, asking you to solve the problem. Then a suggested solution is shown, with an explanation of some of the pitfalls you might have encountered with your answer. Many of these scenarios include configuration and EXEC commands, but some do not. These scenarios are designed so that if you don't have access to real hardware, you can still learn more about the commands on routers and switches. These same scenarios can also be performed using NetSim!

Labs

This book also includes "lab" exercises, which follow a format typical of labs used in networking courses. These labs give you more guidance than do the scenarios. For instance, the scenarios simply state a goal, such as "Configure these three routers to support a full mesh of PVCs," whereas a lab gives you instructions for each step you need to take to configure the network. You simply read the lab instructions, and the lab guides you through the steps required to configure a network based on a stated set of requirements.

As with the scenarios, you can perform these labs on real gear or using the special NetSim build included with the CD that comes with this book. You can also just read through the labs and their solutions if your time is limited, but you might want to at least try to write down the solution before looking at the answer!

Configuration Sections of Chapters 3 and 10

Chapter 3, "Virtual LANs and Trunking," covers VLAN and trunking configuration. NetSim includes a "lab" that essentially mirrors the topology of the example used in the configuration section of Chapter 3. NetSim has a topology that matches the topology used for the configuration examples in Chapter 3, so you can simply repeat and experiment with those commands using that NetSim lab.

Similarly, Chapter 10, "ISDN and Dial-on-Demand Routing," covers how to configure dial-on-demand routing, which can also be performed using NetSim.

Listing of the Hands-on Exercises

To best use NetSim, you should first pick a particular lab or scenario. You might even want to print a copy if the lab or scenario is in one of the CD-only appendixes. Then you can bring up NetSim and select the corresponding NetSim lab topology that matches the lab or scenario. NetSim creates a simulated network that matches the lab or scenario, so all you have to do is start entering commands, just as if it were a real network with real gear!

The scenarios and labs are located in a couple different places. First, Chapter 13, "Final Preparation," includes two scenarios. They cover a lot of different topics from the book. The CD contains a scenarios appendix (CD-only Appendix B, "Scenarios") and a lab appendix (CD-only Appendix C, "Hands-on Lab Exercises"). These scenarios and labs focus on a more specific set of topics. If you plan to use NetSim frequently, you should probably print the CD-only Appendixes B and C.

In CD-only Appendix B, the scenarios are numbered in a way to help remind you of the corresponding chapter in the book. For instance, Scenario 4 reinforces topics covered in Chapter 5, "RIP, IGRP, and Static Route Concepts and Configuration."

Table C-1 lists the different scenarios and labs from this book that can be performed using NetSim. Note that some of the scenarios in CD-only Appendix B cannot be performed on the simulator, mainly because those scenarios do not ask you to implement anything on a network, making the simulator unnecessary. So Table C-1 lists the scenarios and labs that can be performed using NetSim.

Table C-1   *Scenarios and Labs That Can Be Performed Using NetSim*

Scenario or Lab	Location	Topic	NetSim Lab Number
Scenario 1*	Chapter 13	Comprehensive scenario 1 for topics in this book	7
Scenario 2*	Chapter 13	Comprehensive scenario 2 for topics in this book	8
Scenario 2	CD-only Appendix B	Subnet design with a Class B network	9
Scenario 3	CD-only Appendix B	Subnet design with a Class C network	10
Scenario 4	CD-only Appendix B	IP configuration 1	11
Scenario 5	CD-only Appendix B	IP configuration 2	12
Scenario 8	CD-only Appendix B	Frame Relay configuration	13
Scenario 9	CD-only Appendix B	Frame Relay configuration dissection	14
Scenario 10	CD-only Appendix B	IP filtering sample 1	15
Scenario 11	CD-only Appendix B	IP filtering sample 2	16
Scenario 12	CD-only Appendix B	IP filtering sample 3	17
Lab 1*	CD-only Appendix C	IP routing configuration	18
Lab 2*	CD-only Appendix C	IP access list configuration	19
Lab 3*	CD-only Appendix C	WAN configuration	20
VLAN and trunk configuration*	Chapter 3	Lab that simply supports the topology and commands in this part of Chapter 3	21
DDR and ISDN configuration	Chapter 10	Lab that simply supports the topology and commands in this part of Chapter 10	22

* Labs with an asterisk can be performed with the limited-function version of NetSim included with this book. To perform the other lab scenarios, you will need to purchase the full version of NetSim.

How You Should Proceed with NetSim

You can bring up NetSim and dive right in. However, here are a few suggestions before you are ready to do all the labs:

■ Bring up NetSim now, and make sure you can at least get to a router command prompt, using the PC you will most likely use when studying. That way, when you are ready to do your first lab or scenario, you know you have worked out any installation issues.

- If you intend to do most of the labs and scenarios, you might want to print CD-only Appendixes B and C.
- Decide if you prefer to do the labs and scenarios after reading the book or as you go along.
- If you want to do the labs as you progress through the book, refer to Table C-2 for my suggestions on the best time to do the labs and scenarios.

Table C-2 *The Best Time to Do Each Lab or Scenario Using NetSim*

Scenario or Lab	Location	Topic	After Reading Which Chapter
Scenario 1	Chapter 13	Comprehensive scenario 1 for topics in this book	13
Scenario 2	Chapter 13	Comprehensive scenario 2 for topics in this book	13
Scenario 2	CD-only Appendix B	Subnet design with a Class B network	4
Scenario 3	CD-only Appendix B	Subnet design with a Class C network	4
Scenario 4	CD-only Appendix B	IP configuration 1	5
Scenario 5	CD-only Appendix B	IP configuration 2	5
Scenario 8	CD-only Appendix B	Frame Relay configuration	11
Scenario 9	CD-only Appendix B	Frame Relay configuration dissection	11
Scenario 10	CD-only Appendix B	IP filtering sample 1	12
Scenario 11	CD-only Appendix B	IP filtering sample 2	12
Scenario 12	CD-only Appendix B	IP filtering sample 3	12
Lab 1	CD-only Appendix C	IP routing configuration	4
Lab 2	CD-only Appendix C	IP access list configuration	12
Lab 3	CD-only Appendix C	WAN configuration	10
VLAN and trunk configuration	Chapter 3	Lab that simply supports the topology and commands in this part of Chapter 3	3
DDR and ISDN configuration	Chapter 10	Lab that simply supports the topology and commands in this part of Chapter 10	10

Considerations When Using NetSim

NetSim is a wonderful product, and you can certainly get a lot of good hands-on experience using the NetSim product that is included with the book. However, like any simulator product, it does not mimic a network with 100% accuracy. Some situations are difficult to simulate. For instance, it is very challenging to simulate the output of debug commands, because the simulator is not actually running IOS. If you intend to use NetSim, please download the latest list of hints, tips, and caveats from www.ciscopress.com/158720083x.

This appendix covers the following subjects:

- Select an appropriate routing protocol based on user requirements

Comparisons of Dynamic Routing Protocols

The United States Postal Service routes a huge number of letters and packages each day. To do so, the postal sorting machines run fast, sorting lots of letters. Then the letters are placed in the correct container and onto the correct truck or plane to reach the final destination. However, if no one programs the letter-sorting machines to know where letters to each ZIP code should be sent, the sorter can't do its job. Similarly, Cisco routers can route many packets, but if the router doesn't know any routes, it can't do its job.

Chapters 5, "RIP, IGRP, and Static Route Concepts and Configuration", and 6, "OSPF and EIGRP Concepts and Configuration", in this book cover the details of four different routing protocols – RIP, IGRP, EIGRP, and OSPF. However, the ICND exam lists one exam topic that implies that you should be able to pick the right routing protocol, given a set of requirements. So, this appendix contains an excerpt from the INTRO Exam Certification Guide that lists some definitions, lists comparisons of the routing protocols, as well as giving a few insights into two other IP routing protocols.

For those of you who have a copy of the INTRO exam certification guide: all the information in this chapter is taken from that book, specifically from chapter 14.

Routing Protocol Overview

IP routing protocols have one primary goal—to fill the IP routing table with the current best routes it can find. The goal is simple, but the process and options can be complicated.

Terminology can get in the way when you're learning about routing protocols. This book's terminology relating to routing and routing protocols is consistent with the authorized Cisco courses, as well as with most Cisco documentation. So, just to make sure you have the terminology straight before diving into the details, a quick review of a few related terms might be helpful:

- A *routing protocol* fills the routing table with routing information. Examples include RIP and IGRP.

- A *routed protocol* is a protocol with OSI Layer 3 characteristics that define logical addressing and routing. The packets defined by the network layer (Layer 3) portion of these protocols can be routed. Examples of routed protocols include IP and IPX.

- The term *routing type* has been used in other Cisco courses, so you should also know this term. It refers to the type of routing protocol, such as link-state or distance vector.

IP routing protocols fill the IP routing table with valid, (hopefully) loop-free routes. Although the primary goal is to build a routing table, each routing protocol has a very important secondary goal of preventing loops. The routes added to the routing table include a subnet number, the interface out which to forward packets so that they are delivered to that subnet, and the IP address of the next router that should receive packets destined for that subnet (if needed).

An analogy about routing protocols can help. Imagine that a stubborn man is taking a trip to somewhere he has never been. He might look for a road sign referring to the destination town and pointing him to the next turn. By repeating the process at each intersection, he eventually should make it to the correct town. Of course, if a routing loop occurs (in other words, he's lost!) and he stubbornly never asks for directions, he could drive around forever—or at least until he runs out of gas. In this analogy, the guy in the car is like a routed protocol—it travels through the network from the source to the destination. The routing protocol is like the fellow whose job it is to decide what to paint on the various road signs. As long as all the road signs have correct information, the guy in the car should make it to the right town just by reading the road signs. Likewise, as long as the routing protocol puts the right routes in the various routing tables, the routers should deliver packets successfully.

All routing protocols have several general goals, as summarized in the following list:

- To dynamically learn and fill the routing table with a route to all subnets in the network.

- If more than one route to a subnet is available, to place the best route in the routing table.

- To notice when routes in the table are no longer valid, and to remove those routes from the routing table.

- If a route is removed from the routing table and another route through another neighboring router is available, to add the route to the routing table. (Many people view this goal and the preceding one as a single goal.)

- To add new routes, or to replace lost routes with the best currently available route, as quickly as possible. The time between losing the route and finding a working replacement route is called *convergence time*.

- To prevent routing loops.

So, all routing protocols have the same general goals. Cisco IOS Software supports a large variety of IP routing protocols. IP's long history and continued popularity have resulted in the specification and creation of several different competing routing protocol options. So, classifying IP routing protocols based on their differences is useful.

Comparing and Contrasting IP Routing Protocols

Routing protocols can be categorized in several ways. One distinction is whether the protocol is more useful between two companies or inside a single company. Only one IP routing protocol that is popular today, the Border Gateway Protocol (BGP), is designed specifically for use between two different organizations. In fact, BGP distributes routing information between ISPs worldwide today and between ISPs and their customers as need be.

Routing protocols that are best used to distribute routes between companies and organizations, such as BGP, are called *exterior routing protocols*. Routing protocols designed to distribute routing information inside a single organization are called *interior routing protocols*. The comparison is like the U.S. Department of Transportation (DOT) versus the local government's transportation department. The U.S. DOT plans the large interstate highways, but it could care less that someone just sold a farm to a developer and the local government has given the developer the approval to pave a new street so that he can build some houses. The U.S. DOT could be compared to exterior routing protocols—they care about overall worldwide connectivity, but they could care less when a single company adds a new LAN and a new subnet. However, the interior routing protocols do care, so when the packet gets to the company, all the routers will have learned about any new subnets, and the packet can be delivered successfully.

Table D-1 lists some of the major comparison points for Routing Protocols.

Table D-1 *Major Comparison Points Between Interior Routing Protocols*

Point of Comparison	Description
Type of routing protocol	Each interior routing protocol covered in this chapter can be characterized based on the underlying logic used by the routing protocol. This underlying logic often is referred to as the type of routing protocol. The three types are *distance vector*, *link-state*, and *hybrid*.
Full/partial updates	Some interior routing protocols send their entire routing tables regularly, which is called *full routing updates*. Other routing protocols send only a subset of the routing table in updates, typically just the information about any changed routes. This subset is referred to as *partial routing updates*. Partial routing updates require less overhead in the network.
Convergence	*Convergence* refers to the time required for routers to react to changes (for example, link failures and router failures) in the network, removing bad routes and adding new, better routes so that the current best routes are in all the routers' routing tables.

continues

Table D-1 *Major Comparison Points Between Interior Routing Protocols (Continued)*

Point of Comparison	Description
Metric	The *metric* refers to the numeric value that describes how good a particular route is. The lower the value is, the better the route is. Some metrics provide a more realistic perspective on which routes are truly the best routes.
Support for VLSM	*Variable-length subnet masking (VLSM)* means that, in a single Class A, B, or C network, multiple subnet masks can be used. The advantage of VLSM is that it enables you to vary the size of each subnet, based on the needs of that subnet. For instance, a point-to-point serial link needs only two IP addresses, so a subnet mask of 255.255.255.252, which allows only two valid IP addresses, meets the requirements but does not waste IP addresses. A mask allowing a much larger number of IP addresses then can be used on each LAN-based subnet. Some routing protocols support VLSM, and some do not.
Classless or classful	*Classless routing protocols* transmit the subnet mask along with each route in the routing updates sent by that protocol. *Classful routing protocols* do not transmit mask information. So, only classless routing protocols support VLSM. To say that a routing protocol is classless is to say that it supports VLSM, and vice versa.

You will see lots of coverage for most of the IP routing protocols in chapters 5 and 6. For the few that are not covered in depth on the ICND exam, the next few sections outline the basics..

Routing Through the Internet with the Border Gateway Protocol

ISPs use BGP today to exchange routing information between themselves and other ISPs and customers. Whereas interior routing protocols might be concerned about advertising all subnets inside a single organization, with a large network having a few thousand routes in the IP routing table, exterior routing protocols try to make sure that advertising routes reach every organization's network. Exterior routing protocols also deal with routing tables that, with a lot of work done to keep the size down, still exceed 100,000 routes.

BGP advertises only routing information to specifically defined peers using TCP. By using TCP, a router knows that any routing updates will be re-sent if they happen to get lost in transit.

BGP uses a concept called *autonomous systems* when describing each route. An autonomous system (AS) is a group of devices under the control of a single organization—in other words, that organization has autonomy from the other interconnected parts of the Internet. An AS number (ASN) is assigned to each AS, uniquely identifying each AS in the Internet. BGP includes the ASNs in the routing updates to prevent loops. Figure D-1 shows the general idea.

Figure D-1 *BGP Uses ASNs to Prevent Routing Loops*

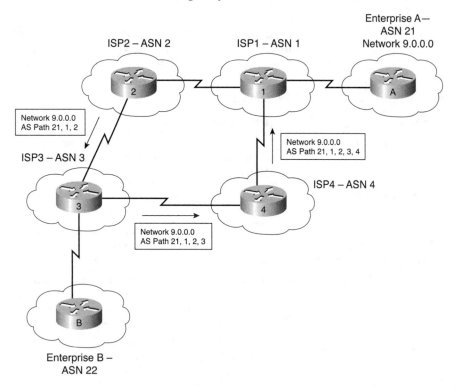

Notice that in the figure, the BGP updates sent to each successive AS show the ASNs in the route. When R1 receives the BGP update from R4, it notices that its own ASN in found inside the AS path and ignores that particular route.

BGP does not use a metric like internal routing protocols. Because BGP expects to be used between different ISPs and between ISPs and customers, BGP allows for a very robust set of alternatives for deciding what route to use; these alternatives are called *policies*. Routing policy can be based on the fact that an ISP might have a better business relationship with a particular ISP. For instance, in Figure D-1, packets from Enterprise B toward Enterprise A can take the "high" route (from ASN 3, to ASN 2, and then to ASN 1) if ISP3 has a better business relationship with ISP2, as compared with ISP4.

RIP Version 2

RIP Version 2 (RIP-2), as currently defined in RFC 2453, defines several enhancements to the original RIP protocol, which is called RIP Version 1. (Chapter 5 covers RIP Version 1 details.) Like RIP-1, RIP-2 uses distance vector logic; uses hop count for the metric; sends full, periodic updates; and still converges relatively slowly.

RIP-2 does add support for VLSM, as compared with RIP-1, making it a classless routing protocol, with RIP-2 including the subnet mask for each subnet in the routing updates. Table D-2 outlines the improvements made to RIP with the creation of RIP-2.

Table D-2 *Improvements Made to RIP by RIP V2*

Feature	Description
Transmits subnet mask with route	This feature allows VLSM by passing the mask along with each route so that the subnet is defined exactly. It allows VLSM, making RIP-2 a classless routing protocol.
Provides authentication	Both clear text (RFC-defined) and MD5 encryption (Cisco-added feature) can be used to authenticate the source of a routing update.
Includes a next-hop router IP address in its routing update	A router can advertise a route but direct any listeners to a different router on that same subnet.
Uses external route tags	RIP can pass information about routes learned from an external source and redistributed into RIP. Another router then can pass these external tags to that same routing protocol in a difference part of the network, effectively helping that other routing protocol pass information.
Uses multicast routing updates	Instead of broadcasting updates to 255.255.255.255 like RIP-1, the destination IP address is 224.0.0.9, an IP multicast address. 224.0.0.9 is reserved specifically for use by RIP-2. This reduces the amount of processing required on non–RIP-speaking hosts on a common subnet.

The most important feature comparing the two is that RIP-2 supports VLSM. Today, when choosing a routing protocol, RIP-1 would not be the best choice—in fact, the RIP-1 RFC has been designated for historic status. Both protocols work well, but RIP-2 is more functional. If you want a routing protocol that uses a public standard and you want to avoid the complexity of link-state protocols, RIP-2 is your best choice today.

The Integrated IS-IS Link State Routing Protocol

Once upon a time, the world of networking consisted of proprietary networking protocols from the various computer vendors. For companies that bought computers from only that one vendor, there was no problem. However, when you used multiple vendor's computers, networking became more problematic.

One solution to the problem was the development of a standardized networking protocol, such as TCP/IP. Skipping a few dozen years of history, you get to today's networking environment, where a computer vendor couldn't sell a computer without it also supporting TCP/IP. Problem solved!

Well, before TCP/IP became the networking protocol standard solving all these problems, the International Organization for Standardization (ISO) worked hard on a set of protocols that together fit into an architecture called *Open System Interconnection (OSI)*. OSI defined its own protocols for Layers 3 through 7, relying on other standards for Layers 1 and 2, much like TCP/IP does today. OSI did not become commercially viable, whereas TCP/IP did—the victory going to the nimbler, more flexible TCP/IP.

So, why bother telling you all this now? Well, OSI defines a network layer protocol called the Connectionless Network Protocol (CLNP). It also defines a routing protocol—a routing protocol used to advertise CLNP routes, called Intermediate System-to-Intermediate System (IS-IS). IS-IS advertises CLNP routes between "intermediate systems," which is what OSI calls *routers*.

Later in life, IS-IS was updated to include the capability to advertise IP routes as well as CLNP routes. To distinguish it from the older IS-IS, this new updated IS-IS is called *Integrated IS-IS*. The word *integrated* identifies the fact that the routing protocol can exchange routing information for multiple Layer 3 routed protocols.

IS-IS and OSPF are Link State protocols. Link-state protocols prevent loops from occurring easily because each router essentially has a complete map of the network. If you take a trip in your car and you have a map, you are a lot less likely to get lost than someone else who is just reading the signs by the side of the road. Likewise, the detailed topological information helps link-state protocols easily avoid loops. As you will in chapter 5, the main reasons that distance vector protocols converge slowly are related to the loop-avoidance features. With link-state protocols, those same loop-avoidance features are not needed, allowing for fast convergence—often in less than 10 seconds.

Integrated IS-IS has an advantage over OSPF because it supports both CLNP and IP route advertisement, but most installations could not care less about CLNP, so that advantage is minor. Table D-3 outlines the key comparison points with all Interior routing protocols for both Integrated IS-IS and OSPF.

Table D-3   *IP Link-State Protocols Compared*

Feature	OSPF	Integrated IS-IS
Period for individual reflooding of routing information	30 minutes	15 minutes
Metric	Cost	Metric
Supports VLSM	Yes	Yes
Convergence	Fast	Fast

Summary of Interior Routing Protocols

Before finishing your study for the INTRO or CCNA exam, you will learn a lot more about RIP-1, IGRP, EIGRP, and OSPF. This appendix has introduced you to some of the key terms and points of comparison for these routing protocols, as well covering a few details about other routing protocols. Table D-4 summarizes the most important points of comparison between the interior routing protocols, and Table D-5 lists some of the key terminology.

Table D-4   *Interior IP Routing Protocols Compared: Summary*

Routing Protocol	Metric	Convergence Speed	Supports VLSM and Is a Classless Routing Protocol	Default Period for Full Routing Updates
RIP-1	Hop count	Slow	No	30 seconds
RIP-2	Hop count	Slow	Yes	30 seconds
IGRP	Calculated based on constraining bandwidth and cumulative delay	Slow	No	90 seconds
EIGRP	Same as IGRP, except multiplied by 256	Very fast	Yes	N/A
OSPF	Cost, as derived from bandwidth by default	Fast	Yes	N/A
Integrated IS-IS	Metric	Fast	Yes	N/A

Table D-5 *Routing Protocol Terminology*

Term	Definition
Routing protocol	A protocol whose purpose is to learn the available routes, place the best routes into the routing table, and remove routes when they are no longer valid.
Exterior routing protocol	A routing protocol designed for use between two different organizations. These typically are used between ISPs or between a company and an ISP. For example, a company would run BGP, an exterior routing protocol, between one of its routers and a router inside an ISP.
Interior routing protocol	A routing protocol designed for use within a single organization. For example, an entire company might choose the IGRP routing protocol, which is an interior routing protocol.
Distance vector	The logic behind the behavior of some interior routing protocols, such as RIP and IGRP.
Link state	The logic behind the behavior of some interior routing protocols, such as OSPF.
Balanced hybrid	The logic behind the behavior of EIGRP, which is more like distance vector than link state but is different from these other two types of routing protocols.
Dijkstra Shortest Path First (SPF) algorithm	Magic math used by link-state protocols, such as OSPF, when the routing table is calculated.
Diffusing Update Algorithm (DUAL)	The process by which EIGRP routers collectively calculate the routes to place into the routing tables.
Convergence	The time required for routers to react to changes in the network, removing bad routes and adding new, better routes so that the current best routes are in all the routers' routing tables.
Metric	The numeric value that describes how good a particular route is. The lower the value is, the better the route is.

Configuring Cisco 1900 Switches

In years past, Cisco used the Catalyst 1900 switch line as the recommended switches in their courses relating to CCNA. The 1900 series is no longer a reasonable choice when purchasing a new switch from Cisco – in fact, you cannot even buy a new one any more. So, Cisco has added coverage of both 1900's and 2950 series switches to their courses, so the Cisco Learning Partner teaching the course can effectively use an older lab, or update their labs and use the more modern 2950 switches. In the end, Cisco simply wants you to learn the types of things you configure on a switch – so using an older model can still be useful for learning.

We strive to ensure that all possible exam topics are included somewhere in these books, even the ones that may be less likely to be on the exams. So, while you'll find lots of coverage of 2950's in the main chapters, the 1900 coverage is relegated to this appendix. Simply put, the topics in this appendix could be covered on one of the exams, but the investment of study time in these topics may not be worth the return. For those of you who want to be super-prepared, this appendix lists some pertinent details about 1900 series switches.

Basic 1900 Switch Configuration

On the Catalyst 1900 switch, three different configuration methods exist:

- Menu-driven interface from the console port
- Web-based Visual Switch Manager (VSM)
- IOS command-line interface (CLI)

As mentioned earlier, this chapter focuses on using the CLI to configure the switch. Table E-1 lists the switch commands referred to in this section.

Table E-1 *Commands for Catalyst 1900 Switch Configuration*

Command	Description
ip address *address subnet-mask*	Sets the IP address for in-band management of the switch
ip default-gateway	Sets the default gateway so that the management interface can be reached from a remote network
show ip	Displays IP address configuration
show interfaces	Displays interface information
mac-address-table permanent *mac-address type module/port*	Sets a permanent MAC address
mac-address-table restricted static *mac-address type module/port src-if-list*	Sets a restricted static MAC address
port secure [**max-mac-count** *count*]	Sets port security
show mac-address-table {**security**}	Displays the MAC address table; the **security** option displays information about the restricted or static settings
address-violation {**suspend** | **disable** | **ignore**}	Sets the action to be taken by the switch if there is a security address violation
show version	Displays version information
copy tftp://host/src_ file {**opcode** [*type module*] | **nvram**}	Copies a configuration file from the TFTP server into NVRAM
copy nvram tftp://host/dst_ file	Saves a configuration file to the TFTP server
delete nvram [*type module*]	Removes all configuration parameters and returns the switch to factory default settings

Default 1900 Configuration

The default values vary depending on the features of the switch. The following list provides some of the default settings for the Catalyst 1900 switch. (Not all the defaults are shown in this example.)

- IP address: 0.0.0.0
- CDP: Enabled

- Switching mode: FragmentFree

- 100BaseT port: Autonegotiate duplex mode

- 10BaseT port: Half duplex

- Spanning Tree: Enabled

- Console password: None

Numbering Ports (Interfaces)

The terms *interface* and *port* both are used to describe the physical connectors on the switch hardware. For instance, the **show running-config** command uses the term *interface*; the **show spantree** command uses the term *port*. The numbering of the interfaces is relatively straightforward; the interface numbering convention for the 1912 and 1924 switches is shown in Table E-2. Example E-1 shows three exec commands and highlights the use of the terms *interface* and *port*.

Table E-2 *Catalyst 1912 and 1924 Interface/Port Numbering*

	Catalyst 1912	**Catalyst 1924**
10BaseT ports	12 total (e0/1 to e0/12)	24 total (e0/1 to e0/24)
AUI port	e0/25	e0/25
100BaseT uplink ports	fa0/26 (port A)	fa0/26 (port A)
	fa0/27 (port B)	fa0/27 (port B)

Example E-1 **show run** *Output Refers to Port e0/1 as Interface Ethernet 0/1*

```
wg_sw_d#show running-config

Building configuration...
Current configuration:
!
!
interface Ethernet 0/1
!
interface Ethernet 0/2
! Portions omitted for brevity...

wg_sw_d#show spantree

Port Ethernet 0/1 of VLAN1 is Forwarding
   Port path cost 100, Port priority 128
   Designated root has priority 32768, address 0090.8673.3340
   Designated bridge has priority 32768, address 0090.8673.3340
```

continues

Example E-1   **show run** *Output Refers to Port e0/1 as Interface Ethernet 0/1 (Continued)*

```
    Designated port is Ethernet 0/1, path cost 0
    Timers: message age 20, forward delay 15, hold 1
! Portions omitted for brevity...
wg_sw_a#show vlan-membership


Port  VLAN  Membership Type    Port  VLAN  Membership Type
------------------------------------------------------------------
1      5       Static         13     1        Static
2      1       Static         14     1        Static
3      1       Static         15     1        Static
```

Basic IP and Port Duplex Configuration

Two features commonly configured during switch installation are TCP/IP support and the setting of duplex on key switch ports. Switches support IP, but in a different way than a router. The switch acts more like a normal IP host, with a single address/mask for the switch and a default router. Each port/interface does not need an IP address because the switch is not performing Layer 3 routing. In fact, if there were no need to manage the switch, IP would not be needed on the switch at all.

The second feature typically configured at installation time is to preconfigure some ports to always use half- or full-duplex operation rather than allow negotiation. At times, autonegotia- tion can produce unpredictable results. For example, if a device attached to the switch does not support autonegotiation, the Catalyst switch sets the corresponding switch port to half-duplex mode by default. If the attached device is configured for full-duplex operation, a duplex mismatch occurs. To avoid this situation, manually set the duplex parameters of the switch to match the attached device.

Similar to the router IOS, the Catalyst 1900 switch has various configuration modes. Example E-2 shows the initial configuration of IP and duplex, with the actual prompts showing the familiar exec and configuration modes.

Example E-2   *Configuration Modes for Configuring IP and Duplex*

```
wg_sw_a#configure terminal
wg_sw_a(config)#ip address 10.5.5.11 255.255.255.0
wg_sw_a(config)#ip default-gateway 10.5.5.3
wg_sw_a(config)# interface e0/1
wg_sw_a(config-if)#duplex  half
wg_sw_a(config-if)#end
wg_sw_a
```

In the example, the duplex could have been set to one of the following modes:

- **Auto**—Sets autonegotiation of duplex mode. This is the default option for 100-Mbps TX ports.

- **Full**—Sets full-duplex mode.

- **Full-flow-control**—Sets full-duplex mode with flow control.

- **Half**—Sets half-duplex mode. This is the default option for 10-Mbps TX ports.

To verify the IP configuration and duplex settings on a given interface, use the **show ip** and **show interface** commands, as shown in Example E-3.

Example E-3   show ip *and* show interfaces *Output*

```
wg_sw_a#show ip
IP address: 10.5.5.11
Subnet mask: 255.255.255.0
Default gateway: 10.5.5.3
Management VLAN:   1
Domain name:
Name server 1: 0.0.0.0
Name server 2: 0.0.0.0
HTTP server: Enabled
HTTP port:  80
RIP: Enabled


wg_sw_a#show interfaces


Ethernet 0/1 is Enabled
Hardware is Built-in 10Base-T
Address is 0090.8673.3341
MTU 1500 bytes, BW 10000 Kbits
802.1d STP State:  Forwarding      Forward Transitions:  1
Port monitoring: Disabled
Unknown unicast flooding: Enabled
Unregistered multicast flooding:  Enabled
Description:
Duplex setting: Half duplex
Back pressure: Disabled

    Receive Statistics                    Transmit Statistics
 -----------------------------------    ------------------------------------
Total good frames            44841    Total frames                404502
Total octets               4944550    Total octets              29591574
Broadcast/multicast frames   31011    Broadcast/multicast frames  390913
Broadcast/multicast octets 3865029    Broadcast/multicast octets 28478154
Good frames forwarded        44832    Deferrals                        0
```

continues

Example E-3   show ip *and* show interfaces *Output (Continued)*

Frames filtered	9	Single collisions	0
Runt frames	0	Multiple collisions	0
No buffer discards	0	Excessive collisions	0
		Queue full discards	0
Errors:		Errors:	
FCS errors	0	Late collisions	0
Alignment errors	0	Excessive deferrals	0
Giant frames	0	Jabber errors	0
Address violations	0	Other transmit errors	0

No IP address is in the **show interface** output because the IP address is associated with the entire switch, not just a single interface. The spanning-tree state of the interface is shown, as is the duplex setting. If duplex was mismatched with the device on the other end, the late collisions counter most likely would increment rapidly.

Viewing and Configuring Entries in the MAC Address Table

The switching/bridging table concept discussed earlier in this chapter is called the *MAC address table* on the 1900 family of switches. The MAC address table contains dynamic entries, which are learned when the switch receives frames and examines the source MAC address. Two other variations of entries in the MAC address table are important to switch configuration and are outlined along with dynamic entries in the following list:

■ **Dynamic addresses**—MAC addresses are added to the MAC address table through normal bridge/switch processing. In other words, when a frame is received, the source MAC of the frame is associated with the incoming port/interface. These entries in the table time out with disuse (default 300 seconds on a 1900 series switch) and are cleared whenever the entire table is cleared.

■ **Permanent MAC addresses**—Through configuration, a MAC address is associated with a port, just as it would have been associated as a dynamic address. However, permanent entries in the table never time out.

■ **Restricted-static entries**—Through configuration, a MAC address is configured to be associated only with a particular port, with an additional restriction: Frames destined to that MAC address must have entered through a particular set of incoming ports.

Figure E-1 provides a simple example to show the use of permanent and restricted-static addresses. A popular server (Server 1) is on port E0/3, and there is never a case when its MAC address should not be in the table. The payroll server is also on this switch, and only the company comptroller is allowed access. The configuration and resulting MAC address table are shown in Example E-4, which follows the figure.

Figure E-1 *MAC Address Table Manipulation—Sample Network*

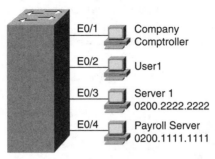

E0/1	Company Comptroller
E0/2	User1
E0/3	Server 1 0200.2222.2222
E0/4	Payroll Server 0200.1111.1111

Example E-4 *The MAC Address Table, with Dynamic, Permanent, and Restricted Static Entries*

```
wg_sw_a(config)#mac-address-table permanent 0200.2222.2222 ethernet 0/3
wg_sw_a(config)#mac-address-table restricted static 0200.1111.1111 e0/4 e0/1
wg_sw_a(config)#End
wg_sw_a#
wg_sw_a#show mac-address-table
Number of permanent addresses : 1
Number of restricted static addresses : 1
Number of dynamic addresses : 5


Address            Dest Interface      Type         Source Interface List
-------------------------------------------------------------------------
0200.4444.4444     Ethernet 0/1        Dynamic      All
00E0.1E5D.AE2F     Ethernet 0/2        Dynamic      All
0200.2222.2222     Ethernet 0/3        Permanent    All
0200 1111.1111     Ethernet 0/4        Static       Et0/1
00D0.588F.B604     FastEthernet 0/26   Dynamic      All
00E0.1E5D.AE2B     FastEthernet 0/26   Dynamic      All
00D0.5892.38C4     FastEthernet 0/27   Dynamic      All
```

In the example, Server 1 is always in the address table as the permanent entry. The payroll server is always in the table off port 0/4, and only devices on port 0/1 are allowed to send frames to it.

Another feature affecting the MAC address table is called *port security*. Port security is a feature that, when enabled, limits the number of MAC addresses associated with a port in the MAC address table. In other words, there is a preset limit to the number of sources that can forward frames into that switch port.

An example is particularly useful for understanding this concept; the configuration is straightforward. Consider Figure E-2, which shows a similar configuration to Figure E-1, except that the finance department has increased to three employees. These three employees are on the same shared hub, which then is cabled to switch port 0/1.

Figure E-2   *Figure E-2 Sample Network with Port Security*

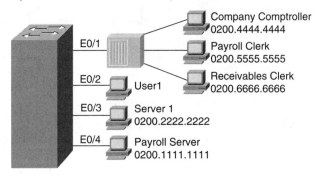

Port security can be used to restrict port 0/1 so that only three MAC addresses can source frames that enter port 0/1; this is because only the finance department is expected to use the shared hub. Any permanent or restricted-static MAC addresses count against this total of three. Example E-5 shows a sample configuration, with **show** commands.

Example E-5   *Port Security Example*

```
wg_sw_a(config)#mac-address-table permanent 0200.2222.2222 ethernet 0/3
wg_sw_a(config)#mac-address-table permanent 0200.4444.4444 ethernet 0/1
wg_sw_a(config)#mac-address-table restricted static 0200.1111.1111 e0/4 e0/1
wg_sw_a(config)#interface ethernet 0/1
wg_sw_a(config-if)#port secure max-mac-count 3
wg_sw_a(config-if)#End
wg_sw_a#
wg_sw_a#show mac-address-table
Number of permanent addresses : 2
Number of restricted static addresses : 1
Number of dynamic addresses : 6


Address            Dest Interface     Type        Source Interface List
---------------------------------------------------------------------------
0200.4444.4444     Ethernet 0/1       Permanent   All
0200.5555.5555     Ethernet 0/1       Dynamic     All
0200.6666.6666     Ethernet 0/1       Dynamic     All
00E0.1E5D.AE2F     Ethernet 0/2       Dynamic     All
0200.2222.2222     Ethernet 0/3       Permanent   All
0200.1111.1111     Ethernet 0/4       Static      Et0/1
00D0.588F.B604     FastEthernet 0/26  Dynamic     All
```

Example E-5 *Port Security Example (Continued)*

```
00E0.1E5D.AE2B    FastEthernet 0/26  Dynamic      All
00D0.5892.38C4    FastEthernet 0/27  Dynamic      All
wg_sw_a#show mac-address-table security
Action upon address violation : Suspend

Interface          Addressing Security      Address Table Size
- - - - - - - - - - - - - - - - - - - - - - - - - - - - - - - - - - - - - -
Ethernet 0/1       Enabled                  3
Ethernet 0/2       Disabled                 N/A
Ethernet 0/3       Disabled                 N/A
Ethernet 0/4       Disabled                 N/A
Ethernet 0/5       Disabled                 N/A
Ethernet 0/6       Disabled                 N/A
Ethernet 0/7       Disabled                 N/A
Ethernet 0/8       Disabled                 N/A
Ethernet 0/9       Disabled                 N/A
Ethernet 0/10      Disabled                 N/A
Ethernet 0/11      Disabled                 N/A
Ethernet 0/12      Disabled                 N/A
```

In this example, the permanently defined MAC address of 0200.4444.444, the comptroller's MAC address, is always associated with port e0/1. Notice that the two new employees' MAC addresses are also in the MAC address table. The **port secure max-mac-count 3** command means that a total of three addresses can be learned on this port.

What should the switch do when a fourth MAC address sources a frame that enters E0/1? An address violation occurs when a secured port receives a frame from a new source address that, if added to the MAC table, would cause the switch to exceed its address table size limit for that port. When a port security address violation occurs, the options for action to be taken on a port include suspending, ignoring, or disabling the port. When a port is suspended, it is re-enabled when a frame containing a valid address is received. When a port is disabled, it must be manually re-enabled. If the action is ignored, the switch ignores the security violation and keeps the port enabled.

Use the **address-violation** global configuration command to specify the action for a port address violation. The syntax for this command is as follows:

```
address-violation {suspend | disable | ignore}
```

Use the **no address-violation** command to set the switch to its default value, which is **suspend**.

Managing Configuration and System Files

Commands that are used to manage and control the configuration and system software files are slightly different on the 1900 switch family than on IOS-based routers. One of the reasons for the difference is that the switch does not actually run IOS—it has many features similar to IOS, including the IOS CLI, but there are and probably always will be some differences. For example, in Example E-6, the familiar **show version** command is used to display uptime and software levels, but it does not show the IOS level because IOS is not running.

Example E-6 show version *Output Displays Switch Hardware and Cisco IOS Software Information*

```
wg_sw_a#show version
Cisco Catalyst 1900/2820 Enterprise Edition Software
Version V9.00.00(12) written from 171.071.114.222
Copyright  Cisco Systems, Inc.  1993-1999
DS2820-1 uptime is 2day(s) 19hour(s) 34minute(s) 41second(s)
cisco Catalyst 2820 (486sxl) processor with 2048K/1024K bytes of memory
Hardware board revision is 1
Upgrade Status: No upgrade currently in progress.
Config File Status: No configuration upload/download is in progress
25 Fixed Ethernet/IEEE 802.3 interface(s)
SLOT A:
 FDDI (Fiber DAS Model), Version 00
  v1.14 written from 172.031.004.151: valid
SLOT B:
 100Base-TX(1 Port UTP Model), Version 0
Base Ethernet Address: 00-E0-1E-87-21-40
```

Another difference is that when the configuration is changed, the running config is modified but the startup config file in NVRAM is automatically updated. In other words, there is no need for a **copy running-config startup-config** command on the 1900 family of switches, as there would be on a router. Configuration files can be copied to an external TFTP server, but instead of using the keyword **startup-config** (used by routers), NVRAM is used.

The syntax of the command used to copy the NVRAM configuration file to host 10.1.1.1 into file mybackup.cfg is **copy nvram tftp://10.1.1.1/mybackup.cfg**. Unlike the router IOS, the switch IOS CLI will not prompt for the server name or IP address or the name of the file. Instead, the address or server host name and the filename are entered at the command line. The fact that the command does not prompt you is certainly different than with the router IOS. However, the same general syntax is available on the router IOS as of Cisco IOS Software release 12.0. For example, a similar, valid router IOS command would be **copy startup-config tftp://10.1.1.1/myrouter.cfg**.

Table E-3 summarizes some of the key differences between the router IOS CLI and the 1900 IOS CLI.

Table E-3 *IOS CLI Differences: Router Versus 1900 Switch*

Function	Router Command, Features	Switch Command, Features
Finding software version	**show version** command; shows IOS version.	**show version** command; shows switch software version.
Copying configuration files to TFTP server	**copy startup-config tftp** command; router IOS prompts for TFTP parameters.	**copy nvram tftp://server/file** command; switch IOS CLI does not prompt for TFTP parameters. "Server" can be IP address or host name.
Updating the config file used at reload time	**copy running-config startup- config** command.	Changes made to running configuration using config mode automatically are reflected in NVRAM config file.
Erasing the config file used at reload time	**write erase** or **erase startup- config** command.	**delete nvram** command.

VLAN and Trunking Configuration

This section covers VLAN configuration, as well as VTP configuration, on a 1900 series switch.

Basic VLAN Configuration

You should remember several items before you begin VLAN configuration:

- The maximum number of VLANs is switch-dependent. The Catalyst 1900 supports 64 VLANs with a separate spanning tree per VLAN.
- VLAN 1 is one of the factory-default VLANs.
- CDP and VTP advertisements are sent on VLAN 1.
- Catalyst 1900 IP address is in the VLAN 1 broadcast domain.
- The switch must be in VTP server mode or transparent mode to create, add, or delete VLANs.

Table E-4 represents the commands covered in this section and gives a brief description of each command's function.

Table E-4 *VLAN Command List*

Command	Description
delete vtp	Resets all VTP parameters to defaults and resets the configuration revision number to 1
vtp [server | transparent | client] [domain *domain-name*] [trap {enable | disable}] [password *password*] [pruning {enable | disable}]	Defines VTP parameters
vtp trunk pruning-disable *vlan-list*	Disables pruning for specified VLANs on a particular trunk interface (interface subcommand)
show vtp	Displays VTP status
trunk [on | off | desirable | auto | nonegotiate]	Configures a trunk interface
show trunk {A | B | port-channel} [allowed-vlans | prune-eligible | joined-vlans | joining-vlans]	Displays trunk status
vlan *vlan* [name *vlan-name*] [state {operational | suspended}]	Defines a VLAN and its name
show vlan [*vlan*]	Displays VLAN information
vlan-membership {static {*vlan*} | dynamic}	Assigns a port to a VLAN
show vlan-membership	Displays VLAN membership
show spantree [*bridge-group* | *vlan*]	Displays spanning tree information for a VLAN

VLAN Configuration for a Single Switch

If only one switch is in use, there is no real benefit to using VTP. However, VTP is on in server mode by default. Because VTP does not help when using a single switch, the first example shows VTP functions being turned off by enabling VTP transparent mode. The steps taken in this example are listed here:

1. Enabling VTP transparent mode

2. Creating the VLAN numbers and names

3. Configuring each port's assigned VLAN

First, use the **vtp** global configuration command to configure VTP transparent mode. Use the **vlan** global command to define each VLAN number (required) and associated name (optional). Then assign each port to its associated VLAN using the **vlan-membership** interface subcommand. Example E-7 shows an example based on Figure E-3.

Figure E-3 *Sample Network with One Switch and Three VLANs*

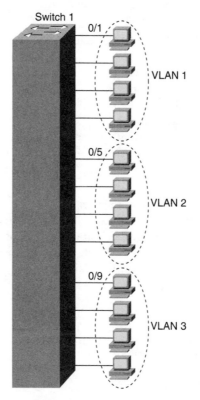

Example E-7 *Single-Switch VLAN Configuration Matching Figure E-3*

```
switch(config)# vtp transparent domain dummy
switch(config)# vlan 2 name VLAN2
switch1(config)# vlan 3 name VLAN3
switch1(config)# interface e 0/5
switch1(config-if)# vlan-membership static 2
switch1(config-if)# interface e 0/6
switch1(config-if)# vlan-membership static 2
switch1(config-if)# interface e 0/7
switch1(config-if)# vlan-membership static 2
switch1(config-if)# interface e 0/8
switch1(config-if)# vlan-membership static 2
```

continues

Example E-7 *Single-Switch VLAN Configuration Matching Figure E-3 (Continued)*

```
switch1(config-if)# interface e 0/9
switch1(config-if)# vlan-membership static 3
switch1(config-if)# interface e 0/10
switch1(config-if)# vlan-membership static 3
switch1(config-if)# interface e 0/11
switch1(config-if)# vlan-membership static 3
switch1(config-if)# interface e 0/12
switch1(config-if)# vlan-membership static 3
```

Notice that some configuration seems to be missing. VLAN 1, with name VLAN 1, is not configured because it is configured automatically. In fact, the name cannot be changed. Also, any ports without a specific static VLAN configuration are considered to be in VLAN 1. Also, the IP address of the switch is considered to be in VLAN 1's broadcast domain. Ports 5 through 8 are statically configured for VLAN 2; similarly, VLAN 3 comprises ports 9 through 12. In addition, VTP is set to transparent mode, with a meaningless domain name of dummy.

After the VLANs are configured, the parameters for that VLAN should be confirmed to ensure validity. To verify the parameters of a VLAN, use the **show vlan** *vlan#* privileged exec command to display information about a particular VLAN. Use **show vlan** to show all configured VLANs. Example E-8 demonstrates the **show** command output, which shows the switch ports assigned to the VLAN.

Example E-8 show vlan *Output*

```
Switch1#show vlan 3

VLAN Name          Status    Ports
------------------------------------------------------
3   VLAN3          Enabled   9-12
------------------------------------------------------


VLAN Type          SAID    MTU    Parent RingNo BridgeNo Stp  Trans1 Trans2
----------------------------------------------------------------------------
3   Ethernet       100003 1500       0     1        1    Unkn    0      0
----------------------------------------------------------------------------
```

Other VLAN parameters shown in Example E-8 include the type (default is Ethernet), SAID (used for FDDI trunk), MTU (default is 1500 for Ethernet VLAN), Spanning-Tree Protocol (the 1900 supports only the 802.1D Spanning-Tree Protocol standard), and other parameters used for Token Ring or FDDI VLANs.

Sample Configuration for Multiple Switches

To allow VLANs to span multiple switches, you must configure *trunks* to interconnect the switches. Trunks are simply LAN segments that connect switches and use one of two methods of tagging the frames with the VLAN number. Cisco calls the use of a trunking protocol such as ISL or 802.1Q *trunking*, so the command to enable these protocols is **trunk**.

Use the **trunk** interface configuration command to set a Fast Ethernet port to trunk mode. On the Catalyst 1900, the two Fast Ethernet ports are interfaces fa0/26 and fa0/27. Enabling and defining the type of *trunking* protocol can be done statically or dynamically for ISL. The syntax for the **trunk** Fast Ethernet interface configuration subcommand is as follows:

```
switch(config-if)# trunk [on | off | desirable | auto | nonnegotiate]
```

The options for the **trunk** command function are as follows:

- **on**—Configures the port into permanent ISL trunk mode and negotiates with the connected device to convert the link to trunk mode.
- **off**—Disables port trunk mode and negotiates with the connected device to convert the link to nontrunk.
- **desirable**—Triggers the port to negotiate the link from nontrunking to trunk mode. The port negotiates to a trunk port if the connected device is either in the **on, desirable,** or **auto** states. Otherwise, the port becomes a nontrunk port.
- **auto**—Enables a port to become a trunk only if the connected device has the state set to **on** or **desirable.**
- **nonegotiate**—Configures a port to permanent ISL trunk mode, and no negotiation takes place with the partner.

As seen in the list, many options exist. Choices for these options are mostly personal preference. Because trunks seldom change, my preference is to configure either **on** or **off.**

Figure E-4 and Examples E-9 and E-10 provide an expanded sample network, along with the additional configuration required for trunking and VTP server configuration.

Figure E-4 *Sample Network with Two Switches and Three VLANs*

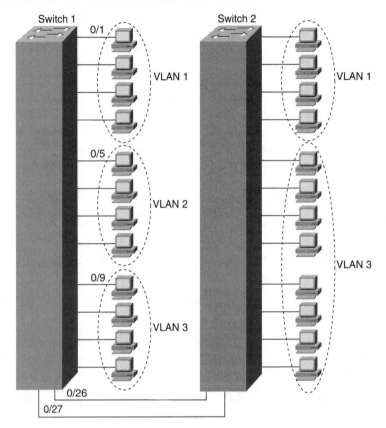

Example E-9 *Switch 1 Complete Configuration as VTP Server*

```
switch1# configure terminal
switch1(config)#ip address 10.5.5.11 255.255.255.0
switch1(config)#ip default-gateway 10.5.5.3
switch1(config)# vtp server domain Hartsfield pruning enable
switch1(config)# vlan 2 name VLAN2
switch1(config)# vlan 3 name VLAN3
switch1(config)# interface e 0/5
switch1(config-if)# vlan-membership static 2
switch1(config-if)# interface e 0/6
switch1(config-if)# vlan-membership static 2
switch1(config-if)# interface e 0/7
switch1(config-if)# vlan-membership static 2
switch1(config-if)# interface e 0/8
switch1(config-if)# vlan-membership static 2
switch1(config-if)# interface e 0/9
```

Example E-9   *Switch 1 Complete Configuration as VTP Server (Continued)*

```
switch1(config-if)# vlan-membership static 3
switch1(config-if)# interface e 0/10
switch1(config-if)# vlan-membership static 3
switch1(config-if)# interface e 0/11
switch1(config-if)# vlan-membership static 3
switch1(config-if)# interface e 0/12
switch1(config-if)# vlan-membership static 3
Switch1(config)# interface fa 0/26
switch1(config-if)# trunk on
switch1(config-if)# vlan-membership static 1
switch1(config-if)# vlan-membership static 2
switch1(config-if)# vlan-membership static 3
switch1(config-if)# interface fa 0/27
switch1(config-if)# trunk on
switch1(config-if)# vlan-membership static 1
switch1(config-if)# vlan-membership static 2
switch1(config-if)# vlan-membership static 3
```

Example E-10   *Switch 2 Complete Configuration as VTP Client*

```
switch2# configure terminal
switch2(config)#ip address 10.5.5.12 255.255.255.0
switch2(config)#ip default-gateway 10.5.5.3
switch2(config)# vtp client
switch2(config)# interface e 0/5
switch2(config-if)# vlan-membership static 3
switch2(config-if)# interface e 0/6
switch2(config-if)# vlan-membership static 3
switch2(config-if)# interface e 0/7
switch2(config-if)# vlan-membership static 3
switch2(config-if)# interface e 0/8
switch2(config-if)# vlan-membership static 3
switch2(config-if)# interface e 0/9
switch2(config-if)# vlan-membership static 3
switch2(config-if)# interface e 0/10
switch2(config-if)# vlan-membership static 3
switch2(config-if)# interface e 0/11
switch2(config-if)# vlan-membership static 3
switch2(config-if)# interface e 0/12
switch2(config-if)# vlan-membership static 3
switch2(config-if)# interface fa 0/27
switch2(config-if)# trunk on
switch2(config-if)# vlan-membership static 1
switch2(config-if)# vlan-membership static 3
```

Several items are particularly important in these configurations. The **vtp** global command in Example E-9 shows Switch 1 as the server, with domain Hartsfield. No password is used in this case. Switch 2 is not configured with the domain name but will learn it with the first advertisement. Missing from Example E-10 is the definition of the VLANs, which not only is unnecessary but also is not allowed when in VTP client mode. And because pruning was enabled in the **vtp** command on Switch 1, VTP prunes VLAN 2 from Switch 2 because Switch 2 has no ports in VLAN 2. VLAN 2 broadcasts received by Switch 1 are not forwarded to Switch 2.

Notice that not only was trunking enabled on both Fast Ethernet ports, but each of the three VLANs was statically configured on those ports. By also configuring the VLANs, the switch treats the trunk ports as part of those VLANs.

To verify a recent configuration change, or to just view the VTP configuration information, use the **show vtp** privileged exec command, as demonstrated in Example E-11. Also displayed is the IP address of the device that last modified the configuration and a time stamp of the time the modification was made. VTP has two versions: VTP Version 1 supports only Ethernet; VTP Version 2 supports Ethernet and Token Ring.

Example E-11   show vtp *Command Output*

```
switch1# show vtp
VTP version: 1
Configuration revision: 4
Maximum VLANs supported locally: 1005
Number of existing VLANs: 3
VTP domain name:Hartsfield
VTP password:
VTP operating mode: Server
VTP pruning mode: Enabled
VTP traps generation: Enabled
Configuration last modified by: 10.5.5.3 at 00-00-0000 00:00:00
```

To verify a trunk configuration, use the show trunk privileged exec command to display the trunk parameters, as demonstrated in Example E-12. The syntax is as follows:

```
switch1# show trunk [a | b]
```

The parameters a and b represent the Fast Ethernet ports:

- Port a represents Fast Ethernet 0/26.
- Port b represents Fast Ethernet 0/27.

Example E-12 shows a sample of the **show trunk** command as well as the **show vlan-membership** command.

Example E-12   show trunk *and* show vlan-membership *Sample Output*

```
Switch1# show trunk a
DISL state: Off, Trunking: On, Encapsulation type: ISL


Switch1#show vlan-membership


   Port  VLAN   Membership Type        Port    VLAN    Membership Type
   .........................................................................
   1     1      Static                 14      1       Static
   2     1      Static                 15      1       Static
   3     1      Static                 16      1       Static
   4     1      Static                 17      1       Static
   5     2      Static                 18      1       Static
   6     2      Static                 19      1       Static
   7     2      Static                 20      1       Static
   8     2      Static                 21      1       Static
   9     3      Static                 22      1       Static
   10    3      Static                 23      1       Static
   11    3      Static                 24      1       Static
   12    3      Static                 AUI     1       Static
   13    1      Static
   A     1-3    Static
   B     1-3    Static
```

You can see some basic information about STP using the **show spantree** privileged exec command, as demonstrated in Example E-13.

Example E-13   show spantree *Output*

```
switch1# show spantree 1
VLAN1 is executing the IEEE compatible Spanning-Tree Protocol
   Bridge Identifier has priority 32768, address 0050.F037.DA00
   Configured hello time 2, max age 20, forward delay 15
   Current root has priority 0, address 00D0.588F.B600
   Root port is FastEthernet 0/27, cost of root path is 10
   Topology change flag not set, detected flag not set
   Topology changes 53, last topology change occurred 0d00h17m14s ago
   Times:  hold 1, topology change 8960
           hello 2, max age 20, forward delay 15
   Timers: hello 2, topology change 35, notification 2
Port Ethernet 0/1 of VLAN1 is Forwarding
   Port path cost 100, Port priority 128
   Designated root has priority 0, address 00D0.588F.B600
```

continues

Example E-13 show spantree *Output (Continued)*

```
Designated bridge has priority 32768, address 0050.F037.DA00
Designated port is Ethernet 0/1, path cost 10
Timers: message age 20, forward delay 15, hold 1
```

Example E-13 displays various spanning tree information for VLAN 1, including the following:

- Port e0/1 is in the forwarding state for VLAN 1.

- The root bridge for VLAN 1 has a bridge priority of 0, with a MAC address of 00D0.588F.B600.

- The switch is running the IEEE 802.1d Spanning Tree Protocol.

ICND Exam Updates: Version 1.0

Over time, reader feedback allows Cisco Press to gauge which topics give our readers the most problems when taking the exams. To assist readers with those topics, the author creates new materials clarifying and expanding upon those troublesome exam topics. As mentioned in the introduction to the *CCNA ICND Exam Certification Guide*, the additional content about the exam is contained in a PDF document on this book's companion website located at http://www.ciscopress.com/title/158720083X.

This appendix presents all the latest update information available at the time of this book's printing. To make sure you have the latest version of this document, be sure to visit the companion website to learn whether any more recent versions have been posted since this printing went to press.

This appendix attempts to fill the void that occurs with any print book. In particular, this appendix

- Mentions technical items that might not have been mentioned elsewhere in the book.

- Emphasizes points that might have been mentioned briefly inside the book.

- Reviews several related topics that might have been under separate headings in the original chapters.

- Provides a way to get up-to-the-minute current information about content for the exam.

Always Get the Latest at the Companion Website

You are reading the version of this appendix that was available when your book was printed. However, given that the main purpose of this appendix is to be a living, changing document, it is very important that you look for the latest version on-line at the book's companion website. To do so do the following:

1. Browse to http://www.ciscopress.com/title/158720083X.

2. Select the **Downloads** option under the **More Information** box.

3.   Download the latest "ICND Appendix F" document

> **NOTE**   Note that the downloaded document has a version number. Compare the version of this print Appendix F (version 1.0) with the latest online version of this appendix, and follow this advice:
>
> ■ **Same version**—Ignore the PDF that you downloaded from the companion website.
>
> ■ **Website has a later version**—Ignore this Appendix F in your book, and just read the latest version that you downloaded from the companion website.

Technical Content

The topics in this appendix provide clarifications, technical tidbits, points of emphasis, and the like. The section titles for each topic identify the corresponding chapters of the book relevant to that topic.

Additionally, one section at the end of this appendix is covered in Chapter 7, "Operating Cisco Routers," of the *CCNA INTRO Exam Certification Guide*. This material is included here for those of you who might have a copy of the *CCNA ICND Exam Certification Guide* but not a copy of the *CCNA INTRO Exam Certification Guide*.

VLAN, Trunking, and VTP (Chapter 3)

Chapter 3, "Virtual LANs and Trunking," covers virtual LANs (VLANs) and VLAN Trunking Protocol (VTP). This section provides additional information about configuration for VLANs and VTP, including some of the nuances and potential problems when using VTP.

VLAN and VTP Configuration

Chapter 3 shows how to configure VLANs and VTP from VLAN database mode. You can also configure these features directly from configuration mode. Example F-1 shows how to configure VLANs and VTP; you can compare the equivalent configuration in Examples 3-1 and 3-2 from Chapter 3.

Example F-1   *VLAN and VTP Configuration from Configuration Mode*

```
sw1-2950#configure terminal
Enter configuration commands, one per line.  End with CNTL/Z.
sw1-2950(config)#interface range fastethernet 0/5 - 8
sw1-2950(config-if)#switchport access vlan 2
% Access VLAN does not exist. Creating vlan 2
sw1-2950(config-if)#exit
!!!!!!!!!!!!!!!!!!!!!!!!!!!!!!!!!!!!!!!!!!!!!!!!!!!!!!!!!!!!!!!!!!!!!!!!!!!!!!!!!!!!!
```

Example F-1 *VLAN and VTP Configuration from Configuration Mode*

```
! Above, VLAN 2 did not yet exist. When the switchport access vlan 2 command was
! used, the switch automatically created VLAN 2.
! Below, VLAN 3 is created explicitly, and given the correct name. At that point,
! when interfaces 9 - 12 are added to VLAN 3, the switch does not issue a message
! saying it is creating a VLAN, because VLAN 3 already exists.
!!!!!!!!!!!!!!!!!!!!!!!!!!!!!!!!!!!!!!!!!!!!!!!!!!!!!!!!!!!!!!!!!!!!!!!!!!!!!!!!!!!!
sw1-2950(config)#vlan 3
sw1-2950(config-vlan)#name Wilma-3
sw1-2950(config-vlan)#exit
sw1-2950(config)#interface range fastethernet 0/9 - 12
sw1-2950(config-if)#switchport access vlan 3
!!!!!!!!!!!!!!!!!!!!!!!!!!!!!!!!!!!!!!!!!!!!!!!!!!!!!!!!!!!!!!!!!!!!!!!!!!!!!!!!!!!!
! Below, the VTP domain name is set to "fred".
!!!!!!!!!!!!!!!!!!!!!!!!!!!!!!!!!!!!!!!!!!!!!!!!!!!!!!!!!!!!!!!!!!!!!!!!!!!!!!!!!!!!
sw1-2950#conf t
Enter configuration commands, one per line.  End with CNTL/Z.
sw1-2950(config)#vtp domain fred
Changing VTP domain name from NULL to fred
sw1-2950(config)#^Z
```

The commands shown in the example are very similar to those used in VLAN database mode. For instance, the **vtp domain fred** command is the same in both VLAN database mode and configuration mode. In configuration mode, however, you must use the **name** command to configure a VLAN name inside VLAN configuration mode, in contrast to treating the VLAN name as a parameter in the VLAN database mode **vlan** command. The meaning of the command options in each mode are relatively similar. The generic command syntax for the **vtp** command in configuration mode is as follows:

```
vtp {domain domain-name | password password | pruning | v2-mode | {server | client
     | transparent}}
```

For instance, from configuration mode, the **vtp server** command sets the switch to be a VTP server, and the **vtp pruning** command tells the switch to attempt pruning.

VTP Requirements

VTP must meet the following requirements to work on a set of switches:

- VLAN trunking (802.1Q or inter-switch link [ISL]) must be operational on the segments connecting the switches.
- At least one switch must be in VTP server mode.
- The switches must have the same case-sensitive domain name.

■   If a password is configured, the switches must have the same case-sensitive password configured.

When you receive a new Cisco 2950 switch, it defaults to VTP server mode, with a null domain name, and with trunking defaulting to "dynamic desirable." Seemingly, when you connect two brand new 2950 switches with a crossover cable, a trunk would form—and that is true. It also seems that because both switches are VTP servers, any VLAN information configured on either switch would be exchanged automatically with the other switch. As it turns out, with the default VTP server's VTP domain name of null, VTP does not send any VTP updates; instead, it waits until a domain name has been set. Therefore, to actually use VTP to dynamically distribute VLAN configuration information between these two switches, the following must happen:

■   Trunking must be operational between the two switches. (With the default of "dynamic desirable," this should happen as soon as a crossover cable connects the two switches.)

■   A VTP domain name must be defined on one of the VTP server switches.

If the preceding two conditions are met, the VTP server with its domain name set will send VTP advertisements. Interestingly, any VTP server or client switch with a null domain name actually updates its domain name based on the VTP update from the server. For instance, if you remove two brand new 2950s from their cardboard boxes, connect them with a crossover cable, and give switch1 a VTP domain name, switch2 will hear switch1's VTP update and change its domain name to match. A VTP client behaves the same way. *However, a good practice is to go ahead and set the VTP domain name on VTP clients and servers and to set VTP password on all switches.*

The Danger of Multiple VTP Servers

The support of multiple VTP servers introduces the possibility of either accidentally or purposefully eliminating the VLAN configuration for the network. When a VTP client or VTP transparent switch first connects to a switched network, using a trunk, it cannot destroy the VLAN configuration in other switches, because in these modes, the switch does not originate VTP updates. When a newly added VTP server switch attaches via trunk, however, it could replace the VLAN configuration of the other switches with its own—assuming the following are true about this new switch:

■   The VTP server switch has the same VTP domain name as all of the other switches.

■   The new VTP server switch has a higher revision number in VTP advertisement as compared with the existing switches.

■   The new VTP server switch has the same password as the existing switches (if configured).

You can easily determine the revision number and VTP domain name with a Sniffer trace. If a password is used, the Sniffer sees only an MD5 hash of the password, preventing the password from being stolen. Therefore, VTP passwords you can use to prevent denial of service attacks with VTP, where a new switch could essentially delete all VLAN information.

Changing the Allowed VLAN List

Each LAN trunk has a feature called the *allowed VLAN* list. By default, the allowed VLAN list on 2950 switches includes VLANs 1 through 1005 when using standard software, or 1 through 4094 when using the more expensive enhanced software. The **show interfaces** *interface-id* **trunk** command displays the VLAN allowed list. For instance, Example 3-2 in Chapter 3 includes the **show interfaces trunk** command, and shows that the default VLANs 1 through 4094 are allowed.

You can configure switch trunk interfaces to disallow a particular VLAN from the VLAN allowed list on a trunk by using the following interface subcommand:

```
switchport trunk allowed vlan {add | all | except | remove} vlan-list
```

For instance, the **add** option permits the switch to add VLANs to the existing list, and the **remove** option permits the switch to remove VLANs from the existing list. The **all** option means all VLANs, so you can use it to reset the switch to its original default setting (permitting VLANs 1–1005 or 1–4094 on the trunk, depending on the software). The **except** option is rather tricky—it adds all VLANs to the list that are not part of the command. For instance, on an enhanced software switch, the **switchport trunk allowed vlan except 100-200** interface subcommand adds VLANs 1 through 99 and 201 through 4094 to the existing allowed VLAN list on that trunk.

Subnetting (Chapter 4)

To complete your CCNA certification, you need to have a fairly deep, confident, and fast ability to answer subnetting questions. With subnetting, you must be very accurate, as well as fast. When practicing, first make sure that you can consistently get the right answer. At that point, in my humble opinion, for the ICND exam, you should be able to answer the following style of questions in 45 seconds or less in order to lessen time pressure on the ICND exam. And for each of these, assume that any subnet mask supplied by the question has one octet that is not a 0 or 255.

■ Given a subnet number and mask, what router command configures a router interface with the last valid IP address in the subnet?

- Given an IP address and mask, what is the subnet number?

- Given an IP address and mask, what is the range of valid IP addresses?

- Given a mask and a class (A, B, or C) for the network, into how many subnets can the network be divided?

- Given a mask and a class (A, B, or C) for the network, how many hosts are there on each subnet?

- Given a requirement of x hosts per subnet, a total of y subnets of the network, and a class (A, B, or C), which valid subnet masks meet this requirement?

My suggestion of 45 seconds to answer these questions is indeed subjective. If such questions require you to take more than 45 seconds for thought and computation, I recommend that you spend some time improving your speed. The CD-only appendix that supplies 25 more subnetting practice questions to help you get faster.

Expect questions that require you to perform multiple subnetting steps. You should be able to answer them within 60 to 90 seconds.

- Given a network diagram showing four Ethernets and three serial links, with five PCs shown with their IP addresses and masks, and with router IP addresses and masks listed, select an answer that shows the IP addressing misconfiguration of a single device.

- Figure out what happens in a network when an IP address or mask is misconfigured.

- In general, questions that require the math behind finding the subnet number, broadcast address, and range of valid IP addresses, for three to four subnets, to answer a single question.

In short, know subnetting! Know it well, and do it confidently and fast.

Improvement for Finding the Last Valid Subnet

The section "What Are the Other Subnet Numbers?" in Chapter 4, "IP Addressing and Subnetting," explains how to find the list of subnets, given a network number and a static mask used throughout the network. Another easy trick to find the last subnet number is as follows:

For the last subnet number (called the broadcast subnet), the interesting octet's value is the same number as the subnet mask's value in that same octet.

For instance, for network 172.16.0.0, with mask 255.255.255.0, the first subnet (the zero subnet) is 172.16.0.0. The next subnet is 172.16.1.0, then 172.16.2.0, and so on, with the very last subnet (the broadcast subnet) being 172.16.255.0. Note that the interesting octet (third octet) of the last subnet number matches the subnet mask's third octet. Consider another example. For network 192.168.1.0, with mask

255.255.255.192, the subnets are 192.168.1.0 (zero subnet), 192.168.1.64, 192.168.1.128, and 192.168.1.192 (last and broadcast subnet). The fourth (interesting) octet is 192 in both the last subnet number and in the subnet mask.

Number of Subnets: Subtract 2, or Not?

When choosing a subnet mask, the mask value implies the number of host bits and the number of subnet bits. The number of valid hosts per subnet is found using the formula $2^n - 2$, where n is the number of host bits. That formula is always true.

To find the number of possible subnets, however, you can use one of two formulas. Choosing which formula to use depends on what routing protocol is in use for that question. In short, if the question states or implies that a classful routing protocol is used, then use the formula $2^n - 2$, where n is the number of subnet bits. If the question states or implies that a classless routing protocol is used, use the formula of 2^n.

For a good reference of classless and classful routing protocols, and related terminology, refer to Table 7-3 in Chapter 7.

Table F-1 discusses the clues in the question that would imply which of the two formulas to use.

Table F-1   *When to Use Which Formula for the Number of Subnets*

If the question mentions...	Use the $2^n - 2$ rule when the questions says...	Use the 2^n rule when the questions says...
Classless or classful rules	Classful rules	Classless rules
Routing protocol being used	RIP version 1, IGRP	RIP version 2, EIGRP, OSPF
Whether VLSM is used	When VLSM is not used	When VLSM is used

Administrative Distance and Static Routes (Chapter 5)

Chapter 5 covers the concept of *administrative distance*, which is used by a single router when multiple routing protocols discover the same route. Table 5-14 in Chapter 5, "RIP, IGRP, and Static Route Concepts and Configuration," summarizes the default administrative distance values. Not mentioned in Chapter 5, however, is the fact that you can override administrative distance values in a couple of ways:

- A router can be configured to change a routing protocol's administrative distance via the **distance** routing protocol subcommand.

- The **ip route** command, which creates static routes, can set the administrative distance for the statically-configured route.

Example F-2 shows an example with the distance changed in several cases.

Example F-2 *Changing the Administrative Distance of a Route or Routing Protocol*

```
router eigrp 1
distance eigrp 121 170
!
ip route 172.31.101.0 255.255.255.0 172.31.3.2 11
ip route 172.31.102.0 255.255.255.0 serial0/0.2 12
!!!!!!!!!!!!!!!!!!!!!!!!!!!!!!!!!!!!!!!!!!!!!!!!!!!!!!!!!!!!!!!!!!!!!!!!!!!!
! Above, EIGRP has been changed to use AD 121 for internal routes and
! AD 170 (the default) for external routes. Also, two static routes
! are shown, one referencing a next-hop IP address, and the other
! referencing an outgoing point-to-point subinterface. Each ip route
! command sets the AD at the end of the command.
! Below, the show ip route command lists the  updated AD values.
!!!!!!!!!!!!!!!!!!!!!!!!!!!!!!!!!!!!!!!!!!!!!!!!!!!!!!!!!!!!!!!!!!!!!!!!!!!!
Router1#show ip route
Mar  1 00:22:40.050: %SYS-5-CONFIG_I: Configured from console by consoleute
Codes: C - connected, S - static, R - RIP, M - mobile, B - BGP
       D - EIGRP, EX - EIGRP external, O - OSPF, IA - OSPF inter area
       N1 - OSPF NSSA external type 1, N2 - OSPF NSSA external type 2
       E1 - OSPF external type 1, E2 - OSPF external type 2
       i - IS-IS, L1 - IS-IS level-1, L2 - IS-IS level-2, ia - IS-IS inter area
       * - candidate default, U - per-user static route, o - ODR
       P - periodic downloaded static route

Gateway of last resort is not set

     172.31.0.0/24 is subnetted, 10 subnets
C       172.31.130.0 is directly connected, Serial0/0.1
C       172.31.140.0 is directly connected, Serial0/0.2
C       172.31.3.0 is directly connected, Serial0/1
C       172.31.2.0 is directly connected, FastEthernet0/0
D       172.31.4.0 [121/2172416] via 172.31.3.2, 00:01:05, Serial0/1
D       172.31.103.0 [121/2195456] via 172.31.130.3, 00:01:05, Serial0/0.1
S       172.31.102.0 is directly connected, Serial0/0.2
S       172.31.101.0 [11/0] via 172.31.3.2
Router1#show ip route 172.31.102.0
Routing entry for 172.31.102.0/24
  Known via "static", distance 12, metric 0 (connected)
  Redistributing via eigrp 1
  Advertised by eigrp 1
  Routing Descriptor Blocks:
  * directly connected, via Serial0/0.2
      Route metric is 0, traffic share count is 1
```

Note also that the **show ip route** command lists the administrative distance values for EIGRP and one of the static routes, but not the other static route. IOS considers any static routes that use the outgoing interface option, rather than the next-hop address, as being *directly connected* static routes, and in that case, the administrative distance is not displayed in the **show ip route** command output. To see the associated administrative distance for those routes, use the **show ip route** *subnet-number* command, as shown at the end of the example.

RIP Version 2 Configuration (Chapter 5)

As mentioned in the introduction to Chapter 5 of this book, Appendix D of the *ICND Exam Certification Guide* provides some background information on and compares regarding the popular interior IP routing protocols. (Appendix D is a reprint of Chapter 14 from the INTRO Exam Certification Guide; if you have not yet read Appendix D, or Chapter 14 from the INTRO Exam Certification Guide, definately do so before taking the exam.) Appendix D covers some information about RIP version 2, including comparisons with RIP version 1, but it does not include information regarding RIP version 2 configuration; the configuration basics are covered here.

To configure a router to use only RIP version 2, and not version 1, use the **version 2** router subcommand. Back in Chapter 5, Figure 5-11 and Example 5-7 display a network diagram and the related configuration, **show**, and **debug** commands with RIP version 1. Example F-3 that follows shows the RIP version 2 configuration for the same design, with two small changes. In this case, all the links are up, plus the subnet mask used on the LAN at Seville uses a /26 prefix rather than a /24 as shown in Chapter 5. By using a different mask, Example F-3 can show RIP version 2 working with VLSM. Example F-3 also shows a sample RIP **debug** on the Albuquerque router.

Example F-3   *RIP-2 Sample Configuration for Routers in Figure 5-11 from Chapter 5*

```
router rip
network 10.0.0.0
version 2
Albuquerque#debug ip rip
RIP protocol debugging is on
00:36:04: RIP: received v2 update from 10.1.4.252 on Serial0
00:36:04:        10.1.2.0/24 -> 0.0.0.0 in 1 hops
00:36:04:        10.1.5.0/24 -> 0.0.0.0 in 1 hops
00:36:04:        10.1.3.192/26 -> 0.0.0.0 in 2 hops
00:36:08: RIP: sending v2 update to 224.0.0.9 via Serial0 (10.1.4.251)
00:36:08:        10.1.1.0/24 -> 0.0.0.0, metric 1, tag 0
00:36:08:        10.1.6.0/24 -> 0.0.0.0, metric 1, tag 0
00:36:08:        10.1.3.192/26 -> 0.0.0.0, metric 2, tag 0
```

Note a couple of important items in the **debug** output of Example F-3. RIP version 2 sends updates to multicast IP address 224.0.0.9, as opposed to a broadcast IP address of 255.255.255.255 used by RIP version 1. By multicasting the RIP-2 updates, RIP-2 allows the devices that are not using RIP-2 to ignore the updates and not waste processing cycles. The **debug** messages show the subnet masks as part of the routing updates, in prefix style, reaffirming RIP-2's support of VLSM. Note that Seville's Ethernet subnet (10.1.3.192/26) is shown, with the correct subnet mask.

Configuring routers to use only RIP-1, or only RIP-2, is easy—just ignore or include the **version 2** subcommand, respectively. However, IOS can run both RIP versions in the same internetwork, using the **ip rip send version** interface subcommand. Essentially, the configuration tells the router whether to send RIP-1 style updates, RIP-2 style updates, or both, for each interface. For instance, in that same Figure 5-11 from Chapter 5 again, suppose that the Yosemite router (lower left) will use RIP-1, and the other two routers will use RIP-2. Examples F-4 and F-5 show the configurations on Albuquerque and Yosemite to accomplish the feat.

Example F-4 *Configuration on Albuquerque for RIP-Version Coexistence*

```
interface ethernet 0
ip addr 10.1.1.251 255.255.255.0
interface serial 0
ip addr 10.1.4.251 255.255.255.0
ip rip send version 1
ip rip receive version 1
interface serial 1
ip address 10.1.6.251 255.255.255.0
!
router rip
network 10.0.0.0
version 2
```

Example F-5 *Configuration on Yosemite for RIP-Version Coexistence*

```
interface ethernet 0
ip addr 10.1.2.252 255.255.255.0
interface serial 0
ip addr 10.1.4.252 255.255.255.0
interface serial 1
ip address 10.1.5.252 255.255.255.0
!
router rip
network 10.0.0.0
```

The RIP-2 configuration logic works just like RIP-1—RIP-2 updates are sent and received on each interface that is matched by a **network** command. Because Yosemite will send and receive only RIP-1 updates, however, the other two routers need the appropriate interface subcommands to tell the router to send and receive RIP-1 updates to and from Yosemite. For instance, on Albuquerque, with the **version 2** command configured, the router sends RIP-2 updates and expects to receive only RIP-2 updates. The **ip rip send version 1** and **ip rip receive version 1** commands override those defaults, telling IOS to both send and receive RIP-1 updates on that interface.

IGRP and EIGRP Metric Comparison (Chapters 5 and 6)

IGRP computes its metric based on the bandwidth, delay, reliability, load, and maximum transmission unit (MTU). With default settings, only the bandwidth and delay are considered, and the calculation reduces to the following:

$$\text{Metric} = \frac{10^7}{\text{least-bandwidth (kbps)}} + \text{cumulative delay}$$

In this formula, the term *least-bandwidth* represents the lowest-bandwidth link in the route; this value uses a unit of kilobits per second. For instance, if the slowest link in a route is a 10 Mbps Ethernet link, the first part of the formula is $10^7 / 10^4$, which equals 1000, because 10 Mbps is equal to 10,000 kbps (10^4 kbps). The delay value used by the formula is the sum of all the delay values for all links in the route, with a unit of "tens of microseconds." You can set both bandwidth and delay for each link, using the cleverly named **bandwidth** and **delay** interface subcommands.

Example F-6 shows an example of the bandwidth, delay, and calculated metrics. The output comes from the familiar three-router network, as shown in Figure F-1. In this case, all links are up, plus EIGRP is in use. That means that the calculation includes an additional multiplier of 256, essentially making the formula EIGRP_metric = IGRP_metric * 256.

Figure F-1 *Network Showing Bandwidth and Delay for EIGRP Metric Calculation*

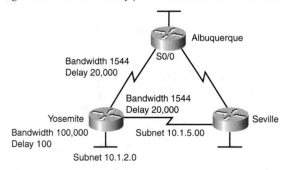

Example F-6 *EIGRP Metric Calculation Example (Albuquerque)*

```
Albuquerque#show interfaces s 0/0
Serial0/0 is up, line protocol is up
  Hardware is PowerQUICC Serial
  Internet address is 10.1.4.1/24
  MTU 1500 bytes, BW 1544 Kbit, DLY 20000 usec,
     reliability 255/255, txload 1/255, rxload 1/255
! lines omitted for brevity
!!!!!!!!!!!!!!!!!!!!!!!!!!!!!!!!!!!!!!!!!!!!!!!!!!!!!!!!!!!!!!!!!!!!!!!
! Above, the show interfaces command shows the bandwidth and delay
! values for Albuquerque's S0/0 interface. Note that the bandwidth
! is shown in Kbps, and the delay in microseconds.
! Below, the show ip route command lists the calculated metrics.
!!!!!!!!!!!!!!!!!!!!!!!!!!!!!!!!!!!!!!!!!!!!!!!!!!!!!!!!!!!!!!!!!!!!!!!
Albuquerque#show ip route          _____
Codes: C - connected, S - static, R - RIP, M - mobile, B - BGP
       D - EIGRP, EX - EIGRP external, O - OSPF, IA - OSPF inter area
       N1 - OSPF NSSA external type 1, N2 - OSPF NSSA external type 2
       E1 - OSPF external type 1, E2 - OSPF external type 2
       i - IS-IS, L1 - IS-IS level-1, L2 - IS-IS level-2, ia - IS-IS inter area
       * - candidate default, U - per-user static route, o - ODR
       P - periodic downloaded static route

Gateway of last resort is not set

     10.0.0.0/24 is subnetted, 5 subnets
D       10.1.2.0 [90/2172416] via 10.1.4.2, 00:10:54, Serial0/0
C       10.1.1.0 is directly connected, Ethernet0/0
C       10.1.6.0 is directly connected, Serial0/1
D       10.1.5.0 [90/2681856] via 10.1.4.2, 00:10:54, Serial0/0
C       10.1.4.0 is directly connected, Serial0/0
```

First, consider the route from Albuquerque to 10.1.2.0/24. The constraining bandwidth is 1544, meaning 1544 kbps, on Albuquerque's S0/0 interface. So, the first part of the formula is 10^7 / 1544, rounded down to an integer value of 6476. Next, the cumulative delay is added, with a unit of "tens of microseconds." Note that the **show interfaces** command output lists delay in microseconds. So, Albuquerque's delay of 20,000 microseconds counts as a delay of 2000, and Yosemite's fa0/0 delay of 100 microseconds counts as a delay of 10. So, the "cumulative delay" in the formula is 2000 + 10 = 2010, which is added to the 6476 calculated for bandwidth—giving a total of 8486. Finally, because EIGRP is used, the formula multiplies 8486 times 256, giving 2,172,416, which is the metric shown in Example F-6 for subnet 10.1.2.0.

The calculation for Albuquerque's route to 10.1.5.0 through Yosemite follows the same kind of logic, with the constraining bandwidth still being 1544 kbps, but a cumulative delay total of 4000: 2000 from Albuquerque's S0/0 interface plus 2000 more from Yosemite's S0/1 interface. So, the formula computes to the following:

(6476 + 2000 + 2000) * 256 = 2,681,856

The result is the same number shown for subnet 10.1.5.0/24 in the **show ip route** command output in Example F-6.

Finally, although neither IGRP nor EIGRP uses hop count in its calculations, they both actually include a hop count mechanism to help prevent loops. You might recall that RIP allows a maximum valid hop count of 15, with 16 implying an infinite metric (or failed) route. Similarly, IGRP has a maximum valid hop count of 255, and EIGRP uses a maximum of 224, with both values defaulting to 100, although neither hop-count value is used to calculate the metric.

Route Summarization Terminology (Chapter 7)

Chapter 7 covers a topic described as *route summarization*, as well as a topic called *autosummarization*. Some texts use the term *manual summarization* to mean the same thing as what Chapter 7 calls *route summarization*. The use of the word *manual* emphasizes a key difference compared with autosummarization, because manual summarization relies on the explicit configuration of the routing protocol to know exactly what summarized route to advertise. Conversely, with autosummarization, the routing protocol automatically figures out the classful network to summarize, plus autosummarization is enabled by default for those routing protocols that support it. Table F-2 lists the routing protocols and some of the key details of support for manual summarization and autosummarization.

Table F-2 *Manual Summarization and Autosummarization Summary*

Feature	RIP-1	IGRP	RIP-2	EIGRP	OSPF
Supports autosummarization	Yes	Yes	Yes	Yes	No
Autosummarization can be disabled	No	No	Yes	Yes	N/A
Supports Manual Route Summarization	No	No	Yes	Yes	Yes

ISDN DDR Names and PPP CHAP Authentication (Chapter 10)

Most dial-on-demand routing (DDR) implementations also use Point-to-Point Protocol (PPP) Challenge Handshake Authentication Protocol (CHAP) for authentication. When a router uses DDR to dial multiple different sites, good security practices suggest that each remote site should use a different CHAP name and password. This section reviews some of the interrelationships between DDR configuration and the associated CHAP configuration.

Imagine a router named Core, with 10 branch routers named BR1, BR2, and so on. Router Core's configuration includes 10 **username** commands, one for each branch router, for example, **username BR1 password fred**. Then, when router Core dials BR1's phone number, router Core could be configured to only accept the user name BR1 for that call; thus, you configure better security than if router Core accepts any of the names configured in the 10 **username** commands.

You can configure a router to require a particular name when calling each particular site when using two of the three styles of DDR configuration shown back in Chapter 10, "ISDN and Dial-on-Demand Routing." First, when using legacy DDR with the **dialer map** command, you can configure the rquired name using the **dialer map** interface subcommand. Additionally, when using DDR dialer profiles, you can configure the required name with the **dialer remote-name** dialer interface subcommand. (The configuration option to use Legacy DDR with the **dialer string** command does not provide a way to define what name the remote site should supply.)

Example 10-5 in Chapter 10 shows a classic case of configuring the name required when dialing each site, along with the related PPP CHAP configuration. The following list shows the progression of events when a dial is made in the network explained in Example 10-5, and shows how IOS uses the names configured in the **dialer map**, **dialer remote-name**, and **username** commands of that example.

1. SanFrancisco dials 14045551234 based on some interesting traffic occurring.

2. The ISDN call is set up.

3. PPP then begins initialization, including CHAP, with LosAngeles sending its CHAP username, random number, and hash back to SanFrancisco. (You might want to refer back to Chapter 9, "Point-to-Point Leased-Line Implementation," for a review of CHAP.)

4. SanFrancisco's logic first checks to make sure the CHAP name is LosAngeles because of the *name* parameter in the **dialer map broadcast name LosAngeles 14045551234** command.

5. SanFrancisco then performs normal PPP CHAP processing of the received information, using SanFrancisco's **username LosAngeles password Clark** command to find the password associated with the name LosAngeles.

6. If the CHAP processing completes, PPP continues and completes initialization of PPP LCP, along with any Layer 3 control protocols such as IP Control Protocol (IPCP).

   For dialer profiles, the same steps occur, except that the name checked at Step 4 is configured with the **dialer remote-name** dialer interface subcommand. (See Example 10-10 in Chapter 10.)

NOTE   For anyone with a book that is printing 4 or earlier: Example 10-10 was updated due to errors. Go to http://www.ciscopress.com/title/158720083X, click the **Errata** link in the **More Information** box, and download the errata file to get the latest and most accurate Example 10-10.

Interestingly, the **dialer map** *name* parameter can be omitted, essentially skipping Step 4 in the preceding process. Likewise, when configuring dialer profiles, omitting the **dialer remote-name** command also essentially skips Step 4's logic.

NOTE   The names and passwords used with DDR and PPP CHAP are case-sensitive.

The DDR process is rather involved. You can find examples of many of the most useful **show** and **debug** commands related to DDR in Chapter 10 in the section titled "ISDN and DDR **show** and **debug** Commands," particularly in Example 10-7. Example F-7 adds a few more commands that are not in Example 10-7. In particular, note the **debug ppp negotiation** command, which supplies messages relating to all facets of PPP negotiation, and **debug ppp authentication**, which only lists CHAP or PAP-related messages.

Example F-7 follows the same style as Chapter 10's Example 10-7 in that one **debug** is enabled, the dial is made and then taken down, and then the dial is repeated with only the other **debug** setting enabled. By doing so, you can see exactly what messages are generated by each debug.

Example F-7   *Additional DDR Troubleshooting Commands*

```
SanFrancisco#debug ppp negotiation
PPP protocol negotiation debugging is on
SanFrancisco#ping 172.16.2.1

Type escape sequence to abort.
Sending 5, 100-byte ICMP Echos to 122.16.2.1, timeout is 2 seconds:
!!!!!!!!!!!!!!!!!!!!!!!!!!!!!!!!!!!!!!!!!!!!!!!!!!!!!!!!!!!!!!!!!!!!!!!!!!!!!!!!!!!
! Above, a debug is enabled, and the dial trigger with the ping command.
! Below, the debug messages start with PPP, then LCP, then followed by the CHAP
! related messages. Note that challenge and response messages are sent in pairs,
! one for each direction.
!!!!!!!!!!!!!!!!!!!!!!!!!!!!!!!!!!!!!!!!!!!!!!!!!!!!!!!!!!!!!!!!!!!!!!!!!!!!!!!!!!!
00:43:05: %LINK-3-UPDOWN: Interface BRI0/0:1, changed state to up
00:43:05: BR0/0:1 PPP: Using dialer call direction
00:43:05: BR0/0:1 PPP: Treating connection as a callout
00:43:05: BR0/0:1 PPP: Phase is ESTABLISHING, Active Open [0 sess, 0 load]
00:43:05: BR0/0:1 LCP: O CONFREQ [Closed] id 5 len 15
00:43:05: BR0/0:1 LCP:    AuthProto CHAP (0x0305C22305)
00:43:05: BR0/0:1 LCP:    MagicNumber 0x07AD731A (0x050607AD731A).
00:43:07: BR0/0:1 LCP: I CONFREQ [REQsent] id 3 len 15
00:43:07: BR0/0:1 LCP:    AuthProto CHAP (0x0305C22305)
00:43:07: BR0/0:1 LCP:    MagicNumber 0x0272DFDC (0x05060272DFDC)
00:43:07: BR0/0:1 LCP: O CONFACK [REQsent] id 3 len 15
00:43:07: BR0/0:1 LCP:    AuthProto CHAP (0x0305C22305)
00:43:07: BR0/0:1 LCP:    MagicNumber 0x0272DFDC (0x05060272DFDC)
00:43:07: BR0/0:1 LCP: TIMEout: State ACKsent
00:43:07: BR0/0:1 LCP: O CONFREQ [ACKsent] id 6 len 15
00:43:07: BR0/0:1 LCP:    AuthProto CHAP (0x0305C22305)
00:43:07: BR0/0:1 LCP:    MagicNumber 0x07AD731A (0x050607AD731A)
00:43:07: BR0/0:1 LCP: I CONFACK [ACKsent] id 6 len 15
00:43:07: BR0/0:1 LCP:    AuthProto CHAP (0x0305C22305)
00:43:07: BR0/0:1 LCP:    MagicNumber 0x07AD731A (0x050607AD731A)
00:43:07: BR0/0:1 LCP: State is Open
00:43:07: BR0/0:1 PPP: Phase is AUTHENTICATING, by both [0 sess, 0 load]
00:43:07: BR0/0:1 CHAP: O CHALLENGE id 3 len 28 from "SanFrancisco"
00:43:07: BR0/0:1 CHAP: I CHALLENGE id 3 len 27 from "LosAngeles"
00:43:07: BR0/0:1 CHAP: O RESPONSE id 3 len 28 from "SanFrancisco"
00:43:07: BR0/0:1 CHAP: I SUCCESS id 3 len 4
00:43:07: BR0/0:1 CHAP: I RESPONSE id 3 len 27 from "LosAngeles"
00:43:07: BR0/0:1 CHAP: O SUCCESS id 3 len 4
00:43:07: BR0/0:1 PPP: Phase is UP [0 sess, 0 load]
```

Example F-7   *Additional DDR Troubleshooting Commands (Continued)*

```
00:43:07: BR0/0:1 IPCP: O CONFREQ [Closed] id 3 len 10
00:43:07: BR0/0:1 IPCP:    Address 172.16.2.2 (0x0306C00A0001)
00:43:07: BR0/0:1 CDPCP: O CONFREQ [Closed] id 3 len 4
00:43:07: BR0/0:1 IPCP: I CONFREQ [REQsent] id 3 len 10
00:43:07: BR0/0:1 IPCP:    Address 172.16.2.1 (0x0306C00A0002)
00:43:07: BR0/0:1 IPCP: O CONFACK [REQsent] id 3 len 10
00:43:07: BR0/0:1 IPCP:    Address 172.16.2.1 (0x0306C00A0002)
00:43:07: BR0/0:1 CDPCP: I CONFREQ [REQsent] id 3 len 4
00:43:07: BR0/0:1 CDPCP: O CONFACK [REQsent] id 3 len 4
00:43:07: BR0/0:1 IPCP: I CONFACK [ACKsent] id 3 len 10
00:43:07: BR0/0:1 IPCP:    Address 172.16.2.1 (0x0306C00A0001)
00:43:07: BR0/0:1 IPCP: State is Open
00:43:07: BR0/0:1 CDPCP: I CONFACK [ACKsent] id 3 len 4
00:43:07: BR0/0:1 CDPCP: State is Open
00:43:07: BR0/0 IPCP: Install route to 172.16.2.1
00:43:08: %LINEPROTO-5-UPDOWN: Line protocol on Interface BRI0/0:1, changed state to up
!!!!!!!!!!!!!!!!!!!!!!!!!!!!!!!!!!!!!!!!!!!!!!!!!!!!!!!!!!!!!!!!!!!!!!!!!!!!!!!!!!!!!!
! Above, the last two highlighted lines show the completion of higher-layer PPP
! protocols IPCP and CDPCP.
! Below, show dialer interface lists signaling info under "BRI0/0", which is
! the D channel; the current call under "BRI0/0:1", which is one of the B
! channels; and "BRI0/0:2, which is the other B channel, which is currently idle.
! It also shows the reason why the dial was made.
!!!!!!!!!!!!!!!!!!!!!!!!!!!!!!!!!!!!!!!!!!!!!!!!!!!!!!!!!!!!!!!!!!!!!!!!!!!!!!!!!!!!!!
SanFrancisco#show dialer interface bri0/0

BRI0/0 - dialer type = ISDN

Dial String     Successes    Failures    Last DNIS   Last status
14045551234         2           0        00:00:07    successful
0 incoming call(s) have been screened.
0 incoming call(s) rejected for callback.

BRI0/0:1 - dialer type = ISDN
Idle timer (150 secs), Fast idle timer (20 secs)
Wait for carrier (30 secs), Re-enable (15 secs)
Dialer state is data link layer up
Dial reason: ip (s=172.16.2.2, d=172.16.2.1)
Time until disconnect 146 secs
Connected to 14045551234 (LosAngeles)

BRI0/0:2 - dialer type = ISDN
Idle timer (150 secs), Fast idle timer (20 secs)
Wait for carrier (30 secs), Re-enable (15 secs)
Dialer state is idle
!!!!!!!!!!!!!!!!!!!!!!!!!!!!!!!!!!!!!!!!!!!!!!!!!!!!!!!!!!!!!!!!!!!!!!!!!!!!!!!!!!!!!!!!
! Next, but not shown, the dial is taken down, and the old debug disabled.
```

continues

Example F-7 *Additional DDR Troubleshooting Commands (Continued)*

```
! Below, a new debug is enabled, and a new dial triggered. Note that the messages
! are the same ones shown with debug ppp negotiation, but in this case, only
! authentication messages are shown.
!!!!!!!!!!!!!!!!!!!!!!!!!!!!!!!!!!!!!!!!!!!!!!!!!!!!!!!!!!!!!!!!!!!!!!!!!!!!!!!!!!!!
SanFrancisco#debug ppp authentication
PPP authentication debugging is on
SanFrancisco#ping 172.16.2.1

Type escape sequence to abort.
Sending 5, 100-byte ICMP Echos to 172.16.2.1, timeout is 2 seconds:

00:39:33: %LINK-3-UPDOWN: Interface BRI0/0:1, changed state to up
00:39:33: BR0/0:1 PPP: Using dialer call direction
00:39:33: BR0/0:1 PPP: Treating connection as a callout.
00:39:35: BR0/0:1 CHAP: O CHALLENGE id 1 len 28 from "SanFrancisco"
00:39:35: BR0/0:1 AUTH: Started process 0 pid 99
00:39:35: BR0/0:1 CHAP: I CHALLENGE id 1 len 27 from "LosAngeles"
00:39:35: BR0/0:1 CHAP: O RESPONSE id 1 len 28 from "SanFrancisco"
00:39:35: BR0/0:1 CHAP: I SUCCESS id 1 len 4
00:39:35: BR0/0:1 CHAP: I RESPONSE id 1 len 27 from "LosAngeles"
00:39:35: BR0/0:1 CHAP: O SUCCESS id 1 len 4.
```

Clarifications on Frame Relay Local and Global DLCI Addressing (Chapter 11)

Chapter 11, "Frame Relay," explains the fact that data-link connection identifiers (DLCIs) are locally significant. In other words, DLCIs have meaning only on the local access link between a router (Frame Relay DTE) and the Frame Relay switch (Frame Relay DCE) to which it connects. However, some Frame Relay providers assign DLCIs such that you can think of them as global values, more like LAN MAC addresses. These details are described in the section "DLCI Addressing Details," in Chapter 11.

When taking the Cisco exams, if a figure for a question shows three or more routers, you should be able to easily decide whether the figure implies local or global DLCI values. For instance, Figure 11-10 (in Chapter 11) shows a main site with four permanent virtual circuits (PVCs), one to each remote site. However, only one DLCI is shown beside the main site router, implying the use of global addressing. If local DLCIs were used, the figure would need to show a DLCI per PVC beside the main site router. Figure 11-7 depicts how local DLCIs are typically shown, with a DLCI beside each PVC.

In cases where a figure for a question shows only two routers, the figure might not imply whether local or global DLCI addressing is used. In those cases, look for clues in the question, answers, and any configuration. The best clues relate to the following fact:

On any given router, only local DLCI values are in the configuration or **show** commands.

For instance, from Chapter 11, Figure 11-19 shows global DLCIs, with DLCI 51 beside the Atlanta router. However, the **frame-relay interface-dlci** commands in Example 11-8 and the Atlanta **show** commands in Example 11-12 list DLCIs 52, 53, and 54. Although Figure 11-19 makes it obvious that global addressing is used, even if only two routers had been shown, the **show** commands and configuration commands could have helped identify the correct DLCIs to use.

Frame Relay FECN and BECN (Chapter 11)

If a router has a T1 Frame Relay access link, but only a 128-kbps committed information rate (CIR), the router can send a lot more data into the Frame Relay network than the business contract with the Frame Relay provider allows. The Frame Relay provider can forward traffic beyond the 128-kbps CIR rate, but they guarantee to forward an average of only 128 kbps. So, IOS includes a feature called *Traffic Shaping*, which enables a router to send some packets, wait, send more, wait again, and so on, so that the average sending rate is slower than the actual clock rate of the interface. For instance, with a T1 access link and a 128-kbps CIR, Traffic Shaping could be defined to only send an average of 256 kbps over time. The idea is that the Frame Relay provider will probably discard a lot of traffic if the router averages sending data at close to T1 speed, but maybe the provider will not discard any traffic if the average rate is only 256 kbps.

You can set Traffic Shaping to use a single speed, or to adapt and range between two speed settings. When configured to adapt between two speeds, if the network is not congested, the higher speed is used; when the network is congested, the router adapts so that it shapes using the lower rate.

To adapt the shaping rates, the routers need a way to know whether congestion is occurring—and that's where Forward Explicit Correction Notification (FECN) and Backward Explicit Correction Notification (BECN) are used. Figure F-2 shows the basic use of the FECN and BECN bits.

Figure F-2   *Basic Operation of FECN and BECN*

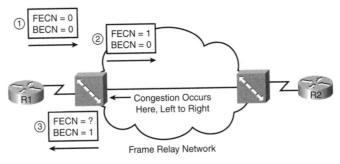

FECN and BECN are bits in the Frame Relay header. At any point—either in a router or inside the Frame Relay cloud—a device can set the FECN bit, meaning that this frame itself has experienced congestion. In other words, there is congestion in the forward direction of that frame. In Figure F-2, at Step 1, the router sends a frame, with FECN=0. The Frame Relay switch notices congestion, and sets FECN=1 at Step 2.

The goal of the whole process, however, is to get the sending router—R1 in this figure—to slow down. So, knowing that it set FECN in a frame at step 2 in the figure, the Frame Relay switch *can* set the BECN bit in the next frame going back to R1 on that virtual circuit (VC), shown as Step 3 in the figure. The BECN tells R1 that congestion occurred in the direction opposite, or backward, from the direction of the frame—in other words, that congestion occurred for the frame sent by R1 to R2. R1 can then choose to slow down (or not), depending on how Traffic Shaping is configured.

Interface Status (Various Chapters)

Several IOS commands, most notably the **show interfaces** command, supply two words or phrases to identify whether an interface is working. To be functional, the command output must list "up and up." This short section covers a few scenarios that affect the settings of these two indicators.

Although not always true, the first word or phrase typically refers to the OSI Layer 1 status, with the second word or phrase referring to the Layer 2 status. For instance, the first indicator would list "down" when

- There is no cable installed.
- The other end of the cable is not connected to anything else.
- The other end of the cable is installed, but the interface on the other devices is administratively disabled—for example, a router could be cabled to the switch, but the switch might have a **shutdown** command on that interface.
- For a serial link, the CSU/DSU might be installed and configured, but the link from the phone company might be down.

  The first indicator can be "up," but the second indicator might be "down," under several conditions, including the following:

- Mismatched configuration for the Data Link protocol. (For instance, for a router and switch using Ethernet, one might have been configured for ISL trunking, whereas the other had not.)
- For a serial link, one end might be configured for Frame Relay, the other defaulting to HDLC.

- For point-to-point serial links created with a DCE and DTE cable, a missing **clock rate** command on the DCE side.

- For Frame Relay, the access link might be up, but the Frame Relay switch and router might be using different LMI protocols.

- For PPP, CHAP authentication failure, which causes PPP LCP to fail.

- Anything that causes a router to cease to hear keepalive messages on the link.

The Configuration Register and the Boot Sequence (Chapter 7 of the *CCNA INTRO Exam Certification Guide*)

For those who have the *CCNA ICND Exam Certification Guide* but not the *CCNA INTRO Exam Certification Guide*, this section contains a short description of the configuration register and boot process of routers. The following text is derived from the *CCNA INTRO Exam Certification Guide*, Chapter 7.

The *configuration register* is a 16-bit software register in a router, and its value is set using the **config-register** global configuration command. This register tells the router at boot time whether to use a full-featured IOS, ROMMON (a rudimentary small OS with no IP routing function), or RXBOOT (a limited-feature IOS with some IP capabilities). In fact, only the low-order 4 bits of the configuration register direct the router as to what IOS to load; because of that, the last 4 bits are together called the *boot field* of the configuration register. If the boot field is hex 0, ROMMON is loaded. If the boot field is hex 1, RXBOOT mode is used. For anything else, the router attempts to load a full-featured IOS.

Other configuration register bits are interesting as well. (The configuration register's bits are numbered right to left, 0 through 15, so bit 0 is on the right when viewed in Cisco documents.) You can set the speed of the console port to a speed other than the default of 9600 bps. Also, with a value of 0x2142, bit 6 is set—which tells the router to ignore the startup-config file in NVRAM upon next reboot. Ignoring the startup-config file is a key part of the password-recovery process. (For more information on password recovery, go to Cisco.com and search on "password"; typically the first URL listed contains password recovery procedures.) You can also browse to the URL http://www.cisco.com/warp/customer/474/. Note that these web pages require a valid login.

At boot time, assuming the boot field of the configuration register is not a hex 0 or 1, the router will attempt to load a fully functional IOS image. To pick the IOS to load, the router then looks for **boot system** configuration commands in the startup configuration file. If there are no **boot system** commands, the router takes the default action, which is to load the first IOS file in Flash memory. Table F-3 summarizes how a router uses the various options for the **boot system** command.

Table F-3 *Impact of the **boot system** Command on Choice of IOS*

Boot System Commands	Result
No **boot system** command	Tries loading the following, in order: first file in Flash memory; broadcasts looking for TFTP server and a default filename; IOS in ROM; or uses ROM Monitor.
boot system ROM	IOS from ROM is loaded.
boot system flash	The first file from Flash memory is loaded.
boot system flash *filename*	IOS with the name filename is loaded from Flash memory.
boot system tftp *filename* 10.1.1.1	IOS with the name filename is loaded from the TFTP server.
Multiple boot system commands, any variety	An attempt occurs to load IOS based on the first boot command in the configuration. If that fails, the second boot command is used, and so on, until one succeeds.

802.1Q   The IEEE standardized protocol for VLAN trunking.

access link   The leased line between the Frame Relay DTE and DCE.

ACL   Access Control List. A list configured on a router to control packet flow through the router, such as to prevent packets with a certain IP address from leaving a particular interface on the router.

AR   access rate. The speed at which the access link is clocked. This choice affects the connection's price.

ARP   Address Resolution Protocol. An Internet protocol used to map an IP address to a MAC address. Defined in RFC 826.

asynchronous   Describes digital signals that are transmitted without precise clocking. Such signals generally have different frequencies and phase relationships. Asynchronous transmissions usually encapsulate individual characters in control bits (called start and stop bits) that designate the beginning and end of each character.

autosummarization   When advertised on an interface whose IP address is not in network X, routes related to subnets in network X are summarized and advertised as one route. That route is for the entire Class A, B, or C network X. Autosummarization is a feature of some IP routing protocols.

balanced hybrid   Refers to a third general type of routing protocol algorithm—the other two being distance vector and link-state. EIGRP is the only routing protocol that Cisco classifies as using a balanced hybrid algorithm.

Bc   committed burst. Over time, Bc defines the number of bits that can be sent consecutively at the access rate without exceeding the traffic contract.

BECN   backward explicit congestion notification. The bit in the Frame Relay header that signals to anything receiving the frame (switches and DTEs) that congestion is occurring in the opposite (backward) direction from the frame. Switches and DTEs can react by slowing the rate at which data is sent in that direction.

blocking state   A Spanning Tree Protocol port state in which the bridge or switch does not process any frames (input or output) on the interface, with the exception of STP messages.

Boolean AND   A math operation performed on a pair of one-digit binary numbers. The result is another one-digit binary number. 1 AND 1 yields 1; all other combinations yield 0.

BRI   Basic Rate Interface. An ISDN interface composed of two bearer (B) channels and one data (D) channel for circuit-switched communication of voice, video, and data.

bridge ID   An 8-byte value, defined for use by Spanning Tree Protocol, that represents a bridge or switch. The first 2 bytes consist of a priority value, and the last 6 bytes typically consist of a MAC address on the bridge or switch.

broadcast address   An IP address in each subnet is considered the broadcast address for that subnet. It is the highest numerical value in the range of numbers for the subnet. The broadcast address cannot be assigned as an IP address to a computer. Packets sent to this address are delivered to all hosts in the subnet.

broadcast domain   A set of all devices that receive broadcast frames originating from any device in the set. Devices in the same VLAN are in the same broadcast domain.

broadcast subnet   When subnetting a Class A, B, or C network, two subnet numbers are "discouraged" from use; one of these two subnets is the broadcast subnet. It is the subnet number for which the subnet bits all have a value of binary 1.

CHAP   Challenge Handshake Authentication Protocol. A security feature supported on lines using PPP encapsulation that prevents unauthorized access. CHAP does not itself prevent unauthorized access; it merely identifies the remote end. The router or access server then determines whether that user is allowed access.

CIDR   classless interdomain routing. A technique supported by BGP-4 and based on route aggregation. CIDR allows routers to group routes to reduce the quantity of routing information carried by the core routers. With CIDR, several IP networks appear to networks outside the group as a single, larger entity.

CIR   committed information rate. The rate at which the DTE can send data for an individual VC, for which the provider commits to deliver that amount of data. The provider sends any data in excess of this rate for this VC if its network has capacity at the time. This choice typically affects the price of each VC.

circuit switching   The switching system in which a dedicated physical circuit path must exist between the sender and the receiver for the duration of the "call." Used heavily in the telephone company network.

classful routing   Routing logic that first matches the Class A, B, or C network in the routing table. If the network number is matched, and then the correct subnet number matching a packet's destination IP address is not found, any existing default route is not used.

classful routing protocol   Does not transmit the mask information along with the subnet number. Therefore, it must consider Class A, B, and C network boundaries and perform autosummarization at Class A, B, and C network boundaries. Does not support VLSM.

classless routing   Routing logic that does not bother matching the Class A, B, or C network in the routing table. If the correct subnet number matching a packet's destination IP address is not found, any existing default route is used.

classless routing protocol   Transmits the mask information along with the subnet number, which means that it does not have to consider Class A, B, and C network boundaries. Although autosummarization at Class A, B, and C network boundaries may be supported, it is not required. Does not support VLSM.

CSU/DSU   channel service unit/data service unit. The CSU component is a digital interface device that connects end-user equipment to the local digital telephone loop. The DSU component is a device used in digital transmission that adapts the physical interface on a data terminal equipment (DTE) device to a transmission facility, such as T1 or E1. The DSU also is responsible for functions such as signal timing.

DCE   data communications equipment. From a physical layer perspective, the device providing the clocking on a WAN link, typically a CSU/DSU, is the DCE. From a packet switching perspective, the Service Provider's switch, to which a router might connect, is considered the DCE.

DDR   dial-on-demand routing. A technique whereby a router can automatically initiate and close a circuit-switched session as transmitting stations demand. The router spoofs keepalives so that end stations treat the session as active. DDR permits routing over ISDN or telephone lines.

DE   discard eligible. The bit in the Frame Relay header that, if frames must be discarded, signals a switch to choose this frame to discard instead of another frame without the DE bit set.

deny   An action taken with an ACL that implies that the packet is discarded.

designated port   The port (interface) on a bridge or switch that advertises the best spanning-tree BPDU (hello message) onto a LAN segment.

directed broadcast address   The same as a broadcast address.

discarding state   A Rapid Spanning Tree Protocol port state that is used instead of the blocking, listening, and disabled states in STP.

distance vector   The logic behind the behavior of some interior routing protocols, such as RIP and IGRP. Distance vector routing algorithms call for each router to send its entire routing table in each update, but only to its neighbors. Distance vector routing algorithms can be prone to routing loops but are computationally simpler than link-state routing algorithms. Also called *Bellman-Ford routing algorithm*.

DLCI   data-link connection identifier. A Frame Relay address used in Frame Relay headers to identify the VC.

DTE   data terminal equipment. From a Layer 1 perspective, the DTE synchronizes its clock based on the clock sent by the DCE. From a Packet Switching perspective, the DTE is the device outside the Service Provider's network, typically a router.

DUAL   Diffusing Update Algorithm. A convergence algorithm used in EIGRP that provides loop-free operation at every instant throughout a route computation. Allows routers involved in a topology change to synchronize at the same time, while not involving routers that are unaffected by the change.

EIGRP   Enhanced Interior Gateway Routing Protocol. An advanced version of IGRP developed by Cisco. Provides superior convergence properties and operating efficiency and combines the advantages of link-state protocols with those of distance vector protocols.

encoding   The conventions for how a device varies the electrical or optical signals sent over a cable to imply a particular binary code. For instance, a modem might encode a binary 1 or 0 by using one frequency to mean 1 and another to mean 0.

EtherChannel   Developed and copyrighted by Cisco Systems. A logical aggregation of multiple Ethernet interfaces used to form a single higher-bandwidth routing or bridging endpoint.

feasible successor   To converge quickly, EIGRP keeps track of possible alternative next-hop routers for each route. A feasible successor is a neighboring router that can be used as a replacement next-hop router for a particular route when it fails.

FECN forward explicit congestion notification. The bit in the Frame Relay header that signals to anything receiving the frame (switches and DTEs) that congestion is occurring in the same direction as the frame.

filter Generally, a process or a device that screens network traffic for certain characteristics, such as source address, destination address, or protocol, and determines whether to forward or discard that traffic based on the established criteria.

forward To send a frame toward its ultimate destination by way of an internetworking device.

Forward Delay timer A timer that sets the amount of time an interface spends in the STP listening and learning states. In other words, an interface stays in each of these two states for the Forward Delay amount of time.

forwarding state A Spanning Tree Protocol port state in which the bridge or switch processes frames (input or output) on the interface, with the exception of STP messages.

framing The conventions for how the bits sent according to OSI Layer 1 are interpreted by Layer 2. For instance, after an electrical signal has been received and converted to binary, framing identifies the information fields inside the data.

FTP File Transfer Protocol. An application protocol, part of the TCP/IP protocol stack, used to transfer files between network nodes. FTP is defined in RFC 959.

function group An ISDN term that generically refers to a set of functions that a piece of hardware or software must perform. Because the ITU wanted several options for the customer, it defined multiple different function groups. *See also* reference point.

HDLC High-Level Data Link Control. A bit-oriented synchronous data link layer protocol developed by the International Organization for Standardization (ISO). Derived from synchronous data link control (SDLC), HDLC specifies a data encapsulation method on synchronous serial links using frame characters and checksums.

hello timer An STP timer that dictates how often the root bridge or switch sends STP hello messages. It also dictates how often nonroot bridges and switches should expect to hear these hello messages. This term may also refer to the Hello timer used by OSPF, which defines how often a router sends OSPF Hello messages.

Hello A protocol used by OSPF systems to establish and maintain neighbor relationships. Can also refer to the STP Hello BPDU message generates by the root bridge in a Spanning Tree.

holddown A state into which a route is placed so that routers neither advertise the route nor accept advertisements about it for a specific length of time (the hold-down period). Holddown is used to flush bad information about a route from all routers in the network. A route typically is placed in holddown when a link in that route fails.

IGRP Interior Gateway Routing Protocol. An Interior Gateway Protocol (IGP) developed by Cisco to address the issues associated with routing in large, heterogeneous networks.

ISDN Integrated Services Digital Network. A communication protocol offered by telephone companies that permits telephone networks to carry data, voice, and other source traffic.

ISL Inter-Switch Link. A Cisco-proprietary protocol that maintains VLAN information as traffic flows between switches and routers.

LAPD Link Access Procedure D-Channel. The data link protocol used to control ISDN D-channels.

LAPF Link Access Procedure Frame Bearer Services. Defines the basic Frame Relay header and trailer. The header includes DLCI, FECN, BECN, and DE bits.

learn Transparent bridges and switches learn MAC addresses by examining the source MAC addresses of frames they receive. They add each new MAC address, along with the port number of the port on which it learned of the MAC address, to an address table.

leased line A transmission line reserved by a communications carrier for a customer's private use. A leased line is a type of dedicated line.

link-state A type of routing protocol which sends full topology information about the network to all routers, so they all have a consistent view of the network topology and status. Link-state algorithms create a consistent view of the network and therefore are not prone to routing loops. However, they achieve this at the cost of relatively greater computational difficulty and more-widespread traffic (compared with distance vector routing algorithms).

LMI Local Management Interface. The protocol used between a Frame Relay DCE and DTE to manage the connection. Signaling messages for SVCs, PVC status messages, and keepalives are all LMI messages.

LSA Link-State Advertisement. A packet used by link-state protocols that contains information about neighbors and path costs. LSAs are used by the receiving routers to maintain their routing tables.

mask *See* subnet mask.

MaxAge timer An STP timer that defines how long a bridge or switch should wait after the last received hello message before believing that the network topology has changed, and it can no longer hear the hello messages sent by the root bridge or switch.

metric   A unit of measure used by routing protocol algorithms to determine the best pathway for traffic to use to reach a particular destination.

MLP   Multilink Point-to-Point Protocol. A method of splitting, recombining, and sequencing datagrams across multiple point-to-point WAN links.

MTU   maximum transmission unit. The maximum packet size, in bytes, that a particular interface can handle.

NAT   Network Address Translation. A mechanism for reducing the need for globally unique IP addresses. NAT allows an organization with addresses that are not globally unique to connect to the Internet by translating those addresses into globally routable address space.

NBMA   nonbroadcast multiaccess. A network in which broadcasts are not supported, but more than two devices can be connected.

neighbor   A router that has an interface to a common network.

OSPF   Open Shortest Path First. A link-state, hierarchical Interior Gateway Protocol (IGP) routing algorithm proposed as a successor to Routing Information Protocol (RIP) in the Internet community. OSPF features include least-cost routing, multipath routing, and load balancing. OSPF was derived from an early version of the Intermediate System-to-Intermediate System (IS-IS) protocol.

packet switching   Service in which each DTE device connects to a telco using a single physical line, with the possibility of being able to forward traffic to all other sites. The telco switch makes the forwarding decision based on an address in the packet header.

PAP   Password Authentication Protocol. An authentication protocol that allows PPP peers to authenticate one another. Unlike Challenge Handshake Authentication Protocol (CHAP), PAP passes the password and the host name or username in the clear (unencrypted). PAP is supported only on PPP lines.

permit   An action taken with an ACL that implies that the packet is allowed to proceed through the router and be forwarded.

poison reverse   A routing update that explicitly indicates that a network or subnet is unreachable, rather than implying that a network is unreachable by not including it in updates. Poison reverse updates are sent to defeat large routing loops.

port   A TCP/IP transport layer header field found in TCP and UDP headers. Ports are numbers, and each numbered port is associated with a specific process. For example, SMTP is associated with port 25.

PPP   Point-to-Point Protocol. A data-link protocol that provides router-to-router and host-to-network connections over synchronous and asynchronous circuits. PPP was designed to work with several network layer protocols, such as IP, IPX, and AppleTalk Remote Access (ARA).

PRI   Primary Rate Interface. An ISDN interface to primary rate access. Primary rate access consists of a single 64-kbps D channel plus 23 (T1) or 30 (E1) B channels for voice or data.

private addresses   IP addresses in several Class A, B, and C networks that are set aside for use inside private organizations. These addresses, as defined in RFC 1918, are not routable through the Internet.

protocol type   A field in the IP header that identifies the type of header that follows the IP header, typically a Layer 4 header, such as TCP or UDP. ACLs can examine the protocol type to match packets with a particular value in this header field.

PVC   permanent virtual circuit. A predefined VC. A PVC can be equated to a leased line in concept.

Q.921   An ITU-T specification for the ISDN User-Network Interface (UNI) data link layer.

Q.931   An ITU-T specification for signaling to establish, maintain, and clear ISDN network connections.

reference point   An ISDN term that refers to the various interfaces between ISDN devices that implement different ISDN function groups.

RIP   Routing Information Protocol. An Interior Gateway Protocol (IGP) supplied with UNIX Berkeley Standard Distribution (BSD) systems. RIP is the most common IGP in the Internet. It uses hop count as a routing metric.

root bridge   A bridge that exchanges topology information with designated bridges in a spanning-tree implementation to notify all other bridges in the network when topology changes are required.

route summarization   A consolidation of advertised addresses which causes a single summary route to be advertised.

RSTP   Rapid Spanning Tree Protocol, defined in IEEE 802.1w, defines an improved version of STP that converges much more quickly and consistently than STP (802.1d).

SLSM   Static-length subnet mask. The usage of the same subnet mask for all subnets of a single Class A, B, or C network.

Spanning Tree Protocol   A bridge protocol that uses the Spanning Tree algorithm, allowing a learning bridge to dynamically work around loops in a network topology by creating a spanning tree. Bridges exchange bridge protocol data unit (BPDU) messages with other bridges to detect loops and then remove the loops by shutting down selected bridge interfaces. Refers to both the IEEE 802.1d Spanning Tree Protocol standard and the earlier Digital Equipment Corporation Spanning Tree Protocol upon which it is based. The IEEE version supports bridge domains and allows the bridge to construct a loop-free topology across an extended LAN. The IEEE version generally is preferred over the Digital version.

split horizon   A routing technique in which information about routes is prevented from exiting the router interface through which that information was received. Split-horizon updates are useful in preventing routing loops.

subinterface   One of the virtual interfaces on a single physical interface.

subnet   Subnets are subdivisions of a Class A, B, or C network, as configured by a network administrator. Subnets allow a single Class A, B, or C network to be used and still allow for a large number of groups of IP addresses, as is required for efficient IP routing.

subnet broadcast address   The same as a broadcast address.

subnet mask   A 32-bit address mask used to indicate the bits of an IP address that are being used for the subnet part of the address. Sometimes simply called a mask.

successor   In EIGRP, a neighboring router that could possibly be an alternative next-hop router to reach a particular subnet. Successors might or might not be feasible successors.

SVC   switched virtual circuit. A VC that is set up dynamically when needed. An SVC can be equated to a dial connection in concept.

switch   A network device that filters, forwards, and floods frames based on each frame's destination address. The switch operates at the data link layer of the Open System Interconnection (OSI) reference model.

synchronous   The imposition of time ordering on a bit stream. Practically, a device will try to use the same speed as another device on the other end of a serial link. However, by examining transitions between voltage states on the link, the device can notice slight variations in the speed on each end and can adjust its speed accordingly.

TFTP   Trivial File Transfer Protocol. A simplified version of File Transfer Protocol (FTP) that allows files to be transferred from one computer to another over a network, usually without the use of client authentication (for example, username and password).

topology database   The structured data that describes the network topology to a routing protocol. Link-state and balanced hybrid routing protocols use topology tables, from which they build the entries in the routing table.

trunking   Also called VLAN trunking. A method (using either Cisco's ISL protocol or the IEEE 802.1Q protocol) to support multiple VLANs that have members on more than one switch.

update timer   The time interval that regulates how often a routing protocol sends its next periodic routing updates. Distance vector routing protocols send full routing updates every update interval.

variance   IGRP and EIGRP compute their metrics, so the metrics for different routes to the same subnet seldom have the exact same value. The variance value is multiplied with the lower metric when multiple routes to the same subnet exist. If the product is larger than the metrics for other routes, the routes are considered of "equal" metric, allowing multiple routes to be added to the routing table.

VC   virtual circuit. A logical concept that represents the path that frames travel between DTEs. VCs are particularly useful when comparing Frame Relay to leased physical circuits.

VLAN   Virtual LAN. A group of devices on one or more LANs that are configured (using management software) so that they can communicate as if they were attached to the same wire when in fact they are located on a number of different LAN segments. Because VLANs are based on logical instead of physical connections, they are extremely flexible.

VLSM   Variable-length subnet mask(ing). The capability to specify a different subnet mask for the same Class A, B, or C network number on different subnets. VLSM can help optimize available address space.

VTP   VLAN Trunking Protocol. Cisco switches use this proprietary protocol to exchange VLAN configuration information between switches. VTP defines a Layer 2 messaging protocol that allows the switches to exchange VLAN configuration information so that the VLAN configuration stays consistent throughout a network. VTP manages the additions, deletions, and name changes of VLANs across multiple switches. It also reduces broadcast overhead through the use of VTP pruning.

zero subnet   When subnetting a Class A, B, or C network, two subnet numbers are "discouraged" from use; the zero subnet is one of these two subnets. It is the subnet number for which the subnet bits all have a value of binary 0.

Index

G–H

I

O

P

Q–R

U–V

W

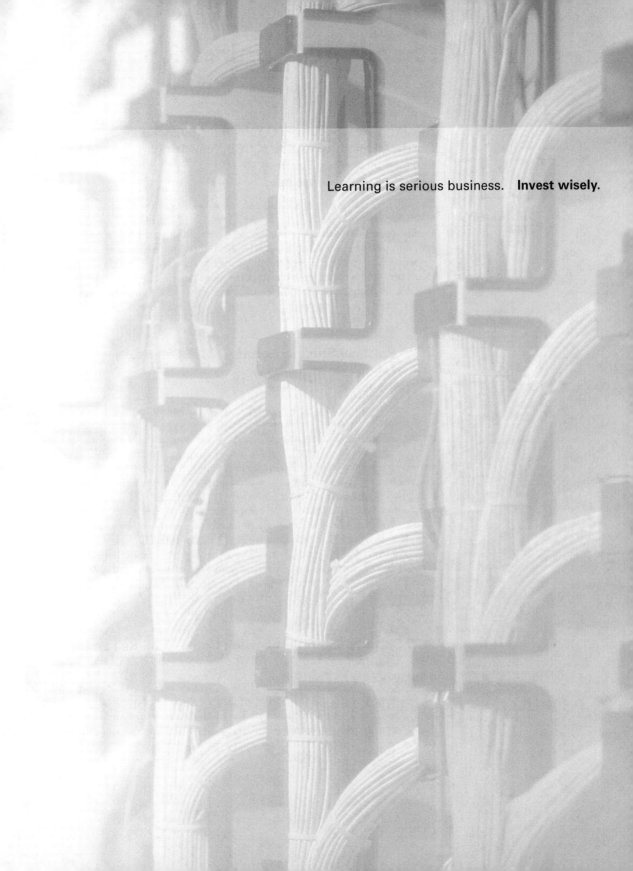

Learning is serious business.   **Invest wisely.**

Cisco Security Certification

CCSP™ Cisco Secure PIX® Firewall Advanced Exam Certification Guide (CCSP Self-Study)

Christian Degu, Greg Bastien

1-58720-067-8 • **Available Now**

The CSPFA exam is one of the five component exams to the CCSP certification. *CCSP Cisco Secure PIX Firewall Advanced Exam Certification Guide* provides CSPFA exam candidates with a comprehensive preparation tool for testing success. With pre- and post-chapter tests, a CD-ROM-based testing engine with more than 200 questions, and comprehensive training on all exam topics, this title brings the proven exam preparation tools from the popular Cisco Press Exam Certification Guide series to the CSPFA candidate. It also serves as a learning guide for networkers interested in learning more about working with the PIX Firewall line of products.

CCIE® Practical Studies: Security (CCIE Self-Study)

Andrew Mason, Dmitry Bokotey

1-58705-110-9 • **Available June 2003**

The Cisco Certified Internetworking Expert (CCIE) Certification from Cisco Systems is the most prestigious certification in the networking industry. In 2001, Cisco introduced the CCIE in Security. This exam, a combination of a written qualification exam with a one-day intensive lab exam is a highly sought after affirmation of a networkers security skills. A key to success in the intensive lab exam is hands-on understanding of how the security principles and concepts are executed in a real network. *CCIE Practical Studies: Security* provides a series of lab scenarios that help a CCIE candidate or advanced-level networker gain that expertise. The labs show how, with or without a lab of actual equipment, different concepts are applied. Chapters include background and technology overviews, directions on how to set up a practice lab, case study-based scenarios that show the step-by-step implementation of these concepts, and comprehensive labs that mimic those in the one-day lab exam. *CCIE Practical Studies: Security* serves as an invaluable guide in gaining networking security experience and in CCIE testing success.

CCIE Security Exam Certification Guide (CCIE Self-Study)

Henry Benjamin

1-58720-065-1 • **Available Now**

CCIE Security Exam Certification Guide is a valuable self-study aid in preparing for the Security Qualification Exam. The book covers security and application protocols, security technologies, general and Cisco-specific security applications, as well as related general networking and operating system issues.

CCIE Professional Development

Network Security Principles and Practices (CCIE Professional Development)

Saadat Malik

1-58705-025-0 • Available Now

Network Security Principles and Practices is a comprehensive guide to network security threats and the policies and tools developed specifically to combat those threats. Starting with a general discussion of network security concepts and design philosophy, the book shows readers how they can build secure network architectures from the ground up. Taking a practical, applied approach to building security into networks, the book focuses on showing readers how to implement and verify security features and products in a variety of environments. Security aspects of routing protocols are discussed and various options for choosing and using them analyzed. The book goes into a detailed discussion of the security threats posed by increasingly prevalent LAN to LAN Virtual Private Networks and remote access VPN installations and how to minimize large vulnerabilities caused by these non-traditional network portals. Firewalls, including the PIX and IOS® firewalls, and underlying protocols are presented in depth. Intrusion detection is fully examined. The book shows the reader how to control dial-in access by setting up access servers with AAA, PPP, TACACS+, and Radius. Finally, protections at the service provider are discussed by showing the reader how to provision security at the service provider level.

ciscopress.com

Cisco BGP-4 Command and Configuration Handbook
(CCIE Professional Development)

William R. Parkhurst

1-58705-017-X • **Available Now**

Cisco BGP-4 Command and Configuration Handbook is an exhaustive practical reference to the commands contained within BGP-4. For each command/subcommand, author Bill Parkhurst explains the intended use or function and how to properly configure it. Then, he presents scenarios to demonstrate every facet of the command and its use, along with appropriate show and debug commands. Through the discussion of functionality and the scenario-based configuration examples, Cisco BGP-4 Command and Configuration Handbook helps you gain a thorough understanding of the practical side of BGP-4.

Routing TCP/IP, Volume II
(CCIE Professional Development)

Jeff Doyle, Jennifer DeHaven Carroll

1-57870-089-2 • **Available Now**

This book presents a detailed examination of exterior routing protocols (EGP and BGP) and advanced IP routing issues, such as multicast routing, quality of service routing, IPv6, and router management. Students learn IP design and management techniques for implementing routing protocols efficiently. Network planning, design, implementation, operation, and optimization are stressed in each chapter.

Cisco CCNP BSCI Certification

CCNP® BSCI Exam Certification Guide (CCNP Self-Study), Second Edition

Clare Gough

1-58720-078-3 • **Available Now**

CCNP BSCI Exam Certification Guide, Second Edition, is a comprehensive exam self-study tool for the CCNP/CCDP/CCIP BSCI exam, which evaluates a networkers ability to build scalable, routed Cisco internetworks. This book, updated with more than 100 pages of IS-IS protocol coverage, addresses all the major topics on the most recent BSCI #640-901 exam. This guide enables readers to master the concepts and technologies upon which they will be tested, including extending IP addresses, routing principles, scalable routing protocols, managing traffic and access, and optimizing scalable internetworks. CCNP candidates will seek out *CCNP BSCI Exam Certification Guide* as timely and expert late-stage exam preparation tool and useful post-exam reference.

CCNP Self-Study: Building Scalable Cisco Internetworks (BSCI)

Catherine Paquet, Diane Teare

1-58705-084-6 • **Available Now**

CCNP Self-Study: Building Scalable Cisco Internetworks (BSCI) is a Cisco authorized, self-paced learning tool for CCNP, CCDP, and CCIP preparation. The book teaches readers how to design, configure, maintain, and scale routed networks that are growing in size and complexity. The book focuses on using Cisco routers connected in LANs and WANs typically found at medium-to-large network sites. Upon completing this book, readers will be able to select and implement the appropriate Cisco IOS® Software services required to build a scalable, routed network.

Cisco CCNP Certification

CCNP Preparation Library (CCNP Self-Study), Third Edition
Various Authors
1-58705-131-1 • **Available Now**

CCNP Preparation Library, Third Edition, is a Cisco authorized library of self-paced learning tools for the four component exams of the CCNP certification. These books teach readers the skills in professional level routing, switching, remote access and support as recommended for their respective exams, including for the new Building Scalable Cisco Internetworks (BSCI) exam.

Based on the four component exams of the CCNP certification, this four-book library contains *CCNP Self-Study: Building Scalable Cisco Internetworks* (BSCI), *Building Cisco Multilayer Switched Networks*, *Building Cisco Remote Access Networks*, and *Cisco Internetwork Troubleshooting*. These books serve as valuable study guides and supplements to the instuctor-led courses for certification candidates. They are also valuable to any intermediate level networker who wants to master the implementation of Cisco networking devices in medium to large networks.

Cisco CCNP Certification Library (CCNP Self-Study), Second Edition
Various Authors
1-58720-080-5 • **Available Now**

Cisco Certified Network Professional (CCNP) is the intermediate-level Cisco certification for network support. This is the next step for networking professionals who wish to validate their skills beyond the Cisco Certified Network Associate (CCNA®) level or who want to have a path to the expert level certification of CCIE. CCNP tests a candidates skill in installing, configuring, operating, and troubleshooting complex routed LANs, routed WANs, switched LANs, and dial access services. Where CCNA requires candidates to pass a single exam, CCNP requires candidates to pass four written exams, including 640-901 BSCI, 640-604 Switching, 640-605 Remote Access, and 640-606 Support.

The official exam self-study guides for each of these exams are now available in this value priced bundle. These books, *CCNP BSCI Exam Certification Guide*, *CCNP Switching Exam Certification Guide*, *CCNP Remote Access Exam Certification Guide*, and *CCNP Support Exam Certification Guide*, present the certification candidate with comprehensive review and practice of all the key topics that appear on each of the CCNP exams.

Cisco CCNP Certification

Internetworking Technologies Handbook, Third Edition

Cisco Systems, Inc.

1-58705-001-3 • **Available Now**

Internetworking Technologies Handbook, Third Edition, is an essential reference for every network professional. *Internetworking Technologies Handbook* has been one of Cisco Press' best-selling and most popular books since the first edition was published in 1997. Network engineers, administrators, technicians, and support personnel use this book to understand and implement many different internetworking and Cisco technologies. Beyond the on-the-job use, *Internetworking Technologies Handbook* is also a core training component for CCNA and CCDA® certifications. It is a comprehensive reference that enables networking professionals to understand and implement contemporary internetworking technologies. You will master terms, concepts, technologies, and devices used in today's networking industry, and will learn how to incorporate internetworking technologies into a LAN/WAN environment.

This Third Edition features new chapters on cable technologies, wireless technologies, and voice/data integration. After reading this book, networking professionals will possess a greater understanding of local and wide-area networking and the hardware, protocols, and services involved. *Internetworking Technologies Handbook* offers system optimization techniques that will strengthen results, increase productivity, and improve efficiency--helping you make more intelligent, cost-effective decisions for your network environment.

ciscopress.com

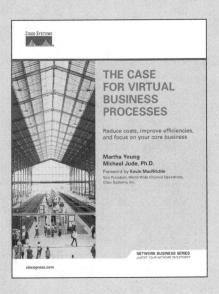

CISCO SYSTEMS

Cisco Press

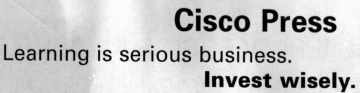

Cisco Press

Learning is serious business.

Invest wisely.

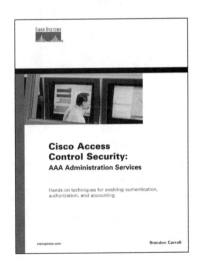

SEARCH THOUSANDS OF BOOKS FROM LEADING PUBLISHERS

Safari® Bookshelf is a searchable electronic reference library for IT professionals that features more than 2,000 titles from technical publishers, including Cisco Press.

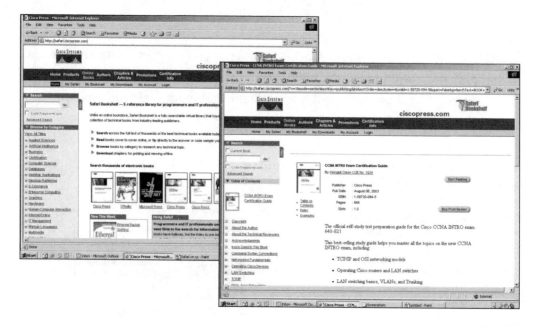

With Safari Bookshelf you can

- **Search** the full text of thousands of technical books, including more than 70 Cisco Press titles from authors such as Wendell Odom, Jeff Doyle, Bill Parkhurst, Sam Halabi, and Karl Solie.

- **Read** the books on My Bookshelf from cover to cover, or just flip to the information you need.

- **Browse** books by category to research any technical topic.

- **Download** chapters for printing and viewing offline.

With a customized library, you'll have access to your books when and where you need them—and all you need is a user name and password.

3 STEPS TO LEARNING

STEP 1   **STEP 2**   **STEP 3**

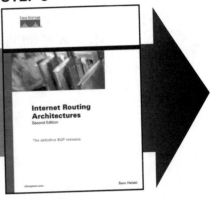

First-Step   **Fundamentals**   **Networking Technology Guides**

STEP 1   **First-Step**—Benefit from easy-to-grasp explanations. No experience required!

STEP 2   **Fundamentals**—Understand the purpose, application, and management of technology.

STEP 3   **Networking Technology Guides**—Gain the knowledge to master the challenge of the network.

NETWORK BUSINESS SERIES

The Network Business series helps professionals tackle the business issues surrounding the network. Whether you are a seasoned IT professional or a business manager with minimal technical expertise, this series will help you understand the business case for technologies.

Justify Your Network Investment.

DISCUSS

NETWORKING PRODUCTS AND TECHNOLOGIES WITH CISCO EXPERTS AND NETWORKING PROFESSIONALS WORLDWIDE

**VISIT NETWORKING PROFESSIONALS
A CISCO ONLINE COMMUNITY
WWW.CISCO.COM/GO/DISCUSS**

THIS IS THE POWER OF THE NETWORK. now.

CISCO SYSTEMS

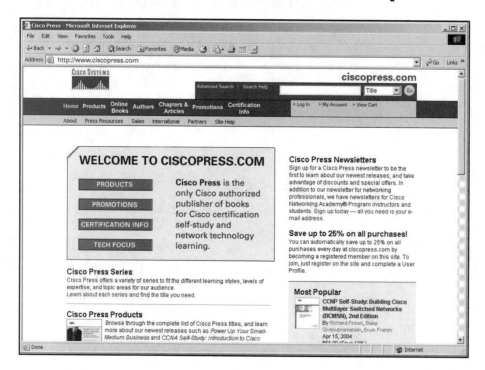
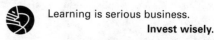